15th Conference on Computational Natural Language Learning 2011

(CoNLL 2011)

AA005979

Co-Located with ACL HLT 2011

Portland, Oregon, USA
23-24 June 2011

ISBN: 978-1-61839-235-0

Printed from e-media with permission by:

Curran Associates, Inc.
57 Morehouse Lane
Red Hook, NY 12571

CURRAN ASSOCIATES INC. proceedings.com

Some format issues inherent in the e-media version may also appear in this print version.

Printed by Curran Associates, Inc. (2011)

Association for Computational Linguistics
209 N. Eighth Street
Stroudsburg, Pennsylvania 18360

Phone: 1-570-476-8006
Fax: 1-570-476-0860

acl@aclweb.org

Additional copies of this publication are available from:

Curran Associates, Inc.
57 Morehouse Lane
Red Hook, NY 12571 USA
Phone: 845-758-0400
Fax: 845-758-2634
Email: curran@proceedings.com
Web: www.proceedings.com

Table of Contents

Preface

The 2011 Conference on Computational Natural Language Learning is the fifteenth in the series of annual meetings organized by SIGNLL, the ACL special interest group on natural language learning. CONLL-2011 will be held in Portland, Oregon, USA, June 23-24 2011, in conjunction with ACL-HLT.

For our special focus this year in the main session of CoNLL, we invited papers relating to massive, linked text data. We received 82 submissions on these and other relevant topics, of which 4 were eventually withdrawn. Of the remaining 78 papers, 13 were selected to appear in the conference program as oral presentations, and 14 were chosen as posters. All accepted papers appear here in the proceedings. Each accepted paper was allowed eight content pages plus any number of pages containing only bibliographic references.

As in previous years, CoNLL-2011 has a shared task, *Modeling unrestricted coreference in OntoNotes*. The Shared Task papers are collected in a companion volume of CoNLL-2011.

We begin by thanking all of the authors who submitted their work to CoNLL-2011, as well as the program committee for helping us select from among the many strong submissions. We are also grateful to our invited speakers, Bruce Hayes and Yee Whye Teh, who graciously agreed to give talks at CoNLL. Special thanks to the SIGNLL board members, Lluís Màrquez and Joakim Nivre, for their valuable advice and assistance in putting together this year's program, and to the SIGNLL information officer, Erik Tjong Kim Sang, for publicity and maintaining the CoNLL-2011 web page. We also appreciate the additional help we received from the ACL program chairs, workshop chairs, and publication chairs.

Finally, many thanks to Google for sponsoring the best paper award at CoNLL-2011.

We hope you enjoy the conference!

Sharon Goldwater and Christopher Manning

CoNLL 2011 Conference Chairs

Program Chairs:

Sharon Goldwater (University of Edinburgh, United Kingdom)
Christopher Manning (Stanford University, United States)

Program Committee:

Steven Abney (University of Michigan, United States)
Eneko Agirre (University of the Basque Country, Spain)
Afra Alishahi (Saarland University, Germany)
Lourdes Araujo (Universidad Nacional de Educación a Distancia, Spain)
Jason Baldridge (University of Texas at Austin, United States)
Steven Bethard (Katholieke Universiteit Leuven, Belgium)
Steven Bird (University of Melbourne, Australia)
Phil Blunsom (University of Oxford, United Kingdom)
Thorsten Brants (Google Inc., United States)
Chris Brew (Ohio State University, United States)
David Burkett (University of California at Berkeley, United States)
Yunbo Cao (Microsoft Research Asia, China)
Xavier Carreras (Technical University of Catalonia, Spain)
Nathanael Chambers (Stanford University, United States)
Ming-Wei Chang (University of Illinois at Urbana-Champaign, United States)
Colin Cherry (National Research Council, Canada)
Massimiliano Ciaramita (Google Research, Switzerland)
Alexander Clark (Royal Holloway, University of London, United Kingdom)
Stephen Clark (University of Cambridge, United Kingdom)
Shay Cohen (Carnegie Mellon University, United States)
Trevor Cohn (University of Sheffield, United Kingdom)
James Curran (University of Sydney, Australia)
Walter Daelemans (University of Antwerp, Belgium)
Mark Dras (Macquarie University, Australia)
Amit Dubey (University of Edinburgh, United Kingdom)
Chris Dyer (Carnegie Mellon University, United States)
Jacob Eisenstein (Carnegie Mellon University, United States)
Micha Elsner (University of Edinburgh, United Kingdom)
Jenny Finkel (Columbia University, United States)
Radu Florian (IBM Watson Research Center, United States)
Robert Frank (Yale University, United States)
Stella Frank (University of Edinburgh, United Kingdom)
Michel Galley (Microsoft Research, United States)
Kevin Gimpel (Carnegie Mellon University, United States)
Yoav Goldberg (Ben Gurion University of the Negev, Israel)
Cyril Goutte (National Research Council, Canada)

Spence Green (Stanford University, United States)
Gholamreza Haffari (BC Cancer Research Center, Canada)
Keith Hall (Google Research, Switzerland)
James Henderson (University of Geneva, Switzerland)
Julia Hockenmaier (University of Illinois at Urbana-Champaign, United States)
Fei Huang (IBM Research, United States)
Rebecca Hwa (University of Pittsburgh, United States)
Richard Johansson (University of Trento, Italy)
Mark Johnson (Macquarie University, Australia)
Rohit Kate (University of Wisconsin at Milwaukee, United States)
Philipp Koehn (University of Edinburgh, United Kingdom)
Mamoru Komachi (Nara Institute of Science and Technology, Japan)
Terry Koo (Google Inc., United States)
Shankar Kumar (Google Inc., United States)
Tom Kwiatkowski (University of Edinburgh, United Kingdom)
Mirella Lapata (University of Edinburgh, United Kingdom)
Shalom Lappin (Kings College London, United Kingdom)
Lillian Lee (Cornell Universiy, United States)
Percy Liang (University of California at Berkeley, United States)
Adam Lopez (Johns Hopkins University, United States)
Rob Malouf (San Diego State University, United States)
André Martins (Carnegie Mellon University, United States)
Yuji Matsumoto (Nara Institute of Science and Technology, Japan)
Takuya Matsuzaki (University of Tokyo, Japan)
David McClosky (Stanford University, United States)
Ryan McDonald (Google Inc., United States)
Paola Merlo (University of Geneva, Switzerland)
Haitao Mi (Institute of Computing Technology, Chinese Academy of Sciences, China)
Yusuke Miyao (University of Tokyo, Japan)
Alessandro Moschitti (University of Trento, Italy)
Lluís Màrquez (Technical University of Catalonia, Spain)
Tahira Naseem (Massachusetts Institute of Technology, United States)
Mark-Jan Nederhof (University of St. Andrews, United Kingdom)
Hwee Tou Ng (National University of Singapore, Singapore)
Vincent Ng (University of Texas at Dallas, United States)
Joakim Nivre (Uppsala University, Sweden)
Miles Osborne (University of Edinburgh, United Kingdom)
Christopher Parisien (University of Toronto, Canada)
Amy Perfors (University of Adelaide, Australia)
Slav Petrov (Google Research, United States)
Hoifung Poon (University of Washington, United States)
Vasin Punyakanok (BBN Technologies, United States)
Chris Quirk (Microsoft Research, United States)
Ari Rappoport (The Hebrew University, Israel)
Lev Ratinov (University of Illinois at Urbana-Champaign, United States)
Roi Reichart (Massachusetts Institute of Technology, United States)

Joseph Reisinger (University of Texas at Austin, United States)
Sebastian Riedel (University of Massachusetts, United States)
Dan Roth (University of Illinois at Urbana-Champaign, United States)
William Sakas (Hunter College, United States)
Anoop Sarkar (Simon Fraser University, Canada)
William Schuler (The Ohio State University, United States)
Libin Shen (Akamai, United States)
Khalil Sima'an (University of Amsterdam, Netherlands)
Noah Smith (Carnegie Mellon University, United States)
Benjamin Snyder (University of Wisconsin-Madison, United States Richard Socher (Stanford University, United States)
Valentin Spitkovsky (Stanford University, United States)
Mark Steedman (University of Edinburgh, United Kingdom)
Mihai Surdeanu (Stanford University, United States)
Jun Suzuki (NTT Communication Science Laboratories, Japan)
Hiroya Takamura (Tokyo Institute of Technology, Japan)
Ivan Titov (Saarland University, Germany)
Kristina Toutanova (Microsoft Research, United States)
Antal van den Bosch (Tilburg University, Netherlands)
Theresa Wilson (Johns Hopkins University, United States)
Peng Xu (Google Inc., United States)
Charles Yang (University of Pennsylvania, United States)
Chen Yu (Indiana University, United States)
Daniel Zeman (Charles University in Prague, Czech Republic)
Luke Zettlemoyer (University of Washington at Seattle, United States)

Invited Speakers:

Bruce Hayes (University of California, Los Angeles, United States)
Yee Whye Teh (Gatsby Unit, University College London, United Kingdom)

Modeling Syntactic Context Improves Morphological Segmentation

Yoong Keok Lee **Aria Haghighi** **Regina Barzilay**
Computer Science and Artificial Intelligence Laboratory
Massachusetts Institute of Technology
{yklee, aria42, regina}@csail.mit.edu

Abstract

The connection between part-of-speech (POS) categories and morphological properties is well-documented in linguistics but underutilized in text processing systems. This paper proposes a novel model for morphological segmentation that is driven by this connection. Our model learns that words with common affixes are likely to be in the same syntactic category and uses learned syntactic categories to refine the segmentation boundaries of words. Our results demonstrate that incorporating POS categorization yields substantial performance gains on morphological segmentation of Arabic. [1]

1 Introduction

A tight connection between morphology and syntax is well-documented in linguistic literature. In many languages, morphology plays a central role in marking syntactic structure, while syntactic relations help to reduce morphological ambiguity (Harley and Phillips, 1994). Therefore, in an unsupervised linguistic setting which is rife with ambiguity, modeling this connection can be particularly beneficial.

However, existing unsupervised morphological analyzers take little advantage of this linguistic property. In fact, most of them operate at the vocabulary level, completely ignoring sentence context. This design is not surprising: a typical morphological analyzer does not have access to syntactic information, because morphological segmentation precedes other forms of sentence analysis.

In this paper, we demonstrate that morphological analysis can utilize this connection without assuming access to full-fledged syntactic information. In particular, we focus on two aspects of the morpho-syntactic connection:

- **Morphological consistency within POS categories.** Words within the same syntactic category tend to select similar affixes. This linguistic property significantly reduces the space of possible morphological analyses, ruling out assignments that are incompatible with a syntactic category.

- **Morphological realization of grammatical agreement.** In many morphologically rich languages, agreement between syntactic dependents is expressed via correlated morphological markers. For instance, in Semitic languages, gender and number agreement between nouns and adjectives is expressed using matching suffixes. Enforcing mutually consistent segmentations can greatly reduce ambiguity of word-level analysis.

In both cases, we do not assume that the relevant syntactic information is provided, but instead jointly induce it as part of morphological analysis.

We capture morpho-syntactic relations in a Bayesian model that grounds intra-word decisions in sentence-level context. Like traditional unsupervised models, we generate morphological structure from a latent lexicon of prefixes, stems, and suffixes.

[1] The source code for the work presented in this paper is available at http://groups.csail.mit.edu/rbg/code/morphsyn/.

Proceedings of the Fifteenth Conference on Computational Natural Language Learning, pages 1–9,
Portland, Oregon, USA, 23–24 June 2011.

In addition, morphological analysis is guided by a latent variable that clusters together words with similar affixes, acting as a proxy for POS tags. Moreover, a sequence-level component further refines the analysis by correlating segmentation decisions between adjacent words that exhibit morphological agreement. We encourage this behavior by encoding a transition distribution over adjacent words, using string match cues as a proxy for grammatical agreement.

We evaluate our model on the standard Arabic treebank. Our full model yields 86.2% accuracy, outperforming the best published results (Poon et al., 2009) by 8.5%. We also found that modeling morphological agreement between adjacent words yields greater improvement than modeling syntactic categories. Overall, our results demonstrate that incorporating syntactic information is a promising direction for improving morphological analysis.

2 Related Work

Research in unsupervised morphological segmentation has gained momentum in recent years bringing about significant developments to the area. These advances include novel Bayesian formulations (Goldwater et al., 2006; Creutz and Lagus, 2007; Johnson, 2008), methods for incorporating rich features in unsupervised log-linear models (Poon et al., 2009) and the development of multilingual morphological segmenters (Snyder and Barzilay, 2008a).

Our work most closely relates to approaches that aim to incorporate syntactic information into morphological analysis. Surprisingly, the research in this area is relatively sparse, despite multiple results that demonstrate the connection between morphology and syntax in the context of part-of-speech tagging (Toutanova and Johnson, 2008; Habash and Rambow, 2005; Dasgupta and Ng, 2007; Adler and Elhadad, 2006). Toutanova and Cherry (2009) were the first to systematically study how to incorporate part-of-speech information into lemmatization and empirically demonstrate the benefits of this combination. While our high-level goal is similar, our respective problem formulations are distinct. Toutanova and Cherry (2009) have considered a semi-supervised setting where an initial morphological dictionary and tagging lexicon are provided but the model also has access to unlabeled data. Since a lemmatizer and tagger trained in isolation may produce mutually inconsistent assignments, and their method employs a log-linear reranker to reconcile these decisions. This reranking method is not suitable for the unsupervised scenario considered in our paper.

Our work is most closely related to the approach of Can and Manandhar (2009). Their method also incorporates POS-based clustering into morphological analysis. These clusters, however, are learned as a separate preprocessing step using distributional similarity. For each of the clusters, the model selects a set of affixes, driven by the frequency of their occurrences in the cluster. In contrast, we model morpho-syntactic decisions jointly, thereby enabling tighter integration between the two. This design also enables us to capture additional linguistic phenomena such as agreement. While this technique yields performance improvement in the context of their system, the final results does not exceed state-of-the-art systems that do not exploit this information (for e.g., (Creutz and Lagus, 2007)).

3 Model

Given a corpus of unannotated and unsegmented sentences, our goal is to infer the segmentation boundaries of all words. We represent segmentations and syntactic categories as latent variables with a directed graphical model, and we perform Bayesian inference to recover the latent variables of interest. Apart from learning a compact morpheme lexicon that explains the corpus well, we also model morpho-syntactic relations both within each word and between adjacent words to improve segmentation performance. In the remaining section, we first provide the key linguistic intuitions on which our model is based before describing the complete generative process.

3.1 Linguistic Intuition

While morpho-syntactic interface spans a range of linguistic phenomena, we focus on two facets of this connection. Both of them provide powerful constraints on morphological analysis and can be modeled without explicit access to syntactic annotations.

Morphological consistency within syntactic category. Words that belong to the same syntactic category tend to select similar affixes. In fact, the power of affix-related features has been empirically shown in the task of POS tag prediction (Habash and Rambow, 2005). We hypothesize that this regularity can also benefit morphological analyzers by eliminating assignments with incompatible prefixes and suffixes. For instance, a state-of-the-art segmenter erroneously divides the word "Al{ntxAbAt" into four morphemes "Al-{ntxAb-A-t" instead of three "Al-{ntxAb-At" (translated as "the-election-s".) The affix assignment here is clearly incompatible — determiner "Al" is commonly associated with nouns, while suffix "A" mostly occurs with verbs.

Since POS information is not available to the model, we introduce a latent variable that encodes affix-based clustering. In addition, we consider a variant of the model that captures dependencies between latent variables of adjacent words (analogous to POS transitions).

Morphological realization of grammatical agreement. In morphologically rich languages, agreement is commonly realized using matching suffices. In many cases, members of a dependent pair such as adjective and noun have the exact same suffix. A common example in the Arabic Treebank is the bigram "Al-Df-p Al-grby-p" (which is translated word-for-word as "the-bank the-west") where the last morpheme "p" is a feminine singular noun suffix.

Fully incorporating agreement constraints in the model is difficult, since we do not have access to syntactic dependencies. Therefore, we limit our attention to adjacent words which end with similar strings – for e.g., "p" in the example above. The model encourages consistent segmentation of such pairs. While our string-based cue is a simple proxy for agreement relation, it turns to be highly effective in practice. On the Penn Arabic treebank corpus, our cue has a precision of around 94% at the token-level.

3.2 Generative Process

The high-level generative process proceeds in four phases:

(a) **Lexicon Model**: We begin by generating morpheme lexicons $\boldsymbol{L}$ using parameters γ. This set of lexicons consists of separate lexicons for prefixes, stems, and suffixes generated in a hierarchical fashion.

(b) **Segmentation Model**: Conditioned on $\boldsymbol{L}$, we draw word types, their segmentations, and also their syntactic categories $(\boldsymbol{W}, \boldsymbol{S}, \boldsymbol{T})$.

(c) **Token-POS Model**: Next, we generate the unsegmented tokens in the corpus and their syntactic classes $(\boldsymbol{w}, \boldsymbol{t})$ from a standard first-order HMM which has dependencies between adjacent syntactic categories.

(d) **Token-Seg Model**: Lastly, we generate token segmentations $\boldsymbol{s}$ from a first-order Markov chain that has dependencies between adjacent segmentations.

The complete generative story can be summarized by the following equation:

$$
\begin{aligned}
P(\boldsymbol{w},\boldsymbol{s},\boldsymbol{t},\boldsymbol{W},\boldsymbol{S},\boldsymbol{T},\boldsymbol{L},\boldsymbol{\Theta},\boldsymbol{\theta}|\boldsymbol{\gamma},\boldsymbol{\alpha},\boldsymbol{\beta}) = \\
& P(\boldsymbol{L}|\boldsymbol{\gamma}) && \text{(a)} \\
& P(\boldsymbol{W},\boldsymbol{S},\boldsymbol{T},\boldsymbol{\Theta}|\boldsymbol{L},\boldsymbol{\gamma},\boldsymbol{\alpha}) && \text{(b)} \\
& P_{\text{pos}}(\boldsymbol{w},\boldsymbol{t},\boldsymbol{\theta}|\boldsymbol{W},\boldsymbol{S},\boldsymbol{T},\boldsymbol{L},\boldsymbol{\alpha}) && \text{(c)} \\
& P_{\text{seg}}(\boldsymbol{s}|\boldsymbol{W},\boldsymbol{S},\boldsymbol{T},\boldsymbol{L},\boldsymbol{\beta},\boldsymbol{\alpha}) && \text{(d)}
\end{aligned}
$$

where $\boldsymbol{\gamma}, \boldsymbol{\alpha}, \boldsymbol{\Theta}, \boldsymbol{\theta}, \boldsymbol{\beta}$ are hyperparameters and parameters whose roles we shall detail shortly.

Our lexicon model captures the desirability of compact lexicon representation proposed by prior work by using parameters $\boldsymbol{\gamma}$ that favors small lexicons. Furthermore, if we set the number of syntactic categories in the segmentation model to one and exclude the token-based models, we recover a segmenter that is very similar to the unigram Dirichlet Process model (Goldwater et al., 2006; Snyder and Barzilay, 2008a; Snyder and Barzilay, 2008b). We shall elaborate on this point in Section 4.

The segmentation model captures morphological consistency within syntactic categories (POS tag), whereas the Token-POS model captures POS tag dependencies between adjacent tokens. Lastly, the Token-Seg model encourages consistent segmentations between adjacent tokens that exhibit morphological agreement.

Lexicon Model The design goal is to encourage morpheme types to be short and the set of affixes (i.e. prefixes and suffixes) to be much smaller than the set of stems. To achieve this, we first draw each morpheme σ in the master lexicon L^* according to a geometric distribution which assigns monotonically smaller probability to longer morpheme lengths:

$$|\sigma| \sim \text{Geometric}(\gamma_l)$$

The parameter γ_l for the geometric distribution is fixed and specified beforehand. We then draw the prefix, the stem, and suffix lexicons (denoted by L_-, L_0, L_+ respectively) from morphemes in L^*. Generating the lexicons in such a hierarchical fashion allows morphemes to be shared among the lower-level lexicons. For instance, once determiner "Al" is generated in the master lexicon, it can be used to generate prefixes or stems later on. To favor compact lexicons, we again make use of a geometric distribution that assigns smaller probability to lexicons that contain more morphemes:

$$\begin{aligned} \text{prefix:} \quad & |L_-| \sim \text{Geometric}(\gamma_-) \\ \text{stem:} \quad & |L_0| \sim \text{Geometric}(\gamma_0) \\ \text{suffix:} \quad & |L_+| \sim \text{Geometric}(\gamma_+) \end{aligned}$$

By separating morphemes into affixes and stems, we can control the relative sizes of their lexicons with different parameters.

Segmentation Model The model independently generates each word type using only morphemes in the affix and stem lexicons, such that each word has exactly one stem and is encouraged to have few morphemes. We fix the number of syntactic categories (tags) to K and begin the process by generating multinomial distribution parameters for the POS tag prior from a Dirichlet prior:

$$\Theta_T \sim \text{Dirichlet}(\alpha_T, \{1, \ldots, K\})$$

Next, for each possible value of the tag $T \in \{1, \ldots, K\}$, we generate parameters for a multinomial distribution (again from a Dirichlet prior) for each of the prefix and the suffix lexicons:

$$\begin{aligned} \Theta_{-|T} &\sim \text{Dirichlet}(\alpha_-, L_-) \\ \Theta_0 &\sim \text{Dirichlet}(\alpha_0, L_0) \\ \Theta_{+|T} &\sim \text{Dirichlet}(\alpha_+, L_+) \end{aligned}$$

By generating parameters in this manner, we allow the multinomial distributions to generate only morphemes that are present in the lexicon. Also, at inference time, only morphemes in the lexicons receive pseudo-counts. Note that the affixes are generated conditioned on the tag; But the stem are not.[2]

Now, we are ready to generate each word type W, its segmentation S, and its syntactic category T. First, we draw the number of morpheme segments $|S|$ from a geometric distribution truncated to generate at most five morphemes:

$$|S| \sim \text{Truncated-Geometric}(\gamma_{|S|})$$

Next, we pick one of the morphemes to be the stem uniformly at random, and thus determine the number of prefixes and suffixes. Then, we draw the syntactic category T for the word. (Note that T is a latent variable which we recover during inference.)

$$T \sim \text{Multinomial}(\Theta_T)$$

After that, we generate each stem σ_0, prefix σ_-, and suffix σ_+ independently:

$$\begin{aligned} \sigma_0 &\sim \text{Multinomial}(\Theta_0) \\ \sigma_-|T &\sim \text{Multinomial}(\Theta_{-|T}) \\ \sigma_+|T &\sim \text{Multinomial}(\Theta_{+|T}) \end{aligned}$$

Token-POS Model This model captures the dependencies between the syntactic categories of adjacent tokens with a first-order HMM. Conditioned on the type-level assignments, we generate (unsegmented) tokens $\boldsymbol{w}$ and their POS tags $\boldsymbol{t}$:

$$\begin{aligned} & P_{\text{pos}}(\boldsymbol{w}, \boldsymbol{t}|\boldsymbol{W}, \boldsymbol{T}, \boldsymbol{\theta}) \\ & = \prod_{w_i, t_i} P(t_{i-1}|t_i, \theta_{t|t}) P(w_i|t_i, \theta_{w|t}) \end{aligned}$$

where the parameters of the multinomial distributions are generated by Dirichlet priors:

$$\begin{aligned} \theta_{t|t} &\sim \text{Dirichlet}(\alpha_{t|t}, \{1, \ldots, K\}) \\ \theta_{w|t} &\sim \text{Dirichlet}(\alpha_{w|t}, \boldsymbol{W_t}) \end{aligned}$$

[2]We design the model as such since the dependencies between affixes and the POS tag are much stronger than those between the stems and tags. In our preliminary experiments, when stems are also generated conditioned on the tag, spurious stems are easily created and associated with garbage-collecting tags.

Here, $\boldsymbol{W}_t$ refers to the set of word types that are generated by tag t. In other words, conditioned on tag t, we can only generate word w from the set of word types in $\boldsymbol{W}_t$ which is generated earlier (Lee et al., 2010).

Token-Seg Model The model captures the morphological agreement between adjacent segmentations using a first-order Markov chain. The probability of drawing a sequence of segmentations $\boldsymbol{s}$ is given by

$$P_{\text{seg}}(\boldsymbol{s}|\boldsymbol{W},\boldsymbol{S},\boldsymbol{T},\boldsymbol{L},\boldsymbol{\beta},\boldsymbol{\alpha}) = \prod_{(s_{i-1},s_i)} p(s_i|s_{i-1})$$

For each pair of segmentations s_{i-1} and s_i, we determine: (1) if they should exhibit morpho-syntactic agreement, and (2) if their morphological segmentations are consistent. To answer the first question, we first obtain the final suffix for each of them. Next, we obtain n, the length of the longer suffix. For each segmentation, we define the *ending* to be the last n characters of the word. We then use matching endings as a proxy for morpho-syntactic agreement between the two words. To answer the second question, we use matching final suffixes as a cue for consistent morphological segmentations. To encode the linguistic intuition that words that exhibit morpho-syntactic agreement are likely to be morphological consistent, we define the above probability distribution to be:

$$p(s_i|s_{i-1}) = \begin{cases} \beta_1 & \text{if same endings and same final suffix} \\ \beta_2 & \text{if same endings but different final suffixes} \\ \beta_3 & \text{otherwise (e.g. no suffix)} \end{cases}$$

where $\beta_1 + \beta_2 + \beta_3 = 1$, with $\beta_1 > \beta_3 > \beta_2$. By setting β_1 to a high value, we encourage adjacent tokens that are likely to exhibit morpho-syntactic agreement to have the same final suffix. And by setting $\beta_3 > \beta_2$, we also discourage adjacent tokens with the same endings to be segmented differently.[3]

4 Inference

Given a corpus of unsegmented and unannotated word tokens $\boldsymbol{w}$, the objective is to recover values of all latent variables, including the segmentations $\boldsymbol{s}$.

$$\begin{aligned} &P(\boldsymbol{s},\boldsymbol{t},\boldsymbol{S},\boldsymbol{T},\boldsymbol{L}|\boldsymbol{w},\boldsymbol{W},\boldsymbol{\gamma},\boldsymbol{\alpha},\boldsymbol{\beta}) \\ &\propto \int P(\boldsymbol{w},\boldsymbol{s},\boldsymbol{t},\boldsymbol{W},\boldsymbol{S},\boldsymbol{T},\boldsymbol{L},\boldsymbol{\Theta},\boldsymbol{\theta}|\boldsymbol{\gamma},\boldsymbol{\alpha},\boldsymbol{\beta})d\boldsymbol{\Theta}d\boldsymbol{\theta} \end{aligned}$$

We want to sample from the above distribution using collapsed Gibbs sampling ($\boldsymbol{\Theta}$ and $\boldsymbol{\theta}$ integrated out.) In each iteration, we loop over each word type W_i and sample the following latent variables: its tag T_i, its segmentation S_i, the segmentations and tags for all of its token occurrences $(\boldsymbol{s}_i, \boldsymbol{t}_i)$, and also the morpheme lexicons $\boldsymbol{L}$:

$$\begin{aligned} &P(\boldsymbol{L}, T_i, S_i, \boldsymbol{s}_i, \boldsymbol{t}_i| \\ &\quad \boldsymbol{s}_{-i}, \boldsymbol{t}_{-i}, \boldsymbol{S}_{-i}, \boldsymbol{T}_{-i}, \boldsymbol{w}_{-i}, \boldsymbol{W}_{-i}, \boldsymbol{\gamma}, \boldsymbol{\alpha}, \boldsymbol{\beta}) \end{aligned} \quad (1)$$

such that the type and token-level assignments are consistent, i.e. for all $t \in \boldsymbol{t}_i$ we have $t = T_i$, and for all $s \in \boldsymbol{s}_i$ we have $s = S_i$.

4.1 Approximate Inference

Naively sampling the lexicons $\boldsymbol{L}$ is computationally infeasible since their sizes are unbounded. Therefore, we employ an approximation which turns is similar to performing inference with a Dirichlet Process segmentation model. In our approximation scheme, for each possible segmentation and tag hypothesis $(T_i, S_i, \boldsymbol{s}_i, \boldsymbol{t}_i)$, we only consider one possible value for $\boldsymbol{L}$, which we denote the *minimal lexicons*. Hence, the total number of hypothesis that we have to consider is only as large as the number of possibilities for $(T_i, S_i, \boldsymbol{s}_i, \boldsymbol{t}_i)$.

Specifically, we recover the minimal lexicons as follows: for each segmentation and tag hypothesis, we determine the set of distinct affix and stem types in the whole corpus, including the morphemes introduced by segmentation hypothesis under consideration. This set of lexicons, which we call the minimal lexicons, is the most compact ones that are needed to generate all morphemes proposed by the current hypothesis.

Furthermore, we set the number of possible POS tags $K = 5$.[4] For each possible value of the tag, we consider all possible segmentations with at most five segments. We further restrict the stem to have no

[3] Although p sums to one, it makes the model deficient since, conditioned everything already generated, it places some probability mass on invalid segmentation sequences.

[4] We find that increasing K to 10 does not yield improvement.

more than two prefixes or suffixes and also that the stem cannot be shorter than the affixes. This further restricts the space of segmentation and tag hypotheses, and hence makes the inference tractable.

4.2 Sampling equations

Suppose we are considering the hypothesis with segmentation S and POS tag T for word type W_i. Let $\boldsymbol{L} = (L^*, L_-, L_0, L_+)$ be the minimal lexicons for this hypothesis (S, T). We sample the hypothesis $(S, T, s = S, t = T, \boldsymbol{L})$ proportional to the product of the following four equations.

Lexicon Model

$$\begin{aligned}
&\prod_{\sigma \in L^*} \gamma_l (1-\gamma_l)^{|\sigma|} && \times \\
&\gamma_-(1-\gamma_-)^{|L_-|} && \times \\
&\gamma_0(1-\gamma_0)^{|L_0|} && \times \\
&\gamma_+(1-\gamma_+)^{|L_+|} && (2)
\end{aligned}$$

This is a product of geometric distributions involving the length of each morpheme σ and the size of each of the prefix, the stem, and the suffix lexicons (denoted as $|L_-|, |L_0|, |L_+|$ respectively.) Suppose, a new morpheme type σ_0 is introduced as a stem. Relative to a hypothesis that introduces none, this one incurs an additional cost of $(1 - \gamma_0)$ and $\gamma_l(1-\gamma_l)^{|\sigma_0|}$. In other words, the hypothesis is penalized for increasing the stem lexicon size and generating a new morpheme of length $|\sigma_0|$. In this way, the first and second terms play a role similar to the concentration parameter and base distribution in a DP-based model.

Segmentation Model

$$\begin{aligned}
&\frac{\gamma_{|S|}(1-\gamma_{|S|})^{|S|}}{\sum_{j=0}^{5} \gamma_{|S|}(1-\gamma_{|S|})^{j}} && \times \\
&\frac{n_T^{-i} + \alpha}{N^{-i} + \alpha K} && \times \\
&\frac{n_{\sigma_0}^{-i} + \alpha_0}{N_0^{-i} + \alpha_0 |L_0|} && \times \\
&\frac{n_{\sigma_-|T}^{-i} + \alpha_-}{N_{-|T}^{-i} + \alpha_- |L_-|} && \times \\
&\frac{n_{\sigma_+|T}^{-i} + \alpha_+}{N_{+|T}^{-i} + \alpha_+ |L_+|} && (3)
\end{aligned}$$

The first factor is the truncated geometric distribution of the number of segmentations $|S|$, and the second factor is the probability of generate the tag T. The rest are the probabilities of generating the stem σ_0, the prefix σ_-, and the suffix σ_+ (where the parameters of the multinomial distribution collapsed out). n_T^{-1} is the number of word types with tag T and N^{-i} is the total number of word types. $n_{\sigma_-|T}^{-i}$ refers to the number of times prefix σ_- is seen in all word types that are tagged with T, and $N_{-|T}^{-i}$ is the total number of prefixes in all word types that has tag T. All counts exclude the word type W_i whose segmentation we are sampling. If there is another prefix, $N_{-|T}^{-i}$ is incremented (and also $n_{\sigma_-|T}^{-i}$ if the second prefix is the same as the first one.) Integrating out the parameters introduces dependencies between prefixes. The rest of the notations read analogously.

Token-POS Model

$$\frac{\alpha_{w|t}{}^{(m^i)}}{(M_t^{-i} + \alpha_{w|t}|\boldsymbol{W_t}|)^{(m^i)}} \times \prod_{t=1}^{K}\prod_{t'=1}^{K} \frac{(m_{t'|t}^{-i} + \alpha_{t|t})^{(m_{t'|t}^{i})}}{(M_t^{-i} + \alpha_{t|t})^{(m_{t'|t}^{i})}} \quad (4)$$

The two terms are the token-level emission and transition probabilities with parameters integrated out. The integration induces dependences between all token occurrences of word type W which results in ascending factorials defined as $\alpha^{(m)} = \alpha(\alpha + 1)\cdots(\alpha + m - 1)$ (Liang et al., 2010). M_t^{-i} is the number of tokens that have POS tag t, m^i is the number of tokens w_i, and $m_{t'|t}^{-i}$ is the number of tokens t-to-t' transitions. (Both exclude counts contributed by tokens belong to word type W_i.) $|\boldsymbol{W_t}|$ is the number of word types with tag t.

Token-Seg Model

$$\beta_1^{m_{\beta_1}^i} \beta_2^{m_{\beta_2}^i} \beta_3^{m_{\beta_3}^i} \quad (5)$$

Here, $m_{\beta_1}^i$ refers to the number of transitions involving token occurrences of word type W_i that exhibit morphological agreement. This does not result in ascending factorials since the parameters of transition probabilities are fixed and not generated from Dirichlet priors, and so are not integrated out.

4.3 Staged Training

Although the Gibbs sampler mixes regardless of the initial state in theory, good initialization heuristics often speed up convergence in practice. We therefore train a series of models of increasing complexity (see section 6 for more details), each with 50 iterations of Gibbs sampling, and use the output of the preceding model to initialize the subsequent model. The initial model is initialized such that all words are not segmented. When POS tags are first introduced, they are initialized uniformly at random.

5 Experimental Setup

Performance metrics To enable comparison with previous approaches, we adopt the evaluation set-up of Poon et al. (2009). They evaluate segmentation accuracy on a per token basis, using recall, precision and F1-score computed on segmentation points. We also follow a transductive testing scenario where the same (unlabeled) data is used for both training and testing the model.

Data set We evaluate segmentation performance on the Penn Arabic Treebank (ATB).[5] It consists of about 4,500 sentences of modern Arabic obtained from newswire articles. Following the preprocessing procedures of Poon et al. (2009) that exclude certain word types (such as abbreviations and digits), we obtain a corpus of 120,000 tokens and 20,000 word types. Since our full model operates over sentences, we train the model on the entire ATB, but evaluate on the exact portion used by Poon et al. (2009).

Pre-defined tunable parameters and testing regime In all our experiments, we set $\gamma_l = \frac{1}{2}$ (for length of morpheme types) and $\gamma_{|S|} = \frac{1}{2}$ (for number of morpheme segments of each word.) To encourage a small set of affix types relative to stem types, we set $\gamma_- = \gamma_+ = \frac{1}{1.1}$ (for sizes of the affix lexicons) and $\gamma_0 = \frac{1}{10{,}000}$ (for size of the stem lexicon.) We employ a sparse Dirichlet prior for the type-level models (for morphemes and POS tag) by setting $\alpha = 0.1$. For the token-level models, we set hyperparameters for Dirichlet priors $\alpha_{w|t} = 10^{-5}$ (for unsegmented tokens) and $\alpha_{t|t} = 1.0$ (for POS tags transition.) To encourage adjacent words that exhibit morphological agreement to have the same final suffix, we set $\beta_1 = 0.6, \beta_2 = 0.1, \beta_1 = 0.3$.

In all the experiments, we perform five runs using different random seeds and report the mean score and the standard deviation.

[5] Our evaluation does not include the Hebrew and Arabic Bible datasets (Snyder and Barzilay, 2008a; Poon et al., 2009) since these corpora consists of short phrases that omit sentence context.

Model	R	P	F1	t-test
PCT 09	69.2	88.5	77.7	-
Morfessor	72.6	77.4	74.9	-
BASIC	71.4	86.7	78.3 (2.9)	-
+POS	75.4	87.4	81.0 (1.5)	+
+TOKEN-POS	75.7	88.5	81.6 (0.7)	~
+TOKEN-SEG	**82.1**	**90.8**	**86.2 (0.4)**	++

Table 1: Results on the Arabic Treebank (ATB) data set: We compare our models against Poon et al. (2009) (PCT09) and the Morfessor system (Morfessor-CAT). For our full model (+TOKEN-SEG) and its simplifications (BASIC, +POS, +TOKEN-POS), we perform five random restarts and show the mean scores. The sample standard deviations are shown in brackets. The last column shows results of a paired t-test against the preceding model: ++ (significant at 1%), + (significant at 5%), ~ (not significant), - (test not applicable).

Baselines Our primary comparison is against the morphological segmenter of Poon et al. (2009) which yields the best published results on the ATB corpus. In addition, we compare against the Morfessor Categories-MAP system (Creutz and Lagus, 2007). Similar to our model, their system uses latent variables to induce clustering over morphemes. The difference is in the nature of the clustering: the Morfessor algorithm associates a latent variable for each morpheme, grouping morphemes into four broad categories (prefix, stem, suffix, and non-morpheme) but not introducing dependencies between affixes directly. For both systems, we quote their performance reported by Poon et al. (2009).

6 Results

Comparison with the baselines Table 1 shows that our full model (denoted +TOKEN-SEG) yields a mean F1-score of 86.2, compared to 77.7 and 74.9 obtained by the baselines. This performance gap corresponds to an error reduction of 38.1% over the best published results.

Ablation Analysis To assess relative impact of various components, we consider several simplified variants of the model:

- BASIC is the type-based segmentation model that is solely driven by the lexicon.[6]

- +POS adds latent variables but does not capture transitions and agreement constraints.

- +TOKEN-POS is equivalent to the full model, without agreement constraints.

Our results in Table 1 clearly demonstrate that modeling morpho-syntactic constraints greatly improves the accuracy of morphological segmentation.

We further examine the performance gains arising from improvements due to (1) encouraging morphological consistency within syntactic categories, and (2) morphological realization of grammatical agreement.

We evaluate our models on a subset of words that exhibit morphological consistency. Table 2 shows the accuracies for words that begin with the prefix "Al" (determiner) and end with a suffix "At" (plural noun suffix.) An example is the word "Al-{ntxAb-At" which is translated as "the-election-s". Such words make up about 1% of tokens used for evaluation, and the two affix boundaries constitute about 3% of the all gold segmentation points. By introducing a latent variable to capture dependencies between affixes, +POS is able to improve segmentation performance over BASIC. When dependencies between latent variables are introduced, +TOKEN-POS yields additional improvements.

We also examine the performance gains due to morphological realization of grammatical agreement. We select the set of tokens that share the same final suffix as the preceding token, such as the bigram "Al-Df-p Al-grby-p" (which is translated word-for-word as "the-bank the-west") where the last morpheme "p" is a feminine singular noun suffix. This subset makes up about 4% of the evaluation set, and the boundaries of the final suffixes take up about 5% of the total gold segmentation boundaries.

[6]The resulting model is similar in spirit to the unigram DP-based segmenter (Goldwater et al., 2006; Snyder and Barzilay, 2008a; Snyder and Barzilay, 2008b).

Model	Token		Type	
	F1	Acc.	F1	Acc.
BASIC	68.3	13.9	73.8	24.3
+POS	75.4	26.4	78.5	38.0
+TOKEN-POS	76.5	34.9	82.0	49.6
+TOKEN-SEG	84.0	49.5	85.4	57.7

Table 2: Segmentation performance on words that begin with prefix "Al" (determiner) and end with suffix "At" (plural noun suffix). The mean F1 scores are computed using all boundaries of words in this set. For each word, we also determine if both affixes are recovered while ignoring any other boundaries between them. The other two columns report this accuracy at both the type-level and the token-level.

Model	Token		Type	
	F1	Acc.	F1	Acc.
BASIC	85.6	70.6	79.5	58.6
+POS	87.6	76.4	82.3	66.3
+TOKEN-POS	87.5	75.2	82.2	65.3
+TOKEN-SEG	92.8	91.1	88.9	84.4

Table 3: Segmentation performance on words that have the same final suffix as their preceding words. The F1 scores are computed based on all boundaries within the words, but the accuracies are obtained using only the final suffixes.

Table 3 reveals this category of errors persisted until the final component (+TOKEN-SEG) was introduced.

7 Conclusion

Although the connection between syntactic (POS) categories and morphological structure is well-known, this relation is rarely exploited to improve morphological segmentation performance. The performance gains motivate further investigation into morpho-syntactic models for unsupervised language analysis.

Acknowledgements

This material is based upon work supported by the U.S. Army Research Laboratory and the U.S. Army Research Office under contract/grant number W911NF-10-1-0533. Thanks to the MIT NLP group and the reviewers for their comments.

References

Meni Adler and Michael Elhadad. 2006. An unsupervised morpheme-based hmm for hebrew morphological disambiguation. In *Proceedings of the ACL/CONLL*, pages 665–672.

Burcu. Can and Suresh Manandhar. 2009. Unsupervised learning of morphology by using syntactic categories. In *Working Notes, CLEF 2009 Workshop*.

Mathias Creutz and Krista Lagus. 2007. Unsupervised models for morpheme segmentation and morphology learning. *ACM Transactions on Speech and Language Processing*, 4(1).

Sajib Dasgupta and Vincent Ng. 2007. Unsupervised part-of-speech acquisition for resource-scarce languages. In *Proceedings of the EMNLP-CoNLL*, pages 218–227.

Sharon Goldwater, Thomas L. Griffiths, and Mark Johnson. 2006. Contextual dependencies in unsupervised word segmentation. In *Proceedings of the ACL*, pages 673–680.

Nizar Habash and Owen Rambow. 2005. Arabic tokenization, part-of-speech tagging and morphological disambiguation in one fell swoop. In *Proceedings of the 43rd Annual Meeting of the Association for Computational Linguistics (ACL'05)*, pages 573–580, Ann Arbor, Michigan, June. Association for Computational Linguistics.

Heidi Harley and Colin Phillips, editors. 1994. *The Morphology-Syntax Connection*. Number 22 in MIT Working Papers in Linguistics. MIT Press.

Mark Johnson. 2008. Unsupervised word segmentation for Sesotho using adaptor grammars. In *Proceedings of the Tenth Meeting of ACL Special Interest Group on Computational Morphology and Phonology*, pages 20–27, Columbus, Ohio, June. Association for Computational Linguistics.

Yoong Keok Lee, Aria Haghighi, and Regina Barzilay. 2010. Simple type-level unsupervised POS tagging. In *Proceedings of the 2010 Conference on Empirical Methods in Natural Language Processing*, pages 853–861, Cambridge, MA, October. Association for Computational Linguistics.

Percy Liang, Michael I. Jordan, and Dan Klein. 2010. Type-based mcmc. In *Human Language Technologies: The 2010 Annual Conference of the North American Chapter of the Association for Computational Linguistics*, pages 573–581, Los Angeles, California, June. Association for Computational Linguistics.

Hoifung Poon, Colin Cherry, and Kristina Toutanova. 2009. Unsupervised morphological segmentation with log-linear models. In *Proceedings of HLT-NAACL 2009*, pages 209–217, Boulder, Colorado, June. Association for Computational Linguistics.

Benjamin Snyder and Regina Barzilay. 2008a. Crosslingual propagation for morphological analysis. In *Proceedings of the AAAI*, pages 848–854.

Benjamin Snyder and Regina Barzilay. 2008b. Unsupervised multilingual learning for morphological segmentation. In *Proceedings of ACL-08: HLT*, pages 737–745, Columbus, Ohio, June. Association for Computational Linguistics.

Kristina Toutanova and Colin Cherry. 2009. A global model for joint lemmatization and part-of-speech prediction. In *Proceedings of the Joint Conference of the 47th Annual Meeting of the ACL and the 4th International Joint Conference on Natural Language Processing of the AFNLP*, pages 486–494, Suntec, Singapore, August. Association for Computational Linguistics.

Kristina Toutanova and Mark Johnson. 2008. A bayesian lda-based model for semi-supervised part-of-speech tagging. In J.C. Platt, D. Koller, Y. Singer, and S. Roweis, editors, *Advances in Neural Information Processing Systems 20*, pages 1521–1528. MIT Press, Cambridge, MA.

The Effect of Automatic Tokenization, Vocalization, Stemming, and POS Tagging on Arabic Dependency Parsing

Emad Mohamed
Suez Canal University
Suez, Egypt
emohamed@umail.iu.edu

Abstract

We use an automatic pipeline of word tokenization, stemming, POS tagging, and vocalization to perform real-world Arabic dependency parsing. In spite of the high accuracy on the modules, the very few errors in tokenization, which reaches an accuracy of 99.34%, lead to a drop of more than 10% in parsing, indicating that no high quality dependency parsing of Arabic, and possibly other morphologically rich languages, can be reached without (semi-)perfect tokenization. The other module components, stemming, vocalization, and part of speech tagging, do not have the same profound effect on the dependency parsing process.

1. Introduction

Arabic is a morphologically rich language in which words may be composed of several tokens and hold several syntactic relations. We define *word* to be a whitespace delimited unit and token to be (part of) a word that has a syntactic function. For example, the word *wsytzwjhA* (وسيتزوجها)(English: And he will marry her) consists of 4 tokens: a conjunction *w*, a future marker *s*, a verb inflected for the singular masculine in the perfective form *ytzwj*, and a feminine singular 3rd person object pronoun. Parsing such a word requires tokenization, and performing dependency parsing in the tradition of the CoNLL-X (Buchholz and Marsi, 2006) and CoNLL 2007 shared task (Nivre et al, 2007) also requires part of speech tagging, lemmatization, linguistic features, and vocalization, all of which were in the human annotated gold standard form in the shared task.

The current study aims at measuring the effect of a pipeline of non gold standard tokenization, lemmatization, vocalization, linguistic features and POS tagging on the quality of Arabic dependency parsing. We only assume that we have gold standard sentence boundaries since we do not agree with the sentence boundaries in the data, and introducing our own will have a complicating effect on evaluation. The CoNLL shared tasks of 2006 and 2007 used gold standard components in all fields, which is not realistic for Arabic, or for any other language. For Arabic and other morphologically rich languages, it may be more unrealistic than it is for English, for example, since the CoNLL 2007 Arabic dataset has tokens, rather than white space delimited words, as entries. A single word may have more than one syntactically functional token. Dependency parsing has been selected in belief that it is more suitable for Arabic than constituent-based parsing. All grammatical relations in Arabic are binary asymmetrical relations that exist between the tokens of a sentence. According to Jonathan Owens (1997: 52): "In general the Arabic notion of dependency and that defined in certain modern versions e.g. Tesniere (1959) rest on common principles".

With a tokenization accuracy of 99.34%, a POS tagging accuracy of 96.39%, and with the absence of linguistic features and the use of word stems instead of lemmas, the Labeled Attachment Score drops from 74.75% in the gold standard experiment to 63.10% in the completely automatic experiment. Most errors are a direct result of tokenization errors, which indicates that despite the high accuracy on tokenization, it is still not enough to produce satisfactory parsing numbers.

2. Related Studies

The bulk of literature on Arabic Dependency Parsing stems from the two CoNLL shared tasks of 2006 and 2007. In CoNLL-X (Buchholz and

Proceedings of the Fifteenth Conference on Computational Natural Language Learning, pages 10–18,
Portland, Oregon, USA, 23–24 June 2011. ©2011 Association for Computational Linguistics

Marsi, 2006), the average Labeled Attachment Score on Arabic across all results presented by the 19 participating teams was 59.9% with a standard deviation of 6.5. The best results were obtained by McDonald et al (2006) with a score of 66.9% followed by Nivre et al (2006) with 66.7%.

The best results on Arabic in the CoNLL 2007 shared task were obtained by Hall et al (2007) as they obtained a Labeled Attachment Score of 76.52%, 9.6 percentage points above the highest score of the 2006 shared task. Hall et al used an ensemble system, based on the MaltParser dependency parser that extrapolates from a single MaltParser system. The settings with the Single MaltParser led to a Labeled Accuracy Score of 74.75% on Arabic. The Single MaltParser is the one used in the current paper. All the papers in both shared tasks used gold standard tokenization, vocalization, lemmatization, POS tags, and linguistic features.

A more recent study is that by Marton et al (2010). Although Marton et al varied the POS distribution and linguistic features, they still used gold standard tokenization. They also used the Columbia Arabic Treebank, which makes both the methods and data different from those presented here.

3. Data, Methods, and Evaluation

3.1.Data

The data used for the current study is the same data set used for the CoNLL (2007) shared task, with the same division into training set, and test set. This design helps in comparing results in a way that enables us to measure the effect of automatic pre-processing on parsing accuracy. The data is in the CoNLL column format. In this format, each token is represented through columns each of which has some specific information. The first column is the ID, the second the token, the third the lemma, the fourth the coarse-grained POS tag, the fifth the POS tag, and the sixth column is a list of linguistic features. The last two columns of the vector include the head of the token and the dependency relation between the token and its head. Linguistic features are an unordered set of syntactic and/or morphological features, separated by a vertical bar (|), or an underscore if not available. The features in the CoNLL 2007 Arabic dataset represent case, mood, definiteness, voice, number, gender and person.

The data used for training the stemmer/tokenizer is taken from the Arabic Treebank (Maamouri and Bies, 2004). Care has been taken not to use the parts of the ATB that are also used in the Prague Arabic Dependency Treebank (Haijc et al 2004) since the PADT and the ATB share material.

3.2. Methods

We implement a pipeline as follows

(1) We build a memory-based word segmenter using TIMBL (Daelemans et al, 2007) which treats segmentation as a per letter classification in which each word segment is delimited by a + sign whether it is syntactic or inflectional. A set of hand-written rules then produces tokens and stems based on this. Tokens are syntactically functional units, and stems are the tokens without the inflectional segments, For example, the word *wsytzwjhA* above is segmented as *w+s+y+tzwj+hA*. The tokenizer splits this into four tokens *w*, *s*, *ytzwj*, and *hA*, and the stemmer strips the inflectional prefix from *ytzwj* to produce *tzwj*. In the segmentation experiments, the best results were obtained with the IB1 algorithm with similarity computed as weighted overlap, relevance weights computed with gain ratio, and the number of *k* nearest distances equal to 1.

(2) The tokens are passed to the part of speech tagger. We use the Memory-based Tagger, MBT, (Daelemans et al: 2007). The MBT features for known words include the two context words to the left along with their disambiguated POS tags, the focus word itself, and one word to the right along with its ambitag (the set of all possible tags it can take). For unknown words, the features include the first five letters and the last three letters of the word, the, the left context tag, the right context

ambitag, one word to the left, the focus word itself, one ambitag to the right, and one word to the right.

(3) The column containing the linguistic features in the real world dependency experiment will have to remain vacant due to the fact that it is hard to produce these features automatically given only naturally occurring text.

(4) The dependency parser (MaltParser 1.3.1) takes all the information above and produces the data with head and dependency annotations.

Although the purpose of this experiment is to perform dependency parsing of Arabic without any assumptions, one assumption we cannot avoid is that the input text should be divided into sentences. For this purpose, we use the gold standard division of text into sentences without trying to detect the sentence boundaries, although this would be necessary in actual real-world use of dependency parsing. The reason for this is that it is not clear how sentence boundaries are marked in the data as there are sentences whose length exceeds 300 tokens. If we detected the boundaries automatically, then we would face the problem of aligning our sentences with those of the test set for evaluation, and many of the dependencies would not still hold.

In the parsing experiments below, we will use the dependency parser MaltParser (Nivre et al., 2006). We will use Single MaltParser, as used by Hall et al (2007), with the same settings for Arabic that were used in the CoNLL 2007 shared task on the same data to be as close as possible to the original results in order to be able to compare the effect of non gold standard elements in the parsing process.

3.3.Evaluation

The official evaluation metric in the CoNLL 2007 shared task on dependency parsing was the **labeled attachment score** (LAS), i.e., the percentage of tokens for which a system has predicted the correct HEAD and DEPREL, but results reported also included **unlabeled attachment score** (UAS), i.e., the percentage of tokens with correct HEAD, and the **label accuracy** (LA), i.e., the percentage of tokens with correct DEPREL. We will use the same metrics here.

One major difference between the parsing experiments which were performed in the 2007 shared task and the ones performed here is vocalization. The data set which was used in the shared task was completely vocalized with both word-internal short vowels and case markings. Since vocalization in such a perfect form is almost impossible to produce automatically, we have decided to primarily use unvocalized data instead. We have removed the word internal short vowels as well as the case markings from both the training set and the test set. This has the advantage of representing naturally occurring Arabic more closely, and the disadvantage of losing information that is only available through vocalization. We will, however, report on the effect of vocalization on dependency parsing in the discussion.

To give an estimate of the effects vocalization has on dependency parsing, we have replicated the original task with the vocalized data, and then re-run the experiment with the unvocalized version. Table 1 presents the results:

	Vocalized	**Unvocalized**
LAS	74.77%	74.16%
UAS	84.09%	83.53%
LA	85.68%	85.44%

Table 1: Vocalized versus unvocalized dependency parsing

The results of the experiment indicate that vocalization has a positive effect on the quality of the parsing output, which may be due to the fact that ambiguity decreases with vocalization. Labeled attachment score drops from 74.77% on the vocalized data to 74.16% on unvocalized data. Unlabeled attachment score drops from 84.09% to 83.53% and labeled accuracy score from 85.68% to 85.44%. The difference is minimal, and is expected to be even smaller with automatic vocalization

4. Results and discussion

4.1.Tokenization

We obtain an accuracy of 99.34%. Out of the 4550 words which the test set comprises, there are only 30 errors affecting 21 out of the 132 sentences in the test set. 17 of the errors can be characterized as over-tokenization while the other 13 are under-tokenization. 13 of the over- tokenization cases are different tokens of the word *blywn* (Eng. billion) as the initial *b* in the words was treated as a preposition while it is an original part of the word.

A closer examination of the errors in the tokenization process reveals that most of the words which are incorrectly tokenized do not occur in the training set, or occur there only in the form produced by the tokenizer. For example, the word *blywn* does not occur in the training set, but the form *b+lywn+p* occurs in the training set, and this is the reason the word is tokenized erroneously. Another example is the word *bAsm*, which is ambiguous between a one-token word *bAsm* (Eng. smiling), and a two-token word, *b+Asm* (Eng. in the name of). Although the word should be tokenized as *b+Asm*, the word occurs in the training set as *bAsm*, which is a personal name.

In fact, only five words in the 30 mis-tokenized words are available in the training set, which means that the tokenizer has a very high accuracy on known words. There are yet two examples that are worthy of discussion. The first one involves suboptimal orthography. The word *r>smAl* (Eng. capital in the financial sense) is in the training set but is nonetheless incorrectly tokenized in our experiments because it is written as *brAsmAl* (with the preposition *b*) but with an *alif* instead of the *hamza*. The word was thus not tokenized correctly. The other example involves an error in the tokenization in the Prague Arabic Dependency Treebank. The word *>wjh* (Eng. I give/address) has been tokenized in the Prague Arabic dependency treebank as >wj+h (Eng. its utmost/prime), which is not the correct tokenization in this context as the *h* is part of the word and is not a different token. The classifier did nonetheless tokenize it correctly but it was counted as wrong in the evaluation since it does not agree with the PADT gold standard.

4.2.Stemming

Since stemming involves removing all the inflectional prefixes and suffixes from the words, and since inflectional affixes are not demarcated in the PADT data set used in the CoNLL shared tasks, there is no way to know the exact accuracy of the stemming process in that specific experiment, but since stemming is a by-product of segmentation, and since segmentation in general reaches an accuracy in excess of 98%, stemming should be trusted as an accurate process.

4.3.Part of speech tagging

The performance of the tagger on gold standard data with gold standard tokenization is shown in table 2. The experiment yields an accuracy of 96.39% on all tokens. Known tokens reach an accuracy of 97.49% while unknown tokens reach an accuracy of 81.48%. These numbers constitute the ceiling for accuracy since the real-world experiment makes use of automatic tokenization, which definitely leads to lower numbers.

Unknown	Known	Total
81.48%	97.49%	96.39%

Table 2: Part of speech tagging on gold standard tokenization

When we run the experiment using automatic tokenization we obtain an accuracy of 95.70% which is less than 1% lower than the gold standard accuracy. This indicates that part of speech tagging has been affected by tokenization quality. The drop in quality in part of speech tagging is almost identical to the drop in quality in tokenization.

While some of the errors made by the part of speech tagger are due to the fact that nouns, adjectives, and proper nouns cannot be distinguished by any formal features, a large number of the nominal class annotation in the gold standard data can hardly be justified. For example, the expression الاتحاد الأوروبي (Eng. the European Union) is annotated once in the training data as proper noun and adjective, and another time as a noun and adjective. A similar confusion holds for the names of the months and the weekdays, which are sometimes tagged as nouns and sometimes as proper nouns.

4.4. Dependency parsing

Now that we have stems, tokens, and part of speech tags, we can proceed with the parsing experiment, the final step and the ultimate goal of the preprocessing modules we have introduced so far. In order to prepare the training data, we have replaced the lemmas in the training and testing sets with the stems since we do not have access to lemmas in real-world experiments. While this introduces an automatic element in the training set, it guarantees the similarity between the features in the training set and those in the test set.

In order to discover whether the fine-grained POS tagset is necessary, we have run two parsing experiments using gold standard parts of speech with stems instead of lemmas, but without any of the linguistic features included in the gold standard: the first experiment has the two distinct part of speech tags and the other one has only the coarse-grained part of speech tags. Table 3 outlines the results.

	LAS	UAS	LA
CPOS+POS	72.54%	82.92%	84.04%
CPOS	73.11%	83.31%	84.39%
CoNLL2007	74.75%	84.21%	84.21%

Table 3: effect of fine-grained POS

As can be seen from table 3, using two part of speech tagsets harms the performance of the dependency parser. While the one-tag dependency parser obtains a Labeled Accuracy Score of 73.11%, the number goes down to 72.54% when we used the fine-grained part of speech set. In Unlabeled Attachment Score, the one tag parser achieves an accuracy of 83.31% compared to 82.92% on two tag parser. The same is also true for Label Accuracy Score as the numbers go down from 84.39% when using only one tagset compared to 84.04% when using two tagsets. This means that the fine-grained tagset is not needed to perform real world parsing. We have thus decided to use the coarse-grained tagset in the two positions of the part of speech tags. We can also see that this setting produces results that are 1.64% lower than those of the Single MaltParser results reported in the CoNLL 2007 shared task in terms of Labeled Accuracy Score. The difference can be attributed to the lack of linguistic features, vocalization, and the use of stems instead of lemmas. The LAS of 73.11% now constitutes the upper bound for real world experiments where also parts of speech and tokens have to be obtained automatically (since vocalization has been removed, linguistic features have been removed, and lemmas have been replaced with automatic stems). It should be noted that our experiments, with the complete set of gold standard features, achieve higher results than those reported in the CoNLL 2007 shared task: a LAS of 74.77 (here) versus a LAS of 74.75 (CoNLL, 2007). This may be attributed to the change of the parser since we use the 1.3.1 version whereas the parser used in the 2007 shared task was the 0.4 version.

Using the settings above, we have run an experiment to parse the test set, which is now automatic in terms of tokenization, lemmatization, and part of speech tags, and in the absence of the linguistic features that enrich the gold standard training and test sets. Table 4 presents the results of this experiment.

	Automatic	Gold Standard
LAS	63.10%	73.11%
UAS	72.19%	83.31%
LA	82.61%	84.39%

Table 4: Automatic dependency parsing experiment

The LAS drops more than 10 percentage points from 73.11 to 63.10. This considerable drop in accuracy is expected since there is a mismatch in the tokenization which leads to mismatch in the sentences. The 30 errors in tokenization affect 21 sentences out of a total of 129 in the test set. When we evaluate the dependency parsing output on the correctly tokenized sentences only, we obtain much better results (shown in Table 5). Labeled Attachment Score on correctly tokenized sentences is 71.56%, Unlabeled Attachment Score 81.91%, and Label Accuracy Score is 83.22%. This indicates that no good quality parsing can be obtained if there are problems in the tokenization. A drop of a half percent in the quality of tokenization causes a drop of ten percentage points in the quality of parsing, whereas automatic POS tags and stemming, and the lack of linguistic features do not cause the same negative effect.

	Correctly-tokenized Sentences	Incorrectly-Tokenized Sentences
LAS	71.56%	33.60%
UAS	81.91%	38.32%
LA	83.22%	80.49%

Table 5: Dependency parsing Evaluation on Correctly vs. Incorrectly Tokenized Sentences

While correctly tokenized sentences yield results that are not extremely different from those using gold standard information, and the drop in accuracy in them can be attributed to the differences introduced through stemming and automatic parts of speech as well as the absence of the linguistic features, incorrectly tokenized sentences show a completely different picture as the Labeled Attachment Score now plummets to 33.6%, which is 37.96 percentage points below that on correctly tokenized sentences. The Unlabeled Attachment Score also drops from 81.91% in correctly tokenized sentences to 38.32% on incorrectly tokenized sentences with a difference of 43.59 percentage points.

Error Analysis

Considering the total number of errors, out of the 5124 tokens in the test set, there are 1425 head errors (28%), and 891 dependency errors (17%). In addition, there are 8% of the tokens in which both the dependency and the head are incorrectly assigned by the parser. The POS tag with the largest percentage of head errors is the Adverb (D) with an error rate of 57%, followed by Preposition (P) at 34%, and Conjunctions at 34%. The preposition and conjunction errors are common among all experiments: those with gold standard and those with automatic information. These results also show that assigning the correct head is more difficult than assigning the correct dependency. This is reasonable since some tokens will have specific dependency types. Also, while there are a limited number of dependency relations, the number of potential heads is much larger.

If we look at the lexicon and examine the tokens in which most errors occur, we can see one conjunction and five prepositions. The conjunction *w* (Eng. and) tops the list, followed by the preposition *l* (Eng. for, to), followed by the preposition *fy* (Eng. in), then the preposition *b* (Eng. with), then the preposition *ElY* (Eng. on), and finally the preposition *mn* (Eng. from, of). We conclude this section by examining a very short sentence in which we can see the effect of tokenization on dependency parsing. Table 6 is a sentence that has an instance of incorrect tokenization.

Arabic	المساعدات الأمريكية الاستثنائية لمصر بليون دولار حتى مارس
English	The American exceptional aid to Egypt is a billion dollars until March.
Buckwalter (Gold Standard Tokenization)	AlmsAEdAt Al>mrykyp AlAstvnA}yp l mSr **blywn** dwlAr HtY |*Ar
Buckwalter (Automatic Tokenization)	AlmsAEdAt Al>mrykyp AlAstvnA}yp l mSr **b lywn** dwlAr HtY |*Ar

Table 6: A sentence showing the effect of tokenization

The sentence has 8 words one of which comprises two tokens. The word *lmSr* comprises a preposition *l*, and the proper noun *mSr* (Eng. Egypt). The tokenizer succeeds in splitting the word into two tokens, but it fails on the one-token word *blywn* (Eng. billion) and splits it into two tokens *b* and *lywn*. The word is ambiguous between *blywn* (Eng. one billion) and *b+lywn* (Eng. in the city of Lyon), and since the second solution is much more frequent in the training set, it is the one incorrectly selected by the tokenizer.

This tokenization decision leads to an ill-alignment between the gold standard sentence and the automatic one as the gold standard has 8 tokens while the automatically produced one has 9. This thus affects the POS tagging decisions as *blywn*, which in the gold standard is a NOUN, has been now tagged as b/PREPOSITION and lywn/PROPER_NOUN. This has also affected the assignment of heads and dependency relations. While *blywn* is a predicate dependent on the root of the sentence, it has been annotated as two tokens: *b* is a preposition dependent on the subject, and *lywn* is an attribute dependent on *b*.

Using the Penn Tags

So far, we have used only the POS tags of the PADT, and have not discussed the possibility of using the Penn Arabic Treebank. The difference is that the PADT tags are basic while the ATB ones have detailed representations of inflections. While the word *AlmtHdp* is given the tag ADJ in the PADT, it is tagged as DET+ADJ+FEMININE_SINGULAR_MARKER in the ATB. Table 7 shows the effect of using the Penn tagset with the gold standard full-featured dataset in three different experiments as compared with the PADT tagset:

(1) The original Unvocalized Experiment with the full set of features and gold standard components. The Penn tagset is not used in this experiment, and it is provided for reference purposes only.
(2) Unvocalized experiment with Penn tags as CPOS tags. In this experiment, the Penn tagset is used instead of the coarse grained POS tagset, while the fine-grained pos tagset remains unchanged.
(3) Using Penn tags as fine grained POS tags, while the CPOS tags remain unchanged.
(4) Using the Penn POS tags in both positions.

In the four experiments, the only features that change are the POS and CPOS features.

Experiment	**LAS**	**UAS**
Unvocalized Original	74.16%	83.53 %
Using Penn Tags as CPOS tags	74.12%	83.43 %
Using Penn tags as POS	72.40%	81.79 %
Using Penn tags in both positions	69.63%	79.33 %

Table 7: Using the ATB tagset with the PADT dataset

As can be seen from Table 7, in all three cases the Penn tagset produces lower results than the PADT tagset. The reason for this may be that the tagset is automatic in both cases, and the perfect accuracy of the PADT tags helps the classifier embedded in the MaltParser parser to choose the correct label and head. The results also show that when we use the Penn tagset as the CPOS tagset, the results are almost no different from the gold standard PADT tagset (74.12% vs. 74.16%). The fact that the Penn tagset does not harm the results encourages the inclusion of the Penn tags as CPOS tags in the automatic experiments that have been used throughout this chapter. The worst results are those obtained by using the Penn tags in both positions (POS and CPOS).

Using the Penn tagset with the reduced experiments, those without the linguistic features, gives a different picture from that in the full standard experiments, as detailed in table 8.

Experiment	**LAS**	**UAS**
Reduced with both PADT tags	72.54%	82.92 %
Reduced with Penn tags as CPOS	73.09%	83.16 %
Reduced with Penn tags as CPOS and automatic tokenization	63.11%	72.38 %

Table 8: Including the Penn full tagset in the reduced experiments

While the Penn tagset does not help improve parsing accuracy with the full-featured parsing experiments, it helps with the reduced experiments. While the experiment without the Penn tags score an LAS of 72.54%, replacing the CPOS tags in this experiment with the Penn tagset raises the accuracy to 73.09%, with an increase of 0.55%. This may be due to the fact that the full tagset gives more information that helps the parser. The increase is not as noticeable in the automatic tokenization experiment where the accuracy minimally changes from 63.10% to 63.11%.

Effect of Vocalization

We have stated in the methodology section that we use unvocalized data since naturally occurring Arabic is hardly vocalized. While this is a reasonable approach, it is worth checking the effect of vocalization on dependency parsing. Table 9 presents the results of vocalization effect in three experiments: (a) All the gold standard features with vocalization. This is the experiment reported in the literature on Arabic dependency parsing in CoNLL (2007), (b) All the gold standard features without the vocalization, (c) All gold standard features except for vocalization which is automatic, and (d) the automatic experiment with automatic vocalization. The vocalizer in the latter 2 experiments is trained on the PADT. The TIMBL memory-based learner is used in the experiment. The best results are obtained with the IB1 algorithm with similarity computed as weighted overlap,. Relevance weights are computed with gain ratio, and the number of *k* nearest neighbors is set to 1. The vocalizer has an accuracy of 93.8% on the PADT test set.

Experiment	LAS	UAS
Fully Gold Standard Vocalized	74.77%	84.09 %
Fully Gold Standard Unvocalized	74.16%	83.53 %
Full-featured with automatic vocalization	74.43%	83.88 %
Completely automatic (with automatic vocalization)	63.11%	72.19 %
Completely automatic without vocalization	63.11%	72.38 %

Table 9: Vocalization Effect on Dependency Parsing

As can be seen from Table 9, gold standard vocalization with gold standard features produces the best results (LAS: 74.77%) followed by the same settings, but with automatic vocalization with a LAS of 74.43%, then unvocalized gold standard with a LAS of 74.16%. The fact that even automatic vocalization produces better results than unvocalized text given the same conditions, in spite of a token error rate of 6.2%, may be attributed to the ability of vocalization to disambiguate text even when it is not perfect. We can also notice that the LAS for the Automatic experiment is the same whether or not vocalization is used. This indicates that vocalization, in spite of its imperfections, does not harm performance, although it also does not help the parser. Tokenization sets a ceiling for parsing accuracy.

5. Conclusion

We have presented an experiment in real world dependency parsing of Arabic using the same data, algorithm and settings used in the CoNLL (2007) shared task on dependency parsing. The real world experiment included performing tokenization, stemming, and part of speech tagging of the data before it was passed to MaltParser.

Tokenization was performed using the memory-based segmenter/tokenizer/stemmer and it reached an accuracy of 99.34% on the CoNLL 2007 test set. We performed stemming rather than lemmatization due to the many problems and difficulties involved in obtaining the lemmas.

Part of speech tagging scored 96.39% on all tokens on gold standard tokenization, but the accuracy dropped to 95.70% on automatic tokens. We also found that using the coarse grained POS tagset alone yielded better results than using it in combination with the fine-grained POS tagset.

The tokens, stems, and CPOS tags were then fed into the dependency parser, but the linguistic features were not since it was not feasible to obtain these automatically. The parser yielded a Labeled Accuracy Score of 63.10%, more than 10% below the accuracy obtained on when all the components are gold standard. The main reason behind the accuracy drop is the tokenization module, since tokenization is responsible for creating the nodes that carry syntactic functions. Since this process was not perfect, many nodes were wrong, and the right heads were missing. When we evaluated the parser on correctly tokenized sentences, we obtained a Labeled Accuracy Score of 71.56%. On incorrectly tokenized sentences, however, the LAS score drops to 33.60%.

We have also found that the full tagset of the Penn Arabic Treebank improves parsing results minimally in the automatic experiments, but not in the gold standard experiments.

Vocalization does not help in the real world experiment unlike in the gold standard one.

These results show that tokenization is the major hindrance to obtaining high quality parsing in Arabic. Arabic computational linguistics should thus focus on ways to perfect tokenization, or try to find ways to parsing without having to perform tokenization.

Acknowledgment

We would like to thank Joakim Nivre for his helpful answers to our questions concerning MaltParser.

References

Buchholz, Sabine and Marsi, Erwin (2006). *CoNLL-X shared task on multilingual dependency parsing*. In Proceedings of the 10th Conference on Computational Natural Language Learning (CoNLL), pages 149–164.

Daelemans, Walter; Zavrel, Jakub; van der Sloot, Ko and van den Bosch, Antal (2007). *TiMBL: Tilburg memory based learner – version 6.1 – reference guide*. Technical Report ILK 07-09, Induction of Linguistic Knowledge, Computational Linguistics, Tilburg University.

Daelemans, Walter,; Zavrel, Jakub; an den Bosch, Antal, and van der Sloot, Ko (2007). MBT: Memory-Based Tagger- Version 3.1. Reference Guide. Technical Report ILK 07-09, Induction of Linguistic Knowledge, Computational Linguistics, Tilburg University.

Hajič, Jan; Smrž, Otakar; Zemánek, Petr; Šnaidauf, Jan, and Beška, Emanuel (2004). *Prague Arabic Dependency Treebank: Development in Data and Tools*. In *Proceedings of the EMLAR International Conference on Arabic Language Resources and Tools*, pages 110-117, Cairo, Egypt, September 2004.

Hall, Johan; Nilsson, Jens; Nivre, Joakim; Eryigit, Gülsen; Megyesi, Beáta; Nilsson, Mattias and Saers, Markus (2007). Single Malt or Blended? A Study in Multilingual Parser Optimization. In *Proceedings of the CoNLL Shared Task Session of EMNLP-CoNLL 2007*, 933-939.

Maamouri, Mohamed and Bies, Ann (2004) *Developing an Arabic Treebank: Methods, Guidelines, Procedures, and Tools.* In Proceedings of the Workshop on Computational Approaches to Arabic Script-based Languages, COLING 2004, Geneva, August 28, 2004.

Marton, Yuval; Habash, Nizar; and Rambow, Owen (2010). Improving Arabic Dependency Parsing with Lexical and Inflectional Morphological Features. In *Proceddings of The FirstWorkshop on Statistical Parsing of Morphologically Rich Languages* (SPMRL 2010), LA, California.

McDonald, Ryan; Lerman, Kevin and Pereira, Fernando (2006). *Multilingual dependency analysis with a two-stage discriminative parser*. CoNLLX shared task on multilingual dependency parsing. In Proceedings of the 10th Conference on Computational Natural Language Learning

Nivre, Joakim; Hall, Jonathan; Nilsson, Jens; Eryigit, Gülsen and Marinov, Svetsolav (2006). Labeled Pseudo-Projective Dependency Parsing with Support Vector Machines. In *Proceedings of the Tenth Conference on Computational Natural Language Learning (CoNLL)*

Nivre, Joakim; Hall, Johan; Kübler, Sandra; McDonald, Ryan; Nilsson, Jens; Riedel, Sebastian, and Yuret, Deniz. (2007). *The CoNLL 2007 shared task on dependency parsing*. In Proceedings of the CoNLL Shared Task of EMNLP-CoNLL 2007, pages 915–932

Owen, Jonathan. *The Arabic Grammatical Tradition*. In Hetzron, Robert (ed.) (1997). *The Semitic Languages*. Routledge, London.

Punctuation: Making a Point in Unsupervised Dependency Parsing

Valentin I. Spitkovsky
Computer Science Department
Stanford University and Google Inc.
valentin@cs.stanford.edu

Hiyan Alshawi
Google Inc.
Mountain View, CA, 94043, USA
hiyan@google.com

Daniel Jurafsky
Departments of Linguistics and Computer Science
Stanford University, Stanford, CA, 94305, USA
jurafsky@stanford.edu

Abstract

We show how punctuation can be used to improve unsupervised dependency parsing. Our linguistic analysis confirms the strong connection between English punctuation and phrase boundaries in the Penn Treebank. However, approaches that naively include punctuation marks in the grammar (as if they were words) do not perform well with Klein and Manning's Dependency Model with Valence (DMV). Instead, we split a sentence at punctuation and impose parsing restrictions over its fragments. Our grammar inducer is trained on the Wall Street Journal (WSJ) and achieves 59.5% accuracy out-of-domain (Brown sentences with 100 or fewer words), more than 6% higher than the previous best results. Further evaluation, using the 2006/7 CoNLL sets, reveals that punctuation aids grammar induction in 17 of 18 languages, for an overall average net gain of 1.3%. Some of this improvement is from training, but more than half is from parsing with induced constraints, in inference. Punctuation-aware decoding works with existing (even already-trained) parsing models and always increased accuracy in our experiments.

1 Introduction

Unsupervised dependency parsing is a type of grammar induction — a central problem in computational linguistics. It aims to uncover hidden relations between head words and their dependents in free-form text. Despite decades of significant research efforts, the task still poses a challenge, as sentence structure is underdetermined by only raw, unannotated words.

Structure can be clearer in *formatted* text, which typically includes proper capitalization and punctuation (Gravano et al., 2009). Raw word streams, such as utterances transcribed by speech recognizers, are often difficult even for humans (Kim and Woodland, 2002). Therefore, one would expect grammar inducers to exploit any available linguistic meta-data. And yet in unsupervised dependency parsing, sentence-internal punctuation has long been ignored (Carroll and Charniak, 1992; Paskin, 2001; Klein and Manning, 2004; Blunsom and Cohn, 2010, *inter alia*).

HTML is another kind of meta-data that is ordinarily stripped out in pre-processing. However, recently Spitkovsky et al. (2010b) demonstrated that web markup can successfully guide hierarchical syntactic structure discovery, observing, for example, that anchors often match linguistic constituents:

> ..., whereas McCain is secure on the topic, Obama <a>$[_{\text{VP}}$ worries about winning the pro-Israel vote$]$</a>.

We propose exploring punctuation's potential to aid grammar induction. Consider a motivating example (all of our examples are from WSJ), in which all (six) marks align with constituent boundaries:

> $[_{\text{SBAR}}$ Although it probably has reduced the level of expenditures for some purchasers$]$, $[_{\text{NP}}$ utilization management$]$ — $[_{\text{PP}}$ like most other cost containment strategies$]$ — $[_{\text{VP}}$ doesn't appear to have altered the long-term rate of increase in health-care costs$]$, $[_{\text{NP}}$ the Institute of Medicine$]$, $[_{\text{NP}}$ an affiliate of the National Academy of Sciences$]$, $[_{\text{VP}}$ concluded after a two-year study$]$.

This link between punctuation and constituent boundaries suggests that we could approximate parsing by treating inter-punctuation fragments independently. In training, our algorithm first parses each fragment separately, then parses the sequence of the resulting head words. In inference, we use a better approximation that allows heads of fragments to be attached by arbitrary external words, e.g.:

> The Soviets complicated the issue by offering to $[_{\text{VP}}$ include light tanks$]$, $[_{\text{SBAR}}$ which are as light as ... $]$.

Proceedings of the Fifteenth Conference on Computational Natural Language Learning, pages 19–28,
Portland, Oregon, USA, 23–24 June 2011.

	Count	POS Sequence	Frac	Cum
1	3,492	NNP	2.8%	
2	2,716	CD CD	2.2	5.0
3	2,519	NNP NNP	2.0	7.1
4	2,512	RB	2.0	9.1
5	1,495	CD	1.2	10.3
6	1,025	NN	0.8	11.1
7	1,023	NNP NNP NNP	0.8	11.9
8	916	IN NN	0.7	12.7
9	795	VBZ NNP NNP	0.6	13.3
10	748	CC	0.6	13.9
11	730	CD DT NN	0.6	14.5
12	705	PRP VBD	0.6	15.1
13	652	JJ NN	0.5	15.6
14	648	DT NN	0.5	16.1
15	627	IN DT NN	0.5	16.6
WSJ	+103,148	*more with Count* ≤ 621	83.4%	

Table 1: Top 15 fragments of POS tag sequences in WSJ.

	Count	Non-Terminal	Frac	Cum
1	40,223	S	32.5%	
2	33,607	NP	27.2	59.7
3	16,413	VP	13.3	72.9
4	12,441	PP	10.1	83.0
5	8,350	SBAR	6.7	89.7
6	4,085	ADVP	3.3	93.0
7	3,080	QP	2.5	95.5
8	2,480	SINV	2.0	97.5
9	1,257	ADJP	1.0	98.5
10	369	PRN	0.3	98.8
WSJ	+1,446	*more with Count* ≤ 356	1.2%	

Table 2: Top 99% of the lowest dominating non-terminals deriving complete inter-punctuation fragments in WSJ.

2 Definitions, Analyses and Constraints

Punctuation and syntax are related (Nunberg, 1990; Briscoe, 1994; Jones, 1994; Doran, 1998, *inter alia*). But are there simple enough connections between the two to aid in grammar induction? This section explores the regularities. Our study of punctuation in WSJ (Marcus et al., 1993) parallels Spitkovsky et al.'s (2010b, §5) analysis of markup from a weblog, since their proposed constraints turn out to be useful. Throughout, we define an inter-punctuation ***fragment*** as a maximal (non-empty) consecutive sequence of words that does not cross punctuation boundaries and is shorter than its source sentence.

2.1 A Linguistic Analysis

Out of 51,558 sentences, most — 37,076 (71.9%) — contain sentence-internal punctuation. These punctuated sentences contain 123,751 fragments, nearly all — 111,774 (90.3%) — of them multi-token. Common part-of-speech (POS) sequences comprising fragments are diverse (note also their flat distribution — see Table 1). The plurality of fragments are dominated by a clause, but most are dominated by one of several kinds of phrases (see Table 2). As expected, punctuation does not occur at all constituent boundaries: Of the top 15 productions that yield fragments, five do *not* match the exact bracketing of their lowest dominating non-terminal (see ranks 6, 11, 12, 14 and 15 in Table 3, left). Four of them miss a left-adjacent clause, e.g., S → S NP VP:

$[_S$ $[_S$ It's an overwhelming job$]$, $[_{NP}$ she$]$ $[_{VP}$ says.$]]$

This production is flagged because the fragment NP VP is not *a* constituent — it is two; still, **49.4**% of all fragments do align with whole constituents.

Inter-punctuation fragments correspond more strongly to dependencies (see Table 3, right). Only one production (rank 14) shows a daughter outside her mother's fragment. Some number of such productions is inevitable and expected, since fragments must coalesce (i.e., the root of at least one fragment — in every sentence with sentence-internal punctuation — must be attached by some word from a different, external fragment). We find it noteworthy that in 14 of the 15 most common cases, a word in an inter-punctuation fragment derives precisely the rest of that fragment, attaching none of the other, external words. This is true for **39.2**% of all fragments, and if we include fragments whose heads attach other fragments' heads, agreement increases to **74.0**% (see *strict* and *loose* constraints in §2.2, next).

2.2 Five Parsing Constraints

Spitkovsky et al. (2010b, §5.3) showed how to express similar correspondences with markup as parsing constraints. They proposed four constraints but employed only the strictest three, omitting implementation details. We revisit their constraints, specifying precise logical formulations that we use in our code, and introduce a fifth (most relaxed) constraint.

Let $[x, y]$ be a fragment (or markup) spanning positions x through y (inclusive, with $1 \leq x < y \leq l$), in a sentence of length l. And let $[i, j]_h$ be a sealed span headed by h ($1 \leq i \leq h \leq j \leq l$), i.e., the word at position h dominates precisely $i \ldots j$ (but none other):

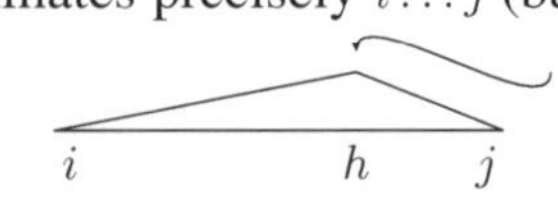

	Count	Constituent Production	Frac	Cum
1	7,115	PP → IN NP	5.7%	
2	5,950	S → NP VP	4.8	10.6
3	3,450	NP → NP PP	2.8	13.3
4	2,799	SBAR → WHNP S	2.3	15.6
5	2,695	NP → NNP	2.2	17.8
6	2,615	S → S NP VP	2.1	19.9
7	2,480	SBAR → IN S	2.0	21.9
8	2,392	NP → NNP NNP	1.9	23.8
9	2,354	ADVP → RB	1.9	25.7
10	2,334	QP → CD CD	1.9	27.6
11	2,213	S → PP NP VP	1.8	29.4
12	1,441	S → S CC S	1.2	30.6
13	1,317	NP → NP NP	1.1	31.6
14	1,314	S → SBAR NP VP	1.1	32.7
15	1,172	SINV → S VP NP NP	0.9	33.6
WSJ	+82,110	*more with Count* ≤ 976	66.4%	

	Count	Head-Outward Spawn	Frac	Cum
1	11,928	IN	9.6%	
2	8,852	NN	7.2	16.8
3	7,802	NNP	6.3	23.1
4	4,750	CD	3.8	26.9
5	3,914	VBD	3.2	30.1
6	3,672	VBZ	3.0	33.1
7	3,436	RB	2.8	35.8
8	2,691	VBG	2.2	38.0
9	2,304	VBP	1.9	39.9
10	2,251	NNS	1.8	41.7
11	1,955	WDT	1.6	43.3
12	1,409	MD	1.1	44.4
13	1,377	VBN	1.1	45.5
14	1,204	IN VBD	1.0	46.5
15	927	JJ	0.7	47.3
WSJ	+65,279	*more with Count* ≤ 846	52.8%	

Table 3: Top 15 productions yielding punctuation-induced fragments in WSJ, viewed as constituents (left) and as dependencies (right). For constituents, we recursively expanded any internal nodes that did not align with the associated fragmentation (underlined). For dependencies we dropped all daughters that fell entirely in the same region as their mother (i.e., both inside a fragment, both to its left or both to its right), keeping only crossing attachments (just one).

Define $inside(h, x, y)$ as true iff $x \leq h \leq y$; and let $cross(i, j, x, y)$ be true iff $(i < x \wedge j \geq x \wedge j < y) \vee (i > x \wedge i \leq y \wedge j > y)$. The three tightest constraints impose conditions which, when satisfied, disallow sealing $[i, j]_h$ in the presence of an annotation $[x, y]$:

strict — requires $[x, y]$ itself to be sealed in the parse tree, voiding all seals that straddle exactly one of $\{x, y\}$ or protrude beyond $[x, y]$ if their head is inside. This constraint holds for **39.2%** of fragments. By contrast, only 35.6% of HTML annotations, such as anchor texts and italics, agree with it (Spitkovsky et al., 2010b). This necessarily fails in every sentence with internal punctuation (since there, *some* fragment must take charge and attach another), when $cross(i, j, x, y) \vee (inside(h, x, y) \wedge (i < x \vee j > y))$.

... the British daily newspaper, The Financial Times .
$x = i$ $h = j = y$

loose — if $h \in [x, y]$, requires that everything in $x \ldots y$ fall under h, with only h allowed external attachments. This holds for **74.0%** of fragments — 87.5% of markup, failing when $cross(i, j, x, y)$.

... arrests followed a " Snake Day " at Utrecht ...
i x $h = j = y$

sprawl — still requires that h derive $x \ldots y$ but lifts restrictions on external attachments. Holding for **92.9%** of fragments (95.1% of markup), it fails when $cross(i, j, x, y) \wedge \neg inside(h, x, y)$.

Maryland Club also distributes tea , which ...
$x = i$ h y j

These three strictest constraints lend themselves to a straight-forward implementation as an $O(l^5)$ chart-based decoder. Ordinarily, the probability of $[i, j]_h$ is computed by multiplying the probability of the associated *un*sealed span by two stopping probabilities — that of the word at h on the left (adjacent if $i = h$; non-adjacent if $i < h$) and on the right (adjacent if $h = j$; non-adjacent if $h < j$). To impose a constraint, we ran through all of the annotations $[x, y]$ associated with a sentence and zeroed out this probability if any of them satisfied disallowed conditions.

There are faster — e.g., $O(l^4)$, and even $O(l^3)$ — recognizers for split head automaton grammars (Eisner and Satta, 1999). Perhaps a more practical, but still clear, approach would be to generate n-best lists using a more efficient unconstrained algorithm, then apply the constraints as a post-filtering step.

Relaxed constraints disallow joining adjacent subtrees, e.g., preventing the seal $[i, j]_h$ from merging below the *un*sealed span $[j+1, J]_H$, on the left:

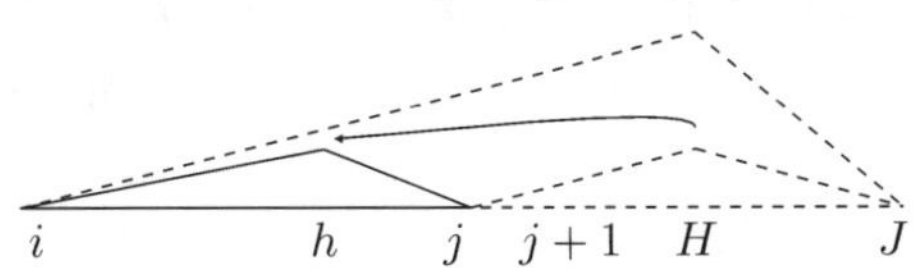

tear — prevents $x \ldots y$ from being torn apart by external heads from *opposite* sides. It holds for **94.7**% of fragments (97.9% of markup), and is violated when $(x \leq j \wedge y > j \wedge h < x)$, in this case.

... they "were not consulted about the [Ridley decision]

in advance and were surprised at the action taken .

thread — requires only that no path from the root to a leaf enter $[x, y]$ twice. This holds for **95.0**% of all fragments (98.5% of markup); it is violated when $(x \leq j \wedge y > j \wedge h < x) \wedge (H \leq y)$, again, in this case. Example that satisfies *thread* but violates *tear*:

The ... changes "all make a lot of sense to me," he added.

The case when $[i, j]_h$ is to the right is entirely symmetric, and these constraints could be incorporated in a more sophisticated decoder (since i and J do not appear in the formulae, above). We implemented them by zeroing out the probability of the word at H attaching that at h (to its left), in case of a violation.

Note that all five constraints are nested. In particular, this means that it does not make sense to combine them, for a given annotation $[x, y]$, since the result would just match the strictest one. Our markup number for *tear* is lower (97.9 versus 98.9%) than Spitkovsky et al.'s (2010b), because theirs allowed cases where markup was *neither* torn nor threaded.

Common structures that violate *thread* (and, consequently, all five of the constraints) include, e.g., "seamless" quotations and even ordinary lists:

Her recent report classifies the stock as a "hold."

The company said its directors, management and subsidiaries will remain long-term investors and ...

2.3 Comparison with Markup

Most punctuation-induced constraints are less accurate than the corresponding markup-induced constraints (e.g., *sprawl*: 92.9 vs. 95.1%; *loose*: 74.0 vs. 87.5%; but not *strict*: 39.2 vs. 35.6%). However, markup is rare: Spitkovsky et al. (2010b, §5.1) observed that only 10% of the sentences in their blog were annotated; in contrast, over 70% of the sentences in WSJ are fragmented by punctuation.

Fragments are more than 40% likely to be dominated by a clause; for markup, this number is below 10% — nearly 75% of it covered by noun phrases. Further, inter-punctuation fragments are spread more evenly under noun, verb, prepositional, adverbial and adjectival phrases (approximately 27:13:10:3:1 versus 75:13:2:1:1) than markup.[1]

3 The Model, Methods and Metrics

We model grammar via Klein and Manning's (2004) Dependency Model with Valence (DMV), which ordinarily strips out punctuation. Since this step already requires identification of marks, our techniques are just as "unsupervised." We would have preferred to test punctuation in their original set-up, but this approach wasn't optimal, for several reasons. First, Klein and Manning (2004) trained with short sentences (up to only ten words, on WSJ10), whereas most punctuation appears in longer sentences. And second, although we could augment the training data (say, to WSJ45), Spitkovsky et al. (2010a) showed that classic EM struggles with longer sentences. For this reason, we use Viterbi EM and the scaffolding suggested by Spitkovsky et al. (2010a) — also the setting in which Spitkovsky et al. (2010b) tested their markup-induced constraints.

3.1 A Basic System

Our system is based on Laplace-smoothed Viterbi EM, following Spitkovsky et al.'s (2010a) two-stage scaffolding: the first stage trains with just the sentences up to length 15; the second stage then retrains on nearly all sentences — those with up to 45 words.

Initialization

Klein and Manning's (2004) "ad-hoc harmonic" initializer does not work very well for longer sentences, particularly with Viterbi training (Spitkovsky et al., 2010a, Figure 3). Instead, we use an improved initializer that approximates the attachment probability between two words as an average, over all sentences, of their normalized aggregate *weighted* distances. Our weighting function is $w(d) = 1 + 1/\lg(1 + d)$.[2]

Termination

Spitkovsky et al. (2010a) iterated until successive changes in overall (best parse) per-token cross-entropy dropped below 2^{-20} bits. Since smoothing can (and does, at times) increase the objective, we found it more efficient to terminate early, after ten

[1]Markup and fragments are as likely to be in verb phrases.

[2]Integer $d \geq 1$ is a distance between two tokens; lg is $\log_2$.

steps of suboptimal models. We used the lowest-perplexity (not necessarily the last) model found, as measured by the cross-entropy of the training data.

Constrained Training

Training with punctuation replaces ordinary Viterbi parse trees, at every iteration of EM, with the output of a constrained decoder. In all experiments other than #2 (§5) we train with the *loose* constraint. Spitkovsky et al. (2010b) found this setting to be best for markup-induced constraints. We apply it to constraints induced by inter-punctuation fragments.

Constrained Inference

Spitkovsky et al. (2010b) recommended using the *sprawl* constraint in inference. Once again, we follow their advice in all experiments except #2 (§5).

3.2 Data Sets and Scoring

We trained on the Penn English Treebank's Wall Street Journal portion (Marcus et al., 1993). To evaluate, we automatically converted its labeled constituents into unlabeled dependencies, using deterministic "head-percolation" rules (Collins, 1999), discarding punctuation, any empty nodes, etc., as is standard practice (Paskin, 2001; Klein and Manning, 2004). We also evaluated against the parsed portion of the Brown corpus (Francis and Kučera, 1979), used as a blind, out-of-domain evaluation set,[3] similarly derived from labeled constituent parse trees.

We report directed accuracies — fractions of correctly guessed arcs, including the root, in unlabeled reference dependency parse trees, as is also standard practice (Paskin, 2001; Klein and Manning, 2004). One of our baseline systems (§3.3) produces dependency trees containing punctuation. In this case we do not score the heads assigned to punctuation and use *forgiving scoring* for regular words: crediting correct heads separated from their children by punctuation alone (from the point of view of the child, looking up to the nearest non-punctuation ancestor).

3.3 Baseline Systems

Our primary baseline is the basic system without constraints (*standard training*). It ignores punctuation, as is standard, scoring 52.0% against WSJ45.

A secondary (*punctuation as words*) baseline incorporates punctuation into the grammar as if it were words, as in *supervised* dependency parsing (Nivre et al., 2007b; Lin, 1998; Sleator and Temperley, 1993, *inter alia*). It is worse, scoring only 41.0%.[4,5]

4 Experiment #1: Default Constraints

Our first experiment compares "punctuation as constraints" to the baseline systems. We use default settings, as recommended by Spitkovsky et al. (2010b): *loose* in training; and *sprawl* in inference. Evaluation is on Section 23 of WSJ (all sentence lengths). To facilitate comparison with prior work, we also report accuracies against shorter sentences, with up to ten non-punctuation tokens (WSJ10 — see Table 4).

We find that both constrained regimes improve performance. Constrained decoding alone increases the accuracy of a standardly-trained system from 52.0% to 54.0%. And constrained training yields 55.6% — 57.4% in combination with inference.

	WSJ^{∞}	WSJ10
Supervised DMV	69.8	83.6
w/Constrained Inference	73.0	84.3
Punctuation as Words	41.7	54.8
Standard Training	52.0	63.2
w/Constrained Inference	54.0	63.6
Constrained Training	55.6	67.0
w/Constrained Inference	**57.4**	**67.5**

Table 4: Directed accuracies on Section 23 of WSJ^{∞} and WSJ10 for the supervised DMV, our baseline systems and the punctuation runs (all using the weighted initializer).

[3]Note that WSJ$\{15, 45\}$ overlap with Section 23 — training on the test set is standard practice in unsupervised learning.

[4]We were careful to use exactly the same data sets in both cases, not counting punctuation towards sentence lengths. And we used forgiving scoring (§3.2) when evaluating these trees.

[5]To get this particular number we forced punctuation to be tacked on, as a layer below the tree of words, to fairly compare systems (using the same initializer). Since improved initialization strategies — both ours and Klein and Manning's (2004) "ad-hoc harmonic" initializer — rely on distances between tokens, they could be unfairly biased towards one approach or the other, if punctuation counted towards length. We also trained similar baselines without restrictions, allowing punctuation to appear anywhere in the tree (still with forgiving scoring — see §3.2), using the uninformed uniform initializer (Spitkovsky et al., 2010a). Disallowing punctuation as a parent of a real word made things worse, suggesting that not all marks belong near the leaves (sentence stops, semicolons, colons, etc. make more sense as roots and heads). We tried the weighted initializer also without restrictions and repeated all experiments without scaffolding, on WSJ15 and WSJ45 alone, but treating punctuation as words never came within even 5% of (comparable) standard training. Punctuation, as words, reliably disrupted learning.

These are multi-point increases, but they could disappear in a more accurate state-of-the-art system.

To test this hypothesis, we applied constrained decoding to a *supervised* system. We found that this (ideal) instantiation of the DMV benefits as much or more than the unsupervised systems: accuracy increases from 69.8% to 73.0%. Punctuation seems to capture the kinds of, perhaps long-distance, regularities that are not accessible to the model, possibly because of its unrealistic independence assumptions.

5 Experiment #2: Optimal Settings

Spitkovsky et al. (2010b) recommended training with *loose* and decoding with *sprawl* based on their experiments with markup. But are these the right settings for punctuation? Inter-punctuation fragments are quite different from markup — they are more prevalent but less accurate. Furthermore, we introduced a new constraint, *thread*, that Spitkovsky et al. (2010b) had not considered (along with *tear*).

We next re-examined the choices of constraints. Our full factorial analysis was similar, but significantly smaller, than Spitkovsky et al.'s (2010b): we excluded their larger-scale news and web data sets that are not publicly available. Nevertheless, we still tried every meaningful combination of settings, testing both *thread* and *tear* (instead of *strict*, since it can't work with sentences containing sentence-internal punctuation), in both training and inference. We did not find better settings than *loose* for training, and *sprawl* for decoding, among our options.

A full analysis is omitted due to space constraints. Our first observation is that constrained inference, using punctuation, is helpful and robust. It boosted accuracy (on WSJ45) by approximately 1.5%, on average, with all settings. Indeed, *sprawl* was consistently (but only slightly, at 1.6%, on average) better than the rest. Second, constrained training hurt more often than it helped. It degraded accuracy in all but one case, *loose*, where it gained approximately 0.4%, on average. Both improvements are statistically significant: $p \approx 0.036$ for training with *loose*; and $p \approx 5.6 \times 10^{-12}$ for decoding with *sprawl*.

6 More Advanced Methods

So far, punctuation has improved grammar induction in a toy setting. But would it help a modern system? Our next two experiments employ a slightly more complicated set-up, compared with the one used up until now (§3.1). The key difference is that this system is lexicalized, as is standard among the more accurate grammar inducers (Blunsom and Cohn, 2010; Gillenwater et al., 2010; Headden et al., 2009).

Lexicalization

We lexicalize only in the second (full data) stage, using the method of Headden et al. (2009). For words seen at least 100 times in the training corpus, we augment their gold POS tag with the lexical item. The first (data poor) stage remains entirely unlexicalized, with gold POS tags for word classes, as in the earlier systems (Klein and Manning, 2004).

Smoothing

We do not use smoothing in the second stage except at the end, for the final lexicalized model. Stage one still applies "add-one" smoothing at every iteration.

7 Experiment #3: State-of-the-Art

The purpose of these experiments is to compare the punctuation-enhanced DMV with other, recent state-of-the-art systems. We find that, lexicalized (§6), our approach performs better, by a wide margin; without lexicalization (§3.1), it was already better for longer, but not for shorter, sentences (see Tables 5 and 4).

We trained a variant of our system *without* gold part-of-speech tags, using the unsupervised word clusters (Clark, 2000) computed by Finkel and Manning (2009).[6] Accuracy decreased slightly, to 58.2% on Section 23 of WSJ (down only 0.2%). This result improves over substantial performance degradations previously observed for unsupervised dependency parsing with induced word categories (Klein and Manning, 2004; Headden et al., 2008, *inter alia*).

[6] Available from `http://nlp.stanford.edu/software/stanford-postagger-2008-09-28.tar.gz:models/egw.bnc.200`

	Brown	WSJ^{∞}	WSJ10
(Headden et al., 2009)	—	—	68.8
(Spitkovsky et al., 2010b)	53.3	50.4	69.3
(Gillenwater et al., 2010)	—	53.3	64.3
(Blunsom and Cohn, 2010)	—	55.7	67.7
Constrained Training	58.4	58.0	69.3
w/Constrained Inference	**59.5**	**58.4**	**69.5**

Table 5: Accuracies on the out-of-domain Brown100 set and Section 23 of WSJ^{∞} and WSJ10, for the lexicalized punctuation run and other recent state-of-the-art systems.

	Unlexicalized, Unpunctuated				*Lexicalized*		... ***and** Punctuated*		
CoNLL Year	*Initialization @15*		*Training @15*		*Retraining @45*		*Retraining @45*		*Net*
& Language	*1.*	*w/Inference*	*2.*	*w/Inference*	*3.*	*w/Inference*	*3′.*	*w/Inference*	*Gain*
Arabic 2006	23.3	23.6 (+0.3)	32.8	33.1 (+0.4)	31.5	31.6 (+0.1)	32.1	32.6 (+0.5)	+1.1
'7	25.6	26.4 (+0.8)	33.7	34.2 (+0.5)	32.7	33.6 (+0.9)	34.9	35.3 (+0.4)	+2.6
Basque '7	19.3	20.8 (+1.5)	29.9	30.9 (+1.0)	29.3	30.1 (+0.8)	29.3	29.9 (+0.6)	+0.6
Bulgarian '6	23.7	24.7 (+1.0)	39.3	40.7 (+1.4)	38.8	39.9 (+1.1)	39.9	40.5 (+0.6)	+1.6
Catalan '7	33.2	34.1 (+0.8)	54.8	55.5 (+0.7)	54.3	55.1 (+0.8)	54.3	55.2 (+0.9)	+0.9
Czech '6	18.6	19.6 (+1.0)	34.6	35.8 (+1.2)	34.8	35.7 (+0.9)	37.0	37.8 (+0.8)	+3.0
'7	17.6	18.4 (+0.8)	33.5	35.4 (+1.9)	33.4	34.4 (+1.0)	35.2	36.2 (+1.0)	+2.7
Danish '6	22.9	24.0 (+1.1)	35.6	36.7 (+1.2)	36.9	37.8 (+0.9)	36.5	37.1 (+0.6)	+0.2
Dutch '6	15.8	16.5 (+0.7)	*11.2*	12.5 (+1.3)	11.0	11.9 (+1.0)	13.7	14.0 (+0.3)	+3.0
English '7	25.0	25.4 (+0.5)	47.2	49.5 (+2.3)	47.5	48.8 (+1.3)	49.3	50.3 (+0.9)	+2.8
German '6	19.2	19.6 (+0.4)	27.4	28.0 (+0.7)	27.0	27.8 (+0.8)	28.2	28.6 (+0.4)	+1.6
Greek '7	18.5	18.8 (+0.3)	20.7	21.4 (+0.7)	20.5	21.0 (+0.5)	20.9	21.2 (+0.3)	+0.7
Hungarian '7	17.4	17.7 (+0.3)	*6.7*	7.2 (+0.5)	6.6	7.0 (+0.4)	7.8	8.0 (+0.2)	+1.4
Italian '7	25.0	26.3 (+1.2)	29.6	29.9 (+0.3)	29.7	29.7 (+0.1)	28.3	28.8 (+0.5)	*-0.8*
Japanese '6	30.0	30.0 (+0.0)	*27.3*	27.3 (+0.0)	27.4	27.4 (+0.0)	27.5	27.5 (+0.0)	+0.1
Portuguese '6	27.3	27.5 (+0.2)	32.8	33.7 (+0.9)	32.7	33.4 (+0.7)	33.3	33.5 (+0.3)	+0.8
Slovenian '6	21.8	21.9 (+0.2)	28.3	30.4 (+2.1)	28.4	30.4 (+2.0)	29.8	31.2 (+1.4)	+2.8
Spanish '6	25.3	26.2 (+0.9)	31.7	32.4 (+0.7)	31.6	32.3 (+0.8)	31.9	32.3 (+0.5)	+0.8
Swedish '6	31.0	31.5 (+0.6)	44.1	45.2 (+1.1)	45.6	46.1 (+0.5)	46.1	46.4 (+0.3)	+0.8
Turkish '6	22.3	22.9 (+0.6)	39.1	39.5 (+0.4)	39.9	39.9 (+0.1)	40.6	40.9 (+0.3)	+1.0
'7	22.7	23.3 (+0.6)	41.7	42.3 (+0.6)	41.9	42.1 (+0.2)	41.6	42.0 (+0.4)	+0.1
Average:	23.4	24.0 (**+0.7**)	31.9	32.9 (**+1.0**)	31.9	32.6 (**+0.7**)	32.6	33.2 (**+0.5**)	**+1.3**

Table 6: Multi-lingual evaluation for CoNLL sets, measured at all three stages of training, with and without constraints.

8 Experiment #4: Multi-Lingual Testing

This final batch of experiments probes the generalization of our approach (§6) across languages. The data are from 2006/7 CoNLL shared tasks (Buchholz and Marsi, 2006; Nivre et al., 2007a), where punctuation was identified by the organizers, who also furnished disjoint train/test splits. We tested against all sentences in their evaluation sets.[7,8]

The gains are *not* English-specific (see Table 6). Every language improves with constrained decoding (more so without constrained training); and all but Italian benefit in combination. Averaged across all eighteen languages, the net change in accuracy is 1.3%. After standard training, constrained decoding alone delivers a 0.7% gain, on average, never causing harm in any of our experiments. These gains are statistically significant: $p \approx 1.59 \times 10^{-5}$ for constrained training; and $p \approx 4.27 \times 10^{-7}$ for inference.

[7]With the exception of Arabic '07, from which we discarded one sentence with 145 tokens. We down-weighed languages appearing in both years by 50% in our analyses, and excluded Chinese entirely, since it had already been cut up at punctuation.

[8]Note that punctuation was treated differently in the two years: in '06, it was always at the leaves of the dependency trees; in '07, it matched original annotations of the source treebanks. For both, we used punctuation-insensitive scoring (§3.2).

We did not detect synergy between the two improvements. However, note that without constrained training, "full" data sets do not help, on average, despite having more data and lexicalization. Furthermore, *after* constrained training, we detected no evidence of benefits to additional retraining: not with the relaxed *sprawl* constraint, nor unconstrained.

9 Related Work

Punctuation has been used to improve parsing since rule-based systems (Jones, 1994). Statistical parsers reap dramatic gains from punctuation (Engel et al., 2002; Roark, 2001; Charniak, 2000; Johnson, 1998; Collins, 1997, *inter alia*). And it is even known to help in *unsupervised* constituent parsing (Seginer, 2007). But for *dependency* grammar induction, until now, punctuation remained unexploited.

Parsing Techniques Most-Similar to Constraints A "divide-and-rule" strategy that relies on punctuation has been used in supervised constituent parsing of long Chinese sentences (Li et al., 2005). For English, there has been interest in *balanced* punctuation (Briscoe, 1994), more recently using rule-based filters (White and Rajkumar, 2008) in a combinatory categorial grammar (CCG). Our focus is specifically on *unsupervised* learning of *dependency* grammars and is similar, in spirit, to Eisner and Smith's (2005) "vine grammar" formalism. An important difference is that instead of imposing static limits on allowed dependency lengths, our restrictions are dynamic — they disallow some long (and some short) arcs that would have otherwise crossed nearby punctuation.

Incorporating partial bracketings into grammar induction is an idea tracing back to Pereira and Schabes (1992). It inspired Spitkovsky et al. (2010b) to mine parsing constraints from the web. In that same vein, we prospected a more abundant and natural language-resource — punctuation, using constraint-based techniques they developed for web markup.

Modern Unsupervised Dependency Parsing

State-of-the-art in unsupervised dependency parsing (Blunsom and Cohn, 2010) uses tree substitution grammars. These are powerful models, capable of learning large dependency fragments. To help prevent overfitting, a non-parametric Bayesian prior, defined by a hierarchical Pitman-Yor process (Pitman and Yor, 1997), is trusted to nudge training towards fewer and smaller grammatical productions.

We pursued a complementary strategy: using Klein and Manning's (2004) much simpler Dependency Model with Valence (DMV), but persistently steering training away from certain constructions, as guided by punctuation, to help prevent *underfitting*.

Various Other Uses of Punctuation in NLP

Punctuation is hard to predict,[9] partly because it can signal long-range dependences (Lu and Ng, 2010). It often provides valuable cues to NLP tasks such as part-of-speech tagging and named-entity recognition (Hillard et al., 2006), information extraction (Favre et al., 2008) and machine translation (Lee et al., 2006; Matusov et al., 2006). Other applications have included Japanese sentence analysis (Ohyama et al., 1986), genre detection (Stamatatos et al., 2000), bilingual sentence alignment (Yeh, 2003), semantic role labeling (Pradhan et al., 2005), Chinese creation-title recognition (Chen and Chen, 2005) and word segmentation (Li and Sun, 2009), plus, recently, automatic vandalism detection in Wikipedia (Wang and McKeown, 2010).

10 Conclusions and Future Work

Punctuation improves dependency grammar induction. Many unsupervised (and supervised) parsers could be easily modified to use *sprawl*-constrained decoding in inference. It applies to pre-trained models and, so far, helped every data set and language.

Tightly interwoven into the fabric of writing systems, punctuation frames most unannotated plaintext. We showed that rules for converting markup into accurate parsing constraints are still optimal for inter-punctuation fragments. Punctuation marks are more ubiquitous and natural than web markup: what little punctuation-induced constraints lack in precision, they more than make up in recall — perhaps both types of constraints would work better yet in tandem. For language acquisition, a natural question is whether prosody could similarly aid grammar induction from speech (Kahn et al., 2005).

Our results underscore the power of simple models and algorithms, combined with common-sense constraints. They reinforce insights from *joint* modeling in *supervised* learning, where simplified, independent models, Viterbi decoding and expressive constraints excel at sequence labeling tasks (Roth and Yih, 2005). Such evidence is particularly welcome in *unsupervised* settings (Punyakanok et al., 2005), where it is crucial that systems scale gracefully to volumes of data, on top of the usual desiderata — ease of implementation, extension, understanding and debugging. Future work could explore softening constraints (Hayes and Mouradian, 1980; Chang et al., 2007), perhaps using features (Eisner and Smith, 2005; Berg-Kirkpatrick et al., 2010) or by learning to associate different settings with various marks: Simply adding a hidden tag for "ordinary" versus "divide" types of punctuation (Li et al., 2005) may already usefully extend our model.

Acknowledgments

Partially funded by the Air Force Research Laboratory (AFRL), under prime contract no. FA8750-09-C-0181, and by NSF, via award #IIS-0811974. We thank Omri Abend, Slav Petrov and anonymous reviewers for many helpful suggestions, and we are especially grateful to Jenny R. Finkel for shaming us into using punctuation, to Christopher D. Manning for reminding us to explore "punctuation as words" baselines, and to Noah A. Smith for encouraging us to test against languages other than English.

[9] Punctuation has high semantic entropy (Melamed, 1997); for an analysis of the many roles played in the WSJ by the comma — the most frequent and unpredictable punctuation mark in that data set — see Beeferman et al. (1998, Table 2).

References

D. Beeferman, A. Berger, and J. Lafferty. 1998. CYBERPUNC: A lightweight punctuation annotation system for speech. In *ICASSP*.

T. Berg-Kirkpatrick, A. Bouchard-Côté, J. DeNero, and D. Klein. 2010. Painless unsupervised learning with features. In *NAACL-HLT*.

P. Blunsom and T. Cohn. 2010. Unsupervised induction of tree substitution grammars for dependency parsing. In *EMNLP*.

E. J. Briscoe. 1994. Parsing (with) punctuation, etc. Technical report, Xerox European Research Laboratory.

S. Buchholz and E. Marsi. 2006. CoNLL-X shared task on multilingual dependency parsing. In *CoNLL*.

G. Carroll and E. Charniak. 1992. Two experiments on learning probabilistic dependency grammars from corpora. Technical report, Brown University.

M.-W. Chang, L. Ratinov, and D. Roth. 2007. Guiding semi-supervision with constraint-driven learning. In *ACL*.

E. Charniak. 2000. A maximum-entropy-inspired parser. In *NAACL*.

C. Chen and H.-H. Chen. 2005. Integrating punctuation rules and naïve Bayesian model for Chinese creation title recognition. In *IJCNLP*.

A. Clark. 2000. Inducing syntactic categories by context distribution clustering. In *CoNLL-LLL*.

M. Collins. 1997. Three generative, lexicalised models for statistical parsing. In *ACL*.

M. Collins. 1999. *Head-Driven Statistical Models for Natural Language Parsing*. Ph.D. thesis, University of Pennsylvania.

C. D. Doran. 1998. *Incorporating Punctuation into the Sentence Grammar: A Lexicalized Tree Adjoining Grammar Perspective*. Ph.D. thesis, University of Pennsylvania.

J. Eisner and G. Satta. 1999. Efficient parsing for bilexical context-free grammars and head-automaton grammars. In *ACL*.

J. Eisner and N. A. Smith. 2005. Parsing with soft and hard constraints on dependency length. In *IWPT*.

D. Engel, E. Charniak, and M. Johnson. 2002. Parsing and disfluency placement. In *EMNLP*.

B. Favre, R. Grishman, D. Hillard, H. Ji, D. Hakkani-Tür, and M. Ostendorf. 2008. Punctuating speech for information extraction. In *ICASSP*.

J. R. Finkel and C. D. Manning. 2009. Joint parsing and named entity recognition. In *NAACL-HLT*.

W. N. Francis and H. Kučera, 1979. *Manual of Information to Accompany a Standard Corpus of Present-Day Edited American English, for use with Digital Computers*. Department of Linguistics, Brown University.

J. Gillenwater, K. Ganchev, J. Graça, F. Pereira, and B. Taskar. 2010. Posterior sparsity in unsupervised dependency parsing. Technical report, University of Pennsylvania.

A. Gravano, M. Jansche, and M. Bacchiani. 2009. Restoring punctuation and capitalization in transcribed speech. In *ICASSP*.

P. J. Hayes and G. V. Mouradian. 1980. Flexible parsing. In *ACL*.

W. P. Headden, III, D. McClosky, and E. Charniak. 2008. Evaluating unsupervised part-of-speech tagging for grammar induction. In *COLING*.

W. P. Headden, III, M. Johnson, and D. McClosky. 2009. Improving unsupervised dependency parsing with richer contexts and smoothing. In *NAACL-HLT*.

D. Hillard, Z. Huang, H. Ji, R. Grishman, D. Hakkani-Tür, M. Harper, M. Ostendorf, and W. Wang. 2006. Impact of automatic comma prediction on POS/name tagging of speech. In *IEEE/ACL: SLT*.

M. Johnson. 1998. PCFG models of linguistic tree representations. *Computational Linguistics*, 24.

B. E. M. Jones. 1994. Exploring the role of punctuation in parsing natural text. *COLING*.

J. G. Kahn, M. Lease, E. Charniak, M. Johnson, and M. Ostendorf. 2005. Effective use of prosody in parsing conversational speech. In *HLT-EMNLP*.

J.-H. Kim and P. C. Woodland. 2002. Implementation of automatic capitalisation generation systems for speech input. In *ICASSP*.

D. Klein and C. D. Manning. 2004. Corpus-based induction of syntactic structure: Models of dependency and constituency. In *ACL*.

Y.-S. Lee, S. Roukos, Y. Al-Onaizan, and K. Papineni. 2006. IBM spoken language translation system. In *TC-STAR: Speech-to-Speech Translation*.

Z. Li and M. Sun. 2009. Punctuation as implicit annotations for Chinese word segmentation. *Computational Linguistics*, 35.

X. Li, C. Zong, and R. Hu. 2005. A hierarchical parsing approach with punctuation processing for long Chinese sentences. In *IJCNLP*.

D. Lin. 1998. Dependency-based evaluation of MINIPAR. In *Evaluation of Parsing Systems*.

W. Lu and H. T. Ng. 2010. Better punctuation prediction with dynamic conditional random fields. In *EMNLP*.

M. P. Marcus, B. Santorini, and M. A. Marcinkiewicz. 1993. Building a large annotated corpus of English: The Penn Treebank. *Computational Linguistics*, 19.

E. Matusov, A. Mauser, and H. Ney. 2006. Automatic sentence segmentation and punctuation prediction for spoken language translation. In *IWSLT*.

I. D. Melamed. 1997. Measuring semantic entropy. In *ACL-SIGLEX: Tagging Text with Lexical Semantics*.

J. Nivre, J. Hall, S. Kübler, R. McDonald, J. Nilsson, S. Riedel, and D. Yuret. 2007a. The CoNLL 2007 shared task on dependency parsing. In *EMNLP-CoNLL*.

J. Nivre, J. Hall, J. Nilsson, A. Chanev, G. Eryiğit, S. Kübler, S. Marinov, and E. Marsi. 2007b. Malt-Parser: A language-independent system for data-driven dependency parsing. *Natural Language Engineering*, 13.

G. Nunberg. 1990. *The Linguistics of Punctuation*. CSLI Publications.

Y. Ohyama, T. Fukushima, T. Shutoh, and M. Shutoh. 1986. A sentence analysis method for a Japanese book reading machine for the blind. In *ACL*.

M. A. Paskin. 2001. Grammatical bigrams. In *NIPS*.

F. Pereira and Y. Schabes. 1992. Inside-outside reestimation from partially bracketed corpora. In *ACL*.

J. Pitman and M. Yor. 1997. The two-parameter Poisson-Dirichlet distribution derived from a stable subordinator. *Annals of Probability*, 25.

S. Pradhan, K. Hacioglu, W. Ward, J. H. Martin, and D. Jurafsky. 2005. Semantic role chunking combining complementary syntactic views. In *CoNLL*.

V. Punyakanok, D. Roth, W.-t. Yih, and D. Zimak. 2005. Learning and inference over constrained output. In *IJCAI*.

B. E. Roark. 2001. *Robust Probabilistic Predictive Syntactic Processing: Motivations, Models, and Applications*. Ph.D. thesis, Brown University.

D. Roth and W.-t. Yih. 2005. Integer linear programming inference for conditional random fields. In *ICML*.

Y. Seginer. 2007. Fast unsupervised incremental parsing. In *ACL*.

D. D. Sleator and D. Temperley. 1993. Parsing English with a link grammar. In *IWPT*.

V. I. Spitkovsky, H. Alshawi, D. Jurafsky, and C. D. Manning. 2010a. Viterbi training improves unsupervised dependency parsing. In *CoNLL*.

V. I. Spitkovsky, D. Jurafsky, and H. Alshawi. 2010b. Profiting from mark-up: Hyper-text annotations for guided parsing. In *ACL*.

E. Stamatatos, N. Fakotakis, and G. Kokkinakis. 2000. Text genre detection using common word frequencies. In *COLING*.

W. Y. Wang and K. R. McKeown. 2010. "Got you!": Automatic vandalism detection in Wikipedia with web-based shallow syntactic-semantic modeling. In *COLING*.

M. White and R. Rajkumar. 2008. A more precise analysis of punctuation for broad-coverage surface realization with CCG. In *GEAF*.

K. C. Yeh. 2003. Bilingual sentence alignment based on punctuation marks. In *ROCLING: Student*.

Modeling Infant Word Segmentation

Constantine Lignos
Department of Computer and Information Science
University of Pennsylvania
lignos@cis.upenn.edu

Abstract

While many computational models have been created to explore how children might learn to segment words, the focus has largely been on achieving higher levels of performance and exploring cues suggested by artificial learning experiments. We propose a broader focus that includes designing models that display properties of infants' performance as they begin to segment words. We develop an efficient bootstrapping online learner with this focus in mind, and evaluate it on child-directed speech. In addition to attaining a high level of performance, this model predicts the error patterns seen in infants learning to segment words.

1 Introduction

The last fifteen years have seen an increased interest in the problem of how infants learn to segment a continuous stream of speech into words. Much of this work has been inspired by experiments with infants focusing on what capabilities infants have and which cues they attend to. While experimental work provides insight into the types of cues infants may be using, computational modeling of the task provides a unique opportunity to test proposed cues on representative data and validate potential approaches to using them.

While there are many potential approaches to the problem, a desirable solution to the problem should demonstrate acceptable performance in a simulation of the task, rely on cues in the input that an infant learner is able to detect at the relevant age, and exhibit learning patterns similar to those of infant learners. Most work in computational modeling of language acquisition has primarily focused on achieving acceptable performance using a single cue, transitional probabilities, but little effort has been made in that work to try to connect these learning solutions to the actual learning patterns observed in children outside of performance on short artificial language learning experiments.

In this work we present a simple, easily extended algorithm for unsupervised word segmentation that, in addition to achieving a high level of performance in the task, correlates with the developmental patterns observed in infants. We discuss the connections between the design and behavior of our algorithm and the cognitive capabilities of infants at the age at which they appear to begin segmenting words. We also discuss how our technique can easily be extended to accept additional cues to word segmentation beyond those implemented in our learner.

2 Related Work

As this paper examines the intersection of infants' capabilities and computational modeling, we discuss work in both domains, beginning with experimental approaches to understanding how infants may perform the task of word segmentation.

2.1 Infant Word Segmentation

A potential account of how infants learn to identify words in fluent speech is that they learn words in isolation and then use those words to segment longer utterances (Peters, 1983; Pinker et al., 1984). It is not clear, however, that infant-directed speech provides enough detectable words in isolation for

Proceedings of the Fifteenth Conference on Computational Natural Language Learning, pages 29–38,
Portland, Oregon, USA, 23–24 June 2011. ©2011 Association for Computational Linguistics

such a strategy (Aslin et al., 1996). Whatever isolated words children do hear, they appear to attend to them; whether a word is heard in isolation is a better predictor of whether a child has learned a word than the word's frequency (Brent and Siskind, 2001).

A more plausible alternative account to assume children attend to patterns in the input, using them to identify likely word units. Much experimental work has followed from the finding that in artificial learning tasks, infants and adults appear to prefer word-like units that match statistical patterns in the input (Saffran et al., 1996b; Saffran et al., 1996a). Saffran et al. and the authors of following studies (Aslin et al., 1998; Saffran, 2001, among many others) suggest that participants used transitional probabilities to succeed in these experiments, but the actual strategy used is unclear and may even be an artifact of the perceptual system (Perruchet and Vinter, 1998; Hewlett and Cohen, 2009).

More recent work using real language data has not shown transitional probabilities to be as useful a cue as originally suggested. Lew-Williams et al. (2011) found that 9-month-old English-learning infants were not able to learn high-transitional probability words in fluent Italian speech unless those words were also presented in isolation. Given this finding and the extensive exisiting modeling work focusing on the used of transitional probabilities, we believe it is crucial to additionally explore segmentation strategies that rely on other cues in the input.

2.2 Modeling Word Segmentation

While experimental work has posited simple algorithms that infants might use to accomplish the task of word segmentation, when applied to real language data these techniques have yielded very poor results (Yang, 2004). This problem has created a challenge for researchers modeling language acquisition to suggest more sophisticated strategies that infants might use. These approaches have fallen into two primary categories: optimization-based and bootstrapping algorithm strategies.

Optimization-based strategies have focused on techniques that a learner might use to arrive at an optimal segmentation, either through a dynamic programming approach (Brent, 1999), online learning (Venkataraman, 2001), or nonparametric Bayesian inference (Goldwater et al., 2009; Johnson and Goldwater, 2009). These approaches fit within standard statistical approaches to natural language processing, defining statistical objectives and inference strategies, with the learners trying to optimize some combination of the quality of its lexicon and representations of the corpus.

In contrast, bootstrapping approaches (Gambell and Yang, 2004; Lignos and Yang, 2010) to word segmentation have focused on simple heuristics for populating a lexicon and strategies for using the contents of the lexicon to segment utterances. These approaches have focused on a procedure for segmentation rather than defining an optimal segmentation explicitly, and do not define a formal objective that is to be optimized.

While bootstrapping approaches have generally made stronger attempts to align with infants abilities to process the speech signal (Gambell and Yang, 2004) than other approaches, little effort has been made to connect the details of an implemented segmentation strategy with children's learning patterns since the earliest computational models of the task (Olivier, 1968). It is important to draw a contrast here between attempts to match patterns of human development with regard to word segmentation with attempts to model performance in artificial language learning experiments whose goal is to probe word segmentation abilities in humans (Frank et al., 2010). In this paper we are focused on matching the progression of development and performance in naturalistic experiments to characteristics of a segmentation strategy, an approach similar to that employed in English past tense learning (Rumelhart and McClelland, 1986; Pinker, 2000; Yang, 2002).

We will now discuss the patterns of development for children learning to segment English words, which form the motivation for the design of our segmenter.

3 Infant Performance in Word Segmentation

While the developmental patterns of English-learning infants have been broadly studied, it has been difficult to identify errors that must be caused by failures to correctly segment words and not other cognitive limitations, issues of morphological productivity, or syntactic competency issues.

Brown (1973) offers one of the most comprehensive examinations of the types of errors that young infants make regarding word segmentation. He notes that Adam's common errors included treating *it's-a, that-a, get-a, put-a, want-to*, and *at-that* as single words, as judged by various misproductions that involved these items. A possible analysis of these errors is that in addition to the high level of frequency with which those syllables co-occur, elements such as *a* and *to* do not carry any identifiable amount of stress in natural speech.

In addition to the undersegmentations that Brown identifies, Peters (1983) identifies the pattern of oversegmenting function words begin other words, including this famous dialog between a parent and child, where in the child's response *have* is pronounced in the same way as the second syllable of *behave*: Parent: Behave! Child: I *am* have!

The response by the child indicates that they have analyzed *behave* as *be have*. There are two major factors that could contribute to such an analysis: the high frequency of *be* leading to it being treated as a separate word (Saffran et al., 1996b), and the lack of stress on *be* but stress on *have* which forms a word contrary to the dominant pattern of stress in English (Cutler and Butterfield, 1992).

Infants appear to use the ends of utterances to aid segmentation, and as early at 7.5 months old they are able to recognize novel words in fluent speech if the novel words are presented at the ends of an utterance and not utterance medially (Seidl and Johnson, 2006). Thus the reliable boundaries presented by the edge of an utterance should be treated as informative for a learner.

Most crucially, the syllable seems to be the unit children use to form words. Experiments that have been performed to gauge adult and infant competency in word segmentation have been designed with the assumption that the only possible segmentation points are at syllable boundaries. That infants should be able to operate on syllables is unsurprising; infants as young as 4-days-old are able to discriminate words based on syllable length (Bijeljac-Babic et al., 1993) and phonotactic cues to syllable boundaries seem to be rapidly acquired by infants (Onishi et al., 2002). The use of the syllable in experimental work on word segmentation stands in contrast to many computational models that have operated at the phoneme level (Brent, 1999; Venkataraman, 2001; Goldwater et al., 2009). An exception to the focus on phoneme-based segmentation is the joint learning model proposed by Johnson (2008) that learns syllabification and other levels of representation jointly with word segmentation, but that model poses problems as a developmentally relevant approach in that it predicts unattested joint syllabification/segmentation errors by infants and problems as a linguistically relevant approach due to its non-phonotactic approach to learning syllabification.

From this survey, we see some relevant phenomena that a good model of infant word segmentation should replicate. (1) The learner should operate on syllables. (2) At some stage of learning, undersegmentation function word collocations (e.g., *that-a* should occur. (3) At some stage of learning, oversegmentation of function words that may begin other words (e.g., *be-have*) should occur. (4) The learner should attend to the ends of utterances as use them to help identify novel words.

4 An Algorithm for Segmentation

The algorithm we propose is similar in style to previous online bootstrapping segmenters (Gambell and Yang, 2004; Lignos and Yang, 2010) but varies in a few crucial aspects. First, it inserts word boundaries in a left-to-right fashion as it processes each utterance (i.e., in temporal order), unlike previous models which have worked from the outside in. Second, it can handle cases where the segmentation is ambiguous given the current lexicon and score multiple possible segmentations. Finally, the use of word-level stress information is an optional part of the model, and not an essential part of the segmentation process. This allows us to examine the additional power that stress provides on top of a subtractive segmentation system and allows the model to generalize to languages where word-level stress is not present in the same fashion as English (e.g., French). We first discuss the individual operations the algorithm uses to segment an utterance, and then discuss how they are combined in the segmenter.

4.1 The Lexicon

The learner we propose will primarily use items in its lexicon to help identify new possible words. The structure of the lexicon is as follows:

Lexicon. *The lexicon contains the phonological material of each word that the learner has previously hypothesized. The lexicon stores a score along with each word, which the segmenter may increment or decrement.*

The score assigned to each entry in the lexicon represents the relative confidence that it is a true word of the language. Each increment simply adds to the score of an individual word and each decrement subtracts from it.

4.2 Subtractive Segmentation

Subtractive segmentation is the process of using known words to segment the speech signal, which infants appear to be able to do as young as at six months of age (Bortfeld et al., 2005).

Subtractive Segmentation. *When possible, remove a known word in the lexicon from the front of the utterance being segmented.*

One way to apply subtractive segmentation is a greedy score-based heuristic for subtractive segmentation (Lignos and Yang, 2010), such that whenever multiple words in the lexicon could be subtracted from an utterance, the entry with the highest score will deterministically be used. This greedy approach results in a "rich get richer" effect of the sort seen in Dirichlet processes (Goldwater et al., 2009). We will first discuss this approach and then later extend this greedy search to a beam search.

Figure 1 gives the implementation of subtractive segmentation in our algorithm. This algorithm results in the following properties:

Initially, utterances are treated as words in isolation. When the lexicon is empty, no word boundaries will be inserted and the full contents of each utterance will be added to the lexicon as a word.

High-frequency words are preferred. When presented with a choice of multiple words to subtract, the highest scored word will be subtracted, which will prefer higher frequency words over lower frequency words in segmentation.

Syllables between words are not necessarily considered words. Syllables that occur between subtractions are not added as words in the lexicon. For example, if *play* and *please* are in the lexicon but *checkers* is not, the utterance *play checkers please* will be correctly segmented, but *checkers* will not be added to the lexicon. Much like infants appear to do, the learner does not place as much weight on less reliable boundaries hypothesized in the middle of an utterance (Seidl and Johnson, 2006).

4.3 Incorporating Stress Information

A particularly useful constraint for defining a word, introduced to the problem of word segmentation by Yang (2004) but previously discussed by Halle and Vergnaud (1987), is as follows:

Unique Stress Constraint (USC): A word can bear at most one primary stress.

Yang (2004) evaluated the effectiveness of the USC in conjunction with a simple approach to using transitional probabilities, showing significant performance improvements. The availability of such stress cues is not, however, an uncontroversial assumption; there are no language-universal cues to stress and even within a single language automatic detection of word-level stress is still unreliable (Van Kuijk and Boves, 1999), making automatic capture of such data for simulation purposes difficult.

Before taking advantage of word-level stress information, the infant learner would need to identify the acoustic correlates to word-level stress in her language, and we will not address the specific mechanisms that an infant learner may use to accomplish the task of identifying word-level stress in this paper. Based on strong experimental evidence that infants discriminate between weakly and strongly stressed syllables and use it to group syllables into word-like units (Jusczyk et al., 1999), we assume that an infant may attend to this cue and we evaluate our model with and without it.

We adopt the USC for segmentation in the following fashion:

Unique Stress Segmentation (USS). *Insert word boundaries such that no word contains two strong stresses. Do so in a lazy fashion, inserting boundaries as a last resort just before adding another syllable to the current would cause it to contain two strong stresses.*

```
u ← the syllables of the utterance, initially with no word boundaries
i ← 0
while i < len(u) do
    if u starts with one or more words in the lexicon then
        Choose the highest scoring word w and remove it from the front of u by inserting a word boundary before and after it.
        Increment the score of w
        Advance i to the last word boundary inserted
    else
        Advance i by one syllable
    end if
end while
Add the syllables between the last boundary inserted (or the beginning of the utterance if no boundaries were inserted) and the
end of the utterance as a word in the lexicon with a score of 1
```

Figure 1: Subtractive segmentation procedure

```
u ← the syllables of the utterance, initally with no word boundaries
i ← 0
seenStress ← False
while i < len(u) − 1 do
    if u[i] is stressed then
        seenStress ← True
    end if
    if seenStress and u[i + 1] is stressed then
        Insert a word boundary between u[i] and u[i + 1]
        w ← the syllables between the previous boundary inserted (or the beginning of the utterance if no boundaries were inserted)
        and the boundary just inserted
        Increment w's score in the lexicon, adding it to the lexicon if needed
        seenStress ← False
    end if
    i ← i + 1
end while
w ← the syllables between the last boundary inserted (or the beginning of the utterance if no boundaries were inserted) and the
end of the utterance
Increment w's score in the lexicon, adding it to the lexicon if needed
```

Figure 2: A Unique Stress Segmentation Algorithm

This strategy is expressed in an algorithmic form in Figure 2. The learner uses USS as a last resort to prevent creating a segmentation with an impossible amount of stress in a single word. For example consider an unsegmented English utterance with the stressed syllables underlined: *Givemetheball*. Applying USS would create the following segmentation: *Givemethe ball*.

A USS-based algorithm would note the stress on the first syllable, then keep scanning until another stress is located on the fourth syllable, inserting a break between the two. *Givemethe* and *ball* would be added to the lexicon. While this is not a perfect segmentation, it can be used to aid subtractive segmentation by seeding the lexicon, even if not all entries added to the lexicon are not correct.

4.4 Combining Subtraction and Stress Information

Given our bootstrapping methodology, it is highly desirable to be able to integrate USS along with subtractive segmentation. An algorithm that combines both is shown in Figure 3.

4.5 Extending to Beam Search

The greedy segmentation proposed is limited in its ability to find a good segmentation by its reliance on local decisions. A frequent undersegmentation error of the greedy segmenter is of this type: *partof an apple*. Because *partof* has a higher score than *part* at the point in learning where this utterance is encountered, the greedy segmenter will always choose *partof*.

An alternative approach is to let the segmenter

```
u ← the syllables of the utterance, initally with no word boundaries
i ← 0
while i < len(u) do
   if USS requires a word boundary then
      Insert a word boundary and advance i, updating the lexicon as needed
   else if Subtractive Segmentation can be performed then
      Subtract the highest scoring word and advance i, updating the lexicon as needed
   else
      Advance i by one syllable
   end if
end while
w ← the syllables between the last boundary inserted (or the beginning of the utterance if no boundaries were inserted) and the end of the utterance
Increment w's score in the lexicon, adding it to the lexicon if needed
```

Figure 3: An algorithm combining USS and Subtractive Segmentation

explore multiple hypotheses at once, using a simple beam search. New hypotheses are added to support multiple possible subtractive segmentations. For example, using the utterance above, at the beginning of segmentation either *part* or *partof* could be subtracted from the utterance, and both possible segmentations can be evaluated. The learner scores these hypotheses in a fashion similar to the greedy segmentation, but using a function based on the score of all words used in the utterance. The geometric mean has been used in compound splitting (Koehn and Knight, 2003), a task in many ways similar to word segmentation, so we adopt it as the criterion for selecting the best hypothesis. For a hypothesized segmentation H comprised of words $w_i \dots w_n$, a hypothesis is chosen as follows:

$$\arg\max_{H}\left(\prod_{w_i \in H} score(w_i)\right)^{\frac{1}{n}}$$

For any w not found in the lexicon we must assign a score; we assign it a score of one as that would be its value assuming it had just been added to the lexicon, an approach similar to Laplace smoothing.

Returning to the previous example, while the score of *partof* is greater than that of *part*, the score of *of* is much higher than either, so if both *partof an apple* and *part of an apple* are considered, the high score of *of* causes the latter to be chosen. When beam search is employed, only words used in the winning hypothesis are rewarded, similar to the greedy case where there are no other hypotheses.

In addition to preferring segmentations that use words of higher score, it is useful to reduce the score of words that led to the consideration of a losing hypothesis. In the previous example we may want to penalize *partof* so that we are less likely to choose a future segmentation that includes it. Setting the beam size to be two, forcing each hypothesis to develop greedily after an ambiguous subtraction causes two hypotheses to form, we are guaranteed a unique word to penalize. In the previous example *partof* causes the split between the two hypotheses in the beam, and thus the learner penalizes it to discourage using it in the future.

Algorithm	**Word Boundaries**		
	Precision	Recall	F-Score
No Stress Information			
Syllable Baseline	81.68	**100.0**	89.91
Subtractive Seg.	91.66	89.13	90.37
Subtractive Seg. + Beam 2	**92.74**	88.69	**90.67**
Word-level Stress			
USS Only	91.53	18.82	31.21
USS + Subtractive Seg.	93.76	**92.02**	92.88
USS + Subtractive Seg. + Beam 2	**94.20**	91.87	**93.02**

Table 1: Learner and baseline performance

5 Results

5.1 Evaluation

To evaluate the performance of our model, we measured performance on child-directed speech, using the same corpus used in a number of previous studies that used syllabified input (Yang, 2004; Gambell and Yang, 2004; Lignos and Yang, 2010). The evaluation set was comprised of adult utterances from the Brown (1973) data of the CHILDES database (MacWhinney, 2000).[1] Phonemic transcriptions of words from the Carnegie Mellon Pronouncing Dictionary (CMUdict) Version 0.7 (Weide, 1998), using the first pronunciation for each word and marking syllables with level 1 stress as strong syllables. The corpus was syllabified using onset maximization. Any utterance in which a word could not be transcribed using CMUDICT was excluded, leaving 55,840 utterances. We applied a probabilistic recall function to the lexicon to simulate the fact that a child learner will not perfectly recall all hypothesized words either due to memory limitations, variability in the input, or any other possible source of failure. We used the same function and constant as used by Lignos and Yang (2010).

To adjust the word-level stress information to better reflect natural speech, the stress information obtained from CMUdict was post-processed in the context of each utterance using the technique of Lignos and Yang (2010). For any n adjacent primary-stress syllables, only the nth syllable retains primary stress; all others are made into weak syllables. This reflects the fact that stress clash is avoided in English and that infants may not reliably detect acoustic correlates of stress in the input.

In addition to variations of our algorithm, we evaluated a baseline segmenter which marks every syllable boundary as a word boundary, treating each syllable as a word. We tested five variants of our algorithm, adding combinations of USS, subtractive segmentation, and adding beam search with a beam size of two[2] to subtractive segmentation.

Precision and recall metrics were calculated over all word boundaries over all utterances in the corpus. The segmenter's task is effectively to classify each syllable boundary as a word boundary or not. As single-syllable utterances are unambiguously a single word with no possible boundaries, they are excluded from evaluation but still given as input.

Evaluation was performed by giving each algorithm a single pass over the data set, with the performance on every utterance included in the total score. This is the most challenging metric for an online segmenter, as early mistakes made when the learner has been exposed to no data still count against it.

5.2 Performance

The performance of several variations of our algorithm is given in Table 1. The most surprising result is the high performance provided by the syllable baseline. This good performance is both an artifact of English and the metrics used to evaluate the segmenters. In English, there are larger number of monosyllabic words than in other languages, resulting in high precision in addition to the guaranteed 100% recall because it predicts every possible word boundary. The standard metric of evaluating precision and recall over word boundaries rather than words identified in each utterance also contributes to this performance; when this baseline is evaluated with a word-level precision and recall it does not perform as well (Lignos and Yang, 2010).

Subtractive Segmentation provides an improvement in utterance evaluation over the Syllable Baseline, and adding beam search to it slightly improves F-score, sacrificing precision for recall. This is to be expected from the penalization step in beam search; as the penalization penalizes some good words in addition to undesirable ones, the purification of the utterance segmentation and the lexicon comes at the cost of recall from over-penalization.

While USS alone is clearly not a sufficiently rich segmentation technique, it is important to note that it is a high precision indicator of word boundaries, suggesting that stress information can be useful to the learner even when used in this simple way. More importantly, USS contributes unique information to subtractive segmentation, as the utterance F-score of subtractive segmentation improves from 90.37 to 92.88.

While the performance numbers show that the segmenter performs competently at the task, the more significant question at hand is whether the errors committed by the learner match developmental patterns of infants. As the design of the segmenter predicts, the main error types of the Subtractive Seg-

[1] A separate set of previous studies have used a corpus selected by Brent (1999) for evaluation. Due to length limitations and the fact that the results presented here cannot be meaningfully compared to those studies, we only present results on the Brown (1973) data here.

[2] As larger beam sizes did not lead to any benefits, partly because they do not straightforwardly allow for penalization, we do not report results for larger beam sizes.

mentation + USS algorithm fall into two classes:

Function word collocations. For example, the third highest-scored non-word in the lexicon is *that'sa*, congruent with observations of function word collocations seen in children (Brown, 1973).

Oversegmentation of function words. The greedy approach used for segmenting the words of highest score results in function words being aggressively segmented off the front of words, for example *a nother*. The highest scored non-word in the lexicon is *nother* as a result.

Adding beam search reduces the number of function word collocations in the segmenter's output; the learner's most commonly penalized lexicon entry is *isthat*. However, beam search also penalizes a lot of words, such as *another*. Thus the strategy used in beam search predicts an early use of function word collocations, followed by later oversegmentation.

6 Discussion

In the discussion of related work, we identified two major paradigms in modeling word segmentation: optimization and bootstrapping approaches. The algorithm presented here combines elements of both. Its behavior over time and across utterances is that of a bootstrapping learner, but when processing each utterance it selects a segmentation based on a simple, cognitively plausible beam search.

By using a beam search of the kind suggested, it is easy to see how a variety of other cues could be integrated into the learning process. We have given a simple function for selecting the best hypothesis that only relies on lexicon scores, but more sophisticated functions could take multiple cues into account. For example it has been observed that 7-month-olds attend more to distributional cues while 9-month-olds attend more to stress cues (Thiessen and Saffran, 2003). A learner in which the weight placed on stress cues increases as the learner receives more data would match this pattern. Other research has suggested a more complex hierarchy of cues (Mattys et al., 2005), but how the weighting of the various cues can be adjusted with more input remains an open question.

A crucial frontier in word segmentation is the expansion of evaluation to include other languages. As with many other tasks, creating solutions that perform well in a broad variety of languages is important but has not yet been pursued. Future work should attempt to match developmental patterns in other languages, which will require adding morphological complexity to the system; the techniques developed for English are unlikely to succeed unchanged in other languages.

Comparing with other algorithms' published results is difficult because of varying choices of data sets and metrics. For example, other syllable-based algorithms have evaluated their performance using word-level, as opposed to boundary-level, precision and recall (Gambell and Yang, 2004; Lignos and Yang, 2010). We have adopted the more popular boundary-based metric here, but there is no way to directly compare with work that does not use syllabified input. The variety of possible evaluation metrics obviates the need for a longer-form exploration of how existing approaches perform when evaluated against varying metrics. Additionally, a more standard set of evaluation data in many languages would greatly improve the ability to compare different approaches to this task.

7 Conclusion

The work presented here represents a step toward bringing together developmental knowledge regarding word segmentation and computational modeling. Rather than focusing on cues in artificial learning experiments which may or may not generalize to the natural development of word segmentation in children, we have shown how a simple algorithm for segmentation mimics many of the patterns seen in infants' developing competence. We believe this work opens the door to a promising line of research that will make a stronger effort to see simulations of language acquisition as not just an unsupervised learning task but rather a modeling task that must take into account a broad variety of phenomena.

8 Acknowledgments

I would like to thank Charles Yang and Mitch Marcus for many enlightening discussions regarding this work. The author was supported by an NSF IGERT grant to the University of Pennsylvania Institute for Research in Cognitive Science.

References

R.N. Aslin, J.Z. Woodward, N.P. LaMendola, and T.G. Bever. 1996. Models of word segmentation in fluent maternal speech to infants. *Signal to syntax: Bootstrapping from speech to grammar in early acquisition*, pages 117–134.

R.N. Aslin, J.R. Saffran, and E.L. Newport. 1998. Computation of conditional probability statistics by 8-month-old infants. *Psychological Science*, 9(4):321.

R. Bijeljac-Babic, J. Bertoncini, and J. Mehler. 1993. How do 4-day-old infants categorize multisyllabic utterances? *Developmental Psychology*, 29:711–711.

H. Bortfeld, J.L. Morgan, R.M. Golinkoff, and K. Rathbun. 2005. Mommy and me. *Psychological Science*, 16(4):298.

M.R. Brent and J.M. Siskind. 2001. The role of exposure to isolated words in early vocabulary development. *Cognition*, 81(2):B33–B44.

M.R. Brent. 1999. An efficient, probabilistically sound algorithm for segmentation and word discovery. *Machine Learning*, 34(1):71–105.

R. Brown. 1973. *A First Language: The Early Stages.* Harvard Univ. Press, Cambridge, Massachusetts 02138.

A. Cutler and S. Butterfield. 1992. Rhythmic cues to speech segmentation: Evidence from juncture misperception. *Journal of Memory and Language*, 31(2):218–236.

M.C. Frank, S. Goldwater, T.L. Griffiths, and J.B. Tenenbaum. 2010. Modeling human performance in statistical word segmentation. *Cognition*.

T. Gambell and C. Yang. 2004. Statistics learning and universal grammar: Modeling word segmentation. In *First Workshop on Psycho-computational Models of Human Language Acquisition*, page 49.

S. Goldwater, T.L. Griffiths, and M. Johnson. 2009. A Bayesian framework for word segmentation: Exploring the effects of context. *Cognition*.

M. Halle and J.R. Vergnaud. 1987. *An essay on stress.* MIT Press.

D. Hewlett and P. Cohen. 2009. Word segmentation as general chunking. In *Psychocomputational Models of Language Acquisition Workshop (PsychoCompLA)*, July 29, 2009.

M. Johnson and S. Goldwater. 2009. Improving nonparameteric Bayesian inference: experiments on unsupervised word segmentation with adaptor grammars. In *Proceedings of Human Language Technologies: The 2009 Annual Conference of the North American Chapter of the Association for Computational Linguistics*, pages 317–325. Association for Computational Linguistics.

M. Johnson. 2008. Using adaptor grammars to identify synergies in the unsupervised acquisition of linguistic structure. In *46th Annual Meeting of the ACL*, pages 398–406. Citeseer.

P.W. Jusczyk, D.M. Houston, and M. Newsome. 1999. The Beginnings of Word Segmentation in English-Learning Infants. *Cognitive Psychology*, 39(3-4):159–207.

P. Koehn and K. Knight. 2003. Empirical methods for compound splitting. In *Proceedings of the tenth conference on European chapter of the Association for Computational Linguistics-Volume 1*, pages 187–193. Association for Computational Linguistics.

C. Lew-Williams, B. Pelucchi, and J. Saffran. 2011. Isolated words enhance statistical learning by 9-month-old infants. In *Budapest CEU Conference on Cognitive Development 2011*.

C. Lignos and C. Yang. 2010. Recession Segmentation: Simpler Online Word Segmentation Using Limited Resources. In *Proceedings of CoNLL-2010*, pages 88–97.

B. MacWhinney. 2000. *The CHILDES Project: Tools for Analyzing Talk.* Lawrence Erlbaum Associates.

S.L. Mattys, L. White, and J.F. Melhorn. 2005. Integration of multiple speech segmentation cues: A hierarchical framework. *Journal of Experimental Psychology-General*, 134(4):477–500.

D.C. Olivier. 1968. *Stochastic grammars and language acquisition mechanisms: a thesis.* Ph.D. thesis, Harvard University.

K.H. Onishi, K.E. Chambers, and C. Fisher. 2002. Learning phonotactic constraints from brief auditory experience. *Cognition*, 83(1):B13–B23.

P. Perruchet and A. Vinter. 1998. PARSER: A model for word segmentation. *Journal of Memory and Language*, 39:246–263.

A.M. Peters. 1983. *The units of language acquisition.* CUP Archive.

S. Pinker, Harvard University. The President, and Fellows of Harvard College. 1984. *Language learnability and language development.* Harvard University Press Cambridge, MA.

S. Pinker. 2000. *Words and rules: The ingredients of language.* Harper Perennial.

D.E. Rumelhart and J.L. McClelland. 1986. *Parallel distributed processing: Explorations in the microstructure of cognition.* MIT Press, Cambridge, MA.

J.R. Saffran, R.N. Aslin, and E.L. Newport. 1996a. Statistical Learning by 8-month-old Infants. *Science*, 274(5294):1926.

J.R. Saffran, E.L. Newport, and R.N. Aslin. 1996b. Word Segmentation: The Role of Distributional Cues. *Journal of Memory and Language*, 35(4):606–621.

J.R. Saffran. 2001. Words in a sea of sounds: The output of infant statistical learning. *Cognition*, 81(2):149–169.

A. Seidl and E.K. Johnson. 2006. Infant word segmentation revisited: edge alignment facilitates target extraction. *Developmental Science*, 9(6):565–573.

E.D. Thiessen and J.R. Saffran. 2003. When cues collide: Use of stress and statistical cues to word boundaries by 7-to 9-month-old infants. *Developmental Psychology*, 39(4):706–716.

D. Van Kuijk and L. Boves. 1999. Acoustic characteristics of lexical stress in continuous telephone speech. *Speech Communication*, 27(2):95–111.

A. Venkataraman. 2001. A statistical model for word discovery in transcribed speech. *Computational Linguistics*, 27(3):351–372.

R.L. Weide. 1998. The Carnegie Mellon Pronouncing Dictionary [cmudict. 0.6].

C.D. Yang. 2002. *Knowledge and learning in natural language*. Oxford University Press, USA.

C.D. Yang. 2004. Universal Grammar, statistics or both? *Trends in Cognitive Sciences*, 8(10):451–456.

Word Segmentation as General Chunking

Daniel Hewlett and **Paul Cohen**
Department of Computer Science
University of Arizona
Tucson, AZ 85721
{dhewlett,cohen}@cs.arizona.edu

Abstract

During language acquisition, children learn to segment speech into phonemes, syllables, morphemes, and words. We examine word segmentation specifically, and explore the possibility that children might have general-purpose chunking mechanisms to perform word segmentation. The Voting Experts (VE) and Bootstrapped Voting Experts (BVE) algorithms serve as computational models of this chunking ability. VE finds chunks by searching for a particular information-theoretic signature: low internal entropy and high boundary entropy. BVE adds to VE the ability to incorporate information about word boundaries previously found by the algorithm into future segmentations. We evaluate the general chunking model on phonemically-encoded corpora of child-directed speech, and show that it is consistent with empirical results in the developmental literature. We argue that it offers a parsimonious alternative to special-purpose linguistic models.

1 Introduction

The ability to extract words from fluent speech appears as early as the seventh month in human development (Jusczyk et al., 1999). Models of this ability have emerged from such diverse fields as linguistics, psychology and computer science. Many of these models make unrealistic assumptions about child language learning, or rely on supervision, or are specific to speech or language. Here we present an alternative: a general unsupervised model of chunking that performs very well on word segmentation tasks. We will examine the Voting Experts, Bootstrapped Voting Experts, and Phoneme to Morpheme algorithms in Section 2. Each searches for a general, information-theoretic signature of chunks. Each can operate in either a fully unsupervised setting, where the input is a single continuous sequence of phonemes, or a semi-supervised setting, where the input is a sequence of sentences. In Section 4, we evaluate these general chunking methods on phonetically-encoded corpora of child-directed speech, and compare them to a representative set of computational models of early word segmentation. Section 4.4 presents evidence that words optimize the information-theoretic signature of chunks. Section 5 discusses segmentation methods in light of what is known about the segmentation abilities of children.

2 General Chunking

The Voting Experts algorithm (Cohen and Adams, 2001) defines the *chunk* operationally as a sequence with the property that elements within the sequence predict one another but do not predict elements outside the sequence. In information-theoretic terms, chunks have low entropy internally and high entropy at their boundaries. Voting Experts (VE) is a local, greedy algorithm that works by sliding a relatively small window along a relatively long input sequence, calculating the internal and boundary entropies of sequences within the window.

The name *Voting Experts* refers to the two "experts" that vote on possible boundary locations: One expert votes to place boundaries after sequences that have low internal entropy (also called *surprisal*), given by $H_I(seq) = -\log P(seq)$. The other places votes after sequences that have

Proceedings of the Fifteenth Conference on Computational Natural Language Learning, pages 39–47,
Portland, Oregon, USA, 23–24 June 2011.

high *branching entropy*, given by $H_B(seq) = -\sum_{c \in S} P(c|seq) \log P(c|seq)$, where S is the set of successors to seq. In a modified version of VE, a third expert "looks backward" and computes the branching entropy at locations before, rather than after, seq.

The statistics required to calculate H_I and H_B are stored efficiently using an n-gram trie, which is typically constructed in a single pass over the corpus. The trie depth is 1 greater than the size of the sliding window. Importantly, all statistics in the trie are normalized so as to be expressed in standard deviation units. This allows statistics from sequences of different lengths to be compared.

The sliding window is then passed over the corpus, and each expert votes once per window for the boundary location that best matches that expert's criteria. After voting is complete, the algorithm yields an array of vote counts, each element of which is the number of times some expert voted to segment at that location. The result of voting on the string `thisisacat` could be represented in the following way, where the number between each letter is the number of votes that location received, as in `t0h0i1s3i1s4a4c1a0t`.

With the final vote totals in place, the boundaries are placed at locations where the number of votes exceeds a chosen threshold. For further details of the Voting Experts algorithm see Cohen et al. (2007), and also Miller and Stoytchev (2008).

2.1 Generality of the Chunk Signature

The information-theoretic properties of chunks upon which VE depends are present in every non-random sequence, of which sequences of speech sounds are only one example. Cohen et al. (2007) explored word segmentation in a variety of languages, as well as segmenting sequences of robot actions. Hewlett and Cohen (2010) demonstrated high performance for a version of VE that segmented sequences of utterances between a human teacher and an AI student. Miller and Stoytchev (2008) applied VE in a kind of bootstrapping procedure to perform a vision task similar to OCR: first to chunk columns of pixels into letters, then to chunk sequences of these discovered letters into words. Of particular relevance to the present discussion are the results of Miller et al. (2009), who showed that VE was able to segment a continuous audio speech stream into phonemes. The input in that experiment was generated to mimic the input presented to infants by Saffran et al. (1996), and was discretized for VE with a Self-Organizing Map (Kohonen, 1988).

2.2 Similar Chunk Signatures

Harris (1955) noticed that if one proceeds incrementally through a sequence of letters and asks speakers of the language to list all the letters that could appear next in the sequence (today called the *successor count*), the points where the number *increases* often correspond to morpheme boundaries. Tanaka-Ishii and Jin (2006) correctly recognized that this idea was an early version of branching entropy, one of the experts in VE, and they developed an algorithm called Phoneme to Morpheme (PtM) around it. PtM calculates branching entropy in both directions, but it does not use internal entropy, as VE does. It detects change-points in the absolute branching entropy rather than local maxima in the standardized entropy. PtM achieved scores similar to those of VE on word segmentation in phonetically-encoded English and Chinese.

Within the morphology domain, Johnson and Martin's HubMorph algorithm (2003) constructs a trie from a set of words, and then converts it into a DFA by the process of minimization. HubMorph searches for *stretched hubs* in this DFA, which are sequences of states in the DFA that have a low branching factor internally, and high branching factor at the edges (shown in Figure 1). This is a nearly identical chunk signature to that of VE, only with successor/predecessor count approximating branching entropy. The generality of this idea was not lost on Johnson and Martin, either: Speaking with respect to the morphology problem, Johnson and Martin close by saying "We believe that hub-automata will be the basis of a general solution for Indo-European languages as well as for Inuktitut." [1]

2.3 Chunking and Bootstrapping

Bootstrapped Voting Experts (BVE) is an extension to VE that incorporates knowledge gained from prior segmentation attempts when segmenting new input, a process known as *bootstrapping*. This

[1] Inuktitut is a polysynthetic Inuit language known for its highly complex morphology.

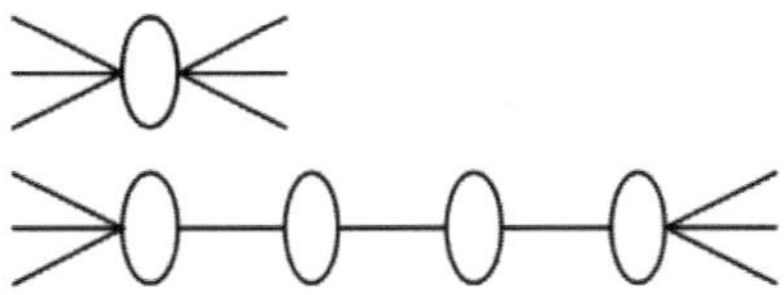

Figure 1: The DFA signature of a *hub* (top) and *stretched hub* in the HubMorph algorithm. Figure from Johnson and Martin (2003).

knowledge does not consist in the memorization of whole words (chunks), but rather in statistics describing the beginnings and endings of chunks. In the word segmentation domain, these statistics effectively correspond to phonotactic constraints that are inferred from hypothesized segmentations. Inferred boundaries are stored in a data structure called a *knowledge trie* (shown in Figure 2), which is essentially a generalized prefix or suffix trie.

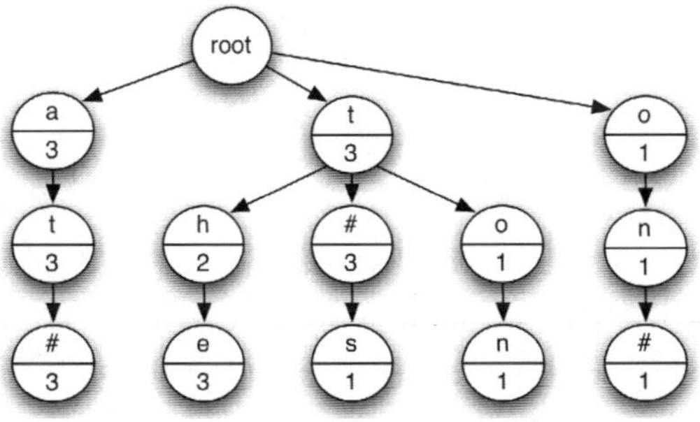

Figure 2: A portion of the knowledge trie built from `#the#cat#sat#on#the#mat#`. Numbers within each node are frequency counts.

BVE was tested on a phonemically-encoded corpus of child-directed speech and achieved a higher level of performance than any other unsupervised algorithm (Hewlett and Cohen, 2009). We reproduce these results in Section 4.

3 Computational Models of Word Segmentation

While many algorithms exist for solving the word segmentation problem, few have been proposed specifically as computational models of word segmentation in language acquisition. One of the most widely cited is MBDP-1 (Model-Based Dynamic Programming) by Brent (1999). Brent describes three features that an algorithm should have to qualify as an algorithm that "children could use for segmentation and word discovery during language acquisition." Algorithms should learn in a completely unsupervised fashion, should segment incrementally (i.e., segment each utterance before considering the next one), and should not have any built-in knowledge about specific natural languages (Brent, 1999).

However, the word segmentation paradigm Brent describes as "completely unsupervised" is actually *semi-supervised*, because the boundaries at the beginning and end of each utterance are known to be true boundaries. A fully unsupervised paradigm would include no boundary information at all, meaning that the input is, or is treated as, a continuous sequences of phonemes. The MBDP-1 algorithm was not designed for operation in this continuous condition, as it relies on having at least some true boundary information to generalize.

MBDP-1 achieves a robust form of bootstrapping through the use of Bayesian maximum-likelihood estimation of the parameters of a language model. More recent algorithms in the same tradition, including the refined MBDP-1 of Venkataraman (2001), the WordEnds algorithm of Fleck (2008), and the Hierarchical Dirichlet Process (HDP) algorithm of Goldwater (2007), share this limitation. However, infants are able to discover words in a single stream of continuous speech, as shown by the seminal series of studies by Saffran et al. (1996; 1998; 2003). In these studies, Saffran et al. show that both adults and 8-month-old infants quickly learn to extract words of a simple artificial language from a continuous speech stream containing no pauses.

The general chunking algorithms VE, BVE, and PtM work in either condition. The unsupervised, continuous condition is the norm (Cohen et al., 2007; Hewlett and Cohen, 2009; Tanaka-Ishii and Jin, 2006) but these algorithms are easily adapted to the semi-supervised, incremental condition. Recall that these methods make one pass over the entire corpus to gather statistics, and then make a second pass to segment the corpus, thus violating Brent's requirement of incremental segmentation. To adhere to the incremental requirement, the algorithms simply must segment each sentence as it is seen, and then update their trie(s) with statistics from that sentence. While VE and PtM have no natural way to store true boundary information, and so cannot benefit from the supervision inherent in the incremental paradigm, BVE has the knowledge trie which serves exactly this purpose. In the incremental paradigm, BVE simply adds each segmented sentence to the knowledge trie, which will inform the segmentation of future sentences. This way it learns from its own decisions as well as the ground truth boundaries surrounding each utterance, much like MBDP-1 does. BVE and VE were first tested in the incremental paradigm by Hewlett and Cohen (2009), though only on sentences from a literary corpus, George Orwell's *1984*.

4 Evaluation of Computational Models

In this section, we evaluate the general chunking algorithms VE, BVE, and PtM in both the continuous, unsupervised paradigm of Saffran et al. (1996) and the incremental, semi-supervised paradigm assumed by bootstrapping algorithms like MBDP-1. We briefly describe the artificial input used by Saffran et al., and then turn to the broader problem of word segmentation in natural languages by evaluating against corpora drawn from the CHILDES database (MacWhinney and Snow, 1985).

We evaluate segmentation quality at two levels: boundaries and words. At the boundary level, we compute the Boundary Precision (BP), which is simply the percentage of induced boundaries that were correct, and Boundary Recall (BR), which is the percentage of true boundaries that were recovered by the algorithm. These measures are commonly combined into a single metric, the Boundary F-score (BF), which is the harmonic mean of BP and BR: $\text{BF} = (2 \times \text{BP} \times \text{BR})/(\text{BP} + \text{BR})$. Generally, higher BF scores correlate with finding correct chunks more frequently, but for completeness we also compute the Word Precision (WP), which is the percentage of induced words that were correct, and the Word Recall (WR), which is the percentage of true words that were recovered exactly by the algorithm. These measures can naturally be combined into a single F-score, the Word F-score (WF): $\text{WF} = (2 \times \text{WP} \times \text{WR})/(\text{WP} + \text{WR})$.

4.1 Artificial Language Results

To simulate the input children heard during Saffran et al.'s 1996 experiment, we generated a corpus of 400 words, each chosen from the four artificial words from that experiment (`dapiku`, `tilado`, `burobi`, and `pagotu`). As in the original study, the only condition imposed on the random sequence was that no word would appear twice in succession. VE, BVE, and PtM all achieve a boundary F-score of 1.0 whether the input is syllabified or considered simply as a stream of phonemes, suggesting that a child equipped with a chunking ability similar to VE could succeed even without syllabification.

4.2 CHILDES: Phonemes

To evaluate these algorithms on data that is closer to the language children hear, we used corpora of child-directed speech taken from the CHILDES database (MacWhinney and Snow, 1985). Two corpora have been examined repeatedly in prior studies: the Bernstein Ratner corpus (Bernstein Ratner, 1987), abbreviated BR87, used by Brent (1999), Venkataraman (2001), Fleck (2008), and Goldwater et al. (2009), and the Brown corpus (Brown, 1973), used by Gambell and Yang (2006).

Before segmentation, all corpora were encoded into a phonemic representation, to better simulate the segmentation problem facing children. The BR87 corpus has a traditional phonemic encoding created by Brent (1999), which facilitates comparison with other published results. Otherwise, the corpora are translated into a phonemic representation using the CMU Pronouncing Dictionary, with unknown words discarded.

The BR87 corpus consists of speech from nine different mothers to their children, who had an average age of 18 months (Brent, 1999). BR87 consists of 9790 utterances, with a total of 36441 words, yielding an average of 3.72 words per utterance. We evaluate word segmentation models against BR87 in two different paradigms, the incremental paradigm discussed above and an unconstrained paradigm. Many of the results in the literature do not constrain the number of times algorithms can process the corpus, meaning that algorithms generally process the entire corpus once to gather statistics, and then at least one more time to actually segment it. Results of VE and other algorithms in this unconstrained setting are presented below in Table 1. In this test, the general chunking algorithms were given one continuous corpus with no boundaries, while the results for bootstrapping algorithms were reported in a semi-supervised condition.

Algorithm	BP	BR	BF	WP	WR	WF
PtM	0.861	**0.897**	0.879	0.676	0.704	0.690
VE	0.875	0.803	0.838	0.614	0.563	0.587
BVE	**0.949**	0.879	**0.913**	**0.793**	**0.734**	**0.762**
MBDP-1	0.803	0.843	0.823	0.670	0.694	0.682
HDP	0.903	0.808	0.852	0.752	0.696	0.723
WordEnds	0.946	0.737	0.829	NR	NR	0.707

Table 1: Results for the BR87 corpus with unconstrained processing of the corpus. Algorithms in italics are semi-supervised.

In the incremental setting, the corpus is treated as a series of utterances and the algorithm must segment each one before moving on to the next. This is designed to better simulate the learning process, as a child would normally listen to a series of utterances produced by adults, analyzing each one in turn. To perform this test, we used the incremental versions of PtM, VE, and BVE described in Section 3, and compared them with MBDP-1 on the BR87 corpus. Each point in Figure 3 shows the boundary F-score of each algorithm on the last 500 utterances. Note that VE and PtM do not benefit from the information about boundaries at the beginnings and endings of utterances, yet they achieve levels of performance not very inferior to MBDP-1 and BVE, which do leverage true boundary information.

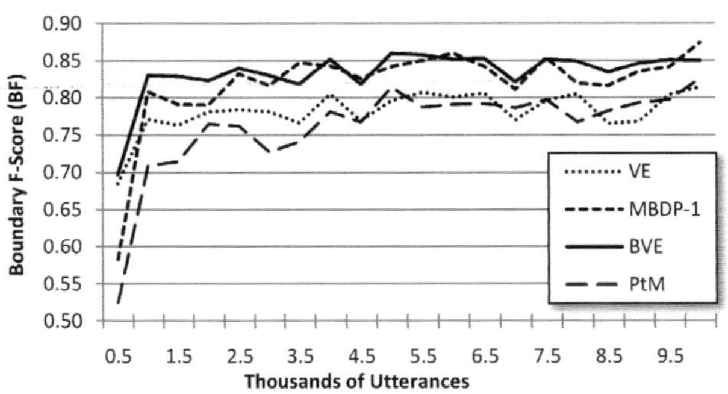

Figure 3: Results for three chunking algorithms and MBDP-1 on BR87 in the incremental paradigm.

We also produced a phonemic encoding of the BR87 and Bloom73 (Bloom, 1973) corpora from CHILDES with the CMU pronouncing dictionary, which encodes stress information (primary, secondary, or unstressed) on phonemes that serve as syllable nuclei. Stress information is known to be a useful factor in word segmentation, and infants appear to be sensitive to stress patterns by as early as 8 months of age (Jusczyk et al., 1999). Results with these corpora are shown below in Figures 4 and 5. For each of the general chunking algorithms, a window size of 4 was used, meaning decisions were made in a highly local manner. Even so, BVE outperforms MBDP-1 in this arguably more realistic setting, while VE and PtM rival it or even surpass it. Note that the quite different results shown in Figure 3 and Figure 4 are for the same corpus, under two different phonemic encodings, illustrating the importance of accurately representing the input children receive.

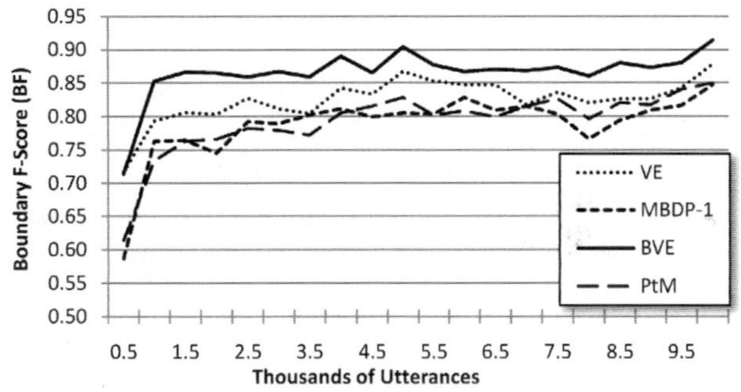

Figure 4: Results for chunking algorithms and MBDP-1 on BR87 (CMU) in the incremental paradigm.

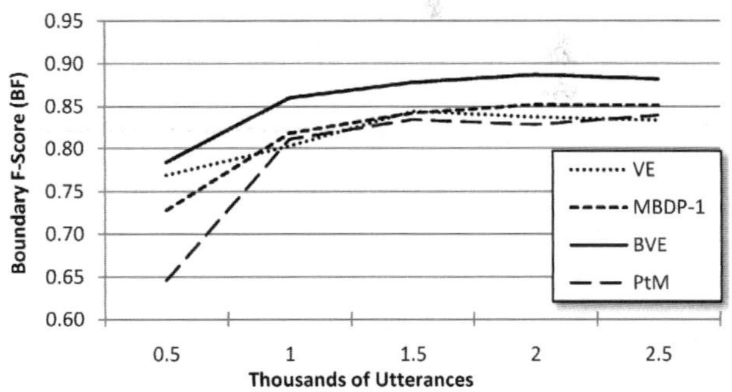

Figure 5: Results for chunking algorithms and MBDP-1 on Bloom73 (CMU) in the incremental paradigm.

4.3 CHILDES: Syllables

In many empirical studies of word segmentation in children, especially after Saffran et al. (1996), the problem is treated as though syllables were the basic units of the stream to be segmented, rather than phonemes. If we assume children can syllabify their phonemic representation, and that word boundaries only occur at syllable boundaries, then word segmentation becomes a very different, and potentially much easier, problem. This must be the case, as the process of syllabification removes a high percentage of the potential boundary locations, and all of the locations it removes would be incorrect choices. Table 2 supports this argument. In the CHILDES corpora examined here, over 85% of the words directed to the child are monosyllabic. This means that the trivial All-Locations baseline, which segments at every possible location, achieves an F-measure of 0.913 when working with syllabic input, compared to only 0.524 for phonemic input.

Gambell and Yang (2006) present an algorithm for word segmentation that achieves a boundary F-score of 0.946 on correctly syllabified input. In order to achieve this level of performance, Gambell and Yang use a form of bootstrapping combined with a rule called the "Unique Stress Constraint," or USC, which simply requires that each word contain exactly one stressed syllable. Gambell and Yang developed this algorithm partially as a response to a hypothesis put forward by Saffran et al. (1996) to explain their own experimental results. Saffran et al. concluded that young infants can attend to the transitional probabilities between syllables, and posit word boundaries where transitional probability (TP) is low. The TP from syllable X to syllable Y is simply given by:

$$P(Y|X) = \text{frequency of } XY/\text{frequency of } X \quad (1)$$

While TP is sufficient to explain the results of Saffran et al.'s 1996 study, it performs very poorly on actual child-directed speech, regardless of whether the probabilities are calculated between phonemes (Brent, 1999) or syllables. Because of the dramatic performance gains shown by the addition of USC in testing, as well as the poor performance of TP, Gambell and Yang conclude that the USC is required for word segmentation and thus is a likely candidate for inclusion in Universal Grammar (Gambell and Yang, 2006).

However, as the results in Table 2 show, VE is capable of slightly superior performance on syllable input, without assuming any prior constraints on syllable stress distribution. Moreover, the performance of both algorithms is also only a few points above the baseline of segmenting at every possible boundary location (i.e., at every syllable). These results show the limitations of simple statistics like TP, but also show that segmenting a sequence of syllables is a simple problem for more powerful statistical algorithms like VE. The fact that a very high percentage of the words found by VE have one stressed syllable suggest that a rule like the USC could be emergent rather than innate.

Algorithm	BP	BR	BF
TP	0.416	0.233	0.298
TP + USC	0.735	0.712	0.723
Bootstrapping + USC	0.959	0.934	0.946
Voting Experts	0.918	0.992	0.953
All Points	0.839	1.000	0.913

Table 2: Performance of various algorithms on the Brown corpus from CHILDES. Other than VE and All Points, values are taken from (Gambell and Yang, 2006).

4.4 Optimality of the VE Chunk Signature

It is one thing to find chunks in sequences, another to have a theory or model of chunks. The question addressed in this section is whether the chunk signature – low internal entropy and high boundary entropy – is merely a good detector of chunk boundaries, or whether it characterizes chunks, themselves. Is the chunk signature merely a good detector of word boundaries, or are words those objects that maximize the signal from the signature? One way to answer the question is to define a "chunkiness score" and show that words maximize the score while other objects do not.

The chunkiness score is:

$$Ch(s) = \frac{H_f(s) + H_b(s)}{2} - \log Pr(s) \quad (2)$$

It is just the average of the forward and backward boundary entropies, which our theory says should be high at true boundaries, minus the internal entropy between the boundaries, which should be low. $Ch(s)$ can be calculated for any segment of any sequence for which we can build a trie.

Our prediction is that words have higher chunkiness scores than other objects. Given a sequence, such as the letters in this sentence, we can generate other objects by segmenting the sequence in every possible way (there are 2^{n-1} of these for a sequence of length n). Every segmentation will produce some chunks, each of which will have a chunkiness score.

For each 5-word sequence (usually between 18 and 27 characters long) in the Bloom73 corpus from CHILDES, we generated all possible chunks and ranked them by their chunkiness. The average rank of true words was the 98.7th percentile of the distribution of chunkiness. It appears that syntax is the primary reason that true chunks do not rank higher: When the word-order in the training corpus is scrambled, the rank of true words is the 99.6th percentile of the chunkiness distribution. These early results, based on a corpus of child-directed speech, strongly suggest that words are objects that maximize chunkiness. Keep in mind that the chunkiness score knows nothing of words: The probabilities and entropies on which it is based are estimated from continuous sequences that contain no boundaries. It is therefore not obvious or necessary that the objects that maximize chunkiness scores should be words. It might be that letters, or phones, or morphemes, or syllables, or something altogether novel maximize chunkiness scores. However, empirically, the chunkiest objects in the corpus are words.

5 Discussion

Whether segmentation is performed on phonemic or syllabic sequences, and whether it is unsupervised or provided information such as utterance boundaries and pauses, information-theoretic algorithms such as VE, PtM and especially BVE perform segmentation very well. The performance of VE on BR87 is on par with other state-of-the-art semi-supervised segmentation algorithms such as WordEnds (Fleck, 2008) and HDP (Goldwater et al., 2009). The performance of BVE on corpora of child-directed speech is unmatched in the unconstrained case, to the best of our knowledge.

These results suggest that BVE provides a single, general chunking ability that that accounts for word segmentation in both scenarios, and potentially a wide variety of other cognitive tasks as well. We now consider other properties of BVE that are especially relevant to natural language learning. Over time, BVE's knowledge trie comes to represent the distribution of phoneme sequences that begin and end words it has found. We now discuss how this knowledge trie models phonotactic constraints, and ultimately becomes an emergent lexicon.

5.1 Phonotactic Constraints

Every language has a set of constraints on how phonemes can combine together into syllables, called phonotactic constraints. These constraints affect the distribution of phonemes found at the beginnings and ends of words. For example, words in English never begin with /ts/, because it is not a valid syllable onset in English. Knowledge of these constraints allows a language learner to simplify the segmentation problem by eliminating many possible segmentations, as demonstrated in Section 4.3. This approach has inspired algorithms in the literature, such as WordEnds (Fleck, 2008), which builds a statistical model of phoneme distributions at the beginnings and ends of words. BVE also learns a model of phonotactics at word boundaries by keeping similar statistics in its knowledge trie, but can do so in a fully unsupervised setting by inferring its own set of high-precision word boundaries with the chunk signature.

5.2 An Emergent Lexicon

VE does not represent explicitly a "lexicon" of chunks that it has discovered. VE produces chunks when applied to a sequence, but its internal data structures do not represent the chunks it has discovered explicitly. By contrast, BVE stores boundary information in the knowledge trie and refines it over time. Simply by storing the beginnings and endings of segments, the knowledge trie comes to store sequences like `#cat#`, where # represents a word boundary. The set of such bounded sequences constitutes an emergent lexicon. After segmenting a corpus of child-directed speech, the ten most frequent words of this lexicon are *you, the, that, what, is, it, this, what's, to*, and *look*. Of the 100 most frequent words, 93 are correct. The 7 errors include splitting off morphemes such as *ing*, and merging frequently co-occurring word pairs such as *do you*.

6 Implications for Cognitive Science

Recently, researchers have begun to empirically assess the degree to which segmentation algorithms accurately model human performance. In particular,

Frank et al. (2010) compared the segmentation predictions made by TP and a Bayesian Lexical model against the segmentation performance of adults, and found that the predictions of the Bayesian model were a better match for the human data. As mentioned in Section 4.3, computational evaluation has demonstrated repeatedly that TP provides a poor model of segmentation ability in natural language. Any of the entropic chunking methods investigated here can explain the artificial language results motivating TP, as well as the segmentation of natural language, which argues for their inclusion in future empirical investigations of human segmentation ability.

6.1 Innate Knowledge

The word segmentation problem provides a revealing case study of the relationship between nativism and statistical learning. The initial statistical proposals, such as TP, were too simple to explain the phenomenon. However, robust statistical methods were eventually developed that perform the linguistic task successfully. With statistical learning models in place that perform as well as (or better than) models based on innate knowledge, the argument for an impoverished stimulus becomes difficult to maintain, and thus the need for a nativist explanation is removed.

Importantly, it should be noted that the success of a statistical learning method is not an argument that nothing is innate in the domain of word segmentation, but simply that it is the learning *procedure*, rather than any specific *linguistic knowledge*, that is innate. The position that a statistical segmentation ability is innate is bolstered by speech segmentation experiments with cotton-top tamarins (Hauser et al., 2001) that have yielded similar results to Saffran's experiments with human infants, suggesting that the ability may be present in the common ancestor of humans and cotton-top tamarins.

Further evidence for a domain-general chunking ability can be found in experiments where human subjects proved capable of discovering chunks in a single continuous sequence of non-linguistic inputs. Saffran et al. (1999) found that adults and 8-month-old infants were able to segment sequences of tones at the level of performance previously established for syllable sequences (Saffran et al., 1996). Hunt and Aslin (1998) measured the reaction time of adults when responding to a single continuous sequence of light patterns, and found that subjects quickly learned to exploit predictive subsequences with quicker reactions, while delaying reaction at subsequence boundaries where prediction was uncertain. In both of these results, as well as the word segmentation experiments of Saffran et al., humans learned to segment the sequences quickly, usually within minutes, just as general chunking algorithms quickly reach high levels of performance.

7 Conclusion

We have shown that a domain-independent theory of chunking can be applied effectively to the problem of word segmentation, and can explain the ability of children to segment a continuous sequence, which other computational models examined here do not attempt to explain. The human ability to segment continuous sequences extends to non-linguistic domains as well, which further strengthens the general chunking account, as these chunking algorithms have been successfully applied to a diverse array of non-linguistic sequences. In particular, BVE combines the power of the information-theoretic chunk signature with a bootstrapping capability to achieve high levels of performance in both the continuous and incremental paradigms.

8 Future Work

Within the CHILDES corpus, our results have only been demonstrated for English, which leaves open the possibility that other languages may present a more serious segmentation problem. In English, where many words in child-directed speech are mono-morphemic, the difference between finding words and finding morphs is small. In some languages, ignoring the word/morph distinction is likely to be a more costly assumption, especially for highly agglutinative or even polysynthetic languages. One possibility that merits further exploration is that, in such languages, morphs rather than words are the units that optimize chunkiness.

Acknowledgements

This work was supported by the Office of Naval Research under contract ONR N00141010117. Any views expressed in this publication are solely those of the authors and do not necessarily reflect the views of the ONR.

References

Richard N. Aslin, Jenny R. Saffran, and Elissa L. Newport. 1998. Computation of Conditional Probability Statistics by 8-Month-Old Infants. *Psychological Science*, 9(4):321–324.

Nan Bernstein Ratner, 1987. *The phonology of parent-child speech*, pages 159–174. Erlbaum, Hillsdale, NJ.

Lois Bloom. 1973. *One Word at a Time*. Mouton, Paris.

Michael R. Brent. 1999. An Efficient, Probabilistically Sound Algorithm for Segmentation and Word Discovery. *Machine Learning*, (34):71–105.

Roger Brown. 1973. *A first language: The early stages*. Harvard University, Cambridge, MA.

Paul Cohen and Niall Adams. 2001. An algorithm for segmenting categorical time series into meaningful episodes. In *Proceedings of the Fourth Symposium on Intelligent Data Analysis*.

Paul Cohen, Niall Adams, and Brent Heeringa. 2007. Voting Experts: An Unsupervised Algorithm for Segmenting Sequences. *Intelligent Data Analysis*, 11(6):607–625.

Margaret M. Fleck. 2008. Lexicalized phonotactic word segmentation. In *Proceedings of The 49th Annual Meeting of the Association for Computational Linguistics: Human Language Technologies*, pages 130–138, Columbus, Ohio, USA. Association for Computational Linguistics.

Michael C Frank, Harry Tily, Inbal Arnon, and Sharon Goldwater. 2010. Beyond Transitional Probabilities : Human Learners Impose a Parsimony Bias in Statistical Word Segmentation. In *Proceedings of the 32nd Annual Meeting of the Cognitive Science Society*.

Timothy Gambell and Charles Yang. 2006. Statistics Learning and Universal Grammar: Modeling Word Segmentation. In *Workshop on Psycho-computational Models of Human Language*.

Sharon Goldwater, Thomas L Griffiths, and Mark Johnson. 2009. A Bayesian Framework for Word Segmentation: Exploring the Effects of Context. *Cognition*, 112(1):21–54.

Sharon Goldwater. 2007. *Nonparametric Bayesian models of lexical acquisition*. Ph.D. dissertation, Brown University.

Zellig S. Harris. 1955. From Phoneme to Morpheme. *Language*, 31(2):190–222.

Marc D. Hauser, Elissa L. Newport, and Richard N. Aslin. 2001. Segmentation of the speech stream in a non-human primate: statistical learning in cotton-top tamarins. *Cognition*, 78(3):B53–64.

Daniel Hewlett and Paul Cohen. 2009. Bootstrap Voting Experts. In *Proceedings of the Twenty-first International Joint Conference on Artificial Intelligence*.

Daniel Hewlett and Paul Cohen. 2010. Artificial General Segmentation. In *The Third Conference on Artificial General Intelligence*.

Ruskin H. Hunt and Richard N. Aslin. 1998. Statistical learning of visuomotor sequences: Implicit acquisition of sub-patterns. In *Proceedings of the Twentieth Annual Conference of the Cognitive Science Society*, Mahwah, NJ. Lawrence Erlbaum Associates.

Howard Johnson and Joel Martin. 2003. Unsupervised learning of morphology for English and Inuktitut. *Proceedings of the 2003 Conference of the North American Chapter of the Association for Computational Linguistics on Human Language Technology (HLT-NAACL 2003)*, pages 43–45.

Peter W. Jusczyk, Derek M. Houston, and Mary Newsome. 1999. The Beginnings of Word Segmentation in English-Learning Infants. *Cognitive Psychology*, 39(3-4):159–207.

Teuvo Kohonen. 1988. *Self-organized formation of topologically correct feature maps*.

Brian MacWhinney and Catherine E Snow. 1985. The child language data exchange system (CHILDES). *Journal of Child Language*.

Matthew Miller and Alexander Stoytchev. 2008. Hierarchical Voting Experts: An Unsupervised Algorithm for Hierarchical Sequence Segmentation. In *Proceedings of the 7th IEEE International Conference on Development and Learning*, pages 186–191.

Matthew Miller, Peter Wong, and Alexander Stoytchev. 2009. Unsupervised Segmentation of Audio Speech Using the Voting Experts Algorithm. *Proceedings of the 2nd Conference on Artificial General Intelligence (AGI 2009)*.

Jenny R. Saffran and Erik D. Thiessen. 2003. Pattern induction by infant language learners. *Developmental Psychology*, 39(3):484–494.

Jenny R. Saffran, Richard N. Aslin, and Elissa L. Newport. 1996. Statistical Learning by 8-Month-Old Infants. *Science*, 274(December):926–928.

Jenny R. Saffran, Elizabeth K Johnson, Richard N. Aslin, and Elissa L. Newport. 1999. Statistical learning of tone sequences by human infants and adults. *Cognition*, 70(1):27–52.

Kumiko Tanaka-Ishii and Zhihui Jin. 2006. From Phoneme to Morpheme: Another Verification Using a Corpus. In *Proceedings of the 21st International Conference on Computer Processing of Oriental Languages*, pages 234–244.

Anand Venkataraman. 2001. A procedure for unsupervised lexicon learning. In *Proceedings of the Eighteenth International Conference on Machine Learning*.

Computational Linguistics for Studying Language in People: Principles, Applications and Research Problems

Invited talk

Bruce Hayes
Department of Linguistics, UCLA
bhayes@humnet.ucla.edu

One of the goals of computational linguistics is to create automated systems that can learn, generate, and understand language at all levels of structure (semantics, syntax, morphology, phonology, phonetics). This is a very demanding task whose complete fulfillment lies far in the future. Human beings can learn, generate, and understand language at all levels of structure, and the study of how they do it can be pursued by computational modeling. Indeed, one sort of "acid test" for theories in linguistics is whether they can serve as the basis for successful models of this kind. A research strategy for theoretical linguistics based on modeling thus invites close collaboration between "mainstream" linguists and their computational colleagues.

Such collaborations make the job of the computationalists, already very demanding, even harder. The collision between a computational model and human data arises when we apply the Turing test: the model ought to behave like a human, not just in generating a correct output, but in every conceivable sense: generating alternative outputs for a single input, (often with a nuanced sense of preferences among them), generating human-like mistakes, generating child-like mistakes when given incomplete information, and so on. I suggest that linguists could serve as good Turing testers, because it is their daily practice in professional life to interrogate their models in the most ingenious ways they can find, probing for deficiencies though comparison to complex human intuitions and behavior.

With this as backdrop, I offers a series of case studies, of three different kinds: (1) **Turing tests**: cases where interrogation by linguists revealed non-humanlike traits in computational models that performed well by traditional computational criteria (precision, recall, etc.); (2) **Success stories**: particular results of computational linguistics that have proven useful so far in modeling language in humans; (3) **Suggestions for future work**: proposals in linguistic theory that look promising and would benefit from computational analysis.

Proceedings of the Fifteenth Conference on Computational Natural Language Learning, page 48,
Portland, Oregon, USA, 23–24 June 2011. ©2011 Association for Computational Linguistics

Search-based Structured Prediction applied to Biomedical Event Extraction

Andreas Vlachos and **Mark Craven**
Department of Biostatistics and Medical Informatics
University of Wisconsin-Madison
{vlachos,craven}@biostat.wisc.edu

Abstract

We develop an approach to biomedical event extraction using a search-based structured prediction framework, SEARN, which converts the task into cost-sensitive classification tasks whose models are learned jointly. We show that SEARN improves on a simple yet strong pipeline by 8.6 points in F-score on the BioNLP 2009 shared task, while achieving the best reported performance by a joint inference method. Additionally, we consider the issue of cost estimation during learning and present an approach called *focused costing* that improves improves efficiency and predictive accuracy.

1 Introduction

The term *biomedical event extraction* is used to refer to the task of extracting descriptions of actions and relations involving one or more entities from the biomedical literature. The recent BioNLP 2009 shared task (BioNLP09ST) on event extraction (Kim et al., 2009) focused on event types of varying complexity. Each event consists of a *trigger* and one or more *arguments*, the latter being proteins or other events. Any token in a sentence can be a trigger for one of the nine event types and, depending on their associated event types, triggers are assigned appropriate arguments. Thus, the task can be viewed as a structured prediction problem in which the output for a given instance is a (possibly disconnected) directed acyclic graph (not necessarily a tree) in which vertices correspond to triggers or protein arguments, and edges represent relations between them.

Despite being a structured prediction task, most of the systems that have been applied to BioNLP09ST to date are pipelines that decompose event extraction into a set of simpler classification tasks. Classifiers for these tasks are typically learned independently, thereby ignoring event structure during training. Typically in such systems, the relationships among these tasks are taken into account by incorporating post-processing rules that enforce certain constraints when combining their predictions, and by tuning classification thresholds to improve the accuracy of joint predictions. Pipelines are appealing as they are relatively easy to implement and they often achieve state-of-the-art performance (Bjorne et al., 2009; Miwa et al., 2010).

Because of the nature of the output space, the task is not amenable to sequential or grammar-based approaches (e.g. linear CRFs, HMMs, PCFGs) which employ dynamic programming in order to do efficient inference. The only joint inference framework that has been applied to BioNLP09ST to date is Markov Logic Networks (MLNs) (Riedel et al., 2009; Poon and Vanderwende, 2010). However, MLNs require task-dependent approximate inference and substantial computational resources in order to achieve state-of-the-art performance.

In this work we explore an alternative joint inference approach to biomedical event extraction using a search-based structured prediction framework, SEARN (Daumé III et al., 2009). SEARN is an algorithm that converts the problem of learning a model for structured prediction into learning a set of models for cost-sensitive classification (CSC). CSC is a task in which each training instance has a vector of misclassification costs associated with it, thus rendering some mistakes on some instances to be more expensive than others (Domingos, 1999). Compared to a standard pipeline, SEARN is able to

Proceedings of the Fifteenth Conference on Computational Natural Language Learning, pages 49–57,
Portland, Oregon, USA, 23–24 June 2011.

achieve better performance because its models are learned jointly. Thus, each of them is able to use features representing the predictions made by the others, while taking into account possible mistakes.

In this paper, we make the following contributions. Using the SEARN framework, we develop a joint inference approach to biomedical event extraction. We evaluate our approach on the BioNLP09ST dataset and show that SEARN improves on a simple yet strong pipeline by 8.6 points in F-score, while achieving the best reported performance on the task by a joint inference method. Additionally, we consider the issue of cost estimation and present an approach called *focused costing* that improves performance. We believe that these contributions are likely to be relevant to applications of SEARN to other natural language processing tasks that involve structured prediction in complex output spaces.

2 BioNLP 2009 shared task description

BioNLP09ST focused on the extraction of events involving proteins whose names are annotated in advance. Each event has two types of arguments, *Theme* and *Cause*, which correspond respectively to the *Agent* and *Patient* roles in semantic role labeling (Gildea and Jurafsky, 2002). Nine event types are defined which can be broadly classified in three categories, namely *Simple*, *Binding* and *Regulation*. *Simple* events include *Gene_expression*, *Transcription*, *Protein_catabolism*, *Phosphorylation*, and *Localization* events. These have only one *Theme* argument which is a protein. *Binding* events have one or more protein *Themes*. Finally, *Regulation* events, which include *Positive_regulation*, *Negative_regulation* and *Regulation*, have one obligatory *Theme* and one optional *Cause*, each of which can be either a protein or another event. Each event has a trigger which is a contiguous string that can span over one or more tokens. Triggers and arguments can be shared across events. In an example demonstrating the complexity of the task, given the passage "...SQ 22536 suppressed gp41-induced IL-10 production in monocytes", systems should extract the three appropriately nested events listed in Fig. 1d.

Performance is measured using Recall, Precision and F-score over complete events, i.e. the trigger, the event type and the arguments all must be correct in order to obtain a true positive. It is important to note that if either the trigger, the type, or an argument of a predicted event is incorrect then this event will result in one false positive and one false negative. In the example of Fig. 1, if "suppressed" is recognized incorrectly as a *Regulation* trigger then it is better to not assign a *Theme* to it so that we avoid a false positive due to extracting an event with incorrect type. Finally, the evaluation ignores triggers that do not form events.

3 Event extraction decomposition

Figure 1 describes the event extraction decomposition that we use throughout the paper. We assume that the sentences to be processed are parsed into syntactic dependencies and lemmatized. Each stage has its own module, which is either a learned classifier (trigger recognition, *Theme*/*Cause* assignment) or a rule-based component (event construction).

3.1 Trigger recognition

In trigger recognition the system decides whether a token acts as a trigger for one of the nine event types or not. Thus it is a 10-way classification task. We only consider tokens that are tagged as nouns, verbs or adjectives by the parser, as they cover the majority of the triggers in the BioNLP09ST data. The main features used in the classifier represent the lemma of the token which is sufficient to predict the event type correctly in most cases. In addition, we include features that conjoin each lemma with its part-of-speech tag. This allows us to handle words with the same nominal and verbal form that have different meanings, such as "lead". While the domain restricts most lemmas to one event type, there are some whose event type is determined by the context, e.g. "regulation" on its own denotes a *Regulation* event but in "positive regulation" it denotes a *Positive_regulation* event instead. In order to capture this phenomenon, we add as features the conjunction of each lemma with the lemma of the tokens immediately surrounding it, as well as with the lemmas of the tokens with which it has syntactic dependencies.

3.2 *Theme* and *Cause* assignment

In *Theme* assignment, we form an agenda of candidate trigger-argument pairs for all trigger-protein combinations in the sentence and classify them as

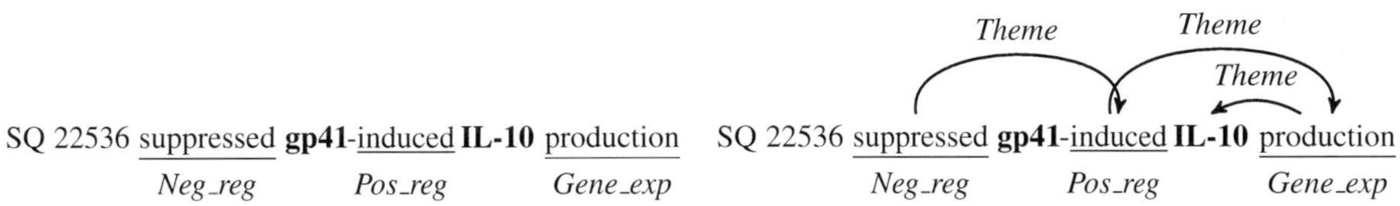

(a) Trigger recognition

(b) *Theme* assignment

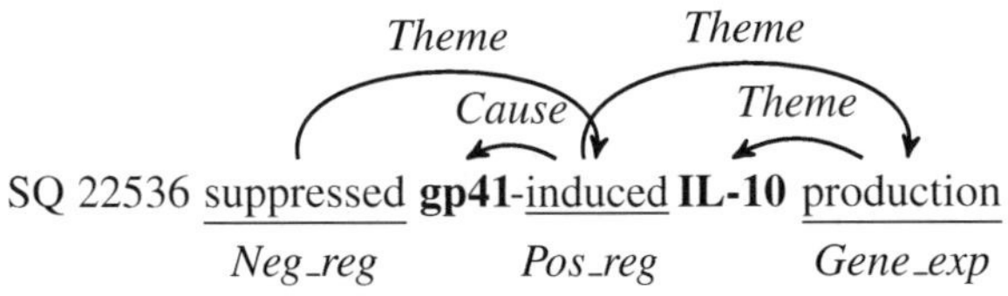

(c) *Cause* assignment

ID	type	*Trigger*	*Theme*	*Cause*
E1	*Neg_reg*	suppressed	*E2*	
E2	*Pos_reg*	induced	*E3*	gp41
E3	*Gene_exp*	production	IL-10	

(d) Event construction

Figure 1: The stages of our event extraction decomposition. Protein names are shown in bold.

Themes or not. Whenever a trigger is predicted to be associated with a *Theme*, we form candidate pairs between all the *Regulation* triggers in the sentence and that trigger as the argument, thus allowing the prediction of nested events. Also, we remove candidate pairs that could result in directed cycles, as they are not allowed by the task.

The features used to predict whether a trigger-argument pair should be classified as a *Theme* are extracted from the syntactic dependency path and the textual string between them. In particular, we extract the shortest unlexicalized dependency path connecting each trigger-argument pair, allowing the paths to follow either dependency direction. One set of features represents these paths, and in addition, we have sets of features representing each path conjoined with the lemma, the PoS tag and the event type of the trigger, the type of the argument and the first and last lemmas in the dependency path. The latter help by providing some mild lexicalization. We also add features representing the textual string between the trigger and the argument, combined with the event type of the trigger. While not as informative as dependency paths, such features help in sentences where the parse is incorrect, as triggers and their arguments tend to appear near each other.

In *Cause* assignment, we form an agenda of candidate trigger-argument pairs using only the *Regulation* class triggers that were assigned at least one *Theme*. These are combined with protein names and other triggers that were assigned a *Theme*. We extract features as in *Theme* assignment, further features representing the conjunction of the dependency path of the candidate pair with the path(s) from the trigger to its *Theme(s)*.

3.3 Event construction

In event construction, we convert the predictions of the previous stages into a set of legal events. If a *Binding* trigger is assigned multiple *Themes*, we choose to form either one event per *Theme* or one event with multiple *Themes*. Following Bjorne et al. (2009), we group the arguments of each *Binding* trigger according to the first label in their syntactic dependency path and generate events using the cross-product of these groups. For example, assuming the parse was correct and all the *Themes* recognized, "interactions of **A** and **B** with **C**" results in two *Binding* events with two *Themes* each, **A** with **C**, and **B** with **C** respectively. We add the exception that if two *Themes* are in the same token (e.g. "**A/B** interactions") or the lemma of the trigger is "bind" then they form one *Binding* event with two *Themes*.

4 Structured prediction with SEARN

SEARN (Daumé III et al., 2009) forms the structured output prediction for an instance s as a sequence of T multiclass predictions $\hat{y}_{1:T}$ made by a hypothesis h. The latter consists of a set of classifiers that are learned jointly. Each prediction $\hat{y}_t$ can use features from s as well as from all the previous predictions $\hat{y}_{1:t-1}$. These predictions are referred to as *actions* and we adopt this term in order to distinguish them from the structured output predictions.

The SEARN algorithm is presented in Alg. 1. It initializes hypothesis h to the *optimal policy* π (step 2) which predicts the optimal action in each step t according to the gold standard. The optimal action at step t is the one that minimizes the overall loss over s assuming that all future actions $\hat{y}_{t+1:T}$ are also made optimally. The loss function ℓ is defined by the structured prediction task considered. Each iteration begins by making predictions for all instances s in the training data $\mathcal{S}$ (step 6). For each s and each action $\hat{y}_t$, a cost-sensitive classification (CSC) example is generated (steps 8-12). The features are extracted from s and the previous actions $\hat{y}_{1:t-1}$ (step 8). The cost for each possible action y_t^i is estimated by predicting the remaining actions $y'_{t+1:T}$ in s using h (step 10) and evaluating the cost incurred given that action (step 11). Using a CSC learning algorithm, a new hypothesis is learned (step 13) which is combined with the current one according to the interpolation parameter β.

Algorithm 1 SEARN

```
1: Input: labeled instances S, optimal policy π, CSC
   learning algorithm CSCL, loss function ℓ
2: current policy h = π
3: while h depends significantly on π do
4:   Examples E = ∅
5:   for s in S do
6:     Predict h(s) = ŷ_{1:T}
7:     for ŷ_t in h(s) do
8:       Extract features Φ_t = f(s, ŷ_{1:t-1})
9:       for each possible action y_t^i do
10:        Predict y'_{t+1:T} = h(s|ŷ_{1:t-1}, y_t^i)
11:        Estimate c_t^i = ℓ(ŷ_{1:t-1}, y_t^i, y'_{t+1:T})
12:      Add (Φ_t, c_t) to E
13:  Learn a hypothesis h_new = CSCL(E)
14:  h = β h_new + (1 − β)h
15: Output: policy h without π
```

In each iteration, SEARN moves away from the optimal policy and uses the learned hypotheses instead when predicting (steps 6 and 10). Thus, each h_{new} is adapted to the actions chosen by h instead of those of the optimal policy. When the dependence on the latter becomes insignificant, the algorithm terminates and returns the weighted ensemble of learned hypotheses without the optimal policy. Note though that the estimation of the costs in step 11 is always performed using the gold standard.

The interpolation parameter β determines how fast SEARN moves away from the optimal policy and as a result how many iterations will be needed to minimize the dependence on it. Dependence in this context refers to the probability of using the optimal policy instead of the learned hypothesis in choosing an action during prediction. In each iteration, the features extracted Φ_t are progressively corrupted with the actions chosen by the learned hypotheses instead of those of the optimal policy.

Structural information under SEARN is incorporated in two ways. First, via the costs that are estimated using the loss over the instance rather than isolated actions (e.g. in PoS tagging, the loss would be the number of incorrect PoS tags predicted in a sentence if a token is tagged as noun). Second, via the features extracted from the previous actions ($\hat{y}_{1:t-1}$) (e.g. the PoS tag predicted for the previous token can be a feature). These types of features are possible in a standard pipeline as well, but during training they would have to be extracted using the gold standard instead of the actual predictions made by the learned hypotheses, as during testing. Since the prediction for each instance ($\hat{y}_{1:T}$ in step 6) changes in every iteration, the structure features used to predict the actions have to be extracted anew.

The extraction of features from previous actions implies a search order. For some tasks, such as PoS tagging, there is a natural left-to-right order in which the tokens are treated, however for many tasks this is not the case.

Finally, SEARN can be used to learn a pipeline of independently trained classifiers. This is achieved using only one iteration in which the cost for each action is set to 0 if it follows from the gold standard and to 1 otherwise. This adaptation allows for a fair comparison between SEARN and a pipeline.

5 SEARN for biomedical event extraction

In this section we discuss how we learn the event extraction decomposition described in Sec. 3 under SEARN. Each instance is a sentence consisting of the tokens, the protein names and the syntactic parsing output. The hypothesis learned in each iteration consists of a classifier for each stage of the pipeline, excluding event construction which is rule-based.

Unlike PoS tagging, there is no natural ordering of the actions in event extraction. Ideally, the actions predicted earlier should be less dependent on structural features and/or easier so that they can inform the more structure dependent/harder ones. In trigger recognition, we process the tokens from left to right since modifiers appearing before nouns tend to affect the meaning of the latter, e.g. "binding activity". In *Theme* and *Cause* assignment, we predict trigger-argument pairs in order of increasing dependency path length, assuming that since dependency paths are the main source of features at this stage and shorter paths are less sparse, pairs containing shorter ones should be more reliable to predict.

In addition to the features mentioned in Sec. 3, SEARN allows us to extract and learn weights for structural features for each action from the previous ones. During trigger recognition, we add as features the combination of the lemma of the current token combined with the event type (if any) assigned to the previous and the next token, as well as to the tokens that have syntactic dependencies with it. During *Theme* assignment, when considering a trigger-argument pair, we add features based on whether it forms an undirected cycle with previously predicted *Themes*, whether the trigger has been assigned a protein as a *Theme* and the candidate *Theme* is an event trigger (and the reverse) and whether the argument has become the *Theme* of a trigger with the same event type. We also add a feature indicating whether the trigger has three *Themes* predicted already. During *Cause* assignment, we add features representing whether the trigger has been assigned a protein as a *Cause* and the candidate *Cause* is an event trigger.

The loss function ℓ sums the number of false positive and false negative events, which is the evaluation measure of BioNLP09ST. The optimal policy is derived from the gold standard and returns the action that minimizes this loss over the sentence given the previous actions and assuming that all future actions are optimal. In trigger recognition, it returns either the event type for tokens that are triggers or a "notrigger" label otherwise. In *Theme* assignment, for a given trigger-argument pair the optimal policy returns *Theme* only if the trigger is recognized correctly and the argument is indeed a *Theme* for that trigger according to the gold standard. In case the argument is another event, we require that at least one of its *Themes* to be recognized correctly as well. In *Cause* assignment, the requirements are the same as those for the *Themes*, but we also require that at least one *Theme* of the trigger in the trigger-argument pair to be considered correct. These additional checks follow from the task definition, under which events must have all their elements identified correctly.

5.1 Cost estimation

Cost estimation (steps 5-12 in Alg. 1) is crucial to the successful application of SEARN. In order to highlight its importance, consider the example of Fig. 2 focusing on trigger recognition.

In the first iteration (Fig. 2a), the actions for the sentence will be made using the optimal policy only, thus replicating the gold standard. During costing, if a token is not a trigger according to the gold standard (e.g. "SQ"), then the cost for incorrectly predicting that it is a trigger is 0, as the optimal policy will not assign *Themes* to a trigger with incorrect event type. Such instances are ignored by the cost-sensitive learner. If a token is a trigger according to the gold standard, then the cost for not predicting it as such or predicting its type incorrectly is equal to the number of the events that are dependent on it, as they will become false negatives. False positives are avoided as we are using the optimal policy in this iteration.

In the second iteration (Fig. 2b), the optimal policy is interpolated with the learned hypothesis, thus some of the actions are likely to be incorrect. Assume that "SQ" is incorrectly predicted to be a *Neg_reg* trigger and assigned a *Theme*. During costing, the action of labeling "SQ" as *Neg_reg* has a cost of 1, as it would result in a false positive event. Thus the learned hypothesis will be informed that it should not label "SQ" as a trigger as it would assign *Themes* to it incorrectly and it is adapted to handle its own mistakes. Similarly, the action of labeling "production" as *Neg_reg* in this iteration would incur a cost of 6, as the learned hypothesis would assign a *Theme* incorrectly, thus resulting in 3 false negative and 3 false positive events. Therefore, the learned hypothesis will be informed that assigning the wrong event type to "production" is worse than not predicting a trigger.

By evaluating the cost of each action according to

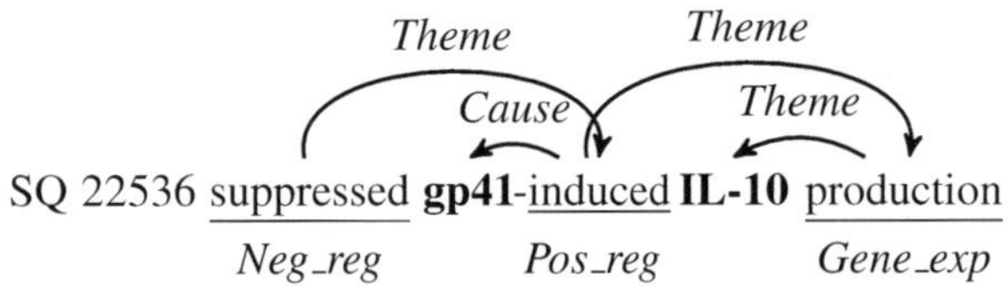

token	*No*	*Gene_exp*	*Pos_reg*	*Neg_reg*
SQ	0	0	0	0
suppressed	1	1	1	0
-induced	2	2	0	2
production	3	0	3	3

(a) First iteration (optimal policy only)

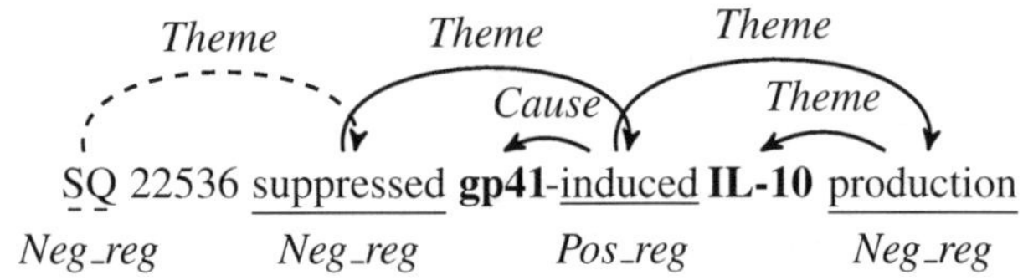

token	*No*	*Gene_exp*	*Pos_reg*	*Neg_reg*
SQ	0	0	0	1
suppressed	1	1	1	0
-induced	2	2	0	2
production	3	0	3	6

(b) Second iteration (interpolation)

Figure 2: Prediction (top) and CSC examples for trigger recognition actions (bottom) in the first two SEARN iterations. Each CSC example has its own vector of misclassification costs.

its effect on the prediction for the whole sentence, we are able to take into account steps in the prediction process that are not learned as actions. For example, if the *Binding* event construction heuristic described in Sec. 3.3 cannot produce the correct events for a token that is a *Binding* trigger despite the *Themes* being assigned correctly, then this will increase the cost for tagging that trigger as *Binding*.

The interpolation between the optimal policy and the learned hypothesis is stochastic, thus affecting the cost estimates obtained. In order to obtain more reliable estimates, one can average multiple samples for each action by repeating steps 10 and 11 of Alg. 1. However, the computational cost is effectively multiplied by the number of samples.

In step 11 of Alg. 1, the cost of each action is estimated over the whole sentence. While this allows us to take structure into account, it can result in costs being affected by a part of the output that is not related to that action. This is likely to occur in event extraction, as sentences can often be long and contain disconnected event components in their output graphs. For this reason, we refine the cost estimation of each action to take into account only the events that are connected to it through either gold standard or predicted events. For example, in Fig. 2 the cost estimation for "SQ" will ignore the predicted events in the first iteration and the gold standard, while it will take them into account in the second one. We refer to this refinement as *focused costing*.

A different approach proposed by Daumé III et al. (2009) is to assume that all actions following the one we are costing are going to be optimal and use the optimal policy to approximate the prediction of the learned hypothesis in step 10 of Alg. 1. In tasks where the learned hypothesis is accurate enough, this has no performance loss and it is computationally efficient as the optimal policy is deterministic. However, in event extraction the learned hypothesis is likely to make mistakes, thus the optimal policy does not provide a good approximation for it.

5.2 CSC learning with passive-aggressive algorithms

The SEARN framework requires a multiclass CSC algorithm to learn how to predict actions. This algorithm must be computationally fast during parameter learning and prediction, as in every iteration we need to learn a new hypothesis and to consider each possible action for each instance in order to construct the cost-sensitive examples. Daumé III et al. (2009) showed that any binary classification algorithm can be used to perform multiclass CSC by employing an appropriate conversion between the tasks. The main drawback of this approach is its reliance on multiple subsamplings of the training data, which can be inefficient for large datasets and many classes.

With these considerations in mind, we implement a multiclass CSC learning algorithm using the generalization of the online passive-aggressive (PA) algorithm for binary classification proposed by Crammer et al. (2006). For each training example x_t, the K-class linear classifier with K weight vectors $w_t^{(k)}$ makes a prediction $\hat{y}_t$ and suffers a loss ℓ_t. In the case of multiclass CSC learning, each example has its own cost vector c_t. If the loss is 0 then the weight vectors of the classifier are not updated (passive). Otherwise, the weight vectors are updated minimally so that the prediction on example x_t is corrected (aggressive). The update takes into account the loss and the aggressiveness parameter $\mathcal{C}$. Crammer et al. (2006) describe three variants to perform the updates which differ in how the learning rate τ_t is set. In our experiments we use the variant named PA-II with prediction-based updates (Alg. 2). Since we are operating in a batch learning setting (i.e. we have access to all the training examples and their order is not meaningful), we perform multiple rounds over the training examples shuffling their order, and average the weight vectors obtained.

Algorithm 2 Passive-aggressive CSC learning

Input: training examples $\mathcal{X} = x_1 \dots x_T$, cost vectors $c_1 \dots c_T \geq 0$, rounds R, aggressiveness $\mathcal{C}$
Initialize weights $w_0^{(k)} = (0, ..., 0)$
for $r = 1, ..., R$ **do**
  Shuffle $\mathcal{X}$
  for $x_t \in \mathcal{X}$ **do**
    Predict $\hat{y}_t = argmax_k(w_t^{(k)} \cdot x_t)$
    Receive cost vector $c_t \geq 0$
    if $c_t^{(\hat{y}_t)} > 0$ **then**
      Suffer loss $\ell_t = w_t^{(\hat{y}_t)} \cdot x_t - w_t^{(y_t)} \cdot x_t + \sqrt{c_t^{(\hat{y}_t)}}$
      Set learning rate $\tau_t = \frac{\ell_t}{||x_t||^2 + \frac{1}{2\mathcal{C}}}$
      Update $w_{t+1}^{(y_t)} = w_t + \tau_t x_t$
      Update $w_{t+1}^{(\hat{y}_t)} = w_t - \tau_t x_t$
Average $w_{avg} = \frac{1}{T \times R} \sum_{i=0}^{T \times R} w_i$

6 Experiments

BioNLP09ST comprises three datasets – training, development and test – which consist of 800, 150 and 260 abstracts respectively. After the end of the shared task, an on-line evaluation server was activated in order to allow the evaluation on the test data once per day, without allowing access to the data itself. We report results using Recall/Precision/F-score over complete events using the approximate span matching/approximate recursive matching variant which was the primary performance criterion in BioNLP09ST. This variant counts a predicted event as a true positive if its trigger is extracted within a one-token extension of the gold-standard trigger. Also, in the case of nested events, those events below the top-level need their trigger, event type and *Theme* but not their *Cause* to be correctly identified for the top-level event to be considered correct. The same event matching variant was used in defining the loss as described in Sec. 5.

A pre-processing step we perform on the training data is to reduce the multi-token triggers in the gold standard to their syntactic heads. This procedure simplifies the task of assigning arguments to triggers and, as the evaluation variant used allows approximate trigger matching, it does not result in a performance loss. For syntactic parsing, we use the output of the BLLIP re-ranking parser adapted to the biomedical domain by McClosky and Charniak (2008), as provided by the shared task organizers in the Stanford collapsed dependency format with conjunct dependency propagation. Lemmatization is performed using *morpha* (Minnen et al., 2001).

In all our experiments, for CSC learning with PA, the C parameter is set by tuning on 10% of the training data and the number of rounds is fixed to 10. For SEARN, we set the interpolation parameter β to 0.3 and the number of iterations to 12. The costs for each action are obtained by averaging three samples as described in Sec. 5.1. β and the number of samples are the only parameters that need tuning and we use the development data for this purpose.

First we compare against a pipeline of independently learned classifiers obtained as described in Sec. 4 in order to assess the benefits of joint learning under SEARN using focused costing. The results shown in Table 1 demonstrate that SEARN obtains better event extraction performance on both the development and test sets by 7.7 and 8.6 F-score points respectively. The pipeline baseline employed in our experiments is a strong one: it would have ranked fifth in BioNLP09ST and it is 20 F-score points better than the baseline MLN employed by Poon and Vanderwende (2010). Nevertheless, the independently learned classifier for triggers misses almost half of the event triggers, from which the subsequent stages cannot recover. On the other hand, the trigger classifier learned with SEARN overpredicts, but since the *Theme* and *Cause* classifiers are learned jointly with it they maintain relatively high precision with substantially higher recall compared to their in-

	pipeline			SEARN_focus			SEARN_default		
	R	P	F	R	P	F	R	P	F
trigger_{dev}	53.0	61.1	56.8	81.8	34.2	48.2	84.9	12.0	21.0
$Theme_{dev}$	44.2	79.6	56.9	62.0	69.1	65.4	59.0	65.1	61.9
$Cause_{dev}$	18.1	59.2	27.8	30.6	45.0	36.4	31.9	45.5	37.5
Event_{dev}	35.8	68.9	47.1	50.8	59.5	54.8	47.4	54.3	50.6
Event_{test}	30.8	67.4	42.2	44.5	59.1	50.8	41.3	53.6	46.6

Table 1: Recall / Precision / F-score on BioNLP09ST development and test data. Left-to-right: pipeline of independently learned classifiers, SEARN with focused costing, SEARN with default costing.

dependently learned counterparts. The benefits of SEARN are more pronounced in *Regulation* events which are more complex. For these events, it improves on the pipeline on both the development and test sets by 11 and 14.2 F-score points respectively.

The focused costing approach we proposed contributes to the success of SEARN. If we replace it with the default costing approach which uses the whole sentence, the F-score drops by 4.2 points on both development and test datasets. The default costing approach mainly affects the trigger recognition stage, which takes place first. Trigger overprediction is more extreme in this case and renders the *Theme* assignment stage harder to learn. While the joint learning of the classifiers ameliorates this issue and the event extraction performance is eventually higher than that of the pipeline, the use of focused costing improves the performance even further. Note that trigger overprediction also makes training slower, as it results in evaluating more actions for each sentence. Finally, using one instead of three samples per action decreases the F-score by 1.3 points on the development data.

Compared with the MLN approaches applied to BioNLP09ST, our predictive accuracy is better than that of Poon and Vanderwende (2010) which is the best joint inference performance to date and substantially better than that of Riedel et al. (2009) (50 and 44.4 in F-score respectively). Recently, McClosky et al. (2011) combined multiple decoders for a dependency parser with a reranker, achieving 48.6 in F-score. While they also extracted structure features for *Theme* and *Cause* assignment, their model is restricted to trees (ours can output directed acyclic graphs) and their trigger recognizer is learned independently.

When we train SEARN combining the training and the development sets, we reach 52.3 in F-score, which is better than the performance of the top system in BioNLP09ST (51.95) by Bjorne et al. (2009) which was trained in the same way. The best performance to date is reported by Miwa et al. (2010) (56.3 in F-score), who experimented with six parsers, three dependency representations and various combinations of these. They found that different parser/dependency combinations provided the best results on the development and test sets.

A direct comparison between learning frameworks is difficult due to the differences in task decomposition and feature extraction. In particular, event extraction results depend substantially on the quality of the syntactic parsing. For example, Poon and Vanderwende (2010) heuristically correct the syntactic parsing used and report that this improved their performance by four F-score points.

7 Conclusions

We developed a joint inference approach to biomedical event extraction using the SEARN framework which converts a structured prediction task into a set of CSC tasks whose models are learned jointly. Our approach employs the PA algorithm for CSC learning and a focused cost estimation procedure which improves the efficiency and accuracy of the standard cost estimation method. Our approach provides the best reported results for a joint inference method on the BioNLP09ST task. With respect to the experiments presented by Daumé III et al. (2009), we empirically demonstrate the gains of using SEARN on a problem harder than sequential tagging.

Acknowledgments

The authors were funded by NIH/NLM grant R01 / LM07050.

References

Jari Bjorne, Juho Heimonen, Filip Ginter, Antti Airola, Tapio Pahikkala, and Tapio Salakoski. 2009. Extracting complex biological events with rich graph-based feature sets. In *Proceedings of the BioNLP 2009 Workshop Companion Volume for Shared Task*, pages 10–18.

Koby Crammer, Ofer Dekel, Joseph Keshet, Shai Shalev-Shwartz, and Yoram Singer. 2006. Online passive-aggressive algorithms. *Journal of Machine Learning Research*, 7:551–585.

Hal Daumé III, John Langford, and Daniel Marcu. 2009. Search-based structured prediction. *Machine Learning*, 75:297–325.

Pedro Domingos. 1999. Metacost: a general method for making classifiers cost-sensitive. In *Proceedings of the 5th International Conference on Knowledge Discovery and Data Mining*, pages 155–164.

Daniel Gildea and Daniel Jurafsky. 2002. Automatic labeling of semantic roles. *Computational Linguistics*, 28:245–288.

Jin-Dong Kim, Tomoko Ohta, Sampo Pyysalo, Yoshinobu Kano, and Jun'ichi Tsujii. 2009. Overview of BioNLP'09 shared task on event extraction. In *Proceedings of the BioNLP 2009 Workshop Companion Volume for Shared Task*, pages 1–9.

David McClosky and Eugene Charniak. 2008. Self-training for biomedical parsing. In *Proceedings of the 46th Annual Meeting of the Association of Computational Linguistics: Human Language Technologies*, pages 101–104.

David McClosky, Mihai Surdeanu, and Christopher D. Manning. 2011. Event extraction as dependency parsing. In *Proceedings of the 49th Annual Meeting of the Association for Computational Linguistics: Human Language Technologies*.

Guido Minnen, John Carroll, and Darren Pearce. 2001. Applied morphological processing of English. *Natural Language Engineering*, 7(3):207–223.

Makoto Miwa, Sampo Pyysalo, Tadayoshi Hara, and Jun'ichi Tsujii. 2010. Evaluating dependency representation for event extraction. In *Proceedings of the 23rd International Conference on Computational Linguistics*, pages 779–787.

Hoifung Poon and Lucy Vanderwende. 2010. Joint inference for knowledge extraction from biomedical literature. In *Proceedings of the Human Language Technologies: The 2010 Annual Conference of the North American Chapter of the Association for Computational Linguistics*, pages 813–821.

Sebastian Riedel, Hong-Woo Chun, Toshihisa Takagi, and Jun'ichi Tsujii. 2009. A Markov logic approach to bio-molecular event extraction. In *Proceedings of the BioNLP 2009 Workshop Companion Volume for Shared Task*, pages 41–49.

Using Sequence Kernels to identify Opinion Entities in Urdu

Smruthi Mukund[†] **and Debanjan Ghosh**[*]
[†]SUNY at Buffalo, NY
smukund@buffalo.edu
[*]Thomson Reuters Corporate R&D
debanjan.ghosh@thomsonreuters.com

Rohini K Srihari
SUNY at Buffalo, NY
rohini@cedar.buffalo.edu

Abstract

Automatic extraction of opinion holders and targets (together referred to as opinion entities) is an important subtask of sentiment analysis. In this work, we attempt to accurately extract opinion entities from Urdu newswire. Due to the lack of resources required for training role labelers and dependency parsers (as in English) for Urdu, a more robust approach based on (i) generating candidate word sequences corresponding to opinion entities, and (ii) subsequently disambiguating these sequences as opinion holders or targets is presented. Detecting the boundaries of such candidate sequences in Urdu is very different than in English since in Urdu, grammatical categories such as tense, gender and case are captured in word inflections. In this work, we exploit the morphological inflections associated with nouns and verbs to correctly identify sequence boundaries. Different levels of information that capture context are encoded to train standard linear and sequence kernels. To this end the best performance obtained for opinion entity detection for Urdu sentiment analysis is 58.06% F-Score using sequence kernels and 61.55% F-Score using a combination of sequence and linear kernels.

1 Introduction

Performing sentiment analysis on newswire data facilitates the development of systems capable of answering perspective questions like "*How did people react to the latest presidential speech?*" and "*Does General Musharraf support the Indo-Pak peace treaty?*". The components involved in developing such systems require accurate identification of opinion expressions and opinion entities. Several of the approaches proposed in the literature to automatically extract the opinion entities rely on the use of thematic role labels and dependency parsers to provide new lexical features for opinion words (Bethard *et al.,* 2004). Semantic roles (SRL) also help to mark the semantic constituents (*agent, theme, proposition*) of a sentence. Such features are extremely valuable for a task like opinion entity detection.

English is a privileged language when it comes to the availability of resources needed to contribute features for opinion entity detection. There are other widely spoken, resource poor languages, which are still in the infantile stage of automatic natural language processing (NLP). Urdu is one such language. The main objective of our research is to provide a solution for opinion entity detection in the Urdu language. Despite Urdu lacking NLP resources required to contribute features similar to what works for the English language, the performance of our approach is comparable with English for this task (compared with the work of Weigand and Klalow, 2010 ~ 62.61% F1). The morphological richness of the Urdu language enables us to extract features based on noun and verb inflections that effectively contribute to the opinion entity extraction task. Most importantly, these features can be generalized to other Indic languages (Hindi, Bengali etc.) owing to the grammatical similarity between the languages.

Proceedings of the Fifteenth Conference on Computational Natural Language Learning, pages 58–67,
Portland, Oregon, USA, 23–24 June 2011.

English has seen extensive use of sequence kernels (string and tree kernels) for tasks such as relation extraction (Culotta and Sorensen, 2004) and semantic role labeling (Moschitti *et al.,* 2008). But, the application of these kernels to a task like opinion entity detection is scarcely explored (Weigand and Klalow, 2010). Moreover, existing works in English perform only opinion holder identification using these kernels. What makes our approach unique is that we use the power of sequence kernels to simultaneously identify opinion holders and targets in the Urdu language.

Sequence kernels allow efficient use of the learning algorithm exploiting massive number of features without the traditional explicit feature representation (such as, Bag of Words). Often, in case of sequence kernels, the challenge lies in choosing meaningful subsequences as training samples instead of utilizing the whole sequence. In Urdu newswire data, generating candidate sequences usable for training is complicated. Not only are the opinion entities diverse in that they can be contained within noun phrases or clauses, the clues that help to identify these components can be contained within any word group - speech events, opinion words, predicates and connectors.

1	***Pakistan ke swaat sarhad ke janoobi shahar Banno ka havayi adda*** *zarayye ablaagk tavvju ka markaz ban gaya hai.* ***[Pakistan's provincial border's south city's airbase*** *has become the center of attraction for all reporters.]* Here, the opinion target spans across four noun chunks, "**Pakistan's | provincial border's | south city's | airbase**". The case markers (connectors) "***ke***"and"***ka***" indicate the span.
2	***Habib miyan ka*** *ghussa bad gaya aur wo* ***apne aurat*** *ko* ***maara.*** ***[Habib miya's*** *anger increased and he* ***hit*** *his own* ***wife.]*** Here, the gender (Masculine) inflection of the verb ***"maara"*** *(hit)* indicates that the agent performing this action is **"Habib miya"** (Masculine)
3	*Ansari ne* ***kaha*** ***"mere rayee mein*** *Aamir Sohail eek badimaak aur Ziddi insaan hai".* *[Ansari said, "****according to me*** *Aamir Sohail is one crazy and stubborn man"]* Here, cues similar to English such as ***"mere rayee mein"*** *(according to)* indicate the opinion holder. Another interesting behavior here is the presence of nested opinion holders. ***"kaha"*** *(said)* indicates that this statement was made by Ansari only.
4	*Sutlan bahut khush tha,* ***naseer key kaam se.*** *[Sultan was very happy with* ***Naseer's work****]* Here, the target of the expression ***"khush"*** is after the verb ***"khush tha"****(was happy) – SVO structure*

Table 1: Examples to outline the complexity of the task

Another contributing factor is the free word order of the Urdu language. Although the accepted form is SOV, there are several instances where the object comes after the verb or the object is before the subject. In Urdu newswire data, the average number of words in a sentence is 42 (Table 3). This generates a large number of candidate sequences that are not opinion entities, on account of which the data used for training is highly unbalanced. The lack of tools such as dependency parsers makes boundary detection for Urdu different from English, which in turn makes opinion entity extraction a much harder task. Examples shown in table 1 illustrate the complexity of the task.

One safe assumption that can be made for opinion entities is that they are always contained in a phrase (or clause) that contains a noun (common noun, proper noun or pronoun), which is either the subject or the object of the predicate. Based on this, we generate candidate sequences by considering contextual information around noun phrases. In example 1 of Table 1, the subsequence that is generated will consider all four noun phrases **"Pakistan's | provincial border's | south city's | airbase"** as a single group for opinion entity.

We demonstrate that investigating postpositions to capture semantic relations between nouns and predicates is crucial in opinion entity identification. Our approach shows encouraging performance.

2 Related Work

Choi *et al.,* (2005) consider opinion entity identification as an information extraction task and the opinion holders are identified using a conditional random field (Lafferty *et al.,* 2001) based sequence-labeling approach. Patterns are extracted using AutoSlog (Riloff *et al.,* 2003). Bloom *et al.,* (2006) use hand built lexicons for opinion entity identification. Their method is dependent on a combination of heuristic shallow parsing and dependency parsing information. Kim and Hovy

(2006) map the semantic frames of FrameNet (Baker *et al.,* 1998) into opinion holder and target for adjectives and verbs to identify these components. Stoyanov and Cardie (2008) treat the task of identifying opinion holders and targets as a co-reference resolution problem. Kim *et al.,* (2008) used a set of communication words, appraisal words from Senti-WordNet (Esuli and Sebastiani, 2006) and NLP tools such as NE taggers and syntactic parsers to identify opinion holders accurately. Kim and Hovy (2006) use structural features of the language to identify opinion entities. Their technique is based on syntactic path and dependency features along with heuristic features such as topic words and named entities. Weigand and Klalow (2010) use convolution kernels that use predicate argument structure and parse trees.

For Urdu specifically, work in the area of classifying subjective and objective sentences is attempted by Mukund and Srihari, (2010) using a vector space model. NLP tools that include POS taggers, shallow parser, NE tagger and morphological analyzer for Urdu is provided by Mukund *et al.,* (2010). This is the only extensive work done for automating Urdu NLP, although other efforts to generate semantic role labels and dependency parsers are underway.

3 Linguistic Analysis for Opinion Entities

In this section we introduce the different cues used to capture the contextual information for creating candidate sequences in Urdu by exploiting the morphological richness of the language.

Case	Clitic Form	Examples
Ergative	(ne)	*Ali **ne** ghussa dikhaya ~ Ali showed anger*
Accusative	(ko)	*Ali **ko** mainey maara ~ I hit Ali*
Dative	(ko,ke)	Similar to accusative
Instrumental	(se)	*Yeh kaam Ali **se** hua ~ This work was done by Ali*
Genitive	(ka, ke, ki)	*Ali **ka** ghussa, baap re baap! ~ Ali's anger, oh my God!*
Locative	(mein, par, tak, tale, talak)	*Ali **mein** ghussa zyaada hai ~ there is a lot of anger in Ali*

Table 2: Case Inflections on Nouns

Urdu is a head final language with post-positional case markers. Some post-positions are associated with grammatical functions and some with specific roles associated with the meaning of verbs (Davison, 1999). Case markers play a very important role in determining the case inflections of nouns. The case inflections that are useful in the context of opinion entity detection are *"ergative", "dative", "genitive", "instrumental"* and *"locative"*. Table 2 outlines the constructs.

Consider example 1 below. (a) is a case where *"Ali"* is nominative. However, in (b) *"Ali"* is dative. The case marker *"ko"* helps to identify subjects of certain experiential and psychological predicates: sensations, psychological or mental states and obligation or compulsion. Such predicates clearly require the subject to be sentient, and further, indicate that they are affected in some manner, correlating with the semantic properties ascribed to the dative's primary use (Grimm, 2007).

Example (1):

*(a) Ali khush **hua** (Ali became happy)*

*(b) Ali **ko** khushi **hui** (Ali became happy)*

Example (2):

(a) ***Sadaf*** *kaam karne ki koshish* ***karti hai*** *(Sadaf tries to do work)*

Semantic information in Urdu is encoded in a way that is very different from English. Aspect, tense and gender depend on the noun that a verb governs. Example 2 shows the dependency that verbs have on nouns without addressing the linguistic details associated with complex predicates.

In example 2, the verb *"karti"(do)* is *feminine* and the noun it governs *~Sadaf* is also *feminine*. The doer for the predicate *"karti hai"(does)* is *"Sadaf"* and there exists a gender match. This shows that we can obtain strong features if we are able to accurately (i) identify the predicates, (ii) find the governing noun, and (iii) determine the gender.

In this work, for the purpose of generating candidate sequences, we encompass the post-position responsible for case inflection in nouns, into the noun phrase and group the entire chunk as one single candidate. In example 1, the dative inflection on *'Ali'* is due to the case marker *'ko'*. Here, *'Ali ko'* will always be considered together in all candidate sequences that this sentence generates. This behavior can also be observed in example 1 of table 1.

We use Semantex™ (Srihari *et al.,* 2008) - an end to end NLP framework for Urdu that provides POS, NE, shallow parser and morphological analyzer, to mark tense, mood, aspect, gender and number inflections of verbs and case inflections of nouns. For ease of parsing, we enclose dative and accusative inflected nouns and the respective case markers in a tag called *POSSESS*. We also enclose locative, genitive and ergative inflections and case markers in a tag called *DOER*.

4 Methodology

Sequence boundaries are first constructed based on the POSSESS, DOER and NP (noun chunk) tags prioritized by the position of the tag while parsing. We refer to these chunks as *"candidates"* as they are the possible opinion entity candidates. We generate candidate sequences by combining these candidates with opinion expressions (Mukund and Srihari, 2010) and the predicates that contain or follow the expression words (*~khushi* in (b) of example 1 above).

We evaluate our approach in two steps:

(i) Boundary Detection - detecting opinion entities that contain both holders and targets

(ii) Entity Disambiguation - disambiguating opinion holders from opinion targets

In the following sections, we briefly describe our research methodology including sequence creation, choice of kernels and the challenges thus encountered.

4.1 Data Set

The data used for the experiments are newswire articles from BBC Urdu[1] that are manually annotated to reflect opinion holders, targets, and expressions (emotion bearing words).

Number of subjective sentences	824
Average word length of each sentence	42
Number of opinion holders	974
Number of opinion targets	833
Number of opinion expressions	894

Table 3: Corpus Statistics

Table 3 summarizes the corpus statistics. The inter annotator agreement established between two annotators over 30 documents was found to be 0.85 using Cohen's Kappa score (averaged over all tags). The agreement is acceptable as tagging emotions is a difficult and a personalized task.

4.2 Support Vector Machines (SVM) and Kernel Methods

SVMs belong to a class of supervised machine learning techniques that merge the nuances of statistical learning theory, kernel mapping and optimization techniques to discover separating hyperplanes. Given a set of positive and negative data points, based on structural risk minimization, SVMs attempt to find not only a separating hyperplane that separates two categories (Vapnik and Kotz, 2006) but also maximize the boundary between them (maximal margin separation technique). In this work, we propose to use a variation of sequence kernels for opinion entity detection.

4.3 Sequence Kernels

The lack of parsers that capture dependencies in Urdu sentences inhibit the use of 'tree kernels' (Weigand and Klalow, 2010). In this work, we exploit the power of a set of sequence kernels known as 'gap sequence string kernels' (Lodhi *et al.*, 2002). These kernels provide numerical comparison of phrases as entire sequences rather than a probability at the chunk level. Gap sequence kernels measure the similarity between two sequences (in this case a sequence of Urdu words) by counting the number of common subsequences. Gaps between words are penalized with suitable use of decay factor $(\lambda; 0 < \lambda < 1)$ to compensate for matches between lengthy word sequences.

Formally, let Σ_i be the feature space over words. Consequently, we declare other disjoint feature spaces $\Sigma_j, \Sigma_k ... \Sigma_l$ (stem words, POS, chunks, gender inflections, etc.) and $\Sigma_x = \Sigma_i \times \Sigma_j \times \Sigma_k ... \Sigma_l$. For any two-feature vectors $s, t \in \Sigma_x$ let $f(s,t)$ compute the number of common features between *s* and *t*. Table 5 lists the features used to compute $f(s,t)$.

Given two sequences, *s* and *t* and the kernel function $K_{es}(s,t,\lambda)$ that calculates the number of

[1] www.bbc.co.uk/urdu/

weighted sparse subsequences of length n (say, n=2: bigram) common to both s and t, then $K_{es}(s,t,\lambda)$ is as shown in eq 1 (Bunescu and Mooney, 2005).

$$K_{es}(s,t,\lambda) = \sum_{\mathbf{i}:|\mathbf{i}|=n} \sum_{\mathbf{j}:|\mathbf{j}|=n} \prod_{k=1}^{n} s(s_{i_k}, t_{j_k}) \lambda^{l(\mathbf{i})+l(\mathbf{j})}$$

(i,j,k are dimensions) ------ Eq 1.

Generating correct sequences is a prior requirement for sequence kernels. For example, in the task of relation extraction, features included in the shortest path between the mentions of the two sequences (which hold the relation) play a decisive role (Bunescu and Mooney, 2005). Similarly, in the task of role labeling (SRL - Moschitti *et al.*, 2008), syntactic sub-trees containing the arguments are crucial in finding the correct associations. Our approach to create candidate sequences for opinion entity detection in Urdu is explained in the next section.

4.4 Candidate Sequence Generation

Each subjective sentence in Urdu contains several noun phrases with one or more opinion expressions. The words that express opinions (expression words) can be contained within a verb predicate (if the predicate is complex) or precede the verb predicate. These subjective sentences are first pre-processed to mark the morphological inflections as mentioned in §3.

1	A sentence is parsed to extract all likely candidate chunks – POSSESS, DOER, NP in that order.
2	<expression, predicate> tuples are first selected based on nearest neighbor rule : 1. Predicates that are paired with the expression words either contain the expressions or follow the expressions. 2. Stand alone predicates are simply ignored as they do not contribute to the holder identification task (they contribute to either the sentence topic or the reason for the emotion).
3	For each candidate, <candidate, expression, predicate> tuples are generated without changing the word order. (Fig. 1 – example candidates maintain the same word order)

Table 4: Candidate Sequence Generation

We define training candidate sequences as the shortest substring t which is a tuple that contains the candidate noun phrase (POSSESS, DOER or NP), an emotion expression and the closest predicate. Table 4 outlines the steps taken to create the candidate sequences and figure 1 illustrates the different tuples for a sample sentence.

Experiments conducted by Weigand and Klakow (2010) consider <candidate, predicate> and <candidate, expression> tuples. However, in Urdu the sense of expression and predicate are so tightly coupled (in many examples they subsume each other and hence inseparable), that specifically trying to gauge the influence of predicate and expression separately on candidates is impossible.

There are three advantages in our approach to creating candidate sequences: (i) by pairing expressions with their nearest predicates, several unnecessary candidate sequences are eliminated, (ii) phrases that do not contain nouns are automatically not considered (see RBP chunk in figure 1), and (iii) by considering only one candidate chunk at a time in generating the candidate sequence, we ensure that the sequence that is generated is short for better sequence kernel performance.

4.4.1 Linear Kernel features

For linear kernels we define features explicitly based on the lexical relationship between the candidate and its context. Table 5 outlines the features used.

Feature Sets and Description	
Set 1 **Baseline**	1. head word of candidate 2. case marker contained within candidate? 3. expression words 4. head word of predicate 5. POS sequence of predicate words 6. # of NPs between candidate and emotion
Set 2	7. the DOER 8. expression right after candidate?
Set 3	9. gender match between candidate and predicate 10. predicate contains emotion words?
Set 4	11. POS sequence of candidate
Set 5	12. *"kah"* feature in the predicate 13. locative feature? 14. genitive feature on noun?

Table 5: Linear Kernel Features

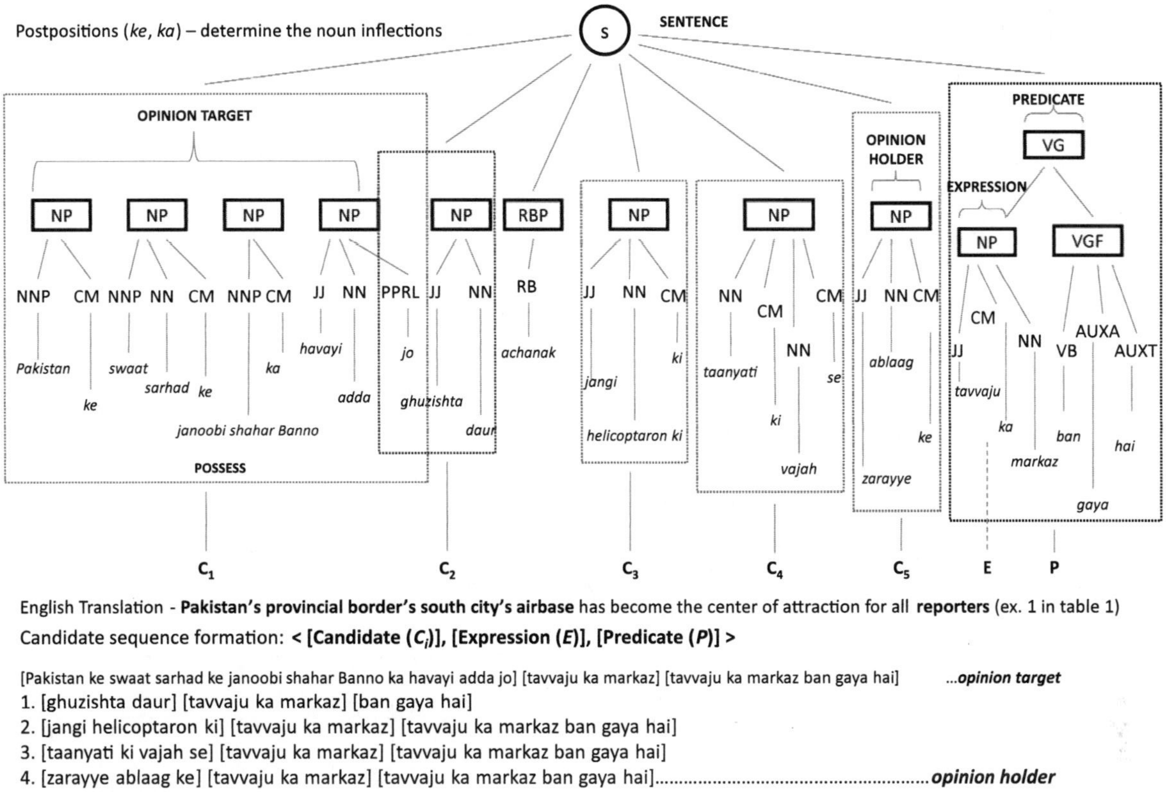

Figure 1: Illustration of candidate sequences

4.4.1 Sequence Kernel features

Features commonly used for sequence kernels are based on words (such as character-based or word-based sequence kernels). In this work, we consider Σ_i to be a feature space over Urdu words along with other disjoint features such as POS, gender, case inflections. In the kernel, however, for each combination (see table 6) the similarity matching function $f(s,t)$ that computes the number of similar features remains the same.

KID	Kernel Type
1	word based kernel (baseline)
2	word + POS (parts of speech)
3	word + POS + chunk
4	word + POS + chunk + gender inflection

Table 6: Disjoint feature set for sequence kernels

Sequence kernels are robust and can deal with complex structures. There are several overlapping features between the feature sets used for linear kernel and sequence kernel. Consider the POS path information feature. This is an important feature for the linear kernel. However this feature need not be explicitly mentioned for the sequence kernel as the model internally learns the path information. In addition, several Boolean features explicitly described for the linear kernel (2 and 13 in table 5) are also learned automatically in the sequence kernel by matching subsequences.

5 Experiments

The data used for our experiments is explained in §4.1. Figure 2 gives a flow diagram of the entire process. LIBSVM's (Chang and Lin, 2001) linear kernel is trained using the manually coded features mentioned in table 5. We integrated our proposed sequence kernel with the same toolkit. This sequence kernel uses the features mentioned in table 6 and the decay factor λ is set to 0.5.

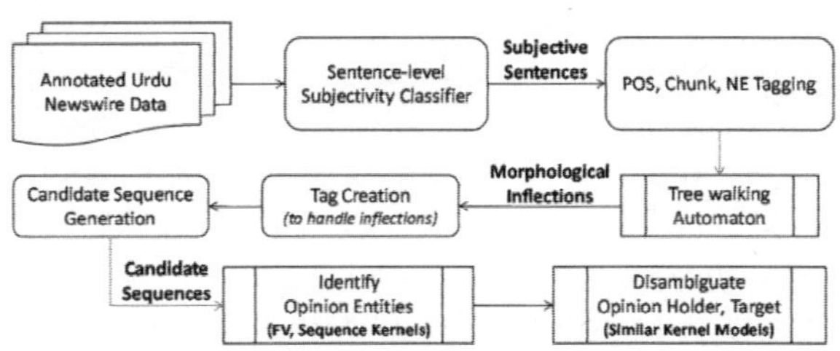

Figure 2: Overall Process

The candidate sequence generation algorithm generated 8,329 candidate sequences (contains all opinion holders and targets – table 3) that are used for training both the kernels. The data is parsed using Semantex™ to apply POS, chunk and morphology information. Our evaluation is based on the exact candidate boundary (whether the candidate is enclosed in a POSSESS, DOER or NP chunk).All scores are averaged over a 5-fold cross validation set.

5.1 Comparison of Kernels

We apply both linear kernels (LK) and sequence kernels (SK) to identify the entities as well as disambiguate between the opinion holders and targets. Table 7 illustrates the baselines and the best results for boundary detection of opinion entities. ID 1 of table 7 represents the result of using LK with feature set 1 (table 5). We interpret this as our baseline result. The best F1 score for this classifier is 50.17%.

ID	Kernel	Features (table 5/6)	Prec. (%)	Rec. (%)	F1 (%)
1	LK	Baseline (Set 1)	39.58	51.49	44.75
2	LK(best)	Set 1, 2, 3, 4, 5	44.20	57.99	50.17
3	SK	Baseline (KID 1)	58.22	42.75	49.30
4	SK (best)	KID 4	54.00	62.79	58.06
5	Best LK + best SK	KID 4, Set 1, 2, 3, 4, 5	**58.43**	**65.04**	**61.55**

Table 7: Boundary detection of Opinion Entities

Table 8 compares various kernels and combinations. Set 1 of table 8 shows the relative effect of feature sets for LK and how each set contributes to detecting opinion entity boundaries. Although several features are inspired by similar classification techniques (features used for SRL and opinion mining by Choi *et al.,* (2005) ~ set 1, table 5), the free word nature of Urdu language renders these features futile. Moreover, due to larger average length of each sentence and high occurrences of NPs (candidates) in each sentence, the number of candidate instances (our algorithm creates 10 sequences per sentence on average) is also very high as compared to any English corpus. This makes the training corpus highly imbalanced. Interestingly, when features like – *occurrence of postpositions, "kah" predicate, gender inflections etc.* are used, classification improves (set 1, Feature set 1,2,3,4,5, table 8).

Set	Kernel	KID	Prec. (%)	Rec. (%)	F1 (%)
1	LK	Baseline (Set 1)	39.58	51.49	44.75
		Set 1,2	39.91	52.57	45.38
		Set 1, 2, 3	43.55	57.72	49.65
		Set 1,2,3,4	44.10	56.90	49.68
		Feature set 1,2,3,4,5	**44.20**	**57.99**	**50.17**
2	SK	Baseline - KID 1	58.22	42.75	49.30
		KID 2	**58.98**	47.55	52.65
		KID 3	58.18	49.62	53.59
		KID 4	54.00	**62.79**	**58.06**
3	SK + LK	KID 1 + best LK	51.44	**68.89**	58.90
		KID 2 + best LK	**59.18**	62.98	61.02
		KID 3 + best LK	55.18	68.38	61.07
		KID 4 + best LK	58.43	65.04	**61.55**

Table 8: Kernel Performance

ID 3 of table 7 displays the baseline result for SK. Interestingly enough, the baseline F1 for SK is very close to the best LK performance. This shows the robustness of SK and its capability to learn complex substructures with only words. A sequence kernel considers all possible subsequence matching and therefore implements a concept of partial (fuzzy) matching. Because of its tendency to learn all fuzzy matches while penalizing the gaps between words intelligently, the performance of SK in general has better recall (Wang, 2008). To explain the recall situation, consider set 2 of table 8. This illustrates the effect of disjoint feature scopes of each feature (POS, chunk, gender). Each feature adds up and expands the feature space of sequence kernel and allows fuzzy matching thereby improving the recall. Hence KID 4 has almost 20% recall gain over the baseline (SK baseline). However, in many cases, this fuzzy matching accumulates in wrong classification and lowers precision. A fairly straightforward approach to overcome this problem is to employ a high precision kernel in addition to sequence kernel. Another limitation of SK is its inability to capture complex grammatical structure and dependencies making it highly dependent on only the order of the string sequence that is supplied.

We also combine the similarity scores of SK and LK to obtain the benefits of both kernels. This permits SK to expand the feature space by naturally adding structural features (POS, chunk) resulting in high recall. At the same time, LK with strict features (such as the use of *"kah"* verb) or rigid word orders (several Boolean features) will help maintain acceptable precision. By summing the contribution of both kernels, we achieve an F1 of 61.55% (Set 3, table 8), which is 17.8%, more (relative gain – around 40%) than the LK baseline results (ID 1, table 7).

Kernel	Opinion Entity	Prec. (%)	Rec. (%)	F1 (%)
LK (best)	Holder	58.71	66.67	62.44
	Target	**65.53**	57.48	61.23
SK	Holder	60.26	69.46	64.54
	Target	59.75	49.73	54.28
Both kernels	Holder	62.90	**69.81**	**65.26**
	Target	60.71	55.44	57.96

Table 9: Opinion entity disambiguation for best features

Our next sets of experiments are conducted to disambiguate opinion holders and targets. A large number of candidate sequences that are created are not candidates for opinion entities. This results in a huge imbalance in the data set. Jointly classify opinion holders, opinion targets and false candidates with one model can be attempted if this imbalance in the data set due to false candidates can be reduced. However, this has not been attempted in this work. In order to showcase the feasibility of our method, we train our model only on the gold standard candidate sequences that contain opinion entities for entity disambiguation.

The two kernels are applied on just the two classes (opinion holder vs. opinion target). Combined kernels identify holders with a 65.26% F1 (table 9). However, LK performs best for target identification (61.23%). We believe that this is due to opinion holders and targets sharing similar syntactic structures. Hence, the sequence information that SK learns affects accuracy but improves recall.

6 Challenges

Based on the error analysis, we observe some common mistakes and provide some examples.

1. Mistakes resulting due to POS tagger and shallow chunker errors.
2. Errors due to heuristic rules for morphological analysis.
3. Mistakes due to inaccurate identification of expression words by the subjectivity classifier.
4. Errors due to complex and unusual sentence structures which the kernels failed to capture.

Example (3):

Is ***na-insaafi ka badla*** **hamein** zaroor layna chahiye.

[**we** have to certainly take ***revenge for this injustice.***]

Example (4):

Kya ***hum*** ***dayshadgardi*** ka shikar banna chahatein hai?

[Do **we** want to become victims of **terrorism**?]

Example (5):

Jab ***secretary*** kisi aur say baat karke husthi hai, tho ***Pinto*** ko ghussa aata hai.

[When the ***secretary*** talks to someone and laughs, **Pinto** gets angry.]

Example 3 is a false positive. The emotion is "anger", indicated by ***"na-insaafi ka badla"*** *(revenge for injustice)* and ***"zaroor"*** *(certainly)*. But only the second expression word is identified accurately. The sequence kernel model determines *na-insaafi (injustice)* to be the opinion holder when it is actually the reason for the emotion. However, it also identifies the correct opinion holder - *hamein (we)*. Emotions associated with interrogative sentences are not marked (example 4) as there exists no one word that captures the overall emotion. However, the subjectivity classifier identifies such sentences as subjective candidates. This results in false negatives for opinion entity detection. The target (*secretary*) in example 5, fails to be detected as no candidate sequence that we generate indicates the noun *"secretary"* to be the target. We propose to address these issues in our future work.

7 Conclusion

We describe an approach to identify opinion entities in Urdu using a combination of kernels. To the best of our knowledge this is the first attempt where such an approach is used to identify opinion entities in a language lacking the availability of resources for automatic text processing. The performance for this task for Urdu is equivalent to the state of the art performance for English (Weigand and Klakow, 2010) on the same task.

References

Collin F. Baker, Charles J. Fillmore, John B. Lowe. 1998. The Berkeley FrameNet Project, Proceedings of the 17th international conference on Computational linguistics, August 10-14. Montreal, Quebec, Canada

Steven Bethard, Hong Yu, Ashley Thornton, Vasileios Hatzivassiloglou, and Dan Jurafsky. 2004. Automatic Extraction of Opinion Propositions and their Holders, AAAI Spring Symposium on Exploring Attitude and Affect in Text: Theories and Applications.

Kenneth Bloom, Sterling Stein, and Shlomo Argamon. 2007. Appraisal Extraction for News Opinion Analysis at NTCIR-6. In Proceedings of NTCIR-6 Workshop Meeting, Tokyo, Japan.

R. C. Bunescu and R. J. Mooney. 2005. A shortest path dependency kernel for relation extraction. In Proceedings of HLT/EMNLP.

R. C. Bunescu and R. J. Mooney. 2005. Subsequence Kernels for Relation Extraction. NIPS. Vancouver. December.

Chih-Chung Chang and Chih-Jen Lin. 2001. LIBSVM: a library for support vector machines. Software available at http://www.csie.ntu.edu.tw/~cjlin/libsvm

Yejin Choi, Claire Cardie, Ellen Riloff, and Siddharth Patwardhan. 2005. Identifying Sources of Opinions with Conditional Random Fields and Extraction Patterns. In Proceedings of the Conference on Human Language Technology and Empirical Methods in Natural Language Processing (HLT/EMNLP), Vancouver, Canada.

Aaron Culotta and Jeffery Sorensen. 2004. Dependency tree kernels for relation extraction. In Proceedings of the 42rd Annual Meeting of the Association for Computational Linguistics. pp. 423-429.

Alice Davison. 1999. Syntax and Morphology in Hindi and Urdu: A Lexical Resource. University of Iowa.

Andrea Esuli and Fabrizio Sebastiani. 2006. SentiWordNet: A publicly available lexical resource for opinion mining. In Proc of LREC. Vol 6, pp 417-422.

Scott Gimm. 2007. Subject Marking in Hindi/Urdu: A Study in Case and Agency. ESSLLI Student Session. Malaga, Spain.

Youngho Kim, Seaongchan Kim and Sun-Hyon Myaeng. 2008. Extracting Topic-related Opinions and their Targets in NTCIR-7. In Proceedings of the 7th NTCIR Workshop Meeting. Tokyo. Japan.

John Lafferty, Andrew McCallum and F. Pereira. 2001. Conditional random fields: Probabilistic models for segmenting and labeling sequence data. In: Proc. 18th International Conf. on Machine Learning, Morgan Kaufmann, San Francisco, CA . pp. 282–289

Huma Lodhi, Craig Saunders, John Shawe-Taylor, Nello Cristianini, Chris Watkins. 2002. Text classification using string kernels. J. Mach. Learn. Res. 2 (March 2002), 419-44.

Kim, Soo-Min. and Eduard Hovy. 2006. Extracting Opinions, Opinion Holders, and Topics Expressed in Online News Media Text. In ACL Workshop on Sentiment and Subjectivity in Text.

Alessandro Moschitti, Daniele Pighin, Roberto Basili. 2008. Tree kernels for semantic role labeling. Computational Linguistics. Vol 34, num 2, pp 193-224.

Smruthi Mukund and Rohini K. Srihari. 2010. A Vector Space Model for Subjectivity Classification in Urdu aided by Co-Training, In Proceedings of the 23rd International Conference on Computational Linguistics, Beijing, China.

Smruthi Mukund, Rohini K. Srihari and Erik Peterson. 2010. An Information Extraction System for Urdu – A Resource Poor Language. Special Issue on Information Retrieval for Indian Languages.

Ellen Riloff, Janyce Wiebe and Theresa Wilson. 2003. Learning subjective nouns using extraction pattern bootstrapping. In Proceedings of the Seventh Conference on Natural Language Learning (CoNLL-03).

Rohini K. Srihari, W. Li, C. Niu, and T. Cornell. 2008. InfoXtract: A Customizable Intermediate Level Information Extraction Engine, Journal of Natural Language Engineering, Cambridge U. Press, 14(1), pp. 33-69.

Veselin Stoyanov and Claire Cardie. 2008. Annotating Topic Opinions. In Proceedings of the Sixth International Conference on Language Resources and Evaluation (LREC 2008), Marrakech, Morocco.

John Shawe-Taylor and Nello Cristianni. 2004. Kernel methods for pattern analysis. Cambridge University Press.

Mengqiu Wang. 2008. A Re-examination of Dependency Path Kernels for Relation Extraction, In Proceedings of IJCNLP 2008.

Michael Wiegand and Dietrich Klalow. 2010. Convolution kernels for opinion holder extraction. In Proc. of Human Language Technologies: The 2010 Annual Conference of the North American Chapter of the Association for Computational Linguistics. pp 795-803, ACL

Vladimir Vapnik, S.Kotz. 2006. Estimation of Dependences Based on Empirical Data. Springer, 510 pages.

Subword and spatiotemporal models for identifying actionable information in Haitian Kreyol

Robert Munro
Department of Linguistics
Stanford University
Stanford, CA, 94305
rmunro@stanford.edu

Abstract

Crisis-affected populations are often able to maintain digital communications but in a sudden-onset crisis any aid organizations will have the least free resources to process such communications. Information that aid agencies can actually act on, 'actionable' information, will be sparse so there is great potential to (semi)automatically identify actionable communications. However, there are hurdles as the languages spoken will often be under-resourced, have orthographic variation, and the precise definition of 'actionable' will be response-specific and evolving. We present a novel system that addresses this, drawing on 40,000 emergency text messages sent in Haiti following the January 12, 2010 earthquake, predominantly in Haitian Kreyol. We show that keyword/ngram-based models using streaming MaxEnt achieve up to F=0.21 accuracy. Further, we find current state-of-the-art subword models increase this substantially to F=0.33 accuracy, while modeling the spatial, temporal, topic and source contexts of the messages can increase this to a very accurate F=0.86 over direct text messages and F=0.90-0.97 over social media, making it a viable strategy for message prioritization.

1 Introduction

The recent proliferation of cellphone technologies has resulted in rapid increases in the volume of information coming out of crisis-affected regions. In the wake of the January 12, 2010 earthquake in Haiti local emergency response services were inoperable but 70-80% of cell-towers were quickly restored. With 83%/67% of men/women possessing a cellphone, the nation remained largely connected. People within Haiti were texting, calling and interacting with social media, but aid agencies were not equipped to process so much information. This is because in any sudden onset crisis, this flood of information out of the region coincides with crisis-response organizations already working at capacity as they move in. The problem definition is clear: *how can we filter this information to identify actionable intelligence to support relief efforts?*

The solution is complicated. There may be few resources for the language(s) of the crisis-affected population and the ratio of actionable to non-actionable information will often be very large, especially when reported through social-media and other non-official channels. In the absence of existing electronic resources models must be built on-the-fly and account for substantial spelling variations. The definition of what constitutes actionable intelligence will often be context-specific and changing, too. In the data used here 'actionable' changed quickly from Search and Rescue to any medical emergency and then to include clusters of requests for food and water. The models will therefore need to be time-sensitive or otherwise adaptive.

The system presented here attempts to address these problems, finding that the accurate identification of actionable information can be achieved with subword models, the automatic identification of topics (categories), and spatiotemporal clustering, all within a streaming architecture. It is evaluated using 40,811 emergency text messages sent in Haiti following the January 12, 2010 earthquake.

Proceedings of the Fifteenth Conference on Computational Natural Language Learning, pages 68–77,
Portland, Oregon, USA, 23–24 June 2011. ©2011 Association for Computational Linguistics

2 Evaluation data

Three sets of short-messages are used, all from between January 12 and May 12, 2010:

1. *Mission 4636.* 40,811 text-messages sent to a free number, '4636', in Haiti.
2. *Radio Station.* 7,528 text-messages sent to a Haitian radio station.
3. *Twitter.* 63,195 Haiti-related tweets.

The *Mission 4636* messages were translated, geolocated and categorized by a volunteer online crowdsourced workforce, predominantly from the Haitian diaspora, and by paid workers within Haiti (Munro, 2010). English-speaking crisis-mappers identified actionable messages and refined the coordinates and categories. The categories are a standard set of UN-defined emergency categories with some additions (48 total). The definition of an 'actionable' message was defined by the main responders to the messages, the US Coast Guard and the US Marines working with Southern Command, and included any messages with an identifiable location that contained a request for medical assistance, Search and Rescue, water-shortages, clusters of requests for food in areas not known to aid workers, security, and reports of unaccompanied minors.

The radio station and Twitter messages are not structured or geolocated. They are used here as potential false-positives in a needle-in-a-haystack scenario where the majority of messages are irrelevant. A recent Red Cross survey (2010) found that nearly half the respondents would use social media to report emergencies, so this is a realistic scenario.

3 Streaming models

Supervised streaming-models attempt to classify an incoming stream of unlabeled items by building up training-data on past items (Aggarwal, 2006; Hulten et al., 2001; Babcock et al., 2002). The models are often time-sensitive with training data either weighted towards or exclusively consisting of more recently seem items, especially in the context of concept drift or bounded memory (Zhang et al., 2008).

There is a penalty for applying GOLD labels to past items for training: either only a subset can be labeled or there is a time-delay. When only a subset can be labeled the scenario is similar to that of *active learning* (Cohn et al., 1996; Tong and Koller, 2002). When there is a delay not all past items are immediately available, meaning that short-term concept drifts might not be adapted to. In both cases, accuracy is continually evaluated over incoming items.

Here, the time-delay penalty was used for all Mission 4636 messages as it is closer to the actual scenario where each potential emergency message is ultimately read by a person but with potential delays from sudden bursts and backlogs.

The messages were divided into 100 temporally ordered sets. Each set belongs to one epoch i in the streaming architecture, R, such that R_i is evaluated on $R_0, \ldots, R_{i-1}$ (R_1 is evaluated on a model trained on R_0; R_2 is evaluated on a model trained on $\{R_0, R_1\}$; R_3 is evaluated on a model trained on $\{R_0, R_1, R_2\}$, etc.). The accuracy is therefore calculated over $R_1, \ldots, R_{99}$ (all but the first set).

The results here report a system using a MaxEnt learning algorithm with Quasi-Newton optimization and a convergence tolerance of 10^{-4}. Changing parameter settings or swapping out the learning algorithm with linear and quadratic kernel SVMs made little difference in accuracy (see discussion of other models below).

4 Features (F)

G : Words and ngrams.

W : Subword patterns (extended definition below).

P : Source of the message (phone number).

T : Time received.

C : Categories ($c_{0,\ldots,47}$).

L : Location (longitude and latitude).

$L_\exists$: Has-location (there is an identifiable location within the message).

G, W, P and T were calculated directly from the messages. C and $L_\exists$ were predicted using independent streaming models and L was clustered through tiling (see below).

4.1 Hierarchical streaming models for has-location ($L_\exists$) and category (C)

The SMS protocol does not encode locations or categories. The streaming model was extended to a two-level hierarchical architecture so that we could use (predicted) locations and categories as features.

Nou tigwav,nou pa gen manje nou pa gen kay. m.			
'We are Petit Goave, we don't have food, we don't have a house. Thanks.			
Actionable	-72.86537, 18.43264	1/22/2010 16:59	2a. Food Shortage, 2b. Water shortage
Lopital Sacre-Coeur ki nan vil Milot, 14 km nan sid vil Okap, pre pou li resevwa moun malad e l'ap mande pou moun ki malad yo ale la.			
'Sacre-Coeur Hospital which located in this village Milot 14 km south of Oakp is ready to receive those who are injured. Therefore, we are asking those who are sick to report to that hospital.'			
Actionable	-72.21272, 19.60869	2/13/2010 22:33	4a. Health services
Mwen se [FIRST NAME] [LAST NAME] depi jeremi mwen ta renmen jwenm travay.			
'My name is [FIRST NAME] [LAST NAME], I'm in Jeremi and I would like to find work.'			
Not Actionable	-74.1179, 18.6423	1/22/2010 18:29	5. Other
Rue Casseus no 9 gen yon sant kap bay swen ak moun ki blese e moun ki brile.			
'Street Casseus no 9, there is a center that helps people that are wounded or burnt.'			
Actionable	-72.32857,18.53019	1/19/2010 11:21	4a. Health services
Paket moun delmas 32 ki forme organisation kap mache pran manje sou non pep yo ankesel lakay			
'People in Delmas 32 formed an association that takes food in the name of everyone in the neighborhood'			
Not Actionable	-72.30815,18.54414	2/4/2010 1:21	5. Other

Table 1: Examples of messages, with translation, actionable flag, location, timestamp and categories. The final two were a consistent false negative and false positive respectively. The former likely because of sparsity - places offering services were rare - and the latter because reports of possible corruption were not, unfortunately, considered actionable.

A set S, of 49 base streaming models predicted the has-location, $L_\exists$, feature and categories, $c_{0,\ldots,47}$. That is, unlike the main model, R, which predicts the 'Actionable'/'Not Actionable' division, each model S predicts either the existence of a location within the text or binary per-category membership. The predictions for each message were added to the final model as feature confidence values per-label. This is richer than simply using the best-guess labels for each model S and it was clear in early processing that confidence features produced consistently more accurate final models than binary predicted labels. In fact, using model confidence features for $L_\exists$ actually outperforms an oracle binary has-location feature, $O(L_\exists)$ (see results).

The same G, W, P and T features were used for the S and R models.

As the final model R requires the outputs from S for training, and S are themselves predictive models, the $L_\exists$ and C features are not included until the second training epoch R_1. In the context of machine-learning for sudden onset humanitarian information processing any delay could be significant. One simple solution is starting with smaller epoch sizes.

4.2 Subword features

A typical former creole, Haitian Kreyol has very simple morphology but the text message-language produces many compounds and reductions ('my family': *fanmi mwen, fanmwen, fanmi m, fanmi'm, fanmim', fanmim*), so it requires segmentation. There is also substantial variation due to lack of spelling conventions, geographic variation, varying literacy, more-or-less French spellings for cognates, and character sets/accents ('thank you': *mesi, mési, méci meci, merci*). See Table 2 for further examples and common subword patterns that were discovered across very different surface forms.

The approach here builds on the earlier work of Munro and Manning (2010), adapted from Goldwater et al. (2009), where unsupervised methods were used to segment and phonologically normalize the words. For example, the process might turn all variants of 'thank you' into *'mesi'* and all variants of 'my family' into *'fan mwen'*. This regularization allows a model to generalize over the different

Abbrev.	Full Form	Pattern	Meaning
s'on	se yon	*sVn*	is a
avèn	avèknou	*VvVn*	with us
relem	rele mwen	*relem*	call me
wap	ouap	*uVp*	you are
map	mwen ap	*map*	I will be
zanmim	zanmi mwen	*zanmim*	my friend
lavel	lave li	*lavel*	to wash (it)

Table 2: Abbreviations and full forms of words, showing substantial variation but common subword patterns and character alternations (V=any vowel).

forms even in the event of singleton word variants. Here we incorporated the segmentation into the supervised learning task rather than model the phonological/orthographic variation as a pre-learning normalization step, as in Munro and Manning. A set of candidate segmentations and normalizations were added to our final model as features representing both the pre and post-normalization, allowing the model to arrive at the optimal training weights between the unnormalized/unsegmented and normalized/segmented variants.

This meant that rather than optimizing the subword segmentation according to a Gaussian prior over unlabeled data we optimized the segmentation according to the predictive ability of a given segmentation *per model*. This is further from the linguistic reality of the segments than our earlier approach but the richer feature space led to an increase in accuracy in all test cases here.

The subword models were only applied to the original messages. The English translations were not included among the features as it is not realistic to assume manual translation of every message before the less labor-intensive task of identifying actionable items.

4.3 Oracle features

While the SMS protocol does not encode the geographical origin of the message, other protocols/systems do, especially those used by smartphones. Similarly, cell-tower granularity of locations might be available, phone numbers might be *a priori* associated with locations, or locations could be formalized within the text using methods like 'Tweak the Tweet' (Starbird and Stamberger, 2010). Therefore, it is reasonable to also simulate a scenario where the messages come pre-geocoded. We compared our results to models also containing the oracle longitude and latitude of the messages, $O(L)$ (no attempt was made to predict L, the precise longitude and latitude - a challenging but interesting task) and the oracle existence of a location $O(L_\exists)$.

It is less likely that messages come precategorized but oracle features for the categories were also evaluated to compare the performance for models containing the predictive categories to ones containing the actual categories, $O(c_{0,\ldots,47})$.

4.4 Spatial clustering

In addition to identifying locations, we also used the latitude and longitude to geographically cluster messages. This was to capture two phenomena:

1. *Hot spots:* some areas were in greater need of aid than others.

2. *Clustered food requests:* the definition of 'actionable' extended to clustered requests for food, but not requests from lone individuals.

Figure 1 shows a Port-au-Prince (Pótoprens) neighborhood with incident reports from the text messages. The x, y axes (latitude, longitude) show the clusters given by the Ushahidi map and the z axis shows the temporal distribution of messages over a two month period. Both the spatial and temporal distributions clearly show a high frequency of both clusters and outliers.

The most accurate clustering divided the messages by longitude and latitude into tiles approximating $100m^2$, $1km^2$ and $10km^2$. At each granularity, tiling was repeated with an offset by half on each dimension to partially smooth the arbitrariness of tile boundaries. This resulted in each geolocated messages being a member of 12 tiles in total, which were included as 12 features L. We were not able to find an unsupervised spatial clustering algorithm that improved the results beyond this bruteforce method of multiple tiles at different granularities (see discussion of other models tested below).

4.5 Temporal modeling and discounting

It is common to calculate a discounting function over training epochs in streaming models (Aggar-

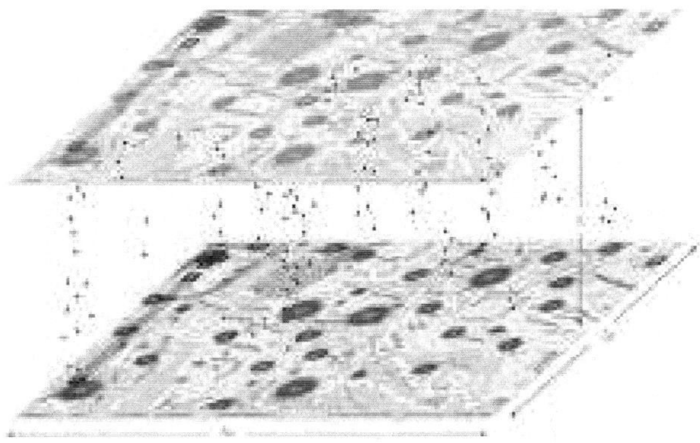

Figure 1: Map of a Port-au-Prince neighborhood with incident reports from text messages, with spatial clusters on the latitudinal and longitudinal axes and temporal distributions on the time axis, showing both spatial and temporal clustering, with frequent outliers.

wal, 2006; Hulten et al., 2001; Babcock et al., 2002).

We used a slightly different method here where the time-stamp feature, T, performs this function, arriving at the relative probability for a given time period t in the final model, R (Zhang et al., 2008). It has several advantages over a simple weighted discounting function. First, t is calculated incrementally, not per training epoch, meaning that the weight θ for t is calculated until the most recently seen items. Second, it frees T to cluster according to temporal divisions other than the (arbitrary) divisions of training epochs. Finally, it allows unconstrained weights for different temporal clusters, permitting the final distribution of weights over different ts to define complex and possibly nonmonotonic discounting functions. Modeling time as a feature rather than a discounting function also made it simpler to combine temporal and spatial clustering. The feature T consisted of multiple buckets of time-stamps per message and also composite features with the $O(L)$ tiles when present.

4.6 Other models tested

Several other machine-learning methods were tested but ultimately not reported here.

Intuitively, SVMs with non-linear kernels could more accurately model geographic divisions in the latitude and longitude dimensions and discover different combinations of features like *has-location=true* and *category=emergency*. However, we were not able to find a combination of kernels and parameter settings that demonstrated this. It is possible that we could not avoid over-fitting or that the composite features had already sufficiently captured the combinations.

Munro and Manning (2010) also found gains using supervised LDA (Ramage et al., 2009), which has also previously been used for disaster response clustering (Kireyev et al., 2009). We implemented supervised LDA and unsupervised LDA topic models, but they showed modest improvements over the baseline model only. We presume that this is because when we add the predicted categories from our (supervised) category learning task, they already contained enough information about topic divisions.

We looked at several methods for spatio-temporal clustering including cliques (Zhang et al., 2004), k-means (Wagstaff et al., 2001), and targeted low frequency clusters (Huang et al., 2003). The change in accuracy was negligible but the exploration of methods was by no means exhaustive. One exception was using nearest-neighbor spatiotemporal clustering, however the gains were predominantly repeated messages from the same person and thus already captured by the source feature, P.

Several systems have been built by humanitarian organizations for filtering/prioritizing messages, mostly keyword and memory-based. All are currently less accurate than the baseline system here and their predicted outputs gave no gains as features. The *SwiftRiver* system built on NLTK library (Bird et al., 2009) was the most promising, only underperforming the baseline by F=0.01.

5 Results

The results in Table 3 show that a combination of streaming models with subword models improves the accuracy of identifying actionable messages. All increases in accuracy are significant relative to the baseline.

The temporal feature, T, alone gives F=0.045 increase in accuracy indicating that there is substantial concept drift and an adaptive model is necessary for accurate classification.

The subword models, W, increase the gain to 0.119 showing that despite Kreyol being a morphologically simple language the variation in spellings and compounds is significant.

Model	Precision	Recall	F-value	F-Gain
Words/Ngrams (G)	0.622	0.124	0.207	*n/a*
Temporal feature (G, T)	0.716	0.153	0.252	0.045
Subwords and Source (G, T, W, P)	0.548	0.233	0.326	0.119
Categories (predicted: G, T, C, P)	0.464	0.240	0.316	0.109
Location (predicted: $G, T, L_{\exists}, P$)	0.572	0.212	0.310	0.103
Categories (oracle: $G, T, O(C), P$)	0.565	0.225	0.322	0.115
Location (oracle: $G, T, O(L_{\exists}), P$)	0.746	0.168	0.274	0.067
Spatial clusters (L)	0.896	0.653	0.756	0.549
All non-oracle and spatial clusters	0.872	0.840	**0.855**	0.648
Pre-filtered spatial clusters	0.613	0.328	0.428	0.221
Radio station	0.961	0.854	0.904	*n/a*
Twitter	0.950	0.989	0.969	*n/a*

Table 3: The final results for the different models. The first three and *Location (oracle)* contain only single streaming models. The others use a hierarchical streaming model combining features with the outputs from the base streaming models S. The model combining all features is the most accurate at F=0.855, 0.648 above the baseline model optimized over words and word sequences (ngrams). The *Pre-filtered spatial clusters* contains the same architecture/features as the most accurate model, but with those messages not containing an identifiable location (and therefore automatically non-actionable) stripped from the training and test data. The final *Radio station* and *Twitter* models used the messages sent to a radio station and Twitter as the non-actionable items, using the same training model as *All non-oracle and spatial clusters*.

5.1 Oracle vs predicted outputs

Comparing the oracle values and predicted outputs from the categories and the identification of messages containing locations, $O(C), O(L_{\exists}), C, L_{\exists}$, we see that the predictive model for categories only slightly underperforms the oracle, but the predictive model for locations *out*performs the oracle model. We suspect that this is because the predictions are probabilities, not binary indicators of the existence of a location. Therefore, the richer real-valued feature space led to greater information for the final model despite any predictive errors in this base model. Another reason can be clearly seen in the precision, 0.746 for the $O(L)$ model, one of the highest precision-to-recall ratios. The final model is clearly giving too much weight to the existence of a location as a predictor of an actionable label. Smoothing $O(L)$ makes little difference as it is a high-frequency binary feature, but the greater range of probability values in L are necessarily more sparse and therefore more de-weighted by smoothing.

Identifying locations is one area that could be expanded on greatly. Initial experiments with named-entity recognition were abandoned when it was clear that the data was too sparse and too different from existing data sets, but perhaps text-message-specific named-entity recognition methods could lead to even more accurate results for identifying locations.

5.2 Spatial clustering

By adding spatial clusters we get the greatest leap in accuracy: F=0.756, a substantial F=0.549 over the baseline. This is strong evidence in favor of extending text-only messaging to location-aware messaging. As with the prediction of locations, it is likely that methods for spatial clustering other than brute-force bucketing could lead to more accurate results, but as stated earlier we were not able to identify any.

Combining the base streaming model outputs with all features leads to the most accurate model. It is expected that this would produce the best results, but at F=0.855 we have a *very* significant gain over any of the models implementing only single-stream learning, or without the full feature space.

5.3 Pre-filtering

Somewhat counterintuitively, pre-filtering messages without known locations (in both training and test data) decreased the accuracy to F=0.428. Oracle filtering of true-negative test items will not change recall and can only increase precision, so clearly there is 'signal' in the 'noise' here. Analysis of the messages showed that many non-actionable messages were not related to emergencies at all (general questions, requests for work, etc), as were many messages without identifiable locations. That is, people who tended to not send actionable information also tended to not include locations. Because of this correlation, the content of messages without locations becomes useful information for the model.

A careful analysis of the training models confirms this: the word and subword features for non-actionable messages with no locations had non-zero weights. Pre-filtering them therefore resulted in an impoverished training set.

It is standard practice in the humanitarian industry to pre-filter messages that are easily identified as non-actionable (for obvious reasons: it reduces the manual processing), which is what occurred in Haiti - only about 5% of messages were treated as 'actionable' candidates. The results here indicate that if manual processing is extended to automated or semi-automated processing this strategy needs to change, with all potential training items included in the models.

5.4 Comparison to non-emergency messages

For the social media scenarios where we combined the actionable test items with the messages sent to a radio station and Twitter the accuracy was highest of all. This is a promising result for seeking actionable information in non-traditional sources. The radio station is particularly promising as almost all the messages where in Haitian Kreyol and spoke about the same locations as the 4636 messages.

While the Twitter messages were extremely accurate at F=0.969, the majority of the tweets were in English or French from people outside of Haiti, so this model was at least in part about language identification, a much simpler task and less novel from a research perspective. Nonetheless, while at least part of the accuracy is easily explained this was the most sparse test set with only 0.025% actionable items, so the application scenario is very promising.

5.5 Prioritization

Applying ROC analysis, the methods here could speed up the prioritization of actionable messages by a factor of 10 to 1 based on content alone. That is, on average an actionable message falls within the 90th percentile for probability of being actionable. By including spatial clustering this becomes the 98th percentile. There is great potential for improvements but the methods reported here could already be used to efficiently prioritize the triage of the most important messages within a semi-automated system.

6 Related Work

6.1 trillion text messages were sent in 2010 - more than emails and social network communications combined (ITU, 2010), especially in areas of great linguistic diversity (Maffi, 2005). This easily makes it the *least* well-studied method for digital communication relative to the amount digital information being generated.

The lack of research is probably due to obstacles in obtaining data. By contrast Twitter's API has led to much recent research, primarily in sentiment analysis (O'Connor et al., 2010; Alexander Pak, 2010; Sriram et al., 2010) and unsupervised event detection (Petrović et al., 2010). The task of identifying sentiment is different to filtering actionable intelligence, we were not training on tweets, and Twitter-language is reportedly different from text-message-language (Krishnamurthy et al., 2008). However, there are similarities relating to problems of message brevity and the ability to extend the feature-space. For example, Sriram et al. (2010) also found that modeling the source of a message improved accuracy. Eisenstein et al. (Eisenstein et al., 2010) show promising results in identifying an author's geographic location from micro-blogs, but the locations are course-grained and rely on a substantial message history per-source.

In recent work with medical text messages in the Chichewa language, we compared the accuracy of rule-based and unsupervised phonological normalization and morphological segmentation when applied to a classification task over medical labels, showing substantial gains from subword models (Munro and Manning, 2010).

A cluster of earlier work looked at SMS-SPAM in English (Healy et al., 2005; Hidalgo et al., 2006; Cormack et al., 2007) and Beaufort et al. (2010) used a similar preprocessing method for normalizing text-messages in French, combining rule-based models with a finite-state framework. The accuracy was calculated relative to BLEU scores for 'correct' French, not as a classification task.

Machine-translation into a more well-spoken language can extend the potential workforce. Early results are promising (Lewis, 2010) but still leave some latency in deployment.

For streaming architectures, Zhang et al. (2008) proposed a similar method for calculating per epoch weights as an alternative to a discounting function with significant gains. Wang et al. (2007) also looked at multiple parallel streams of text from different newspapers reporting the same events but we couldn't apply their method here as there were few instances of the same pairs of people independently reporting two distinct events. The two-tiered architecture used here is similar to a hierarchical model, the main difference being epoch-based retraining and the temporal offset of the base models feeding into the final one. Joint learning over hierarchical models has been successful in NLP (Finkel and Manning, 2010) but to our best knowledge no one has published work on joint learning over hierarchical streaming models, in NLP or otherwise.

7 Conclusions

From models optimized over words and ngrams to one including temporal clustering and subword models the accuracy rises from F=0.207 to F=0.326. Clearly, the words that someone has chosen to express a message is just one small aspect of the context in which that message is understood and by combining different learning models with richer features we can prioritize actionable reports with some accuracy. With spatial clustering this rises to F=0.885, indicating that geographic location was the single most important factor for prioritizing actionable messages.

These results are only a first step as there is great potential for research identifying more accurate and efficient learning paradigms. A growing number of our communications are real-time text with frequent spelling variants and a spatial component (tweets, location-based 'check-ins', instant messaging, etc) so there will be increasingly more data available in an increasing variety of languages.

It is easy to imagine many humanitarian applications for classifying text-messages with spatiotemporal information. Social development organizations are already using text messaging to support health (Leach-Lemens, 2009), banking (Peevers et al., 2008), access to market information (Jagun et al., 2008), literacy (Isbrandt, 2009), and there is the potential to aid many of them. Even more importantly, this work can contribute to information processing strategies in future crises. Had a system like the one presented here been in place for Haiti then the identification of actionable messages could have been expedited considerably and a greater volume processed. I coordinated the Mission 4636 volunteers who were translating and mapping the messages in real-time, so this research is partially motivated by the need to see what I could have done better, with a view to being better prepared for future crises.

The results for social media are especially promising. In total, the tweets contained 1,178,444 words - the size of approximately 10 novels - but if there was just one real emergency among them, there was a 97% chance it would rise to the top when ordered by actionable confidence.

Acknowledgments

With thanks to the volunteers of Mission 4636. Their work translating, categorizing and mapping communications showed the humanitarian community the benefits of crowdsourcing/microtasking and is now also helping us prepare for higher-volume semi-automated systems. Thanks also to the volunteers and workers of Samasource/FATEM in Haiti, Ushahidi Haiti in Boston, and to the engineers at CrowdFlower and Ushahidi who built the platforms we used for translation and mapping.

This work was supported by a Stanford Graduate Fellowship and owes thanks to collaborative work and conversations with Chris Manning and colleagues in the Stanford NLP Research Group.

References

Charu C. Aggarwal. 2006. *Data Streams: Models and Algorithms (Advances in Database Systems)*. Springer-Verlag, New York.

Patrick Paroubek Alexander Pak. 2010. Twitter as a corpus for sentiment analysis and opinion mining. In *Proceeding of the 2010 International Conference on Language Resources and Evaluation (LREC 2010)*.

Brian Babcock, Shivnath Babu, Mayur Datar, Rajeev Motwani, and Jennifer Widom. 2002. Models and issues in data stream systems. In *Proceedings of the twenty-first ACM SIGMOD-SIGACT-SIGART symposium on Principles of database systems*, pages 1–16. ACM.

Richard Beaufort, Sophie Roekhaut, Louise-Amélie Cougnon, and Cédrick Fairon. 2010. A hybrid rule/model-based finite-state framework for normalizing sms messages. In *Proceedings of the 48th Annual Meeting of the Association for Computational Linguistics ACL 2010*.

BSteven Bird, Ewan Klein, and Edward Loper. 2009. *Natural language processing with Python*. Oreilly & Associates Inc.

David A. Cohn, Zoubin Ghahramani, and Michael Jordan. 1996. Active learning with statistical models. *Arxiv preprint cs/9603104*.

Gordon V. Cormack, José Mara Gómez Hidalgo, and Enrique Puertas Sánz. 2007. Feature engineering for mobile (SMS) spam filtering. In *The 30th annual international ACM SIGIR conference on research and development in information retrieval*.

The American Red Cross. 2010. Social media in disasters and emergencies. Presentation.

Jacob Eisenstein, Brendan O'Connor, Noah A. Smith, and Eric P. Xing. 2010. A latent variable model for geographic lexical variation. In *Proceedings of the Conference on Empirical Methods in Natural Language Processing (EMNLP 2010)*.

Jenny Rose Finkel and Christopher D. Manning. 2010. Hierarchical joint learning: Improving joint parsing and named entity recognition with non-jointly labeled data. In *Annual Conference of the Association for Computational Linguistics (ACL 2010)*.

Sharon Goldwater, Thomas L. Griffiths, and Mark Johnson. 2009. A bayesian framework for word segmentation: Exploring the effects of context. *Cognition*, 112(1):21–54.

Matt Healy, Sarah Jane Delany, and Anton Zamolotskikh. 2005. An assessment of case-based reasoning for Short Text Message Classification. In *The 16th Irish Conference on Artificial Intelligence & Cognitive Science*.

José Mara Gómez Hidalgo, Guillermo Cajigas Bringas, Enrique Puertas Sánz, and Francisco Carrero Garca. 2006. Content based SMS spam filtering. In *ACM symposium on Document engineering*.

Yan Huang, Hui Xiong, Shashi Shekhar, and Jian Pei. 2003. Mining confident co-location rules without a support threshold. In *Proceedings of the 2003 ACM symposium on Applied computing*.

Geoff Hulten, Laurie Spencer, and Pedro Domingos. 2001. Mining time-changing data streams. In *Proceedings of the seventh ACM SIGKDD international conference on Knowledge discovery and data mining*. ACM.

Scott Isbrandt. 2009. Cell Phones in West Africa: improving literacy and agricultural market information systems in Niger. White paper: Projet Alphabétisation de Base par Cellulaire.

ITU. 2010. The world in 2010: ICT facts and figures. *International Telecommunication Union*.

Abi Jagun, Richard Heeks, and Jason Whalley. 2008. The impact of mobile telephony on developing country micro-enterprise: A Nigerian case study. *Information Technologies and International Development*, 4.

Kirill Kireyev, Leysia Palen, and Kenneth M. Anderson. 2009. Applications of topics models to analysis of disaster-related Twitter data. In *Proceedings of the NIPS Workshop on Applications for Topic Models: Text and Beyond*.

Balachander Krishnamurthy, Phillipa Gill, and Martin Arlitt. 2008. A few chirps about Twitter. In *Proceedings of the first workshop on Online social networks*, New York.

Carole Leach-Lemens. 2009. Using mobile phones in HIV care and prevention. *HIV and AIDS Treatment in Practice*, 137.

Will Lewis. 2010. Haitian Creole: How to Build and Ship an MT Engine from Scratch in 4 days, 17 hours, & 30 minutes. In *14th Annual Conference of the European Association for Machine Translation*.

Luisa Maffi. 2005. Linguistic, cultural, and biological diversity. *Annual Review of Anthropology*, 34:599–617.

Robert Munro and Christopher D. Manning. 2010. Subword variation in text message classification. In *Proceedings of the Annual Conference of the North American Chapter of the Association for Computational Linguistics (NAACL 2010)*.

Robert Munro. 2010. Crowdsourced translation for emergency response in Haiti: the global collaboration of local knowledge. In *AMTA Workshop on Collaborative Crowdsourcing for Translation*.

Brendan O'Connor, Ramnath Balasubramanyan, Bryan R. Routledge, and Noah A. Smith. 2010.

From tweets to polls: Linking text sentiment to public opinion time series. In *Proceedings of the Fourth International AAAI Conference on Weblogs and Social Media*.

Gareth Peevers, Gary Douglas, and Mervyn A. Jack. 2008. A usability comparison of three alternative message formats for an SMS banking service. *International Journal of Human-Computer Studies*, 66.

Sasa Petrović, Miles Osborne, and Victor Lavrenko. 2010. Streaming first story detection with application to twitter. In *Proceedings of the Annual Conference of the North American Chapter of the Association for Computational Linguistics (NAACL 2010)*.

Daniel Ramage, David Hall, Ramesh Nallapati, and Christopher D. Manning. 2009. Labeled LDA: A supervised topic model for credit attribution in multi-labeled corpora. In *Proceedings of the 2009 Conference on Empirical Methods in Natural Language Processing*, Singapore.

Bharath Sriram, Dave Fuhry, Engin Demir, Hakan Ferhatosmanoglu, and Murat Demirbas. 2010. Short text classification in twitter to improve information filtering. In *Proceeding of the 33rd international ACM SIGIR conference on research and development in information retrieval*.

Kate Starbird and Jeannie Stamberger. 2010. Tweak the Tweet: Leveraging Microblogging Proliferation with a Prescriptive Syntax to Support Citizen Reporting. In *Proceedings of the 7th International ISCRAM Conference*.

Simon Tong and Daphne Koller. 2002. Support vector machine active learning with applications to text classification. *The Journal of Machine Learning Research*, 2:45–66.

Kiri Wagstaff, Claire Cardie, Seth Rogers, and Stefan Schr
"odl. 2001. Constrained k-means clustering with background knowledge. In *Proceedings of the Eighteenth International Conference on Machine Learning*, volume 577, page 584. Citeseer.

Xuanhui Wang, Cheng Xiang Zhai, Xiao Hu, and Richard Sproat. 2007. Mining correlated bursty topic patterns from coordinated text streams. In *Proceedings of the 13th ACM SIGKDD international conference on Knowledge discovery and data mining*.

Xin Zhang, Nikos Mamoulis, David W. Cheung, and Yutao Shou. 2004. Fast mining of spatial collocations. In *Proceedings of the tenth ACM SIGKDD international conference on Knowledge discovery and data mining*, pages 384–393. ACM.

Peng Zhang, Xingquan Zhu, and Yong Shi. 2008. Categorizing and mining concept drifting data streams. In *Proceedings of the 14th ACM SIGKDD international conference on Knowledge discovery and data mining*.

Gender Attribution: Tracing Stylometric Evidence Beyond Topic and Genre

Ruchita Sarawgi, Kailash Gajulapalli, and Yejin Choi
Department of Computer Science
Stony Brook University
NY 11794, USA
{rsarawgi, kgajulapalli, ychoi}@cs.stonybrook.edu

Abstract

Sociolinguistic theories (e.g., Lakoff (1973)) postulate that women's language styles differ from that of men. In this paper, we explore statistical techniques that can learn to identify the gender of authors in modern English text, such as web blogs and scientific papers. Although recent work has shown the efficacy of statistical approaches to gender attribution, we conjecture that the reported performance might be overly optimistic due to non-stylistic factors such as topic bias in gender that can make the gender detection task easier. Our work is the first that consciously avoids gender bias in topics, thereby providing stronger evidence to gender-specific styles in language beyond topic. In addition, our comparative study provides new insights into robustness of various stylometric techniques across topic and genre.

1 Introduction

Sociolinguistic theories (e.g., Lakoff (1973)) postulate that women's language styles differ from that of men with respect to various aspects of communication, such as discourse behavior, body language, lexical choices, and linguistic cues (e.g., Crosby and Nyquist (1977), Tannen (1991), Argamon et al. (2003), Eckert and McConnell-Ginet (2003), Argamon et al. (2007)). In this paper, we explore statistical techniques that can learn to identify the gender of authors in modern English text, such as web blogs and scientific papers, motivated by sociolinguistic theories for gender attribution.

There is a broad range of potential applications across computational linguistics and social science where statistical techniques for gender attribution can be useful: e.g., they can help understanding demographic characteristics of user-created web text today, which can provide new insight to social science as well as intelligent marketing and opinion mining. Models for gender attribution can also help tracking changes to gender-specific styles in language over different domain and time. Gender detectors can be useful to guide the style of writing as well, if one needs to assume the style of a specific gender for imaginative writing.

Although some recent work has shown the efficacy of machine learning techniques to gender attribution (e.g., Koppel et al. (2002), Mukherjee and Liu (2010)), we conjecture that the reported performance might be overly optimistic under scrutiny due to non-stylistic factors such as topic bias in gender that can make the gender detection task easier. Indeed, recent research on web blogs reports that there is substantial gender bias in topics (e.g., Janssen and Murachver (2004), Argamon et al. (2007)) as well as in genre (e.g., Herring and Paolillo (2006)).

In order to address this concern, we perform the first comparative study of machine learning techniques for gender attribution after deliberately removing gender bias in topics and genre. Furthermore, making the task even more realistic (and challenging), we experiment with *cross-topic* and *cross-genre* gender attribution, and provide statistical evidence to gender-specific styles in language beyond topic and genre. Five specific questions we aim to investigate are:

Proceedings of the Fifteenth Conference on Computational Natural Language Learning, pages 78–86,
Portland, Oregon, USA, 23–24 June 2011.

Q1 Are there truly gender-specific characteristics in language? or are they confused with gender preferences in topics and genre?

Q2 Are there deep-syntactic patterns in women's language beyond words and shallow patterns?

Q3 Which stylometric analysis techniques are effective in detecting characteristics in women's language?

Q4 Which stylometric analysis techniques are robust against domain change with respect to topics and genre?

Q5 Are there gender-specific language characteristics even in modern scientific text?

From our comparative study of various techniques for gender attribution, including two publicly available systems - Gender Genie[1] and Gender Guesser[2] we find that (1) despite strong evidence for deep syntactic structure that characterizes gender-specific language styles, such deep patterns are not as robust as shallow morphology-level patterns when faced with topic and genre change, and that (2) there are indeed gender-specific linguistic signals that go beyond topics and genre, even in modern and scientific literature.

2 Related Work

The work of Lakoff (1973) initiated the research on women's language, where ten basic characteristics of women's language were listed. Some exemplary ones are as follows:

1 Hedges: e.g., "kind of", "it seems to be"

2 Empty adjectives: e.g., "lovely", "adorable", "gorgeous"

3 Hyper-polite: e.g., "would you mind ...", "I'd much appreciate if ..."

4 Apologetic: e.g., "I am very sorry, but I think that ..."

5 Tag questions: e.g., "you don't mind, do you?"

Many sociolinguists and psychologists consequently investigated on the validity of each of the above assumptions and extended sociolinguistic theories on women's language based on various controlled experiments and psychological analysis (e.g., Crosby and Nyquist (1977), McHugh and Hambaugh (2010)).

While most theories in socioliguistics and psychology focus on a small set of cognitively identifiable patterns in women's language (e.g., the use of tag questions), some recent studies in computer science focus on investigating the use of machine learning techniques that can learn to identify women's language from a bag of features (e.g., Koppel et al. (2002), Mukherjee and Liu (2010)).

Our work differs from most previous work in that we consciously avoid gender bias in topics and genre in order to provide more accurate analysis of statistically identifiable patterns in women's language. Furthermore, we compare various techniques in stylometric analysis within and beyond topics and genre.

3 Dataset without Unwanted Gender Bias

In this section, we describe how we prepared our dataset to avoid unwanted gender bias in topics and genre. Much of previous work has focused on formal writings, such as English literature, newswire articles and the British Natural Corpus(BNC) (e.g., Argamon et al. (2003)), while recent studies expanded toward more informal writing such as web blogs (e.g., Mukherjee and Liu (2010)). In this work, we chose two very different and prominent genre electronically available today: *web blogs* and *scientific papers*.

Blogs: We downloaded blogs from popular blog sites for 7 distinctive topics:[3] *education, travel, spirituality, entertainment, book reviews, history* and *politics*. Within each topic, we find 20 articles written by male authors, and additional 20 articles written by female authors. We took the effort to match articles written by different gender even at the subtopic level. For example, if we take a blog written about the TV show "How I met your mother" by a female author, then we also find a blog written by a

[1] http://bookblog.net/gender/genie.php

[2] Available at http://www.hackerfactor.com/GenderGuesser.php

[3] wordpress.com, blogspot.com & nytimes.com/interactive/blogs/directory.html

male author on the same show. Note that previous research on web blogs does not purposefully maintain balanced topics between gender, thereby benefiting from topic bias inadvertently. From each blog, we keep the first 450 (+/- 20) words preserving the sentence boundaries.[4] We plan to make this data publically available.

Scientific Papers: Scientific papers have not been studied in previous research on gender attribution. Scientific papers correspond to very formal writing where gender-specific language styles are not likely to be conspicuous (e.g., Janssen and Murachver (2004)).

For this dataset, we collected papers from the researchers in our own Natural Language Processing community. We randomly selected 5 female and 5 male authors, and collected 20 papers from each author. We tried to select these authors across a variety of subtopics within NLP research, so as to reduce potential topic-bias in gender even in research. It is also worthwhile to mention that authors in our selection are highly established ones who have published over multiple subtopics in NLP.

Similarly as the blog dataset, we keep the first 450 (+/- 20) words preserving the sentence boundaries. Some papers are co-authored by researchers of mixed gender. In those cases, we rely on the gender of the advisory person as she or he is likely to influence on the abstract and intro the most.

4 Statistical Techniques

In this section, we describe three different types of statistical language models that learn patterns at different depth. The first kind is based on probabilistic context-free grammars (PCFG) that learn *deep long-distance syntactic patterns* (Section 4.1). The second kind is based on token-level language models that learn *shallow lexico-syntactic patterns* (Section 4.2). The last kind is based on character-level language models that learn *morphological patterns* on extremely short text spans (Section 4.3). Finally, we describe the bag-of-word approach using the maximum entropy classifier (Section 4.4).

[4]Note that existing gender detection tools require a minimum 300 words for appropriate identification.

4.1 Deep Syntactic Patterns using Probabilistic Context free Grammar

A probabilistic context-free grammar (PCFG) captures syntactic regularities beyond shallow ngram-based lexico-syntactic patterns. Raghavan et al. (2010) recently introduced the use of PCFG for authorship attribution for the first time, and demonstrated that it is highly effective for learning stylistic patterns for authorship attribution. We therefore explore the use of PCFG for gender attribution. We give a very concise description here, referring to Raghavan et al. (2010) for more details.

(1) Train a generic PCFG parser G_o on manually tree-banked corpus such as WSJ or Brown.

(2) Given training corpus D for gender attribution, tree-bank each training document $d_i \in D$ using the PCFG parser G_o.

(3) For each gender γ, train a new gender-specific PCFG parser G_γ using only those tree-banked documents in D that correspond to gender γ.

(4) For each test document, compare the likelihood of the document determined by each gender-specific PCFG parser G_γ, and the gender corresponding to the higher score.

Note that PCFG models can be considered as a kind of language models, where probabilistic context-free grammars are used to find the patterns in language, rather than n-grams. We use the implementation of Klein and Manning (2003) for PCFG models.

4.2 Shallow Lexico-Syntactic Patterns using Token-level Language Models

Token-based (i.e. word-based) language models have been employed in a wide variety of NLP applications, including those that require stylometric analysis, e.g., authorship attribution (e.g., Uzner and Katz (2005)), and Wikipedia vandalism detection (Wang and McKeown, 2010). We expect that token-based language models will be effective in learning shallow lexico-syntactic patterns of gender specific language styles. We therefore experiment with unigram, bigram, and trigram token-level models, and name them as TLM(n=1), TLM(n=2), TLM(n=3), respectively, where TLM stands for **T**oken-based

	lexicon based		deep syntax	morphology			b.o.w.	shallow lex-syntax		
	Gender	Gender	PCFG	CLM	CLM	CLM	ME	TLM	TLM	TLM
Data Type	Genie	Guesser		n=1	n=2	n=3		n=1	n=2	n=3
Male Only	**72.1**	68.6	53.4	65.8	69.0	63.4	57.6	67.1	67.8	66.2
Female Only	27.1	06.4	**74.8**	57.6	73.6	76.8	73.8	60.1	64.2	64.2
All	50.0	37.5	64.1	61.70	**71.3**	70.3	65.8	63.7	66.1	65.4

Table 1: Overall Accuracy of Topic-Balanced Gender Attribution on Blog Data **(Experiment-I)**

Language **M**odels. We use the LingPipe package[5] for experiments.

4.3 Shallow Morphological Patterns using Character-level Language Models

Next we explore the use of character-level language models to investigate whether there are morphological patterns that characterize gender-specific styles in language. Despite its simplicity, previous research have reported that character-level language models are effective for authorship attribution (e.g., Peng et al. (2003b)) as well as genre classification (e.g., Peng et al. (2003a), Wu et al. (2010)). We experiment with unigram, bigram, and trigram character-level models, and name them as CLM(n=1), CLM(n=2), CLM(n=3), respectively, where CLM stands for **C**haracter-based **L**anguage **M**odels. We again make use of the LingPipe package for experiments.

Note that there has been no previous research that directly compares the performance of character-level language models to that of PCFG based models for author attribution, not to mention for gender attribution.

4.4 Bag of Words using Maximum Entropy (MaxEnt) Classifier

We include Maximum Entropy classifier using simple unigram features (bag-of-words) for comparison purposes, and name it as ME. We use the MALLET package (McCallum, 2002) for experiments.

5 Experimental Results

Note that our two datasets are created to specifically answer the following question: *are there gender-specific characteristics in language beyond gender preferences in topics and genre?* One way to answer this question is to test whether statistical models can detect gender attribution on a dataset that is drastically different from the training data in topic and genre. Of course, it is a known fact that machine learning techniques do not transfer well across different domains (e.g., Blitzer et al. (2006)). However, if they can still perform considerably better than random prediction, then it would prove that there is indeed gender-specific stylometric characteristics beyond topic and genre. In what follows, we present five different experimental settings across two different dataset to compare in-domain and cross-domain performance of various techniques for gender attribution.

5.1 Experiments with Blog Dataset

First we conduct two different experiments using the blog data in the order of increasing difficulty.

[Experiment-I: Balanced Topic] Using the web blog dataset introduced in Section 3, we perform gender attribution (classification) task on balanced topics. For each topic, 80% of the documents are used for training and remaining ones are used for testing, yielding 5-fold cross validation. Both training and test data have balanced class distributions so that random guess would yield 50% of accuracy. The results are given in Table 1. Note that the "overall accuracy" corresponds to the average across the five folds.

The PCFG model achieves prediction accuracy 64.1%, demonstrating statistical evidence to gender-specific characteristics in syntactic structure. The PCFG model outperforms two publicly available systems - Gender Genie and Gender Guesser, which are based on a fixed list of indicator words. The difference is statistically significant ($p = 0.01 < 0.05$)

[5]Available at `http://alias-i.com/lingpipe/`

	lexicon based		deep syntax	morphology			b.o.w.	shallow lex-syntax		
Topic	Gender Genie	Gender Guesser	PCFG	CLM n=1	CLM n=2	CLM n=3	ME	TLM n=1	TLM n=2	TLM n=3
Per Topic Accuracy (%) for All Authors										
Entertain	50.0	42.5	50.0	52.5	**67.5**	**67.5**	60.0	57.5	57.5	57.5
Book	50.0	42.5	65.0	57.5	67.5	**72.5**	55.0	60.0	67.5	67.5
Politics	35.0	30.0	50.0	47.5	**52.5**	50.0	45.0	**52.5**	**52.5**	**52.5**
History	40.0	35.0	77.5	65.0	**80.0**	**80.0**	55.0	65.0	65.0	65.0
Education	62.5	42.5	55.0	63.0	65.0	**70.0**	63.0	55.0	57.5	52.5
Travel	62.5	37.5	63.0	**65.0**	63.0	63.0	63.0	62.5	**65.0**	**65.0**
Spirituality	50.0	32.5	53.0	**78.0**	**78.0**	**78.0**	50.0	65.0	70.0	72.5
Avg	50.0	37.5	59.0	61.2	**68.3**	**68.3**	55.87	60.0	61.3	61.5
Per Topic Accuracy (%) for Female Authors										
Entertain	25.0	10.0	**85.0**	70.0	50.0	**85.0**	70.0	75.0	75.0	75.0
Book	15.0	15.0	**95.0**	80.0	**95.0**	90.0	85.0	75.0	90.0	90.0
Politics	10.0	05.0	**65.0**	00.0	05.0	00.0	35.0	30.0	30.0	25.0
History	10.0	05.0	**90.0**	70.0	80.0	75.0	70.0	50.0	50.0	50.0
Education	45.0	10.0	80.0	95.0	85.0	90.0	**100.0**	50.0	55.0	50.0
Travel	65.0	00.0	85.0	90.0	**100.0**	**100.0**	**100.0**	85.0	95.0	90.0
Spirituality	20.0	00.0	60.0	65.0	65.0	**70.0**	45.0	50.0	50.0	50.0
Avg	27.1	06.4	**80.0**	67.1	68.6	72.9	72.1	59.3	63.6	61.4
Per Topic Accuracy (%) for Male Authors										
Entertain	75.0	75.0	15.0	35.0	**85.0**	50.0	50.0	40.0	40.0	40.0
Book	**80.0**	70.0	35.0	35.0	40.0	55.0	25.0	45.0	45.0	45.0
Politics	60.0	55.0	35.0	95.0	**100.0**	**100.0**	55.0	75.0	75.0	80.0
History	70.0	65.0	65.0	60.0	80.0	**85.0**	40.0	80.0	80.0	80.0
Education	**80.0**	75.0	30.0	30.0	45.0	50.0	25.0	60.0	60.0	55.0
Travel	60.0	**75.0**	40.0	40.0	25.0	25.0	25.0	40.0	35.0	40.0
Spirituality	80.0	65.0	45.0	**90.0**	**90.0**	85.0	55.0	80.0	90.0	95.0
Avg	**72.1**	68.6	37.9	55.0	66.4	64.2	39.3	60.0	60.8	62.1

Table 2: Per-Topic & Per-Gender Accuracy of Cross-Topic Gender Attribution on Blog Data **(Experiment-II)**

using paired student's t-test.[6]

Interestingly, the best performing approaches are character-level language models, performing substantially better (71.30% for n=2) than both the token-level language models (66.1% for n=2) and the PCFG model (64.10%). The difference between CLM(n=2) and PCFG is statistically significant ($p = 0.015 < 0.05$) using paired student's t-test, while the difference between TLM(n=2) and PCFG is not.

As will be seen in the following experiment (**Experiment-II**) using the Blog dataset as well, the performance of PCFG models is very close to that of unigram language models. As a result, one might wonder whether PCFG models are learning any useful syntactic pattern beyond terminal productions that can help discriminating gender-specific styles in language. This question will be partially answered in the fourth experiment (**Experiment-IV**) using the Scientific Paper dataset, where PCFG models demonstrate considerably better performance over the unigram language models.

Following Raghavan et al. (2010), we also exper-

[6]We also experimented with the interpolated PCFG model following Raghavan et al. (2010) using various interpolation dataset, but we were not able to achieve a better result in our experiments. We omit the results of interpolated PCFG models for brevity.

Data Type	lexicon based Gender Genie	Gender Guesser	deep syntax PCFG	morphology CLM n=1	CLM n=2	CLM n=3	b.o.w. ME	shallow lex-syntax TLM n=1	TLM n=2	TLM n=3
Male Only	85.0	63.0	59.0	96.0	94.0	**99.0**	62.0	68.0	68.0	68.0
Female Only	9.0	0.0	36.0	10.0	8.0	18.0	**61.0**	34.0	32.0	32.0
All	47.0	31.5	47.5	53.0	51.0	58.5	**61.5**	51.0	50.0	50.0

Table 3: Overall Accuracy of Cross-Topic /Cross-Genre Gender Attribution on Scientific Papers **(Experiment-III)**

imented with ensemble methods that linearly combine the output of different classifiers, but we omit the results in Table 1, as we were not able to obtain consistently higher performance than the simple character-level language models in our dataset.

[Experiment-II: Cross-Topic] Next we perform cross-topic experiments using the same blog dataset, in order to quantify the robustness of different techniques against topic change. We train on 6 topics, and test on the remaining 1 topic, making 7-fold cross validation. The results are shown in Table 2, where the top one third shows the performance for all authors, the next one third shows the performance with respect to only female authors, the bottom one third shows the performance with respect to only male authors.

Again, the best performing approaches are based on character-level language models, achieving upto 68.3% in accuracy. PCFG models and token-level language models achieve substantially lower accuracy of 59.0% and 61.5% respectively. Per-gender analysis in Table 1 reveals interesting insights into different approaches. In particular, we find that Gender Genie and Gender Guesser are biased toward male authors, attributing the majority authors as male. PCFG and ME on the other hand are biased toward female authors. Both character-level and token-level language models show balanced distribution between gender. We also experimented with ensemble methods, but omit the results as we were not able to obtain higher scores than simple character-level language models.

From these two experiments so far, we find that PCFG models and word-level language models are neither as effective, nor as robust as character-level language models for gender attribution. Despite overall low performance of PCFG models, this result suggests that PCFG models are able to learn gender-specific syntactic patterns, albeit the signals from deep syntax seem much weaker than those of very shallow morphological patterns.

5.2 Experiments with Scientific Papers

Next we present three different experiments using the scientific data, in the order of decreasing difficulty.

[Experiment-III: Cross-Topic & Cross-Genre] In this experiment, we challenge statistical techniques for gender attribution by changing both topics and genre across training and testing. To do so, we train models on the blog dataset and test on the scientific paper dataset. Notice that this is a dramatically harder task than the previous two experiments.

Note also that previous research thus far has not reported experiments such as this, or even like the previous one. It is worthwhile to mention that our goal in this paper is not domain adaptation for gender attribution, but merely to quantify to what degree the gender-specific language styles can be traced across different topics and genre, and which techniques are robust against domain change.

The results are shown in Table 5. Precisely as expected, the performance of all models drop significantly in this scenario. The two baseline systems – Gender Genie and Gender Guesser, which are not designed for formal scientific writings also perform worse in this dataset. Table 4 discussed in the next experiment will provide more insight into this by providing per-gender accuracy of these baseline systems.

From this experiment, we find a rather surprising message: although the performance of most statistical approaches decreases significantly, notice that most approaches perform still better than random (50%) prediction, achieving upto 61.5% accuracy.

	lexicon based		deep syntax	morphology			b.o.w.	shallow lex-syntax		
	Gender	Gender	PCFG	CLM	CLM	CLM	ME	TLM	TLM	TLM
Data Type	Genie	Guesser		n=1	n=2	n=3		n=1	n=2	n=3
Per Author Accuracy (%) for All Authors										
All	47.0	31.5	**76.0**	73.0	72.0	**76.0**	70.50	63.5	62.5	62.5
Per Author Accuracy (%) for Male Authors										
A	80.0	55.0	75.0	**100.0**	**100.0**	**100.0**	45.0	45.0	40.0	40.0
B	90.0	75.0	75.0	80.0	70.0	**85.0**	55.0	45.0	40.0	40.0
C	95.0	55.0	85.0	85.0	90.0	**95.0**	90.0	90.0	90.0	90.0
D	85.0	65.0	**100.0**	95.0	**100.0**	**100.0**	**100.0**	**100.0**	**100.0**	**100.0**
E	75.0	65.0	**90.0**	70.0	85.0	80.0	70.0	70.0	70.0	60.0
Avg	85.0	63.0	85.0	86.0	89.0	**92.0**	72.0	70.0	68.0	66.0
Per Author Accuracy (%) for Female Authors										
F	15.0	0.0	95.0	05.0	30.0	75.0	**100.0**	85.0	85.0	85.0
G	5.0	0.0	25.0	55.0	70.0	**85.0**	75.0	80.0	**85.0**	**85.0**
H	10.0	0.0	65.0	**70.0**	45.0	35.0	40.0	35.0	30.0	30.0
I	15.0	0.0	80.0	**85.0**	45.0	50.0	65.0	35.0	35.0	35.0
J	0.0	0.0	70.0	**85.0**	**85.0**	**85.0**	65.0	50.0	50.0	60.0
Avg	9.0	0.0	67.0	60.0	55.0	66.0	**69.0**	57.0	57.0	59.0

Table 4: Per-Author Accuracy of Cross-Topic Gender Attribution for Scientific Papers **(Experiment-IV)**

Considering that the models are trained on drastically different topics and genre, this result suggests that there are indeed gender-specific linguistic signals beyond different topics and genre. This is particularly interesting given that scientific papers correspond to very formal writing where gender-specific language styles are not likely to be conspicuous (e.g., Janssen and Murachver (2004)).

[Experiment-IV: Cross-Topic] Next we perform cross-topic experiment, only using the scientific paper dataset. Because the stylistic difference in genre is significantly more prominent than the stylistic difference in topics, this should be a substantially easier task than the previous experiment. Nevertheless, previous research to date has not attempted to evaluate gender attribution techniques across different topics. Here we train on 4 authors per gender (8 authors in total), and test on the remaining 2 authors, making 5-fold cross validation. As before, the class distributions are balanced in both training and test data.

The experimental results are shown in Table 4, where we report per-author, per-gender, and overall average accuracy. As expected, the overall performance increase dramatically, as models are trained on articles in the same genre. It is interesting to see how Gender Genie and Gender Guesser are extremely biased toward male authors, achieving almost zero accuracy with respect to articles written by female authors. Here the best performing models are PCFG and CLM(n=3), both achieving 76.0% in accuracy. Token-level language models on the other hand achieve significantly lower performance.

Remind that in the first two experiments based on the blog data, PCFG models and token-level language models performed similarly. Given that, it is very interesting that PCFG models now perform just as good as character-level language models, while outperforming token-level language models significantly. We conjecture following two reasons to explain this:

- First, scientific papers use very formal language, thereby suppressing gender-specific lexical cues that are easier to detect (e.g., empty words such as "lovely", "gorgeous" (Lakoff, 1973)). In such data, deep syntactic patterns play a much stronger role in detecting gender specific language styles. This also indirectly

	lexicon based		deep syntax	morphology			b.o.w.	shallow lex-syntax		
	Gender	Gender	PCFG	CLM	CLM	CLM	ME	TLM	TLM	TLM
Data Type	Genie	Guesser		n=1	n=2	n=3		n=1	n=2	n=3
Male Only	85.0	63.0	86.0	**92.0**	**92.0**	91.0	86.0	86.0	87.0	88.0
Female Only	9.0	0.0	84.0	88.0	87.0	**92.0**	91.0	83.0	84.0	86.0
All	47.0	31.5	85.0	90.0	88.50	**91.50**	88.50	85.0	85.5	87.0

Table 5: Overall Accuracy of Topic-Balanced Gender Attribution on Scientific Papers **(Experiment-V)**

addresses the concern raised in **Experiment-I & II** as to whether the PCFG models are learning any syntactic pattern beyond terminal productions that are similar to unigram language models.

- Second, our dataset is constructed in such a way that the training and test data do not share articles written by the same authors. Furthermore, the authors are chosen so that the main research topics are substantially different from each other. Therefore, token-based language models are likely to learn topical words and phrases, and suffer when the topics change dramatically between training and testing.

[Experiment-V: Balanced Topic] Finally, we present the conventional experimental set up, where topic distribution is balanced between training and test dataset. This is not as interesting as the previous two scenarios, however, we include this experiment in order to provide a loose upper bound. Because we choose each different author from each different sub-topic of research, we need to split articles by the same author into training and testing to ensure balanced topic distribution. We select 80% of articles from each author as training data, and use the remaining 20% as test data, resulting in 5-fold cross validation.

This is the easiest task among the three experiments using the scientific paper data, hence the performance increases substantially. As before, character-level language models perform the best, with CLM n=3 reaching extremely high accuracy of 91.50%. All other statistical approaches perform very well achieving at least 85% or higher accuracy.

Note that token-level language models perform very poorly in the previous experimental setting, while performing close to the top performer in this experiment. We make the following two conclusions based on the last two experiments:

- Token-level language models have the tendency of learning topics words, rather than just stylometric cues.

- When performing cross-topic gender attribution (as in **Experiment-IV**), PCFG models are more robust than token-level language models.

6 Conclusions

We postulate that previous study in gender attribution might have been overly optimistic due to gender specific preference on topics and genre. We perform the first comparative study of machine learning techniques for gender attribution consciously removing gender bias in topics. Rather unexpectedly, we find that the most robust approach is based on character-level language models that learn morphological patterns, rather than token-level language models that learn shallow lexico-syntactic patterns, or PCFG models that learn deep syntactic patterns. Another surprising finding is that we can trace statistical evidence of gender-specific language styles beyond topics and genre, and even in modern scientific papers.

Acknowledgments

We thank reviewers for giving us highly insightful and valuable comments.

References

Shlomo Argamon, Moshe Koppel, Jonathan Fine, and Anat Rachel Shimoni. 2003. Gender, genre, and writing style in formal written texts. *Text*, 23.

Shlomo Argamon, Moshe Koppel, James W. Pennebaker, and Jonathan Schler. 2007. Mining the blogosphere:

Age, gender and the varieties of selfexpression. In *First Monday, Vol. 12, No. 9.*

John Blitzer, Ryan McDonald, and Fernando Pereira. 2006. Domain adaptation with structural correspondence learning. In *Conference on Empirical Methods in Natural Language Processing*, Sydney, Australia.

Faye Crosby and Linda Nyquist. 1977. The female register: an empirical study of lakoff's hypotheses. In *Language in Society, 6*, pages 313 – 322.

Penelope Eckert and Sally McConnell-Ginet. 2003. Language and gender. Cambridge University Press.

Susan C. Herring and John C. Paolillo. 2006. Gender and genre variations in weblogs. In *Journal of Sociolinguistics, Vol. 10, No. 4.*, pages 439 –459.

Anna Janssen and Tamar Murachver. 2004. The relationship between gender and topic in gender-preferential language use. In *Written Communication, 21*, pages 344– 367.

Dan Klein and Christopher D. Manning. 2003. Accurate unlexicalized parsing. In *Proceedings of the 41st Annual Meeting on Association for Computational Linguistics*, pages 423–430. Association for Computational Linguistics.

Moshe Koppel, Shlomo Argamon, and Anat Shimoni. 2002. Automatically categorizing written texts by author gender. *Literary and Linguistic Computing*, 17(4):401–412, June.

Robin T. Lakoff. 1973. Language and woman's place. In *Language in Society, Vol. 2, No. 1*, pages 45 – 80.

Andrew Kachites McCallum. 2002. Mallet: A machine learning for language toolkit. http://www.cs.umass.edu/ mccallum/mallet.

Maureen C. McHugh and Jennifer Hambaugh. 2010. She said, he said: Gender, language, and power. In *Handbook of Gender Research in Psychology. Volume 1: Gender Research in General and Experimental Psychology*, pages 379 – 410.

Arjun Mukherjee and Bing Liu. 2010. Improving gender classification of blog authors. In *Proceedings of the 2010 Conference on Empirical Methods in Natural Language Processing*, EMNLP '10, pages 207–217, Stroudsburg, PA, USA. Association for Computational Linguistics.

Fuchun Peng, Dale Schuurmans, Vlado Keselj, and Shaojun Wang. 2003a. Language independent authorship attribution with character level n-grams. In *EACL*.

Funchun Peng, Dale Schuurmans, and Shaojun Wang. 2003b. Language and task independent text categorization with simple language models. In *Proceedings of the 2003 Human Language Technology Conference of the North American Chapter of the Association for Computational Linguistics*.

Sindhu Raghavan, Adriana Kovashka, and Raymond Mooney. 2010. Authorship attribution using probabilistic context-free grammars. In *Proceedings of the ACL*, pages 38–42, Uppsala, Sweden, July. Association for Computational Linguistics.

Deborah Tannen. 1991. You just don't understand: Women and men in conversation. Ballantine Books.

Ozlem Uzner and Boris Katz. 2005. A Comparative Study of Language Models for Book And Author Recognition. In *Second International Joint Conference on Natural Language Processing:Full Papers*, pages 1969–980. Association for Computational Linguistics.

William Yang Wang and Kathleen R. McKeown. 2010. "got you!": Automatic vandalism detection in wikipedia with web-based shallow syntactic-semantic modeling. In *23rd International Conference on Computational Linguistics (Coling 2010)*, page 1146?1154.

Zhili Wu, Katja Markert, and Serge Sharoff. 2010. Fine-grained genre classification using structural learning algorithms. In *Proceedings of the 48th Annual Meeting of the Association for Computational Linguistics*, pages 749–759, Uppsala, Sweden, July. Association for Computational Linguistics.

Improving the Impact of Subjectivity Word Sense Disambiguation on Contextual Opinion Analysis

Cem Akkaya, Janyce Wiebe, Alexander Conrad
University of Pittsburgh
Pittsburgh PA, 15260, USA
{cem,wiebe,conrada}@cs.pitt.edu

Rada Mihalcea
University of North Texas
Denton TX, 76207, USA
rada@cs.unt.edu

Abstract

Subjectivity word sense disambiguation (SWSD) is automatically determining which word instances in a corpus are being used with subjective senses, and which are being used with objective senses. SWSD has been shown to improve the performance of contextual opinion analysis, but only on a small scale and using manually developed integration rules. In this paper, we scale up the integration of SWSD into contextual opinion analysis and still obtain improvements in performance, by successfully gathering data annotated by non-expert annotators. Further, by improving the method for integrating SWSD into contextual opinion analysis, even greater benefits from SWSD are achieved than in previous work. We thus more firmly demonstrate the potential of SWSD to improve contextual opinion analysis.

1 Introduction

Often, methods for opinion, sentiment, and subjectivity analysis rely on lexicons of subjective (opinion-carrying) words (e.g., (Turney, 2002; Whitelaw et al., 2005; Riloff and Wiebe, 2003; Yu and Hatzivassiloglou, 2003; Kim and Hovy, 2004; Bloom et al., 2007; Andreevskaia and Bergler, 2008; Agarwal et al., 2009)). Examples of such words are the following (in bold):

(1) He is a **disease** to every team he has gone to.
Converting to SMF is a **headache**.
The concert left me **cold**.
That guy is such a **pain**.

However, even manually developed subjectivity lexicons have significant degrees of subjectivity sense ambiguity (Su and Markert, 2008; Gyamfi et al., 2009). That is, many clues in these lexicons have both subjective and objective senses. This ambiguity leads to errors in opinion and sentiment analysis, because objective instances represent false hits of subjectivity clues. For example, the following sentence contains the keywords from (1) used with objective senses:

(2) Early symptoms of the **disease** include severe **headaches**, red eyes, fevers and **cold** chills, body **pain**, and vomiting.

Recently, in (Akkaya et al., 2009), we introduced the task of *subjectivity word sense disambiguation (SWSD)*, which is to automatically determine which word instances in a corpus are being used with subjective senses, and which are being used with objective senses. We developed a supervised system for SWSD, and exploited the SWSD output to improve the performance of multiple contextual opinion analysis tasks.

Although the reported results are promising, there are three obvious shortcomings. First, we were able to apply SWSD to contextual opinion analysis only on a very small scale, due to a shortage of annotated data. While the experiments show that SWSD improves contextual opinion analysis, this was only on the small amount of opinion-annotated data that was in the coverage of our system. Two questions arise: is it feasible to obtain greater amounts of the needed data, and do SWSD performance improvements on contextual opinion analysis hold on a

Proceedings of the Fifteenth Conference on Computational Natural Language Learning, pages 87–96,
Portland, Oregon, USA, 23–24 June 2011.

larger scale. Second, the annotations in (Akkaya et al., 2009) are piggy-backed on SENSEVAL sense-tagged data, which are fine-grained word sense annotations created by trained annotators. A concern is that SWSD performance improvements on contextual opinion analysis can only be achieved using such fine-grained expert annotations, the availability of which is limited. Third, (Akkaya et al., 2009) uses manual rules to apply SWSD to contextual opinion analysis. Although these rules have the advantage that they transparently show the effects of SWSD, they are somewhat ad hoc. Likely, they are not optimal and are holding back the potential of SWSD to improve contextual opinion analysis.

To address these shortcomings, in this paper, we investigate (1) the feasibility of obtaining a substantial amount of annotated data, (2) whether performance improvements on contextual opinion analysis can be realized on a larger scale, and (3) whether those improvements can be realized with subjectivity sense tagged data that is not built on expert full-inventory sense annotations. In addition, we explore better methods for applying SWSD to contextual opinion analysis.

2 Subjectivity Word Sense Disambiguation

2.1 Annotation Tasks

We adopt the definitions of *subjective* (*S*) and *objective* (*O*) from (Wiebe et al., 2005; Wiebe and Mihalcea, 2006; Wilson, 2007). Subjective expressions are words and phrases being used to express mental and emotional states, such as speculations, evaluations, sentiments, and beliefs. A general covering term for such states is *private state* (Quirk et al., 1985), an internal state that cannot be directly observed or verified by others. Objective expressions instead are words and phrases that lack subjectivity.

The contextual opinion analysis experiments described in Section 3 include both *S/O* and polarity (positive,negative, neutral) classifications. The opinion-annotated data used in those experiments is from the MPQA Corpus (Wiebe et al., 2005; Wilson, 2007),[1] which consists of news articles annotated for subjective expressions, including polarity.

[1]Available at http://www.cs.pitt.edu/mpqa

2.1.1 Subjectivity Sense Labeling

For SWSD, we need the notions of subjective and objective *senses* of words in a dictionary. We adopt the definitions from (Wiebe and Mihalcea, 2006), who describe the annotation scheme as follows. Classifying a sense as *S* means that, when the sense is used in a text or conversation, one expects it to express subjectivity, and also that the phrase or sentence containing it expresses subjectivity. As noted in (Wiebe and Mihalcea, 2006), sentences containing objective senses may not be objective. Thus, objective senses are defined as follows: Classifying a sense as *O* means that, when the sense is used in a text or conversation, one does not expect it to express subjectivity and, if the phrase or sentence containing it is subjective, the subjectivity is due to something else.

Both (Wiebe and Mihalcea, 2006) and (Su and Markert, 2008) performed agreement studies of the scheme and report that good agreement can be achieved between human annotators labeling the subjectivity of senses (κ values of 0.74 and 0.79, respectively).

(Akkaya et al., 2009) followed the same annotation scheme to annotate the senses of the words used in the experiments. For this paper, we again use the same scheme and annotate WordNet senses of 90 new words (the process of selecting the words is described in Section 2.4).

2.1.2 Subjectivity Sense Tagging

The training and test data for SWSD consists of word instances in a corpus labeled as *S* or *O*, indicating whether they are used with a subjective or objective sense.

Because there was no such tagged data at the time, (Akkaya et al., 2009) created a data set by combining two types of sense annotations: (1) labels of senses within a dictionary as *S* or *O* (i.e., the subjectivity sense labels of the previous section), and (2) sense tags of word instances in a corpus (i.e., SENSEVAL sense-tagged data).[2] The subjectivity sense labels were used to collapse the sense labels in the sense-tagged data into the two new senses, *S* and *O*. The target words (Akkaya et al., 2009) chose are the words tagged in SENSEVAL that are also members

[2]Please see the paper for details on the SENSEVAL data used in the experiments.

Sense_Set1 (Subjective)

{ **attack**, round, assail, lash_out, snipe, assault } – attack in speech or writing; "The editors attacked the House Speaker"

{ assail, assault, set_on, **attack** } – attack someone emotionally; "Nightmares assailed him regularly"

Sense_Set2 (Objective)

{ **attack** } – begin to injure; "The cancer cells are attacking his liver"; "Rust is attacking the metal"

{ **attack**, aggress } – take the initiative and go on the offensive; "The visiting team started to attack"

Figure 1: Sense sets for target word "attack" (abridged).

of the subjectivity lexicon of (Wilson et al., 2005; Wilson, 2007).[3] There are 39 such words. (Akkaya et al., 2009) chose words from a subjectivity lexicon because such words are known to have subjective usages.

For this paper, subjectivity sense-tagged data was obtained from the MTurk workers using the annotation scheme of (Akkaya et al., 2010). A goal is to keep the annotation task as simple as possible. Thus, the workers are not directly asked if the instance of a target word has a subjective or an objective sense, because the concept of subjectivity would be difficult to explain in this setting. Instead the workers are shown two sets of senses – one subjective set and one objective set – for a specific target word and a text passage in which the target word appears. Their job is to select the set that best reflects the meaning of the target word in the text passage. The set they choose gives us the subjectivity label of the instance.

A sample annotation task is shown below. An MTurk worker has access to two sense sets of the target word "attack" as seen in Figure 1. The S and O labels appear here only for the purpose of this paper; the workers do not see them. The worker is presented with the following text passage holding the target word "attack":

> Ivkovic had been a target of intra-party feuding that has shaken the party. He was **attacked** by Milosevic for attempting to carve out a new party from the Socialists.

In this passage, the use of "attack" is most similar to the first entry in sense set one; thus, the correct answer for this problem is Sense_Set-1.

[3]Available at http://www.cs.pitt.edu/mpqa

(Akkaya et al., 2010) carried out a pilot study where a subjectivity sense-tagged dataset was created for eight SENSEVAL words through MTurk. (Akkaya et al., 2010) evaluated the non-expert label quality against gold-standard expert labels which were obtained from (Akkaya et al., 2009) relying on SENSEVAL. The non-expert annotations are reliable, achieving κ scores around 0.74 with the expert annotations.

For some words, there may not be a clean split between the subjective and objective senses. For these, we opted for another strategy for obtaining MTurk annotations. Rather than presenting the workers with WordNet senses, we show them a set of objective usages, a set of subjective usages, and a text passage in which the target word appears. The workers' job is to judge which set of usages the target instance is most similar to.

2.2 SWSD System

We follow the same approach as in (Akkaya et al., 2009) to build our SWSD system. We train a different supervised SWSD classifier for each target word separately. This means the overall SWSD system consists of as many SWSD classifiers as there are target words. We utilize the same machine learning features as in (Akkaya et al., 2009), which are commonly used in *Word Sense Disambiguation (WSD)*.

2.3 Expert SWSD vs. Non-expert SWSD

Before creating a large subjectivity sense-tagged corpus via MTurk, we want to make sure that non-expert annotations are good enough to train reliable SWSD classifiers. Thus, we decided to compare the performance of a SWSD system trained on non-expert annotations and on expert annotations. For this purpose, we need a subjectivity sense-tagged corpus where word instances are tagged both by expert and non-expert annotations. Fortunately, we have such a corpus. As discussed in Section 3, (Akkaya et al., 2009) created a subjecvitivity sense-tagged corpus piggybacked on SENSEVAL. This gives us a gold-standard corpus tagged by experts. There is also a small subjectivity sense-tagged corpus consisting of eight target words obtained from non-expert annotators in (Akkaya et al., 2010). This corpus is a subset of the gold-standard corpus from (Akkaya et al., 2009) and it consists of 60 tagged

	Acc	p-value
$SWSD_{GOLD}$	79.2	-
$SWSD_{MJL}$	78.4	0.542
$SWSD_{MJC}$	78.8	0.754

Table 1: Comparison of SWSD systems

instances for each target word.

Actually, (Akkaya et al., 2010) gathered three labels for each instance. This gives us two options to train the non-expert SWSD system: (1) training the system on the majority vote labels *($SWSD_{MJL}$)* (2) training three systems on the three separate label sets and taking the majority vote prediction *($SWSD_{MJC}$)*. Additionally, we train an expert SWSD system *($SWSD_{GOLD}$)* – a system trained on gold standard expert annotations. All these systems are trained on 60 instances of the eight target words for which we have both non-expert and expert annotations and are evaluated on the remaining instances of the gold-standard corpus. This makes a total of 923 test instances for the eight target words with a majority class baseline of 61.8.

Table 1 reports micro-average accuracy of each system and the two-tailed p-value between the expert SWSD system and the two non-expert SWSD systems. The p-value is calculated with McNemar's test. It shows that there is no statistically significant difference between classifiers trained on expert gold-standard annotations and non-expert annotations. We adopt $SWSD_{MJL}$ in all our following experiments, because it is more efficient.

2.4 Corpus Creation

For our experiments, we have multiple goals, which effect our decisions on how to create the subjectivity sense-tagged corpus via MTurk. First, we want to be able to disambiguate more target words than (Akkaya et al., 2009). This way, SWSD will be able to disambiguate a larger portion of the MPQA Corpus allowing us to evaluate the effect of SWSD on contextual opinion analysis on a larger scale. This will also allow us to investigate additional integration methods of SWSD into contextual opinion analysis rather than simple ad hoc manual rules utilized in (Akkaya et al., 2009). Second, we want to show that we can rely on non-expert annotations instead of expert annotations, which will make an annotation effort on a larger-scale both practical and feasible, timewise and costwise. Optimally, we could have annotated via MTurk the same subjectivity sense-tagged corpus from (Akkaya et al., 2009) in order to compare the effect of a non-expert SWSD system on contextual opinion analysis directly with the results reported for an expert SWSD system in (Akkaya et al., 2009). But, this would have diverted our resources to reproduce the same corpus and contradict our goal to extend the subjectivity sense-tagged corpus to new target words. Moreover, we have already shown in Section 2.3 that non-expert annotations can be utilized to train reliable SWSD classifiers. It is reasonable to believe that similar performance on the SWSD task will reflect to similar improvements on contextual opinion analysis. Thus, we decided to prioritize creating a subjectivity sense-tagged corpus for a totally new set of words. We aim to show that the favourable results reported in (Akkaya et al., 2009) will still hold on new target words relying on non-expert annotations.

We chose our target words from the subjectivity lexicon of (Wilson et al., 2005), because we know they have subjective usages. The contextual opinion systems we want to improve rely on this lexicon. We call the words in the lexicon *subjectivity clues*. At this stage, we want to concentrate on the frequent and ambiguous subjectivity clues. We chose frequent ones, because they will have larger coverage in the MPQA Corpus. We chose ambiguous ones, because these clues are the ones that are most important for SWSD. Choosing most frequent and ambiguous subjectivity clues guarantees that we utilize our limited resources in the most efficient way. We judge a clue to be ambiguous if it appears more than 25% and less than 75% of the times in a subjective expression. We get these statistics by simply counting occurrences in the MPQA Corpus inside and outside of subjective expressions.

There are 680 subjectivity clues that appear in the MPQA Corpus and are ambiguous. Out of those, we selected the 90 most frequent that have to some extent distinct objective and subjective senses in WordNet, as judged by the co-authors. The co-authors annotated the WordNet senses of those 90 target words. For each target word, we selected approximately 120 instances randomly from the *GIGAWORD Corpus*. In a first phase, we collected three sets of MTurk annotations for the selected instances. In this phase, MTurk workers base their judgements on two sense sets they observe. This way, we get training data to build SWSD classifiers for these 90 target words.

The quality of these classifiers is important, because we will exploit them for contextual opinion analysis. Thus, we evaluate them by 10-fold cross-validation. We split the target words into three groups. If the majority class baseline of a word is higher than 90%, it is considered as *skewed* (skewed words have a performance at least as good as the majority class baseline). If a target word improves over its majority class baseline by 25% in accuracy, it is considered as *good*. Otherwise, it is considered as *mediocre*. This way, we end up with 24 skewed, 35 good, and 31 mediocre words. There are many possible reasons for the less reliable performance for the mediocre group. We hypothesize that a major problem is the similarity between the objective and subjective sense sets of a word, thus leading to poor annotation quality. To check this, we calculate the agreement between three annotation sets and report averages. The agreement in the mediocre group is 78.68%, with a κ value of 0.57, whereas the average agreement in the good group is 87.51%, with a κ value of 0.75. These findings support our hypothesis. Thus, the co-authors created usage inventories for the words in the mediocre group as described in Section 2.1.1. We initiated a second phase of MTurk annotations. We collect for the mediocre group another three sets of MTurk annotations for 120 instances, this time utilizing usage inventories. The 10-fold cross-validation experiments show that nine of the 31 words in the mediocre group shift to the good group. Only for these nine words, we accept the annotations collected via usage inventories. For all other words, we use the annotations collected via sense inventories. From now on, we will refer to this non-expert subjectivity sense-tagged corpus consisting of the tagged data for all 90 target words as the *MTurkSWSD Corpus* (agreement on the entire MTurkSWSD corpus is 85.54%, κ:0.71).

3 SWSD Integration

Now that we have the MTurkSWSD Corpus, we are ready to evaluate the effect of SWSD on contextual opinion analysis. In this section, we apply our SWSD system trained on MTurkSWSD to both expression-level classifiers from (Akkaya et al., 2009): (1) the subjective/objective (S/O) classifier and (2) the contextual polarity classifier. Both classifiers are introduced in Section 3.1

Our SWSD system can disambiguate 90 target words, which have 3737 instances in the MPQA Corpus. We refer to this subset of the MPQA Corpus as *MTurkMPQA*. This subset makes up the coverage of our SWSD system. Note that MTurkMPQA is 5.2 times larger than the covered MPQA subset in (Akkaya et al., 2009) referred as *senMPQA*. We try different strategies to integrate SWSD into the contextual classifiers. In Section 3.2, we follow the same rule-based strategy as in (Akkaya et al., 2009) for completeness. In Section 3.3, we introduce two new learning strategies for SWSD integration outperforming existing rule-based strategy. We evaluate the improvement gained by SWSD on MTurkMPQA.

3.1 Contextual Classifiers

The original contextual polarity classifier is introduced in (Wilson et al., 2005). We use the same implementation as in (Akkaya et al., 2009). This classifier labels clue instances in text as contextually negative/positive/neutral. The gold standard is defined on the MPQA Corpus as follows. If a clue instance appears in a positive expression, it is contextually positive (Ps). If it appears in a negative expression, it is contextually negative (Ng). If it is in an objective expression or in a neutral subjective expression, it is contextually neutral (N). The contextual polarity classifier consists of two separate steps. The first step is an expression-level neutral/polar (N/P) classifier. The second step classifies only polar instances further into positive and negative classes. This way, the overall system performs a three-way classification (Ng/Ps/N).

The subjective/objective classifier is introduced in (Akkaya et al., 2009). It relies on the same machine learning features as the N/P classifier (i.e. the first step of the contextual polarity classifier). The only difference is that the classes are S/O instead of N/P. The gold standard is defined on the MPQA Corpus in the following way. If a clue instance appears in a subjective expression, it is contextually S. If it appears in an objective expression, it is contextually O. Both contextual classifiers are supervised.

	Baseline		Acc	OF	SF
MTurkMPQA	52.4% (O)	$O_{S/O}$	67.1	68.9	65.0
		R1R2	**71.1**	72.7	69.2
senMPQA	63.1% (O)	$O_{S/O}$	75.4	65.4	80.9
		R1R2	81.3	75.9	84.8

Table 2: S/O classifier with and without SWSD.

	Baseline		Acc	NF	PF
MTurkMPQA	70.6% (P)	$O_{N/P}$	72.3	82.0	39.8
		R4	**74.5**	84.0	37.8
senMPQA	73.9% (P)	$O_{N/P}$	79.0	86.7	50.3
		R4	81.6	88.6	52.3

Table 3: N/P classifier with and without SWSD

3.2 Rule-Based SWSD Integration

(Akkaya et al., 2009) integrates SWSD into a contextual classifier by simple rules. The rules flip the output of the contextual classifier if some conditions hold. They make use of following information: (1) SWSD output, (2) the contextual classifier's confidence and (3) the presence of another subjectivity clue – any clue from the subjectivity lexicon – in the same expression.

For the contextual S/O classifier, (Akkaya et al., 2009) defines two rules: one flipping the S/O classifier's output from O to S *(R1)* and one flipping from S to O *(R2)*. R1 is defined as follows : if the contextual classifier decides a target word instance is contextually O and SWSD decides that it is used in a S sense, then SWSD overrules the contextual S/O classifier's output and flips it from O to S, because an instance in a S sense will make the surrounding expression subjective. R2 is a little bit more complex. It is defined as follows: If the contextual classifier labels a clue instance as S but (1) SWSD decides that it is used in an O sense, (2) the contextual classifier's confidence is low, and (3) there is no other subjectivity clue in the same expression, then R2 flips the contextual classifier's output from S to O. The rationale behind R2 is that even if the target word instance has an O sense, there might be another reason (e.g. the presence of another subjectivity clue in the same expression) for the expression enclosing it to be subjective.

We use the exact same rules and adopt the same confidence threshold. Table 2 holds the comparison of the original contextual classifier and the classifier with SWSD support on senMPQA as reported in (Akkaya et al., 2009) and on MTurkMPQA. $O_{S/O}$ is the original S/O classifier; R1R2 is the system with SWSD support utilizing both rules. We report only R1R2, since (Akkaya et al., 2009) gets highest improvement utilizing both rules.

In Table 2 we see that R1R2 achieves 4% percentage points improvement in accuracy over $O_{S/O}$ on MTurkMPQA. The improvement is statistically significant at the $p < .01$ level with McNemar's test. It is accompanied with improvements both in subjective F-measure (SF) and objective F-measure (OF). It is not possible to directly compare improvements on senMPQA and MTurkMPQA since they are different subsets of the MPQA Corpus. SWSD support brings 24% error reduction on senMPQA over the original S/O classifier. In comparison, on MTurkMPQA, the error reduction is 12%. We see that the improvements on the large MTurkMPQA set still hold, but not as strong as in (Akkaya et al., 2009).

(Akkaya et al., 2009) uses a similar rule to make the contextual polarity classifier sense-aware. Specifically, the rule is applied to the output of the first step (N/P classifier). The rule, R4, flips P to N and is analogous to R2. If the contextual classifier labels a clue instance as P but (1) SWSD decides that it is used in an O sense, (2) the contextual classifier's confidence is low, and (3) there is no other clue instance in the same expression, then R4 flips the contextual classifier's output from P to N.

Table 3 holds the comparison of the original N/P classifier with and without SWSD support on senMPQA as reported in (Akkaya et al., 2009) and on MTurkMPQA. $O_{N/P}$ is the original N/P classifier; R4 is the system with SWSD support utilizing rule R4. Since our main focus is not rule-based integration, we did not run the second step of the polarity classifier. We report the second step result below for the learning-based SWSD integration in section 3.4.

In Table 3, we see that R4 achieves 2.2 percentage points improvement in accuracy over $O_{N/P}$ on MTurkMPQA. The improvement is statistically significant at the $p < .01$ level with McNemar's test. It is accompanied with improvement only in objective F-measure (OF). SWSD support brings 12.4% error reduction on senMPQA (Akkaya et al., 2009).

On MTurkMPQA, the error reduction is 8%. We see that the rule-based SWSD integration still improves both contextual classifiers on MTurkMPQA, but the gain is not as large as on senMPQA. This might be due to the brittleness of the rule-based integration.

3.3 Learning SWSD Integration

Now that we can disambiguate a larger portion of the MPQA Corpus than in (Akkaya et al., 2009), we can investigate machine learning methods for SWSD integration to deal with the brittleness of the rule-based integration. In this section, we introduce two learning methods to apply SWSD to the contextual classifiers. For the learning methods, we rely on exactly the same information as the rule-based integration: (1) SWSD output, (2) the contextual classifier's output, (3) the contextual classifier's confidence, and (4) the presence of another clue instance in the same expression. The rationale is the same as for the rule-based integration, namely to relate sense subjectivity and contextual subjectivity.

3.3.1 Method1

In the first method, we extend the machine learning features of the underlying contextual classifiers by adding (1) and (4) from above. We evaluate the extended contextual classifiers on MTurkMPQA via 10-fold cross-validation. Tables 4 and 5 hold the comparison of Method1 ($EXT_{S/O}$, $EXT_{N/P}$) to the original contextual classifiers ($O_{S/O}$, $O_{N/P}$) and to the rule-based SWSD integration (R1R2, R4). We see substantial improvement for Method1. It achieves 39% error reduction over $O_{S/O}$ and 25% error reduction over $O_{N/P}$. For both classifiers, the improvement in accuracy over the rule-based integration is statistically significant at the $p < .01$ level with McNemar's test.

3.3.2 Method2

This method defines a third classifier that accepts as input the contextual classifier's output and the SWSD output and predicts what the contextual classifier's output should have been. We can think of this third classifier as the learning counterpart of the manual rules from Section 3.2, since it actually learns when to flip the contextual classifier's output considering SWSD evidence. Specifically, this merger classifier relies on four machine learning features (1), (2), (3), (4) from above (the exact same information used in rule-based integration). Because it is a supervised classifier, we need training data where we have clue instances with corresponding contextual classifier and SWSD predictions. Fortunately, we can use senMPQA for this purpose. We train our merger classifier on senMPQA (we get contextual classifier predictions via 10-fold cross-validation on the MPQA Corpus) and apply it to MTurkMPQA. We use SVM classifier from the Weka package (Witten and Frank., 2005) with its default settings. Tables 4 and 5 hold the comparison of Method2 ($MERGER_{S/O}$, $MERGER_{N/P}$) to the original contextual classifiers (Oo/s, $O_{N/P}$) and the rule-based SWSD integration (R1R2, R4). It achieves 29% error reduction over $O_{S/O}$ and 29% error reduction over $O_{N/P}$. The improvement on the rule-based integration is statistically significant at the $p < .01$ level with McNemar's test. Method2 performs better (statistically significant at the $p < .05$ level) than Method1 for the N/P classifier but worse (statistically significant at the $p < .01$ level) for the S/O classifier.

	Acc	OF	SF
$O_{S/O}$	67.1	68.9	65.0
R1R2	71.1	72.7	69.2
$EXT_{S/O}$	**80.0**	81.4	78.3
$MERGER_{S/O}$	78.2	80.3	75.5

Table 4: S/O classifier with learned SWSD integration

	Acc	NF	PF
$O_{N/P}$	72.3	82.0	39.8
R4	74.5	84.0	37.8
$EXT_{N/P}$	79.1	85.7	61.1
$MERGER_{N/P}$	**80.4**	86.7	62.8

Table 5: N/P classifier with learned SWSD integration

3.4 Improving Contextual Polarity Classification

We have seen that Method2 is the best method to improve the N/P classifier, which is the first step of the contextual polarity classifier. To assess the overall improvement in polarity classification, we run the second step of the contextual polarity classifier after correcting the first step with Method2. Table 6 summarizes the improvement propagated to

		Acc	NF	NgF	PsF
MTurkMPQA	$O_{Ps/Ng/N}$	72.1	83.0	34.2	15.0
	$MERGER_{N/P}$	**77.8**	87.4	53.0	27.7
senMPQA	$O_{Ps/Ng/N}$	77.6	87.2	39.5	40.0
	R4	80.6	89.1	43.2	44.0

Table 6: Polarity classifier with and without SWSD.

Ps/Ng/N classification. For comparison, we also include results from (Akkaya et al., 2009) on senMPQA. Method2 results in 20% error reduction in accuracy over $O_{Ps/Ng/N}$ (R4 achieves 13.4% error reduction on senMPQA). The improvement on the rule-based integration is statistically significant at the $p < .01$ level with McNemar's test. More importantly, the F-measure for all the labels improves. This indicates that non-expert MTurk annotations can replace expert annotations for our end-goal – improving contextual opinion analysis – while reducing time and cost requirements by a large margin. Moreover, we see that the improvements in (Akkaya et al., 2009) scale up to new subjectivity clues.

4 Related Work

One related line of research is to automatically assign subjectivity and/or polarity labels to word senses in a dictionary (Valitutti et al., 2004; Andreevskaia and Bergler, 2006; Wiebe and Mihalcea, 2006; Esuli and Sebastiani, 2007; Su and Markert, 2009). In contrast, the task in our paper is to automatically assign labels to word instances in a corpus.

Recently, some researchers have exploited full word sense disambiguation in methods for opinion-related tasks. For example, (Martín-Wanton et al., 2010) exploit WSD for recognizing quotation polarities, and (Rentoumi et al., 2009; Martín-Wanton et al., 2010) exploit WSD for recognizing headline polarities. None of this previous work investigates performing a coarse-grained variation of WSD such as SWSD to improve their application results, as we do in this work.

A notable exception is (Su and Markert, 2010), who exploit SWSD to improve the performance on a contextual NLP task, as we do. While the task in our paper is subjectivity and sentiment analysis, their task is English-Chinese lexical substitution. As (Akkaya et al., 2009) did, they annotated word senses, and exploited SENSEVAL data as training data for SWSD. They did not directly annotate words in context with S/O labels, as we do in our work. Further, they did not separately evaluate a SWSD system component.

Many researchers work on reducing the granularity of sense inventories for WSD (e.g., (Palmer et al., 2004; Navigli, 2006; Snow et al., 2007; Hovy et al., 2006)). Their criteria for grouping senses are syntactic and semantic similarities, while the groupings in work on SWSD are driven by the goals to improve contextual subjectivity and sentiment analysis.

5 Conclusions and Future Work

In this paper, we utilized a large pool of non-expert annotators (MTurk) to collect subjectivity sense-tagged data for SWSD. We showed that non-expert annotations are as good as expert annotations for training SWSD classifiers. Moreover, we demonstrated that SWSD classifiers trained on non-expert annotations can be exploited to improve contextual opinion analysis.

The additional subjectivity sense-tagged data enabled us to evaluate the benefits of SWSD on contextual opinion analysis on a corpus of opinion-annotated data that is five times larger. Using the same rule-based integration strategies as in (Akkaya et al., 2009), we found that contextual opinion analysis is improved by SWSD on the larger datasets. We also experimented with new learning strategies for integrating SWSD into contextual opinion analysis. With the learning strategies, we achieved greater benefits from SWSD than the rule-based integration strategies on all of the contextual opinion analysis tasks.

Overall, we more firmly demonstrated the potential of SWSD to improve contextual opinion analysis. We will continue to gather subjectivity sense-tagged data, using sense inventories for words that are well represented in WordNet for our purposes, and with usage inventories for those that are not.

6 Acknowledgments

This material is based in part upon work supported by National Science Foundation awards #0917170 and #0916046.

References

Apoorv Agarwal, Fadi Biadsy, and Kathleen Mckeown. 2009. Contextual phrase-level polarity analysis using lexical affect scoring and syntactic N-grams. In *Proceedings of the 12th Conference of the European Chapter of the ACL (EACL 2009)*, pages 24–32. Association for Computational Linguistics.

Cem Akkaya, Janyce Wiebe, and Rada Mihalcea. 2009. Subjectivity word sense disambiguation. In *Proceedings of the 2009 Conference on Empirical Methods in Natural Language Processing*, pages 190–199, Singapore, August. Association for Computational Linguistics.

Cem Akkaya, Alexander Conrad, Janyce Wiebe, and Rada Mihalcea. 2010. Amazon mechanical turk for subjectivity word sense disambiguation. In *Proceedings of the NAACL HLT 2010 Workshop on Creating Speech and Language Data with Amazon's Mechanical Turk*, pages 195–203, Los Angeles, June. Association for Computational Linguistics.

Alina Andreevskaia and Sabine Bergler. 2006. Mining wordnet for a fuzzy sentiment: Sentiment tag extraction from wordnet glosses. In *Proceedings of the 11rd Conference of the European Chapter of the Association for Computational Linguistics (EACL-2006)*.

Alina Andreevskaia and Sabine Bergler. 2008. When specialists and generalists work together: Overcoming domain dependence in sentiment tagging. In *Proceedings of ACL-08: HLT*, pages 290–298, Columbus, Ohio, June. Association for Computational Linguistics.

Kenneth Bloom, Navendu Garg, and Shlomo Argamon. 2007. Extracting appraisal expressions. In *HLT-NAACL 2007*, pages 308–315, Rochester, NY.

Andrea Esuli and Fabrizio Sebastiani. 2007. Pageranking wordnet synsets: An application to opinion mining. In *Proceedings of the 45th Annual Meeting of the Association of Computational Linguistics*, pages 424–431, Prague, Czech Republic, June. Association for Computational Linguistics.

Yaw Gyamfi, Janyce Wiebe, Rada Mihalcea, and Cem Akkaya. 2009. Integrating knowledge for subjectivity sense labeling. In *Proceedings of Human Language Technologies: The 2009 Annual Conference of the North American Chapter of the Association for Computational Linguistics (NAACL-HLT 2009)*, pages 10–18, Boulder, Colorado, June. Association for Computational Linguistics.

E. Hovy, M. Marcus, M. Palmer, L. Ramshaw, and R. Weischedel. 2006. Ontonotes: The 90% solution. In *Proceedings of the Human Language Technology Conference of the NAACL, Companion Volume: Short Papers*, New York City.

Soo-Min Kim and Eduard Hovy. 2004. Determining the sentiment of opinions. In *Proceedings of the Twentieth International Conference on Computational Linguistics (COLING 2004)*, pages 1267–1373, Geneva, Switzerland.

Tamara Martín-Wanton, Aurora Pons-Porrata, Andrés Montoyo-Guijarro, and Alexandra Balahur. 2010. Opinion polarity detection - using word sense disambiguation to determine the polarity of opinions. In *ICAART 2010 - Proceedings of the International Conference on Agents and Artificial Intelligence, Volume 1*, pages 483–486.

R. Navigli. 2006. Meaningful clustering of senses helps boost word sense disambiguation performance. In *Proceedings of the Annual Meeting of the Association for Computational Linguistics*, Sydney, Australia.

M. Palmer, O. Babko-Malaya, and H. T. Dang. 2004. Different sense granularities for different applications. In *HLT-NAACL 2004 Workshop: 2nd Workshop on Scalable Natural Language Understanding*, Boston, Massachusetts.

Randolph Quirk, Sidney Greenbaum, Geoffry Leech, and Jan Svartvik. 1985. *A Comprehensive Grammar of the English Language.* Longman, New York.

Vassiliki Rentoumi, George Giannakopoulos, Vangelis Karkaletsis, and George A. Vouros. 2009. Sentiment analysis of figurative language using a word sense disambiguation approach. In *Proceedings of the International Conference RANLP-2009*, pages 370–375, Borovets, Bulgaria, September. Association for Computational Linguistics.

Ellen Riloff and Janyce Wiebe. 2003. Learning extraction patterns for subjective expressions. In *Proceedings of the Conference on Empirical Methods in Natural Language Processing (EMNLP-2003)*, pages 105–112, Sapporo, Japan.

R. Snow, S. Prakash, D. Jurafsky, and A. Ng. 2007. Learning to merge word senses. In *Proceedings of the Joint Conference on Empirical Methods in Natural Language Processing and Computational Natural Language Learning (EMNLP-CoNLL)*, Prague, Czech Republic.

Fangzhong Su and Katja Markert. 2008. From word to sense: a case study of subjectivity recognition. In *Proceedings of the 22nd International Conference on Computational Linguistics (COLING-2008)*, Manchester.

Fangzhong Su and Katja Markert. 2009. Subjectivity recognition on word senses via semi-supervised mincuts. In *Proceedings of Human Language Technologies: The 2009 Annual Conference of the North American Chapter of the Association for Computational Linguistics*, pages 1–9, Boulder, Colorado, June. Association for Computational Linguistics.

Fangzhong Su and Katja Markert. 2010. Word sense subjectivity for cross-lingual lexical substitution. In *Human Language Technologies: The 2010 Annual Conference of the North American Chapter of the Association for Computational Linguistics*, pages 357–360, Los Angeles, California, June. Association for Computational Linguistics.

Peter Turney. 2002. Thumbs up or thumbs down? Semantic orientation applied to unsupervised classification of reviews. In *Proceedings of the 40th Annual Meeting of the Association for Computational Linguistics (ACL-02)*, pages 417–424, Philadelphia, Pennsylvania.

Alessandro Valitutti, Carlo Strapparava, and Oliviero Stock. 2004. Developing affective lexical resources. *PsychNology*, 2(1):61–83.

Casey Whitelaw, Navendu Garg, and Shlomo Argamon. 2005. Using appraisal taxonomies for sentiment analysis. In *Proceedings of CIKM-05, the ACM SIGIR Conference on Information and Knowledge Management*, Bremen, DE.

Janyce Wiebe and Rada Mihalcea. 2006. Word sense and subjectivity. In *Proceedings of the 21st International Conference on Computational Linguistics and 44th Annual Meeting of the Association for Computational Linguistics*, pages 1065–1072, Sydney, Australia, July. Association for Computational Linguistics.

Janyce Wiebe, Theresa Wilson, and Claire Cardie. 2005. Annotating expressions of opinions and emotions in language. *Language Resources and Evaluation*, 39(2/3):164–210.

Theresa Wilson, Janyce Wiebe, and Paul Hoffmann. 2005. Recognizing contextual polarity in phrase-level sentiment analysis. In *Proceedings of the Human Language Technologies Conference/Conference on Empirical Methods in Natural Language Processing (HLT/EMNLP-2005)*, pages 347–354, Vancouver, Canada.

Theresa Wilson. 2007. *Fine-grained Subjectivity and Sentiment Analysis: Recognizing the Intensity, Polarity, and Attitudes of private states*. Ph.D. thesis, Intelligent Systems Program, University of Pittsburgh.

I. Witten and E. Frank. 2005. *Data Mining: Practical Machine Learning Tools and Techniques, Second Edition*. Morgan Kaufmann, June.

Hong Yu and Vasileios Hatzivassiloglou. 2003. Towards answering opinion questions: Separating facts from opinions and identifying the polarity of opinion sentences. In *Proceedings of the Conference on Empirical Methods in Natural Language Processing (EMNLP-2003)*, pages 129–136, Sapporo, Japan.

Effects of Meaning-Preserving Corrections on Language Learning

Dana Angluin *
Department of Computer Science
Yale University, USA
dana.angluin@yale.edu

Leonor Becerra-Bonache
Laboratoire Hubert Curien
Université de Saint-Etienne, France
leonor.becerra@univ-st-etienne.fr

Abstract

We present a computational model of language learning via a sequence of interactions between a teacher and a learner. Experiments learning limited sublanguages of 10 natural languages show that the learner achieves a high level of performance after a reasonable number of interactions, the teacher can produce meaning-preserving corrections of the learner's utterances, and the learner can detect them. The learner does not treat corrections specially; nonetheless in several cases, significantly fewer interactions are needed by a learner interacting with a correcting teacher than with a non-correcting teacher.

1 Introduction

A child learning his or her native language typically does so while interacting with other people who are using the language to communicate in shared situations. The correspondence between situations and utterances seems likely to be a very important source of information for the language learner. Once a child begins to produce his or her own utterances, other people's responses to them (or lack thereof) are another source of information about the language. When the child's utterances fall short of adult-level competence, sometimes the other person in the conversation will repeat the child's utterance in a more correct form. A number of studies have focused on the phenomenon of such corrections and questions of their frequency in child-directed speech and whether children can and do make use of them; some of these studies are discussed in the next section.

*Research supported by the National Science Foundation, Grant CCF-0916389.

In this paper we construct a computational model with a learner and a teacher who interact in a sequence of shared situations. In each situation the teacher and learner interact as follows. First the learner uses what it has learned about the language to (attempt to) generate an utterance appropriate to the situation. The teacher then analyzes the correctness of the learner's utterance and either generates an utterance intended as a correction of the learner's utterance, or generates another utterance of its own appropriate to the situation. Finally, the learner uses information given by its own utterance, the teacher's utterance and the situation to update its knowledge of the language. At the conclusion of this interaction, a new interaction is begun with the next situation in the sequence.

Both the learner and the teacher engage in comprehension and production of utterances which are intended to be appropriate to their shared situation. This setting allows us to study several questions: whether the teacher can offer meaningful corrections to the learner, whether the learner can detect intended corrections by the teacher, and whether the presence of corrections by the teacher has an effect on language acquisition by the learner. For our model, the answer to each of these questions is yes, and while the model is in many respects artificial and simplified, we believe it sheds new light on these issues. Additional details are available (Angluin and Becerra-Bonache, 2010).

Proceedings of the Fifteenth Conference on Computational Natural Language Learning, pages 97–105,
Portland, Oregon, USA, 23–24 June 2011.

2 Meaning-preserving corrections

Formal models of language acquisition have mainly focused on learning from positive data, that is, utterances that are grammatically correct. But a question that remains open is: Do children receive negative data and can they make use of it?

Chomsky's poverty of stimulus argument has been used to support the idea of human innate linguistic capacity. It is claimed that there are principles of grammar that cannot be learned from positive data only, and negative evidence is not available to children. Hence, since children do not have enough evidence to induce the grammar of their native language, the additional knowledge language learners need is provided by some form of innate linguistic capacity.

E. M. Gold's negative results in the framework of formal language learning have also been used to support the innateness of language. Gold proved that superfinite classes of languages are not learnable from positive data only, which implies than none of the language classes defined by Chomsky to model natural language is learnable from positive data only (Gold, 1967).

Brown and Hanlon (Brown and Hanlon, 1970) studied negative evidence understood as explicit approvals or disapprovals of a child's utterance (e.g.,"That's right" or "That's wrong.") They showed that there is no dependence between these kinds of answers and the grammaticality of children's utterances. These results were taken as showing that children do not receive negative data. But do these results really show this? It seems evident that parents rarely address their children in that way. During the first stages of language acquisition children make a lot of errors, and parents are not constantly telling them that their sentences are wrong; rather the important thing is that they can communicate with each other. However, it is worth studying whether other sources of negative evidence are provided to children. Is this the only form of negative data? Do adults correct children in a different way?

Some researchers have studied other kinds of negative data based on reply-types (e.g., Hirsh-Pasek et al. (Hirsh-Pasek et al., 1984), Demetras et al. (Demetras et al., 1986) and Morgan and Travis (Morgan and Travis, 1989).) These studies argue that parents provide negative evidence to their children by using different types of reply to grammatical versus ungrammatical sentences. Marcus analyzed such studies and concluded that there is no evidence that this kind of feedback (he called it noisy feedback) is required for language learning, or even that it exists (Marcus, 1993). He argued for the weakness, inconsistency and inherently artificial nature of this kind of feedback. Moreover, he suggested that even if such feedback exists, a child would learn which forms are erroneous only after complex statistical comparisons. Therefore, he concluded that internal mechanisms are necessary to explain how children recover from errors in language acquisition.

Since the publication of the work of Marcus, the consensus seemed to be that children do not have access to negative data. However, a study carried out by Chouinard and Clark shows that this conclusion may be wrong (Chouinard and Clark, 2003). First, they point out that the reply-type approach does not consider whether the reply itself also contains corrective information, and consequently, replies that are corrective are erroneously grouped with those that are not. Moreover, if we consider only reply-types, they may not help to identify the error made. Hence, Chouinard and Clark propose another view of negative evidence that builds on Clark's principle of contrast (Clark, 1987; Clark, 1993). Parents often check up on a child's erroneous utterances, to make sure they have understood them. They do this by reformulating what they think the child intended to express. Hence, the child's utterance and the adult's reformulation have the same meaning, but different forms. Because children attend to contrasts in form, any change in form that does not mark a different meaning will signal to children that they may have produced an utterance that is not acceptable in the target language. In this way, reformulations identify the locus of any error, and hence the existence of an error. Chouinard and Clark analyze longitudinal data from five children between two and four years old, and show that adults reformulate erroneous child utterances often enough to help learning. Moreover, these results show that children not only detect differences between their own utterance and the adult reformulation, but that they make use of that information.

In this paper we explore this new view of negative data proposed by Chouinard and Clark. Corrections (in form of reformulations) have a semantic component that has not been taken into account in previous studies. Hence, we propose a new computational model of language learning that gives an account of *meaning-preserving corrections*, and in which we can address questions such as: What are the effects of corrections on learning syntax? Can corrections facilitate the language learning process?

3 The Model

We describe the components of our model, and give examples drawn from the primary domain we have used to guide the development of the model.

3.1 Situation, meanings and utterances.

A **situation** is composed of some objects and some of their properties and relations, which pick out some aspects of the world of joint interest to the teacher and learner. A situation is represented as a set of ground atoms over some constants (denoting objects) and predicates (giving properties of the objects and relations between them.) For example, a situation s_1 consisting of a big purple circle to the left of a big red star is represented by the following set of ground atoms: $s_1 = \{bi1(t_1), pu1(t_1), ci1(t_1), le2(t_1, t_2), bi1(t_2), re1(t_2), st1(t_2)\}$.

Formally, we have a finite set P of **predicate symbols**, each of a specific arity. We also have a set of **constant symbols** $t_1, t_2, \ldots$, which are used to represent distinct objects. A **ground atom** is an expression formed by applying a predicate symbol to the correct number of constant symbols as arguments.

We also have a set of of **variables** $x_1, x_2, \ldots$. A **variable atom** is an expression formed by applying a predicate symbol to the correct number of variables as arguments. A **meaning** is a finite sequence of variable atoms. Note that the atoms do not contain constants, and the order in which they appear is significant. A meaning is **supported** in a situation if there exists a **support witness**, that is, a mapping of its variables to *distinct* objects in the situation such that the image under the mapping of each atom in the meaning appears in the situation. If a meaning is supported in a situation by a unique support witness then it is **denoting** in the situation. We assume that both the teacher and learner can determine whether a meaning is denoting in a situation.

We also have a finite alphabet W of words. An **utterance** is a finite sequence of words. The **target language** is the set of utterances the teacher may produce in some situation; in our examples, this includes utterances like *the star* or *the star to the right of the purple circle* but not *star of circle small the green*. We assume each utterance in the target language is assigned a unique meaning. An utterance is **denoting** in a situation if the meaning assigned to utterance is denoting in the situation. Intuitively, an utterance is denoting if it uniquely picks out the objects it refers to in a situation.

In our model the goal of the learner is to be able to produce every denoting utterance in any given situation. Our model is probabilistic, and what we require is that the probability of learner errors be reduced to very low levels.

3.2 The target language and meaning transducers.

We represent the linguistic competence of the teacher by a finite state transducer that both recognizes the utterances in the target language and translates each correct utterance to its meaning. Let A denote the set of all variable atoms over P. We define a **meaning transducer** M with input symbols W and output symbols A as follows. M has a finite set Q of states, an initial state $q_0 \in Q$, a finite set $F \subseteq Q$ of final states, a deterministic transition function δ mapping $Q \times W$ to Q, and an output function γ mapping $Q \times W$ to $A \cup \{\varepsilon\}$, where ε denotes the empty sequence.

The transition function δ is extended in the usual way to $\delta(q, u)$. The **language** of M, denoted $L(M)$ is the set of all utterances $u \in W^*$ such that $\delta(q_0, u) \in F$. For each utterance u, we define $M(u)$ to be the **meaning** of u, that is, the finite sequence of non-empty outputs produced by M in processing u. Fig. 1 shows a meaning transducer M_1 for a limited sublanguage of Spanish. M_1 assigns the utterance *el triangulo rojo* the meaning $(tr1(x_1), re1(x_1))$.

3.3 The learning task.

Initially the teacher and learner know the predicates P and are able to determine whether a meaning is

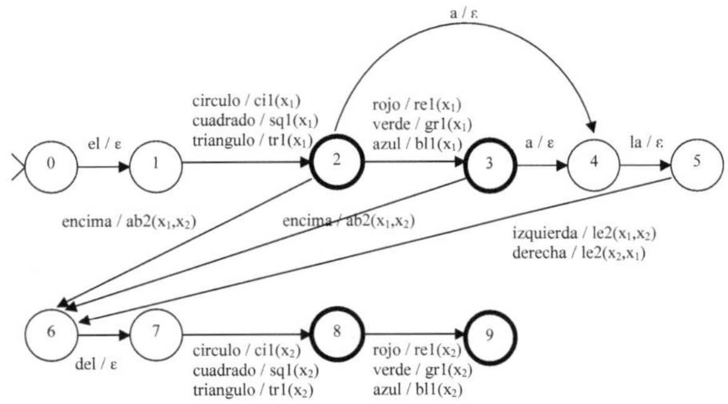

Figure 1: Meaning transducer M_1.

denoting in a situation. The learner and teacher both also know a shared set of **categories** that classify a subset of the predicates into similarity groups. The categories facilitate generalization by the learner and analysis of incorrect learner utterances by the teacher. In our geometric shape domain the categories are shape, size, and color; there is no category for the positional relations. Initially the teacher also has the meaning transducer for the target language, but the learner has no language-specific knowledge.

4 The Interaction of Learner and Teacher

In one interaction of the learner and teacher, a new situation is generated and presented to both of them. The learner attempts to produce a denoting utterance for the situation, and the teacher analyzes the learner's utterance and decides whether to produce a correction of the learner's utterance or a new denoting utterance of its own. Finally, the learner uses the situation and the teacher's utterance to update its current grammar for the language.

In this section we describe the algorithms used by the learner and teacher to carry out the steps of this process.

4.1 Comprehension and the co-occurrence graph.

To process the teacher's utterance, the learner records the words in the utterance and the predicates in the situation in an undirected **co-occurrence graph**. Each node is a word or predicate symbol and there is an edge for each pair of nodes. Each node u has an occurrence count, $c(u)$, recording the number of utterances or situations it has occurred in. Each edge (u, v) also has an occurrence count, $c(u, v)$, recording the number of utterance/situation pairs in which the endpoints of the edge have occurred together. From the co-occurrence graph the learner derives a directed graph with the same nodes, the **implication graph**, parameterized by a noise threshold θ (set at 0.95 in the experiments.) For each ordered pair of nodes u and v, the directed edge (u, v) is included in the implication graph if $c(u, v)/c(u) \geq \theta$. The learner then deletes edges from predicates to words and computes the **transitively reduced implication graph**.

The learner uses the transitively reduced implication graph to try to find the meaning of the teacher's utterance by translating the words of the utterance into a set of sequences of predicates, and determining if there is a unique denoting meaning corresponding to one of the predicate sequences. If so, the unique meaning is generalized into a **general form** by replacing each predicate by its category generalization. For example, if the learner detects the unique meaning $(\mathit{tr1}(x_1), \mathit{re1}(x_1))$, it is generalized to the general form $(\mathit{shape1}(x_1), \mathit{color1}(x_1))$. The learner's set of general forms is the basis for its production.

4.2 Production by the learner.

Each general form denotes the set of possible meanings obtained by substituting appropriate symbols from P for the category symbols. To produce a denoting utterance for a situation, the learner finds all the meanings generated by its general forms using predicates from the situation and tests each meaning to see if it is denoting, producing a set of possible denoting meanings. If the set is empty, the learner produces no utterance. Otherwise, it attempts to translate each denoting meaning into an utterance.

The learner selects one of these utterances with a probability depending on a number stored with the corresponding general form recording the last time a teacher utterance matched it. This ensures that repeatedly matched general forms are selected with asymptotically uniform probability, while general forms that are only matched a few times are selected with probability tending to zero.

4.3 From meaning to utterance.

The process the learner uses to produce an utterance from a denoting meaning is as follows. For a meaning that is a sequence of k atoms, there are two related sequences of positions: the **atom positions** $1, 2, \ldots, k$ and the **gap positions** $0, 1, \ldots, k$. The atom positions refer to the corresponding atoms, and gap position i refers to the position to the right of atom i, (where gap position 0 is to the left of atom a_1.) The learner generates a sequence of zero or more words for each position in left to right order: gap position 0, atom position 1, gap position 1, atom position 2, and so on, until gap position k. The resulting sequences of words are concatenated to form the final utterance.

The choice of what sequence of words to produce for each position is represented by a decision tree. For each variable atom the learner has encountered, there is a decision tree that determines what sequence of words to produce for that atom in the context of the whole meaning. For example, in a sublanguage of Spanish in which there are both masculine and feminine nouns for shapes, the atom $re1(x_1)$ has a decision tree that branches on the value of the shape predicate applied to x_1 to select either *rojo* or *roja* as appropriate. For the gap positions, there are decision trees indexed by the generalizations of all the variable atoms that have occurred; the variable atom at position i is generalized, and the corresponding decision tree is used to generate a sequence of words for gap position i. Gap position 0 does not follow any atom position and has a separate decision tree.

If there is no decision tree associated with a given atom or gap position in a meaning, the learner falls back on a "telegraphic speech" strategy. For a gap position with no decision tree, no words are produced. For an atom position whose atom has no associated decision tree, the learner searches the transitively reduced implication graph for words that approximately imply the predicate of the atom and chooses one of maximum observed frequency.

4.4 The teacher's response.

If the learner produces an utterance, the teacher analyzes it and then chooses its own utterance for the situation. The teacher may find the learner's utterance correct, incorrect but correctable, or incorrect and uncorrectable. If the learner's utterance is incorrect but correctable, the teacher chooses a possible correction for it. The teacher randomly decides whether or not to use the correction as its utterance according to the **correction probability**. If the teacher does not use the correction, then its own utterance is chosen uniformly at random from the denoting utterances for the situation.

If the learner's utterance is one of the correct denoting utterances for the situation, the teacher classifies it as **correct**. If the learner's utterance is not correct, the teacher "translates" the learner's utterance into a sequence of predicates by using the meaning transducer for the language. If the resulting sequence of predicates corresponds to a denoting meaning, the learner's utterance is classified as having an **error in form**. The correction is chosen by considering the denoting utterances with the same sequence of predicates as the learner's utterance, and choosing one that is "most similar" to the learner's utterance. For example, if the learner's utterance was *el elipse pequeno* and $(el1, sm1)$ corresponds to a denoting utterance for the situation, the teacher chooses *la elipse pequena* as the correction. If the learner's utterance is neither correct nor an error in form, the teacher uses a measure of similarity between the learner's sequence of predicates and those of denoting utterances to determine whether there is a "close enough" match. If so, the teacher classifies the learner's utterance as having an **error in meaning** and chooses as the possible correction a denoting utterance whose predicate sequence is "most similar" to the learner's predicate sequence. If the learner produces an utterance and none of these cases apply, then the teacher classifies the learner's utterance as **uninterpretable** and does not offer a correction.

When the teacher has produced an utterance, the learner analyzes it and updates its grammar of the language as reflected in the co-occurrence graph, the general forms, and the decision trees for word choice. The decision trees are updated by computing an alignment between the teacher's utterance and the learner's understanding of the teacher's meaning, which assigns a subsequence of words from the utterance to each atom or gap position in the meaning. Each subsequence of words is then added to the data for the decision tree corresponding to the position of that subsequence.

If the learner has produced an utterance and finds that the teacher's utterance has the same meaning, but is expressed differently, then the learner classifies the teacher's utterance as a **correction**. In the current model, the learner reports this classification, but does not use it in any way.

5 Empirical Results

We have implemented and tested our learning and teaching procedures in order to explore questions about the roles of corrections in language learning. We have used a simplified version of the *Miniature Language Acquisition* task proposed by Feldman et al. (Feldman et al., 1990). Although this task is not as complex as those faced by children, it involves enough complexity to be compared to many real-word tasks.

The questions that we address in this section are the following. (1) Can the learner accomplish the learning task to a high level of correctness and coverage from a "reasonable" number of interactions (that is, well short of the number needed to memorize every legal situation/sentence pair)? (2) What are the effects of correction or non-correction by the teacher on the learner's accomplishment of the learning tasks?

5.1 The specific learning tasks.

Each situation has two objects, each with three attributes (shape, color and size), and one binary relation between the two objects (above or to the left of.) The attribute of shape has six possible values (circle, square, triangle, star, ellipse, and hexagon), that of color has six possible values (red, orange, yellow, green, blue, and purple), and that of size three possible values (big, medium, and small.) There are 108 distinct objects and 23,328 distinct situations. Situations are generated uniformly at random.

For several natural languages we construct a limited sublanguage of utterances related to these situations. A typical utterance in English is *the medium purple star below the small hexagon*. There are 168 meanings referring to a single object and 112,896 meanings referring to two objects, for a total of 113,064 possible meanings. The 113,064 possible meanings are instances of 68 general forms: 4 referring to a single object and 64 referring to two objects. These languages are the **68-form languages**.

We consulted at least one speaker of each language to help us construct a meaning transducer to translate appropriate phrases in the language to all 113,064 possible meanings. Each transducer was constructed to have exactly one accepted phrase for each possible meaning. We also constructed transducers for reduced sublanguages, consisting of the subset of utterances that refer to a single object (168 utterances) and those that refer to two objects, but include all three attributes of both (46,656 utterances.) Each meaning in the reduced sublanguage is an instance of one of 8 general forms, while most of the lexical and syntactic complexity of the 68-form language is preserved. We refer to these reduced sublanguages as the **8-form languages**.

5.2 How many interactions are needed to learn?

The level of performance of a learner is measured using two quantities: the correctness and completeness of the learner's utterances in a given situation. The learning procedure has a test mode in which the learner receives a situation and responds with the set of U utterances it could produce in that situation, with their corresponding production probabilities. The **correctness** of the learner is the sum of the production probabilities of the elements of U that are in the correct denoting set. The **completeness** of the learner is the fraction of all correct denoting utterances that are in U. The averages of correctness and completeness of the learner for 200 randomly generated situations are used to estimate the overall correctness and completeness of the learner. A learner reaches a **level p of performance** if both correctness and completeness are at least p.

In the first set of trials the target level of performance is 0.99 and the learner and teacher engage in a sequence of interactions until the learner first reaches this level of performance. The performance of the learner is tested at intervals of 100 interactions. Fig. 2 shows the number of interactions needed to reach the 0.99 level of performance for each 68-form language with correction probabilities of 0.0 (i.e., the teacher never corrects the learner) and 1.0 (i.e., the teacher offers a correction to the learner every time it classifies the learner's utterance as an error in form or an error in meaning.) For correction probability 1.0, it also shows the number of incorrect utterances by the learner, the number of corrections offered by the teacher, and the percentage of teacher utterances that were corrections. Each entry is the median value of 10 trials except those in the last column. It is worth noting that the learner does not treat corrections specially.

	0.0	1.0	incorrect	corrections	c/u%
English	700	750	25.0	11.5	1.5%
German	800	750	71.5	52.5	7.0%
Greek	3400	2600	344.0	319.0	12.3%
Hebrew	900	900	89.5	62.5	6.9%
Hungarian	750	800	76.5	58.5	7.3%
Mandarin	700	800	50.0	31.5	3.9%
Russian	3700	2900	380.0	357.0	12.3%
Spanish	1000	850	86.0	68.0	8.0%
Swedish	1000	900	54.0	43.5	4.8%
Turkish	800	900	59.0	37.0	4.1%

Figure 2: Interactions, incorrect learner utterances and corrections by the teacher to reach the 0.99 level of performance for 68-form languages.

In the column for correction probability 0.0 there are two clear groups: Greek and Russian, each with at least 3400 interactions and the rest of the languages, each with at most 1000 interactions. The first observation is that the learner achieves correctness and completeness of 0.99 for each of these languages after being exposed to a small fraction of all possible situations and utterances. Even 3700 interactions involve at most 16.5% of all possible situations and at most 3.5% of all possible utterances by the teacher, while 1000 interactions involve fewer than 4.3% of all situations and fewer than 1% of all possible utterances.

5.3 How do corrections affect learning?

In the column for correction probability 1.0 we see the same two groups of languages. For Greek, the number of interactions falls from 3400 to 2600, a decrease of about 24%. For Russian, the number of interactions falls from 3700 to 2900, a decrease of about 21%. Corrections have a clear positive effect in these trials for Greek and Russian, but not for the rest of the languages.

Comparing the numbers of incorrect learner utterances and the number of corrections offered by the teacher, we see that the teacher finds corrections for a substantial fraction of incorrect learner utterances. The last column of Fig. 2 shows the percentage of the total number of teacher utterances that were corrections, from a low of 1.5% to a high of 12.3%.

There are several processes at work in the improvement of the learner's performance. Comprehension improves as more information accumulates about words and predicates. New correct general forms are acquired, and unmatched incorrect general forms decrease in probability. More data improves the decision tree rules for choosing phrases. Attainment of the 0.99 level of performance may be limited by the need to acquire all the correct general forms or by the need to improve the correctness of the phrase choices.

In the case of Greek and Russian, most of the trials had acquired their last general form by the time the 0.90 level of performance was reached, but for the other languages correct general forms were still being acquired between the 0.95 and the 0.99 levels of performance. Thus the acquisition of general forms was not a bottleneck for Greek and Russian, but was for the other languages. Because the teacher's corrections generally do not help with the acquisition of new general forms (the general form in a correction is often the same one the learner just used), but do tend to improve the correctness of phrase choice, we do not expect correction to reduce the number of interactions to attain the 0.99 level of performance when the bottleneck is the acquisition of general forms. This observation led us to construct reduced sublanguages with just 8 general forms to see if correction would have more of an effect when the bottleneck of acquiring general forms was removed.

The reduced sublanguages have just 8 general forms, which are acquired relatively early. Fig. 3 gives the numbers of interactions to reach the 0.99 level of performance (except for Turkish, where the level is 0.95) for the 8-form sublanguages with correction probability 0.0 and 1.0. These numbers are the means of 100 trials (except for Greek and Russian, which each had 20 trials); the performance of the learner was tested every 50 interactions.

Comparing the results for 8-form sublanguages with corresponding 68-form languages, we see that some require notably fewer interactions for 8-form

	0.0	1.0	% reduction
English	247.0	202.0	18.2 %
German	920.0	683.5	25.7 %
Greek	6630.0	4102.5	38.1 %
Hebrew	1052.0	771.5	26.7 %
Hungarian	1632.5	1060.5	35.0 %
Mandarin	340.5	297.5	12.6 %
Russian	6962.5	4640.0	33.4 %
Spanish	908.0	630.5	30.6 %
Swedish	214.0	189.0	11.7 %
Turkish	1112.0*	772.0*	30.6 %

Figure 3: Interactions to reach the 0.99 level of performance for 8-form languages. (For Turkish: the 0.95 level.)

sublanguages (English, Mandarin, and Swedish) while others require notably more (Greek, Hungarian and Russian.) In the case of Turkish, the learner cannot attain the 0.99 level of performance for the 8-form sublanguage at all, though it does so for the 68-form language; this is caused by limitations in learner comprehension as well as the differing frequencies of forms. Thus, the 8-form languages are neither uniformly easier nor uniformly harder than their 68-form counterparts. Arguably, the restrictions that produce the 8-form languages make them "more artificial" than the 68-form languages; however, the artificiality helps us understand more about the possible roles of correction in language learning.

Even though in the case of the 8-form languages there are only 8 correct general forms to acquire, the distribution on utterances with one object versus utterances with two objects is quite different from the case of the 68-form languages. For a situation with two objects of different shapes, there are 40 denoting utterances in the case of 68-form languages, of which 8 refer to one object and 32 refer to two objects. In the case of the 8-form languagues, there are 10 denoting utterances, of which 8 refer to one object and 2 refer to two objects. Thus, in situations of this kind (which are $5/6$ of the total), utterances referring to two objects are 4 times more likely in the case of 68-form languages than in the case of 8-form languages. This means that if the learner needs to see utterances involving two objects in order to master certain aspects of syntax (for example, cases of articles, adjectives and nouns), the waiting time is noticeably longer in the case of 8-form languages.

This longer waiting time emphasizes the effects of correction, because the initial phase of learning is a smaller fraction of the whole. In the third column of Fig. 3 we show the percentage reduction in the number of interactions to reach the 0.99 level of performance (except: 0.95 for Turkish) from correction probability 0.0 to correction probability 1.0 for the 8-form languages. For each language, corrections produce a reduction, ranging from a low of 11.7% for Swedish to a high of 38.1% for Greek. This confirms our hypothesis that corrections can substantially help the learner when the problem of acquiring all the general forms is not the bottleneck.

6 Discussion and Future Work

We show that a simple model of a teacher can offer meaning-preserving corrections to the learner and such corrections can significantly reduce the number of interactions for the learner to reach a high level of performance. This improvement does not depend on the learner's ability to detect corrections: the effect depends on the change in the distribution of teacher utterances in the correcting versus non-correcting conditions. This suggests re-visiting discussions in linguistics that assume that the learner must identify teacher corrections in order for them to have an influence on the learning process.

Our model of language is very simplified, and would have to be modified to deal with issues such as multi-word phrases bearing meaning, morphological relations between words, phonological rules for word choice, words with more than one meaning and meanings that can be expressed in more than one way, languages with freer word-orders and meaning components expressed by non-contiguous sequences of words. Other desirable directions to explore include more sophisticated use of co-occurrence information, more powerful methods of learning the grammars of meanings, feedback to allow the learning of production to improve comprehension, better methods of alignment between utterances and meanings, methods to allow the learner's semantic categories to evolve in response to language learning, and methods allowing the learner to make use of its ability to detect corrections.

References

D. Angluin and L. Becerra-Bonache. 2010. A Model of Semantics and Corrections in Language Learning. Technical Report, Yale University Department of Computer Science, YALE/DCS/TR-1425.

R. Brown and C. Hanlon. 1970. Derivational complexity and the order of acquisition in child speech. In J.R. Hayes (ed.): *Cognition and the Development of Language*. Wiley, New York, NY.

M.M. Chouinard and E.V. Clark. 2003. Adult Reformulations of Child Errors as Negative Evidence. *Journal of Child Language*, 30:637–669.

E.V. Clark 1987. The principle of contrast: a constraint on language acquisition. In B. MacWhinney (ed.): *Mechanisms of language acquisition*. Erlbaum, Hillsdale, NJ.

E.V. Clark 1993. *The Lexicon in Acquisition*. Cambridge University Press, Cambridge, UK.

M. J. Demetras, K. N. Post and C.E. Snow. 1986. Brown and Hanlon revisited: mothers' sensitivity to ungrammatical forms. *Journal of Child Language*, 2:81–88.

J.A. Feldman, G. Lakoff, A. Stolcke and S. Weber 1990. Miniature Language Acquisition: A Touchstone for Cognitive Science. *Annual Conference of the Cognitive Science Society*, 686–693.

E.M. Gold. 1967. Language identification in the limit. *Information and Control*, 10:447–474.

K. Hirsh-Pasek, R.A. Treiman M. and Schneiderman. 1984. Brown and Hanlon revisited: mothers' sensitivity to ungrammatical forms. *Journal of Child Language*, 2:81–88.

G.F. Marcus 1993. Negative evidence in language acquisition. *Cognition*, 46:53–95.

J.L. Morgan and L.L. Travis. 1989. Limits on negative information in language input. *Journal of Child Language*, 16:531–552.

Assessing Benefit from Feature Feedback in Active Learning for Text Classification

Shilpa Arora
Language Technologies Institute
School of Computer Science
Carnegie Mellon University
shilpaa@cs.cmu.edu

Eric Nyberg
Language Technologies Institute
School of Computer Science
Carnegie Mellon University
ehn@cs.cmu.edu

Abstract

Feature feedback is an alternative to instance labeling when seeking supervision from human experts. Combination of instance and feature feedback has been shown to reduce the total annotation cost for supervised learning. However, learning problems may not benefit equally from feature feedback. It is well understood that the benefit from feature feedback reduces as the amount of training data increases. We show that other characteristics such as domain, instance granularity, feature space, instance selection strategy and proportion of relevant text, have a significant effect on benefit from feature feedback. We estimate the maximum benefit feature feedback may provide; our estimate does not depend on how the feedback is solicited and incorporated into the model. We extend the complexity measures proposed in the literature and propose some new ones to categorize learning problems, and find that they are strong indicators of the benefit from feature feedback.

1 Introduction

Linear classifiers model the response as a weighted linear combination of the features in input instances. A supervised approach to learning a linear classifier involves learning the weights for the features from labeled data. A large number of labeled instances may be needed to determine the class association of the features and learn accurate weights for them. Alternatively, the user may directly label the features. For example, for a sentiment classification task, the user may label features, such as words or phrases, as expressing positive or negative sentiment. Prior work (Raghavan et al., 2006; Zaidan et al., 2007) has demonstrated that users are able to reliably provide useful feedback on features.

Direct feedback on a list of features (Raghavan et al., 2006; Druck et al., 2008) is limited to simple features like unigrams. However, unigrams are limited in the linguistic phenomena they can capture. Structured features such as dependency relations, paths in syntactic parse trees, etc., are often needed for learning the target concept (Pradhan et al., 2004; Joshi and Rosé, 2009). It is not clear how direct feature feedback can be extended straightforwardly to structured features, as they are difficult to present visually for feedback and may require special expertise to comprehend. An alternative approach is to seek *indirect feedback* on structured features (Arora and Nyberg, 2009) by asking the user to highlight spans of text, called *rationales*, that support the instance label (Zaidan et al., 2007). For example, when classifying the sentiment of a movie review, rationales are spans of text in the review that support the sentiment label for the review.

Assuming a fixed cost per unit of work, it might be cheaper to ask the user to label a few features, i.e. identify relevant features and their class association, than to label several instances. Prior work (Raghavan et al., 2006; Druck et al., 2008; Druck et al., 2009; Zaidan et al., 2007) has shown that a combination of instance and feature labeling can be used to reduce the total annotation cost required to learn the target concept. However, the benefit from feature feedback may vary across learning problems. If we can estimate the benefit from feature feedback for a

Proceedings of the Fifteenth Conference on Computational Natural Language Learning, pages 106–114,
Portland, Oregon, USA, 23–24 June 2011.

given problem, we can minimize the total annotation cost for achieving the desired performance by selecting the optimal annotation strategy (feature feedback or not) at every stage in learning. In this paper, we present the ground work for this research problem by analyzing how benefit from feature feedback varies across different learning problems and what characteristics of a learning problem have a significant effect on benefit from feature feedback.

We define a *learning problem* ($P = \{D, G, F, L, I, S\}$) as a tuple of the domain (D), instance granularity (G), feature representation (F), labeled data units (L), amount of irrelevant text (I) and instance selection strategy (S).

With enough labeled data, we may not benefit from feature feedback. Benefit from feature feedback also depends on the *features* used to represent the instances. If the feature space is large, we may need several labeled instances to identify the relevant features, while relatively fewer labeled features may help us quickly find these relevant features. Apart from the feature space size, it also matters what types of features are used. When hand crafted features from a domain expert are used (Pradhan et al., 2004) we expect to gain less from feature feedback as most of the features will be relevant. On the other hand, when features are extracted automatically as patterns in annotation graphs (Arora et al., 2010) feature feedback can help to identify relevant features from the large feature space.

In active learning, instances to be labeled are selectively sampled in each iteration. Benefit from feature feedback will depend on the instances that were used to train the model in each iteration. In the case of indirect feature feedback through rationales or direct feature feedback in context, instances selected will also determine what features receive feedback. Hence, *instance selection strategy* should affect the benefit from feature feedback.

In text classification, an instance may contain a large amount of text, and even a simple unigram representation will generate a lot of features. Often only a part of the text is relevant for the classification task. For example, in movie reviews, often the reviewers talk about the plot and characters in addition to providing their opinion about the movie. Often this extra information is not relevant to the classification task and bloats the feature space without adding many useful features. With feature feedback, we hope to filter out some of this noise and improve the model. Thus, the *amount of irrelevant information* in the instance should play an important role in determining the benefit from feature feedback. We expect to see less of such noise when the text instance is more concise. For example, a movie review snippet (about a sentence length) tends to have less irrelevant text than a full movie review (several sentences). In addition to analyzing document instances with varying amount of noise, we also compare the benefit from feature feedback for problems with different *granularity*. Granularity for a learning problem is defined based on the average amount of text in its instances.

Benefit from feature feedback will also depend on how feedback is solicited from the user and how it is incorporated back into the model. Independently from these factors, we estimate the maximum possible benefit and analyze how it varies across problems. Next we describe measures proposed in the literature and propose some new ones for categorizing learning problems. We then discuss our experimental setup and analysis.

2 Related Work

There has been little work on categorizing learning problems and how benefit from feature feedback varies with them. To the best of our knowledge there is only one work in this area by Raghavan et al. (2007). They categorize problems in terms of their *feature complexity*. Feature complexity is defined in terms of the minimum number of features required to learn a good classifier (close to maximum performance). If the concept can be described by a weighted combination of a few well-selected features, it is considered to be of low complexity.

In this estimate of complexity, an assumption is made that the best performance is achieved when the learner has access to all available features and not for any subset of the features. This is a reasonable assumption for text classification problems with robust learners like SVMs together with appropriate regularization and sufficient training data.

Instead of evaluating all possible combinations of features to determine the minimum number of features required to achieve close to the best performance, feature complexity is estimated using an intelligent ranking of the features. This ranking is based on their discriminative ability determined using a large amount of labeled data (referred to as *oracle*) and a feature selection criterion such as Information Gain (Rijsbergen, 1979). It is intuitive that the rate of learning, i.e., the rate at which performance improves as we add more features to the model, is also associated with problem complexity. Raghavan et al. (2007) define the *feature learning convergence profile* (p_{fl}) as the area under the feature learning curve (performance vs. number of features used in training), given by:

$$p_{fl} = \frac{\sum_{t=1}^{log_2 N} F1(M, 2^t)}{log_2 N \times F1(M, N)} \tag{1}$$

where $F1(M, 2^t)$ is the F1 score on the test data when using all M instances for training with top ranked 2^t features. The features are added at an exponentially increasing interval to emphasize the relative increase in feature space size. The three feature complexity measures proposed by Raghavan et al. (2007) are the following: 1) *Feature size complexity (N_f)*: Logarithm (base 2) of the number of features needed to achieve 95% of the best performance (when all instances are available), 2) *Feature profile complexity (F_{pc})*, given by $F_{pc} = 1 - p_{fl}$, and 3) *Combined feature complexity (C_f)*, $C_f = F_{pc} * n_f$, incorporates both the learning profile and the number of features required.

In order to evaluate the benefit from feature feedback, Raghavan et al. (2007) use their tandem learning approach of interleaving instance and feature feedback (Raghavan et al., 2006), referred to as interactive feature selection (ifs). The features are labeled as 'relevant' (feature discriminates well among the classes), or 'non-relevant/don't know'. The labeled features are incorporated into learning by scaling the value of the relevant features by a constant factor in all instances.

Raghavan et al. (2007) measure the benefit from feature feedback as the gain in the learning speed with feature feedback. The learning speed measures the rate of performance improvement with increasing amount of supervision. It is defined in terms of the convergence profile similar to feature learning convergence profile in Equation 1, except in terms of the number of labeled units instead of the number of features. A labeled unit is either a labeled instance or an equivalent set of labeled features with the same annotation time. The benefit from feature feedback is then measured as the difference in the convergence profile with interactive feature selection (p_{ifs}) and with labeled instances only (p_{al}).

Raghavan et al. (2007) analysed 9 corpora and 358 binary classification tasks. Most of these corpora, such as Reuters (Lewis, 1995), 20-newsgroup (Lang, 1995), etc., have topic-based category labels. For all classification tasks, they used simple and fixed feature space containing only unigram features (n-gram features were added where it seemed to improve performance). They observed a negative correlation ($r = -0.65$) between the benefit from feature feedback and combined feature complexity (C_f), i.e., feature feedback accelerates active learning by an amount that is inversely proportional to the feature complexity of the problem. If a concept can be expressed using a few well-selected features from a large feature space, we stand to benefit from feature feedback as few labeled features can provide this information. On the other hand, if learning a concept requires all or most of the features in the feature space, there is little knowledge that feature feedback can provide.

3 Estimating Maximum Benefit & Additional Measures

In this section, we highlight some limitations of the prior work that we address in this work.

Raghavan et al. (2007) only varied the domain among different problems they analyzed, i.e, only the variable D in our problem definition ($P = \{D, G, F, L, I, S\}$). However, as motivated in the introduction, other characteristics are also important when categorizing learning problems and it is not clear if we will observe similar results on problems that differ in these additional characteristics. In this work, we apply their measures to problems that differ in these characteristics in addition to the domain.

Analysis in Raghavan et al. (2007) is specific to their approach for incorporating feature feedback into the model, which may not work well for all domains and datasets as also mentioned in their work (Section 6.1). It is not clear how their results can be extended to alternate approaches for seeking and incorporating feature feedback. Thus, in this work we analyze the maximum benefit a given problem can get from feature feedback independent of the feedback solicitation and incorporation approach.

Raghavan et al. (2007) analyze benefit from feature feedback at a fixed training data size of 42 labeled units. However, the difference between learning problems may vary with the amount of labeled data. Some problems may benefit significantly from feature feedback even at relatively larger amount of labeled data. On the other hand, with very large training set, the benefit from feature feedback can be expected to be small and not significant for all problems and all problems will look similar. Thus, we evaluate the benefit from feature feedback at different amount of labeled data.

Raghavan et al. (2007) evaluate benefit from feature feedback in terms of the gain in learning speed. However, the learning rate does not tell us how much improvement we get in performance at a given stage in learning. In fact, even if at every point in the learning curve performance with feature feedback was lower than performance without feature feedback, the rate of convergence to the corresponding maximum performance may still be higher when using feature feedback. Thus, in this work, in addition to evaluating the improvement in the learning speed, we also evaluate the improvement in the absolute performance at a given stage in learning.

3.1 Determining the Maximum Benefit

Annotating instances with or without feature feedback may require different annotation time. It is only fair to compare different annotation strategies at same annotation cost. Raghavan et al. (2006) found that on average labeling an instance takes the same amount of time as direct feedback on 5 features. Zaidan et al. (2007) found that on average it takes twice as much time to annotate an instance with rationales than to annotate one without rationales. In our analysis, we focus on feedback on features in context of the instance they occur in, i.e., indirect feature feedback through rationales or direct feedback on features that occur in the instance being labeled. Thus, based on the findings in Zaidan et al. (2007), we assume that on average annotating an instance with feature feedback takes twice as much time as annotating an instance without feature feedback. We define a currency for annotation cost as *Annotation cost Units (AUs)*. For an annotation budget of a AUs, we compare two annotation strategies of annotating a instances without feature feedback or $\frac{a}{2}$ instances with feature feedback.

In this work, we only focus on using feature feedback as an alternative to labeled data, i.e., to provide evidence about features in terms of their relevance and class association. Thus, the best feature feedback can do is provide as much evidence about features as evidence from a large amount of labeled data (oracle). Let $F1(k, N_m)$ be the F1 score of a model trained with features that occur in m training instances (N_m) and evidence for these features from k instances ($k \geq m$). For an annotation budget of a AUs, we define the maximum improvement in performance with feature feedback (IP_a) as the difference in performance with feature feedback from oracle on $\frac{a}{2}$ training instances and performance with a training instances without feature feedback.

$$IP_a = F1(o, N_{\frac{a}{2}}) - F1(a, N_a) \qquad (2)$$

where o is the number of instances in the oracle dataset ($o >> a$). We also compare annotation strategies in terms of the learning rate similar to Raghavan et al. (2007), except that we estimate and compare the maximum improvement in the learning rate. For an annotation budget of a AUs, we define the maximum improvement in learning rate from 0 to a AUs (ILR_{0-a}) as follows.

$$ILR_{0-a} = {p_{cp}}^{wFF} - {p_{cp}}^{woFF} \qquad (3)$$

where ${p_{cp}}^{wFF}$ and ${p_{cp}}^{woFF}$ are the convergence profiles with and without feature feedback at same annotation cost, calculated as follows.

$${p_{cp}}^{wFF} = \frac{\sum_{t=1}^{log_2 \frac{a}{2}} F1(o, N_{2^t})}{log_2 \frac{a}{2} \times F1(o, N_{\frac{a}{2}})} \qquad (4)$$

$${p_{cp}}^{woFF} = \frac{\sum_{t=2}^{log_2 a} F1(2^t, N_{2^t})}{(log_2 a - 1) \times F1(a, N_a)} \qquad (5)$$

where 2^t denotes the training data size in iteration t. Like Raghavan et al. (2007), we use exponentially increasing intervals to emphasize the relative increase in the training data size, since adding a few labeled instances earlier in learning will give us significantly more improvement in performance than adding the same number of instances later on.

3.2 Additional Metrics

The feature complexity measures require an 'oracle', simulated using a large amount of labeled data, which is often not available. Thus, we need measures that do not require an oracle.

Benefit from feature feedback will depend on the uncertainty of the model on its predictions, since it suggests uncertainty on the features and hence scope for benefit from feature feedback. We use the probability of the predicted label from the model as an estimate of the model's uncertainty. We evaluate how benefit from feature feedback varies with summary statistics such as mean, median and maximum probability from the model on labels for instances in a held out dataset.

4 Experiments, Results and Observations

In this section, we describe the details of our experimental setup followed by the results.

4.1 Data

We analyzed three datasets: 1) Movie reviews with rationale annotations by Zaidan et al. (2007), where the task is to classify the sentiment (positive/negative) of a review, 2) Movie review snippets from Rotten Tomatoes (Pang and Lee., 2005), and 3) WebKB dataset with the task of classifying whether or not a webpage is a faculty member's homepage. Raghavan et al. (2007) found that the webpage classification task has low feature complexity and benefited the most from feature feedback. We compare our results on this task and the sentiment classification task on the movie review datasets.

4.2 Experimental Setup

Table 1 describes the different variables and their possible values in our experiments. We make a logical distinction for granularity based on whether an instance in the problem is a document (several sentences) or a sentence. Labeled data is composed of instances and their class labels with or without feature feedback. As discussed in Section 3.1, instances with feature feedback take on average twice as much time to annotate as instances without feature feedback. Thus, we measure the labeled data in terms of the number of annotation cost units which may mean different number of labeled instances based on the annotation strategy. We used two feature configurations of "unigram only" and "unigram+dependency triples". The unigram and dependency annotations are derived from the Stanford Dependency Parser (Klein and Manning, 2003).

Rationales by definition are spans of text in a review that convey the sentiment of the reviewer and hence are the part of the document most relevant for the classification task. In order to vary the amount of irrelevant text, we vary the amount of text (measured in terms of the number of characters) around the rationales that is included in the instance representation. We call this the *slack* around rationales. When using the rationales with or without the slack, only features that overlap with the rationales (and the slack, if used) are used to represent the instance. Since we only have rationales for the movie review documents, we only studied the effect of varying the amount of irrelevant text on this dataset.

Variable	**Possible Values**
Domain (D)	{Movie Review classification (MR), Webpage classification (WebKB)}
Instance Granularity (G)	{document (doc), sentence (sent)}
Feature Space (F)	{unigram only (u), unigram+dependency (u+d)}
Labeled Data (#AUs) (L)	{64, 128, 256, 512, 1024}
Irrelevant Text (I)	{0, 200, 400, 600, ∞ }
Instance Selection Strategy (S))	{deterministic (deter), uncertainty (uncert)}

Table 1: Experiment space for analysis of learning problems ($P = \{D, G, F, L, I, S\}$)

For all our experiments, we used Support Vector Machines (SVMs) with linear kernel for learning (libSVM (Chang and Lin, 2001) in Minorthird (Cohen, 2004)). For identifying the discriminative features we used the information gain score. For all datasets we used 1800 total examples with equal number of positive and negative examples. We held out 10% of the data for estimating model's uncertainty as explained in Section 3.2. The results we present are averaged over 10 cross validation folds on the remaining 90% of the data (1620 instances). In a cross validation fold, 10% data is used for testing (162 instances) and all of the remaining 1458 instances are used as the 'oracle' for calculating the feature complexity measures and estimating the maximum benefit from feature feedback as discussed in Sections 2 and 3.1 respectively. The training data size is varied from 64 to 1024 instances (from the total of 1458 instances for training in a fold), based on the annotation cost budget. Instances with their label are added to the training set either in the original order they existed in the dataset, i.e. no selective sampling (deterministic), or in the decreasing order of current model's uncertainty on them. Uncertainty sampling in SVMs (Tong and Koller, 2000) selects the instances closest to the decision boundary since the model is expected to be most uncertain about these instances. In each slice of the data, we ensured that there is equal distribution of the positive and negative class. SVMs do not yield probabilistic output but a decision boundary, a common practice is to fit the decision values from SVMs to a sigmoid curve to estimate the probability of the predicted class (Platt, 1999).

4.3 Results and Analysis

To determine the effect of various factors on benefit from feature feedback, we did an ANOVA analysis with Generalized Linear Model using a 95% confidence interval. The top part of Table 2 shows the average $F1$ score for the two annotation strategies at same annotation cost. As can be seen, with feature feedback, we get a significant improvement in performance.

Next we analyze the significance of the effect of various problem characteristics discussed above on benefit from feature feedback in terms of improvement in performance (IP) at given annotation cost and improvement in learning rate (ILR). Improvement in learning rate is calculated by comparing the learning profile for the two annotation strategies with increasing amount of labeled data, up to the maximum annotation cost of 1024 AUs.

As can be seen from the second part of Table 2, most of the factors have a significant effect on benefit from feature feedback. The benefit is significantly higher for the webpage classification task than the sentiment classification task in the movie review domain. We found that average feature complexity for the webpage classification task ($N_f = 3.07$) to be lower than average feature complexity for the sentiment classification task ($N_f = 5.18$) for 1024 training examples. Lower feature complexity suggests that the webpage classification concept can be expressed with few keywords such as *professor*, *faculty*, etc., and with feature feedback we can quickly identify these features. Sentiment on the other hand can be expressed in a variety of ways which explains the high feature complexity.

The benefit is more for document granularity than sentence granularity, which is intuitive as feature space is substantially larger for documents and we expect to gain more from the user's feedback on which features are important. This difference is significant for improvement in the learning rate and marginally significant for improvement in performance. Note that here we are comparing documents (with or without rationale slack) and sentences. However, documents with low rationale slack should have similar amount of noise as a sentence. Also, a significant difference between domains suggests that documents in WebKB domain might be quite different from those in Movie Review domain. This may explain the marginal significant difference between benefit for documents and sentences. To understand the effect of granularity alone, we compared the benefit from feature feedback for documents (without removing any noise) and sentences in movie review domain only and we found that this difference in also not significant. Thus, contrary to our intuition, sentences and documents seem to benefit equally from feature feedback.

The benefit is more when the feature space is larger and more diverse, i.e., when dependency features are used in addition to unigram features. We found that on average adding dependency features to unigram features increases the feature space by a factor of 10. With larger feature space, feature feedback can help to identify a few relevant features. As can also be seen, feature feedback is more helpful when there is more irrelevant text, i.e., there is noise that feature feedback can help to filter out. Unlike improvement in performance, the improvement in learning rate does not decrease monotonically as the amount of rationale slack decreases. This supports our belief that improvement in performance does not necessarily imply improvement in the learning rate. We saw similar result when comparing benefit from feature feedback at different instance granularity. Improvement in learning rate for problems with different granularity was statistically significant but improvement in performance was not significant. Thus, both metrics should be used when evaluating the benefit from feature feedback.

We also observe that when training examples are selectively sampled as the most uncertain instances, we gain more from feature feedback than without selective sampling. This is intuitive as instances the model is uncertain about are likely to contain features it is uncertain about and hence the model should benefit from feedback on features in these instances. Next we evaluate how well the complexity measures proposed in Raghavan et al. (2007) correlate with improvement in performance and improvement in learning rate.

$Var.$	$Values$	$AvgF1$	Group		
Strat.	wFF	78.2	A		
	woFF	68.2	B		
$Var.$	$Values$	Avg_{IP}	Grp_{IP}	Avg_{ILR}	Grp_{ILR}
D	WebKB	11.9	A	0.32	A
	MR	8.0	B	0.20	B
G	Doc	10.9	A	0.30	A
	Sent	9.0	A	0.22	B
F	u+d	12.1	A	0.30	A
	u	7.8	B	0.22	B
I	∞	12.8	A	0.34	A
	600	11.2	A B	0.23	B
	400	11.1	A B	0.26	A B
	200	9.8	B	0.26	A B
	0	4.8	C	0.21	B
S	Uncer.	12.7	A	0.32	A
	Deter.	7.1	B	0.20	B

Table 2: Effect of variables defined in Table 1 on benefit from feature feedback. Avg_{IP} is the average increase in performance ($F1$) and Avg_{ILR} is the average increase in the learning rate. Different letters in Grp_{IP} and Grp_{ILR} indicate significantly different results.

For a given problem with an annotation cost budget of a AUs, we calculate the benefit from feature feedback by comparing the performance with feature feedback on $\frac{a}{2}$ instances and the performance without feature feedback on a instances as described in Section 3.1. The feature complexity measures are calculated using $\frac{a}{2}$ instances, since it should be the characteristics of these $\frac{a}{2}$ training instances that determine whether we would benefit from feature feedback on these $\frac{a}{2}$ instances or from labeling new $\frac{a}{2}$ instances. As can be seen from Table 3, the correlation of feature complexity measures with both measures of benefit from feature feedback is strong, negative and significant. This suggests that problems with low feature complexity, i.e. concepts that can be expressed with few well-selected features, benefit more from feature feedback.

It is intuitive that the benefit from feature feedback decreases as amount of labeled data increases. We found a significant negative correlation (-0.574) between annotation budget (number of AUs) and improvement in performance with feature feedback. However, note that this correlation is not very strong, which supports our belief that factors other than the amount of labeled data affect benefit from feature feedback.

Measure	**R**(IP)	**R**(ILR)
N_f	-0.625	-0.615
F_{pc}	-0.575	-0.735
C_f	-0.603	-0.629

Table 3: Correlation coefficient (R) for feature size complexity (N_f), feature profile complexity (F_{pc}) and combined feature complexity (C_f) with improvement in performance (IP) and improvement in learning rate (ILR). All results are statistically significant ($p < 0.05$)

Feature complexity measures require an 'oracle' simulated using a large amount of labeled data which is not available for real annotation tasks. In Section 3.2, we proposed measures based on model's uncertainty that do not require an oracle. We calculate the mean, maximum and median of the probability scores from the learned model on instances in the held out dateset. We found a significant but low negative correlation of these measures with improvement in performance with feature feedback ($maxProb = -0.384$, $meanProb = -0.256$, $medianProb = -0.242$). This may seem counter-intuitive. However, note that when the training data is very small, the model might be quite certain about its prediction even when it is wrong and feature feedback may help by correcting the model's beliefs. We observed that these probability measures have only medium and significant positive correlation (around 0.5) with training datasize. Also, the held out dataset we used may not be representative of the whole set and using a larger dataset may give us more accurate estimate of the model's uncertainty. There are also other ways to measure the model's uncertainty, for example, in SVMs the distance of an instance from the decision boundary gives us an estimate of the model's uncertainty about that instance. We plan to explore additional measures for model's uncertainty in the future.

5 Conclusion and Future Work

In this work, we analyze how the benefit from feature feedback varies with different problem characteristics and how measures for categorizing learning problems correlate with benefit from feature feedback. We define a problem instance as a tuple of domain, instance granularity, feature representation, labeled data, amount of irrelevant text and selective sampling strategy.

We compare the two annotation strategies, with and without feature feedback, in terms of both improvement in performance at a given stage in learning and improvement in learning rate. Instead of evaluating the benefit from feature feedback using a specific feedback incorporation approach, we estimate and compare how the maximum benefit from feature feedback varies across different learning problems. This tells us what is the best feature feedback can do for a given learning problem.

We find a strong and significant correlation between feature complexity measures and the two measures of maximum benefit from feature feedback. However, these measures require an 'oracle', simulated using a large amount of labeled data which is not available in real world annotation tasks. We present measures based on the uncertainty of the model on its prediction that do not require an oracle. The proposed measures have a low but significant correlation with benefit from feature feedback. In our current work, we are exploring other measures of uncertainty of the model. It is intuitive that a metric that measures the uncertainty of the model on parameter estimates should correlate strongly with benefit from feature feedback. Variance in parameter estimates is one measure of uncertainty. The Bootstrap or Jacknife method (Efron and Tibshirani, 1994) of resampling from the training data is one way of estimating variance in parameter estimates that we are exploring.

So far only a linear relationship of various measures with benefit from feature feedback has been considered. However, some of these relationships may not be linear or a combination of several measures together may be stronger indicators of the benefit from feature feedback. We plan to do further analysis in this direction in the future.

We only considered one selective sampling strategy based on model's uncertainty which we found to provide more benefit from feature feedback. In the future, we plan to explore other selective sampling strategies. For example, density-based sampling (Donmez and Carbonell, 2008) selects the instances that are representative of clusters of similar instances, and may facilitate more effective feedback on a diverse set of features.

In this work, feature feedback was simulated using an oracle. Feedback from the users, however, might be less accurate. Our next step will be to analyze how the benefit from feature feedback varies as the quality of feature feedback varies.

Our eventual goal is to estimate the benefit from feature feedback for a given problem so that the right annotation strategy can be selected for a given learning problem at a given stage in learning and the total annotation cost for learning the target concept can be minimized. Note that in addition to the characteristics of the labeled data analyzed so far, expected benefit from feature feedback will also depend on the properties of the data to be labeled next for the two annotation strategies - with or without feature feedback.

Acknowledgments

We thank Carolyn P. Rosé, Omid Madani, Hema Raghavan, Jaime Carbonell, Pinar Donmez and Chih-Jen Lin for helpful discussions, and the reviewers for their feedback. This work is supported by DARPA's Machine Reading program under contract FA8750-09-C-0172.

References

Shilpa Arora and Eric Nyberg. 2009. Interactive annotation learning with indirect feature voting. In *Proceedings of NAACL-HLT 2009 (Student Research Workshop)*.

Shilpa Arora, Elijah Mayfield, Carolyn Penstein Rosé, and Eric Nyberg. 2010. Sentiment classification using automatically extracted subgraph features. In *Proceedings of the Workshop on Emotion in Text at NAACL*.

Chih-Chung Chang and Chih-Jen Lin, 2001. *LIBSVM: a library for support vector machines*. Software available at `http://www.csie.ntu.edu.tw/~cjlin/libsvm`.

William W. Cohen. 2004. Minorthird: Methods for identifying names and ontological relations in text using heuristics for inducing regularities from data.

Pinar Donmez and Jaime G. Carbonell. 2008. Paired Sampling in Density-Sensitive Active Learning. In *Proceedings of the International Symposium on Artificial Intelligence and Mathematics*.

Gregory Druck, Gideon Mann, and Andrew McCallum. 2008. Learning from labeled features using generalized expectation criteria. In *SIGIR '08: Proceedings of the 31st annual international ACM SIGIR conference on Research and development in information retrieval*, pages 595–602, New York, NY, USA. ACM.

Gregory Druck, Burr Settles, and Andrew McCallum. 2009. Active learning by labeling features. In *Proceedings of the Conference on Empirical Methods in Natural Language Processing (EMNLP)*. Association for Computational Linguistics.

B. Efron and R.J. Tibshirani. 1994. *An introduction to the bootstrap*. Monographs on Statistics and Applied Probability. Chapman and Hall/CRC, New York.

Mahesh Joshi and Carolyn Penstein Rosé. 2009. Generalizing dependency features for opinion mining. In *ACL-IJCNLP '09: Proceedings of the ACL-IJCNLP 2009 Conference Short Papers*, pages 313–316, Morristown, NJ, USA. Association for Computational Linguistics.

Dan Klein and Christopher D. Manning. 2003. Accurate unlexicalized parsing. In *ACL '03: Proceedings of the 41st Annual Meeting on Association for Computational Linguistics*, pages 423–430, Morristown, NJ, USA. Association for Computational Linguistics.

K. Lang. 1995. NewsWeeder: Learning to filter netnews. In *12th International Conference on Machine Learning (ICML95)*, pages 331–339.

D. Lewis. 1995. The reuters-21578 text categorization test collection.

Bo Pang and Lillian Lee. 2005. Seeing stars: Exploiting class relationships for sentiment categorization with respect to rating scales. In *Proceedings of ACL*.

John C. Platt. 1999. Probabilistic outputs for support vector machines and comparisons to regularized likelihood methods. In *ADVANCES IN LARGE MARGIN CLASSIFIERS*, pages 61–74. MIT Press.

Sameer Pradhan, Wayne Ward, Kadri Hacioglu, James H. Martin, and Dan Jurafsky. 2004. Shallow semantic parsing using support vector machines. In *Proceedings of the Human Language Technology Conference/North American chapter of the Association of Computational Linguistics (HLT/NAACL)*.

Hema Raghavan, Omid Madani, and Rosie Jones. 2006. Active learning with feedback on features and instances. *Journal of Machine Learning Research*, 7:1655–1686.

Hema Raghavan, Omid Madani, and Rosie Jones. 2007. When will feature feedback help? quantifying the complexity of classification problems. In *IJCAI Workshop on Human in the Loop Computing*.

C. J. Van Rijsbergen. 1979. *Information Retrieval*. Butterworths, London, 2 edition.

Simon Tong and Daphne Koller. 2000. Support vector machine active learning with applications to text classification. In *JOURNAL OF MACHINE LEARNING RESEARCH*, pages 999–1006.

Omar Zaidan, Jason Eisner, and Christine Piatko. 2007. Using "annotator rationales" to improve machine learning for text categorization. In *Human Language Technologies: Proceedings of the Annual Conference of the North American Chapter of the Association for Computational Linguistics (NAACL-HLT)*, pages 260–267, Rochester, NY, April.

ULISSE: an Unsupervised Algorithm for Detecting Reliable Dependency Parses

Felice Dell'Orletta, Giulia Venturi and Simonetta Montemagni
Istituto di Linguistica Computazionale "Antonio Zampolli" (ILC–CNR)
via G. Moruzzi, 1 – Pisa (Italy)
{felice.dellorletta,giulia.venturi,simonetta.montemagni}@ilc.cnr.it

Abstract

In this paper we present ULISSE, an unsupervised linguistically–driven algorithm to select reliable parses from the output of a dependency parser. Different experiments were devised to show that the algorithm is robust enough to deal with the output of different parsers and with different languages, as well as to be used across different domains. In all cases, ULISSE appears to outperform the baseline algorithms.

1 Introduction

While the accuracy of state–of–the–art parsers is increasing more and more, this is still not enough for their output to be used in practical NLP–based applications. In fact, when applied to real–world texts (e.g. the web or domain–specific corpora such as bio–medical literature, legal texts, etc.) their accuracy decreases significantly. This is a real problem since it is broadly acknowledged that applications such as Information Extraction, Question Answering, Machine Translation, and so on can benefit significantly from exploiting the output of a syntactic parser. To overcome this problem, over the last few years a growing interest has been shown in assessing the reliability of automatically produced parses: the selection of high quality parses represents nowadays a key and challenging issue. The number of studies devoted to detecting reliable parses from the output of a syntactic parser is spreading. They mainly differ with respect to the kind of selection algorithm they exploit. Depending on whether training data, machine learning classifiers or external parsers are exploited, existing algorithms can be classified into *i)* supervised–based, *ii)* ensemble–based and *iii)* unsupervised–based methods.

The first is the case of the construction of a machine learning classifier to predict the reliability of parses on the basis of different feature types. Yates et al. (2006) exploited semantic features derived from the web to create a statistical model to detect unreliable parses produced by a constituency parser. Kawahara and Uchimoto (2008) relied on features derived from the output of a supervised dependency parser (e.g. dependency lengths, number of unknown words, number of coordinated conjunctions, etc.), whereas Ravi et al. (2008) exploited an external constituency parser to extract text–based features (e.g. sentence length, unknown words, etc.) as well as syntactic features to develop a supervised predictor of the target parser accuracy. The approaches proposed by Reichart and Rappoport (2007a) and Sagae and Tsujii (2007) can be classified as ensemble–based methods. Both select high quality parses by computing the level of agreement among different parser outputs: wheras the former uses several versions of a constituency parser, each trained on a different sample from the training data, the latter uses the parses produced by different dependency parsing algorithms trained on the same data. However, a widely acknowledged problem of both supervised–based and ensemble–based methods is that they are dramatically influenced by a) the selection of the training data and b) the accuracy and the typology of errors of the used parser.

To our knowledge, Reichart and Rappoport (2009a) are the first to address the task of high qual-

Proceedings of the Fifteenth Conference on Computational Natural Language Learning, pages 115–124,
Portland, Oregon, USA, 23–24 June 2011.

ity parse selection by resorting to an unsupervised–based method. The underlying idea is that syntactic structures that are frequently created by a parser are more likely to be correct than structures produced less frequently. For this purpose, their PUPA (*POS–based Unsupervised Parse Assessment Algorithm*) uses statistics about POS tag sequences of parsed sentences produced by an unsupervised constituency parser.

In this paper, we address this unsupervised scenario with two main novelties: unlike Reichart and Rappoport (2009a), a) we address the reliable parses selection task using an unsupervised method in a supervised parsing scenario, and b) we operate on dependency–based representations. Similarly to Reichart and Rappoport (2009a) we exploit text internal statistics: but whereas they rely on features that are closely related to constituency representations, we use linguistic features which are dependency–motivated. The proposed algorithm has been evaluated for selecting reliable parses from English and Italian corpora; to our knowledge, this is the first time that such a task has been applied to a less resourced language such as Italian. The paper is organised as follows: in Section 2 we illustrate the ULISSE algorithm; sections 3 and 4 are devoted to the used parsers and baselines. Section 5 describes the experiments and discusses achieved results.

2 The ULISSE Algorithm

The ULISSE (*Unsupervised LInguiStically–driven Selection of dEpendency parses*) algorithm takes as input a set of parsed sentences and it assigns to each dependency tree a score quantifying its reliability. It operates in two different steps: 1) it collects statistics about a set of linguistically–motivated features extracted from a corpus of parsed sentences; 2) it calculates a quality (or reliability) score for each analyzed sentence using the feature statistics extracted from the whole corpus.

2.1 Selection of features

The features exploited by ULISSE are all linguistically motivated and rely on the dependency tree structure. Different criteria guided their selection. First, as pointed out in Roark et al. (2007), we needed features which could be reliably identified within the automatic output of a parser. Second, we focused on dependency structures that are widely agreed in the literature a) to reflect sentences' syntactic and thus parsing complexity and b) to impose a high cognitive load on the parsing of a complete sentence.

Here follows the list of features used in the experiments reported in this paper, which turned out to be the most effective ones for the task at hand.

Parse tree depth: this feature is a reliable indicator of sentence complexity due to the fact that, with sentences of approximately the same length, parse tree depth can be indicative of increased sentence complexity (Yngve, 1960; Frazier, 1985; Gibson, 1998; Nenkova, 2010).

Depth of embedded complement 'chains': this feature is a subtype of the previous one, focusing on the depth of chains of embedded complements, either prepositional complements or nominal and adjectival modifiers. Long chains of embedded complements make the syntactic structure more complex and their analysis much more difficult.

Arity of verbal predicates: this feature refers to the number of dependency links sharing the same verbal head. Here, there is no obvious relation between the number of dependents and sentence complexity: both a small number and a high number of dependents can make the sentence processing quite complex, although for different reasons (elliptical constructions in the former case, a high number of modifiers in the latter).

Verbal roots: this feature counts the number of verbal roots with respect to number of all sentence roots in the target corpus.

Subordinate vs main clauses: subordination is generally considered to be an index of structural complexity in language. Two distinct features are considered for monitoring this aspect: one measuring the ratio between main and subordinate clauses and the other one focusing on the relative ordering of subordinate clauses with respect to the main clause. It is a widely acknowledged fact that highly complex sentences contain deeply embedded subordinate clauses; however, subordinate clauses are easier to process if they occur in post–verbal rather than in pre–verbal position (Miller, 1998).

Length of dependency links: McDonald and Nivre (2007) report that statistical parsers have a drop in accuracy when analysing long distance dependencies. This is in line with Lin (1996) and Gibson (1998) who claim that the syntactic complexity of sentences can be predicted with measures based on the length of dependency links, given the memory overhead of very long distance dependencies. Here, the dependency length is measured in terms of the words occurring between the syntactic head and the dependent.

Dependency link plausibility (henceforth, ArcPOSFeat): this feature is used to calculate the plausibility of a dependency link given the part–of–speech of the dependent and the head, by also considering the PoS of the head father and the dependency linking the two.

2.2 Computation Score

The quality score (henceforth, QS) of parsed sentences results from a combination of the weights associated with the monitored features. ULISSE is modular and can use several weights combination strategies, which may be customised with respect to the specific task exploiting the output of ULISSE.

For this study, QS is computed as a simple product of the individual feature weights. This follows from the necessity to recognize high quality parses within the input set of parsed sentences: the product combination strategy is able to discard low quality parse trees even in presence of just one low weight feature. Therefore, QS for each sentence i in the set of input parsed sentences I is $QS(S_i) = \prod_{y=1}^{n} Weight(S_i, f_y)$, where S_i is the i–th sentence of I, n is the total number of selected features and $Weight(S_i, f_y)$ is the computed weight for the y–th feature.

Selected features can be divided into two classes, depending on whether they are computed with respect to each sentence and averaged over all sentences in the target corpus (global features), or they are computed with respect to individual dependency links and averaged over all of them (local features). The latter is the case of the ArcPOSFeat feature, whereas the all other ones represent global features.

For the global features, the $Weight(S_i, f_y)$ is defined as:

$$Weight(S_i, f_y) = \frac{F(V(f_y), range(L(S_i), r))}{|range(L(S_i), r)|}, \tag{1}$$

where $V(f_y)$ is the value of the y–th feature (extracted from S_i), $L(S_i)$ is the length of the sentence S_i, $range(L(S_i), r)$ defines a range covering values from $L(S_i) - r$ and $L(S_i) + r$, $F(V(f_y), range(L(S_i), r))$ is the frequency of $V(f_y)$ in all sentences in I that has a value of length in $range(L(S_i), r^1)$ and $|range(L(S_i), r)|$ is the total number of sentences in I with length in $range(L(S_i), r)$. For what concerns the local feature ArcPOSFeat, ULISSE assigns a weight for each arc in S_i: in principle different strategies can be used to compute a unique weight for this feature for S_i. Here, the sentence weight for the feature *ArcPOSFeat* is computed as the minimum weight among the weights of all arcs of S_i. Therefore, $Weight(S_i, ArcPOSFeat) = min\{weight((Pd, Ph, t)), \forall(Pd, Ph, t) \in S_i\}$, where the triple (Pd, Ph, t) is an arc in S_i in which Pd is the POS of the dependent, Ph is the POS of the syntactic head and t is the type of the dependency relation and $weight((Pd, Ph, t))$ is the weight of the specific arc (Pd, Ph, t). The individual arc weight is computed as follows:

$$\begin{aligned} weight((Pd, Ph, t)) = {} & \frac{F((Pd, Ph, t))}{F((Pd, X, t))} \cdot \\ & \cdot \frac{F((Pd, Ph, t))}{F((X, Ph, t))} \cdot \\ & \cdot \frac{F(((Pd, Ph, t)(Ph, Ph2, t2)))}{F((Pd, Ph, t))} \cdot \\ & \cdot \frac{F(((Pd, Ph, t)(Ph, Ph2, t2)))}{F((Ph, Ph2, t2))} \cdot \\ & \cdot \frac{F(((Pd, Ph, t)(Ph, Ph2, t2)))}{F((((Pd, X, t))(X, Ph2, t2)))}, \end{aligned}$$

where $F(x)$ is the frequency of x in I, X is a variable and $(arc1\ arc2)$ represent two consecutive arcs in the tree.

3 The Parsers

ULISSE was tested against the output of two really different data–driven parsers: the first–order Maximum Spanning Tree (MST) parser (McDonald et al., 2006) and the DeSR parser (Attardi, 2006) using Support Vector Machine as learning algorithm. The

[1]We set r=0 in the in–domain experiments and r=2 in the out–of–domain experiment reported in Sec 5.3.

former is a graph–based parser (following the so–called "all–pairs" approach Buchholz et al. (2006)) where every possible arc is considered in the construction of the optimal parse tree and where dependency parsing is represented as the search for a maximum spanning tree in a directed graph. The latter is a Shift–Reduce parser (following a "stepwise" approach, Buchholz et al. (2006)), where the parser is trained and learns the sequence of parsing actions required to build the parse tree.

Although both parser models show a similar accuracy, McDonald and Nivre (2007) demonstrate that the two types of models exhibit different behaviors. Their analysis exemplifies how different the two parsers behave when their accuracies are compared with regard to some linguistic features of the analyzed sentences. To mention only a few, the Shift–Reduce parser tends to perform better on shorter sentences, while the MST parser guarantees a higher accuracy in identifying long distance dependencies. As regards the identification of dependency types, the MST parser shows a better ability to identify the dependents of the sentences' roots whereas the Shift–Reduce tends to better recognize specific relations (e.g. Subject and Object).

McDonald and Nivre (2007) describe how the systems' behavioral differences are due to the different parsing algorithms implemented by the Shift–Reduce and the MST parsing models. The Shift Reduce parser constructs a dependency tree by performing a sequence of parser actions or transitions through a greedy parsing strategy. As a result of this parsing procedure, a Shift Reduce parser creates shorter arcs before longer arcs. The latter could be the reason for the lower accuracy in identifying longer arcs when compared to the MST parser. This also influences a lower level of accuracy in the analysis of longer sentences that usually contain longer arcs than shorter sentences. The MST parser's ability to analyze both short and long arcs is invariant as it employs a graph-based parsing method where every possible arc is considered in the construction of the dependency tree.

4 The Baselines

Three different increasingly complex baseline models were used to evaluate the performance of ULISSE.

The first baseline is constituted by a *Random Selection* (*RS*) of sentences from the test sets. This baseline is calculated in terms of the scores of the parser systems on the test set.

The second baseline is represented by the *Sentence Length* (*SL*), starting from the assumption, demonstrated by McDonald and Nivre (2007), that long sentences are harder to analyse using statistical dependency parsers than short ones. This is a strong unsupervised baseline based on raw text features, ranking the parser results from the shortest sentence to the longest one.

The third and most advanced baseline, exploiting parse features, is the PUPA algorithm (Reichart and Rappoport, 2007a). PUPA uses a set of parsed sentences to compute the statistics on which its scores are based. The PUPA algorithm operates on a constituency based representation and collects statistics about the POS tags of the words in the yield of the constituent and of the words in the yields of neighboring constituents. The sequences of POS tags that are more frequent in target corpus receive higher scores after proper regularization is applied to prevent potential biases. Therefore, the final score assigned to a constituency tree results from a combination of the scores of its extracted sequences of POSs.

In order to use PUPA as a baseline, we implemented a dependency–based version, hencefoth referred to as *dPUPA*. dPUPA uses the same score computation of PUPA and collects statistics about sequences of POS tags: the difference lies in the fact that in this case the POS sequences are not extracted from constituency trees but rather from dependency trees. To be more concrete, rather than representing a sentence as a collection of constituency–based sequences of POSs, dPUPA represents each sentence as a collection of sequences of POSs covering all identified dependency subtrees. In particular, each dependency tree is represented as the set of all subtrees rooted by non–terminal nodes. Each subtree is then represented as the sequence of POS tags of the words in the subtree (reflecting the word order of the original sentence) integrated with the POS of the leftmost and rightmost in the sentence (*NULL* when there are no neighbors). Figure 1 shows the example of the dependency tree for the sentence *I will give you the ball.*

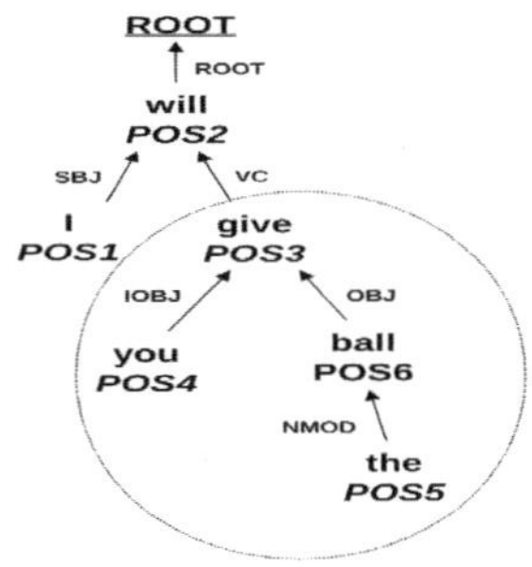

Figure 1: Example of dependency tree.

If we consider the subtree rooted by *give* (in the dotted circle), the resulting POS sequence is as follows: *POS2_POS3_POS4_POS5_POS6_NULL*, where *POS3_POS4_POS5_POS6* is the sequence of POS tags in the subtree, *POS2* is the left neighbor POS tag and *NULL* marks the absence of a right neighbor.

5 Experiments and Results

The experiments were organised as follows: a target corpus was automatically POS tagged (Dell'Orletta, 2009) and dependency–parsed; the ULISSE and baseline algorithms of reliable parse selection were run on the POS–tagged and dependency–parsed target corpus in order to identify high quality parses; results achieved by the selection algorithms were evaluated with respect to a subset of the target corpus of about 5,000 word–tokens (henceforth referred to as "test set") for which gold-standard annotation was available. Different sets of experiments were devised to test the robustness of our algorithm. They were performed with respect to i) the output of the parsers described in Section 3, ii) two different languages, iii) different domains.

For what concerns the languages, we chose Italian and English for two main reasons. First of all, they pose different challenges to a parser since they are characterised by quite different syntactic features. For instance, Italian, as opposed to English, is characterised by a relatively free word order (especially for what concerns subject and object relations with respect to the verb) and by the possible absence of an overt subject. Secondly, as it is shown in Section 5.1, Italian is a less resourced language with respect to English. This is a key issue, since as demonstrated by Reichart and Rappoport (2007b) and McClosky et al. (2008), small and big treebanks pose different problems in the reliable parses selection.

Last but not least, we aimed at demonstrating that ULISSE can be successfully used not only with texts belonging to the same domain as the parser training corpus. For this purpose, ULISSE was tested on a target corpus of Italian legislative texts, whose automatic linguistic analysis poses domain–specific challenges (Venturi, 2010). Out–of–domain experiments are being carried out also for English.

5.1 The Corpora

The Italian corpora Both parsers were trained on ISST–TANL[2], a dependency annotated corpus used in Evalita'09[3], an evaluation campaign carried out for Italian (Bosco et al., 2009). ISST–TANL includes 3,109 sentences (71,285 tokens) and consists of articles from newspapers and periodicals.

Two different target corpora were used for the in–domain and out–of–domain experiments. For the former, we used a corpus of 1,104,237 sentences (22,830,739 word–tokens) of newspapers texts which was extracted from the CLIC-ILC Corpus (Marinelli et al., 2003); for the legal domain, we used a collection of Italian legal texts (2,697,262 word–tokens; 97,564 sentences) regulating a variety of domains, ranging from environment, human rights, disability rights, freedom of expression to privacy, age disclaimer, etc. In the two experiments, the test sets were represented respectively by: a) the test set used in the Evalita'09 evaluation campaign, constituted by 260 sentences and 5,011 tokens from newpapers text; b) a set of 102 sentences (corresponding to 5,691 tokens) from legal texts.

The English corpora For the training of parsers we used the dependency–based version of Sections 2–11 of the Wall Street Journal partition of the Penn Treebank (Marcus et al., 2003), which was developed for the CoNLL 2007 Shared Task on Dependency Parsing (Nivre et al., 2007): it includes 447,000 word tokens and about 18,600 sentences.

As target data we took a corpus of news, specifically the whole Wall Street Journal Section of the

[2] http://medialab.di.unipi.it/wiki/SemaWiki
[3] http://evalita.fbk.eu/index.html

Penn Treebank[4], from which the portion of text corresponding to the training corpus was removed; the English target corpus thus includes 39,285,425 tokens (1,625,606 sentences). For testing we used the test set of the CoNLL 2007 Shared Task, corresponding to a subset of Section 23 of the Wall Street Journal partition of the Penn Treebank (5,003 tokens, 214 sentences).

5.2 Evaluation Methodology

Performances of the ULISSE algorithm have been evaluated i) with respect to the accuracy of ranked parses and ii) in terms of Precision and Recall. First, for each experiment we evaluated how the ULISSE algorithm and the baselines classify the sentences in the test set with respect to the "Labelled Attachment Score" (LAS) obtained by the parsers, i.e. the percentage of tokens for which it has predicted the correct head and dependency relation. In particular, we computed the LAS score of increasingly wider top lists of *k* tokens, where *k* ranges from 500 word tokens to the whole size of the test set (with a step size of 500 word tokens, i.e. k=500, k=1000, k=1500, etc.).

As regards ii), we focused on the set of ranked sentences showing a LAS $\geq \alpha$. Since imposing a 100% LAS was too restrictive, for each experiment we defined a different α threshold taking into account the performance of each parser across the different languages and domains. In particular, we took the top 25% and 50% of the list of ranked sentences and calculated Precision and Recall for each of them. To this specific end, a parse tree showing a LAS $\geq \alpha$ is considered as a *trustworthy analysis*. Precision has been computed as the ratio of the number of trustworthy analyses over the total number of sentences in each top list. Recall has been computed as the ratio of the number of trustworthy analyses which have been retrieved over the total number of trustworthy analyses in the whole test set.

In order to test how the ULISSE algorithm is able to select reliable parses by relying on *parse* features rather than on *raw text* features, we computed the accuracy score (LAS) of a subset of the top list of sentences parsed by both parsers and ranked by ULISSE: in particular, we focused on those sentences which were not shared by the MST and DeSR top lists.

[4]This corpus represents to the unlabelled data set distributed for the CoNLL 2007 Shared Task on Dependency Parsing, domain adaptation track.

5.3 Results

We will refer to the performed experiments as follows: "IT in–domain" and "IT out-of–domain" for the Italian experiments using respectively the ISST–TANL test set (henceforth ISST_TS) and the Legal-Corpus test set (henceforth Legal_TS); "EN in–domain" for the English experiment using the PTB test set (PTB_TS).

As a starting point let us consider the accuracy of DeSR and MST parsers on the whole test sets, reported in Table 1. The accuracy has been computed in terms of LAS and of Unlabelled Attachment Score (UAS), i.e. the percentage of tokens with a correctly identified syntactic head. It can be noticed that the performance of the two parsers is quite similar for Italian (i.e. wrt ISST_TS and Legal_TS), whereas there is a 2.3% difference between the MST and DeSR accuracy as far as English is concerned.

	ISST_TS		Legal_TS		PTB_TS	
Parser	LAS	UAS	LAS	UAS	LAS	UAS
DeSR	80.22	84.96	73.40	76.12	85.95	87.25
MST	79.52	85.43	73.99	78.72	88.25	89.55

Table 1: Overall accuracy of DeSR and MST parsers.

The plots in Figure 2 show the LAS of parses ranked by ULISSE and the baselines across the different experiments. Each plot reports the results of a single experiment: plots in the same row report the LAS of DeSR and MST parsers with respect to the same test set. In all experiments, ULISSE turned out to be the best ranking algorithm since it appears to select top lists characterised by higher LAS scores than the baselines. As Figure 2 shows, all ranking algorithms perform better than Random Selection (RS), i.e. all top lists (for each *k* value) show a LAS higher than the accuracy of DeSR and MST parsers on the whole test sets. In the EN in–domain experiment, the difference between the results of ULISSE and the other ranking algorithms is smaller than in the corresponding Italian experiment, a fact resulting from the higher accuracy of DeSR and MST parsers (i.e. LAS 85.95% and 88.25% respectively) on the PTB_TS. It follows that, for example, the first top list (with *k*=500) of the SL baseline has a

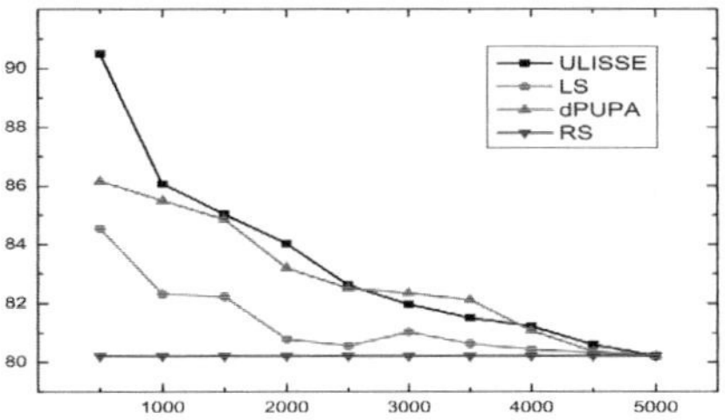

(a) IT in–domain experiment (DeSR).

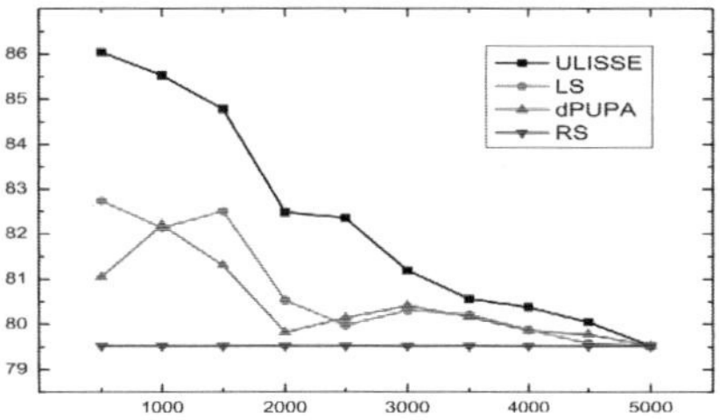

(b) IT in–domain experiment (MST).

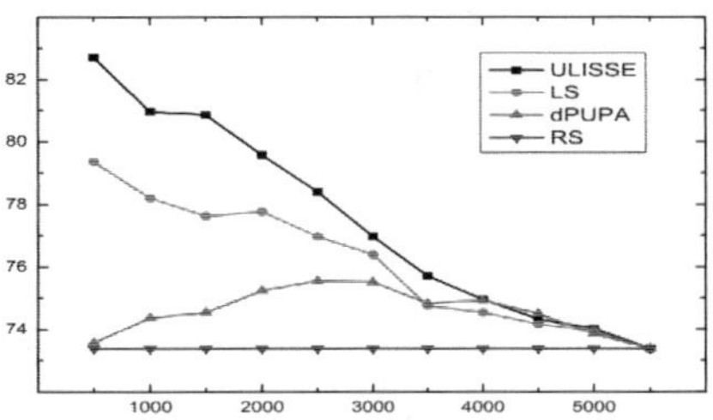

(c) IT out–of–domain experiment (DeSR).

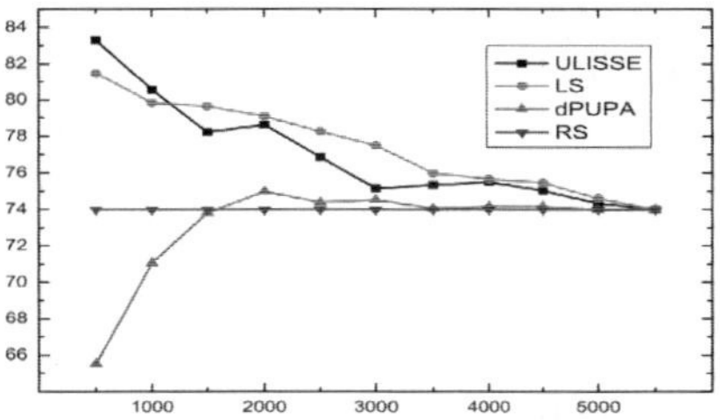

(d) IT out–of–domain experiment (MST).

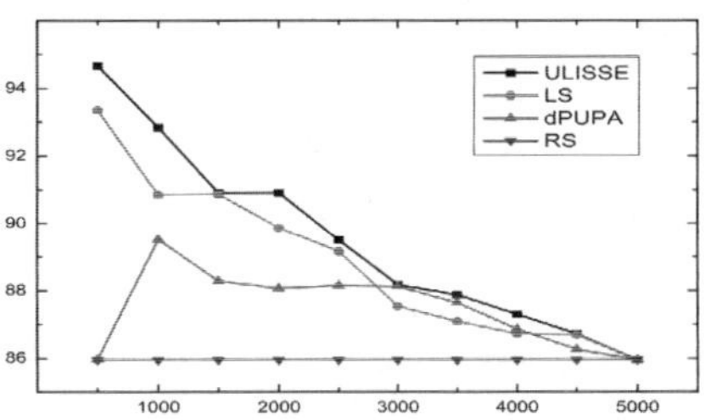

(e) EN in–domain experiment (DeSR).

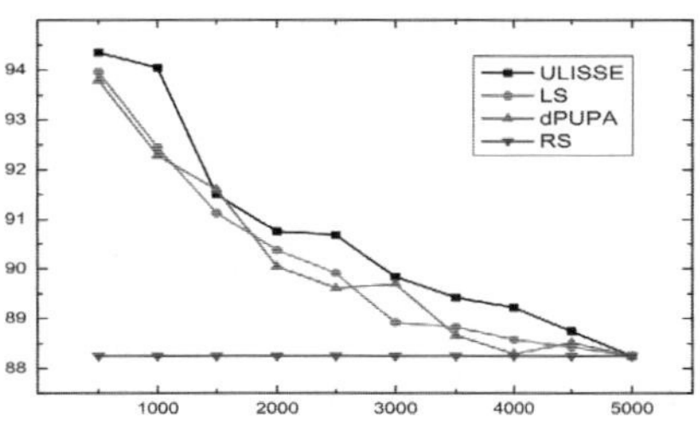

(f) EN in–domain experiment (MST).

Figure 2: LAS of parses ranked by ULISSE algorithm and by the three baselines.

LAS accuracy of 93.36% and 93.96% respectively for DeSR and MST: even in this case, ULISSE outperforms all baselines. This is also the case in the IT out–of–domain experiment. As reported in Table 1, parsing legal texts is a quite challenging task due to a number of domain–specific peculiarities at the level of syntax: this is testified by the average sentence length which in the Legal_TS is 56 word tokens. Nevertheless, ULISSE is able also in this case to highly rank long sentences showing a high LAS. For example, while in the first top list of 500 word tokens the sentences parsed by DeSR and ordered by SL have an average sentence length of 24 words and a LAS of 79.37%, ULISSE includes in the same top list longer sentences (with average sentence length = 29) with a higher LAS (82.72%). Also dPUPA ranks in the same top list quite long sentences (with 27 average sentence length), but compared to ULISSE it shows a lower LAS (i.e. 73.56%).

	IT in–domain		IT out–of–domain		EN in–domain	
	DeSR	MST	DeSR	MST	DeSR	MST
MST top–list	80.93	**80.27**	68.84	74.58	83.37	**90.39**
DeSR top–list	**82.46**	77.82	**75.47**	**74.88**	**86.50**	86.74

Table 3: LAS of not–shared sentences in the DeSR and MST top–lists.

Results in Table 2 show that in the top 25% of the ranked sentences with a LAS $\geq \alpha$ ULISSE has the highest Precision and Recall in all experiments. We believe that the low performance of dPUPA with respect to all other ranking algorithms can be due to

	DeSR								MST							
	25%				50%				25%				50%			
	Prec	Rec	LAS	AvgSL	Prec	Rec	LAS	AvgSL	Prec	Rec	LAS	AvgSL	Prec	Rec	LAS	AvgSL
IT in–domain: LAS $\geq$ 85% (DeSR: 120 sentences; MST: 112 sentences)																
ULISSE	**66.15**	**35.83**	**88.25**	5.25	**59.23**	**64.17**	84.30	14.60	**60**	**34.82**	**86.16**	5.68	**55.38**	**64.29**	**83.39**	15.27
LS	63.08	34.17	84.54	4.15	53.08	57.50	82.07	11.90	58.46	33.93	82.73	4.45	53.08	61.61	82.14	12.75
dPUPA	61.54	33.33	86.89	6.68	**59.23**	**64.17**	**84.36**	14.82	53.85	31.25	82.26	8.61	50.00	58.04	79.94	17.04
IT out–of–domain: LAS $\geq$ 75% (DeSR: 51 sentences; MST: 57 sentences)																
ULISSE	**73.08**	**37.25**	**80.75**	16.71	**69.23**	**70.59**	**79.17**	41.80	**69.23**	**31.58**	**81.47**	13.63	67.31	61.40	78.36	36
LS	53.85	27.45	76.71	12.63	67.31	68.63	78.34	34.14	61.54	28.07	78.42	11.30	**69.23**	**63.16**	**79.78**	30.54
dPUPA	57.69	29.41	73.97	15.67	61.54	62.74	75.24	40.39	46.15	21.05	72.08	22.56	57.69	52.63	74.86	42.91
EN in–domain: LAS $\geq$ 90% (DeSR: 118 sentences; MST: 120 sentences)																
ULISSE	**81.48**	**37.29**	**94.50**	6.31	**69.44**	**63.56**	90.93	16.36	**77.78**	**35**	**93.74**	5.82	**69.44**	**62.5**	**91.20**	16.48
LS	77.78	35.59	93.39	4.87	65.74	60.17	**91.01**	13.67	75.92	34.17	93.55	4.79	68.52	61.67	90.84	13.44
dPUPA	74.07	33.90	89.76	7.95	65.74	60.17	88.37	18.14	**77.78**	**35**	93.43	5.08	68.52	61.67	91.03	14.49

Table 2: **In all Tables**: the number of sentences with a LAS $\geq \alpha$ parsed by DeSr and MST parsers (first row); Precision (Prec), Recall (Rec), the corresponding parser accuracy (LAS) of the top 25% and 50% of the list of sentences and ranked by the ULISSE algorithm, Length of Sentence (LS) and dependency PUPA (dPUPA) and the corresponding average length in tokens of ranked sentence (AvgSL).

the fact that PUPA is based on constituency–specific features that once translated in terms of dependency structures may be not so effective.

In order to show that the ranking of sentences does not follow from raw text features but rather from parse features, we evaluated the accuracy of parsed sentences that are not–shared by MST and DeSR top–lists selected by ULISSE. For each test set we selected a different top list: a set of 100 sentences in the IT and EN in–domain experiments and of 50 sentences in the IT out–of–domain experiment. For each of them we have a different number of not–shared sentences: 24, 15 and 16 in the IT in–domain, IT out–of–domain and EN in–domain experiments respectively. Table 3 reports the LAS of DeSR and MST for these sentences: it can be observed that the LAS of not–shared sentences in the DeSR top list is always higher than the LAS assigned by the same parser to the not–shared sentences in the MST top list, and viceversa. For instance, in the English experiment the LAS achieved by DeSR on the not–shared top list is higher (86.50) than the LAS of DeSR on the not–shared MST top list (83.37); viceversa, the LAS of MST on the not–shared DeSR top list is higher (86.74) than the LAS of MST on the not–shared MST top list (90.39). The unique exception is MST in the IT out–of–domain experiment, but the difference in terms of LAS between the parses is not statistically relevant (p–value < 0.05). These results demonstrate that ULISSE is able to select parsed sentences on the basis of the reliability of the analysis produced by each parser.

6 Conclusion

ULISSE is an unsupervised linguistically–driven method to select reliable parses from the output of dependency parsers. To our knowledge, it represents the first unsupervised ranking algorithm operating on dependency representations which are more and more gaining in popularity and are arguably more useful for some applications than constituency parsers. ULISSE shows a promising performance against the output of two supervised parsers selected for their behavioral differences. In all experiments, ULISSE outperforms all baselines, including dPUPA and Sentence Length (SL), the latter representing a very strong baseline selection method in a supervised scenario, where parsers have a very high performance with short sentences. The fact of carrying out the task of reliable parse selection in a supervised scenario represents an important novelty: however, the unsupervised nature of ULISSE could also be used in an unsupervised scenario (Reichart and Rappoport, 2010). Current direction of research include a careful study of a) the quality score function, in particular for what concerns the combination of individual feature weights, and b) the role and effectivess of the set of linguistic features. This study is being carried out with a specific view to NLP tasks which might benefit from the ULISSE algorithm. This is the case, for instance, of the domain adaptation task in a self–training scenario (McClosky et al., 2006), of the treebank construction process by minimizing the human annotators' efforts (Reichart and Rappoport, 2009b), of *n–best* ranking methods for machine translation (Zhang, 2006).

References

Giuseppe Attardi. 2006. *Experiments with a multilanguage non-projective dependency parser.* In Proceedings of the Tenth Conference on Computational Natural Language Learning (CoNLL-X '06), New York City, New York, pp. 166–170.

Cristina Bosco, Simonetta Montemagni, Alessandro Mazzei, Vincenzo Lombardo, Felice Dell'Orletta and Alessandro Lenci. 2009. Parsing Task: comparing dependency parsers and treebanks. In Proceedings of Evalita'09, Reggio Emilia.

Sabine Buchholz and Erwin Marsi. 2006. *CoNLL-X shared task on multilingual dependency parsing.* In Proceedings of CoNLL.

Felice Dell'Orletta. 2009. *Ensemble system for Part-of-Speech tagging.* In Proceedings of Evalita'09, Evaluation of NLP and Speech Tools for Italian, Reggio Emilia, December.

Lyn Frazier. 1985. *Syntactic complexity.* In D.R. Dowty, L. Karttunen and A.M. Zwicky (eds.), *Natural Language Parsing*, Cambridge University Press, Cambridge, UK.

Edward Gibson. 1998. *Linguistic complexity: Locality of syntactic dependencies.* In *Cognition*, 68(1), pp. 1-76.

Daisuke Kawahara and Kiyotaka Uchimoto. 2008. *Learning Reliability of Parses for Domain Adaptation of Dependency Parsing.* In Proceedings of IJCNLP 2008, pp. 709–714.

Dekan Lin. 1996. *On the structural complexity of natural language sentences.* In Proceedings of COLING 1996, pp. 729–733.

Ryan McDonald, Kevin Lerman, and Fernando Pereira. 2006. *Multilingual dependency analysis with a two-stage discriminative parser.* In Proceedings of CoNLL 2006.

Ryan McDonald and Joakim Nivre. 2007. *Characterizing the Errors of Data-Driven Dependency Parsing Models.* In Proceedings of EMNLP-CoNLL, 2007, pp. 122-131.

Mitchell P. Marcus, Mary Ann Marcinkiewicz and Beatrice Santorini. 1993. *Building a large annotated corpus of English: the penn treebank.* In Comput. Linguist.,vol. 19, issue 2, MIT Press, pp. 313–330.

Rita Marinelli, et al. 2003. *The Italian PAROLE corpus: an overview.* In A. Zampolli et al. (eds.), *Computational Linguistics in Pisa*, XVI–XVII, Pisa–Roma, IEPI., I, 401–421.

David McClosky, Eugene Charniak and Mark Johnson. 2006. *Reranking and self–training for parser adaptation.* In Proceedings of ICCL–ACL 2006, pp. 337–344.

David McClosky, Eugene Charniak and Mark Johnson. 2008. *When is Self–Trainig Effective for parsing?.* In Proceedings of COLING 2008, pp. 561–568.

Jim Miller and Regina Weinert. 1998. *Spontaneous spoken language. Syntax and discourse.* Oxford, Clarendon Press.

Ani Nenkova, Jieun Chae, Annie Louis, and Emily Pitler. 2010. *Structural Features for Predicting the Linguistic Quality of Text Applications to Machine Translation, Automatic Summarization and Human–Authored Text.* In E. Krahmer, M. Theune (eds.), *Empirical Methods in NLG*, LNAI 5790, Springer-Verlag Berlin Heidelberg, pp. 222241.

Joakim Nivre, Johan Hall, Sandra Kübler, Ryan McDonald, Jens Nilsson, Sebastian Riedel, Deniz Yuret. 2007. *The CoNLL 2007 Shared Task on Dependency Parsing.* In Proceedings of the EMNLP-CoNLL, pp. 915–932.

Sujith Ravi, Kevin Knight and Radu Soricut. 2008. *Automatic Prediction of Parser Accuracy.* In Proceedings of the EMNLP 2008, pp. 887–896.

Roi Reichart and Ari Rappoport. 2007a. *An ensemble method for selection of high quality parses.* In Proceedings of ACL 2007, pp. 408–415.

Roi Reichart and Ari Rappoport. 2007b. *Self–Training for Enhancement and Domain Adaptation of Statistical Parsers Trained on Small Datasets.* In Proceedings of ACL 2007, pp. 616–623.

Roi Reichart and Ari Rappoport. 2009a. *Automatic Selection of High Quality Parses Created By a Fully Unsupervised Parser.* In Proceedings of CoNLL 2009, pp. 156–164.

Roi Reichart and Ari Rappoport. 2009b. *Sample Selection for Statistical Parsers: Cognitively Driven Algorithms and Evaluation Measures.* In Proceedings of CoNLL 2009, pp. 3–11.

Roi Reichart and Ari Rappoport. 2010. *Improved Fully Unsupervised Parsing with Zoomed Learning.* In Proceedings of EMNLP 2010.

Brian Roark, Margaret Mitchell and Kristy Hollingshead. 2007. *Syntactic complexity measures for detecting Mild Cognitive Impairment.* In Proceedings of ACL Workshop on Biological, Translational, and Clinical Language Processing (BioNLP'07), pp. 1–8.

Kenji Sagae and Junichi Tsujii. 2007. *Dependency Parsing and Domain Adaptation with LR Models and Parser Ensemble.* In Proceedings of the EMNLP–CoNLL 2007, pp. 1044–1050.

Giulia Venturi. 2010. *Legal Language and Legal Knowledge Management Applications.* In E. Francesconi, S. Montemagni, W. Peters and D. Tiscornia (eds.), *Semantic Processing of Legal Texts*, Lecture Notes in Computer Science, Springer Berlin / Heidelberg, vol. 6036, pp. 3-26.

Alexander Yates, Stefan Schoenmackers and Oren Etzioni. 2006. *Detecting Parser Errors Using Web–based Semantic Filters*. In Proceedings of the EMNLP 2006, pp. 27–34.

Victor H.A. Yngve. 1960. *A model and an hypothesis for language structure*. In Proceedings of the American Philosophical Society, pp. 444-466.

Ying Zhang, Almut Hildebrand and Stephan Vogel. 2006. *Distributed language modeling for N-best list re-ranking*. In Proceedings of the EMNLP 2006, pp. 216–223.

Language Models as Representations for Weakly-Supervised NLP Tasks

Fei Huang and **Alexander Yates**
Temple University
Broad St. and Montgomery Ave.
Philadelphia, PA 19122
fei.huang@temple.edu
yates@temple.edu

Arun Ahuja and **Doug Downey**
Northwestern University
2133 Sheridan Road
Evanston, IL 60208
a-ahuja@northwestern.edu
ddowney@eecs.northwestern.edu

Abstract

Finding the right representation for words is critical for building accurate NLP systems when domain-specific labeled data for the task is scarce. This paper investigates language model representations, in which language models trained on unlabeled corpora are used to generate real-valued feature vectors for words. We investigate ngram models and probabilistic graphical models, including a novel lattice-structured Markov Random Field. Experiments indicate that language model representations outperform traditional representations, and that graphical model representations outperform ngram models, especially on sparse and polysemous words.

1 Introduction

NLP systems often rely on hand-crafted, carefully engineered sets of features to achieve strong performance. Thus, a part-of-speech (POS) tagger would traditionally use a feature like, "the previous token is `the`" to help classify a given token as a noun or adjective. For supervised NLP tasks with sufficient domain-specific training data, these traditional features yield state-of-the-art results. However, NLP systems are increasingly being applied to texts like the Web, scientific domains, and personal communications like emails, all of which have very different characteristics from traditional training corpora. Collecting labeled training data for each new target domain is typically prohibitively expensive. We investigate representations that can be applied when domain-specific labeled training data is scarce.

An increasing body of theoretical and empirical evidence suggests that traditional, manually-crafted features limit systems' performance in this setting for two reasons. First, feature *sparsity* prevents systems from generalizing accurately to words and features not seen during training. Because word frequencies are Zipf distributed, this often means that there is little relevant training data for a substantial fraction of parameters (Bikel, 2004), especially in new domains (Huang and Yates, 2009). For example, word-type features form the backbone of most POS-tagging systems, but types like "gene" and "pathway" show up frequently in biomedical literature, and rarely in newswire text. Thus, a classifier trained on newswire data and tested on biomedical data will have seen few training examples related to sentences with features "gene" and "pathway" (Ben-David et al., 2009; Blitzer et al., 2006).

Further, because words are *polysemous*, word-type features prevent systems from generalizing to situations in which words have different meanings. For instance, the word type "signaling" appears primarily as a present participle (VBG) in Wall Street Journal (WSJ) text, as in, "Interest rates rose, signaling that ..." (Marcus et al., 1993). In biomedical text, however, "signaling" appears primarily in the phrase "signaling pathway," where it is considered a noun (NN) (PennBioIE, 2005); this phrase never appears in the WSJ portion of the Penn Treebank (Huang and Yates, 2010a).

Our response to these problems with traditional NLP representations is to seek new representations that allow systems to generalize more accurately to previously unseen examples. Our approach depends on the well-known *distributional hypothesis*, which states that a word's meaning is identified with the contexts in which it appears (Harris, 1954; Hindle, 1990). Our goal is to develop probabilistic lan-

Proceedings of the Fifteenth Conference on Computational Natural Language Learning, pages 125–134,
Portland, Oregon, USA, 23–24 June 2011.

guage models that describe the contexts of individual words accurately. We then construct *representations*, or mappings from word tokens and types to real-valued vectors, from these language models. Since the language models are designed to model words' contexts, the features they produce can be used to combat problems with polysemy. And by careful design of the language models, we can limit the number of features that they produce, controlling how sparse those features are in training data.

In this paper, we analyze the performance of language-model-based representations on tasks where domain-specific training data is scarce. Our contributions are as follows:

1. We introduce a novel factorial graphical model representation, a Partial-Lattice Markov Random Field (PL-MRF), which is a tractable variation of a Factorial Hidden Markov Model (HMM) for language modeling.
2. In experiments on POS tagging in a domain adaptation setting and on weakly-supervised information extraction (IE), we quantify the performance of representations derived from language models. We show that graphical models outperform ngram representations. The PL-MRF representation achieves a state-of-the-art 93.8% accuracy on the POS tagging task, while the HMM representation improves over the ngram model by 10% on the IE task.
3. We analyze how the performance of the different representations varies due to the fundamental challenges of sparsity and polysemy.

The next section discusses previous work. Sections 3 and 4 present the existing representations we investigate and the new PL-MRF, respectively. Sections 5 and 6 describe our two tasks and the results of using our representations on each of them. Section 7 concludes.

2 Previous Work

There is a long tradition of NLP research on representations, mostly falling into one of four categories: 1) vector space models of meaning based on document-level lexical cooccurrence statistics (Salton and McGill, 1983; Turney and Pantel, 2010; Sahlgren, 2006); 2) dimensionality reduction techniques for vector space models (Deerwester et al., 1990; Honkela, 1997; Kaski, 1998; Sahlgren, 2005; Blei et al., 2003; Väyrynen et al., 2007); 3) using clusters that are induced from distributional similarity (Brown et al., 1992; Pereira et al., 1993; Martin et al., 1998) as non-sparse features (Lin and Wu, 2009; Candito and Crabbe, 2009; Koo et al., 2008; Zhao et al., 2009); 4) and recently, language models (Bengio, 2008; Mnih and Hinton, 2009) as representations (Weston et al., 2008; Collobert and Weston, 2008; Bengio et al., 2009), some of which have already yielded state of the art performance on domain adaptation tasks (Huang and Yates, 2009; Huang and Yates, 2010a; Huang and Yates, 2010b; Turian et al., 2010) and IE (Ahuja and Downey, 2010; Downey et al., 2007b). In contrast to this previous work, we develop a novel Partial Lattice MRF language model that incorporates a factorial representation of latent states, and demonstrate that it outperforms the previous state-of-the-art in POS tagging in a domain adaptation setting. We also analyze the novel PL-MRF representation on an IE task, and several representations along the key dimensions of sparsity and polysemy.

Most previous work on domain adaptation has focused on the case where some labeled data is available in both the source and target domains (Daumé III, 2007; Jiang and Zhai, 2007; Daumé III and Marcu, 2006; Finkel and Manning, 2009; Dredze et al., 2010; Dredze and Crammer, 2008). Learning bounds are known (Blitzer et al., 2007; Mansour et al., 2009). Daumé III *et al.* (2010) use semi-supervised learning to incorporate labeled and unlabeled data from the target domain. In contrast, we investigate a domain adaptation setting where no labeled data is available for the target domain.

3 Representations

A *representation* is a set of features that describe instances for a classifier. Formally, let $\mathcal{X}$ be an instance set, and let $\mathcal{Z}$ be the set of labels for a classification task. A representation is a function $R : \mathcal{X} \to \mathcal{Y}$ for some suitable feature space $\mathcal{Y}$ (such as $\mathbb{R}^d$). We refer to dimensions of $\mathcal{Y}$ as *features*, and for an instance $x \in \mathcal{X}$ we refer to values for particular dimensions of $R(x)$ as features of x.

3.1 Traditional POS-Tagging Representations

As a baseline for POS tagging experiments and an example of our terminology, we describe a representation used in traditional supervised POS taggers. The instance set $\mathcal{X}$ is the set of English sentences, and $\mathcal{Z}$ is the set of POS tag sequences. A traditional representation TRAD-R maps a sentence $\mathbf{x} \in \mathcal{X}$ to a sequence of boolean-valued vectors, one vector per

Representation	Feature
TRAD-R	$\forall_w \mathbf{1}[x_i = w]$ $\forall_{s \in \text{Suffixes}} \mathbf{1}[x_i \text{ ends with } s]$ $\mathbf{1}[x_i \text{ contains a digit}]$
NGRAM-R	$\forall_{\mathbf{w}',\mathbf{w}''} P(\mathbf{w}'w\mathbf{w}'')/P(w)$
HMM-TOKEN-R	$\forall_k \mathbf{1}[y_i* = k]$
HMM-TYPE-R	$\forall_k P(y = k \| x = w)$
I-HMM-TOKEN-R	$\forall_{j,k} \mathbf{1}[y_{i,j}* = k]$
BROWN-TOKEN-R	$\forall_{j \in \{-2,-1,0,1,2\}}$ $\forall_{p \in \{4,6,10,20\}}$ prefix(y_{i+j}, p)
BROWN-TYPE-R	$\forall_p$ prefix(y, p)
LATTICE-TOKEN-R	$\forall_{j,k} \mathbf{1}[y_{i,j}* = k]$
LATTICE-TYPE-R	$\forall_{\mathbf{k}} P(\mathbf{y} = \mathbf{k} \| x = w)$

Table 1: Summary of features provided by our representations. $\forall_a \mathbf{1}[g(a)]$ represents a set of boolean features, one for each value of a, where the feature is true iff $g(a)$ is true. x_i represents a token at position i in sentence $\mathbf{x}$, w represents a word type, Suffixes $=$ $\{$-ing,-ogy,-ed,-s,-ly,-ion,-tion,-ity$\}$, k (and $\mathbf{k}$) represents a value for a latent state (set of latent states) in a latent-variable model, $\mathbf{y}*$ represents the optimal setting of latent states $\mathbf{y}$ for $\mathbf{x}$, y_i is the latent variable for x_i, and $y_{i,j}$ is the latent variable for x_i at layer j. prefix(y,p) is the p-length prefix of the Brown cluster y.

word x_i in the sentence. Dimensions for each latent vector include indicators for the word type of x_i and various orthographic features. Table 1 presents the full list of features in TRAD-R. Since our IE task classifies word types rather than tokens, this baseline is not appropriate for that task. Below, we describe how we can learn representations R by using a variety of language models, for use in both our IE and POS tagging tasks. All representations for POS tagging inherit the features from TRAD-R; all representations for IE do not.

3.2 Ngram Representations

N-gram representations model a word type w in terms of the n-gram contexts in which w appears in a corpus. Specifically, for word w we generate the vector $P(\mathbf{w}'w\mathbf{w}'')/P(w)$, the conditional probability of observing the word sequence $\mathbf{w}'$ to the left and $\mathbf{w}''$ to the right of w. The experimental section describes the particular corpora and language modeling methods used for estimating probabilities.

3.3 HMM-based Representations

In previous work, we have implemented several representations based on HMMs (Rabiner, 1989), which we used for both POS tagging (Huang and Yates, 2009) and IE (Downey et al., 2007b). An HMM is a generative probabilistic model that generates each word x_i in the corpus conditioned on a latent variable y_i. Each y_i in the model takes on integral values from 1 to K, and each one is generated by the latent variable for the preceding word, y_{i-1}. The joint distribution for a corpus $\mathbf{x} = (x_1, \ldots, x_N)$ and a set of state vectors $\mathbf{y} = (y_1, \ldots, y_N)$ is given by: $P(\mathbf{x}, \mathbf{y}) = \prod_i P(x_i|y_i)P(y_i|y_{i-1})$. Using Expectation-Maximization (EM) (Dempster et al., 1977), it is possible to estimate the distributions for $P(x_i|y_i)$ and $P(y_i|y_{i-1})$ from unlabeled data.

We construct two different representations from HMMs, one for POS tagging and one for IE. For POS tagging, we use the Viterbi algorithm to produce the optimal setting $\mathbf{y}*$ of the latent states for a given sentence $\mathbf{x}$, or $\mathbf{y}* = \arg\max_{\mathbf{y}} P(\mathbf{x}, \mathbf{y})$. We use the value of y_i* as a new feature for x_i that represents a cluster of distributionally-similar words. For IE, we require features for word types w, rather than tokens x_i. We use the K-dimensional vector that represents the distribution $P(y|x = w)$ as the feature vector for word type w. This set of features represents a "soft clustering" of w into K different clusters. We refer to these representations as HMM-TOKEN-R and HMM-TYPE-R, respectively.

Because HMM-based representations offer a small number of discrete states as features, they have a much greater potential to combat feature sparsity than do ngram models. Furthermore, for token-based representations, these models can potentially handle polysemy better than ngram language models by providing different features in different contexts.

We also compare against a variation of the HMM from our previous work (Huang and Yates, 2010a), henceforth HY10. This model independently trains M separate HMM models on the same corpus, initializing each one randomly. We can then use the Viterbi-optimal decoded latent state of each independent HMM model as a separate feature for a token. We refer to this language model as an I-HMM, and the representation as I-HMM-TOKEN-R.

Finally, we compare against Brown clusters (Brown et al., 1992) as learned features. Although not traditionally described as such, Brown clustering involves constructing an HMM model in which each type is restricted to having exactly one latent state that may generate it. Brown *et al.* describe a greedy agglomerative clustering algorithm for training this model on unlabeled text. Following Turian *et al.* (2010), we use Percy Liang's implementation of this algorithm for our comparison, and we test runs with 100, 320, and 1000 clusters. We use features from these clusters identical to Turian *et al.*'s.[1] Turian *et al.* have shown that Brown clusters match or exceed the performance of neural network-based language models in domain adaptation experiments for named-entity recognition, as well as in-domain experiments for NER and chunking.

4 A Novel Lattice Language Model Representation

Our final language model is a novel latent-variable language model with rich latent structure, shown in Figure 1. The model contains a lattice of $M \times N$ latent states, where N is the number of words in a sentence and M is the number of layers in the model. We can justify the choice of this model from a linguistic perspective as a way to capture the multi-dimensional nature of words. Linguists have long argued that words have many different features in a high dimensional space: they can be separately described by part of speech, gender, number, case, person, tense, voice, aspect, mass vs. count, and a host of semantic categories (agency, animate vs. inanimate, physical vs. abstract, etc.), to name a few (Sag et al., 2003). Our model seeks to capture a multi-dimensional representation of words by creating a separate layer of latent variables for each dimension. The values of the M layers of latent variables for a single word can be used as M distinct features in our representation. The I-HMM attempts to model the same intuition, but unlike a lattice model the I-HMM layers are entirely independent, and as a result there is no mechanism to enforce that the layers model different dimensions. Duh (2005) previously used a 2-layer lattice for tagging and chunking, but in a supervised setting rather than for representation learning.

Let $Cliq(\mathbf{x}, \mathbf{y})$ represent the set of all maximal cliques in the graph of the MRF model for $\mathbf{x}$ and $\mathbf{y}$.

[1]Percy Liang's implementation is available at *http://metaoptimize.com/projects/wordreprs/*. Turian *et al.* also tested a run with 3200 clusters in their experiments, which we have been training for months, but which has not finished in time for publication.

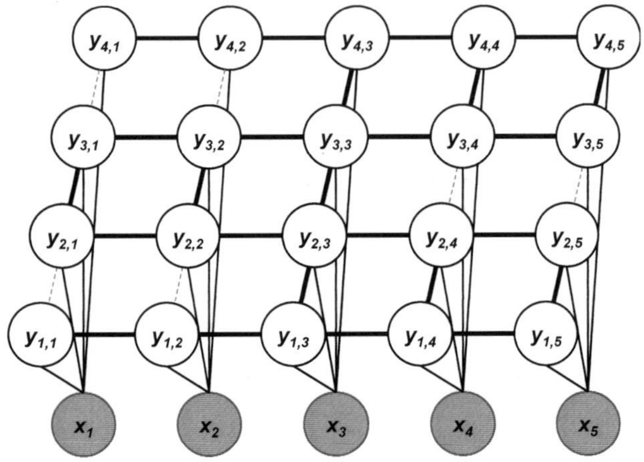

Figure 1: The Partial Lattice MRF (PL-MRF) Model for a 5-word sentence and a 4-layer lattice. Dashed gray edges are part of a full lattice, but not the PL-MRF.

Expressing the lattice model in log-linear form, we can write the marginal probability $P(\mathbf{x})$ of a given sentence $\mathbf{x}$ as:

$$\sum_{\mathbf{y}} \frac{\prod_{c \in Cliq(\mathbf{x},\mathbf{y})} \text{score}(c, \mathbf{x}, \mathbf{y})}{\sum_{\mathbf{x}',\mathbf{y}'} \prod_{c \in Cliq(\mathbf{x}',\mathbf{y}')} \text{score}(c, \mathbf{x}', \mathbf{y}')}$$

where $\text{score}(c, \mathbf{x}, \mathbf{y}) = \exp(\theta_c \cdot \mathbf{f}_c(\mathbf{x}_c, \mathbf{y}_c))$. Our model includes parameters for transitions between two adjacent latent variables on layer j: $\theta^{trans}_{i,s,i+1,s',j}$ for $y_{i,j} = s$ and $y_{i+1,j} = s'$. It also includes observation parameters for latent variables and tokens, as well as for pairs of adjacent latent variables in different layers and their tokens: $\theta^{obs}_{i,j,s,w}$ and $\theta^{obs}_{i,j,s,j+1,s',w}$ for $y_{i,j} = s$, $y_{i,j+1} = s'$, and $x_i = w$.

Computationally, the lattice MRF is preferable to a naïve Factorial HMM (Ghahramani and Jordan, 1997) representation, which would require $O(2^M)$ parameters for an M-layer model. However, exact training and inference in supervised settings are still intractable for this model (Sutton et al., 2007), and thus it has not yet been explored as a language model, which requires even more difficult, unsupervised training. Training is intractable in part because of the difficulty in enumerating and summing over the exponentially-many configurations $\mathbf{y}$ for a given $\mathbf{x}$. We address this difficulty in two ways: by modifying the model, and by modifying the training procedure.

4.1 Partial Lattice MRF

Instead of the full lattice model, we construct a *Partial Lattice MRF* (PL-MRF) model by deleting certain edges between latent layers of the model (dashed gray edges in Figure 1). Let $c = \lfloor \frac{N}{2} \rfloor$, where N is the length of the sentence. If $i < c$ and j is odd, or if j is even and $i > c$, we delete edges between $y_{i,j}$ and $y_{i,j+1}$. The same lattice of nodes remains, but fewer edges and paths. A central "trunk" at $i = c$ connects all layers of the lattice, and branches from this trunk connect either to the branches in the layer above or the layer below (but not both). The result is a model that retains most[2] of the edges of the full model. Additionally, the pruned model makes the branches conditionally independent from one another, except through the trunk. For instance, the right branch at layers 1 and 2 in Figure 1 ($y_{1,4}, y_{1,5}, y_{2,4}$, and $y_{2,5}$) are disconnected from the right branch at layers 3 and 4 ($y_{3,4}, y_{3,5}, y_{4,4}$, and $y_{4,5}$), except through the trunk and the observed nodes. As a result, excluding the observed nodes, this model has a low *tree-width* of 2 (excluding observed nodes), and a variety of efficient dynamic programming and message-passing algorithms for training and inference can be readily applied (Bodlaender, 1988).[3] Our inference algorithm passes information from the branches inwards to the trunk, and then upward along the trunk, in time $O(K^4MN)$.

As with our HMM models, we create two representations from PL-MRFs, one for tokens and one for types. For tokens, we decode the model to compute $\mathbf{y}*$, the matrix of optimal latent state values for sentence $\mathbf{x}$. For each layer j and and each possible latent state value k, we add a boolean feature for token x_i that is true iff $\mathbf{y}*_{i,j} = k$. For types, we compute distributions over the latent state space. Let $\mathbf{y}$ be the column vector of latent variables for word x. For each possible configuration of values $\mathbf{k}$ of the latent variables $\mathbf{y}$, we add a real-valued features for x given by $P(\mathbf{y} = \mathbf{k}|x = w)$. We refer to these two representations as LATTICE-TOKEN-R and LATTICE-TYPE-R, respectively.

4.2 Parameter Estimation

We train the PL-MRF using contrastive estimation, which iteratively optimizes the following objective function on a corpus $\mathbf{X}$:

$$\sum_{\mathbf{x}\in\mathbf{X}} \log \frac{\sum_{\mathbf{y}} \prod_{c\in Cliq(\mathbf{x},\mathbf{y})} \text{score}(c, \mathbf{x}, \mathbf{y})}{\sum_{\mathbf{x}'\in\mathcal{N}(\mathbf{x}),\mathbf{y}'} \prod_{c\in Cliq(\mathbf{x}',\mathbf{y}')} \text{score}(c, \mathbf{x}', \mathbf{y}')}$$

where $\mathcal{N}(\mathbf{x})$, the neighborhood of $\mathbf{x}$, indicates a set of perturbed variations of the original sentence $\mathbf{x}$. Contrastive estimation seeks to move probability mass away from the perturbed neighborhood sentences and onto the original sentence. We use a neighborhood function that includes all sentences which can be obtained from the original sentence by swapping the order of a consecutive pair of words. Training uses gradient descent over this non-convex objective function with a standard software package (Liu and Nocedal, 1989) and converges to a local maximum (Smith and Eisner, 2005).

For tractability, we modify the training procedure to train the PL-MRF one layer at a time. Let θ_i represent the set of parameters relating to features of layer i, and let $\theta_{\neg i}$ represent all other parameters. We fix $\theta_{\neg 0} = \mathbf{0}$, and optimize θ_0 using contrastive estimation. After convergence, we fix $\theta_{\neg 1}$, and optimize θ_1, and so on. We use a convergence threshold of 10^{-6}, and each layer typically converges in under 100 iterations.

5 Domain Adaptation for a POS Tagger

We evaluate the representations described above on a POS tagging task in a domain adaptation setting.

5.1 Experimental Setup

We use the same experimental setup as in HY10: the Penn Treebank (Marcus et al., 1993) Wall Street Journal portion for our labeled training data; 561 MEDLINE sentences (9576 types, 14554 tokens, 23% OOV tokens) from the Penn BioIE project (PennBioIE, 2005) for our labeled test set; and all of the unlabeled text from the Penn Treebank WSJ portion plus a MEDLINE corpus of 71,306 unlabeled sentences to train our language models. The two texts come from two very different domains, making this data a tough test for domain adaptation.

We use an open source Conditional Random Field (CRF) (Lafferty et al., 2001) software package[4] designed by Sunita Sarawagi and William W. Cohen to implement our supervised models. Let $\mathbf{X}$ be a training corpus, $\mathbf{Z}$ the corresponding labels, and R a representation function. For each token x_i in $\mathbf{X}$, we include a parameter in our CRF model for all features $R(x_i)$ and all possible labels in $\mathbf{Z}$. Furthermore, we include transition parameters for pairs of consecutive labels z_i, z_{i+1}.

[2] As $M, N \to \infty$, 5 out of every 6 edges are kept.

[3] *c.f.* a tree-width of min(M,N) for the unpruned model

[4] Available from *http://sourceforge.net/projects/crf/*

For representations, we tested TRAD-R, NGRAM-R, HMM-TOKEN-R, I-HMM-TOKEN-R (between 2 and 8 layers), and LATTICE-TOKEN-R (8, 12, 16, and 20 layers). Following HY10, each latent node in the I-HMMs have 80 possible values, creating $80^8 \approx 10^{15}$ possible configurations of the 8-layer I-HMM for a single word. Each node in the PL-MRF is binary, creating a much smaller number ($2^{20} \approx 10^6$) of possible configurations for each word in a 20-layer representation. NGRAM-R was trained using an unsmoothed trigram model on the Web 1Tgram corpus. To keep the feature set manageable, we included the top 500 most common ngrams for each word type, and then used mutual information on the training data to select the top 10,000 most relevant ngram features for all word types. We incorporated ngram features as binary values indicating whether x_i appeared with the ngram or not. We also report on the performance of Brown clusters and Blitzer *et al.*'s Structural Correspondence Learning (SCL) (2006) technique, which uses manually-selected "pivot" words (like "of", "the") to learn domain-independent features. Finally, we compare against the self-training CRF technique from HY10.

5.2 Results and Discussion

For each representation, we measured the accuracy of the POS tagger on the biomedical test text. Table 2 shows the results for the best variation of each kind of model — 20 layers for the PL-MRF, 7 layers for the I-HMM, and 1000 clusters for the Brown clustering. All language model representations significantly outperform the SCL model and the TRAD-R baseline. The novel PL-MRF model outperforms the previous state of the art, the I-HMM model, and much of the performance increase comes from a 11.3% relative reduction in error on words that appear in biomedical texts but not in newswire texts. Both graphical model representations significantly outperform the ngram model, which is trained on far more text. For comparison, our best model, the PL-MRF, achieved a 96.8% in-domain accuracy on sections 22-24 of the Penn Treebank, about 0.5% shy of a state-of-the-art in-domain system (Shen et al., 2007) with more sophisticated supervised learning.

We expected that language model representations perform well in part because they provide meaningful features for sparse and polysemous words. To test this, we selected 109 polysemous word types

model	% error	OOV % error
TRAD-R	11.7	32.7
TRAD-R+self-training	11.5	29.6
SCL	11.1	-
BROWN-TOKEN-R	10.8	25.4
HMM-TOKEN-R	9.5	24.8
NGRAM-R	6.9	24.4
I-HMM-TOKEN-R	6.7	24
LATTICE-TOKEN-R	**6.2**	**21.3**
SCL+500bio	3.9	-

Table 2: PL-MRF representations reduce error by 7.5% relative to the previous state-of-the-art I-HMM, and approach within 2.3% absolute error a SCL+500bio model with access to 500 labeled sentences from the target domain. 1.8% of the tags in the test set are new tags that do not occur in the WSJ training data, so an error rate of 3.9+1.8 = 5.7% error is a reasonable bound for the best possible performance of a model that has seen no examples from the target domain.

from our test data, along with 296 non-polysemous word types, chosen based on POS tags and manual inspection. We further define sparse word types as those that appear 5 times or fewer in all of our unlabeled data, and non-sparse word types as those that appear at least 50 times in our unlabeled data. Table 3 shows results on these subsets of the data.

As expected, all of our language models outperform the baseline by a larger margin on polysemous words than on non-polysemous words. The margin between graphical model representations and the ngram model also increases on polysemous words, presumably because the Viterbi decoding of these models takes into account the tokens in the surrounding sentence. The same behavior is evident for sparsity: all of the language model representations outperform the baseline by a larger margin on sparse words than not-sparse words, and all of the graphical models perform better relative to the ngram model on sparse words as well. Thus representations based on graphical models address two key issues in building representations for POS tagging.

6 Information Extraction Experiments

In this section, we evaluate our learned representations on a different task that investigates the ability of each representation to capture semantic, rather than syntactic, information. Specifically, we inves-

	POS Tagging				Information Extraction			
	polys.	not polys.	sparse	not sparse	polys.	not polys.	sparse	not sparse
tokens/types	159	4321	463	12194	222	210	266	166
categories	-	-	-	-	12	4	13	3
TRAD-R	59.5	78.5	52.5	89.6	-	-	-	-
Ngram	68.2	85.3	61.8	94.0	0.07	0.17	0.06	0.25
HMM	67.9	83.4	60.2	91.6	**0.14**	**0.26**	**0.15**	**0.32**
(-Ngram)	(-0.3)	(-1.9)	(-1.6)	(-2.4)	**(+0.07)**	**(+0.09)**	**(+0.09)**	**(+0.07)**
I-HMM	**75.6**	85.2	62.9	94.5	-	-	-	-
(-Ngram)	**(+7.4)**	(-0.1)	(+1.1)	(+0.5)	-	-	-	-
PL-MRF	70.5	**86.9**	**65.2**	**94.6**	0.09	0.15	0.1	0.19
(-Ngram)	(+2.3)	**(+1.6)**	**(+3.4)**	**(+0.6)**	(+0.02)	(-0.02)	(+0.04)	(-0.06)

Table 3: Graphical models consistently outperform ngram models by a larger margin on sparse words than not-sparse words. On polysemous words, the difference between graphical model performance and ngram performance grows for POS tagging, where the context surrounding polysemous words is available to the language model, but not for information extraction. For tagging, we show number of tokens and accuracies. For IE, we show number of types, categories, and AUCs.

tigate a *set-expansion* task in which we're given a corpus and a few "seed" noun phrases from a semantic category (e.g. Superheroes), and our goal is to identify other examples of the category in the corpus. This is a *weakly-supervised* task because we are given only a handful of examples of the category, rather than a large sample of positively and negatively labeled training examples.

Existing set-expansion techniques utilize the distributional hypothesis: candidate noun phrases for a given semantic class are ranked based on how similar their contextual distributions are to those of the seeds. Here, we measure how performance on the set-expansion task varies when we employ different representations for the contextual distributions.

6.1 Methods

The set-expansion task we address is formalized as follows: given a corpus, a set of seeds from some semantic category C, and a separate set of candidate phrases P, output a ranking of the phrases in P in decreasing order of likelihood of membership in C.

For any given representation R, the set-expansion algorithm we investigate is straightforward: we create a prototypical "seed representation vector" equal to the mean of the representation vectors for each of the seeds. Then, we rank candidate phrases in increasing order of the distance between the candidate phrase representation and the seed representation vector. As a measure of distance between representations, we compute the average of five standard distance measures, including KL and Jensen-Shannon divergence, and cosine, Euclidean, and L1 distance. In experiments, we found that improving upon this simple averaging was not easy—in fact, tuning a weighted average of the distance measures for each representation did not improve results significantly on held-out data.

Because set expansion is performed at the level of word types rather than tokens, it requires type-based representations. We compare HMM-TYPE-R, NGRAM-R, LATTICE-TYPE-R, and BROWN-TYPE-R in this experiment. We used a 25-state HMM, and the same PL-MRF as in the previous section. Following previous set-expansion experiments with n-grams (Ahuja and Downey, 2010), we employ a trigram model with Kneser-Ney smoothing for NGRAM-R. For Brown clusters, instead of distance metrics like KL divergence (which assume distributions), we rank extractions by the number of matches between a word's BROWN-TYPE-R features and seed features.

6.2 Data Sets

We utilized a set of approximately 100,000 sentences of Web text, joining multi-word named entities in the corpus into single tokens using the Lex algorithm (Downey et al., 2007a). This process enables each named entity (the focus of the set-expansion experiments) to be treated as a single token, with a single representation vector for comparison. We developed all word type representations

model	AUC
HMM-TYPE-R	**0.18**
BROWN-TYPE-R	0.16
LATTICE-TYPE-R	0.11
NGRAM-R	0.10
Random baseline	0.10

Table 4: HMM-TYPE-R outperforms the other methods, improving performance by 12.5% over Brown clusters, and by 80% over the traditional NGRAM-R.

using this corpus.

To obtain examples of multiple semantic categories, we utilized selected Wikipedia "listOf" pages from (Pantel et al., 2009) and augmented these with our own manually defined categories, such that each list contained at least ten distinct examples occurring in our corpus. In all, we had 432 examples across 16 distinct categories such as Countries, Greek Islands, and Police TV Dramas.

6.3 Results

For each semantic category, we tested five different random selections of five seed examples, treating the unselected members of the category as positive examples, and all other candidate phrases as negative examples. We evaluate using the area under the precision-recall curve (AUC) metric.

The results are shown in Table 4. All representations improve performance over a random baseline, equal to the average AUC over five random orderings for each category, and the graphical models outperform the ngram representation. HMM-TYPE-R performs the best overall, and Brown clustering with 1000 clusters is comparable (320 and 100 cluster perform slightly worse).

As with POS tagging, we expect that language model representations improve performance on the IE task by providing informative features for sparse word types. However, because the IE task classifies word types rather than tokens, we expect the representations to provide less benefit for polysemous word types. To test these hypotheses, we measured how IE performance changed in sparse or polysemous settings. We identified polysemous categories as those for which fewer than 90% of the category members had the category as a clear dominant sense (estimated manually); other categories were considered non-polysemous. Categories whose members had a median number of occurrences in the corpus less than 30 were deemed sparse, and others non-sparse. IE performance on these subsets of the data are shown in Table 3. Both graphical model representations outperform the ngram representation more on sparse words, as expected. For polysemy, the picture is mixed: the PL-MRF outperform n-grams on polysemous categories, whereas HMM's performance advantage over n-grams decreases.

One surprise on the IE task is that the LATTICE-TYPE-R performs significantly less well than the HMM-TYPE-R, whereas the reverse is true on POS tagging. We suspect that the difference is due to the issue of classifying types vs. tokens. Because of their more complex structure, PL-MRFs tend to depend more on transition parameters than do HMMs. Furthermore, our decision to train the PL-MRFs using contrastive estimation with a neighborhood that swaps consecutive pairs of words also tends to emphasize transition parameters. As a result, we believe the posterior distribution over latent states given a word type is more informative in our HMM model than the PL-MRF model. We measured the entropy of these distributions for the two models, and found that $H(P_{\text{PL-MRF}}(\mathbf{y}|x = w)) = 9.95$ bits, compared with $H(P_{\text{HMM}}(\mathbf{y}|x = w)) = 2.74$ bits, which supports the hypothesis that the drop in the PL-MRF's performance on IE is due to its dependence on transition parameters. Further experiments are warranted to investigate this issue.

7 Conclusion and Future Work

Our investigation into language models as representations shows that graphical models can be used to combat polysemy and, especially, sparsity in representations for weakly-supervised classifiers. Our novel factorial graphical model yields a state-of-the-art POS tagger for domain adaptation, and HMMs improve significantly over all other representations in an information extraction task. Important directions for future research include models for handling polysemy in IE, and richer language models that incorporate more linguistic intuitions about how words interact with their contexts.

Acknowledgments

This research was supported in part by NSF grant IIS-1065397 and a Microsoft New Faculty Fellowship.

References

Arun Ahuja and Doug Downey. 2010. Improved extraction assessment through better language models. In *Proceedings of the Annual Meeting of the North American Chapter of the Association of Computational Linguistics (NAACL-HLT)*.

Shai Ben-David, John Blitzer, Koby Crammer, Alex Kulesza, Fernando Pereira, and Jenn Wortman. 2009. A theory of learning from different domains. *Machine Learning*, (to appear).

Y. Bengio, J. Louradour, R. Collobert, and J. Weston. 2009. Curriculum learning. In *International Conference on Machine Learning (ICML)*.

Yoshua Bengio. 2008. Neural net language models. *Scholarpedia*, 3(1):3881.

Daniel M. Bikel. 2004. Intricacies of Collins Parsing Model. *Computational Linguistics*, 30(4):479–511.

David M. Blei, Andrew Y. Ng, and Michael I. Jordan. 2003. Latent dirichlet allocation. *Journal of Machine Learning Research*, 3:993–1022, January.

John Blitzer, Ryan McDonald, and Fernando Pereira. 2006. Domain adaptation with structural correspondence learning. In *EMNLP*.

John Blitzer, Koby Crammer, Alex Kulesza, Fernando Pereira, and Jenn Wortman. 2007. Learning bounds for domain adaptation. In *Advances in Neural Information Processing Systems*.

Hans L. Bodlaender. 1988. Dynamic programming on graphs with bounded treewidth. In *Proc. 15th International Colloquium on Automata, Languages and Programming*, pages 105–118.

P. F. Brown, P. V. deSouza, R. L. Mercer, V. J. D. Pietra, and J. C. Lai. 1992. Class-based n-gram models of natural language. *Computational Linguistics*, pages 467–479.

M. Candito and B. Crabbe. 2009. Improving generative statistical parsing with semi-supervised word clustering. In *IWPT*, pages 138–141.

R. Collobert and J. Weston. 2008. A unified architecture for natural language processing: Deep neural networks with multitask learning. In *International Conference on Machine Learning (ICML)*.

Hal Daumé III and Daniel Marcu. 2006. Domain adaptation for statistical classifiers. *Journal of Artificial Intelligence Research*, 26.

Hal Daumé III, Abhishek Kumar, and Avishek Saha. 2010. Frustratingly easy semi-supervised domain adaptation. In *Proceedings of the ACL Workshop on Domain Adaptation (DANLP)*.

Hal Daumé III. 2007. Frustratingly easy domain adaptation. In *ACL*.

S. C. Deerwester, S. T. Dumais, T. K. Landauer, G. W. Furnas, and R. A. Harshman. 1990. Indexing by latent semantic analysis. *Journal of the American Society of Information Science*, 41(6):391–407.

Arthur Dempster, Nan Laird, and Donald Rubin. 1977. Likelihood from incomplete data via the EM algorithm. *Journal of the Royal Statistical Society, Series B*, 39(1):1–38.

D. Downey, M. Broadhead, and O. Etzioni. 2007a. Locating complex named entities in web text. In *Procs. of the 20th International Joint Conference on Artificial Intelligence (IJCAI 2007)*.

Doug Downey, Stefan Schoenmackers, and Oren Etzioni. 2007b. Sparse information extraction: Unsupervised language models to the rescue. In *ACL*.

Mark Dredze and Koby Crammer. 2008. Online methods for multi-domain learning and adaptation. In *Proceedings of EMNLP*, pages 689–697.

Mark Dredze, Alex Kulesza, and Koby Crammer. 2010. Multi-domain learning by confidence weighted parameter combination. *Machine Learning*, 79.

Kevin Duh. 2005. Jointly labeling multiple sequences: A Factorial HMM approach. In *43rd Annual Meeting of the Assoc. for Computational Linguistics (ACL 2005), Student Research Workshop*.

Jenny Rose Finkel and Christopher D. Manning. 2009. Hierarchical bayesian domain adaptation. In *Proceedings of HLT-NAACL*, pages 602–610.

Zoubin Ghahramani and Michael I. Jordan. 1997. Factorial hidden markov models. *Machine Learning*, 29(2-3):245–273.

Z. Harris. 1954. Distributional structure. *Word*, 10(23):146–162.

D. Hindle. 1990. Noun classification from predicage-argument structures. In *ACL*.

T. Honkela. 1997. Self-organizing maps of words for natural language processing applications. In *Proceedings of the International ICSC Symposium on Soft Computing*.

Fei Huang and Alexander Yates. 2009. Distributional representations for handling sparsity in supervised sequence labeling. In *Proceedings of the Annual Meeting of the Association for Computational Linguistics (ACL)*.

Fei Huang and Alexander Yates. 2010a. Exploring representation-learning approaches to domain adaptation. In *Proceedings of the ACL 2010 Workshop on Domain Adaptation for Natural Language Processing (DANLP)*.

Fei Huang and Alexander Yates. 2010b. Open-domain semantic role labeling by modeling word spans. In *Proceedings of the Annual Meeting of the Association for Computational Linguistics (ACL)*.

Jing Jiang and ChengXiang Zhai. 2007. Instance weighting for domain adaptation in NLP. In *ACL*.

S. Kaski. 1998. Dimensionality reduction by random mapping: Fast similarity computation for clustering. In *IJCNN*, pages 413–418.

T. Koo, X. Carreras, and M. Collins. 2008. Simple semi-supervised dependency parsing. In *Proceedings of the Annual Meeting of the Association of Computational Linguistics (ACL)*, pages 595–603.

J. Lafferty, Andrew McCallum, and Fernando Pereira. 2001. Conditional random fields: Probabilistic models for segmenting and labeling sequence data. In *Proceedings of the International Conference on Machine Learning*.

D. Lin and X Wu. 2009. Phrase clustering for discriminative learning. In *ACL-IJCNLP*, pages 1030–1038.

D.C. Liu and J. Nocedal. 1989. On the limited memory method for large scale optimization. *Mathematical Programming B*, 45(3):503–528.

Y. Mansour, M. Mohri, and A. Rostamizadeh. 2009. Domain adaptation with multiple sources. In *Advances in Neural Information Processing Systems*.

Mitchell P. Marcus, Mary Ann Marcinkiewicz, and Beatrice Santorini. 1993. Building a large annotated corpus of English: the Penn Treebank. *Computational Linguistics*, 19(2):313–330.

S. Martin, J. Liermann, and H. Ney. 1998. Algorithms for bigram and trigram word clustering. *Speech Communication*, 24:19–37.

A. Mnih and G. E. Hinton. 2009. A scalable hierarchical distributed language model. In *Neural Information Processing Systems (NIPS)*, pages 1081–1088.

P. Pantel, E. Crestan, A. Borkovsky, A. M. Popescu, and V. Vyas. 2009. Web-scale distributional similarity and entity set expansion. In *Proc. of EMNLP*.

PennBioIE. 2005. Mining the bibliome project. *http://bioie.ldc.upenn.edu/*.

F. Pereira, N. Tishby, and L. Lee. 1993. Distributional clustering of English words. In *Proceedings of the Annual Meeting of the Association for Computational Linguistics (ACL)*, pages 183–190.

Lawrence R. Rabiner. 1989. A tutorial on hidden Markov models and selected applications in speech recognition. *Proceedings of the IEEE*, 77(2):257–285.

Ivan A. Sag, Thomas Wasow, and Emily M. Bender. 2003. *Synactic Theory: A Formal Introduction*. CSLI, Stanford, CA, second edition.

M. Sahlgren. 2005. An introduction to random indexing. In *Methods and Applications of Semantic Indexing Workshop at the 7th International Conference on Terminology and Knowledge Engineering (TKE)*.

M. Sahlgren. 2006. *The word-space model: Using distributional analysis to represent syntagmatic and paradigmatic relations between words in high-dimensional vector spaces*. Ph.D. thesis, Stockholm University.

G. Salton and M.J. McGill. 1983. *Introduction to Modern Information Retrieval*. McGraw-Hill.

L. Shen, G. Satta, and A. Joshi. 2007. Guided learning for bidirectional sequence classification. In *Proceedings of the 45th Annual Meeting of the Association of Computational Linguistics (ACL 2007)*, pages 760–767.

Noah A. Smith and Jason Eisner. 2005. Contrastive estimation: Training log-linear models on unlabeled data. In *Proceedings of the 43rd Annual Meeting of the Association for Computational Linguistics (ACL)*, pages 354–362, Ann Arbor, Michigan, June.

Charles Sutton, Andrew McCallum, and Khashayar Rohanimanesh. 2007. Dynamic conditional random fields: Factorized probabilistic models for labeling and segmenting sequence data. *J. Mach. Learn. Res.*, 8:693–723.

Joseph Turian, Lev Ratinov, and Yoshua Bengio. 2010. Word representations: A simple and general method for semi-supervised learning. In *Proceedings of the Annual Meeting of the Association for Computational Linguistics (ACL)*, pages 384–394.

P. D. Turney and P. Pantel. 2010. From frequency to meaning: Vector space models of semantics. *Journal of Artificial Intelligence Research*, 37:141–188.

J. J. Väyrynen, T. Honkela, and L. Lindqvist. 2007. Towards explicit semantic features using independent component analysis. In *Proceedings of the Workshop Semantic Content Acquisition and Representation (SCAR)*.

Jason Weston, Frederic Ratle, and Ronan Collobert. 2008. Deep learning via semi-supervised embedding. In *Proceedings of the 25th International Conference on Machine Learning*.

Hai Zhao, Wenliang Chen, Chunyu Kit, and Guodong Zhou. 2009. Multilingual dependency learning: A huge feature engineering method to semantic dependency parsing. In *CoNLL 2009 Shared Task*.

Automatic Keyphrase Extraction by Bridging Vocabulary Gap *

Zhiyuan Liu, Xinxiong Chen, Yabin Zheng, Maosong Sun
State Key Laboratory of Intelligent Technology and Systems
Tsinghua National Laboratory for Information Science and Technology
Department of Computer Science and Technology
Tsinghua University, Beijing 100084, China
{lzy.thu, cxx.thu, yabin.zheng}@gmail.com, sms@tsinghua.edu.cn

Abstract

Keyphrase extraction aims to select a set of terms from a document as a short summary of the document. Most methods extract keyphrases according to their statistical properties in the given document. Appropriate keyphrases, however, are not always statistically significant or even do not appear in the given document. This makes a large *vocabulary gap* between a document and its keyphrases. In this paper, we consider that a document and its keyphrases both describe the same object but are written in two different languages. By regarding keyphrase extraction as a problem of translating from the language of documents to the language of keyphrases, we use word alignment models in statistical machine translation to learn translation probabilities between the words in documents and the words in keyphrases. According to the translation model, we suggest keyphrases given a new document. The suggested keyphrases are not necessarily statistically frequent in the document, which indicates that our method is more flexible and reliable. Experiments on news articles demonstrate that our method outperforms existing unsupervised methods on precision, recall and F-measure.

1 Introduction

Information on the Web is emerging with the development of Internet. It is becoming more and more important to effectively search and manage information. Keyphrases, as a brief summary of a document, provide a solution to help organize and retrieve documents, which have been widely used in digital libraries and information retrieval (Turney, 2000; Nguyen and Kan, 2007). Due to the explosion of information, it is ineffective for professional human indexers to manually annotate documents with keyphrases. How to automatically extract keyphrases from documents becomes an important research problem, which is usually referred to as *keyphrase extraction*.

Most methods for keyphrase extraction try to extract keyphrases according to their statistical properties. These methods are susceptible to low performance because many appropriate keyphrases may not be statistically frequent or even not appear in the document, especially for short documents. We name the phenomenon as the *vocabulary gap* between documents and keyphrases. For example, a research paper talking about "machine transliteration" may less or even not mention the phrase "machine translation". However, since "machine transliteration" is a sub-field of "machine translation", the phrase "machine translation" is also reasonable to be suggested as a keyphrase to indicate the topics of this paper. Let us take another example: in a news article talking about "iPad" and "iPhone", the word "Apple" may rarely ever come up. However, it is known that both "iPad" and "iPhone" are the products of "Apple", and the word "Apple" may thus be a proper keyphrase of this article.

We can see that, the essential challenge of keyphrase extraction is the vocabulary gap between documents and keyphrases. Therefore, the task of keyphrase extraction is how to capture the semantic relations between the words in documents and in keyphrases so as to bridge the vocabulary gap. In this paper, we provide a new perspective to

*Zhiyuan Liu and Xinxiong Chen have equal contribution to this work.

Proceedings of the Fifteenth Conference on Computational Natural Language Learning, pages 135–144,
Portland, Oregon, USA, 23–24 June 2011. ©2011 Association for Computational Linguistics

documents and their keyphrases: each document and its keyphrases are descriptions to the same object, but the document is written using one language, while keyphrases are written using another language. Therefore, keyphrase extraction can be regarded as a translation problem from the language of documents into the language of keyphrases.

Based on the idea of translation, we use word alignment models (WAM) (Brown et al., 1993) in statistical machine translation (SMT) (Koehn, 2010) and propose a unified framework for keyphrase extraction: (1) From a collection of translation pairs of two languages, WAM learns translation probabilities between the words in the two languages. (2) According to the translation model, we are able to bridge the vocabulary gap and succeed in suggesting appropriate keyphrases, which may not necessarily frequent in their corresponding documents.

As a promising approach to solve the problem of vocabulary gap, SMT has been widely exploited in many applications such as information retrieval (Berger and Lafferty, 1999; Karimzadehgan and Zhai, 2010), image and video annotation (Duygulu et al., 2002), question answering (Berger et al., 2000; Echihabi and Marcu, 2003; Murdock and Croft, 2004; Soricut and Brill, 2006; Xue et al., 2008), query expansion and rewriting (Riezler et al., 2007; Riezler et al., 2008; Riezler and Liu, 2010), summarization (Banko et al., 2000), collocation extraction (Liu et al., 2009b; Liu et al., 2010b) and paraphrasing (Quirk et al., 2004; Zhao et al., 2010). Although SMT is a widely adopted solution to vocabulary gap, for various applications using SMT, the crucial and non-trivial problem is to find appropriate and enough translation pairs for SMT.

The most straightforward translation pairs for keyphrase extraction is document-keyphrase pairs. In practice, however, it is time-consuming to annotate a large collection of documents with keyphrases for sufficient WAM training. In order to solve the problem, we use titles and summaries to build translation pairs with documents. Titles and summaries are usually accompanying with the corresponding documents. In some special cases, titles or summaries may be unavailable. We are also able to extract one or more important sentences from the corresponding documents to construct sufficient translation pairs.

2 State of the Art

Some researchers (Frank et al., 1999; Witten et al., 1999; Turney, 2000) regarded keyphrase extraction as a binary classification problem (is-keyphrase or non-keyphrase) and learned models for classification using training data. These supervised methods need manually annotated training set, which is time-consuming. In this paper, we focus on unsupervised methods for keyphrase extraction.

The most simple unsupervised method for keyphrase extraction is using TFIDF (Salton and Buckley, 1988) to rank the candidate keyphrases and select the top-ranked ones as keyphrases. TFIDF ranks candidate keyphrases only according to their statistical frequencies, which thus fails to suggest keyphrases with low frequencies.

Starting with TextRank (Mihalcea and Tarau, 2004), graph-based ranking methods are becoming the state-of-the-art methods for keyphrase extraction (Liu et al., 2009a; Liu et al., 2010a). Given a document, TextRank first builds a word graph, in which the links between words indicate their semantic relatedness, which are estimated by the word co-occurrences in the document. By executing PageRank (Page et al., 1998) on the graph, we obtain the PageRank score for each word to rank candidate keyphrases.

In TextRank, a low-frequency word will benefit from its high-frequency neighbor words and thus be ranked higher as compared to using TFIDF. This alleviates the problem of vocabulary gap to some extent. TextRank, however, still tends to extract high-frequency words as keyphrases because these words have more opportunities to get linked with other words and obtain higher PageRank scores. Moreover, TextRank usually constructs a word graph simply according to word co-occurrences as an approximation of the semantic relations between words. This will introduce much noise because of connecting semantically unrelated words and highly influence extraction performance.

Some methods have been proposed to improve TextRank, of which ExpandRank (Wan and Xiao, 2008b; Wan and Xiao, 2008a) uses a small number, namely k, of neighbor documents to provide more information of word relatedness for the construction of word graphs. Compared to TextRank, ExpandRank performs better when facing the vocabulary gap by borrowing the information on *document level*. However, the finding of neighbor documents are usually arbitrary. This process may introduce much noise and result in *topic drift* when the document and its so-called neighbor documents are not exactly talking about the same topics.

Another potential approach to alleviate vocabulary gap is latent topic models (Landauer et al., 1998; Hofmann, 1999; Blei et al., 2003), of which latent Dirichlet allocation (LDA) (Blei et al., 2003) is most popular. Latent topic models learn topics from a collection of documents. Using a topic model, we can represent both documents and words as the distributions over latent topics. The semantic relatedness between a word and a document can be computed using the cosine similarities of their topic distributions. The similarity scores can be used as the ranking criterion for keyphrase extraction (Heinrich, 2005; Blei and Lafferty, 2009). On one hand, latent topic models use topics instead of statistical properties of words for ranking, which abates the vocabulary gap problem on *topic level*. On the other hand, the learned topics are usually very coarse, and topic models tend to suggest general words for a given document. Therefore, the method usually fails to capture the specific topics of the document.

In contract to the above-mentioned methods, our method addresses vocabulary gap on *word level*, which prevents from topic drift and works out better performance. In experiments, we will show our method can better solve the problem of vocabulary gap by comparing with TFIDF, TextRank, ExpandRank and LDA.

3 Keyphrase Extraction by Bridging Vocabulary Gap Using WAM

First, we give a formal definition of keyphrase extraction: given a collection of documents D, for each document $d \in D$, keyphrase extraction aims to rank candidate keyphrases according to their likelihood given the document d, i.e., $\Pr(p|d)$ for all $p \in P$, where P is the candidate keyphrase set. Then we select top-M_d ones as keyphrases, where M_d can be fixed or automatically determined by the system. The document d can be regarded as a sequence of words $\mathbf{w}_d = \{w_i\}_1^{N_d}$, where N_d is the length of d.

In Fig. 1, we demonstrate the framework of keyphrase extraction using WAM. We divide the algorithm into three steps: preparing translation pairs, training translation models and extracting keyphrases for a given document. We will introduce the three steps in details from Section 3.1 to Section 3.3.

Input: A large collection of documents D for keyphrase extraction.

Step 1: Prepare Translation Pairs. For each $d \in D$, we may prepare two types of translation pairs:

- **Title-based Pairs**. Use the title t_d of each document d and prepare translation pairs, denote as $\langle D, T \rangle$.
- **Summary-based Pairs**. Use the summary s_d of each document d and prepare translation pairs, denote as $\langle D, S \rangle$.

Step 2: Train Translation Model. Given translation pairs, e.g., $\langle D, T \rangle$, train word-word translation model $\Pr_{\langle D,T \rangle}(t|w)$ using WAM, where w is the word in document language and t is the word in title language.

Step 3: Keyphrase Extraction. For a document d, extract keyphrases according to a trained translation model, e.g., $\Pr_{\langle D,T \rangle}(t|w)$.

1. Measure the importance score $\Pr(w|d)$ of each word w in document d.
2. Compute the ranking score of candidate keyphrase p by
$$\Pr(p|d) = \sum_{t \in p} \sum_{w \in d} \Pr_{\langle D,T \rangle}(t|w) \Pr(w|d) \quad (1)$$
3. Select top-M_d ranked candidate keyphrases according to $\Pr(p|d)$ as the keyphrases of document d.

Figure 1: WAM for keyphrase extraction.

3.1 Preparing Translation Pairs

Training dataset for WAM consists of a number of translation pairs written in two languages. In keyphrase extraction task, we have to construct sufficient translation pairs to capture the semantic relations between documents and keyphrases. Here we propose to construct two types of translation pairs: title-based pairs and summary-based pairs.

3.1.1 Title-based Pairs

Title is usually a short summary of the given document. In most cases, documents such as research papers and news articles have corresponding titles. Therefore, we can use title to construct translation pairs for a document.

WAM assumes each translation pair should be of comparable length. However, a document is usually much longer than title. It will hurt the performance if we fill the length-unbalanced pairs for WAM training. We propose two methods to address the problem: sampling method and split method.

In sampling method, we perform word sampling for each document to make it comparable to the length of its title. Suppose the lengths of a document and its title are N_d and N_t, respectively. For document d, we first build a bag of words $\mathbf{b}_d = \{(w_i, e_i)\}_{i=1}^{W_d}$, where W_d is the number of *unique* words in d, and e_i is the weights of word w_i in d.

In this paper, we use TFIDF scores as the weights of words. Using $\mathbf{b}_d$, we sample words for N_t times with replacement according to the weights of words, and finally form a new bag with N_t words to represent document d. In the sampling result, we keep the most important words in document d. We can thus construct a document-title pair with balanced length.

In split method, we split each document into sentences which are of comparable length to its title. For each sentence, we compute its semantic similarity with the title. There are various methods to measure semantic similarities. In this paper, we use vector space model to represent sentences and titles, and use cosine scores to compute similarities. If the similarity is smaller than a threshold δ, we will discard the sentence; otherwise, we will regard the sentence and title as a translation pair.

Sampling method and split method have their own characteristics. Compared to split method, sampling method loses the order information of words in documents. While split method generates much more translation pairs, which leads to longer training time of WAM. In experiment section, we will investigate the performance of the two methods.

3.1.2 Summary-based Pairs

For most research articles, authors usually provide abstracts to summarize the articles. Many news articles also have short summaries. Suppose each document itself has a short summary, we can use the summary and document to construct translation pairs using either sampling method or split method. Because each summary usually consists of multiple sentences, split method for constructing summary-based pairs has to split both the document and summary into sentences, and the sentence pairs with similarity scores above the threshold are filled in training dataset for WAM.

3.2 Training Translation Models

Without loss of generality, we take title-based pairs as the example to introduce the training process of translation models, and suppose documents are written in one language and titles are written in another language. In this paper, we use IBM Model-1 (Brown et al., 1993) for WAM training. IBM Model-1 is a widely used word alignment algorithm which does not require linguistic knowledge for two languages [1].

In IBM Model-1, for each translation pair $\langle \mathbf{w}_d, \mathbf{w}_t \rangle$, the relationship of the document language $\mathbf{w}_d = \{w_i\}_{i=0}^{L_d}$ and the title language $\mathbf{w}_t = \{t_i\}_{i=0}^{L_t}$ is connected via a hidden variable $\mathbf{a} = \{a_i\}_{i=1}^{L_d}$ describing an alignment mapping from words of documents to words of titles,

$$\Pr(\mathbf{w}_d|\mathbf{w}_t) = \sum_{\mathbf{a}} \Pr(\mathbf{w}_d, \mathbf{a}|\mathbf{w}_t) \quad (2)$$

For example, $a_j = i$ indicates word w_j in $\mathbf{w}_d$ at position j is aligned to word t_i in $\mathbf{w}_t$ at position i. The alignment $\mathbf{a}$ also contains empty-word alignments $a_j = 0$ which align words of documents to an empty word. IBM Model-1 can be trained using Expectation-Maximization (EM) algorithm (Dempster et al., 1977) in an unsupervised fashion. Using IBM Model-1, we can obtain the translation probabilities of two language-vocabularies, i.e., $\Pr(t|w)$ and $\Pr(w|t)$, where w is a word in document vocabulary and t is a word in title vocabulary.

IBM Model-1 will produce one-to-many alignments from one language to another language, and the trained model is thus asymmetric. Hence, we can

[1] We have also employed more sophisticated WAM algorithms such as IBM Model-3 for keyphrase extraction. However, these methods did not achieve better performance than the simple IBM Model-1. Therefore, in this paper we only demonstrate the experimental results using IBM Model-1.

train two different translation models by assigning translation pairs in two directions, i.e., (document $\rightarrow$ title) and (title $\rightarrow$ document). We denote the former model as $\Pr_{\text{d2t}}$ and the latter as $\Pr_{\text{t2d}}$. We define $\Pr_{\langle D,T \rangle}(t|w)$ in Eq.(1) as the harmonic mean of the two models:

$$\Pr_{\langle D,T \rangle}(t|w) \propto \left(\frac{\lambda}{\Pr_{\text{d2t}}(t|w)} + \frac{(1-\lambda)}{\Pr_{\text{t2d}}(t|w)} \right)^{-1} \quad (3)$$

where λ is the harmonic factor to combine the two models. When $\lambda = 1.0$ or $\lambda = 0.0$, it simply uses model $\Pr_{\text{d2t}}$ or $\Pr_{\text{t2d}}$, correspondingly. Using the translation probabilities $\Pr(t|w)$ we can bridge the vocabulary gap between documents and keyphrases.

3.3 Keyphrase Extraction

Given a document d, we rank candidate keyphrases by computing their likelihood $\Pr(p|d)$. Each candidate keyphrase p may be composed of multiple words. As shown in (Hulth, 2003), most keyphrases are noun phrases. Following (Mihalcea and Tarau, 2004; Wan and Xiao, 2008b), we simply select noun phrases from the given document as candidate keyphrases with the help of POS tags. For each word t, we compute its likelihood given d, $\Pr(t|d) = \sum_{w \in d} \Pr(t|w)\Pr(w|d)$, where $\Pr(w|d)$ is the weight of the word w in d, which is measured using normalized TFIDF scores. $\Pr(t|w)$ is the translation probabilities obtained from WAM training.

Using the scores of all words in candidate keyphrases, we compute the ranking score of each candidate keyphrase by summing up the scores of each word in the candidate keyphrase, i.e., $\Pr(p|d) = \sum_{t \in p} \Pr(t|d)$. In all, the ranking scores of candidate keyphrases is formalized in Eq. (1) of Fig. 1. According to the ranking scores, we can suggest top-M_d ranked candidates as the keyphrases, where M_d is the number of suggested keyphrases to the document d pre-specified by users or systems. We can also consider the number of words in the candidate keyphrase as a normalization factor to Eq. (1), which will be our future work.

4 Experiments

To perform experiments, we crawled a collection of 13,702 Chinese news articles [2] from `www.163.com`, one of the most popular news websites in China. The news articles are composed of various topics including science, technology, politics, sports, arts, society and military. All news articles are manually annotated with keyphrases by website editors, and all these keyphrases come from the corresponding documents. Each news article is also provided with a title and a short summary.

In this dataset, there are 72,900 unique words in documents, and 12,405 unique words in keyphrases. The average lengths of documents, titles and summaries are 971.7 words, 11.6 words, and 45.8 words, respectively. The average number of keyphrases for each document is 2.4. In experiments, we use the annotated titles and summaries to construct translation pairs.

In experiments, we select GIZA++ [3] (Och and Ney, 2003) to train IBM Model-1 using translation pairs. GIZA++, widely used in various applications of statistical machine translation, implements IBM Models 1-5 and an HMM word alignment model.

To evaluate methods, we use the annotated keyphrases by `www.163.com` as the standard keyphrases. If one suggested keyphrase exactly matches one of the standard keyphrases, it is a correct keyphrase. We use precision $p = c_{correct}/c_{method}$, recall $r = c_{correct}/c_{standard}$ and F-measure $f = 2pr/(p+r)$ for evaluation, where $c_{correct}$ is the number of keyphrases correctly suggested by the given method, c_{method} is the number of suggested keyphrases, and $c_{standard}$ is the number of standard keyphrases. The following experiment results are obtained by 5-fold cross validation.

4.1 Evaluation on Keyphrase Extraction

4.1.1 Performance Comparison and Analysis

We use four representative unsupervised methods as baselines for comparison: TFIDF, TextRank (Mihalcea and Tarau, 2004), ExpandRank (Wan and Xiao, 2008b) and LDA (Blei et al., 2003). We denote our method as WAM for short.

In Fig. 2, we demonstrate the precision-recall curves of various methods for keyphrase extraction including TFIDF, TextRank, ExpandRank, LDA and WAM with title-based pairs prepared using

[2] The dataset can be obtained from `http://nlp.csai.tsinghua.edu.cn/~lzy/datasets/ke_wam.html`.

[3] The website for GIZA++ package is `http://code.google.com/p/giza-pp/`.

sampling method (Title-Sa) and split method (Title-Sp), and WAM with summary-based pairs prepared using sampling method (Summ-Sa) and split method (Summ-Sp). For WAM, we set the harmonic factor $\lambda = 1.0$ and threshold $\delta = 0.1$, which is the optimal setting as shown in the later analysis on parameter influence. For TextRank, LDA and ExpandRank, we report their best results after parameter tuning, e.g., the number of topics for LDA is set to 400, and the number of neighbor documents for ExpandRank is set to 5 .

The points on a precision-recall curve represent different numbers of suggested keyphrases from $M_d = 1$ (bottom right) to $M_d = 10$ (upper left), respectively. The closer the curve is to the upper right, the better the overall performance of the method is. In Table 1, we further demonstrate the precision, recall and F-measure scores of various methods when $M_d = 2$ [4]. In Table 1, we also show the statistical variances after $\pm$. From Fig. 2 and Table 1, we have the following observations:

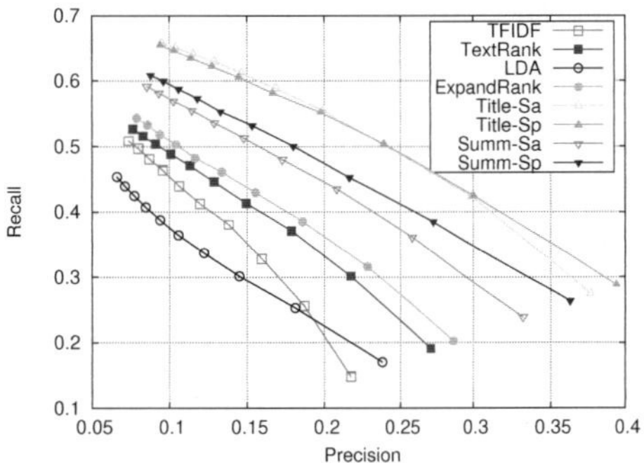

Figure 2: The precision-recall curves of various methods for keyphrase extraction.

First, our method outperforms all baselines. It indicates that the translation perspective is valid for keyphrase extraction. When facing vocabulary gap, TFIDF and TextRank have no solutions, ExpandRank adopts the external information on document level which may introduce noise, and LDA adopts the external information on topic level which may be too coarse. In contrast to these baselines, WAM aims to bridge the vocabulary gap on *word level*, which avoids topic drift effectively.

Method	Precision	Recall	F-measure
TFIDF	0.187	0.256	0.208±0.005
TextRank	0.217	0.301	0.243±0.008
LDA	0.181	0.253	0.203±0.002
ExpandRank	0.228	0.316	0.255±0.007
Title-Sa	0.299	0.424	0.337±0.008
Title-Sp	**0.300**	**0.425**	**0.339±0.010**
Summ-Sa	0.258	0.361	0.289±0.009
Summ-Sp	0.273	0.384	0.307±0.008

Table 1: Precision, recall and F-measure of various methods for keyphrase extraction when $M_d = 2$.

Therefore, our method can better solve the problem of vocabulary gap in keyphrase extraction.

Second, WAM with title-based pairs performs better than summary-based pairs consistently, no matter prepared using sampling method or split method. This indicates the titles are closer to the keyphrase language as compared to summaries. This is also consistent with the intuition that titles are more important than summaries. Meanwhile, we can save training efforts using title-based pairs.

Last but not least, split method achieves better or comparable performance as compared to sampling method on both title-based pairs and summary-based pairs. The reasons are: (1) the split method generates more translation pairs for adequate training than sampling method; and (2) split method also keeps the context of words, which helps to obtain better word alignment, unlike bag-of-words in sampling method.

4.1.2 Influence of Parameters

We also investigate the influence of parameters to WAM with title-based pairs prepared using split method, which achieves the best performance as shown in Fig. 2. The parameters include: harmonic factor λ (described in Eq. 3) and threshold factor δ. Harmonic factor λ controls the weights of the translation models trained in two directions, i.e., $\Pr_{d2t}(t|w)$ and $\Pr_{t2d}(t|w)$ as shown in Eq. (3). As described in Section 3.1.1, using threshold factor δ we filter out the pairs with similarities lower than δ.

In Fig. 3, we show the precision-recall curves of WAM for keyphrase extraction when harmonic factor λ ranges from 0.0 to 1.0 stepped by 0.2. From the figure, we observe that the translation model $\Pr_{d2t}(t|w)$ (i.e., when $\lambda = 1.0$) performs better than

[4] We select $M_d = 2$ because WAM gains the best F-measure score when $M_d = 2$, which is close to the average number of annotated keyphrases for each document 2.4.

$\Pr_{t2d}(t|w)$ (i.e., when $\lambda = 0.0$). This indicates that it is sufficient to simply train a translation model in one direction (i.e., $\Pr_{d2t}(t|w)$) for keyphrase extraction.

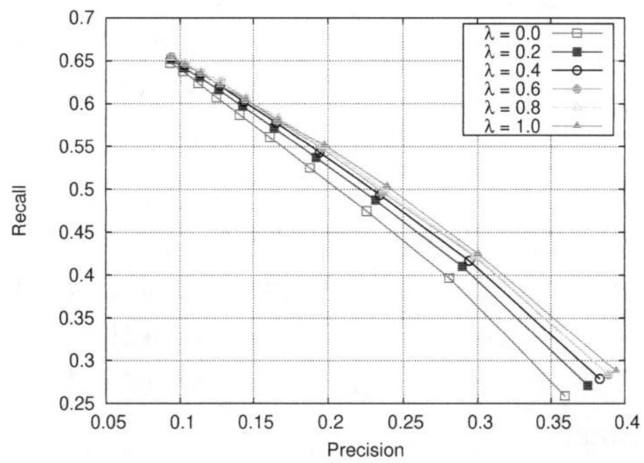

Figure 3: Precision-recall curves of WAM when harmonic factor λ ranges from 0.0 to 1.0.

In Fig. 4, we show the precision-recall curves of WAM for keyphrase extraction when threshold factor δ ranges from 0.01 to 0.90. In title-based pairs using split method, the total number of pairs without filtering any pairs (i.e., $\delta = 0$) is 347,188. When $\delta = 0.01$, 0.10 and 0.90, the numbers of retained translation pairs are 165,023, 148,605 and 41,203, respectively. From Fig. 4, we find that more translation pairs result in better performance. However, more translation pairs also indicate more training time of WAM. Fortunately, we can see that the performance does not drop much when discarding more translation pairs with low similarities. Even when $\delta = 0.9$, our method can still achieve performance with precision $p = 0.277$, recall $r = 0.391$ and F-measure $f = 0.312$ when $M_d = 2$. Meanwhile, we reduce the training efforts by about 50% as compared to $\delta = 0.01$.

In all, based on the above analysis on two parameters, we demonstrate the effectiveness and robustness of our method for keyphrase extraction.

4.1.3 When Titles/Summaries Are Unavailable

Suppose in some special cases, the titles or summaries are unavailable, how can we construct translation pairs? Inspired by extraction-based document summarization (Goldstein et al., 2000; Mihalcea and Tarau, 2004), we can extract one or more important sentences from the given document to construct translation pairs. Unsupervised sentence extraction

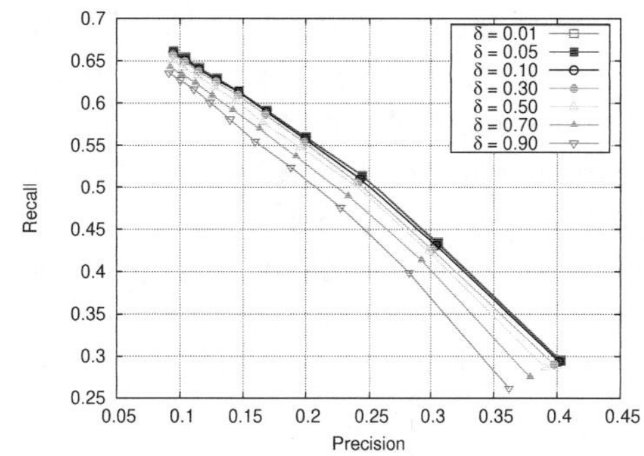

Figure 4: Precision-recall curves of WAM when threshold δ ranges from 0.01 to 0.90.

for document summarization is a well-studied task in natural language processing. As shown in Table 2, we only perform two simple sentence extraction methods to demonstrate the effectiveness: (1) Select the first sentence of a document (denoted as "First"); and (2) Compute the cosine similarities between each sentence and the whole document represented as two bags-of-words (denoted as "Importance").

It is interesting to find that the method of using the first sentence performs similar to using titles. This profits from the characteristic of news articles which tend to give a good summary for the whole article using the first sentence. Although the second method drops much on performance as compared to using titles, it still outperforms than other existing methods. Moreover, the second method will improve much if we use more effective measures to identify the most important sentence.

Method	Precision	Recall	F-measure
First	0.290	0.410	0.327±0.013
Importance	0.260	0.367	0.293±0.010

Table 2: Precision, recall and F-measure of keyphrase extraction when $M_d = 2$ by extracting one sentence to construct translation pairs.

4.2 Beyond Extraction: Keyphrase Generation

In Section 4.1, we evaluate our method on keyphrase extraction by suggesting keyphrases from documents. In fact, our method is also able to suggest keyphrases that have not appeared in the content of given document. The ability is important especially when the length of each document is short, which itself may not contain appropriate keyphrases. We name the new task *keyphrase generation*. To evaluate these methods on keyphrase generation, we perform keyphrase generation for the titles of documents, which are usually much shorter than their corresponding documents. The experiment setting is as follows: the training phase is the same to the previous experiment, but in the test phase we suggest keyphrases only using the titles. LDA and ExpandRank, similar to our method, are also able to select candidate keyphrases beyond the titles. We still use the annotated keyphrases of the corresponding documents as standard answers. In this case, about 59% standard keyphrases do not appear in titles.

In Table 3 we show the evaluation results of various methods for keyphrase generation when $M_d = 2$. For WAM, we only show the results using title-based pairs prepared with split method. From the table, we have three observations: (1) WAM outperforms other methods on keyphrase generation. Moreover, there are about 10% correctly suggested keyphrases by WAM do not appear in titles, which indicates the effectiveness of WAM for keyphrase generation. (2) The performance of TFIDF and TextRank is much lower as compared to Table 1, because the titles are so short that they do not provide enough candidate keyphrases and even the statistical information to rank candidate keyphrases. (3) LDA, ExpandRank and WAM roughly keep comparable performance as in Table 1 (The performance of ExpandRank drops a bit). This indicates the three methods are able to perform keyphrase generation, and verifies again the effectiveness of our method.

Method	Precision	Recall	F-measure
TFIDF	0.105	0.141	0.115±0.004
TextRank	0.107	0.144	0.118±0.005
LDA	0.180	0.256	0.204±0.008
ExpandRank	0.194	0.268	0.216±0.012
WAM	**0.296**	**0.420**	**0.334±0.009**

Table 3: Precision, recall and F-measure of various methods for keyphrase generation when $M_d = 2$.

To demonstrate the features of our method for keyphrase generation, in Table 4 we list top-5 keyphrases suggested by LDA, ExpandRank and WAM for a news article entitled *Israeli Military Claims Iran Can Produce Nuclear Bombs and Considering Military Action against Iran* (We translate the original Chinese title and keyphrases into English for comprehension.). We have the following observations: (1) LDA suggests general words like "negotiation" and "sanction" as keyphrases because the coarse-granularity of topics. (2) ExpandRank suggests some irrelevant words like "Lebanon" as keyphrases, which are introduced by neighbor documents talking about other affairs related to Israel. (3) Our method can generate appropriate keyphrases with less topic-drift. Moreover, our method can find good keyphrases like "nuclear weapon" which even do not appear in the title.

LDA: Iran, U.S.A., negotiation, Israel, sanction
ExpandRank: Iran, Israel, Lebanon, U.S.A., Israeli Military
WAM: Iran, military action, Israeli Military, Israel, nuclear weapon

Table 4: Top-5 keyphrases suggested by LDA, ExpandRank and WAM.

5 Conclusion and Future Work

In this paper, we provide a new perspective to keyphrase extraction: regarding a document and its keyphrases as descriptions to the same object written in two languages. We use IBM Model-1 to bridge the vocabulary gap between the two languages for keyphrase generation. We explore various methods to construct translation pairs. Experiments show that our method can capture the semantic relations between words in documents and keyphrases. Our method is also language-independent, which can be performed on documents in any languages.

We will explore the following two future work: (1) Explore our method on other types of articles and on other languages. (2) Explore more complicated methods to extract important sentences for constructing translation pairs.

Acknowledgments

This work is supported by the National Natural Science Foundation of China (NSFC) under Grant No. 60873174. The authors would like to thank Peng Li and Xiance Si for their suggestions.

References

M. Banko, V.O. Mittal, and M.J. Witbrock. 2000. Headline generation based on statistical translation. In *Proceedings of ACL*, pages 318–325.

A. Berger and J. Lafferty. 1999. Information retrieval as statistical translation. In *Proceedings of SIGIR*, pages 222–229.

A. Berger, R. Caruana, D. Cohn, D. Freitag, and V. Mittal. 2000. Bridging the lexical chasm: statistical approaches to answer-finding. In *Proceedings of SIGIR*, pages 192–199.

D.M. Blei and J.D. Lafferty, 2009. *Text mining: Classification, Clustering, and Applications*, chapter Topic models. Chapman & Hall.

D.M. Blei, A.Y. Ng, and M.I. Jordan. 2003. Latent dirichlet allocation. *Journal of Machine Learning Research*, 3:993–1022, January.

P.F. Brown, V.J.D. Pietra, S.A.D. Pietra, and R.L. Mercer. 1993. The mathematics of statistical machine translation: Parameter estimation. *Computational linguistics*, 19(2):263–311.

A.P. Dempster, N.M. Laird, D.B. Rubin, et al. 1977. Maximum likelihood from incomplete data via the em algorithm. *Journal of the Royal Statistical Society. Series B (Methodological)*, 39(1):1–38.

P. Duygulu, Kobus Barnard, J. F. G. de Freitas, and David A. Forsyth. 2002. Object recognition as machine translation: Learning a lexicon for a fixed image vocabulary. In *Proceedings of ECCV*, pages 97–112.

A. Echihabi and D. Marcu. 2003. A noisy-channel approach to question answering. In *Proceedings of ACL*, pages 16–23.

E. Frank, G.W. Paynter, I.H. Witten, C. Gutwin, and C.G. Nevill-Manning. 1999. Domain-specific keyphrase extraction. In *Proceedings of IJCAI*, pages 668–673.

J. Goldstein, V. Mittal, J. Carbonell, and M. Kantrowitz. 2000. Multi-document summarization by sentence extraction. In *Proceedings of NAACL-ANLP 2000 Workshop on Automatic summarization*, pages 40–48.

G. Heinrich. 2005. Parameter estimation for text analysis. *Web: http://www. arbylon. net/publications/text-est.*

T. Hofmann. 1999. Probabilistic latent semantic indexing. In *Proceedings of SIGIR*, pages 50–57.

A. Hulth. 2003. Improved automatic keyword extraction given more linguistic knowledge. In *Proceedings of EMNLP*, pages 216–223.

M. Karimzadehgan and C.X. Zhai. 2010. Estimation of statistical translation models based on mutual information for ad hoc information retrieval. In *Proceedings of SIGIR*, pages 323–330.

P. Koehn. 2010. *Statistical Machine Translation*. Cambridge University Press.

T.K. Landauer, P.W. Foltz, and D. Laham. 1998. An introduction to latent semantic analysis. *Discourse Processes*, 25:259–284.

Z. Liu, P. Li, Y. Zheng, and M. Sun. 2009a. Clustering to find exemplar terms for keyphrase extraction. In *Proceedings of EMNLP*, pages 257–266.

Z. Liu, H. Wang, H. Wu, and S. Li. 2009b. Collocation extraction using monolingual word alignment method. In *Proceedings of EMNLP*, pages 487–495.

Z. Liu, W. Huang, Y. Zheng, and M. Sun. 2010a. Automatic keyphrase extraction via topic decomposition. In *Proceedings of EMNLP*, pages 366–376.

Z. Liu, H. Wang, H. Wu, and S. Li. 2010b. Improving statistical machine translation with monolingual collocation. In *Proceedings of ACL*, pages 825–833.

R. Mihalcea and P. Tarau. 2004. Textrank: Bringing order into texts. In *Proceedings of EMNLP*, pages 404–411.

V. Murdock and W.B. Croft. 2004. Simple translation models for sentence retrieval in factoid question answering. In *Proceedings of SIGIR*.

T. Nguyen and M.Y. Kan. 2007. Keyphrase extraction in scientific publications. In *Proceedings of the 10th International Conference on Asian Digital Libraries*, pages 317–326.

F.J. Och and H. Ney. 2003. A systematic comparison of various statistical alignment models. *Computational linguistics*, 29(1):19–51.

L. Page, S. Brin, R. Motwani, and T. Winograd. 1998. The pagerank citation ranking: Bringing order to the web. *Technical report, Stanford Digital Library Technologies Project, 1998.*

C. Quirk, C. Brockett, and W. Dolan. 2004. Monolingual machine translation for paraphrase generation. In *Proceedings of EMNLP*, volume 149.

S. Riezler and Y. Liu. 2010. Query rewriting using monolingual statistical machine translation. *Computational Linguistics*, 36(3):569–582.

S. Riezler, A. Vasserman, I. Tsochantaridis, V. Mittal, and Y. Liu. 2007. Statistical machine translation for query expansion in answer retrieval. In *Proccedings of ACL*, pages 464–471.

S. Riezler, Y. Liu, and A. Vasserman. 2008. Translating queries into snippets for improved query expansion. In *Proceedings of COLING*, pages 737–744.

G. Salton and C. Buckley. 1988. Term-weighting approaches in automatic text retrieval. *Information processing and management*, 24(5):513–523.

R. Soricut and E. Brill. 2006. Automatic question answering using the web: Beyond the factoid. *Information Retrieval*, 9(2):191–206.

P.D. Turney. 2000. Learning algorithms for keyphrase extraction. *Information Retrieval*, 2(4):303–336.

X. Wan and J. Xiao. 2008a. Collabrank: towards a collaborative approach to single-document keyphrase extraction. In *Proceedings of COLING*, pages 969–976.

X. Wan and J. Xiao. 2008b. Single document keyphrase extraction using neighborhood knowledge. In *Proceedings of AAAI*, pages 855–860.

I.H. Witten, G.W. Paynter, E. Frank, C. Gutwin, and C.G. Nevill-Manning. 1999. Kea: Practical automatic keyphrase extraction. In *Proceedings of DL*, pages 254–255.

X. Xue, J. Jeon, and W.B. Croft. 2008. Retrieval models for question and answer archives. In *Proceedings of SIGIR*, pages 475–482.

S. Zhao, H. Wang, and T. Liu. 2010. Paraphrasing with search engine query logs. In *Proceedings of COLING*, pages 1317–1325.

Using Second-order Vectors in a Knowledge-based Method for Acronym Disambiguation

Bridget T. McInnes*
College of Pharmacy
University of Minnesota
Minneapolis, MN 55455

Ted Pedersen
Department of Computer Science
University of Minnesota
Duluth, MN 55812

Ying Liu
College of Pharmacy
University of Minnesota
Minneapolis, MN 55455

Serguei V. Pakhomov
College of Pharmacy
University of Minnesota
Minneapolis, MN 55455

Genevieve B. Melton
Institute for Health Informatics
University of Minnesota
Minneapolis, MN 55455

Abstract

In this paper, we introduce a knowledge-based method to disambiguate biomedical acronyms using second-order co-occurrence vectors. We create these vectors using information about a long-form obtained from the Unified Medical Language System and Medline. We evaluate this method on a dataset of 18 acronyms found in biomedical text. Our method achieves an overall accuracy of 89%. The results show that using second-order features provide a distinct representation of the long-form and potentially enhances automated disambiguation.

1 Introduction

Word Sense Disambiguation (WSD) is the task of automatically identifying the appropriate sense of a word with multiple senses. For example, the word *culture* could refer to *anthropological culture* (e.g., the culture of the Mayan civilization), or a *laboratory culture* (e.g., cell culture).

Acronym disambiguation is the task of automatically identifying the contextually appropriate long-form of an ambiguous acronym. For example, the acronym *MS* could refer to the disease *Multiple Sclerosis*, the drug *Morphine Sulfate*, or the state *Mississippi*, among others. Acronym disambiguation can be viewed as a special case of WSD, although, unlike terms, acronyms tend to be complete phrases or expressions, therefore collocation features are not as easily identified. For example, the feature *rate* when disambiguating the term *interest*, as in *interest rate*, may not be available. Acronyms also tend to be noun phrases, therefore syntactic features do not provide relevant information for the purposes of disambiguation.

Identifying the correct long-form of an acronym is important not only for the retrieval of information but the understanding of the information by the recipient. In general English, Park and Byrd (2001) note that acronym disambiguation is not widely studied because acronyms are not as prevalent in literature and newspaper articles as they are in specific domains such as government, law, and biomedicine.

In the biomedical sublanguage domain, acronym disambiguation is an extensively studied problem. Pakhomov (2002) note acronyms in biomedical literature tend to be used much more frequently than in news media or general English literature, and tend to be highly ambiguous. For example, the Unified Medical Language System (UMLS), which includes one of the largest terminology resources in the biomedical domain, contains 11 possible long-forms of the acronym *MS* in addition to the four examples used above. Liu et al. (2001) show that 33% of acronyms are ambiguous in the UMLS. In a subsequent study, Liu et al. (2002a) found that 80% of all acronyms found in Medline, a large repository of abstracts from biomedical journals, are ambiguous. Wren and Garner (2002) found that there exist 174,000 unique acronyms in the Medline abstracts in which 36% of them are ambiguous. The authors also estimated that the number of unique acronyms is increasing at a rate of 11,000 per year.

Supervised and semi-supervised methods have been used successfully for acronym disambiguation

*Contact author : bthomson@umn.edu.

Proceedings of the Fifteenth Conference on Computational Natural Language Learning, pages 145–153,
Portland, Oregon, USA, 23–24 June 2011.

but are limited in scope due to the need for sufficient training data. Liu et al. (2004) state that an acronym could have approximately 16 possible long-forms in Medline but could not obtain a sufficient number of instances for each of the acronym-long-form pairs for their experiments. Stevenson et al. (2009) cite a similar problem indicating that acronym disambiguation methods that do not require training data, regardless if it is created manually or automatically, are needed.

In this paper, we introduce a novel knowledge-based method to disambiguate acronyms using second-order co-occurrence vectors. This method does not rely on training data, and therefore, is not limited to disambiguating only commonly occurring possible long-forms. These vectors are created using the first-order features obtained from the UMLS about the acronym's long-forms and second-order features obtained from Medline. We show that using second-order features provide a distinct representation of the long-form for the purposes of disambiguation and obtains a significantly higher disambiguation accuracy than using first order features.

2 Unified Medical Language System

The Unified Medical Language System (UMLS) is a data warehouse that stores a number of distinct biomedical and clinical resources. One such resource, used in this work, is the Metathesaurus. The Metathesaurus contains biomedical and clinical concepts from over 100 disparate terminology sources that have been semi-automatically integrated into a single resource containing a wide range of biomedical and clinical information. For example, it contains the Systematized Nomenclature of Medicine–Clinical Terms (SNOMED CT), which is a comprehensive clinical terminology created for the electronic exchange of clinical health information, the Foundational Model of Anatomy (FMA), which is an ontology of anatomical concepts created specifically for biomedical and clinical research, and MEDLINEPLUS, which is a terminology source containing health related concepts created specifically for consumers of health services.

The concepts in these sources can overlap. For example, the concept *Autonomic nerve* exists in both SNOMED CT and FMA. The Metathesaurus assigns the synonymous concepts from the various sources a Concept Unique Identifiers (CUIs). Thus both the *Autonomic nerve* concepts in SNOMED CT and FMA are assigned the same CUI (C0206250). This allows multiple sources in the Metathesaurus to be treated as a single resource.

Some sources in the Metathesaurus contain additional information about the concept such as a concept's synonyms, its definition and its related concepts. There are two main types of relations in the Metathesaurus that we use: the parent/child and broader/narrower relations. A parent/child relation is a hierarchical relation between two concepts that has been explicitly defined in one of the sources. For example, the concept *Splanchnic nerve* has an *is-a* relation with the concept *Autonomic nerve* in FMA. This relation is carried forward to the CUI level creating a parent/child relations between the CUIs C0037991 (Splanchnic nerve) and C0206250 (Autonomic nerve) in the Metathesaurus. A broader/narrower relation is a hierarchical relation that does not explicitly come from a source but is created by the UMLS editors. We use the entire UMLS including the RB/RN and PAR/CHD relations in this work.

3 Medline

Medline (*Medical Literature Analysis and Retrieval System Online*) is a bibliographic database containing over 18.5 million citations to journal articles in the biomedical domain which is maintained by the National Library of Medicine (NLM). The 2010 Medline Baseline, used in this study, encompasses approximately 5,200 journals starting from 1948 and is 73 Gigabytes; containing 2,612,767 unique unigrams and 55,286,187 unique bigrams. The majority of the publications are scholarly journals but a small number of newspapers, and magazines are included.

4 Acronym Disambiguation

Existing acronym disambiguation methods can be classified into two categories: form-based and context-based methods. Form-based methods, such as the methods proposed by Taghva and Gilbreth (1999), Pustejovsky et al. (2001), Schwartz and Hearst (2003) and Nadeau and Turney (2005), disambiguate the acronym by comparing its letters directly to the initial letters in the possible long-forms and, therefore, would have difficulties in distinguishing between acronyms with similar long-forms (e.g., RA referring to Refractory anemia or Rheumatoid arthritis).

In contrast, context-based methods disambiguate between acronyms based on the context in which the acronym is used with the assumption that the context surrounding the acronym would be different for each of the possible long-forms. In the remainder of this section, we discuss these types of methods in more detail.

4.1 Context-based Acronym Disambiguation Methods

Liu et al. (2001) and Liu et al. (2002b) introduce a semi-supervised method in which training and test data are automatically created by extracting abstracts from Medline that contain the acronym's long-forms. The authors use collocations and a bag-of-words approach to train a Naive Bayes algorithm and report an accuracy of 97%. This method begins to treat acronym disambiguation as more of a WSD problem by looking at the context in which the acronym exists to determine its long-form, rather than the long-form itself. In a subsequent study, Liu et al. (2004) explore using additional features and machine learning algorithms and report an accuracy of 99% using the Naive Bayes.

Joshi (2006) expands on Liu, et al's work. They evaluate additional machine learning algorithms using unigrams, bigrams and trigrams as features. They found that given their feature set, SVMs obtain the highest accuracy (97%).

Stevenson et al. (2009) re-recreate this dataset using the method described in Liu et al. (2001) to automatically create training data for their method which uses a mixture of linguistics features (e.g., collocations, unigrams, bigrams and trigrams) in combination with the biomedical features CUIs and Medical Subject Headings, which are terms manually assigned to Medline abstracts for indexing purposes. The authors evaluate the Naive Bayes, SVM and Vector Space Model (VSM) described by Agirre and Martinez (2004), and report that VSM obtained the highest accuracy (99%).

Pakhomov (2002) also developed a semi-supervised method in which training data was automatically created by first identifying the long-form found in the text of clinical reports, replacing the long-form with the acronym to use as training data. A maximum entropy model trained and tested on a corpus of 10,000 clinical notes achieved an accuracy of 89%. In a subsequent study, Pakhomov et al. (2005) evaluate obtaining training data from three sources: Medline, clinical records and the world wide web finding using a combination of instances from clinical records and the web obtained the highest accuracy.

Joshi et al. (2006) compare using the Naive Bayes, Decision trees and SVM on ambiguous acronyms found in clinical reports. The authors use the part-of-speech, the unigrams and the bigrams of the context surrounding the acronym as features. They evaluate their method on 7,738 manually disambiguated instances of 15 ambiguous acronyms obtaining an accuracy of over 90% for each acronym.

5 Word Sense Disambiguation

Many knowledge-based WSD methods have been developed to disambiguate terms which are closely related to the work presented in this paper. Lesk (1986) proposes a definition overlap method in which the appropriate sense of an ambiguous term was determined based on the overlap between its definition in a machine readable dictionary (MRD). Ide and Véronis (1998) note that this work provided a basis for most future MRD disambiguation methods; including the one presented in this paper.

Banerjee and Pedersen (2002) use the Lesk's overlap method to determine the relatedness between two concepts (synsets) in WordNet. They extend the method to not only include the definition (gloss) of the two synsets in the overlap but also the glosses of related synsets.

Wilks et al. (1990) expand upon Lesk's method by calculating the number of times the words in the definition co-occur with the ambiguous words. In their method, a vector is created using the co-occurrence information for the ambiguous word and each of its possible senses. The similarity is then calculated between the ambiguous word's vector and each of the sense vectors. The sense whose vector is most similar is assigned to the ambiguous word.

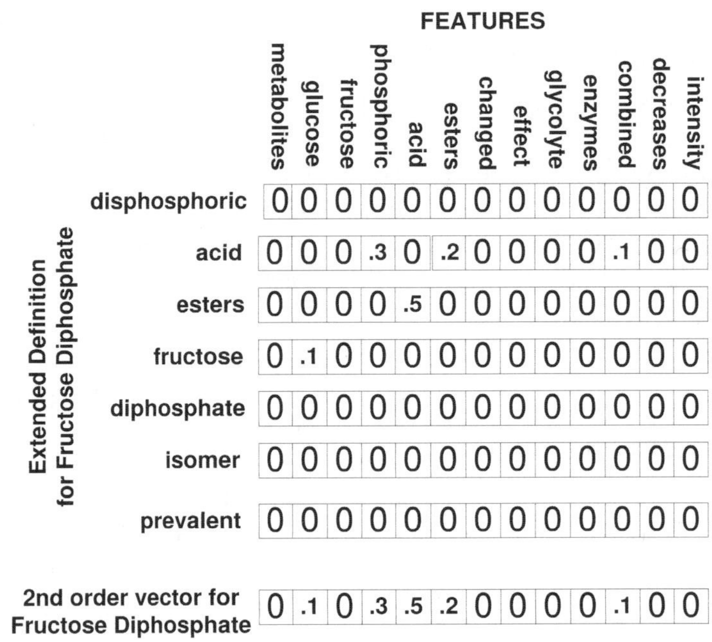

Figure 1: 2nd Order Vector for Fructose Diphosphate (FDP)

Patwardhan and Pedersen (2006) introduce a vector measure to determine the relatedness between pairs of concepts. In this measure, a second order co-occurrence vector is created for each concept using the words in each of the concepts definition and calculating the cosine between the two vectors. This method has been used in the task of WSD by calculating the relatedness between each possible sense of the ambiguous word and its surrounding context. The context whose sum is the most similar is assigned to the ambiguous word.

Second-order co-occurrence vectors were first introduced by Schütze (1992) for the task of word sense *discrimination* and later extended by Purandare and Pedersen (2004). As noted by Pedersen (2010), disambiguation requires a sense-inventory in which the long-forms are known ahead of time, where as in discrimination this information is not known a priori.

6 Method

In our method, a second-order co-occurrence vector is created for each possible long-form of the acronym, and the acronym itself. The appropriate long-form of the acronym is then determined by computing a cosine between the vector representing the ambiguous acronym and each of the vectors representing the long-forms. The long-form whose vector has the smallest angle between it and the acronym vector is chosen as the most likely long-form of the acronym.

To create a second-order vector for a long-form, we first obtain a textual description of the long-form in the UMLS, which we refer to as the *extended definition*. Each long-form, from our evaluation set, was mapped to a concept in the UMLS, therefore, we use the long-form's definition plus the definition of its parent/children and narrow/broader relations and the terms in the long-form.

We include the definition of the related concepts because not all concepts in the UMLS have a definition. In our evaluation dataset, not a single acronym has a definition for each possible long-form. On average, each extended definition contains approximately 453 words. A short example of the extended definition for the acronym FDP when referring to *fructose diphosphate* is: " Diphosphoric acid esters of fructose. The fructose diphosphate isomer is most prevalent. fructose diphosphate."

After the extended definition is obtained, we create the second-order vector by first creating a word by word co-occurrence matrix in which the rows represent the content words in the long-forms, extended definition, and the columns represent words that co-occur in Medline abstracts with the words in the definition. Each cell in this matrix contains the Log Likelihood Ratio (Dunning (1993)) of the word found in the row and the word in the column. Second, each word in the long-forms, extended definition is replaced by its corresponding vector, as given in the co-occurrence matrix. The centroid of these vectors constitutes the second order co-occurrence vector used to represent the long-form.

For example, given the *example corpus* containing two instances: 1) The metabolites, glucose fructose and their phosphoric acid esters are changed due to the effect of glycolytic enzymes, and 2) The phosphoric acid combined with metabolites decreases the intensity. Figure 1 shows how the second-order co-occurrence vector is created for the long-form *fructose diphosphate* using the extended definition and features from our given corpus above.

The second-order co-occurrence vector for the ambiguous acronym is created in a similar fashion, only rather than using words in the extended definition, we use the words surrounding the acronym in the instance.

Vector methods are subject to noise introduced by features that do not distinguish between the different long-forms of the acronym. To reduce this type of noise, we select the features to use in the second order co-occurrence vectors based on the following criteria: 1) second order feature cannot be a stopword, and 2) second order feature must occur at least twice in the feature extraction dataset and not occur more than 150 times. We also experiment with the location of the second-order feature with respect to the first-order feature by varying the window size of zero, four, six and ten words to the right and the left of the first-order feature. The experiments in this paper were conducted using CuiTools v0.15. [1]

Our method is different from other context-based acronym disambiguation methods discussed in the related work because it does not require annotated training data for each acronym that needs to be disambiguated. Our method differs from the method proposed by Wilks et al. (1990) in two fundamental aspects: 1) using the *extended definition* of the possible long-forms of an acronym, and 2) using second-order vectors to represent the instance containing the acronym and each of the acronym's possible long-forms.

7 Data

7.1 Acronym Dataset

We evaluated our method on the "Abbrev" dataset [2] made available by Stevenson et al. (2009). The acronyms and long-forms in the data were initially presented by Liu et al. (2001). Stevenson et al. (2009) automatically re-created this dataset by identifying the acronyms and long-forms in Medline abstracts and replacing the long-form in the abstract with its acronym. Each abstract contains approximately 216 words. The dataset consists of three subsets containing 100 instances, 200 instances and 300 instances of the ambiguous acronym referred to as Abbrev.100, Abbrev.200, Abbrev.300, respectively. The acronyms long-forms were manually mapped to concepts in the UMLS by Stevenson, et al.

A sufficient number of instances were not found for each of the 21 ambiguous acronyms by Stevenson et al. (2009). For example, "ASP" only contained 71 instances and therefore not included in any of the subsets. "ANA" and "FDP" only contained just over 100 instances and therefore, are only included in the Abbrev.100 subset. "ACE", "ASP" and "CSF" were also excluded because several of the acronyms' long-forms did not occur frequently enough in Medline to create a balanced dataset.

We evaluate our method on the same subsets that Stevenson et al. (2009) used to evaluate their supervised method. The average number of long-forms per acronym is 2.6 and the average majority sense across all subsets is 70%.

7.2 Feature Extraction Dataset

We use abstracts from Medline, containing ambiguous acronym or long-form, to create the second-

[1] http://cuitools.sourceforge.net

[2] http://nlp.shef.ac.uk/BioWSD/downloads/corpora

order co-occurrence vectors for our method as described in Section 6. Table 1 shows the number of Medline abstracts extracted for the acronyms.

Acronyms	# Abstracts	Acronym	# Abstracts
ANA	3,267	APC	11,192
BPD	3,260	BSA	10,500
CAT	44,703	CML	8,777
CMV	13,733	DIP	2,912
EMG	16,779	FDP	1,677
LAM	1,572	MAC	6,528
MCP	2,826	PCA	11,044
PCP	5,996	PEG	10,416
PVC	2,780	RSV	5,091

Table 1: Feature Extraction Data for Acronyms

8 Results

Table 2 compares the majority sense baseline and the first-order baseline with the results obtained using our method on the Acronym Datasets (Abbrev.100, Abbrev.200 and Abbrev.300) using a window size of zero, four, six and ten. Differences between the means of disambiguation accuracy produced by various approaches were tested for statistical significance using the pair-wise Student's t-tests with the significance threshold set to 0.01.

	Window Size	Abbrev 100	Abbrev 200	Abbrev 300
Maj. Sense Baseline		0.70	0.70	0.70
1-order Baseline		0.57	0.61	0.61
Our Method	0	0.83	0.83	0.81
	4	0.86	0.87	0.86
	6	0.88	0.90	0.89
	10	0.88	0.90	0.89

Table 2: Overall Disambiguation Results

The majority sense baseline is often used to evaluate supervised learning algorithms and indicates the accuracy that would be achieved by assigning the most frequent sense (long-form) to every instance. The results in Table 2 demonstrate that our method is significantly more accurate than the majority sense baseline ($p \leq 0.01$).

We compare the results using second-order vectors to first-order vectors. Table 2 shows that accuracy of the second-order results is significantly higher than the first-order results ($p \leq 0.01$).

The results in Table 2 also show that, as the window size grows from zero to six, the accuracy of the system increases and plateaus at a window size of ten. There is no statistically significant difference between using a window size of six and ten but there is a significant difference between a window size of zero and six, as well as four and six ($p \leq 0.01$).

Acronym	# Long forms	Abbrev 100	Abbrev 200	Abbrev 300
ANA	3	0.84		
APC	3	0.88	0.87	0.87
BPD	3	0.96	0.95	0.95
BSA	2	0.95	0.93	0.92
CAT	2	0.88	0.87	0.87
CML	2	0.81	0.84	0.83
CMV	2	0.98	0.98	0.98
DIP	2	0.98	0.98	
EMG	2	0.88	0.89	0.88
FDP	4	0.65		
LAM	2	0.86	0.87	0.88
MAC	4	0.94	0.95	0.95
MCP	4	0.73	0.67	0.68
PCA	4	0.78	0.79	0.79
PCP	2	0.97	0.96	0.96
PEG	2	0.89	0.89	0.88
PVC	2	0.95	0.95	
RSV	2	0.97	0.98	0.98

Table 3: Individual Results using a Window Size of 6.

9 Error Analysis

Table 3 shows the results obtained by our method for the individual acronyms using a window size of six, and the number of possible long-forms per acronym. Of the 18 acronyms, three obtain an accuracy below 80 percent: FDP, MCP and PCA.

FPD has four possible long-forms: Fructose Diphosphate (E1), Formycin Diphosphate (E2), Fibrinogen Degradation Product (E3) and Flexor Digitorum Profundus (E4). The confusion matrix in Table 4 shows that the method was unable to distinguish between the two long-forms, E1 and E2, which are both diphosphates, nor E2 and E3.

Long-Form	E1	E2	E3	E4
E1: Fructose Diphosphate				
E2: Formycin Diphosphate	5	2	11	19
E3: Fibrinogen Degradation Product			4	
E4: Flexor Digitorum Profundus				59

Table 4: FDP Confusion Matrix

MCP also has four possible long-forms: Multicatalytic Protease (E1), Metoclopramide (E2), Monocyte Chemoattractant Protein (E3) and Membrane

Cofactor Protein (E4). The confusion matrix in Table 5 shows that the method was not able to distinguish between E3 and E4, which are both proteins, and E1, which is a protease (an enzyme that breaks down a protein).

Long-Form	E1	E2	E3	E4
E1: Multicatalytic Protease	1	5	6	1
E2: Metoclopramide		15		
E3: Monocyte Chemoattractant Protein	1	3	44	11
E4: Membrane Cofactor Protein				13

Table 5: MCP Confusion Matrix

PCA has four possible long-forms: Passive Cutaneous Anaphylaxis (E1), Patient Controlled Analgesia (E2), Principal Component Analysis (E3), and Posterior Cerebral Artery (E4). The confusion matrix in Table 6 shows that the method was not able to distinguish between E2 and E3. Analyzing the extended definitions of the concepts showed that E2 includes the definition to the concept Pain Management. The words in this definition overlap with many of the words used in E3s extended definition.

Long-Form	E1	E2	E3	E4
E1:Passive Cutaneous Anaphylaxis	18		6	1
E2:Patient Controlled Analgesia		5	15	
E3:Principal Component Analysis			48	
E4:Posterior Cerebral Artery				7

Table 6: PCA Confusion Matrix

10 Comparison with Previous Work

Of the previously developed methods, Liu et al. (2004) and Stevenson et al. (2009) evaluated their semi-supervised methods on the same dataset as we used for the current study. A direct comparison can not be made between our method and Liu et al. (2004) because we do not have an exact duplication of the dataset that they use. Their results are comparable to Stevenson et al. (2009) with both reporting results in the high 90s. Our results are directly comparable to Stevenson et al. (2009) who report an overall accuracy of 98%, 98% and 99% on the Abbrev.100, Abbrev.200 and Abbrev.300 datasets respectively. This is approximately 10 percentage points higher than our results.

The advantage of the methods proposed by Stevenson et al. (2009) and Liu et al. (2004) is that they are semi-supervised which have been shown to obtain higher accuracies than methods that do not use statistical machine learning algorithms. The disadvantage is that sufficient training data are required for each possible acronym-long-form pair. Liu et al. (2004) state that an acronym could have approximately 16 possible long-forms in Medline but a sufficient number of instances for each of the acronym-long-form pairs were not found in Medline and, therefore, evaluated their method on 15 out of the original 34 acronyms. Stevenson et al. (2009) cite a similar problem in re-creating this dataset. This shows the limitation to these methods is that a sufficient number of training examples can not be obtained for each acronym that needs to be disambiguated. The method proposed in the paper does not have this limitation and can be used to disambiguate any acronym in Medline.

11 Discussion

In this paper, we presented a novel method to disambiguate acronyms in biomedical text using second-order features extracted from the UMLS and Medline. The results show that using second-order features provide a distinct representation of the long-form that is useful for disambiguation.

We believe that this is because biomedical text contains technical terminology that has a rich source of co-occurrence information associated with them due to their compositionality. Using second-order information works reasonably well because when the terms in the extended definition are broken up into their individual words, information is not being lost. For example, the term Patient Controlled Analgesia can be understood by taking the union of the meanings of the three terms and coming up with an appropriate definition of the term (patient has control over their analgesia).

We evaluated various window sizes to extract the second-order co-occurrence information from, and found using locally occurring words obtains a higher accuracy. This is consistent with the finding reported by Choueka and Lusignan (1985) who conducted an experiment to determine what size window is needed for humans to determine the appropriate sense of an ambiguous word.

The amount of data used to extract the second-order features for each ambiguous acronym varied depending on its occurrence in Medline. Table 1 in Section 7.2 shows the number of abstracts in Medline used for each acronym. We compared the accuracy obtained by our method using a window size of six on the Abbrev.100 dataset with the number of abstracts in the feature extraction data. We found that the accuracy was not correlated with the amount of data used (r = *0.07*). This confirms that it is not the quantity but the content of the contextual information that determines the accuracy of disambiguation.

We compared using second-order features and first-order features showing that the second-order results obtained a significantly higher accuracy. We believe that this is because the definitions of the possible concepts are too sparse to provide enough information to distinguish between them. This finding coincides to that of Purandare and Pedersen (2004) and Pedersen (2010) who found that with large amounts of data, first-order vectors perform better than second-order vectors, but second-order vectors are a good option when large amounts of data are not available.

The results of the error analysis indicate that for some acronyms using the extended definition does not provide sufficient information to make finer grained distinctions between the long-forms. This result also indicates that, although many long-forms of acronyms can be considered coarse-grained senses, this is not always the case. For example, the analysis of MCP showed that two of its possible long-forms are proteins which are difficult to differentiate from given the context.

The results of the error analysis also show that indicative collocation features for acronyms are not easily identified because acronyms tend to be complete phrases. For example, two of the possible long-forms of DF are *Fructose Diphosphate* and *Formycin Diphosphate*.

Two main limitations of this work must be mentioned to facilitate the interpretation of the results. The first is the small number of acronyms and the small number of long-forms per acronym in the dataset; however, the acronyms in this dataset are representative of the kinds of acronyms one would expect to see in biomedical text. The second limitation is that the dataset contains only those acronyms whose long-forms were found in Medline abstracts. The main goal of this paper was to determine if the context found in the long-forms, extended definition was distinct enough to distinguish between them using second-order vectors. For this purpose, we feel that the dataset was sufficient although a more extensive dataset may be needed in the future for improved coverage.

12 Future Work

In the future, we plan to explore three different avenues. The first avenue is to look at obtaining contextual descriptions of the possible long-forms from resources other than the UMLS such as the MetaMapped Medline baseline and WordNet. The second avenue is limiting the features that are used in the instance vectors. The first-order features in the instance vector contain the words from the entire abstract. As previously mentioned, vector methods are subject to noise, therefore, in the future we plan to explore using only those words that are co-located next to the ambiguous acronym. The third avenue is expanding the vector to allow for terms. Currently, we use word vectors, in the future, we plan to extend the method to use terms, as identified by the UMLS, as features rather than single words.

We also plan to test our approach in the clinical domain. We believe that acronym disambiguation may be more difficult in this domain due to the increase amount of long-forms as seen in the datasets used by Joshi et al. (2006) and Pakhomov (2002).

13 Conclusions

Our study constitutes a significant step forward in the area of automatic acronym ambiguity resolution, as it will enable the incorporation of scalable acronym disambiguation into NLP systems used for indexing and retrieval of documents in specialized domains such as medicine. The advantage of our method over previous methods is that it does not require manually annotated training for each acronym to be disambiguated while still obtaining an overall accuracy of 89%.

Acknowledgments

This work was supported by the National Institute of Health, National Library of Medicine Grant #R01LM009623-01.

References

E. Agirre and D. Martinez. 2004. The Basque Country University system: English and Basque tasks. In *Proceedings of the 3rd ACL workshop on the Evaluation of Systems for the Semantic Analysis of Text (SENSEVAL)*, pages 44–48.

S. Banerjee and T. Pedersen. 2002. An adapted lesk algorithm for word sense disambiguation using WordNet. In *Proceedings of the 3rd International Conference on Intelligent Text Processing and Computational Linguistics*, pages 136–145.

Y. Choueka and S. Lusignan. 1985. Disambiguation by short contexts. *Computers and the Humanities*, 19(3):147–157.

T. Dunning. 1993. Accurate methods for the statistics of surprise and coincidence. *Computational Linguistics*, 19(1):61–74.

N. Ide and J. Véronis. 1998. Introduction to the special issue on word sense disambiguation: the state of the art. *Computational Linguistics*, 24(1):2–40.

M. Joshi, S. Pakhomov, T. Pedersen, and C.G. Chute. 2006. A comparative study of supervised learning as applied to acronym expansion in clinical reports. In *Proceedings of the Annual Symposium of AMIA*, pages 399–403.

M. Joshi. 2006. Kernel Methods for Word Sense Disambiguation and Abbreviation Expansion. Master's thesis, University of Minnesota.

M. Lesk. 1986. Automatic sense disambiguation using machine readable dictionaries: how to tell a pine cone from an ice cream cone. *Proceedings of the 5th Annual International Conference on Systems Documentation*, pages 24–26.

H. Liu, YA. Lussier, and C. Friedman. 2001. Disambiguating ambiguous biomedical terms in biomedical narrative text: an unsupervised method. *Journal of Biomedical Informatics*, 34(4):249–261.

H. Liu, A.R. Aronson, and C. Friedman. 2002a. A study of abbreviations in MEDLINE abstracts. In *Proceedings of the Annual Symposium of AMIA*, pages 464–468.

H. Liu, S.B. Johnson, and C. Friedman. 2002b. Automatic resolution of ambiguous terms based on machine learning and conceptual relations in the UMLS. *JAMIA*, 9(6):621–636.

H. Liu, V. Teller, and C. Friedman. 2004. A multi-aspect comparison study of supervised word sense disambiguation. *JAMIA*, 11(4):320–331.

D. Nadeau and P. Turney. 2005. A supervised learning approach to acronym identification. In *Proceedings of the 18th Canadian Conference on Artificial Intelligence*, pages 319–329.

S. Pakhomov, T. Pedersen, and C.G. Chute. 2005. Abbreviation and acronym disambiguation in clinical discourse. In *Proceedings of the Annual Symposium of AMIA*, pages 589–593.

S. Pakhomov. 2002. Semi-supervised maximum entropy based approach to acronym and abbreviation normalization in medical texts. In *Proceedings of the 40th Annual Meeting on Association for Computational Linguistics*, pages 160–167.

Y. Park and R.J. Byrd. 2001. Hybrid text mining for finding abbreviations and their definitions. In *Proceedings of the Conference on Empirical Methods in Natural Language Processing*, pages 126–133.

S. Patwardhan and T. Pedersen. 2006. Using WordNet-based context vectors to estimate the semantic relatedness of concepts. In *Proceedings of the EACL 2006 Workshop Making Sense of Sense - Bringing Computational Linguistics and Psycholinguistics Together*, pages 1–8.

T. Pedersen. 2010. The effect of different context representations on word sense discrimination in biomedical texts. In *Proceedings of the 1st ACM International IHI Symposium*, pages 56–65.

A. Purandare and T. Pedersen. 2004. Word sense discrimination by clustering contexts in vector and similarity spaces. In *Proceedings of the Conference on Computational Natural Language Learning (CoNLL)*, pages 41–48.

J. Pustejovsky, J. Castano, B. Cochran, M. Kotecki, M. Morrell, and A. Rumshisky. 2001. Extraction and disambiguation of acronym-meaning pairs in medline. *Unpublished manuscript*.

H. Schütze. 1992. Dimensions of meaning. In *Proceedings of the 1992 ACM/IEEE Conference on Supercomputing*, pages 787–796.

A.S. Schwartz and M.A. Hearst. 2003. A simple algorithm for identifying abbreviation definitions in biomedical text. In *Proceedings of the Pacific Symposium on Biocomputing (PSB)*, pages 451–462.

M. Stevenson, Y. Guo, A. Al Amri, and R. Gaizauskas. 2009. Disambiguation of biomedical abbreviations. In *Proceedings of the ACL BioNLP Workshop*, pages 71–79.

K. Taghva and J. Gilbreth. 1999. Recognizing acronyms and their definitions. *ISRI UNLV*, 1:191–198.

Y. Wilks, D. Fass, C.M. Guo, J.E. McDonald, T. Plate, and B.M. Slator. 1990. Providing machine tractable dictionary tools. *Machine Translation*, 5(2):99–154.

J.D. Wren and H.R. Garner. 2002. Heuristics for identification of acronym-definition patterns within text: towards an automated construction of comprehensive acronym-definition dictionaries. *Methods of Information in Medicine*, 41(5):426–434.

Using the Mutual k-Nearest Neighbor Graphs for Semi-supervised Classification of Natural Language Data

Kohei Ozaki and **Masashi Shimbo** and **Mamoru Komachi** and **Yuji Matsumoto**
Nara Institute of Science and Technology
8916-5 Takayama, Ikoma, Nara 630-0192, Japan
{kohei-o,shimbo,komachi,matsu}@is.naist.jp

Abstract

The first step in graph-based semi-supervised classification is to construct a graph from input data. While the k-nearest neighbor graphs have been the de facto standard method of graph construction, this paper advocates using the less well-known *mutual* k-nearest neighbor graphs for high-dimensional natural language data. To compare the performance of these two graph construction methods, we run semi-supervised classification methods on both graphs in word sense disambiguation and document classification tasks. The experimental results show that the mutual k-nearest neighbor graphs, if combined with maximum spanning trees, consistently outperform the k-nearest neighbor graphs. We attribute better performance of the mutual k-nearest neighbor graph to its being more resistive to making hub vertices. The mutual k-nearest neighbor graphs also perform equally well or even better in comparison to the state-of-the-art b-matching graph construction, despite their lower computational complexity.

1 Introduction

Semi-supervised classification try to take advantage of a large amount of unlabeled data in addition to a small amount of labeled data, in order to achieve good classification accuracy while reducing the cost of manually annotating data. In particular, graph-based techniques for semi-supervised classification (Zhou et al., 2004; Zhu et al., 2003; Callut et al., 2008; Wang et al., 2008) are recognized as a promising approach. Some of these techniques have been successfully applied for NLP tasks: word sense disambiguation (Alexandrescu and Kirchhoff, 2007; Niu et al., 2005), sentiment analysis (Goldberg and Zhu, 2006), and statistical machine translation (Alexandrescu and Kirchhoff, 2009), to name but a few.

However, the focus of these studies is how to assign accurate labels to vertices in a given graph. By contrast, there has not been much work on how such a graph should be built, and graph construction remains "more of an art than a science" (Zhu, 2005). Yet, it is an essential step for graph-based semi-supervised classification and (unsupervised) clustering, and the input graph affects the quality of final classification/clustering results.

Both for semi-supervised classification and for clustering, the k-nearest neighbor (k-NN) graph construction has been used almost exclusively in the literature. However, k-NN graphs often produce *hubs*, or vertices with extremely high degree (i.e., the number of edges incident to a vertex). This tendency is obvious especially if the original data is high-dimensional—a characteristic typical of natural language data. In a later section, we demonstrate that such hub vertices indeed deteriorate the accuracy of semi-supervised classification.

While not in the context of graph construction, Radovanović et al. (2010) made an insightful observation into the nature of hubs in high-dimensional space; in their context, a hub is a sample close to many other samples in the (high-dimensional) sample space. They state that such hubs inherently emerge in high-dimensional data as a side effect of the "curse of dimensionality," and argue that this is a

Proceedings of the Fifteenth Conference on Computational Natural Language Learning, pages 154–162,
Portland, Oregon, USA, 23–24 June 2011.

reason nearest neighbor classification does not work well in high-dimensional space.

Their observation is insightful for graph construction as well. Most of the graph-based semi-supervised classification methods work by gradually propagating label information of a vertex towards neighboring vertices in a graph, but the neighborhood structure in the graph is basically determined by the proximity of data in the original high-dimensional sample space. Hence, it is very likely that a hub in the sample space also makes a hub in the k-NN graph, since k-NN graph construction greedily connects a pair of vertices if the sample corresponding to one vertex is among the k closest samples of the other sample in the original space. It is therefore desirable to have an efficient graph construction method for high-dimensional data that can produce a graph with reduced hub effects.

To this end, we propose to use the *mutual k-nearest neighbor graphs* (*mutual k-NN graphs*), a less well-known variant of the standard k-NN graphs. All vertices in a mutual k-NN graph have a degree upper-bounded by k, which is not usually the case with standard k-NN graphs. This property helps not to produce vertices with extremely high degree (hub vertices) in the graph. A mutual k-NN graph is easy to build, at a time complexity identical to that of the k-NN graph construction.

We first evaluated the quality of the graphs apart from specific classification algorithms using the ϕ-edge ratio of graphs. Our experimental results show that the mutual k-NN graphs have a smaller number of edges connecting vertices with different labels than the k-NN graphs, thus reducing the possibility of wrong label information to be propagated. We also compare the classification accuracy of two standard semi-supervised classification algorithms on the mutual k-NN graphs and the k-NN graphs. The results show that the mutual k-NN graphs consistently outperorm the k-NN graphs. Moreover, the mutual k-NN graphs achieve equally well or better classification accuracy than the state-of-the-art graph construction method called b-matching (Jebara et al., 2009), while taking much less time to construct.

2 Problem Statement

2.1 Semi-supervised Classification

The problem of semi-supervised classification can be stated as follows. We are given a set of n examples, $X = \{\boldsymbol{x}_1, \ldots, \boldsymbol{x}_n\}$, but only the labels of the first l examples are at hand; the remaining $u = n - l$ examples are unlabeled examples. Let $S = \{1, \ldots, c\}$ be the set of possible labels, and $y_i \in S$ the label of $\boldsymbol{x}_i$, for $i = 1, \ldots, n$. Since we only know the labels of the first l examples, we do not have access to $y_{l+1}, \ldots, y_n$. For later convenience, further let $\boldsymbol{y} = (y_1, \ldots, y_n)$.

The goal of a semi-supervised classification algorithm is to predict the hidden labels $y_{l+1}, \ldots, y_n$ of u unlabeled examples $\boldsymbol{x}_{l+1}, \ldots, \boldsymbol{x}_n$, given these unlabeled examples and l labeled data $(\boldsymbol{x}_1, y_1), \ldots, (\boldsymbol{x}_l, y_l)$. A measure of similarity between examples is also provided to the algorithm. Stated differently, the classifier has access to an all-pair similarity matrix W' of size $n \times n$, with its (i, j)-element W'_{ij} holding the similarity of examples $\boldsymbol{x}_i$ and $\boldsymbol{x}_j$. It is assumed that W' is a symmetric matrix, and the more similar two examples are (with respect to the similarity measure), more likely they are to have the same label. This last assumption is the premise of many semi-supervised classification algorithms and is often called the cluster assumption (Zhou et al., 2004).

2.2 Graph-based Semi-supervised Classification

Graph-based approaches to semi-supervised classification are applicable if examples X are graph vertices. Otherwise, X must first be converted into a graph. This latter case is the focus of this paper. That is, we are interested in how to construct a graph from the examples, so that the subsequent classification works well.

Let $\mathcal{G}$ denote the graph constructed from the examples. Naturally, $\mathcal{G}$ has n vertices, since vertices are identified with examples. Instead of graph $\mathcal{G}$ itself, let us consider its real-valued (weighted) adjacency matrix W, of size $n \times n$. The task of graph construction then reduces to computing W from all-pairs similarity matrix W'.

The simplest way to compute W from W' is to let $W = W'$, which boils down to using a dense, complete graph $\mathcal{G}$ with the unmodified all-pairs similarity as its edge weights. However, it has been observed that a sparse W not only save time needed for classification, but also results in better classification accuracy[1] than the full similarity matrix W' (Zhu, 2008). Thus, we are concerned with how to sparsify W' to obtain a sparse W; i.e., the strategy of zeroing out some elements of W'.

Let the set of binary values be $\mathbb{B} = \{0, 1\}$. A sparsification strategy can be represented by a binary-valued matrix $P \in \mathbb{B}^{n \times n}$, where $P_{ij} = 1$ if W'_{ij} must be retained as W_{ij}, and $P_{ij} = 0$ if $W_{ij} = 0$. Then, the weighted adjacency matrix W of $\mathcal{G}$ is given by $W_{ij} = P_{ij} W'_{ij}$. The $n \times n$ matrices W and P are symmetric, reflecting the fact that most graph-based algorithms require the input graph to be undirected.

3 k-Nearest Neighbor Graphs and the Effect of Hubs

The standard approach to making a sparse graph $\mathcal{G}$ (or equivalently, matrix W) is to construct a k-NN graph from the data (Szummer and Jaakkola, 2002; Niu et al., 2005; Goldberg and Zhu, 2006).

3.1 The k-Nearest Neighbor Graphs

The k-NN graph is a weighted undirected graph connecting each vertex to its k-nearest neighbors in the original sample space. Building a k-NN graph is a two step process. First we solve the following optimization problem.

$$\max_{\hat{P} \in \mathbb{B}^{n \times n}} \sum_{i,j} \hat{P}_{ij} W'_{ij} \tag{1}$$
$$\text{s.t.} \sum_{j} \hat{P}_{ij} = k,\ \hat{P}_{ii} = 0,\ \forall i, j \in \{1, \ldots, n\}$$

Note that we are trying to find $\hat{P}$, and not P. This is an easy problem and we can solve it by greedily assigning $\hat{P}_{ij} = 1$ only if W'_{ij} is among the top k elements in the ith row of W' (in terms of the magnitude of the elements). After $\hat{P}$ is determined, we let $P_{ij} = \max(\hat{P}_{ij}, \hat{P}_{ji})$. Thus P is a symmetric matrix, i.e., $P_{ij} = P_{ji}$ for all i and j, while $\hat{P}$ may not. Finally, weighted adjacency matrix W is determined by $W_{ij} = P_{ij} W'_{ij}$. Matrix W is also symmetric since P and W' are symmetric.

This process is equivalent to retaining all edges from each vertex to its k-nearest neighbor vertices, and then making all edges undirected.

Note the above symmetrization step is necessary because the k-nearest neighbor relation is not symmetric; even if a vertex v_i is a k-nearest neighbor of another vertex v_j, v_j may or may not be a k-nearest neighbor of v_i. Thus, symmetrizing P and W as above makes the graph irregular; i.e., the degree of some vertices may be larger than k, which opens the possibility of hubs to emerge.

[1]See also the experimental results of Section 6.3.2 in which the full similarity matrix W' is used as the baseline.

d	1	2	≥ 3	total
# of vertices	1610	1947	164	3721
original	65.9	65.7	**69.8**	66.0
hub-removed	**66.6**	**66.0**	**69.8**	**66.4**

Table 1: Classification accuracy of vertices around hubs in a k-NN graph, before ("original") and after ("hub-removed") hubs are removed. The value d represents the shortest distance (number of hops) from a vertex to its nearest hub vertex in the graph.

3.2 Effect of Hubs on Classification

In this section, we demonstrate that hubs in k-NN graphs are indeed harmful to semi-supervised classification as we claimed earlier. To this end, we eliminate such high degree vertices from the graph, and compare the classification accuracy of other vertices before and after the elimination. For this preliminary experiment, we used the "line" dataset of a word sense disambiguation task (Leacock et al., 1993). For details of the dataset and the task, see Section 6.

In this experiment, we randomly selected 10 percent of examples as labeled examples. The remaining 90 percent makes the set of unlabeled examples, and the goal is to predict the label (word sense) of these unlabeled examples.

We first built a k-NN graph (with $k = 3$) from the dataset, and ran Gaussian Random Fields (GRF) (Zhu et al., 2003), one of the most widely-used graph-based semi-supervised classification algorithms. Then we removed vertices with degree greater than or equal to 30 from the k-NN graph, and ran GRF again on this "hub-removed" graph.

Table 1 shows the classification accuracy of GRF on the two graphs. The table shows both the overall classification accuracy, and the classification accuracy on the subsets of vertices, stratified by their distance d from the nearest hub vertices (which were eliminated in the "hub-removed" graph). Obviously, overall classification accuracy has improved after hub removal. Also notice that the increase in the classification accuracy on the vertices nearest to hubs ($d = 1, 2$). These results suggest that the presence of hubs in the graph is deteriorating classification accuracy.

4 Mutual k-Nearest Neighbor Graphs for Semi-supervised Classification

As demonstrated in Section 3.2, removing hub vertices in k-NN graphs is an easy way of improving the accuracy of semi-supervised classification. However, this method adds another parameter to the graph construction method, namely, the threshold on the degree of vertices to be removed. The method also does not tell us how to assign labels to the removed (hub) vertices. Hence, it is more desirable to have a graph construction method which has only one parameter just like the k-NN graphs, but is at the same time less prone to produce hub vertices.

In this section, we propose to use mutual k-NN graphs for this purpose.

4.1 Mutual k-Nearest Neighbor Graphs

The mutual k-NN graph is not a new concept and it has been used sometimes in clustering. Even in clustering, however, they are not at all as popular as the ordinary k-NN graphs. A mutual k-NN graph is defined as a graph in which there is an edge between vertices v_i and v_j if each of them belongs to the k-nearest neighbors (in terms of the original similarity metric W) of the other vertex. By contrast, a k-NN graph has an edge between vertices v_i and v_j if one of them belongs to the k-nearest neighbors of the other. Hence, the mutual k-NN graph is a subgraph of the k-NN graph computed from the same data with the same value of k. The mutual k-NN graph first optimizes the same formula as (1), but in mutual k-NN graphs, the binary-valued symmetric matrix P is defined as $P_{ij} = \min(\hat{P}_{ij}, \hat{P}_{ji})$. Since mutual k-NN graph construction guarantees that all vertices in the resulting graph have degree at most k, it is less likely to produce extremely high degree vertices in comparison with k-NN graphs, provided that the value of k is kept adequately small.

4.2 Fixing Weak Connectivity

Because the mutual k-NN graph construction is more selective of edges than the standard k-NN graphs, the resulting graphs often contain many small disconnected components. Disconnected components are not much of a problem for clustering (since its objective is to divide a graph into discrete components eventually), but can be a problem for semi-supervised classification algorithms; if a connected component does not contain a labeled node, the algorithms cannot reliably predict the labels of the vertices in the component; recall that these algorithms infer labels by propagating label information along edges in the graph.

As a simple method for overcoming this problem, we combine the mutual k-NN graph and the maximum spanning tree. To be precise, the minimum number of edges from the maximum spanning tree are added to the mutual k-NN graph to ensure that only one connected component exists in a graph.

4.3 Computational Efficiency

Using a Fibonacci heap-based implementation (Fredman and Tarjan, 1987), one can construct the standard k-NN graph in (amortized) $O(n^2 + kn \log n)$ time. A mutual k-NN graph can also be constructed in the same time complexity as the k-NN graphs. The procedure below transforms a standard k-NN graph into a mutual k-NN graph. It uses Fibonacci heaps once again and assumes that the input k-NN graph is represented as an adjacency matrix in sparse matrix representation.

1. Each vertex is associated with its own heap. For each edge e connecting vertices u and v, insert e to the heaps associated with u and v.

2. Fetch maximum weighted edges from each heap k times, keeping globally the record of the number of times each edge is fetched. Notice that an edge can be fetched at most twice,

once at an end vertex of the edge and once at the other end.

3. A mutual k-NN graph can be constructed by only keeping edges fetched twice in the previous step.

The complexity of this procedure is $O(kn)$. Hence the overall complexity of building a mutual k-NN graph is dominated by the time needed to build the standard k-NN graph input to the system; i.e., $O(n^2 + kn \log n)$.

If we call the above procedure on an *approximate* k-NN graph which can be computed more efficiently (Beygelzimer et al., 2006; Chen et al., 2009; Ram et al., 2010; Tabei et al., 2010), it yields an approximate mutual k-NN graphs. In this case, the overall complexity is identical to that of the approximate k-NN graph construction algorithm, since these approximate algorithms have a complexity at least $O(kn)$.

5 Related Work

5.1 b-Matching Graphs

Recently, Jebara et al. (2009) proposed a new graph construction method called *b-matching*. A b-matching graph is a b-regular graph, meaning that every vertex has the degree b uniformly. It can be obtained by solving the following optimization problem.

$$
\begin{aligned}
\max_{P \in \mathbb{B}^{n \times n}} \quad & \sum_{ij} P_{ij} W'_{ij} \\
\text{s.t.} \quad & \sum_{j} P_{ij} = b, \qquad \forall i \in \{1, \ldots, n\} \quad (2) \\
& P_{ii} = 0, \qquad \forall i \in \{1, \ldots, n\} \quad (3) \\
& P_{ij} = P_{ji}, \qquad \forall i, j \in \{1, \ldots, n\} \quad (4)
\end{aligned}
$$

After P is computed, the weighted adjacency matrix W is determined by $W_{ij} = P_{ij} W'_{ij}$ The constraint (4) makes the binary matrix P symmetric, and (3) is to ignore self-similarity (loops). Also, the constraint (2) ensures that the graph is regular. Note that k-NN graphs are in general not regular. The regularity requirement of the b-matching graphs can be regarded as an effort to avoid the hubness phenomenon discussed by Radovanović et al. (2010).

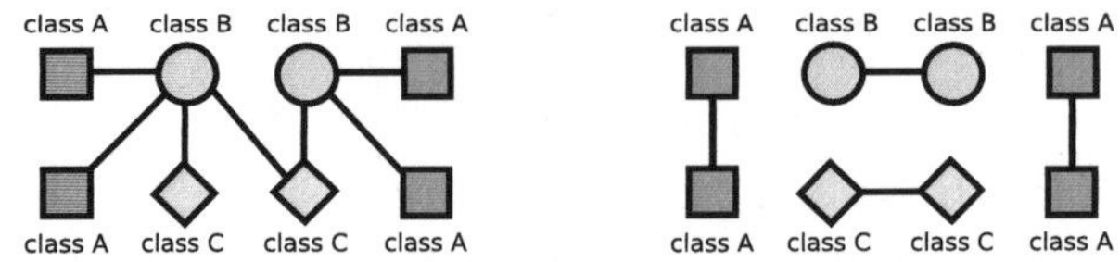

Figure 1: Two extreme cases of ϕ-edge ratio. Vertex shapes (and colors) denote the class labels. The ϕ-edge ratio of the graph on the left is 1, meaning that all edges connect vertices with different labels. The ϕ-edge ratio of the one on the right is 0, because all edges connect vertices of the same class.

Jebara et al. (2009) reported that b-matching graphs achieve semi-supervised classification accuracy higher than k-NN graphs. However, without approximation, building a b-matching graph is prohibitive in terms of computational complexity. Huang and Jebara (2007) developed a fast implementation based on belief propagation, but the guaranteed running time of the implementation is $O(bn^3)$, which is still not practical for large scale graphs. Notice that the k-NN graphs and mutual k-NN graphs can be constructed with much smaller time complexity, as we mentioned in Section 4.3. In Section exp, we empirically compare the performance of mutual k-NN graphs with that of b-matching graphs.

5.2 Mutual Nearest Neighbor in Clustering

In the clustering context, mutual k-NN graphs have been theoretically analyzed by Maier et al. (2009) with Random Geometric Graph Theory. Their study suggests that if one is interested in identifying the most significant clusters only, the mutual k-NN graphs give a better clustering result. However, it is not clear what their results imply in semi-supervised classification settings.

6 Experiments

We compare the k-NN, mutual k-NN, and b-matching graphs in word sense disambiguation and document classification tasks. All of these tasks are multi-class classification problems.

6.1 Datasets

We used two word sense disambiguation datasets in our experiment: "interest" and "line." The "interest" data is originally taken from the POS-tagged

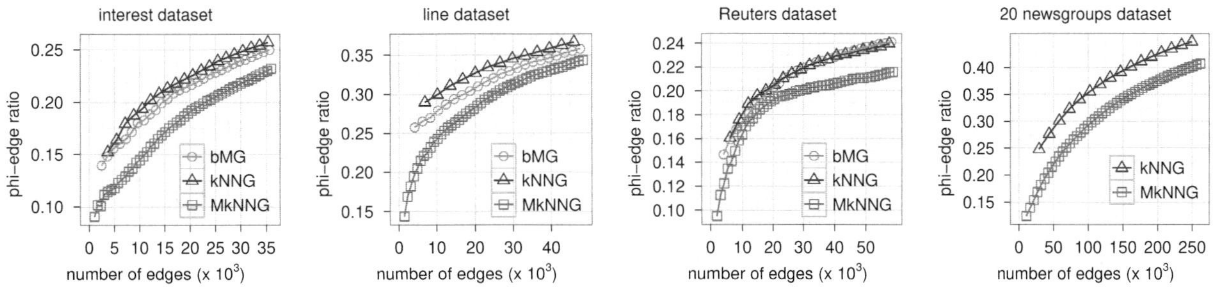

Figure 2: ϕ-edge ratios of the k-NN graph, mutual k-NN graph, and b-matching graphs. The ϕ-edge ratio of a graph is a measure of how much the cluster assumption is violated; hence, smaller the ϕ-edge ratio, the better. The plot for b-matching graph is missing for the 20 newsgroups dataset, because its construction did not finish after one week for this dataset.

dataset	examples	features	labels
interest	2,368	3,689	6
line	4,146	8,009	6
Reuters	4,028	17,143	4
20 newsgroups	19,928	62,061	20

Table 2: Datasets used in experiments.

portion of the Wall Street Journal Corpus. Each instance of the polysemous word "interest" has been tagged with one of the six senses in Longman Dictionary of Contemporary English. The details of the dataset are described in Bruce and Wiebe (1994). The "line" data is originally used in numerous comparative studies of word sense disambiguation. Each instance of the word "line" has been tagged with one of the six senses on the WordNet thesaurus. Further details can be found in the Leacock et al. (1993). Following Niu et al. (2005), we used the following context features in the word sense disambiguation tasks: part-of-speech of neighboring words, single words in the surrounding context, and local collocation. Details of these context features can be found in Lee and Ng (2002).

The Reuters dataset is extracted from RCV1-v2/LYRL2004, a text categorization test collection (Lewis et al., 2004). In the same manner as Crammer et al. (2009), we produced the classification dataset by selecting approximately 4,000 documents from 4 general topics (corporate, economic, government and markets) at random. The features described in Lewis et al. (2004) are used with this dataset.

The 20 newsgroups dataset is a popular dataset frequently used for document classification and clustering. The dataset consists of approximately 20,000 messages on newsgroups and is originally distributed by Lang (1995). Each message is assigned one of the 20 possible labels indicating which newsgroup it has been posted to, and represented as binary bag-of-words features as described in Rennie (2001).

Table 2 summarizes the characteristics of the datasets used in our experiments.

6.2 Experimental Setup

Our focus in this paper is a semi-supervised classification setting in which the dataset contains a small amount of labeled examples and a large amount of unlabeled examples. To simulate such settings, we create 10 sets of labeled examples, with each set consisting of randomly selected l examples from the original dataset, where l is 10 percent of the total number of examples. For each set, the remaining 90 percent constitute the unlabeled examples whose labels must be inferred.

After we build a graph from the data using one of the graph construction methods discussed earlier, a graph-based semi-supervised classification algorithm must be run on the resulting graph to infer labels to the unlabeled examples (vertices). We use two most frequently used classification algorithms: Gaussian Random Fields (GRF) (Zhu et al., 2003) and the Local/Global Consistency algorithm (LGC) (Zhou et al., 2004). Averaged classification accuracy is used as the evaluation metric. For all datasets, co-

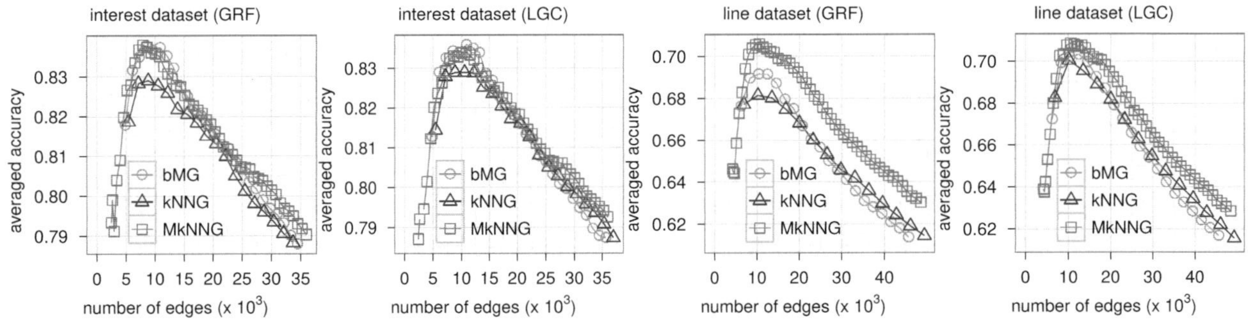

Figure 3: Averaged classification accuracies for k-NN graphs, b-matching graphs and mutual k-NN graphs (+ maximum spanning trees) in the interest and line datasets.

sine similarity is used as the similarity measure between examples.

In "interest" and "line" datasets, we compare the performance of the graph construction methods over the broad range of their parameters; i.e., b in b-matching graphs and k in (mutual) k-NN graphs.

In Reuters and the 20 newsgroups datasets, 2-fold cross validation is used to determine the hyperparameters (k and b) of the graph construction methods; i.e., we split the labeled data into two folds, and used one fold for training and the other for development, and then switch the folds in order to find the optimal hyperparameter among $k, b \in \{2, \ldots, 50\}$. The smoothing parameter μ of LGC is fixed at $\mu = 0.9$.

6.3 Results

6.3.1 Comparison of ϕ-Edge Ratio

We first compared the ϕ-edge ratios of k-NN graphs, mutual k-NN graphs, and b-matching graphs to evaluate the quality of the graphs apart from specific classification algorithms.

For this purpose, we define the *ϕ-edge ratio* as the yardstick to measure the quality of a graph. Here, a *ϕ-edge* of a labeled graph $(\mathcal{G}, \boldsymbol{y})$ is any edge (v_i, v_j) for which $y_i \neq y_j$ (Cesa-Bianchi et al., 2010), and we define the *ϕ-edge ratio* of a graph as the number of ϕ-edges divided by the total number of edges in the graph. Since most graph-based semi-supervised classification methods propagate label information along edges, edges connecting vertices with different labels may lead to misclassification. Hence, a graph with a smaller ϕ-edge ratio is more desirable. Figure 1 illustrates two toy graphs with extreme values of ϕ-edge ratio.

Figure 2 shows the plots of ϕ-edge ratios of the compared graph construction methods when the values of parameters k (for k-NN and mutual k-NN graphs) and b (for b-matching graphs) are varied. In these plots, the y-axes denote the ϕ-edge ratio of the constructed graphs. The x-axes denote the number of edges in the constructed graphs, and not the values of parameters k or b, because setting parameters b and k to an equal value does not achieve the same level of sparsity (number of edges) in the resulting graphs.

As mentioned earlier, the smaller the ϕ-edge ratio, the more desirable. As the figure shows, mutual k-NN graphs achieve smaller ϕ-edge ratio than other graphs if they are compared at the same level of graph sparsity.

The plot for b-matching graph is missing for the 20 newsgroups data, because we were unable to complete its construction in one week[2]. Meanwhile, a k-NN graph and a mutual k-NN graph for the same dataset can be constructed in less than 15 minutes on the same computer.

6.3.2 Classification Results

Figure 3 shows the classification accuracy of GRF and LGC on the different types of graphs constructed for the interest and line datasets. As in Figure 2, the x-axes represent the sparsity of the constructed graphs measured by the number of edges in the graph, which can change as the hyperparameter (b or k) of the compared graph construction methods

[2]All experiments were run on a machine with 2.3 GHz AMD Opteron 8356 processors and 256 GB RAM.

				kNN graph		b-matching graph		mutual kNN graph	
dataset	algorithm	Dense	MST	original	+MST	original	+MST	original	+MST
Reuters	GRF	43.65	72.74	81.70	80.89	84.04	84.04	**85.01**	84.72
Reuters	LGC	43.66	71.78	82.60	82.60	84.42	84.42	84.81	**84.85**
20 newsgroups	GRF	10.18	66.96	75.47	75.47	—	—	76.31	**76.46**
20 newsgroups	LGC	14.51	65.82	75.19	75.19	—	—	75.27	**75.41**

Table 3: Document classification accuracies for k-NN graphs, b-matching graphs, and mutual k-NN graphs. The column for 'Dense' is the result for the graph with the original similarity matrix W' as the adjacency matrix; i.e., without using any graph construction (sparsification) methods. The column for 'MST' is the result the for the maximum spanning tree. b-matching graph construction did not complete after one week on the 20 newsgroups data, and hence no results are shown.

	vs. kNNG		vs. bMG	
dataset (algo)	orig	+MST	orig	+MST
Reuters (GRF)	$\gg$	$\gg$	$>$	$\sim$
Reuters (LGC)	$\gg$	$\gg$	$\sim$	$\sim$
20 newsgroups (GRF)	$\gg$	$\gg$	—	—
20 newsgroups (LGC)	$\sim$	$>$	—	—

Table 4: One-sided paired t-test results of averaged accuracies between using mutual k-NN graphs and other graphs. "$\gg$", "$>$", and "$\sim$" correspond to p-value < 0.01, $(0.01, 0.05]$, and > 0.05 respectively.

are varied.

As shown in the figure, the combination of mutual k-NN graphs and the maximum spanning trees achieves better accuracy than other graph construction methods in most cases, when they are compared at the same levels of graph sparsity (number of edges).

Table 3 summarizes the classification accuracy on the document classification datasets. As a baseline, the table also shows the results ('Dense') on the dense complete graph with the original all-pairs similarity matrix W' as the adjacency matrix (i.e., no graph sparsification), as well as the results for using the maximum spanning tree alone as the graph construction method.

In all cases, mutual k-NN graphs achieve better classification accuracy than other graphs.

Table 4 reports the one-sided paired t-test results of averaged accuracies with k-NN graphs and b-matching graphs against our proposed approach, the combination of mutual k-NN graphs and maximum spanning trees. From Table 4, we see that mutual k-NN graphs perform significantly better than k-NN graphs. On the other hand, theere is no significant difference in the accuracy of the mutual k-NN graphs and b-matching graphs. However, mutual k-NN graphs achieves the same level of accuracy with b-matching graphs, at much less computation time and are applicable to large datasets. As mentioned earlier, mutual k-NN graphs can be computed with less than 15 minutes in the 20 newsgroups data, while b-matching graphs cannot be computed in one week.

7 Conclusion

In this paper, we have proposed to use mutual k-NN graphs instead of the standard k-NN graphs for graph-based semi-supervised learning. In mutual k-NN graphs, all vertices have degree upper bounded by k. We have demonstrated that this type of graph construction alleviates the hub effects stated in Radovanović et al. (2010), which also makes the graph more consistent with the cluster assumption. In addition, we have shown that the weak connectivity of mutual k-NN graphs is not a serious problem if we augment the graph with maximum spanning trees. Experimental results on various natural language processing datasets show that mutual k-NN graphs lead to higher classification accuracy than the standard k-NN graphs, when two popular label inference methods are run on these graphs.

References

Andrei Alexandrescu and Katrin Kirchhoff. 2007. Data-driven graph construction for semi-supervised graph-based learning in NLP. In *Proc. of HLT-NAACL*.

Andrei Alexandrescu and Katrin Kirchhoff. 2009. Graph-based learning for statistical machine translation. In *Proc. of NAACL-HLT*.

Alina Beygelzimer, Sham Kakade, and John Langford. 2006. Cover trees for nearest neighbor. In *Proc. of ICML*.

Rebecca Bruce and Janyce Wiebe. 1994. Word-sense disambiguation using decomposable models. In *Proc. of ACL*.

Jérôme Callut, Kevin Françoisse, Marco Saerens, and Pierre Dupont. 2008. Semi-supervised classification from discriminative random walks. In *Proc. of ECML-PKDD*.

Nicolo Cesa-Bianchi, Claudio Gentile, Fabio Vitale, and Giovanni Zappella. 2010. Random spanning trees and the prediction of weighted graphs. In *Proc. of ICML*.

Jie Chen, Haw-ren Fang, and Yousef Saad. 2009. Fast approximate kNN graph construction for high dimensional data via recursive lanczos bisection. *Journal of Machine Learning Research*, 10.

Koby Crammer, Mark Dredze, and Alex Kulesza. 2009. Multi-class confidence weighted algorithms. In *Proc. of EMNLP*.

Michael L. Fredman and Robert Endre Tarjan. 1987. Fibonacci heaps and their uses in improved network optimization algorithms. *J. ACM*, 34:596–615, July.

Andrew B. Goldberg and Xiaojin Zhu. 2006. Seeing stars when there aren't many stars: graph-based semi-supervised learning for sentiment categorization. In *Proc. of TextGraphs Workshop on HLT-NAACL*.

Bert Huang and Tony Jebara. 2007. Loopy belief propagation for bipartite maximum weight b-matching. In *Proc. of AISTATS*.

Tony Jebara, Jun Wang, and Shih-Fu Chang. 2009. Graph construction and b-matching for semi-supervised learning. In *Proc. of ICML*.

Ken Lang. 1995. Newsweeder: Learning to filter netnews. In *Proc. of ICML*.

Claudia Leacock, Geoffrey Towell, and Ellen Voorhees. 1993. Corpus-based statistical sense resolution. In *Proc. of ARPA Workshop on HLT*.

Yoong Keok Lee and Hwee Tou Ng. 2002. An empirical evaluation of knowledge sources and learning algorithms for word sense disambiguation. In *Proc. of EMNLP*.

David D. Lewis, Yiming Yang, Tony G. Rose, Fan Li, G. Dietterich, and Fan Li. 2004. RCV1: A new benchmark collection for text categorization research. *Journal of Machine Learning Research*, 5.

Markus Maier, Matthias Hein, and Ulrike von Luxburg. 2009. Optimal construction of k-nearest-neighbor graphs for identifying noisy clusters. *Journal of Theoretical Computer Science*, 410.

Zheng-Yu Niu, Dong-Hong Ji, and Chew Lim Tan. 2005. Word sense disambiguation using label propagation based semi-supervised learning. In *Proc. of ACL*.

Miloš Radovanović, Alexandros Nanopoulos, and Mirjana Ivanović. 2010. Hub in space: popular nearest neighbors in high-dimensional data. *Journal of Machine Learning Research*, 11.

Parikshit Ram, Dongryeol Lee, William March, and Alexander Gray. 2010. Linear-time algorithms for pairwise statistical problems. In *Proc. of NIPS*.

Jason D. M. Rennie. 2001. Improving multi-class text classification with naive bayes. Master's thesis, Massachusetts Institute of Technology. AITR-2001-004.

Martin Szummer and Tommi Jaakkola. 2002. Partially labeled classification with markov random walks. In *Proc. of NIPS*.

Yasuo Tabei, Takeaki Uno, Masashi Sugiyama, and Koji Tsuda. 2010. Single versus multiple sorting in all pairs similarity search. In *Proc. of ACML*.

Jun Wang, Tony Jebara, and Shih-Fu. Chang. 2008. Graph transduction via alternating minimization. In *Proc. of ICML*.

Dengyong Zhou, Olivier Bousquet, Thomas Navin Lal, Jason Weston, and Bernhard Schölkopf. 2004. Learning with local and global consistency. In *Proc. of NIPS*.

Xiaojin Zhu, Zoubin Ghahramani, and John D. Lafferty. 2003. Semi-supervised learning using gaussian fields and harmonic functions. In *Proc. of ICML*.

Xiaojin Zhu. 2005. *Semi-Supervised Learning with Graphs*. Ph.D. thesis, Carnegie Mellon University. CMU-LTI-05-192.

Xiaojin Zhu. 2008. Semi-supervised learning literature survey. Technical Report 1530, Computer Sciences, University of Wisconsin-Madison.

Automatically Building Training Examples for Entity Extraction

Marco Pennacchiotti
Yahoo! Labs
Sunnyvale, CA, USA
pennac@yahoo-inc.com

Patrick Pantel
Microsoft Research
Redmond, WA, USA
ppantel@microsoft.com

Abstract

In this paper we present methods for automatically acquiring training examples for the task of entity extraction. Experimental evidence show that: (1) our methods compete with a current heavily supervised state-of-the-art system, within 0.04 absolute mean average precision; and (2) our model significantly outperforms other supervised and unsupervised baselines by between 0.15 and 0.30 in absolute mean average precision.

1 Introduction

Entity extraction is a fundamental task in NLP and related applications. It is broadly defined as the task of extracting entities of a given semantic class from texts (e.g., lists of actors, musicians, cities). Search engines such as Bing, Yahoo, and Google collect large sets of entities to better interpret queries (Tan and Peng, 2006), to improve query suggestions (Cao et al., 2008) and to understand query intents (Hu et al., 2009). In response, automated techniques for entity extraction have been proposed (Paşca, 2007; Wang and Cohen, 2008; Chaudhuri et al., 2009; Pantel et al., 2009).

There is mounting evidence that combining knowledge sources and information extraction systems yield significant improvements over applying each in isolation (Paşca et al., 2006; Mirkin et al., 2006). This intuition is explored by the Ensemble Semantics (ES) framework proposed by Pennacchiotti and Pantel (2009), which outperforms previous state-of-the-art systems. A severe limitation of this type of extraction system is its reliance on editorial judgments for building large training sets for each semantic class to be extracted. This is particularly troublesome for applications such as web search that require large numbers of semantic classes in order to have a sufficient coverage of facts and objects (Tan and Peng, 2006). Hand-crafting training sets across international markets is often infeasible. In an exploratory study we estimated that a pool of editors would need roughly 300 working days to complete a basic set of 100 English classes using the ES framework. Critically needed are methods for automatically building training sets that preserve the extraction quality.

In this paper, we propose simple and intuitively appealing solutions to automatically build training sets. Positive and negative training sets for a target semantic class are acquired by leveraging: i) 'trusted' sources such as structured databases (e.g., IMDB or Wikipedia for acquiring a list of $Actors$); ii) automatically constructed semantic lexicons; and iii) instances of semantic classes other than the target class. Our models focus on extracting training sets that are large, balanced, and representative of the unlabeled data. These models can be used in any extraction setting, where 'trusted' sources of knowledge are available: Today, the popularity of structured and semi-structured sources such as Wikipedia and internet databases, makes this approach widely applicable. As an example, in this paper we show that our methods can be successfully adapted and used in the ES framework. This gives us the possibility to test the methods on a large-scale entity extraction task. We replace the manually built training data in the the ES model with the training data built

Proceedings of the Fifteenth Conference on Computational Natural Language Learning, pages 163–171,
Portland, Oregon, USA, 23–24 June 2011.

by our algorithms. We show by means of a large empirical study that our algorithms perform nearly as good as the fully supervised ES model, within 4% in absolute mean average precision. Further, we compare the performance of our method against both Paşca et al. (2006) and Mirkin et al. (2006), showing 17% and 15% improvements in absolute mean average precision, respectively.

The main contributions of this paper are:

- We propose several general methods for automatically acquiring labeled training data; we show that they can be used in a large-scale extraction framework, namely ES; and
- We show empirical evidence on a large-scale entity extraction task that our system using automatically labeled training data performs nearly as well as the fully-supervised ES model, and that it significantly outperforms state-of-the-art systems.

2 Automatic Acquisition of Training Data

Supervised machine learning algorithms require training data that is: (1) balanced and large enough to correctly model the problem at hand (Kubat and Matwin, 1997; Japkowicz and Stephen, 2002); and (2) representative of the unlabeled data to decode, i.e., training and unlabeled instances should be ideally drawn from the same distribution (Blumer et al., 1989; Blum and Langley, 1997). If these two properties are not met, various learning problems, such as overfitting, can drastically impair predictive accuracy. To address the above properties, a common approach is to select a subset of the unlabeled data (i.e., the instances to be decoded), and manually label them to build the training set.

In this section we propose methods to automate this task by leveraging the multitude of structured knowledge bases available on the Web.

Formally, given a *target class* c, our goal is to implement methods to automatically build a training set $T(c)$, composed of both positive and negative examples, respectively $P(c)$ and $N(c)$; and to apply $T(c)$ to classify (or rank) a set of *unlabeled data* $U(c)$, by using a learning algorithm. For example, in entity extraction, given the class $Actors$, we might have $P(c) = \{Brad\ Pitt,\ Robert\ De\ Niro\}$ and $N(c) = \{Serena\ Williams,\ Rome,\ Robert\ Demiro\}$.

Below, we define the components of a typical knowledge acquisition system as in the ES framework, where our methods can be applied :

Sources. Textual repositories of information, either structured (e.g., Freebase), semi-structured (e.g., HTML tables) or unstructured (e.g., a webcrawl). Information sources serve as inputs to the extraction system, either for the Knowledge Extractors to generate candidate instances, or for the Feature Generators to generate features (see below).

Knowledge Extractors (KE). Algorithms responsible for extracting candidate instances such as entities or facts. Extractors fall into two categories: trusted and untrusted. *Trusted extractors* execute on structured sources where the contents are deemed to be highly accurate. *Untrusted extractors* execute on unstructured or semi-structured sources and generally generate high coverage but noisy knowledge.

Feature Generators. Methods that extract evidence (features) of knowledge in order to decide which extracted candidate instances are correct.

Ranker. A module for ranking the extracted instances using the features generated by the feature generators. In supervised ML-based rankers, labeled training instances are required to train the model. Our goal here is to automatically label training instances thus avoiding the editorial costs.

2.1 Acquiring Positive Examples

Trusted positives: Candidate instances for a class c that are extracted by a trusted Knowledge Extractor (e.g., a wrapper induction system over IMDB), tend to be mostly positive examples. A basic approach to acquiring a set of positive examples is then to sample from the unlabeled set $U(c)$ as follows:

$$P(c) = \{i \in U(c) : (\exists\, KE_i | KE_i\ is\ trusted\} \quad (1)$$

where KE_i is a knowledge extractor that extracted instance i.

The main advantage of this method is that $P(c)$ is guaranteed to be highly accurate, i.e., most instances are true positives. On the downside, instances in $P(c)$ are not necessarily representative of the untrusted KEs. This can highly impact the performance of the learning algorithm, which could overfit the training data on properties that are specific to the trusted KEs, but that are not representative of the true population to be decoded (which is largely coming from untrusted KEs).

We therefore enforce that the instances in $P(c)$ are extracted not only from a trusted KE, but also from any of the untrusted extractors:

$$P(c) = \{i \in U(c) : \exists\, KE_i | KE_i \; is \; trusted \wedge \\ \exists\, KE_j | KE_j \; is \; untrusted\} \quad (2)$$

External positives: This method selects the set of positive examples $P(c)$ from an external repository, such as an ontology, a database, or an automatically harvested source. The main advantage of this method is that such resources are widely available for many knowledge extraction tasks. Yet, the risk is that $P(c)$ is not representative of the unlabeled instances $U(c)$, as they are drawn from different populations.

2.1.1 Acquiring Negative Examples

Acquiring negative training examples is a much more daunting task (Fagni and Sebastiani, 2007). The main challenge is to select a set which is a good representative of the unlabeled negatives in $U(c)$. Various strategies can be adopted, ranging from selecting near-miss examples to acquiring generic ones, each having its own pros and cons. Below we propose our methods, some building on previous work described in Section 5.

Near-class negatives: This method selects $N(c)$ from the population $U(C)$ of the set of classes C which are semantically similar to c. For example, in entity extraction, the classes $Athletes$, $Directors$ and $Musicians$ are semantically similar to the class $Actors$, while $Manufacturers$ and $Products$ are dissimilar. Similar classes allow us to select negative examples that are semantic near-misses for the class c. The hypothesis is the following:

A positive instance extracted for a class similar to the target class c, is likely to be a near-miss incorrect instance for c.

To model this hypothesis, we acquire $N(c)$ from the set of instances having the following two restrictions:

1. The instance is most likely correct for C
2. The instance is most likely incorrect for c

Note that restriction (1) alone is not sufficient, as an instance of C can be at the same time also instance of c. For example, given the target class *Actors*, the instance *'Woody Allen'* $\in$ *Directors*, is not a good negative example for *Actors*, since Woody Allen is both a director and an actor.

In order to enforce restriction (1), we select only instances that have been extracted by a trusted KE of C, i.e., the confidence of them being positive is very high. To enforce (2), we select instances that have never been extracted by any KE of c. More formally, we define $N(c)$ as follows:

$$N(c) = \bigcup_{c_i \in C} P(c_i) \setminus U(c) \quad (3)$$

The main advantage of this method is that it acquires negatives that are semantic near-misses of the target class, thus allowing the learning algorithm to focus on these borderline cases (Fagni and Sebastiani, 2007). This is a very important property, as most incorrect instances extracted by unsupervised KEs are indeed semantic near-misses. On the downside, the extracted examples are not representative of the negative examples of the target class c, since they are drawn from two different distributions.

Generic negatives: This method selects $N(c)$ from the population $U(C)$ of all classes C different from the target class c, i.e., both classes semantically similar and dissimilar to c. The method is very similar to the one above, apart from the selection of C, which now includes any class different from c. The underlying hypothesis is the following:

A positive instance extracted for a class different from the target class c, is likely to be an incorrect instance for c.

This method acquires negatives that are both semantic near-misses and far-misses of the target class. The learning algorithm is then able to focus both on borderline cases and on clear-cut incorrect cases, i.e. the hypothesis space is potentially larger than for the near-class method. On the downside, the distribution of c and C are very different. By enlarging the potential hypothesis space, the risk is then again to capture hypotheses that overfit the training data on properties which are not representative of the true population to be decoded.

Same-class negatives: This method selects the set of negative examples $N(c)$ from the population $U(c)$. The driving hypothesis is the following:

> *If a candidate instance for a class c has been extracted by only one KE and this KE is untrusted, then the instance is likely to be incorrect, i.e., a negative example for c.*

The above hypothesis stems from an intuitive observation common to many ensemble-based paradigms (e.g., ensemble learning in Machine Learning): the more evidence you have of a given fact, the higher is the probability of it being actually true. In our case, the fact that an instance has been extracted by only one untrusted KE, provides weak evidence that the instance is correct. $N(c)$ is defined as follows:

$$N(c) = \{i \in U(c) : \exists!\ KE_i \wedge KE_i\ is\ untrusted\} \quad (4)$$

The main advantage of this method is that the acquired instances in $N(c)$ are good representatives of the negatives that will have to be decoded, i.e., they are drawn from the same distribution $U(c)$. This allows the learning algorithm to focus on the typical properties of the incorrect examples extracted by the pool of KEs.

A drawback of this method is that instances in $N(c)$ are not guaranteed to be true negatives. It follows that the final training set may be noisy. Two main strategies can be applied to mitigate this problem: (1) Use a learning algorithm which is robust to noise in the training data; and (2) Adopt techniques to automatically reduce or eliminate noise. We here adopt the first solution, and leave the second as a possible avenue for future work, as described in Section 6. In Section 4 we demonstrate the amount of noise in our training data, and show that its impact is not detrimental for the overall performance of the system.

3 A Use Case: Entity Extraction

Entity extraction is a fundamental task in NLP (Cimiano and Staab, 2004; McCarthy and Lehnert, 2005) and web search (Chaudhuri et al., 2009; Hu et al., 2009; Tan and Peng, 2006), responsible for extracting instances of semantic classes (e.g., *'Brad Pitt'* and *'Tom Hanks'* are instances of the class *Actors*). In this section we apply our methods for automatically acquiring training data to the ES entity extraction system described in Pennacchiotti and Pantel (2009).[1]

The system relies on the following three **knowledge extractors**. $\boldsymbol{KE_{trs}}$: a 'trusted' database wrapper extractor acquiring entities from sources such as *Yahoo! Movies*, *Yahoo! Music* and *Yahoo! Sports*, for extracting respectively *Actors*, *Musicians* and *Athletes*. $\boldsymbol{KE_{pat}}$: an 'untrusted' pattern-based extractor reimplementing Paşca et al.'s (2006) state-of-the-art web-scale fact extractor. $\boldsymbol{KE_{dis}}$: an 'untrusted' distributional extractor implementing a variant of Pantel et al.'s (2009).

The system includes four **feature generators**, which compute a total of 402 features of various types extracted from the following sources: (1) a body of 600 million documents crawled from the Web at Yahoo! in 2008; (2) one year of web search queries issued to Yahoo! Search; (3) all HTML inner tables extracted from the above web crawl; (4) an official Wikipedia dump from February 2008, consisting of about 2 million articles.

The system adopts as a **ranker** a supervised Gradient Boosted Decision Tree regression model (GBDT) (Friedman, 2001). GBDT is generally considered robust to noisy training data, and hence is a good choice given the errors introduced by our automatic training set construction algorithms.

3.1 Training Data Acquisition

The positive and negative components of the training set for GBDT are built using the methods presented in Section 2, as follows:

Trusted positives (P_{trs} and P_{cls}): According to Eq. 2, we acquire a set of positive instances P_{cls} as a random sample of the instances extracted by both KE_{trs} and either: KE_{dis}, KE_{pat} or both of them. As a basic variant, we also experiment with the simpler definition in Eq. 1, i.e. we acquire a set of positive instances P_{trs} as a random sample of the instances extracted by the trusted extractor KE_{trs}, irrespective of KE_{dis} and KE_{pat}.

External positives (P_{cbc}): Any external repository of positive examples would serve here. In our spe-

[1] We here give a summary description of our implementation of that system. Refer to the original paper for more details.

cific implementation, we select a set of positive examples from the CBC repository (Pantel and Lin, 2002). CBC is a word clustering algorithm that groups instances appearing in similar textual contexts. By manually analyzing the cluster members in the repository created by CBC, it is easy to pick-up the cluster(s) representing a target class.

Same-class negatives (N_{cls}): We select a set of negative instances as a random sample of the instances extracted by only one extractor, which can be either of the two untrusted ones, KE_{dis} or KE_{pat}.

Near-class negatives (N_{oth}): We select a set of negative instances, as a random sample of the instances extracted by any of our three extractors for a class different than the one at hand. We also enforce the condition that instances in N_{oth} must not have been extracted for the class at hand.

Generic negatives (N_{cbc}): We automatically select as generic negatives a random sample of instances appearing in any CBC cluster, except those containing at least one member of the class at hand (i.e., containing at least one instance extracted by one of our KEs for the given class).

4 Experimental Evaluation

In this section, we report experiments comparing the ranking performance of our different methods for acquiring training data presented in Section 3, to three different baselines and a fully supervised upper-bound.

4.1 Experimental Setup

We evaluate over three semantic classes: *Actors* (movie, tv and stage actors); *Athletes* (professional and amateur); *Musicians* (singers, musicians, composers, bands, and orchestras), so to compare with (Pennacchiotti and Pantel, 2009). Ranking performance is tested over the test set described in the above paper, composed of 500 instances, randomly selected from the instances extracted by KE_{pat} and KE_{dis} for each of the classes[2].

We experiment with various instantiations of the ES system, each trained on a different training set obtained from our methods. The different system instantiations (i.e., different training sets) are reported in Table 1 (Columns 1-3). Each training set consists of 500 positive examples, and 500 negative examples.

As an **upper bound**, we use the ES system, where the training consists of 500 manually annotated instances (P_{man} and N_{man}), randomly selected from those extracted by the KEs. This allows us to directly check if our automatically acquired training sets can compete to the human upper-bound. We also compare to the following baselines.

Baseline 1: An unsupervised rule-based ES system, assigning the lowest score to instances extracted by only one KE, when the KE is untrusted; and assigning the highest score to any other instance.

Baseline 2: An unsupervised rule-based ES system, adopting as KEs the two untrusted extractors KE_{pat} and KE_{dis}, and a rule-based *Ranker* that assigns scores to instances according to the sum of their normalized confidence scores.

Baseline 3: An instantiation of our ES system, trained on P_{man} and N_{man}. The only difference with the upper-bound is that it uses only two features, namely the confidence score returned by KE_{dis} and KE_{pat}. This instantiation implements the system presented in (Mirkin et al., 2006).

For evaluation, we use *average precision* (AP), a standard information retrieval measure for evaluating ranking algorithms:

$$AP(L) = \frac{\sum_{i=1}^{|L|} P(i) \cdot corr(i)}{\sum_{i=1}^{|L|} corr(i)} \quad (5)$$

where L is a ranked list produced by a system, $P(i)$ is the precision of L at rank i, and *corr(i)* is 1 if the instance at rank i is correct, and 0 otherwise.

In order to accurately compute statistical significance, we divide the test set in 10-folds, and compute the AP mean and variance obtained over the 10-folds. For each configuration, we perform the random sampling of the training set five times, rebuilding the model each time, to estimate the variance when varying the training sampling.

4.2 Experimental Results

Table 1 reports average precision (AP) results for different ES instantiations, separately on the three

[2]We do not test over instances extracted by KE_{trs}, as they do not go though the decoding phase

System	*Training Set*		*AP*			*MAP*
	Positives	**Negatives**	**Actors**	**Athletes**	**Musicians**	
Baseline1 (unsup.)	-	-	0.562	0.535	0.437	0.511
Baseline2 (unsup.)	-	-	0.676	0.664	0.576	0.639
Baseline3 (sup.)	P_{man}	N_{man}	0.715	0.697	0.576	0.664
Upper-bound (full-sup.)	P_{man}	N_{man}	0.860§	0.901§	0.786§	0.849§
S1.	P_{cls}	N_{oth}	0.751†	**0.880**§	0.642	0.758§
S2.	P_{cls}	N_{cbc}	0.734†	0.854§	0.644	0.744‡
S3.	P_{cls}	N_{cls}	**0.842**§	0.806§	**0.770**§	0.806§
S4.	P_{cls}	$N_{oth} + N_{cbc}$	0.756‡	0.853§	0.693‡	0.767§
S5.	P_{cls}	$N_{cls} + N_{oth}$	0.835§	0.807§	0.763§	0.802§
S6.	P_{cls}	$N_{cls} + N_{cbc}$	0.838§	0.822§	0.768§	**0.809**§
S7.	P_{cls}	$N_{cls} + N_{oth} + N_{cbc}$	0.838§	0.818§	0.764§	0.807§

Table 1: Average precision (AP) results of systems using different training sets, compared to two usupervised Baselines, a supervised Baseline, and a fully supervised upper-bound system. § indicates statistical significance at the 0.95 level wrt all Baselines. ‡ indicates statistical significance at the 0.95 level wrt Baseline1 and Baseline 2. † indicates statistical significance at the 0.95 level wrt Baseline1.

classes; and the mean average precision (MAP) computed across the classes. We report results using P_{cls} as positive training, and varying the negative training composition[3]. Systems S1-S3 use a single method to build the negatives. Systems S4-S6 combine two methods (250 examples from one method, 250 from the other), and S7 combines all three methods. Table 3 reports additional basic results when varying the positive training set composition, and fixing the best performing negative set (namely N_{cls}).

Table 1 shows that all systems outperform the baselines in MAP, with 0.95 statistical significance, but $S2$ which is not significant wrt *Baseline 3*. $S6$ is the best performing system, achieving 0.809 MAP, only 4% below the supervised upper-bound (statistically insignificant at the 0.95 level). These results indicate that our methods for automatically acquiring training data are highly effective and competitive with manually crafted training sets.

A class-by-class analysis reveals similar behavior for *Actors* and *Musicians*. For these two classes, the best negative set is N_{cls} (system $S3$), achieving alone the best AP (respectively 0.842 and 0.770 for *Actors* and *Musicians*, 2.1% and 1.6% points below the upper-bound). N_{oth} and N_{cbc} show a lower accuracy, more than 10% below N_{cls}. This suggest that the most promising strategy for automatically

[3]For space limitation we cannot report exhaustively all combinations.

Negative set	*False Negatives*		
	Actors	**Athletes**	**Musicians**
N_{cls}	5%	45%	30%
N_{oth}	0%	10%	10%
N_{cbc}	0%	0%	15%

Table 2: Percentage of false negatives in different types of negative sets, across the three experimented classes (estimations over a random sample of 20 examples per class).

acquiring negative training data is to collect examples from the target class, as they guarantee to be drawn from the same distribution as the instances to be decoded. The use of near- and far-misses is still valuable (AP results are still better than the baselines), but less effective.

Results for *Athletes* give different evidence: the best performing negative set is N_{oth}, performing significantly better than N_{cls}. To investigate this contrasting result, we manually picked 20 examples from N_{cls}, N_{oth} and N_{cbc} for each class, and checked their degree of noise, i.e., how many false negatives they contain. Table 2 reports the results: these numbers indicate that the N_{cls} is very noisy for the *Athletes* class, while it is more clean for the other two classes. This suggests that the learning algorithm, while being robust enough to cope with the small noise in N_{cls} for *Actors* and *Musicians*, it starts to diverge when too many false negatives are presented for training, as it happens for *Athletes*.

False negatives in N_{cls} are correct instances extracted by one untrusted KE alone. The results in

Table 2 indicates that our untrusted KEs are more accurate in extracting instances for *Athletes* than for the other classes: accurate enough to make our training set too noisy, thus decreasing the performance of $S3$ wrt $S1$ and $S2$. This indicates that the effectiveness of N_{cls} decreases when the accuracy of the untrusted KEs is higher.

A good strategy to avoid the above problem is to pair N_{cls} with another negative set, either N_{cbc} or N_{oth}, as in $S5$ and $S6$, respectively. Then, when the above problem is presented, the learning algorithm can rely on the other negative set to compensate some for the noise. Indeed, when adding N_{cbc} to N_{cls} (system $S6$) the accuracy over *Athletes* improves, while the overall performance across all classes (MAP) is kept constant wrt the system using N_{cls} ($S3$).

It is interesting that in Table 2, N_{cbc} and N_{oth} also have a few false negatives. An intrinsic analysis reveals that these are either: (1) Incorrect instances of the other classes that are actual instances of the target class; (2) Correct instances of other classes that are also instances of the target class. Case (1) is caused by errors of KEs for the other classes (e.g., erroneously extracting *'Matthew Flynt'* as a *Musician*). Case (2) covers cases in which instances are ambiguous across classes, for example *'Kerry Taylor'* is both an *Actor* and a *Musician*. This observation is still surprising, since Eq. 3 explicitly removes from N_{cbc} and N_{oth} any correct instance of the target class extracted by the KEs. The presence of false negatives is then due to the low coverage of the KEs for the target class, e.g. the KEs were not able to extract *'Matthew Flynt'* and *'Kerry Taylor'* as actors.

Correlations. We computed the Spearman correlation coefficient r among the rankings produced by the different system instantiations, to verify how complementary the information enclosed in the training sets are for building the learning model. Among the basic systems $S1 - S3$, the highest correlation is between $S1$ and $S2$ ($r = 0.66$ in average across all classes), which is expected, since they both apply the principle of acquiring negative examples from classes other than the target one. $S3$ exhibits lower correlation with both $S1$ and $S2$, respectively $r = 0.57$ and $r = 0.53$, suggesting that it is complementary to them. Also, the best system $S6$ has higher correlation with $S3$ ($r = 0.94$) than with $S2$ ($r = 0.62$), indicating that in the combination of N_{cls} and N_{cbc}, most of the model is built on N_{cls}.

System	*Training Set*		*AP*			*MAP*
	Pos.	**Neg.**	**Act.**	**Ath.**	**Mus.**	
S3.	P_{cls}	N_{cls}	0.842	0.806	0.770	0.806
S8.	P_{trs}	N_{cls}	0.556	0.779	0.557	0.631
S9.	P_{cbc}	N_{cls}	0.633	0.521	0.561	0.571

Table 3: Comparative average precision (AP) results for systems using different positive sets as training data.

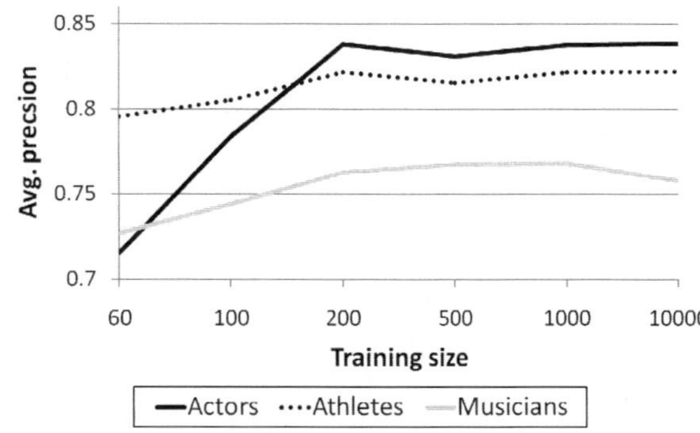

Figure 1: Average precision of system *S6* with different training sizes.

Varying the positive training. Table 3 reports results when fixing the negative set to the best performing N_{cls}, and exploring the use of other positive sets. As expected P_{cls} largely outperforms P_{trs}, confirming that removing the constraint in Eq. 2 and using the simpler Eq. 1 makes the training set unrepresentative of the unlabeled population. A similar observation stands for P_{cbc}. These results indicate that having a good trusted KE, or even an external resource of positives, is effective only when selecting from the training set examples that are also extracted by the untrusted KEs.

Varying the training size. In Figure 1 we report an analysis of the AP achieved by the best performing System ($S6$), when varying the training size, i.e., changing the cardinality of P_{cls} and $N_{cls} + N_{cbc}$. The results show that a relatively small-sized training set offers good performance, the plateau being reached already with 500 training examples. This is an encouraging result, showing that our methods can potentially be applied also in cases where few examples are available, e.g., for rare or not well-represented classes.

5 Related Work

Most relevant are efforts in *semi-supervised learning*. Semi-supervised systems use both labeled and unlabeled data to train a machine learning system. Most common techniques are based on co-training and self-training. *Co-training* uses a small set of labeled examples to train two classifiers at the same time. The classifiers use independent views (i.e. 'conditionally independent' feature sets) to represent the labeled examples. After the learning phase, the most confident predictions of each classifier on the unlabeled data are used to increase the labeled set of the other. These two phases are repeated until a stop condition is met. Co-training has been successfully applied to various applications, such as statistical parsing (Sarkar, 2001) and web pages classification (Yarowsky, 1998). *Self-training* techniques (or bootsrapping) (Yarowsky, 1995) start with a small set of labeled data, and iteratively classify unlabeled data, selecting the most confident predictions as additional training. Self-training has been applied in many NLP tasks, such as word sense disambiguation (Yarowsky, 1995) and relation extraction (Hearst, 1992). Unlike typical semi-supervised approaches, our approach reduces the needed amount of labeled data not by acting on the learning algorithm itself (any algorithm can be used in our approach), but on the method to acquire the labeled training data.

Our work also relates to the automatic acquisition of labeled negative training data. Yangarber et al. (2002) propose a pattern-based bootstrapping approach for harvesting generalized names (e.g., diseases, locations), where labeled negative examples for a given class are taken from positive seed examples of 'competing' classes (e.g. examples of diseases are used as negatives for locations). The approach is semi-supervised, in that it requires some manually annotated seeds. The study shows that using competing categories improves the accuracy of the system, by avoiding *sematic drift*, which is a common cause of divergence in boostrapping approaches. Similar approaches are used among others in (Thelen and Riloff, 2002) for learning semantic lexicons, in (Collins and Singer, 1999) for named-entity recognition, and in (Fagni and Sebastiani, 2007) for hierarchical text categorization. Some of our methods rely on the same intuition described above, i.e., using instances of other classes as negative training examples. Yet, the ES framework allows us to add further restrictions to improve the quality of the data.

6 Conclusion

We presented simple and general techniques for automatically acquiring training data, and then tested them in the context of the Ensemble Semantics framework. Experimental results show that our methods can compete with supervised systems using manually crafted training data. It is our hope that these simple and easy-to-implement methods can alleviate some of the cost of building machine learning architectures for supporting open-domain information extraction, where the potentially very large number of classes to be extracted makes infeasible the use of manually labeled training data.

There are many avenues for future work. Although our reliance on high-quality knowledge sources is not an issue for many head classes, it poses a challenge for tail classes such as 'wine connoisseurs', where finding alternative sources of high precision samples is important. We also plan to explore techniques to automatically identify and eliminate mislabeled examples in the training data as in (Rebbapragada and Brodley, 2007), and relax the boolean assumption of trusted/untrusted extractors into a graded one. Another important issue regards the discovery of 'near-classes' for collecting near-classes negatives: we plan to automate this step by adapting existing techniques as in (McIntosh, 2010). Finally, we plan to experiment on a larger set of classes, to show the generalizability of the approach.

Our current work focuses on leveraging auto-learning to create an extensive taxonomy of classes, which will constitute the foundation of a very large knowledge-base for supporting web search.

References

Avrim L. Blum and Pat Langley. 1997. Selection of relevant features and examples in machine learning. *Artificial Intelligence*, 97:245–271.

A. Blumer, A. Ehrenfeucht, D. Haussler, and M.K. Warmuth. 1989. Proceedings of ltc-07. *Journal of ACM*, 36:929–965.

Huanhuan Cao, Daxin Jiang, Jian Pei, Qi He, Zhen Liao, Enhong Chen, and Hang Li. 2008. Context-aware query suggestion by mining click-through and session data. In *Proceedings of KDD-08*, pages 875–883.

Surajit Chaudhuri, Venkatesh Ganti, and Dong Xin. 2009. Exploiting web search to generate synonyms for entities. In *Proceedings of WWW-09*, pages 151–160.

Philipp Cimiano and Steffen Staab. 2004. Learning by googling. *SIGKDD Explorations*, 6(2):24–34.

M. Collins and Y. Singer. 1999. Unsupervised models for named entity classification. In *Proceedings of WVLC/EMNLP-99*, pages 100–110.

Tiziano Fagni and Fabrizio Sebastiani. 2007. On the selection of negative examples for hierarchical text categorization. In *Proceedings of LTC-07*, pages 24–28.

Jerome H. Friedman. 2001. Greedy function approximation: A gradient boosting machine. *Annals of Statistics*, 29(5):1189–1232.

Marti A. Hearst. 1992. Automatic acquisition of hyponyms from large text corpora. In *Proceedings of COLING-92*, pages 539–545.

Jian Hu, Gang Wang, Fred Lochovsky, Jian tao Sun, and Zheng Chen. 2009. Understanding user's query intent with Wikipedia. In *Proceedings of WWW-09*, pages 471–480.

N. Japkowicz and S. Stephen. 2002. The class imbalance problem: A systematic study. *Intelligent Data Analysis*, 6(5).

M. Kubat and S. Matwin. 1997. Addressing the curse of inbalanced data sets: One-side sampleing. In *Proceedings of the ICML-1997*, pages 179–186. Morgan Kaufmann.

Joseph F. McCarthy and Wendy G Lehnert. 2005. Using decision trees for coreference resolution. In *Proceedings of IJCAI-1995*, pages 1050–1055.

Tara McIntosh. 2010. Unsupervised discovery of negative categories in lexicon bootstrapping. In *Proceedings of the 2010 Conference on Empirical Methods in Natural Language Processing*, pages 356–365, Massachusetts, USA. Association for Computational Linguistics.

Shachar Mirkin, Ido Dagan, and Maayan Geffet. 2006. Integrating pattern-based and distributional similarity methods for lexical entailment acquisition. In *Proceedings of ACL/COLING-06*, pages 579–586.

Marius Paşca, Dekang Lin, Jeffrey Bigham, Andrei Lifchits, and Alpa Jain. 2006. Organizing and searching the world wide web of facts - step one: The one-million fact extraction challenge. In *Proceedings of AAAI-06*, pages 1400–1405.

Marius Paşca. 2007. Weakly-supervised discovery of named entities using web search queries. In *Proceedings of CIKM-07*, pages 683–690, New York, NY, USA.

Patrick Pantel and Dekang Lin. 2002. Discovering word senses from text. In *Proceedings of KDD-02*, pages 613–619.

Patrick Pantel, Eric Crestan, Arkady Borkovsky, Ana-Maria Popescu, and Vishnu Vyas. 2009. Web-scale distributional similarity and entity set expansion. In *Proceedings of EMNLP-09*.

Marco Pennacchiotti and Patrick Pantel. 2009. Entity extraction via ensemble semantics. In *Proceedings of the 2009 Conference on Empirical Methods in Natural Language Processing*, pages 238–247, Singapore. Association for Computational Linguistics.

Umaa Rebbapragada and Carla E. Brodley. 2007. Class noise mitigation through instance weighting. In *Proceedings of the 18th European Conference on Machine Learning*.

Anoop Sarkar. 2001. Applying co-training methods to statistical parsing. In *NAACL-2001*.

Bin Tan and Fuchun Peng. 2006. Unsupervised query segmentation using generative language models and wikipedia. In *Proceedings of WWW-06*, pages 1400–1405.

Michael Thelen and Ellen Riloff. 2002. A bootstrapping method for learning semantic lexicons using extraction pattern contexts. In *Proceedings of the 2002 Conference on Empirical Methods in Natural Language Processing*, pages 214–221, Philadelphia, PA, USA. Association for Computational Linguistics.

Richard C. Wang and William W. Cohen. 2008. Iterative set expansion of named entities using the web. In *ICDM '08: Proceedings of the 2008 Eighth IEEE International Conference on Data Mining*, pages 1091–1096, Washington, DC, USA. IEEE Computer Society.

Roman Yangarber, Winston Lin, and Ralph Grishman. 2002. Unsupervised learning of generalized names. In *COLING-2002*.

David Yarowsky. 1995. Unsupervised word sense disambiguation rivaling supervised methods. In *Proceedings of ACL-1996*, pages 189–196.

David Yarowsky. 1998. Combining labeled and unlabeled data with co-training. In *Proceedings of the Workshop on Computational Learning Theory*, pages 92–100.

Probabilistic Word Alignment under the L_0-norm

Thomas Schoenemann
Center for Mathematical Sciences
Lund University, Sweden

Abstract

This paper makes two contributions to the area of single-word based word alignment for bilingual sentence pairs. Firstly, it integrates the – seemingly rather different – works of (Bodrumlu et al., 2009) and the standard probabilistic ones into a single framework.

Secondly, we present two algorithms to optimize the arising task. The first is an iterative scheme similar to Viterbi training, able to handle large tasks. The second is based on the inexact solution of an integer program. While it can handle only small corpora, it allows more insight into the quality of the model and the performance of the iterative scheme.

Finally, we present an alternative way to handle prior dictionary knowledge and discuss connections to computing IBM-3 Viterbi alignments.

1 Introduction

The training of *single word based* translation models (Brown et al., 1993b; Vogel et al., 1996) is an essential building block for most state-of-the-art translation systems. Indeed, even more refined translation models (Wang and Waibel, 1998; Sumita et al., 2004; Deng and Byrne, 2005; Fraser and Marcu, 2007a) are initialized by the parameters of single word based ones. The exception is here the joint approach of Marcu and Wong (2002), but its refinement by Birch et al. (2006) again relies on the well-known IBM models.

Traditionally (Brown et al., 1993b; Al-Onaizan et al., 1999) single word based models are trained by the EM-algorithm, which has the advantageous property that the collection of counts can be decomposed over the sentences. Refinements that also allow symmetrized models are based on bipartite graph matching (Matusov et al., 2004; Taskar et al., 2005) or quadratic assignment problems (Lacoste-Julien et al., 2006). Recently, Bodrumlu et al. (2009) proposed the first method that treats a non-decomposable problem by handling all sentence pairs at once and via integer linear programming. Their (non-probabilistic) approach finds dictionaries with a minimal number of entries. However, the approach does not include a position model.

In this work we combine the two strategies into a single framework. That is, the dictionary sparsity objective of Bodrumlu et al. will become a *regularity term* in our framework. It is combined with the maximal alignment probability of every sentence pair, where we consider the models IBM-1, IBM-2 and HMM. This allows us to write dictionary sparsity as the (non-convex) L_0 norm of the dictionary parameters of the respective models.

For *supervised* training, regularity terms are quite common, e.g. (Taskar et al., 2005; Lacoste-Julien et al., 2006). For the unsupervised problem addressed in this paper they have recently been introduced in the form of posterior constraints (Ganchev et al., 2010). In related fields of NLP lately Dirichlet priors have been investigated, e.g. (Johnson, 2007).

We present two strategies to handle the objective function addressed in this paper. One of these schemes relies, like (Germann et al., 2004; Lacoste-Julien et al., 2006; DeNero and Klein, 2008; Bodrumlu et al., 2009), on integer linear programming

Proceedings of the Fifteenth Conference on Computational Natural Language Learning, pages 172–180,
Portland, Oregon, USA, 23–24 June 2011.

(see e.g. (Schrijver, 1986; Achterberg, 2007)), but due to the large-scale nature of our problem we solve only the LP-relaxation, followed by successive strengthening. For the latter, we develop our own, exponentially large set of cuts and show that it can be handled as a polynomially sized system, though in practice this is too inefficient.

2 The Models

Before we introduce our objective function we give a brief description of the (standard) models we consider. In all cases, one is given a set of bilingual sentence pairs containing a foreign language and English. The models formalize the probability of obtaining the foreign sentence from a given English sentence, by considering *hidden* variables called alignments:

$$p_{\mathbf{d},\mathbf{l}}(\mathbf{f}_s|\mathbf{e}_s) = \sum_{\mathbf{a}_s} p_{\mathbf{d},\mathbf{l}}(\mathbf{f}_s, \mathbf{a}_s|\mathbf{e}_s) \ .$$

Here, the subscripts $\mathbf{d}$ and $\mathbf{l}$ denote two sets of parameters: whereas the set $\mathbf{l}$ defines the probability of an alignment without knowing any of the sentences, $\mathbf{d}$ describes the translational probability given an alignment and a source sentence.

For a source (English) sentence of length I and a target (foreign) sentence of length J, the set of admissible alignments is generally the set of subsets of $\{1,\ldots,I\} \times \{1,\ldots,J\}$. However, for computational reasons the considered models only allow restricted alignments, where each target word may align to at most one source word. Any such alignment is expressed as a vector $\mathbf{a}_1^J \in \{0,\ldots,I\}^J$.

2.1 Considered models

For a source sentence $\mathbf{e}^s = e_1^I$ and a target sentence $\mathbf{f}^s = f_1^J$, the considered models all factor as follows:

$$p_{\mathbf{d},\mathbf{l}}(\mathbf{f}^s, \mathbf{a}^s|\mathbf{e}^s) = \prod_{j=1}^{J} p_{\mathbf{d}}(f_j|e_{a_j}) \cdot p_{\mathbf{l}}(a_j|a_{j-1}, j, I) \quad (1)$$

In all cases, the translational probability is non-parametric, i.e. $\mathbf{d}$ contains one parameter for every co-occurring pair of source and target words. Since the model is probabilistic, the parameters of all f for a given e have to sum up to one.

With respect to the alignment probability, the models differ. For the IBM-1 the set $\mathbf{l}$ is actually empty, so $p_{\mathbf{l}}(a_j|a_{j-1}, j, I) = 1/(I+1)$. The IBM-2 models[1] $p(a_j|j, I)$, with a respective set of parameters. Finally, the HMM models $p(a_j|a_{j-1}, I)$.

It is common to further reduce the alignment parameters. In this paper we consider a nonparametric distribution for the IBM-2, but both a nonparametric and a parametric one for the HMM. In contrast to GIZA++, we have a parameter for every possible difference, i.e. we do not group differences with absolutes greater than 5. Also, commonly one uses a distribution $p(i|i', I) = r(i-i')/\sum_{i''=1}^{I} r(i''-i')$, but for technical reasons, we drop the denominator and instead constrain the $r(\cdot)$-parameters to sum to 1. In future work we hope to implement both the normalization and the grouping of bins.

2.2 Word Alignment

Originally the considered models were used for the actual translation problem. Hence, the parameters $\mathbf{d}$ and $\mathbf{l}$ had to be inferred from a training corpus, which was based on maximizing the probability

$$\max_{\mathbf{d},\mathbf{l}} \prod_s \sum_{\mathbf{a}} p_{\mathbf{d},\mathbf{l}}(\mathbf{f}^s, \mathbf{a}^s|\mathbf{e}^s) \ . \quad (2)$$

Today the major application of the models lies in *word alignment*. Instead of estimating continuous parameters, one is now faced with the discrete optimization problem of assigning a single alignment to every sentence pair in the corpus. This lead to the recent innovative work of (Bodrumlu et al., 2009) where the alignments are the only unknown quantities.

Nevertheless, the use of probabilistic models remains attractive, in particular since they contribute statistics of likely alignments. In this work, we combine the two concepts into the criterion

$$\min_{\mathbf{d},\mathbf{l}} -\log\left[\prod_s \max_{\mathbf{a}^s} p_{\mathbf{d},\mathbf{l}}(\mathbf{f}^s, \mathbf{a}^s|\mathbf{e}^s)\right] + \lambda \, \|\mathbf{d}\|_0 \ ,$$

where $\lambda \geq 0$ is a weighting parameter and we now estimate a single alignment for every sentence.

The second term denotes the L_0-norm of the translational parameters, i.e. the number of non-zero

[1] The original work considered a dependence on I and J, but it is common to drop J.

parameters. Since we only consider a single alignment per sentence, this term is equivalent to Bodrumlu et al.'s objective function. Minimizing the first term is closely related to the common criterion (2). For parameter estimation it is known as the *maximum approximation*, but for word alignment it is a perfectly valid model.

For the IBM-1 model the first term alone results in a convex, but not strictly convex minimization problem[2]. However, EM-like iterative methods generally do not reach the minimum: they are doing block coordinate descent (Bertsekas, 1999, chap. 2.7) which generally gives the optimum only for *strictly* convex functions. Indeed, our experiments showed a strong dependence on initialization and lead to heavily local solutions.

In the following we present two strategies to minimize the new objective. We start with an iterative method that also handles the regularity term.

3 An Iterative Scheme

To derive our algorithms, we first switch the minimum and maximum in the objective and obtain

$$\min_{\{\mathbf{a}^s\}} \min_{\mathbf{d},\mathbf{l}} - \sum_s \log \left[p_{\mathbf{d},\mathbf{l}}(\mathbf{f}^s, \mathbf{a}^s | \mathbf{e}^s) \right] + \lambda \, \|\mathbf{d}\|_0 \ ,$$

where the notation$\{\mathbf{a}^s\}$ denotes the alignments of all sentence pairs. Ignoring the L_0-term for the moment, we now make use of a result of (Vicente et al., 2009) in their recent work on histogram-based image segmentation: for any *given* set of alignments, the inner minimization over the parameters is solved by relative frequencies. When plugging this solution into the functional, one gets a model that does not decompose over the sentences, but one that is still reasonably easy to handle.

Before we get into details, we observe that this minimizer is valid even when including the L_0 term: if two words are never linked, both terms will set the respective parameter to 0. If they are linked, however, then setting this parameter to 0 would make the first term infinite. All non-zero parameters are treated equally by the L_0 term, so the restriction to relative frequencies does not change the optimal value. In fact, this can be extended to *weighted* L_0 terms, and later on we exploit this to derive an alternative way to handle a dictionary prior. Note that the same principle could also be applied to the work of (Bodrumlu et al., 2009).

3.1 Mathematical Formulation

We detail our scheme for the IBM-1 model, the extension to other models is easy. For given alignments we introduce the counts

$$N_{f,e}(\{\mathbf{a}^s\}) = \sum_s \sum_j \delta(f, f_j) \cdot \delta(e, e_{a_j})$$

$$N_e(\{\mathbf{a}^s\}) = \sum_s \sum_j \delta(e, e_{a_j}) \ ,$$

where $\delta(\cdot,\cdot)$ is the Kronecker-delta. The optimal translation parameters are then given by $N_{f,e}(\{\mathbf{a}^s\})/N_e(\{\mathbf{a}^s\})$, and plugging this into the first term in the objective gives (up to a constant)

$$\min_{\{\mathbf{a}^s\}} \sum_{f,e} -N_{f,e}(\{\mathbf{a}^s\}) \log \left(\frac{N_{f,e}(\{\mathbf{a}^s\})}{N_e(\{\mathbf{a}^s\})} \right) \ .$$

The second term is simply $\lambda \sum_{f,e} \|N_{f,e}(\{\mathbf{a}^s\})\|_0$, and since $N(e) = \sum_f N(f,e)$, in total we get

$$\begin{aligned} \min_{\{\mathbf{a}^s\}} & \sum_{f,e} -N_{f,e}(\{\mathbf{a}^s\}) \log \left(N_{f,e}(\{\mathbf{a}^s\})\right) \\ & + \sum_e N_e(\{\mathbf{a}^s\}) \log \left(N_e(\{\mathbf{a}^s\})\right) \ . \\ & + \lambda \sum_{f,e} \|N_{f,e}(\{\mathbf{a}^s\})\|_0 \end{aligned} \quad (3)$$

In essence we are now dealing with the function $x \log(x)$, where its value for 0 is defined as 0.

3.2 Algorithm

For the new objective, we were able to entirely get rid of the model parameters, leaving only alignment variables. Nevertheless, the algorithm we present maintains these parameters, and it requires an initial choice. While we initialize the alignment parameters uniformly, for the translation parameters we use co-occurrence counts. This performed much better than a uniform initialization. The algorithm, called AM (for alternating minimization), now iterates two steps:

[2] This is due to taking the maximizing alignment. Summing over all alignments is strictly convex.

1. Starting from the current setting of $\mathbf{d}$ and $\mathbf{l}$, derive Viterbi alignments for all sentence pairs. E.g. for the IBM-1 we set $a_j^s = \arg\max_i d(f_j|e_i)$. For the IBM-2 the term is similar, while for the HMM one can use dynamic programming.

   Note that this step does not consider the L_0-term. This term can however not increase.

2. Run the Iterated Conditional Modes (Besag, 1986), i.e. go sequentially over all alignment variables and set them to their optimal value when keeping the others fixed.

   Here, we need to keep track of the current alignment counts. In every step we need to compute the objective cost associated to a count that increases by 1, and (another) one that decreases by 1. For the IBM-2 we need to consider the alignment counts, too, and for the HMM usually two alignment terms are affected. In case of 0-alignments there can be more than two. We presently do not consider these cases and hence do not find the exact optimum there.

   Afterwards, reestimate the parameters $\mathbf{d}$ and $\mathbf{l}$ from the final counts.

4 Integer Linear Programming

The above algorithm is fast and can handle large corpora. However, it still gets stuck in local minima, and there is no way of telling how close to the optimum one got.

This motivates the second algorithm where we cast the objective function as an integer linear program (ILP). In practice it is too large to be solved exactly, so we solve its linear programming relaxation, followed by successive strengthening. Here we derive our own set of cuts. Now we also get a lower bound on the problem and obtain lower energy solutions in practice. But we can handle only small corpora.

We limit this method to the models IBM-1 and IBM-2. Handling an HMM would be possible, but its first order alignment model would introduce many more variables. Handling the IBM-3, based on (Ravi and Knight, 2010; Schoenemann, 2010) seems a more promising direction.

4.1 An ILP for the Regularized IBM-1

The basis of our ILP is the fact that the counts $N_{f,e}$ and N_e can only assume a finite, a-priori known set of integral values, including 0. We introduce a binary variable $n_{f,e}^c \in \{0,1\}$ for each possible value c, where we want $n_{f,e}^c = 1$ if $N_{f,e}(\mathbf{a}^s) = c$, otherwise $n_{f,e}^c = 0$. This is analogous for the variables n_e^c and $N_e(\mathbf{a}^s)$. Finally, since the counts depend on the alignments, we also need binary variables $x_{i,j}^s \in \{0,1\}$ that we want to be 1 if and only if $a_j^s = i$.

The cost function of (3) can now be written as a linear function in terms of the integer variables $n_{f,e}^c$ and n_e^c, with coefficients

$$w_{e,f}^c = -c\log(c) + \lambda\|c\|_0\,, \quad w_e^c = c\log(c) \ .$$

However, we need additional constraints. In particular we need to ensure that for a given f and e exactly one variable $n_{f,e}^c$ is 1. Equivalently we can postulate that the sum of these variables is one. We proceed analogous for each e and the variables n_e^c.

Then, we need to ensure that for each source word in each sentence $\mathbf{f}^s$ an alignment is specified, i.e. that for each given s and j the variables $x_{i,j}^s$ sum to 1. Finally, the count variables have to reflect the counts induced by the alignment variables. For the counts $N_{f,e}$ this is expressed by

$$\sum_{s,i,j:f_j^s=f,e_i^s=e} x_{i,j}^s = \sum_c c\cdot n_{f,e}^c \quad \forall f,e \ ,$$

and likewise for the counts N_e.

Altogether, we arrive at the following system:

$$\begin{aligned}
\min_{\{x_{i,j}^s\},\{n_{f,e}^c\},\{n_e^c\}} \quad & \sum_{e,c} w_e^c n_e^c + \sum_{f,e,c} w_{f,e}^c n_{f,e}^c \\
\text{s.t.} \quad & \sum_i x_{i,j}^s = 1 \quad \forall s,j \\
& \sum_c n_{f,e}^c = 1 \quad \forall f,e \\
& \sum_c n_e^c = 1 \quad \forall e \\
& \sum_{s,i,j:f_j=f,e_i=e} x_{i,j}^s = \sum_c c\cdot n_{f,e}^c \quad \forall f,e \\
& \sum_{s,i,j:e_i=e} x_{i,j}^s = \sum_c c\cdot n_e^c \quad \forall e \\
& x_{i,j}^s \in \{0,1\},\ n_e^c \in \{0,1\},\ n_{e,f}^c \in \{0,1\} \ .
\end{aligned}$$

4.2 Handling the IBM-2

The above mentioned system can be easily adapted to the IBM-2 model. To this end, we introduce variables $n^c_{i,j,I} \in \{0,1\}$ to express how often source word j is aligned to target word i given that there are I words in the target sentence. Note that the number of times source word j is aligned given that the target sentence has I words is known a-priori and does not depend on the alignment to be optimized. We denote it $C_{j,I}$. The cost function of the ILP is augmented by $\sum_{i,j,I,c} w^c_{i,j,I}\, n^c_{i,j,I}$, with $w^c_{i,j,I} = c \log(c/C_{j,I})$. In addition we add the following constraints to the system:

$$\sum_{s:I^s=I} x^s_{i,j} = \sum_c c \cdot n^c_{i,j,I} \quad \forall i,j,I \ .$$

5 Cutting Planes

Integer linear programming is an NP-hard problem (see e.g. (Schrijver, 1986)). While for problems with a few thousand variables it can often be solved exactly via the branch and cut method, in our setting none of the solvers we tried terminated. Already solving the linear programming relaxation requires up to 4 GB of memory for corpora with roughly 3000 sentence pairs.

So instead of looking for an exact solution, we make use of a few iterations of the cutting planes method (Gomory, 1958), where repeatedly an LP-relaxation is solved, then additionally valid inequalities, called *cuts*, are added to the system. Every round gives a tighter relaxation, i.e. a better lower bound on the optimal integral value.

After solving each LP-relaxation we derive an integral solution by starting the iterative method from section 3 from the fractional LP-solution. In the end we output the best found integral solution.

For deriving cuts we tried all the methods implemented in the COIN Cut Generation Library CGL[3], based on the solver Clp from the same project line. However, either the methods were very slow in producing cuts or they produced very few cuts only. So eventually we derived our own set of cuts that will now be presented. Note that they alone do not give an integral solution.

[3] `http://www.coin-or.org/projects/Cgl.xml`

5.1 A Set of Count-based Cuts

The derived ILP contains several constraints of the form

$$\sum_i y_i = \sum_c c \cdot z_c \ , \qquad (4)$$

where all variables are binary. Expressions of this kind arise wherever we need to ensure consistency between alignment variables and count variables. Our cuts aim at strengthening each of these equations individually.

Assume that equation (4) involves the variables $y_1, \ldots, y_K$ and hence also the variables $z_0, \ldots, z_K$. The trouble with the equation is that even if the left hand side is integral, the right-hand side is usually not. As an example, consider the case where $\sum_{i=1}^K y_i = 3$. Then the fractional assignment $z_0 = 1 - 3/K$, $z_K = 3/K$ and $z_c = 0$ for all other c satisfies (4). Indeed, if the cost function for z_c is concave in c, as is the function $-c\,\log(c)$ we use, this will be the optimal solution for the given left hand side.

Hence we want to enforce that for an integral value k of the left hand side, all variables z_c for $0 \le c < k$ are zero. This is ensured by the following system of inequalities that is exponentially large in k:

$$\sum_{i \in \mathcal{K}} y_i + \sum_{c=0}^{k-1} z_c \le k \qquad (5)$$
$$\forall \mathcal{K} \subseteq \{1,\ldots,K\} : |\mathcal{K}| = k \ .$$

It turns out that this system can be formulated quite compactly.

5.2 Polynomial Formulation

We now formalize the result for the compact formulation of (5).

Proposition 1 *The union of the systems (5) for all k can be represented by polynomially many variables and linear constraints.*

Proof: we first observe that it suffices to enforce

$$\left[\max_{\mathcal{K}:|\mathcal{K}|=k} \sum_{i \in \mathcal{K}} y_i\right] + \sum_{c=0}^{k-1} z_c \le k$$

for all k. These are polynomially many equations (one for each k), but each involves a maximization over exponentially many sets. However, this maximization can be expressed by the auxiliary variables

$$\begin{aligned}\tau_l^k &:= \max_{\mathcal{K}\subseteq\{1,\ldots,l\}:|\mathcal{K}|\leq k} \sum_{i\in\mathcal{K}} y_i \\ &= \max\{\tau_{l-1}^{k-1} + y_l \, , \, \tau_{l-1}^k\}\end{aligned}$$

Now we only have to maximize over two linear expressions for each of the new, polynomially many, variables. We can enforce τ_l^k to be an upper bound on the maximum by postulating $\tau_l^k \geq \tau_{l-1}^{k-1} + y_l$ and $\tau_l^k \geq \tau_{l-1}^k$. Since the original maximum occurred on the left hand side of a less-than constraint, this upper bound will be tight wherever this is necessary. □

In practice the arising system is numerically hard to solve. Since usually only polynomially many cuts of the form (5) are actually violated during the cutting planes process, we add them in passes and get significantly lower running times. Moreover, each round of cuts gives a new opportunity to derive a heuristic integral solution.

5.3 Backward Cuts

We call the cuts we have derived above *forward cuts* as they focus on variables that are smaller than k. If we could be sure that the left-hand side of (4) was always integral, they should indeed suffice. In practice this is not the case, so we now also derive *backward cuts* where we focus on all variables that are larger than k, with the following reasoning: once we know that at least $K - k$ variables y_i are inactive (i.e. $y_i = 0$), we can conclude that all z_c with $c > k$ must be zero, too. This can be expressed by the set of inequalities

$$\sum_{i\in\mathcal{K}}(1 - y_i) + \sum_{c=k+1}^{K} z_c \leq K - k$$
$$\forall\mathcal{K} \subseteq \{1,\ldots,K\} : |\mathcal{K}| = K - k \ ,$$

or equivalently

$$\sum_{i\in\mathcal{K}} -y_i + \sum_{c=k+1}^{K} z_c \leq 0 \quad \forall\mathcal{K} : |\mathcal{K}| = K - k \ .$$

5.4 Other Applications

A related constraint system arises in recent work (Ravi and Knight, 2010; Schoenemann, 2010) on computing IBM-3 Viterbi alignments. We implemented[4] the polynomial formulation of the above forward cuts for this system, and got mild speed-ups (224 instead of 237 minutes for the Hansards task reported in the second paper). With an additionally improved fertility exclusion stage[5] this is reduced to 176 minutes.

6 Experiments

We evaluate the proposed strategies on both small scale and (where applicable) large scale tasks. We compare to standard EM with sums over alignments, where for the IBM-1 and the HMM we use GIZA++. In addition, we evaluate several variants (our implementations) of the HMM, with non-parametric and parametric alignment models. Note that for the non-parametric variant we estimate distributions for the first aligned position, for the parametric all initial positions are equally likely. For the IBM-2 we consider the non-parametric variant and hence our implementation. We also evaluate our schemes on the task without regularization.

All experiments in this work were executed on a 3 GHz Core 2 Duo machine with 8 GB of memory, where up to 4 GB were actually used. The iterative scheme was run for 15 iterations, where it was nearly converged. This setting was also used for our own EM-implementations. Solely for GIZA++ we used the standard setting of 5 iterations, and the implemented smoothing process. For the IBM-2 and HMM we follow the standard strategy to first train an IBM-1 with the same objective function.

6.1 Large Scale Tasks

We consider two well-known corpora with publicly available gold alignments, and run both translation directions for each of them. The first task is the Canadian Hansards task (French and English) with roughly 1 million sentences. The second task is Europarl Spanish-English, where we take the first 500000 sentences. Our iterative scheme runs in

[4]based on code available at `www.maths.lth.se/matematiklth/personal/tosch/download.html`.

[5]In (Schoenemann, 2010) we stated that the difference between c_{if}^y and the contribution of i to the bound has to exceed $u - l_3$. This can be tightened if one additionally adds the cost of the best f alignments to i to the cost c_{if}^y.

Canadian Hansards		
	Fr → En	En → Fr
HMM (Giza++)	0.918	0.918
par. HMM (our EM)	0.887	0.896
par. HMM (Viterbi)	0.873	0.897
par. HMM + L_0	0.891	0.907
nonpar. HMM (our EM)	0.873	0.911
nonpar. HMM (Viterbi)	0.881	0.909
nonpar. HMM + L_0	0.902	0.917

Europarl		
	Es → En	En → Es
HMM (Giza++)	0.764	0.754
nonpar. HMM (our EM)	0.738	0.733
nonpar. HMM (Viterbi)	0.726	0.716
nonpar. HMM + L_0	0.729	0.73

Table 1: For large corpora, the proposed scheme outperforms Viterbi training and sometimes even our EM.

roughly 5 hours (with room for improvements), using 2.5 GB memory. We found that an L_0-weight of $\lambda = 5.0$ performs very well. Hence, we will use this for all our experiments.

We compare to the standard GIZA++ implementation and our own HMM implementations with EM. Here we ran 15 iterations for IBM-1 and HMM each.

As shown in Table 1 adding the L_0 term improves the standard Viterbi training. Our method also sometimes beats the simple EM implementation but not GIZA++. This may be due to the special parametric model of GIZA++, its smoothing process or the lower number of iterations. Our deficient parametric model is inferior for the Hansards task, so we did not run it for Europarl.

6.2 Small Scale Tasks

To evaluate the ILP strategy we consider four small scale tasks released by the European Corpus Initiative[6]. See (Schoenemann, 2010) for the corpus statistics. We report weighted f-measures (Fraser and Marcu, 2007b) on gold alignments (sure and possible) specified by one annotator, for 144 and 110 sentences respectively. The number of cut rounds was selected so that the execution times remained below 2 days for all tasks. This was 50 rounds for the IBM-1 and 2 rounds for the IBM-2. In fact, with these numbers the Avalanche task is processed in little less than a day.

We tested a number of LP solvers and found that most of them need several hours to solve the root relaxation. This is different for the commercial solver FICO Xpress, which only needs around 15 minutes. However, it is slower in processing the subsequent cut iterations. Hence, for the IBM-1 we use the open source Clp[7].

The resulting f-measures for the tested strategies are given in Table 2. In all cases, adding the L_0 term greatly improves the standard Viterbi training. Moreover, for the small scale tasks, the parametric HMM is clearly the best choice when using the L_0 penalty. In the majority of cases the ILP strategy performs better than the iterative scheme. In fact, it *always* found the lower energy solution. The most extreme difference we observed for the IBM-2 on the UBS English to German task: here AM finds an energy of 318147, where the ILP gives 303674.

Finally, Table 3 evaluates the effectiveness of the cut strategy exemplarily on one of the tasks. Clearly, the gaps are reduced significantly compared to the LP-relaxation. However, except for the IBM-1 (which is convex for $\lambda = 0$) the lower bounds are still quite loose.

6.3 Handling Dictionary Knowledge

The presented L_0 regularity is easily modified to include dictionary knowledge[8]. To this end, we introduce a *weighted* L_0-norm: whenever a pair of source and target words is listed in the dictionary, the entry is not penalized. All remaining entries are penalized by λ.

Note that this is different from the standard way (Brown et al., 1993a) of handling dictionary knowledge, which appends the dictionary to the corpus (with a proper weighting factor). We tried both schemes with several weighting factors, then chose the best-performing for the UBS task. For the UBS German to English task we get an accuracy of 0.445, which beats GIZA++ both with (0.438) and without (0.398) dictionary knowledge. In the reverse direction both schemes profit from the extra knowledge,

[6] http://www.elsnet.org/eci.html

[7] http://www.coin-or.org/projects/Clp.xml

[8] Our data are based on www.dict.info/uddl.php and www.ilovelanguages.com/idp and the stemming algorithms at snowball.tartarus.org.

Avalanche French → German			
Model	EM	AM	ILP
IBM-1	0.603	0.619	0.591
IBM-1 + L_0	–	0.64	0.625
IBM-2	0.568	0.632	0.60
IBM-2 + L_0	–	0.680	0.636
par. HMM	0.752	0.621	–
par. HMM + L_0	–	0.779	–
nonpar. HMM	0.752	0.655	–
nonpar. HMM + L_0	–	0.714	–

Avalanche German → French			
Model	EM	AM	ILP
IBM-1	0.494	0.485	0.507
IBM-1 + L_0	–	0.497	0.488
IBM-2	0.428	0.459	0.526
IBM-2 + L_0	–	0.483	0.55
par. HMM	0.606	0.49	–
par. HMM + L_0	–	0.592	–
nonpar. HMM	0.582	0.501	–
nonpar. HMM + L_0	–	0.537	–

UBS German → English			
Model	EM	AM	ILP
IBM-1	0.381	0.359	0.335
IBM-1 + L_0	–	0.350	0.442
IBM-2	0.315	0.324	0.340
IBM-2 + L_0	–	0.383	0.462
par. HMM	0.398	0.229	–
par. HMM + L_0	–	0.383	–
nonpar. HMM	0.421	0.29	–
nonpar. HMM + L_0	–	0.371	–

UBS English → German			
Model	EM	AM	ILP
IBM-1	0.515	0.435	0.489
IBM-1 + L_0	–	0.444	0.504
IBM-2	0.417	0.40	0.435
IBM-2 + L_0	–	0.52	0.571
par. HMM	0.625	0.404	–
par. HMM + L_0	–	0.537	–
nonpar. HMM	0.623	0.436	–
nonpar. HMM + L_0	–	0.524	–

Table 2: Alignment accuracy (weighted f-measure) for different algorithms. We use a dictionary penalty of $\lambda = 5$ and the standard EM (GIZA++ for IBM-1 and parametric HMM, our implementation otherwise) training scheme with 5 iterations for each model.

UBS English → German			
	L_0-weight	IBM-1	IBM-2
root relaxation	0.0	1.098	7.697
after cut rounds	0.0	1.081	5.67
root relaxation	5.0	1.16	2.76
after cut rounds	5.0	1.107	2.36

Table 3: Ratios of the best known integer solution and the best known lower bounds for all considered tasks.

but GIZA++ remains the clear winner. Applying the same weights to the above mentioned Hansards task slightly improved GIZA++, whereas it slightly worsened the performance of our scheme in the one direction and slightly improved it in the other. We intend to investigate this more thoroughly in the future.

7 Discussion

In this paper we have shown that an L_0 prior on the dictionary parameters greatly improves Viterbi training. A simple iterative scheme often nearly matches our EM-implementation of the HMM.

We have also derived two algorithms to deal with the new objective. A simple iterative scheme gives quite accurate results on large scale tasks. On small scale tasks our inexact ILP strategy shows that the iterative scheme does not find the optimum in practice, a point that may well carry over to other models trained with the maximum approximation. This strategy also provides lower bounds, but at present they are quite loose.

Moreover, we have presented an alternative way of handling dictionary knowledge. Finally, we have discussed connections to computing IBM-3 Viterbi alignments, where we got mild speed-ups.

In future work we intend to investigate the effect of the generated alignments on the translation quality of phrase-based approaches. We also want to explore strategies to determine the regularity weight. Finally, we want to handle a non-deficient parametric HMM.

Acknowledgements. We thank Ben Taskar and João Graça for helpful discussions. This work was funded by the European Research Council (GlobalVision grant no. 209480).

References

T. Achterberg. 2007. *Constraint Integer Programming*. Ph.D. thesis, Zuse Institut, TU Berlin, Germany, July.

Y. Al-Onaizan, J. Curin, M. Jahr, K. Knight, J. Lafferty, I. D. Melamed, F. J. Och, D. Purdy, N. A. Smith, and D. Yarowsky. 1999. Statistical machine translation, Final report, JHU workshop. `http://www.clsp.jhu.edu/ws99/`.

D.P. Bertsekas. 1999. *Nonlinear Programming, 2nd edition*. Athena Scientific.

J. Besag. 1986. On the statistical analysis of dirty pictures. *Journal of the Royal Statistical Society, Series B*, 48(3):259–302.

A. Birch, C. Callison-Burch, and M. Osborne. 2006. Constraining the phrase-based, joint probability statistical translation model. In *Conference of the Association for Machine Translation in the Americas (AMTA)*, Cambridge, Massachusetts, August.

T. Bodrumlu, K. Knight, and S. Ravi. 2009. A new objective function for word alignment. In *Proceedings of the Workshop on Integer Linear Programming for Natural Language Processing (ILP)*, Boulder, Colorado, June.

P.F. Brown, S.A. Della Pietra, V.J. Della Pietra, M.J. Goldsmith, J. Hajic, R.L. Mercer, and S. Mohanty. 1993a. But dictionaries are data too. In *HLT workshop on Human Language Technology*.

P.F. Brown, S.A. Della Pietra, V.J. Della Pietra, and R.L. Mercer. 1993b. The mathematics of statistical machine translation: Parameter estimation. *Computational Linguistics*, 19(2):263–311, June.

J. DeNero and D. Klein. 2008. The complexity of phrase alignment problems. In *Annual Meeting of the Association for Computational Linguistics (ACL)*, Columbus, Ohio, June.

Y. Deng and W. Byrne. 2005. HMM word and phrase alignment for statistical machine translation. In *HLT-EMNLP*, Vancouver, Canada, October.

A. Fraser and D. Marcu. 2007a. Getting the structure right for word alignment: LEAF. In *Conference on Empirical Methods in Natural Language Processing (EMNLP)*, Prague, Czech Republic, June.

A. Fraser and D. Marcu. 2007b. Measuring word alignment quality for statistical machine translation. *Computational Linguistics*, 33(3):293–303, September.

K. Ganchev, J. Graça, J. Gillenwater, and B. Taskar. 2010. Posterior regularization for structured latent variable models. *Journal of Machine Learning Research*, 11:2001–2049, July.

U. Germann, M. Jahr, K. Knight, D. Marcu, and K. Yamada. 2004. Fast decoding and optimal decoding for machine translation. *Artificial Intelligence*, 154(1–2), April.

R.E. Gomory. 1958. Outline of an algorithm for integer solutions to linear programs. *Bulletin of the American Mathematical Society*, 64:275–278.

M. Johnson. 2007. Why doesn't EM find good HMM POS-taggers? In *Conference on Empirical Methods in Natural Language Processing (EMNLP)*, Prague, Czech Republic, June.

S. Lacoste-Julien, B. Taskar, D. Klein, and M. Jordan. 2006. Word alignment via quadratic assignment. In *Human Language Technology Conference of the North American Chapter of the Association of Computational Linguistics*, New York, New York, June.

D. Marcu and W. Wong. 2002. A phrase-based, joint probability model for statistical machine translation. In *Conference on Empirical Methods in Natural Language Processing (EMNLP)*, Philadelphia, Pennsylvania, July.

E. Matusov, R. Zens, and H. Ney. 2004. Symmetric word alignments for statistical machine translation. In *International Conference on Computational Linguistics (COLING)*, Geneva, Switzerland, August.

S. Ravi and K. Knight. 2010. Does GIZA++ make search errors? *Computational Linguistics*, 36(3).

T. Schoenemann. 2010. Computing optimal alignments for the IBM-3 translation model. In *Conference on Computational Natural Language Learning (CoNLL)*, Uppsala, Sweden, July.

A. Schrijver. 1986. *Theory of Linear and Integer Programming*. Wiley-Interscience Series in Discrete Mathematics and Optimization. John Wiley & Sons.

E. Sumita, Y. Akiba, T. Doi, A. Finch, K. Imamura, H. Okuma, M. Paul, M. Shimohata, and T. Watanabe. 2004. EBMT, SMT, Hybrid and more: ATR spoken language translation system. In *International Workshop on Spoken Language Translation (IWSLT)*, Kyoto, Japan, September.

B. Taskar, S. Lacoste-Julien, and D. Klein. 2005. A discriminative matching approach to word alignment. In *Conference on Empirical Methods in Natural Language Processing (EMNLP)*, Vancouver, Canada, October.

S. Vicente, V.N. Kolmogorov, and C. Rother. 2009. Joint optimization of segmentation and appearance models. In *IEEE International Conference on Computer Vision (ICCV)*, Kyoto, Japan, September.

S. Vogel, H. Ney, and C. Tillmann. 1996. HMM-based word alignment in statistical translation. In *International Conference on Computational Linguistics (COLING)*, pages 836–841, Copenhagen, Denmark, August.

Y.-Y. Wang and A. Waibel. 1998. Modeling with structures in statistical machine translation. In *International Conference on Computational Linguistics (COLING)*, Montreal, Canada, August.

Authorship Attribution with Latent Dirichlet Allocation

Yanir Seroussi **Ingrid Zukerman** **Fabian Bohnert**
Faculty of Information Technology, Monash University
Clayton, Victoria 3800, Australia
firstname.lastname@monash.edu

Abstract

The problem of authorship attribution – attributing texts to their original authors – has been an active research area since the end of the 19th century, attracting increased interest in the last decade. Most of the work on authorship attribution focuses on scenarios with only a few candidate authors, but recently considered cases with tens to thousands of candidate authors were found to be much more challenging. In this paper, we propose ways of employing Latent Dirichlet Allocation in authorship attribution. We show that our approach yields state-of-the-art performance for both a few and many candidate authors, in cases where these authors wrote enough texts to be modelled effectively.

1 Introduction

The problem of authorship attribution – attributing texts to their original authors – has received considerable attention in the last decade (Juola, 2006; Stamatatos, 2009). Most of the work in this field focuses on cases where texts must be attributed to one of a few candidate authors, e.g., (Mosteller and Wallace, 1964; Gamon, 2004). Recently, researchers have turned their attention to scenarios with tens to thousands of candidate authors (Koppel et al., 2011). In this paper, we study authorship attribution with few to many candidate authors, and introduce a new method that achieves state-of-the-art performance in the latter case.

Our approach to authorship attribution consists of building models of authors and their texts using *Latent Dirichlet Allocation* (LDA) (Blei et al., 2003). We compare these models to models built from texts with unknown authors to find the most likely authors of these texts (Section 3.2). Our evaluation shows that our approach yields a higher accuracy than the method recently introduced by Koppel et al. (2011) in several cases where prolific authors are considered, while requiring less runtime (Section 4).

This paper is structured as follows. Related work is surveyed in Section 2. Our LDA-based approach to authorship attribution is described in Section 3, together with the baselines we considered in our evaluation. Section 4 presents and discusses the results of our evaluation, and Section 5 discusses our conclusions and plans for future work.

2 Related Work

The field of authorship attribution predates modern computing. For example, in the late 19th century, Mendenhall (1887) suggested that word length can be used to distinguish works by different authors. In recent years, increased interest in authorship attribution was fuelled by advances in machine learning, information retrieval, and natural language processing (Juola, 2006; Stamatatos, 2009).

Commonly used features in authorship attribution range from "shallow" features, such as token and character n-gram frequencies, to features that require deeper analysis, such as part-of-speech and rewrite rule frequencies (Stamatatos, 2009). As in other text classification tasks, *Support Vector Machines* (SVMs) have delivered high accuracy, as they are designed to handle feature vectors of high dimensionality (Juola, 2006). For example, *one-vs.-all* (OVA) is an effective approach to using binary SVMs for multi-class (i.e., multi-author) problems (Rifkin and Klautau, 2004). Given A authors,

Proceedings of the Fifteenth Conference on Computational Natural Language Learning, pages 181–189,
Portland, Oregon, USA, 23–24 June 2011. ©2011 Association for Computational Linguistics

OVA trains A binary classifiers, where each classifier is trained on texts by one author as positive examples and all the other texts as negative examples. However, if A is large, each classifier has many more negative than positive examples, often yielding poor results due to class imbalance (Raskutti and Kowalczyk, 2004). Other setups, such as *one-vs.-one* or *directed acyclic graph*, require training $O(A^2)$ classifiers, making them impractical where thousands of authors exist. *Multi-class SVMs* have also been suggested, but they generally perform comparably to OVA while taking longer to train (Rifkin and Klautau, 2004). Hence, using SVMs for scenarios with many candidate authors is problematic (Koppel et al., 2011). Recent approaches to employing binary SVMs consider class similarity to improve performance (Bickerstaffe and Zukerman, 2010; Cheng et al., 2007). We leave experiments with such approaches for future work (Section 5).

In this paper, we focus on authorship attribution with many candidate authors. This problem was previously addressed by Madigan et al. (2005) and Luyckx and Daelemans (2008), who worked on datasets with texts by 114 and 145 authors respectively. In both cases, the reported results were much poorer than those reported in the binary case. More recently, Koppel et al. (2011) considered author similarity to handle cases with thousands of candidate authors. Their method, which we use as our baseline, is described in Section 3.1.

Our approach to authorship attribution utilises *Latent Dirichlet Allocation* (LDA) (Blei et al., 2003) to build models of authors from their texts. LDA is a generative probabilistic model that is traditionally used to find topics in textual data. The main idea behind LDA is that each document in a corpus is generated from a distribution of topics, and each word in the document is generated according to the per-topic word distribution. Blei et al. (2003) showed that using LDA for dimensionality reduction can improve performance for supervised text classification. We know of only one case where LDA was used in authorship attribution: Rajkumar et al. (2009) reported preliminary results on using LDA topic distributions as feature vectors for SVMs, but they did not compare the results obtained with LDA-based SVMs to those obtained with SVMs trained on tokens directly. Our comparison shows that both methods perform comparably (Section 4.3).

Nonetheless, the main focus of our work is on authorship attribution with *many* candidate authors, where it is problematic to use SVMs. Our *LDA+Hellinger* approach employs LDA *without* SVM training (Section 3.2), yielding state-of-the-art performance in several scenarios (Section 4).

3 Authorship Attribution Methods

This section describes the authorship attribution methods considered in this paper. While all these methods can employ various representations of documents, e.g., token frequencies or part-of-speech n-gram frequencies, we only experimented with token frequencies.[1] This is because they are simple to extract, and can achieve good performance (Section 4). Further, the focus of this paper is on comparing the performance of our methods to that of the baseline methods. Thus, we leave experiments on other feature types for future work (Section 5).

3.1 Baselines

We consider two baseline methods, depending on whether there are two or many candidate authors. If there are only two, we use *Support Vector Machines* (SVMs), which have been shown to deliver state-of-the-art performance on this task (Juola, 2006). If there are many, we follow Koppel et al.'s (2011) approach, which we denote *KOP*.

The main idea behind KOP is that different pairs of authors may be distinguished by different subsets of the feature space. Hence, KOP randomly chooses k_1 subsets of size k_2F ($k_2 < 1$) from a set of F features; for each of the k_1 subsets, it calculates the cosine similarity between a test document and all the documents by one author (each author is represented by one feature vector); it then outputs the author who had most of the top matches. KOP also includes a threshold σ^* to handle cases where a higher level of precision is required, at the cost of lower recall. If the top-matching author was the top match less than σ^* times, then KOP outputs "unknown author". In our experiments we set $\sigma^* = 0$ to obtain full coverage, as this makes it easier to interpret the results using a single measure of accuracy.

[1] Token frequency is the token count divided by the total number of tokens.

3.2 Authorship Attribution with LDA

In this work, we follow the extended LDA model defined by Griffiths and Steyvers (2004). Under the assumptions of the extended model, given a corpus of M documents, a document i with N tokens is generated by choosing a document topic distribution $\theta_i \sim \text{Dir}(\alpha)$, where $\text{Dir}(\alpha)$ is a T-dimensional symmetric Dirichlet distribution, and α and T are parameters of the model. Then, each token in the document w_{ij} is generated by choosing a topic from the document topic distribution $z_{ij} \sim \text{Multinomial}(\theta_i)$, and choosing a token from the token topic distribution $w_{ij} \sim \text{Multinomial}(\phi_{z_{ij}})$, where $\phi_{z_{ij}} \sim \text{Dir}(\beta)$, and β is a parameter of the model. The model can be inferred from the data using Gibbs sampling, as outlined in (Griffiths and Steyvers, 2004) – an approach we follow in our experiments.

Note that the topics obtained by LDA do not have to correspond to actual, human-interpretable topics. A more appropriate name may be "latent factors", but we adopt the convention of calling these factors "topics" throughout this paper. The meaning of the factors depends on the type of tokens that are used as input to the LDA inference process. For example, if stopwords are removed from the corpus, the resulting factors often, but not necessarily, correspond to topics. However, if only stopwords are retained, as is commonly done in authorship attribution studies, the resulting factors lose their interpretability as topics; rather, they can be seen as stylistic markers. Note that even if stopwords are discarded, nothing forces the factors to stand for actual topics. Indeed, in a preliminary experiment on a corpus of movie reviews and message board posts, we found that some factors correspond to topics, with words such as "noir" and "detective" considered to be highly probable for one topic. However, other factors seemed to correspond to authorship style as reflected by authors' vocabulary, with netspeak words such as "wanna", "alot" and "haha" assigned to one topic, and words such as "compelling" and "beautifully" assigned to a different topic.

We consider two ways of using LDA in authorship attribution: (1) *Topic SVM*, and (2) *LDA+Hellinger*. The LDA part of both approaches consists of applying a frequency filter to the features in the training documents,[2] and then using LDA to reduce the dimensionality of each document to a topic distribution of dimensionality T.

Topic SVM. The topic distributions are used as features for a binary SVM classifier that discriminates between authors. This approach has been employed in the past for document classification, e.g., in (Blei et al., 2003), but it has been applied to authorship attribution only in a limited study that considered just stopwords (Rajkumar et al., 2009). In Section 4.3, we present the results of more thorough experiments in applying this approach to binary authorship attribution. Our results show that the performance of this approach is comparable to that obtained without using LDA. This indicates that we do not lose authorship-related information when employing LDA, even though the dimensionality of the document representations is greatly reduced.

LDA+Hellinger. This method is our main contribution, as it achieves state-of-the-art performance in authorship attribution with many candidate authors, where it is problematic to use SVMs (Section 2).

The main idea of our approach is to use the *Hellinger distance* between document topic distributions to find the most likely author of a document:[3] $D(\theta_1, \theta_2) = \sqrt{\frac{1}{2}\sum_{t=1}^{T}\left(\sqrt{\theta_{1,t}} - \sqrt{\theta_{2,t}}\right)^2}$ where θ_i is a T-dimensional multinomial topic distribution, and $\theta_{i,t}$ is the probability of the t-th topic.

We propose two representations of an author's documents: *multi-document* and *single-document*.

- *Multi-document (LDAH-M).* The LDA model is built based on all the training documents. Given a test document, we measure the Hellinger distance between its topic distribution and the topic distributions of the training documents. The author with the lowest mean distance for all of his/her documents is returned as the most likely author of the test document.

[2] We employed frequency filtering because it has been shown to be a scalable and effective feature selection method for authorship attribution tasks (Stamatatos, 2009). We leave experiments with other feature selection methods for future work.

[3] We considered other measures for comparing topic distributions, including Kullback-Leibler divergence and Bhattacharyya distance. From these measures, only Hellinger distance satisfies all required properties of a distance metric. Hence, we used Hellinger distance.

- *Single-document (LDAH-S).* Each author's documents are concatenated into a single document (the *profile document*), and the LDA model is learned from the profile documents.[4] Given a test document, the Hellinger distance between the topic distributions of the test document and all the profile documents is measured, and the author of the profile document with the shortest distance is returned.

The time it takes to learn the LDA model depends on the number of Gibbs samples S, the number of tokens in the training corpus W, and the number of topics T. For each Gibbs sample, the algorithm iterates through all the tokens in the corpus, and for each token it iterates through all the topics. Thus, the time complexity of learning the model is $O(SWT)$. Once the model is learned, inferring the topic distribution of a test document of length N takes $O(SNT)$. Therefore, the time it takes to classify a document when using LDAH-S is $O(SNT+AT)$, where A is the number of authors, and $O(T)$ is the time complexity of calculating the Hellinger distance between two T-dimensional distributions. The time it takes to classify a document when using LDAH-M is $O(SNT + MT)$, where M is the total number of training documents, and $M \geq A$, because every candidate author has written at least one document.

An advantage of LDAH-S over LDAH-M is that LDAH-S requires much less time to classify a test document when many documents per author are available. However, this improvement in runtime may come at the price of accuracy, as authorship markers that are present only in a few short documents by one author may lose their prominence if these documents are concatenated to longer documents. In our evaluation we found that LDAH-M outperforms LDAH-S when applied to one of the datasets (Section 4.3), while LDAH-S yields a higher accuracy when applied to the other two datasets (Sections 4.4 and 4.5). Hence, we present the results obtained with both variants.

[4]Concatenating all the author documents into one document has been named the *profile-based* approach in previous studies, in contrast to the *instance-based* approach, where each document is considered separately (Stamatatos, 2009).

4 Evaluation

In this section, we describe the experimental setup and datasets used in our experiments, followed by the evaluation of our methods. We evaluate Topic SVM for binary authorship attribution, and LDA+Hellinger on a binary dataset, a dataset with tens of authors, and a dataset with thousands of authors. Our results show that LDA+Hellinger yields a higher accuracy than Koppel et al.'s (2011) baseline method in several cases where prolific authors are considered, while requiring less runtime.

4.1 Experimental Setup

In all the experiments, we perform ten-fold cross validation, employing stratified sampling where possible. The results are evaluated using classification accuracy, i.e., the percentage of test documents that were correctly assigned to their author. Note that we use different accuracy ranges in the figures that present our results for clarity of presentation. Statistically significant differences are reported when $p < 0.05$ according to a paired two-tailed t-test.

We used the LDA implementation from LingPipe (`alias-i.com/lingpipe`) and the SVM implementation from Weka (`www.cs.waikato.ac.nz/ml/weka`). Since our focus is on testing the impact of LDA, we used a linear SVM kernel and the default SVM settings. For the LDA parameters, we followed Griffiths and Steyvers (2004) and the recommendations in LingPipe's documentation, and set the Dirichlet hyperparameters to $\alpha = \min(0.1, 50/T)$ and $\beta = 0.01$, varying only the number of topics T. We ran the Gibbs sampling process for $S = 1000$ iterations, and based the document representations on the last sample. While taking more than one sample is generally considered good practice (Steyvers and Griffiths, 2007), we found that the impact of taking several samples on accuracy is minimal, but it substantially increases the runtime. Hence, we decided to use only one sample in our experiments.

4.2 Datasets

We considered three datasets that cover different writing styles and settings: *Judgement*, *IMDb62* and *Blog*. Table 1 shows a summary of these datasets.

The **Judgement dataset** contains judgements by three judges who served on the Australian High

	Judgement	IMDb62	Blog
Authors	3	62	19,320
Texts	1,342	62,000	678,161
Texts per Author	Dixon: 902 McTiernan: 253 Rich: 187	1,000	Mean: 35.10 Stddev.: 104.99

Table 1: Dataset Statistics

Court from 1913 to 1975: Dixon, McTiernan and Rich (available for download from www.csse.monash.edu.au/research/umnl/data). In this paper, we considered the Dixon/McTiernan and the Dixon/Rich binary classification cases, using judgements from non-overlapping periods (Dixon's 1929–1964 judgements, McTiernan's 1965–1975, and Rich's 1913–1928). We removed numbers from the texts to ensure that dates could not be used to discriminate between judges. We also removed quotes to ensure that the classifiers take into account only the actual author's language use.[5] Employing this dataset in our experiments allows us to test our methods on formal texts with a minimal amount of noise.

The **IMDb62 dataset** contains 62,000 movie reviews by 62 prolific users of the Internet Movie database (IMDb, www.imdb.com, available upon request from the authors of (Seroussi et al., 2010)). Each user wrote 1,000 reviews. This dataset is noisier than the Judgement dataset, since it may contain spelling and grammatical errors, and the reviews are not as professionally edited as judgements. This dataset allows us to test our approach in a setting where all the texts have similar themes, and the number of authors is relatively small, but is already much larger than the number of authors considered in traditional authorship attribution settings.

The **Blog dataset** is the largest dataset we considered, containing 678,161 blog posts by 19,320 authors (Schler et al., 2006) (available for download from u.cs.biu.ac.il/~koppel). In contrast to IMDb reviews, blog posts can be about any topic, but the large number of authors ensures that every topic is likely to interest at least some authors. Koppel et al. (2011) used a different blog dataset consisting of 10,240 authors in their work on authorship attribution with many candidate authors. Unfortunately, their dataset is not publicly available. However, authorship attribution is more challenging on the dataset we used, because they imposed some restrictions on their dataset, such as setting a minimal number of words per author, and truncating the training and testing texts so that they all have the same length. The dataset we use has no such restrictions.

4.3 LDA in Binary Authorship Attribution

In this section, we present the results of our experiments with the Judgement dataset (Section 4.2), testing the use of LDA in producing feature vectors for SVMs and the performance of our LDA+Hellinger methods (Section 3.2).

In all the experiments, we employed a classifier ensemble to address the class imbalance problem present in the Judgement dataset, which contains 5 times more texts by Dixon than by Rich, and over 3 times more texts by Dixon than by McTiernan (Table 1). Dixon's texts are randomly split into 5 or 3 subsets, depending on the other author (Rich or McTiernan respectively), and the base classifiers are trained on each subset of Dixon's texts together with all the texts by the other judge. Given a text by an unknown author, the classifier outputs are combined using majority voting. We found that the accuracies obtained with an ensemble are higher than those obtained with a single classifier. We did not require the vote to be unanimous, even though this increases precision, because we wanted to ensure full coverage of the test dataset. This enables us to compare different methods using only an accuracy measure.[6]

Experiment 1. Figure 1 shows the results of an experiment that compares the accuracy obtained using SVMs with token frequencies as features (*Token SVMs*) with that obtained using LDA topic distributions as features (*Topic SVMs*). We experimented with several filters on token frequency, and different numbers of LDA topics (5, 10, 25, 50, ..., 250). The x-axis labels describe the frequency filters: the minimum and maximum token frequencies, and the approximate number of unique tokens left after filtering (in thousands). We present only the results obtained with 10, 25, 100 and 200 topics, as the re-

[5]We removed numbers and quotes by matching regular expressions for numbers and text in quotation marks, respectively.

[6]For all our experiments, the results for the Dixon/McTiernan case are comparable to those for Dixon/Rich. Therefore, we omit the Dixon/McTiernan results to conserve space.

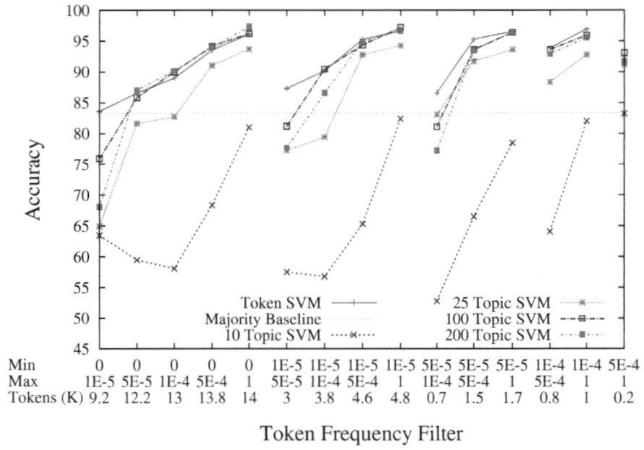

Figure 1: LDA Features for SVMs in Binary Authorship Attribution (Judgement dataset, Dixon/Rich)

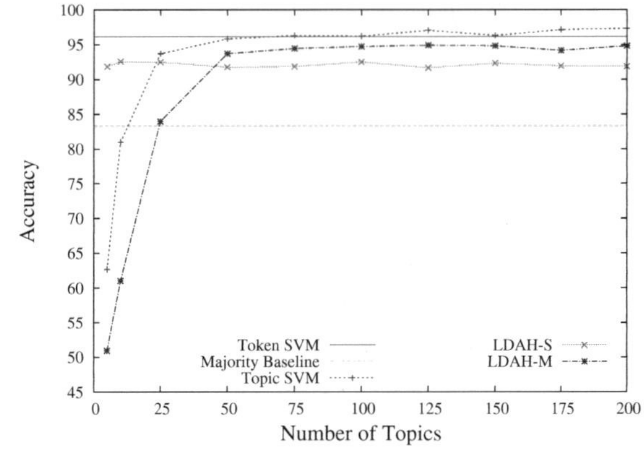

Figure 2: LDA+Hellinger in Binary Authorship Attribution (Judgement dataset, Dixon/Rich)

sults obtained with other topic numbers are consistent with the presented results, and the results obtained with 225 and 250 topics are comparable to the results obtained with 200 topics.

Our results show that setting a maximum bound on token frequency filters out important authorship markers, regardless of whether LDA is used or not (performance drops). This shows that it is unlikely that discriminative LDA topics correspond to actual topics, as the most frequent tokens are mostly non-topical (e.g., punctuation and function words).

An additional conclusion is that using LDA for feature reduction yields results that are comparable to those obtained using tokens directly. While Topic SVMs seem to perform slightly better than Token SVMs, the differences between the best results obtained with the two approaches are not statistically significant. However, the number of features that the SVMs consider when topics are used is usually much smaller than when tokens are used directly, especially when no token filters are used (i.e., when the minimum frequency is 0 and the maximum frequency is 1). This makes it easy to apply LDA to different datasets, since the token filtering parameters may be domain-dependent, and LDA yields good results without filtering tokens.

Experiment 2. Figure 2 shows the results of an experiment that compares the performance of the single profile document (LDAH-S) and multiple author documents (LDAH-M) variants of our LDA+Hellinger approach to the results obtained with Token SVMs and Topic SVMs. As in Experiment 1, we employ classifier ensembles, where the base classifiers are either SVMs or LDA+Hellinger classifiers. We did not filter tokens, since Experiment 1 indicates that filtering has no advantage over not filtering tokens. Instead, Figure 2 presents the accuracy as a function of the number of topics.

Note that we did not expect LDA+Hellinger to outperform SVMs, since LDA+Hellinger does not consider inter-class relationships. Indeed, Figure 2 shows that this is the case (the differences between the best Topic SVM results and the best LDAH-M results are statistically significant). However, LDA+Hellinger still delivers results that are much better than the majority baseline (the differences between LDA+Hellinger and the majority baseline are statistically significant). This leads us to hypothesise that LDA+Hellinger will perform well in cases where it is problematic to use SVMs due to the large number of candidate authors. We verify this hypothesis in the following sections.

One notable result is that LDAH-S delivers high accuracy even when only a few topics are used, while LDAH-M requires about 50 topics to outperform LDAH-S (all the differences between LDAH-S and LDAH-M are statistically significant). This may be because there are only two authors, so LDAH-S builds the LDA model based only on two profile documents. Hence, even 5 topics are enough to obtain two topic distributions that are sufficiently different to discriminate the authors' test documents. The reason LDAH-M outperforms LDAH-S when more topics are considered may be that some important authorship markers lose their prominence in the profile documents created by LDAH-S.

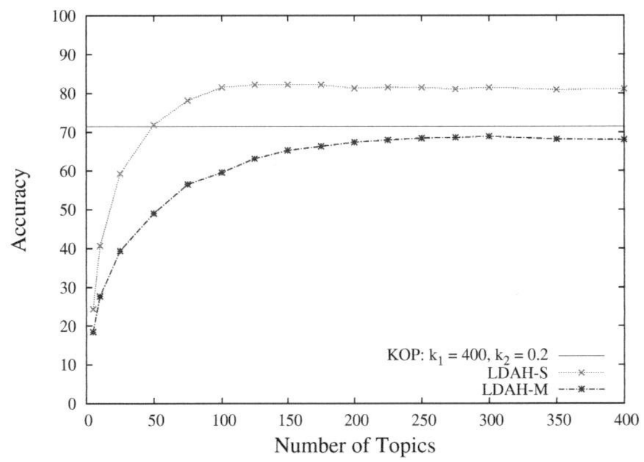

Figure 3: LDA+Hellinger with Tens of Authors (IMDb62 dataset)

4.4 LDA+Hellinger with Tens of Authors

In this section, we apply our LDA+Hellinger approaches to the IMDb62 dataset (Section 4.2), and compare the obtained results to those obtained with Koppel et al.'s (2011) method (KOP). To this effect, we first established a KOP best-performance baseline by performing parameter tuning experiments for KOP. Figure 3 shows the results of the comparison of the accuracies obtained with our LDA+Hellinger methods to the best accuracy yielded by KOP (obtained in the parameter tuning experiment).

For this experiment, we ran our LDA+Hellinger variants with 5, 10, 25, 50, ..., 300, 350 and 400 topics. The highest LDAH-M accuracy was obtained with 300 topics (Figure 3). However, LDAH-S yielded a much higher accuracy than LDAH-M. This may be because the large number of training texts per author (900) may be too noisy for LDAH-M. That is, the differences between individual texts by each author may be too large to yield a meaningful representation of the author if they are considered separately. Finally, LDAH-S requires only 50 topics to outperform KOP, and outperforms KOP by about 15% for 150 topics. All the differences between the methods are statistically significant.

This experiment shows that LDAH-S models the authors in IMDb62 more accurately than KOP. The large improvement in accuracy shows that the compact author representation employed by LDAH-S, which requires only 150 topics to obtain the highest accuracy, has more power to discriminate between authors than KOP's much heavier representation, of 400 subsets with more than 30,000 features each. In addition, the *per-fold* runtime of the KOP baseline was 93 hours, while LDAH-S required only 15 hours per fold to obtain the highest accuracy.

4.5 LDA+Hellinger with Thousands of Authors

In this section, we compare the performance of our LDA+Hellinger variants to the performance of KOP on several subsets of the Blog dataset (Section 4.2). For this purpose, we split the dataset according to the prolificness of the authors, i.e., we ordered the authors by the number of blog posts, and considered subsets that contain all the posts by the 1000, 2000, 5000 and 19320 most prolific authors.[7] Due to the large number of posts, we could not run KOP for more than $k_1 = 10$ iterations on the smallest subset of the dataset and 5 iterations on the other subsets, as the runtime was prohibitive for more iterations. For example, 10 iterations on the smallest subset required about 90 hours per fold (the LDA+Hellinger runtimes were substantially shorter, with maximum runtimes of 56 hours for LDAH-S and 77 hours for LDAH-M, when 200 topics were considered). Interestingly, running KOP for 5 iterations on the larger subsets decreased performance compared to running it for 1 iteration. Thus, on the larger subsets, the most accurate KOP results took less time to obtain than those of our LDA+Hellinger variants.

Figure 4 shows the results of this experiment. For each author subset, it compares the results obtained by LDAH-S and LDAH-M to the best result obtained by KOP. All the differences between the methods are statistically significant. For up to 2000 prolific authors (Figures 4(a), 4(b)), LDAH-S outperforms KOP by up to 50%. For 5000 prolific users (figure omitted due to space limitations), the methods perform comparably, and KOP outperforms LDAH-S by a small margin. However, with all the authors (Figure 4(c)), KOP yields a higher accuracy than both LDA+Hellinger variants. This may be because considering non-prolific authors introduces noise that results in an LDA model that does not capture the differences between authors. However, it is encouraging that LDAH-S outperforms KOP when less than 5000 prolific authors are considered.

[7]These authors make up about 5%, 10%, 25% and exactly 100% of the authors, but they wrote about 50%, 65%, 80% and exactly 100% of the texts, respectively.

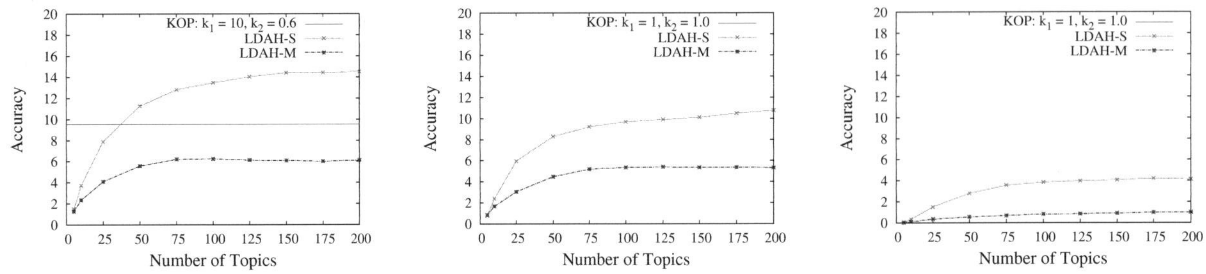

(a) 1,000 Prolific Authors (b) 2,000 Prolific Authors (c) 19,320 (all) Authors

Figure 4: LDA+Hellinger with Thousands of Authors (Blog dataset)

The accuracies obtained in this section are rather low compared to those obtained in the previous sections. This is not surprising, since the authorship attribution problem is much more challenging with thousands of candidate authors. This challenge motivated the introduction of the σ^* threshold in KOP (Section 3.1). Our LDA+Hellinger variants can also be extended to include a threshold: if the Hellinger distance of the best-matching author is greater than the threshold, the LDA+Hellinger algorithm would return "unknown author". We leave experiments with this extension to future work, as our focus in this paper is on comparing LDA+Hellinger to KOP, and we believe that this comparison is clearer when no thresholds are used.

5 Conclusions and Future Work

In this paper, we introduced an approach to authorship attribution that models texts and authors using Latent Dirichlet Allocation (LDA), and considers the distance between the LDA-based representations of the training and test texts when classifying test texts. We showed that our approach yields state-of-the-art performance in terms of classification accuracy when tens or a few thousand authors are considered, and prolific authors exist in the training data. This accuracy improvement was achieved together with a substantial reduction in runtime compared to Koppel et al.'s (2011) baseline method.

While we found that our approach performs well on texts by prolific authors, there is still room for improvement on authors who have not written many texts – an issue that we will address in the future. One approach that may improve performance on such authors involves considering other types of features than tokens, such as parts of speech and character n-grams. Since our approach is based on LDA, it can easily employ different feature types, which makes this a straightforward extension to the work presented in this paper.

In the future, we also plan to explore ways of extending LDA to model authors directly, rather than using it as a black box. Authors were considered by Rosen-Zvi et al. (2004; 2010), who extended LDA to form an author-topic model. However, this model was not used for authorship attribution, and was mostly aimed at topic modelling of multi-authored texts, such as research papers.

Another possible research direction is to improve the scalability of our methods. Our approach, like Koppel et al.'s (2011) baseline, requires linear time in the number of possible authors to classify a single document. One possible way of reducing the time needed for prediction is by employing a hierarchical approach that builds a tree of classifiers based on class similarity, as done by Bickerstaffe and Zukerman (2010) for the sentiment analysis task. Under this framework, class similarity (in our case, author similarity) can be measured using LDA, while small groups of classes can be discriminated using SVMs.

In addition to authorship attribution, we plan to employ text-based author models in user modelling tasks such as rating prediction – a direction that we already started working on by successfully applying our LDA-based approach to model users for the rating prediction task (Seroussi et al., 2011).

Acknowledgements

This research was supported in part by grant LP0883416 from the Australian Research Council. The authors thank Russell Smyth for the collaboration on initial results on the judgement dataset.

References

Adrian Bickerstaffe and Ingrid Zukerman. 2010. A hierarchical classifier applied to multi-way sentiment detection. In *COLING 2010: Proceedings of the 23rd International Conference on Computational Linguistics*, pages 62–70, Beijing, China.

David M. Blei, Andrew Y. Ng, and Michael I. Jordan. 2003. Latent Dirichlet allocation. *Journal of Machine Learning Research*, 3(Jan):993–1022.

Haibin Cheng, Pang-Ning Tan, and Rong Jin. 2007. Localized support vector machine and its efficient algorithm. In *SDM 2007: Proceedings of the 7th SIAM International Conference on Data Mining*, pages 461–466, Minneapolis, MN, USA.

Michael Gamon. 2004. Linguistic correlates of style: Authorship classification with deep linguistic analysis features. In *COLING 2004: Proceedings of the 20th International Conference on Computational Linguistics*, pages 611–617, Geneva, Switzerland.

Thomas L. Griffiths and Mark Steyvers. 2004. Finding scientific topics. *Proceedings of the National Academy of Sciences*, 101(Suppl. 1):5228–5235.

Patrick Juola. 2006. Authorship attribution. *Foundations and Trends in Information Retrieval*, 1(3):233–334.

Moshe Koppel, Jonathan Schler, and Shlomo Argamon. 2011. Authorship attribution in the wild. *Language Resources and Evaluation*, 45(1):83–94.

Kim Luyckx and Walter Daelemans. 2008. Authorship attribution and verification with many authors and limited data. In *COLING 2008: Proceedings of the 22nd International Conference on Computational Linguistics*, pages 513–520, Manchester, UK.

David Madigan, Alexander Genkin, David D. Lewis, Shlomo Argamon, Dmitriy Fradkin, and Li Ye. 2005. Author identification on the large scale. In *Proceedings of the Joint Annual Meeting of the Interface and the Classification Society of North America*, St. Louis, MO, USA.

Thomas C. Mendenhall. 1887. The characteristic curves of composition. *Science*, 9(214S):237–246.

Frederick Mosteller and David L. Wallace. 1964. *Inference and Disputed Authorship: The Federalist*. Addison-Wesley.

Arun Rajkumar, Saradha Ravi, Venkatasubramanian Suresh, M. Narasimha Murthy, and C. E. Veni Madhavan. 2009. Stopwords and stylometry: A latent Dirichlet allocation approach. In *Proceedings of the NIPS 2009 Workshop on Applications for Topic Models: Text and Beyond (Poster Session)*, Whistler, BC, Canada.

Bhavani Raskutti and Adam Kowalczyk. 2004. Extreme re-balancing for SVMs: A case study. *ACM SIGKDD Explorations Newsletter*, 6(1):60–69.

Ryan Rifkin and Aldebaro Klautau. 2004. In defense of one-vs-all classification. *Journal of Machine Learning Research*, 5(Jan):101–141.

Michal Rosen-Zvi, Thomas Griffiths, Mark Steyvers, and Padhraic Smyth. 2004. The author-topic model for authors and documents. In *UAI 2004: Proceedings of the 20th Conference on Uncertainty in Artificial Intelligence*, pages 487–494, Banff, AB, Canada.

Michal Rosen-Zvi, Chaitanya Chemudugunta, Thomas Griffiths, Padhraic Smyth, and Mark Steyvers. 2010. Learning author-topic models from text corpora. *ACM Transactions on Information Systems*, 28(1):1–38.

Jonathan Schler, Moshe Koppel, Shlomo Argamon, and James W. Pennebaker. 2006. Effects of age and gender on blogging. In *Proceedings of AAAI Spring Symposium on Computational Approaches for Analyzing Weblogs*, pages 199–205, Stanford, CA, USA.

Yanir Seroussi, Ingrid Zukerman, and Fabian Bohnert. 2010. Collaborative inference of sentiments from texts. In *UMAP 2010: Proceedings of the 18th International Conference on User Modeling, Adaptation and Personalization*, pages 195–206, Waikoloa, HI, USA.

Yanir Seroussi, Fabian Bohnert, and Ingrid Zukerman. 2011. Personalised rating prediction for new users using latent factor models. In *Hypertext 2011: Proceedings of the 22nd ACM Conference on Hypertext and Hypermedia*, Eindhoven, The Netherlands.

Efstathios Stamatatos. 2009. A survey of modern authorship attribution methods. *Journal of the American Society for Information Science and Technology*, 60(3):538–556.

Mark Steyvers and Tom Griffiths. 2007. Probabilistic topic models. In Thomas K. Landauer, Danielle S. McNamara, Simon Dennis, and Walter Kintsch, editors, *Handbook of Latent Semantic Analysis*, pages 427–448. Lawrence Erlbaum Associates.

Evaluating a Semantic Network Automatically Constructed from Lexical Co-occurrence on a Word Sense Disambiguation Task

Sean Szumlanski
Department of EECS
University of Central Florida
seansz@cs.ucf.edu

Fernando Gomez
Department of EECS
University of Central Florida
gomez@eecs.ucf.edu

Abstract

We describe the extension and objective evaluation of a network[1] of semantically related noun senses (or *concepts*) that has been automatically acquired by analyzing lexical co-occurrence in Wikipedia. The acquisition process makes no use of the metadata or links that have been manually built into the encyclopedia, and nouns in the network are automatically disambiguated to their corresponding noun senses without supervision. For this task, we use the noun sense inventory of WordNet 3.0. Thus, this work can be conceived of as augmenting the WordNet noun ontology with unweighted, undirected *related-to* edges between synsets. Our network contains 208,832 such edges.

We evaluate our network's performance on a word sense disambiguation (WSD) task and show: a) the network is competitive with WordNet when used as a stand-alone knowledge source for two WSD algorithms; b) combining our network with WordNet achieves disambiguation results that exceed the performance of either resource individually; and c) our network outperforms a similar resource that has been automatically derived from semantic annotations in the Wikipedia corpus.

1 Introduction

A growing interest in using semantic relatedness in word sense disambiguation (WSD) tasks has spurred investigations into the limitations of the WordNet ontology (Fellbaum, 1998) for this purpose. Although WordNet comprises a rich set of semantic links between word senses (or *concepts*), indicating semantic similarity through subsumptive hypernymic and hyponymic relations (among others), it lacks a general indication of semantic relatedness.

We present a semantic network that is automatically acquired from lexical co-occurrence in Wikipedia, and indicates general semantic relatedness between noun senses in WordNet 3.0. In this work, the discovery of relatedness is a context-sparse affair that takes place *in absentia* of the semantic annotations of Wikipedia, such as inter-article links, entries in disambiguation pages, the title of the article from which a sentence is extracted, and so on.

We released an earlier version of such a network that was limited by the fact that only relationships involving at least one monosemous noun had been included, and it was not evaluated on a WSD task (Szumlanski and Gomez, 2010).

In contrast, the network we present here has relatedness data for over 4,500 polysemous noun targets and 3,000 monosemous noun targets, each of which are related to an average of 27.5 distinct noun senses. It consists of 208,832 undirected edges – a 181% increase in size over the previous network. The result is a semantic network that has reached maturity and, as we will show, can be successfully applied to a WSD task.

This paper proceeds as follows. In the next section (Section 2), we discuss related work. We then give an overview of the method we use to construct our network (Sections 3 and 4). The network is evaluated through its application to a WSD task (Sections 5–7), where we compare its performance to WordNet and another automatically acquired semantic network called WordNet++ (Ponzetto and Navigli, 2010). A discussion follows (Section 8),

[1] http://www.cs.ucf.edu/~seansz/sem

Proceedings of the Fifteenth Conference on Computational Natural Language Learning, pages 190–199,
Portland, Oregon, USA, 23–24 June 2011.

and we present our conclusions in Section 9.

2 Related Work

Our work bears strong relation to WordNet++ (henceforth WN++), which is constructed automatically from the semantic annotations in Wikipedia (Ponzetto and Navigli, 2010).[2] Links in WN++ are established between words whose articles link to one another. For example, the article on *astronomy* in Wikipedia links to the article on *celestial navigation*, so we find an edge from astronomy#n#1 to celestial_navigation#n#1 in WN++.[3] The nouns related in WN++ are disambiguated automatically using further semantic annotation data from Wikipedia, including sense labels, the titles of other pages linked to by any two related nouns, and the folksonomic categories to which articles belong. These serve as context words that are compared with context words from various WordNet relations in order to map the nouns to their appropriate WordNet senses. The resulting resource contains 1,902,859 unique edges between noun senses.

Augmenting the structure of Wikipedia itself has been the subject of research as well, and involves the discovery of relations between articles. Mihalcea and Csomai (2007), for example, added links between Wikipedia pages after automatically identifying keywords in each article and disambiguating those words to their appropriate Wikipedia concepts (article titles), while Ponzetto and Navigli (2009) used graph theoretic approaches to augment the taxonomic organization of Wikipedia articles.

In terms of automatically discovering semantic relations, many pattern-based approaches have been used to extract specific types of relations from large corpora, e.g., hyponymy, meronymy, and synonymy (Hearst, 1992; Pantel and Pennacchiotti, 2006). Approaches based on distributional similarity have been applied toward the same end (Harris, 1985; Gorman and Curran, 2006), and there are several approaches that rely on the underlying structure of WordNet or Wikipedia to measure the relatedness between two concepts or nouns quantitatively (Hughes and Ramage, 2007; Gabrilovich and Markovitch, 2007; Zaragoza et al., 2007; Patwardhan and Pedersen, 2006; Strube and Ponzetto, 2006; Budanitsky and Hirst, 2006; Resnik, 1995).

Other quantitative approaches have leveraged the large amounts of data available on the Web to discover relatedness. Notably, Agirre and de Lacalle (2004) employed web queries to associate WordNet synsets with representative context words, known as topic signatures. Cuadros and Rigau (2008) have used these data to construct four KnowNets, semantic knowledge bases derived by disambiguating the top 5, 10, 15, and 20 nouns, respectively, from the topic signatures of Agirre and de Lacalle.

3 Automatic Acquisition of the Semantic Network

The semantic network is automatically acquired in three distinct stages (Szumlanski and Gomez, 2010): (1) quantitative measurement of relatedness between nouns that co-occur in a large corpus; (2) categorical determination of whether the quantitative measure indicates strong and mutual semantic relatedness between a given pair of nouns; and (3) unsupervised disambiguation of all the nouns that are found to be semantically related. We provide an overview of each of these steps below (Sections 3.1–3.3), and then discuss how we have expanded this methodology to create a more complete semantic network (Section 4).

3.1 Quantitatively measuring relatedness from lexical co-occurrence

We first measure the semantic relatedness, or **relational strength**, of a target, t, to one of its co-occurring nouns, or co-targets, c, with the following asymmetric function:

$$S_{rel}(t,c) = P(t|c)P(c|t)\log\frac{P(c|t)}{P(c)}$$

where $P(c|t)$ is the relative frequency of c among all nouns co-occurring with t, and vice versa for $P(t|c)$. $P(c)$ is the relative frequency of c among all nouns occurring in the corpus. For these values, we rely on lexical co-occurrence data extracted from Wikipedia. Co-occurrence is considered intra-sententially (as opposed to co-occurrence in entire articles or paragraphs, or co-occurrence within variable-sized windows of context).

[2] http://lcl.uniroma1.it/wordnetplusplus

[3] The notation astronomy#n#1 refers to sense 1 (#1) of the noun (#n) "astronomy" in WordNet. Other parts of speech are denoted by #v (verbs), #a (adjectives), or #r (adverbs).

This function essentially measures the degree to which an occurrence of t in a sentence predicts the co-occurrence of c. It is an adaptation of Resnik's (1999) selectional association measure.

Table 1 shows the results of applying this function to the co-targets of "yoga" and "meditation."

Target (t): yoga		**Target** (t): meditation	
Co-target (c)	$\mathbf{S_{rel}}$	**Co-target** (c)	$\mathbf{S_{rel}}$
hatha yoga	.1801	yoga	.0707
asana	.0761	mindfulness	.0415
meditation	.0673	contemplation	.0165
bhakti	.0508	prayer	.0139
raja	.0410	practice	.0068
tantra	.0148	technique	.0060
yogi	.0132	mantra	.0053
karma	.0125	relaxation	.0048
posture	.0104	retreat	.0047
aerobics	.0093	enlightenment	.0031
tai chi	.0089	monk	.0025
exercise	.0036	posture	.0024
practice	.0032	breathing	.0017
instructor	.0031	- - - - - - - - -	- - - -
- - - - - - - - -	- - - -	exercise	.0015
guru	.0027	teaching	.0014
massage	.0026	practitioner	.0014
exercise	.0019	ascetic	.0014
⋮	⋮	⋮	⋮

Table 1: The most strongly related co-targets of "yoga" and "meditation," sorted by decreasing value of relational strength (S_{rel}). Nouns above dashed lines are the top 5% of the target's most strongly related co-targets.

3.2 Establishing categorical relatedness

We then use a mutual relatedness algorithm to ascertain whether two nouns are semantically related by determining whether the nouns under consideration reciprocate a high degree of relatedness to one another. It proceeds as follows:

For some target noun of interest, t, let $C_x(t)$ be the set of the top $x\%$ of t's co-targets as sorted by $S_{rel}(t, c)$. For each $c \in C_x(t)$, if we have $t \in C_x(c)$, then we say that t and c are categorically related and add the noun pair (t, c) to our semantic network. We then increment x by one and repeat the process: for every $c \in C_{x+1}(t)$ such that (t, c) is not already in our network, we look for t in $C_{x+1}(c)$, and add (t, c) to our network if we find it. This process continues until we have incremented x some number of times without adding any new relations to the semantic network. We then take the symmetric closure of the network, so that if (t, c) is in the network, (c, t) is, as well. (That is, the relation is considered undirected.)

Consider, for example, the nouns in Table 1. Given the target "yoga," we might first examine the top 5% of its most strongly related co-targets (an arbitrary initial threshold chosen simply for illustrative purposes). In this case, we have all the nouns above the dashed line: C_5(*yoga*) = {*hatha yoga, asana, meditation, bhakti, raja, tantra, yogi, karma, posture, aerobics, tai chi, exercise, practice, instructor*}. The algorithm then searches C_5(*hatha yoga*), C_5(*asana*), and so on, for "yoga," adding a new relation to the network every time "yoga" is found. Thus, we can see by the inclusion of "yoga" in C_5(*meditation*) (all nouns above the dashed line in the second column of Table 1), that the pair (*yoga, meditation*) will be included in the network.

This reliance on mutual relatedness ensures that only noun pairs exhibiting strong semantic relatedness are admitted to the network.

3.3 Disambiguation

Disambiguation of the resulting noun-noun pairs is the product of majority-rules voting by the following three algorithms.

Subsumption. The most frequently occurring immediate hypernyms of all nouns related to our target are permitted to disambiguate the polysemous nouns. This is useful because of the semantic clustering that tends to occur among related nouns. (E.g., "astronomer" is related to several terms categorized as celestial bodies in WordNet, such as "planet," "star," "minor planet," and "quasar.")

Glosses. Senses of polysemous co-targets with occurrences of monosemous co-targets in their glosses are preferentially taken as the intended meanings of the polysemous nouns. Monosemous co-targets are matched directly, or by suffix replacement. (E.g., "biology" can be matched by the occurrence of "biologist" in a gloss, "engineering" by "engineers," and so on.)

Selectional Preferences. This method associates a numerical score with all superordinate synsets from the WordNet noun ontology that categorize the monosemous nouns related to a target. For example, the noun "unicorn" strongly predicts related nouns categorized as monsters (monster#1)[4] and mythical beings (mythical_being#1) in WordNet. These selectional preferences are applied to polysemous co-targets in decreasing order of their relational strength to the target noun. A polysemous noun is disambiguated to the first sense or senses subsumed by one of these selectional preferences. For example, "phoenix," as it relates to "unicorn," is disambiguated to phoenix#3 in WordNet (the fiery bird that is reborn from its own ashes) by virtue of its subsumption by mythical_being#1.

4 Creating a More Complete Network

A shortcoming of our previously released network is that it lacked concept-level relations between pairs of polysemous nouns.

When humans encounter a pair of ambiguous but closely related words, like *bus–horn*, we automatically disambiguate to the automobile and the car horn, as opposed to a computer's front-side bus or a rhinoceros's horn. The human ability to perform this disambiguation stems from the fact that human semantic memory relates not just individual words, but specific concepts denoted by those words. But if our goal is to establish such a link in our computational model of semantic relatedness, then we cannot rely on the link to perform that disambiguation for us; another approach is called for.

One reasonable approach (the one taken in our previous work) is to go where the problem no longer exists – to relationships that involve at least one monosemous noun. Monosemous-to-monosemous noun relationships require no disambiguation. Monosemous-to-polysemous noun relationships, on the other hand, require that only one noun be disambiguated. This ameliorates our problem tremendously, because the monosemous noun in the pair anchors the polysemous noun in an unambiguous context where disambiguation can more readily take place. That context includes all the nouns related to our monosemous noun, which, through their transitive relatedness to the polysemous noun in question, can assist in the act of disambiguation *vis-à-vis* the algorithms described in Section 3.3.

Consider, in contrast, the polysemous "batter," which can refer to the baseball player or the cake batter. The algorithm for discovering semantic relatedness yields several nouns related to each of these senses of "batter" (see Table 2). If we wish to disambiguate the pair (batter, cake), we are left with the question: which of the nouns in Table 2 should we take as contextual anchors for the disambiguation?

baking	fastball	inning	strike
ball	flour	outfielder	strikeout
base	glove	pancake	swing
baseball	hitter	pitch	tempura
bat	home plate	pudding	umpire
cake	home run	runner	waffle
dugout	infielder	shortstop	

Table 2: An excerpt of some of the nouns related to "batter" by the algorithm for automatic acquisition.

In considering this question, it is important to note that although the ontological categories that subsume the nouns related to "batter" exhibit greater entropy than we usually observe among the terms related to a monosemous noun, clear delineations still exist. For example, Figure 1 shows the clusters that form as we consider shared hypernymic relationships between all senses of the nouns related to "batter" (gray nodes in the graph). We see that many of the nouns related to "batter" have senses categorized by food#1, cake#3, pitch#2, ballplayer#1, or equipment#1 – the heads of five distinct clusters by semantic similarity.

It is worth noting that some nouns related to "batter" (such as "baking," "swing," and "umpire") do not fall into any of these semantic clusters. In these cases, the WordNet glosses serve as our primary tool for disambiguation. (For example, the glosses of both swing#8 and umpire#1 include mention of "baseball," which is also related to "batter.")

Conversely, some of the polysemous nouns in our example have senses that join semantic clusters unintendedly. For instance, cake#2 ("[a] small flat mass of chopped food," according to WordNet) falls under the cluster headed by food#1. Although this is potentially problematic, cake#2 is discarded in this particular case in favor of cake#3 (the baked good),

[4]We sometimes drop the part of speech from our word sense notation for brevity, but only in the case of noun senses.

which has a greater mass because of its subsumption of waffle#1 and pancake#1, and is indeed the intended meaning of "cake" as it relates to "batter."

Another example of unintended cluster membership comes from bat#4 (the cricket bat), which is categorized by sports_equipment#1. In contrast, the baseball bat does not have its own entry in WordNet, and the most reasonable sense choice, bat#5 ("a club used for hitting a ball in various games"), is categorized as a stick (stick#1), and not as equipment, sports equipment, or game equipment.

These unintended cluster memberships are bound to cause minor errors in our disambiguation efforts. However, our analysis reveals that we do not find such high entropy among the relatives of a polysemous noun that the semantic clustering effect (which is necessary for the success of the disambiguation algorithms described above in Section 3.3) is diminished. Thus, to construct our network, we apply the disambiguation algorithms described above, with the following modification: when confronted with a pair of semantically related polysemous nouns, we apply the disambiguation mechanism described above in both directions, and then fuse the results together. So, in one direction, the various baked goods related to "batter" help us to properly disambiguate "cake" to cake#3 in WordNet, yielding the pair (batter, cake#3). A similar scenario yields the pair (cake, batter#2) when disambiguating in the other direction, and we fuse the results together into the properly disambiguated pair (batter#2, cake#3).

Using this method, we have automatically created a semantic network that has 208,832 pairs of related noun senses – the most extensive semantic network between WordNet noun senses to be derived automatically from a simple lexical co-occurrence measure. For the remainder of this paper, we will refer to our network as the Szumlanski-Gomez network (SGN).

5 Coarse-Grained WSD Experiments

To evaluate our semantic network, and to provide fair comparison to related work, we take our cue from Ponzetto and Navigli (2010), who evaluated the performance of WN++ on the SemEval-2007 (Navigli et al., 2007) coarse-grained all-words WSD task using extended gloss overlaps (Banerjee and

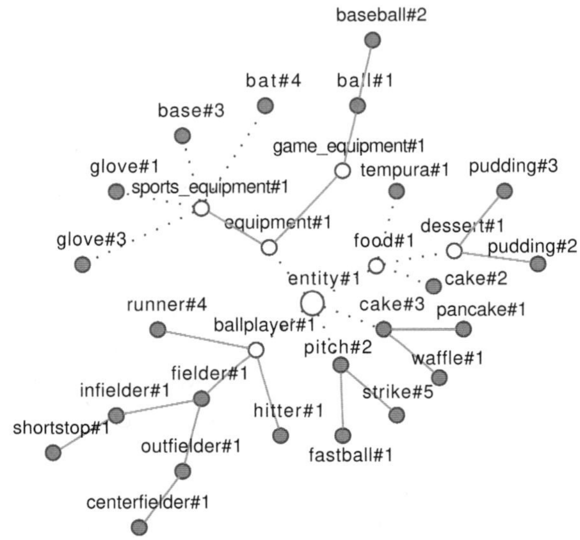

Figure 1: A partial view of the WordNet graph, showing senses of nouns related to "batter" (gray nodes) and intermediary concepts (white nodes) that connect them to the root of the taxonomy through hypernymic relationships.

Pedersen, 2003) and the graph-based degree centrality algorithm (Navigli and Lapata, 2010).

In this particular SemEval task, we are presented with 237 sentences in which lemmatized target words have been flagged for disambiguation. In our experiments, we disambiguate nouns only (as did Ponzetto and Navigli), since both SGN (our network) and WN++ relate only concepts denoted by nouns, and no other parts of speech. In our experimental setup, each sentence is considered in isolation from the rest, and all lemmatized content words in a sentence are provided to the disambiguation algorithms; the verbs, adjectives, and adverbs, although we do not resolve their senses, lend additional context to the disambiguation algorithms.

The coarse-grained nature of the SemEval-2007 task provides that there may be more than one acceptable sense assignment for many of the targets. In the coarse-grained setting, an algorithm's sense assignment is considered correct when it appears in the list of acceptable senses for the given target word.

The algorithms below both allow for multiple disambiguation results to be returned in the event of a tie. In these cases (although they are rare), we adopt the approach of Banerjee and Pedersen (2003), who award partial credit and discredit proportionally for all the senses returned by the algorithm.

6 Extended Gloss Overlaps (ExtLesk)

The first disambiguation algorithm we employ is the extended gloss overlaps measure (henceforth ExtLesk) of Banerjee and Pedersen (2003), which is an extension of the Lesk (1986) gloss overlap measure. Loosely speaking, the algorithm disambiguates a target noun by maximizing the overlap (number of words in common) between the glosses of word senses related[5] to the target's noun senses and those related to all context words (all lemmatized targets in the sentence under consideration other than the target itself). The sense with the greatest overlap is selected as the intended meaning of a target noun.

In the event of a tie, multiple senses may be selected. ExtLesk does not attempt to perform sense assignment if the score for every sense of a target noun is zero, except when dealing with a monosemous noun, in which case we default to the only sense possible.

6.1 Results

We have run ExtLesk on the SemEval-2007 task using five combinations of semantic resources: WordNet only, SGN (our semantic network) only, SGN and WordNet combined (that is, the union of all links contained in both networks), WN++ only, and WN++ combined with WordNet. We include the traditional baselines of most frequent sense (MFS) assignment and random sense assignment for comparison, and measure precision (number of correct sense assignments divided by the number of attempted sense assignments), recall (number of correct sense assignments divided by the number of target nouns to be disambiguated), and the harmonic mean of the two, F_1, defined as:

$$F_1 = \frac{2 * precision * recall}{precision + recall}$$

We present our results in Table 3, and offer the following observations. Firstly, SGN as a stand-alone network rivals the performance of WordNet. This is particularly impressive given the fact that the edges in SGN were derived automatically from a simple lexical co-occurrence measure.

Resource	P	R	F_1
WordNet	78.80	74.82	76.76
SGN	78.64	72.82	75.62
SGN and WordNet	**82.35**	**78.11**	**80.18**
WN++	74.67	61.87	67.67
WN++ and WordNet	77.35	73.38	75.31
MFS Baseline	77.40	77.40	77.40
Random Baseline	63.50	63.50	63.50

Table 3: ExtLesk disambiguation results on the SemEval-2007 all-words coarse-grained WSD task (nouns only).

Equally impressive is the ability of SGN and WordNet, when used in combination, to achieve results that exceed what either network is able to accomplish as a stand-alone knowledge source. When combined, we see improvements of 3.42% and 4.56% over WordNet and SGN as stand-alone resources, respectively. It is also only with these resources combined that we are able to outperform the MFS baseline, and we do so by 2.78%.[6]

In contrast, WN++ fails to perform as a stand-alone resource, falling behind the MFS baseline by 9.73%.[7] Of all the resources tested, WN++ yields the lowest results. When combined with WordNet, WN++ actually diminishes the ability of WordNet to perform on this WSD task by 1.45%. We defer our discussion of factors impacting the performance of WN++ to Section 8 (Discussion).

7 WSD with Degree Centrality

Degree centrality is a graph-based measure of semantic relatedness (Navigli and Lapata, 2010) in which we search through a semantic network for paths of length $l \leq maxLength$ between all sense nodes for all lemmas in our context. The edges along all such paths are added to a new graph, G', and for each target noun to be disambiguated, the sense node with the greatest number of incident edges (highest vertex degree) in G' is taken as its intended sense.

5 We use all relations available in WordNet, as well as a *related-to* relation derived from the links in our semantic network.

6 Other systems have obtained better results on the same dataset, but we focus only on SGN and WN++ because our aim is to compare the resources themselves.

7 Ponzetto and Navigli (2010) report results of $F_1 = 68.3$ and 72.0 for WN and WN++ as stand-alone resources. Space considerations prevent us from discussing this disparity in detail.

In these graphs, nodes represent synsets, as opposed to instantiating separate nodes for different members of the same synset and allowing edges to be constructed between them. We include all lemmas from a sentence in our context, but only return disambiguation results for the nouns.

With SGN and WN++, the implementation of this algorithm is straightforward. We initiate a breadth-first search (BFS)[8] at each target sense node in the network, and proceed through $\lfloor \frac{maxLength+1}{2} \rfloor$ iterations of spreading activation. Whenever the tendrils of this spreading activation from one target sense node in the graph connect to those of another,[9] we add the path between the nodes to our new graph, G', potentially incrementing the degree of the involved target sense nodes in G' as we do so.

Because BFS is an admissible algorithm (guaranteed to find the shortest path from an initial state to a goal), it provides a computationally efficient approach to finding all paths between all target nodes. Also, because any node on a path of length $l \leq maxLength$ between two target nodes is at most $\lfloor \frac{l}{2} \rfloor$ nodes removed from at least one of those target sense nodes, we only need to perform a BFS of depth $\lfloor \frac{maxLength+1}{2} \rfloor$ from every target sense node in order to guarantee that every such path between them will be discovered. Since the time complexity of BFS is exponential with respect to the depth of the search, cutting this depth in half (in comparison to performing a BFS of depth $maxLength$) greatly reduces the running time of our algorithm.

We take the same approach in traversing the WordNet noun graph, using all possible sense relations as edges. In keeping with the approach of Navigli and Lapata (2010), an edge is also induced between synsets if the gloss of one synset contains a monosemous content word. For example, the gloss for leprechaun#n#1, "a mischievous elf in Irish folklore," contains the monosemous noun "folklore;" thus, we have an edge between leprechaun#n#1 and folklore#n#1 in the WordNet graph.

Once we have our new graph, G', constructed in this manner, the vertex degree is considered an indication of the semantic relatedness of a particular synset to all other lemmas in our context. For each target noun, we use its sense node with the highest degree in G' for sense assignment.

7.1 Results

We have tested the degree centrality algorithm with the following combinations of semantic resources: WordNet, SGN, WN++, Refined WN++, SGN and WordNet combined, and Refined WN++ and WordNet combined. (Refined WN++ consists of 79,422 of WN++'s strongest relations, and was created in an unsupervised setting by Ponzetto and Navigli specifically for use with degree centrality when they discovered that WN++ had too many weak relations to perform well with the algorithm.)

We have observed that the performance of degree centrality rapidly levels off as $maxLength$ increases. Ponzetto and Lapata (2010) also report this so-called "plateau" effect, and employ a $maxLength$ of 6 in their experiments, despite finding that results level off around $maxLength = 4$. We, too, find that performance levels off around $maxLength = 4$ in almost all cases, and so only continue up to $maxLength = 5$.

We find that, in all cases tested, degree centrality is unable to outperform the MFS baseline (with respect to F_1) (see Table 4). SGN and WN++ exhibit comparable performance with this algorithm, with maximum F_1 values of 68.4% ($maxLength$ = 2) and 67.3% ($maxLength$ = 3–5), respectively. Neither achieves the performance of WordNet with degree centrality (F_1 = 74.0%), which underperforms the MFS baseline (F_1 = 77.4%) by 3.4%.[10] Ponzetto and Navigli (2010) reported that only performing sense assignment when the max degree exceeded an empirically derived but non-disclosed threshold improved performance, but we have found that implementing such a threshold universally lowers results for all resources we tested with degree centrality.

[8] This is in contrast to the DFS implementation of Navigli and Lapata (2010), so for the sake of posterity, we expound upon our approach in this section.

[9] When $maxLength$ is odd, this requires an additional check to ensure that the intersection is not taking place at a node that is exactly $\lfloor \frac{maxLength+1}{2} \rfloor$ degrees removed from each of the two target nodes it is connecting, as this would result in a path with overall length $maxLength + 1$ between the target nodes.

[10] Although Ponzetto and Navigli (2010) reported similar results with WordNet (F_1 = 74.5), we have been unable to reproduce their results using Refined WN++, either combined with WordNet (F_1 = 79.4) or as a stand-alone resource (F_1 = 57.4).

The lowest performance using degree centrality comes from Refined WN++ as a stand-alone resource. We attribute this to the fact that Refined WN++ is so semantically sparse. On average, noun senses in Refined WN++ are related to only 3.42 other noun senses, while those in WN++ and SGN relate to an average of 44.59 and 10.92 noun senses, respectively. Accordingly, the success of Refined WN++ and WordNet combined is attributable mostly to the success of WordNet as a stand-alone resource; as $maxLength$ increases, the contributions made by the sparse Refined WN++ network rapidly become negligible in comparison to those provided by the WordNet ontology.

l	**P**	**R**	**F$_1$**	**P**	**R**	**F$_1$**
	WordNet			**SGN**		
1	**96.9**	16.8	28.6	79.7	32.9	46.6
2	77.6	45.1	57.0	72.0	64.6	68.4
3	76.7	65.6	70.7	68.7	63.5	66.0
4	76.9	71.0	73.9	68.0	63.9	65.9
5	76.6	71.6	74.0	68.0	64.2	66.1
	SGN & WN			**WN++**		
1	77.4	52.4	62.5	87.2	23.5	37.1
2	74.7	70.7	72.7	71.6	60.2	65.4
3	70.3	67.1	68.7	70.7	64.3	67.3
4	70.5	67.4	68.9	70.4	64.5	67.3
5	70.1	67.0	68.5	70.4	64.5	67.3
	$WN^{++}_{refined}$			**$WN^{++}_{refined}$ & WN**		
1	98.3	15.3	26.5	83.3	31.2	45.4
2	91.4	23.4	37.3	77.5	66.6	71.6
3	88.7	29.9	44.7	77.6	73.6	75.5
4	83.7	32.3	46.7	74.7	71.4	73.0
5	80.2	35.3	49.0	74.7	71.4	73.0
	MFS Baseline			**Random Baseline**		
	77.4	**77.4**	**77.4**	63.5	63.5	63.5

Table 4: Degree centrality disambiguation results on the SemEval-2007 all-words coarse-grained WSD task (nouns only). *l* is maximum path length.

8 Discussion

The fact that the performance of degree centrality quickly plateaus hints at the root cause of its weak performance compared to ExtLesk and the MFS baseline. As the maximum path length is increased in a dense semantic network, all possible edges from our target sense nodes rapidly find themselves involved with paths to other target sense nodes. This is particularly true of WN++ (notice its rapid and stable convergence), where certain "sticky" nodes form bridges between seemingly unrelated concepts. For example, the frequent appearance of "United States" in Wikipedia articles, and its tendency to be linked to the *United States* Wikipage when it occurs, causes the term to serve as a bridge between such diverse concepts as automaton#2 and burrito#1, which one would typically expect to be far removed from one another in a model of semantic relatedness.

Nonetheless, the degree centrality algorithm has no difficulty finding short paths between target sense nodes when traversing any of the semantic networks we tested. In fact, we have discovered that as the results of degree centrality converge, they approach the performance obtained by foregoing the algorithm altogether and simply disambiguating each noun to the sense with the most edges in the network (regardless of whether those edges ultimately connect two word senses from the disambiguation context). The expected values of convergence attained by defaulting to the most semantically well-connected sense of each target noun in each network are $F_1 = 66.3\%$, 67.5%, and 74.6% for SGN, WN++, and WordNet, respectively – remarkably close to the experimentally derived degree centrality results of $F_1 = 66.1\%$, 67.3%, and 74.0%.

9 Conclusion

We have constructed a semantic network of related noun senses automatically from intra-sentential lexical co-occurrence data, and shown that on a WSD task, it outperforms a similar resource, WN++, which is derived from the rich set of semantic annotations available in the Wikipedia corpus. Our network has also shown competitive performance with the WordNet ontology on WSD, and when combined with WordNet, improves disambiguation results in a coarse-grained setting using the ExtLesk disambiguation algorithm.

Acknowledgments

This research was supported in part by the NASA Engineering and Safety Center under Grant/Cooperative Agreement NNX08AJ98A.

References

Eneko Agirre and Oier Lopez de Lacalle. 2004. Publicly available topic signatures for all WordNet nominal senses. In *Proceedings of the 4th International Conference on Language Resources and Evaluations (LREC '04)*, pages 1123–1126, Lisbon, Portugal.

Satanjeev Banerjee and Ted Pedersen. 2003. Extended gloss overlaps as a measure of semantic relatedness. In *Proceedings of the 18th International Joint Conference on Artificial Intelligence (IJCAI '03)*, pages 805–810, Acapulco, Mexico.

Alexander Budanitsky and Graeme Hirst. 2006. Evaluating WordNet-based measures of lexical semantic relatedness. *Computational Linguistics*, 32(1):13–47.

Montse Cuadros and German Rigau. 2008. KnowNet: building a large net of knowledge from the web. In *Proceedings of the 22nd International Conference on Computational Linguistics (COLING '08)*, pages 161–168, Manchester, UK. Association for Computational Linguistics.

Christiane Fellbaum, editor. 1998. *WordNet: An Electronic Lexical Database*. MIT Press.

Evgeniy Gabrilovich and Shaul Markovitch. 2007. Computing semantic relatedness using Wikipedia-based explicit semantic analysis. In *Proceedings of the 20th International Joint Conference on Artificial Intelligence (IJCAI '07)*, pages 1606–1611, Hyderabad, India.

James Gorman and James R. Curran. 2006. Scaling distributional similarity to large corpora. In *Proceedings of the 21st International Conference on Computational Linguistics and the 44th Annual Meeting of the Association for Computational Linguistics (COLING-ACL '06)*, pages 361–368, Sydney, Australia. Association for Computational Linguistics.

Zellig S. Harris. 1985. Distributional structure. In J. J. Katz, editor, *The Philosophy of Linguistics*, pages 26–47. Oxford University Press.

Marti A. Hearst. 1992. Automatic acquisition of hyponyms from large text corpora. In *Proceedings of the 14th International Conference on Computational Linguistics (COLING '92)*, pages 539–545, Nantes, France.

Thad Hughes and Daniel Ramage. 2007. Lexical semantic relatedness with random graph walks. In *Proceedings of the 2007 Joint Conference on Empirical Methods in Natural Language Processing and Computational Natural Language Learning (EMNLP-CoNLL '07)*, pages 581–589, Prague, Czech Republic. Association for Computational Linguistics.

Michael Lesk. 1986. Automatic sense disambiguation using machine readable dictionaries: how to tell a pine cone from an ice cream cone. In *Proceedings of the 5th Annual International Conference on Systems Documentation (SIGDOC '86)*, pages 24–26, Toronto, Ontario, Canada. ACM.

Rada Mihalcea and Andras Csomai. 2007. Wikify!: linking documents to encyclopedic knowledge. In *Proceedings of the 16th ACM Conference on Information and Knowledge Management (CIKM '07)*, pages 233–242, Lisbon, Portugal. ACM.

Roberto Navigli and Mirella Lapata. 2010. An experimental study of graph connectivity for unsupervised word sense disambiguation. *IEEE Transactions on Pattern Analysis and Machine Intelligence*, 32(4):678–692.

Roberto Navigli, Kenneth C. Litkowski, and Orin Hargraves. 2007. SemEval-2007 Task 07: coarse-grained English all-words task. In *Proceedings of the 4th International Workshop on Semantic Evaluations (SemEval '07)*, pages 30–35, Prague, Czech Republic. Association for Computational Linguistics.

Patrick Pantel and Marco Pennacchiotti. 2006. Espresso: leveraging generic patterns for automatically harvesting semantic relations. In *Proceedings of the 21st International Conference on Computational Linguistics and the 44th Annual Meeting of the Association for Computational Linguistics (COLING-ACL '06)*, pages 113–120, Sydney, Australia. Association for Computational Linguistics.

Siddharth Patwardhan and Ted Pedersen. 2006. Using WordNet-based context vectors to estimate the semantic relatedness of concepts. In *Proceedings of the 11th Conference of the European Chapter of the Association for Computational Linguistics Workshop on Making Sense of Sense*, pages 1–8, Trento, Italy.

Simone Paolo Ponzetto and Roberto Navigli. 2009. Large-scale taxonomy mapping for restructuring and integrating Wikipedia. In *Proceedings of the 21st International Joint Conference on Artifical Intelligence (IJCAI '09)*, pages 2083–2088, Pasadena, CA.

Simone Paolo Ponzetto and Roberto Navigli. 2010. Knowledge-rich word sense disambiguation rivaling supervised systems. In *Proceedings of the 48th Annual Meeting of the Association for Computational Linguistics (ACL '10)*, pages 1522–1531, Uppsala, Sweden. Association for Computational Linguistics.

Philip Resnik. 1995. Using information content to evaluate semantic similarity in a taxonomy. In *Proceedings of the 14th International Joint Conference on Artificial Intelligence (IJCAI '95)*, pages 448–453, Montreal, QC.

Philip Resnik. 1999. Semantic similarity in a taxonomy: an information-based measure and its application to problems of ambiguity in natural language. *Journal of Artificial Intelligence Research*, 11:95–130.

Michael Strube and Simone Paolo Ponzetto. 2006. Wikirelate! computing semantic relatedness using wikipedia. In *Proceedings of the 21st National Conference on Artificial Intelligence (AAAI '06)*, pages 1419–1424, Boston, MA. AAAI Press.

Sean Szumlanski and Fernando Gomez. 2010. Automatically acquiring a semantic network of related concepts. In *Proceedings of the 19th ACM Conference on Information and Knowledge Management (CIKM '10)*, pages 19–28, Toronto, Ontario, Canada. ACM.

Hugo Zaragoza, Henning Rode, Peter Mika, Jordi Atserias, Massimiliano Ciaramita, and Giuseppe Attardi. 2007. Ranking very many typed entities on Wikipedia. In *Proceedings of the 16th ACM Conference on Information and Knowledge Management (CIKM '07)*, pages 1015–1018, Lisbon, Portugal. ACM.

Filling the Gap: Semi-Supervised Learning for Opinion Detection Across Domains

Ning Yu
Indiana University
nyu@indiana.edu

Sandra Kübler
Indiana University
skuebler@indiana.edu

Abstract

We investigate the use of Semi-Supervised Learning (SSL) in opinion detection both in sparse data situations and for domain adaptation. We show that co-training reaches the best results in an in-domain setting with small labeled data sets, with a maximum absolute gain of 33.5%. For domain transfer, we show that self-training gains an absolute improvement in labeling accuracy for blog data of 16% over the supervised approach with target domain training data.

1 Introduction

Rich and free opinions published electronically and, more recently, on the WWW offer ample opportunities to discover individual's attitudes towards certain topics, products, or services. To capitalize on this enormous body of opinions, researchers have been working in the area of opinion mining since the late 1990s. Opinion detection seeks to automatically determine the presence or absence of opinions in a text, and it is therefore a fundamental task for opinion mining.

In order to capture subtle and creative opinions, opinion detection systems generally assume that a large body of opinion-labeled data are available. However, collections of opinion-labeled data are often limited, especially at the granularity level of sentences; and manual annotation is tedious, expensive and error-prone. The shortage of opinion-labeled data is less challenging in some data domains (e.g., reviews) than in others (e.g., blog posts). A simple method for improving accuracies in challenging domains would be to borrow opinion-labeled data from a non-target data domain; but this approach often fails because opinion detection strategies designed for one data domain generally do not perform well in another domain. One reason for failure of the simple transfer approach is that the information used for opinion detection is typically lexical, and lexical means of expressing opinions may vary not only from domain to domain, but also from register to register. For example, while the word "awesome" is a good indicator of an opinion in blogs, it is less likely to occur in the same role in newspaper texts.

While it is difficult to obtain opinion-labeled data, one can easily collect almost infinite unlabeled user-generated data that contain opinions. The use of Semi-Supervised Learning (SSL), motivated by limited labeled data and plentiful unlabeled data in the real world, has achieved promising results in various NLP studies (e.g., (Fürstenau and Lapata, 2009; Talukdar and Pereira, 2010)), yet it has not been fully investigated for use in opinion detection. Although studies have shown that simple SSL methods are promising for extracting opinion features or patterns using limited opinion-labeled data (e.g., (Wiebe and Riloff, 2005)), few efforts have been made either to apply SSL directly to opinion detection or to examine more sophisticated SSL methods. This research is intended to fill the gap regarding application of SSL in opinion detection. We investigate a range of SSL algorithms with a focus on self-training and co-training in three types of electronic documents: edited news articles, semi-structured movie reviews, and the informal and unstructured content of the blogosphere. We conclude that SSL is a successful method for handling the shortage of opinion labeled data and the domain transfer problem.

Proceedings of the Fifteenth Conference on Computational Natural Language Learning, pages 200–209,
Portland, Oregon, USA, 23–24 June 2011.

2 Background and Related Work

There is a wide range of literature on opinion detection. We concentrate here on supervised and semi-supervised approaches.

2.1 Supervised Learning for Opinion Detection

Supervised learning algorithms that can automatically learn important opinion-bearing features from an annotated corpus have been adopted and investigated for opinion detection and yielded satisfying results (Wiebe et al., 2004; Yu and Hatzivassiloglou, 2003; Zhang and Yu, 2007). With no classification techniques developed specifically for opinion detection, state-of-the-art topical supervised classification algorithms can achieve performance comparable to complex linguistic approaches when using binary values (i.e., presence or absence) and incorporating different types of features. Commonly used opinion-bearing features include bag-of-words, POS tags, ngrams, low frequency words or unique words (Wiebe et al., 2004; Yang et al., 2007), semantically oriented adjectives (e.g., "great", "poor") and more complex linguistic patterns. Both the scale and quality of the annotated corpus play an important role in the supervised learning approach.

2.2 SSL for Opinion Detection

In contrast to supervised learning, SSL learns from both labeled and unlabeled data. SSL assumes that, although unlabeled data hold no information about classes (e.g., "opinion" or "non-opinion"), they do contain information about joint distribution over classification features. Therefore, when a limited set of labeled data is available in the target domain, using SSL with unlabeled data is expected to achieve an improvement over supervised learning.

Self-training Self-training is the simplest and most commonly adopted form of SSL for opinion detection. Self-training was originally used to facilitate automatic identification of opinion-bearing features. For example, Riloff and Wiebe (2003) proposed a bootstrapping process to automatically identify subjective patterns. Self-training has also been applied directly for identifying subjective sentences by following a standard self-training procedure: (1) train an initial supervised classifier on the labeled data; (2) apply this classifier to unlabeled data and select the most confidently labeled data, as determined by the classifier, to augment the labeled data set; and (3) re-train the classifier by restarting the whole process. Wiebe and Riloff (2005) used a self-trained Naïve Bayes classifier for classifying subjective sentences and achieved better recall with modest precision over several rule-based classifiers.

One shortcoming of self-training is that the resulting data may be biased: That is, the final labeled data may consist of examples that are easiest for this particular opinion detector to identify.

Co-training The core idea of co-training is to use two classifiers and trade additional examples between them, assuming that the resulting union of classified examples is more balanced than examples resulting from using either classifier alone. When labeling new examples, a final decision is made by combining the predictions of the two updated learners. The original co-training algorithm assumes redundancy in the training data and thus more than one view can be used to represent and classify each example independently and successfully (Blum and Mitchell, 1998). For example, an image can be naturally represented by its text description or by its visual attributes. Even when a natural split in the feature set is not available, studies have shown that the key to co-training is the existence of two largely different initial learners, regardless of whether they are built by using two feature sets or two learning algorithms (Wang and Zhou, 2007).

When there are different views for the target examples, co-training is conceptually clearer than self-training, which simply mixes features. Since co-training uses each labeled example twice, it requires less labeled data and converges faster than self-training. However, the lack of natural feature splits has kept researchers from exploring co-training for opinion detection. To the best of our knowledge, the only co-training application for opinion detection was reported by Jin et al. (2009), who created disjoint training sets for building two initial classifiers and successfully identified opinion sentences in camera reviews by selecting auto-labeled sentences agreed upon by both classifiers.

EM-Based SSL Expectation-Maximization (EM) refers to a class of iterative algorithms for maximum-likelihood estimation when dealing with incomplete data. Nigam et al. (1999) combined EM with a Naïve Bayes classifier to resolve the problem of topical classification, where unlabeled data were treated as incomplete data. The EM-NB SSL algorithm yielded better performance than either an unsupervised lexicon-based approach or a supervised approach for sentiment classification in different data domains, including blog data (Aue and Gamon, 2005; Takamura et al., 2006). No opinion detection applications of EM-based SSL have been reported in the literature.

S^3VMs Semi-Supervised Support Vector Machines (S^3VMs) are a natural extension of SVMs in the semi-supervised spectrum. They are designed to find the maximal margin decision boundary in a vector space containing both labeled and unlabeled examples. Although SVMs are the most favored supervised learning method for opinion detection, S^3VMs have not been used in opinion detection. Graph-based SSL learning has been successfully applied to opinion detection (Pang and Lee, 2004) but is not appropriate for dealing with large scale data sets.

2.3 Domain Adaptation for Opinion Detection

When there are few opinion-labeled data in the target domain and/or when the characteristics of the target domain make it challenging to detect opinions, opinion detection systems usually borrow opinion-labeled data from other data domains. This is especially common in opinion detection in the blogosphere (Chesley et al., 2006). To evaluate this shallow approach, Aue and Gamon (2005) compared four strategies for utilizing opinion-labeled data from one or more non-target domains and concluded that using non-targeted labeled data without an adaptation strategy is less efficient than using labeled data from the target domain, even when the majority of labels are assigned automatically by a self-training algorithm.

Blitzer et al. (2007) and Tan et al. (2009) implemented domain adaptation strategies for sentiment analysis. Although promising, their domain adaptation strategies involved sophisticated and computationally expensive methods for selecting general features to link target and non-target domains.

3 Motivation and Objective

While SSL is especially attractive for opinion detection because it only requires a small number of labeled examples, the studies described in the previous section have concentrated on simple SSL methods. We intend to fill this research gap by comparing the feasibility and effectiveness of a range of SSL approaches for opinion detection. Specifically, we aim to achieve the following goals:

First, to gain a more comprehensive understanding of the utility of SSL in opinion detection. We examine four major SSL methods: self-training, co-training, EM-NB, and S^3VM. We focus on self-training and co-training because they are both wrapper approaches that can be easily adopted by any existing opinion detection system.

Second, to design and evaluate co-training strategies for opinion detection. Since recent work has shown that co-training is not restricted by the original multi-view assumption for target data and that it is more robust than self-training, we evaluate new co-training strategies for opinion detection.

Third, to approach domain transfer using SSL, assuming that SSL can overcome the problem of domain-specific features by gradually introducing targeted data and thus diminishing bias from the non-target data set.

4 SSL Experiments

Our research treats opinion detection as a binary classification problem with two categories: subjective sentences and objective sentences. It is evaluated in terms of classification accuracy.

Since a document is normally a mixture of facts and opinions (Wiebe et al., 2001), sub-document level opinion detection is more useful and meaningful than document-level opinion detection. Thus, we conduct all experiments on the sentence level.

The remainder of this section explains the data sets and tools used in this study and presents the experimental design and parameter settings.

4.1 Data Sets

Three types of data sets have been explored in opinion detection studies: news articles, online reviews, and online discourse in blogs or discussion forums. These three types of text differ from one another in terms of structure, text genre (e.g., level of formality), and proportion of opinions found therein. We selected a data set from each type in order to investigate the robustness and adaptability of SSL algorithms for opinion detection and to test the feasibility of SSL for domain adaptation.

Movie Review One of the standard data sets in opinion detection is the movie review data set created by Pang and Lee (2004). It contains 5,000 subjective sentences or snippets from the Rotten Tomatoes pages and 5,000 objective sentences or snippets from IMDB plot summaries, all in lowercase. Sentences containing less than 10 tokens were excluded and the data set was labeled automatically by assuming opinion inheritance: every sentence in an opinion-bearing document expresses an opinion, and every sentence in a factual document is factual. Although this assumption appears to be acceptable for movie review data, it is generally unreliable for other domains.

News Article The Wall Street Journal part of the Penn Treebank III has been manually augmented with opinion related annotations. This set is widely used as a gold-standard corpus in opinion detection research. According to the coding manual (Wiebe et al., 1999), subjective sentences are those expressing evaluations, opinions, emotions, and speculations. For our research, 5,174 objective sentences and 5,297 subjective sentences were selected based on the absence or presence of manually labeled subjective expressions.

JDPA Blog Post The JDPA corpus (Kessler et al., 2010) is a new opinion corpus released in 2010. It consists of blog posts that express opinions about automobile and digital cameras with named entities and sentiments expressed about them manually annotated. For our purpose, we extracted all sentences containing sentiment-bearing expressions as subjective sentences and manually chose objective sentences from the rest by eliminating subjective sentences that were not targeted to any labeled entities. After this process, we had approximately 10,000 subjective sentences and 4,348 objective sentences. To balance the number of subjective and objective sentences, we used 4,348 sentences from each category.

4.2 Data Preparation

We removed a small number of stop words. No stemming was conducted since the literature shows no clear gain from stemming in opinion detection. One reason for this may be that stemming actually erases subtle opinion cues such as past tense verbs. All words were converted to lowercase and numbers were replaced by a placeholder #. Both unigrams and bigrams were generated for each sentence.

Each data set was randomly split into three portions: 5% of the sentences were selected as the evaluation set and were not available during SSL and supervised learning (SL) runs; 90% were treated as unlabeled data (U) for SSL runs and i% ($1 \leq i \leq 5$) as labeled data (L) for both SL and SSL runs. For each SSL run, a baseline SL run was designed with the same number of labeled sentences (i%) and a full SL run was designed with all available sentences (90% + i%). If effective, an SSL run would significantly outperform its corresponding baseline SL run and approach the performance of a full SL run.

4.3 Experimental Design

We conducted three groups of experiments: 1) to investigate the effectiveness of the SSL approach for opinion detection; 2) to explore different co-training strategies; and 3) to evaluate the applicability of SSL for domain adaptation.

4.3.1 General Settings for SSL

The Naïve Bayes classifier was selected as the initial classifier for self-training because of its ability to produce prediction scores and to work well with small labeled data sets. We used binary values for unigram and bigram features, motivated by the brevity of the text unit at the sentence level as well as by the characteristics of opinion detection, where occurrence frequency has proven to be less influential. We implemented two feature selection options: Chi square and Information Gain.

Parameters for SSL included: (1) Threshold k for number of iterations. If k is set to 0, the stopping criterion is convergence; (2) Number of unlabeled sentences available in each iteration u ($u << U$); (3) Number of opinion and non-opinion sentences, p and n, to augment L during each iteration; and (4) Weighting parameter λ for auto-labeled data. When λ is set to 0, auto-labeled and labeled data are treated equally; when λ is set to 1, feature values in an auto-labeled sentence are multiplied by the prediction score assigned to the sentence.

We used the WEKA data mining software (Hall et al., 2009) for data processing and classification of the self-training and co-training experiments. EM implemented in LingPipe (Alias-i, 2008) was used for the EM-NB runs. S^3VMs implemented in SVM^{light} (Joachims, 1999) and based on local search were adopted for the S^3VM runs. Since hyper-parameter optimization for EM-NB and S^3VM is not the focus of this research and preliminary explorations on parameter settings suggested no significant benefit, default settings were applied for EM-NB and S^3VM.

4.3.2 Co-Training Strategies

For co-training, we investigated five strategies for creating two initial classifiers following the criteria that these two classifiers either capture different features or based on different learning assumptions.

Two initial classifiers were generated: (1) Using unigrams and bigrams respectively to create two classifiers based on the assumption that low-order n-grams and high-order n-grams contain redundant information and represent different views of an example: content and context; (2) Randomly splitting feature set into two; (3) Randomly splitting training set into two; (4) Applying two different learning algorithms (i.e., Naïve Bayes and SVM) with different biases; and (5) Applying a character-based language model (CLM) and a bag-of-words (BOW) model where the former takes into consideration the sequence of words while the latter does not. In practice, for strategy (1), bigrams were used in combination with unigrams because bigrams alone are weak features when extracted from limited labeled data at sentence level.

Auto-labeled sentences were selected if they were assigned a label that both classifiers agreed on with highest confidence. Because our initial classifiers violated the original co-training assumptions, forcing agreement between confident predictions improved the maintenance of high precision.

4.3.3 Self-Training for Domain Adaptation

Based on the literature and our preliminary results (Yu and Kübler, 2010), movie reviews achieve the highest accuracy while news articles and blog reviews are considerably more challenging. Thus, we decided to use movie reviews as source data and news articles and blog posts as target data domains. While the data split for the target domain remains the same as in section 4.2, all sentences in the source domain, except for the 5% evaluation data, were treated as labeled data. For example, in order to identify opinion-bearing sentences from the blog data set, all 9,500 movie review sentences and i% of blog sentences were used as labeled data, 90% of blog sentences were used as unlabeled data, and 5% as evaluation data. We also applied a parameter to gradually decrease the weight of the source domain data, similar to the work done by Tan et al. (2009).

	# Labeled Examples					
Type	100	200	300	400	500	all
Self-tr	85.2	86.6	87.0	87.2	86.6	
SL	63.8	73.6	77.2	79.4	80.2	89.4
Co-tr.	92.2	93.8	92.6	93.2	91.4	
SL	75.8	80.8	82.6	85.2	84.8	95.2
EM-NB	88.1	88.7	88.6	88.4	89.0	
SL	73.5	78.7	81.3	82.8	83.9	91.6
S^3VM	59.0	68.4	67.8	67.0	75.2	
SL	70.0	72.8	75.6	76.2	80.0	90.0

Table 1: Classification accuracy(%) of SSL and SL on movie reviews

5 Results and Evaluation

Overall, our results suggest that SSL improves accuracy for opinion detection although the contribution of SSL varies across data domains and different strategies need to be applied to achieve optimized performance. For the movie review data set, almost all SSL runs outperformed their corresponding baseline SL runs and approached full SL runs; for the news article data set, SSL performance followed a similar trend but with only a small rate of increase; for the blog post data set, SSL runs using only blog data showed no benefits over the SL baseline, but with labeled movie review data, SSL runs produced results comparable with full SL result.

5.1 SSL vs. SL

Table 1 reports the performance of SSL and SL runs on movie review data based on different numbers of initial labeled sentences. Both the self- and co-training runs reported here used the same parameter settings: k=0, u=20, p=2, n=2, λ =0, with no feature selection. The co-training results in Table 1 used a CLM and a BOW model (see section 5.2). SL runs for co-training classified sentences based on the highest score generated by two classifiers; SL runs for S^3VM applied the default SVM setting in SVM^{light}; and SL runs for EM-NB used the Naïve Bayes classifier in the EM-NB implementation in LingPipe.

Table 1 shows that, except for S^3VM, SSL always outperforms the corresponding SL baseline on movie reviews: When SSL converges, it achieves improvement in the range of 8% to 34% over the SL baseline. The fewer initial labeled data, the more benefits an SSL run gained from using unlabeled data. For example, using 100 labeled sentences, self-training achieved a classification accuracy of 85.2% and outperformed the baseline SL by 33.5%. Although this SSL run was surpassed by 4.9% by the full SL run using all labeled data, a great amount of effort was saved by labeling only 100 sentences rather than 9,500. Co-training produced the best SSL results. For example, with only 200 labeled sentences, co-training yielded accuracy as high as 93.8%. Overall, SSL for opinion detection on movie reviews shows similar trends to SSL for traditional topical classification (Nigam and Ghani, 2000).

However, the advantages of SSL were not as significant in other data domains. Figure 1 demonstrates the performance of four types of SSL runs relative to corresponding baseline and full SL runs for all three data sets. All SSL runs reported here used 5% data as labeled data. Lines with different patterns indicate different data sets, green triangles mark baseline SL runs, green dots mark full SL runs, and red crosses mark SSL runs. Numbers next to symbols indicate classification accuracy. For each line, if the red cross is located above the triangle, it indicates that the SSL run improved over the SL baseline; and, the closer the red cross to the upper dot, the more effective was the SSL run. Figure 1 shows that S^3VM degrades in performance for all three data sets and we exclude it from the following discussion. From movie reviews to news articles to blog posts, the classification accuracy of baseline SL runs as well as the improvement gained by SSL

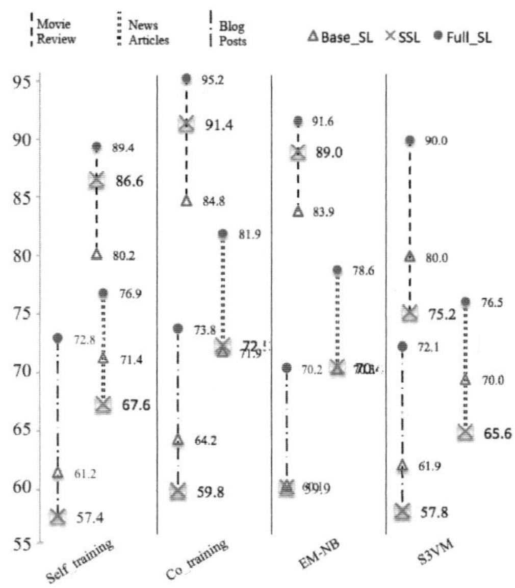

Figure 1: Classification accuracy(%) of SSL and SL on three data sets (i=5)

runs decreased: With greater than 80% baseline accuracy on movie reviews, SSL runs were most effective; with slightly above 70% baseline accuracy on news articles, self-training actually decreased performance of the corresponding SL baseline while co-training and EM-NB outperformed the SL baseline only slightly; and with 60% or so baseline accuracy on blog posts, none of the SSL methods showed improvement. We assume that the lower the baseline accuracy, the worse the quality of auto-labeled data, and, therefore, the less advantages is application of SSL. We also found that the average sentence length in blog posts (17 words) is shorter than the average sentence length in either movie reviews (23.5 words) or news articles (22.5 words), which posed an additional challenge because there is less information for the classifier in terms of numbers of features.

Overall, for movie reviews and news articles, co-training proved to be most robust and effective and EM-NB showed consistent improvement over the SL baseline. For news articles, EM-NB increased accuracy from 63.5% to 68.8% with only 100 labeled sentences. For movie reviews, a close look at EM-NB iterations shows that, with only 32 labeled sentences, EM-NB was able to achieve 88% classification accuracy, which is close to the best performance of simple Naïve Bayes self-training using 300 labeled sentences. This implies that the prob-

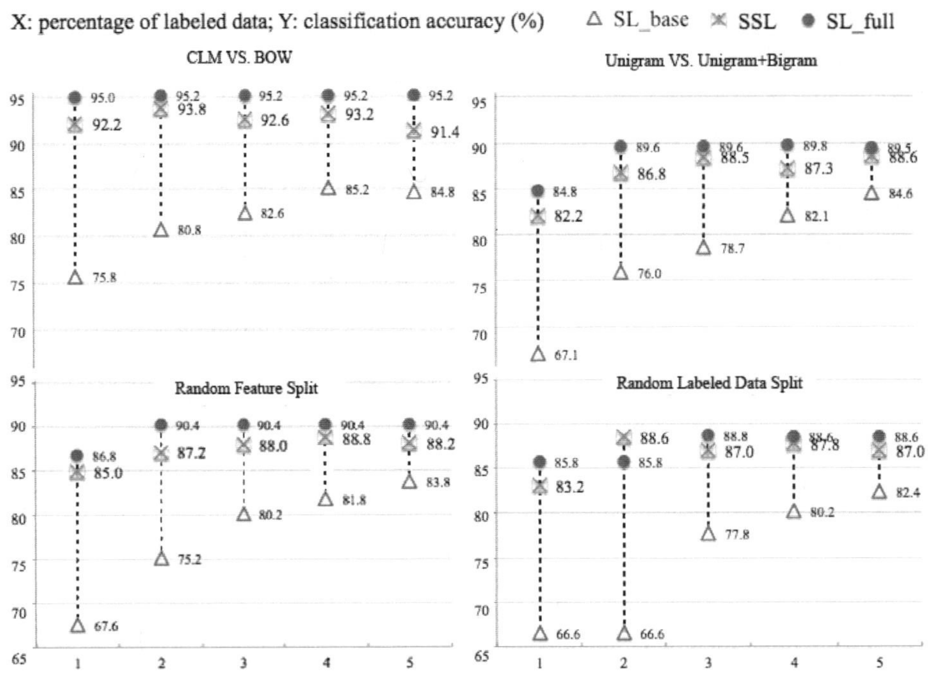

Figure 2: Performance of four co-training strategies on movie review data

lem space of opinion detection may be successfully described by the mixture model assumption of EM. As for blog posts, since the performance of the baseline classifiers was only slightly better than chance (50%), we needed to improve the baseline accuracy in order for SSL to work. One solution was to introduce high quality features. We augmented feature set with domain independent opinion lexicons that have been suggested as effective in creating high precision opinion classifier, but improvement was only minimal. An alternative solution was to borrow more labeled data from non-blog domains(s). Section 5.3 discusses dealing with a 'difficult' data domain using data from an 'easy' domain.

The preliminary exploration of different parameter settings for both self- and co-training showed no significant benefit gained by setting the weight parameter λ or applying feature selection; and using a larger number of unlabeled sentences u available for each iteration did not improve results. Further investigation is needed for an in-depth explanation.

5.2 Co-training

The best co-training runs reported in Table 1 and Figure 1 used an 8-grams CLM to train one classifier and a BOW model to train the other classifier. These two classifiers differ both in feature representation (i.e., character vs. word) and in learning algorithm (language model vs. pure statistical model). To investigate whether the two different classifiers improve each other's performance during iterations, we analyzed the CLM and BOW classifiers individually. When comparing the BOW classifier during co-training iterations to the performance of corresponding SL runs based on BOW, the former using both CLM and BOW classifiers always outperformed the latter, indicating that the BOW classifier learned from CLM. Similarly, the CLM classifier also gained from the BOW classifier during co-training.

Figure 2 shows that for the movie review domain, other simple co-training configurations also produced promising results by using different feature sets (e.g., unigrams and the union of unigrams and bigrams, or randomly split feature sets) or different training sets. In the news domain, we observed similar trends. This shows the robustness and great potential of co-training. Because even with the logistic model to output probabilistic scores for the SVM classifier, the difference in probabilities was too small to select a small number of top predictions, adding an SVM classifier for co-training did not improve accuracy and is not discussed here.

An observation of the performance of self-training and co-training over iterations confirmed that co-training used labeled data more effectively for opinion detection than self-training, as suggested for traditional topical classification. We found that, overall, co-training produces better performance than self-training and reaches optimal performance faster. For instance, with 500 labeled sentences, a self-training run reached an optimal classification accuracy of 88.2% after adding 4,828 automatically annotated sentences for training, while the co-training run reached an optimal performance of 89.4% after adding only 2,588 sentences.

5.3 Domain Transfer

Even without any explicit domain adaptation methods, results indicate that simple self-training alone is promising for tackling domain transfer between the source domain movie reviews and the target domains news articles and blog posts.

Target domain news articles We used 9,500 labeled movie review sentences to train a Naïve Bayes classifier for news articles. Although this classifier produced a fairly good classification accuracy of 89.2% on movie review data, its accuracy was poor (64.1%) on news data (i.e., domain-transfer SL), demonstrating the severity of the domain transfer problem. Self-training with Naïve Bayes using unlabeled data from the news domain (i.e., domain-transfer SSL run) improved the situation somewhat: it achieved a classification accuracy of 75.1% surpassing the domain-transfer SL run by more than 17%. To finvestigate how well SSL handles the domain transfer problem, a full in-domain SL run that used all labeled news sentences was also performed. This full SL run achieved 76.9% classification accuracy, only 1.8% higher than the domain-transfer SSL run, which did not use any labeled news data.

Target domain blog posts Because blog data are more challenging than news data, we kept 5% blog data as labeled data. Both SSL runs with and without out-of-domain data are depicted in Figure 3. Self-training using only blog data decreases SL baseline performance (dashed black line). Keeping the same settings, we added additional labeled data from the movie reviews, and self-training (gray line) came closer to the performance of the full SL run (red line), which used 90% of the labeled blog data. We then added a control factor that reduced the impact of movie review data gradually (i.e., a decrease of 0.001 in each iteration). Using this control, the self-training run (solid black line) reached and occasionally exceeded the performance of the full SL run.

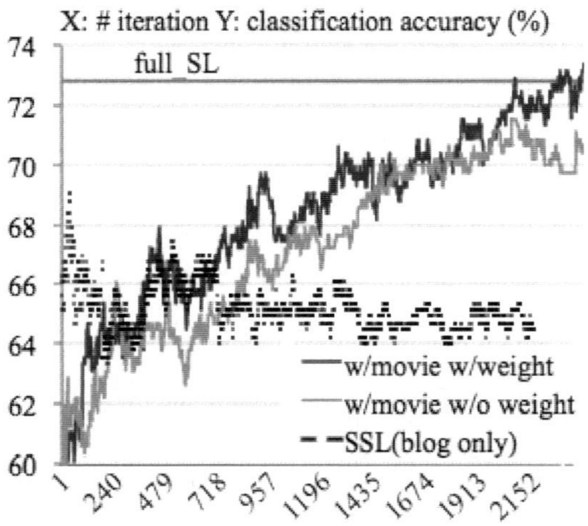

Figure 3: Self-training for domain transfer between movie reviews (source domain) and blogs (target domain)

6 Conclusion and Future Work

We investigated major SSL methods for identifying opinionated sentences in three domains. For movie review data, SSL methods attained state-of-the-art results with a small number of labeled sentences. Even without a natural feature split, different co-training strategies increased the baseline SL performance and outperformed other SSL methods. Due to the nature of the movie review data, we suspect that opinion detection on movie reviews is an 'easy' problem because it relies, strictly speaking, on distinguishing movie reviews from plot summaries, which also involves genre classification. For other manually created data sets that are expected to reflect real opinion characteristics, the SSL approach was impeded by low baseline precision and showed limited improvement. With the addition of out-of-domain labeled data, however, self-training exceeded full SL. This constitutes a successful new approach to domain adaptation.

Future work will include integrating opinion lexicons to bootstrap baseline precision and exploring co-training for domain adaptation.

References

Alias-i. 2008. LingPipe (version 4.0.1). Available from `http://alias-i.com/lingpipe`.

Anthony Aue and Michel Gamon. 2005. Customizing sentiment classifiers to new domains: A case study. In *Proceedings of the International Conference on Recent Advances in Natural Language Processing (RANLP)*, Borovets, Bulgaria.

John Blitzer, Mark Dredze, and Fernando Pereira. 2007. Biographies, Bollywood, boom-boxes and blenders: Domain adaptation for sentiment classification. In *Proceedings of the 45th Annual Meeting of the Association of Computational Linguistics (ACL)*, pages 440–447, Prague, Czech Republic.

Avrim Blum and Tom Mitchell. 1998. Combining labeled and unlabeled data with co-training. In *Proceedings of the 11th Annual Conference on Computational Learning Theory*, pages 92–100, Madison, WI.

Paula Chesley, Bruce Vincent, Li Xu, and Rohini K. Srihari. 2006. Using verbs and adjectives to automatically classify blog sentiment. In *Proceedings of AAAI-CAAW-06, the Spring Symposia on Computational Approaches to Analyzing Weblogs*, Menlo Park, CA.

Hagen Fürstenau and Mirella Lapata. 2009. Semi-supervised semantic role labeling. In *Proceedings of the 12th Conference of the European Chapter of the ACL (EACL)*, pages 220–228, Athens, Greece.

Mark Hall, Eibe Frank, Geoffrey Holmes, Bernhard Pfahringer, Peter Reutemann, and Ian H. Witten. 2009. The WEKA data mining software: An update. *SIGKDD Explorations*, 11(1).

Wei Jin, Hung Hay Ho, and Rohini K. Srihari. 2009. OpinionMiner: A novel machine learning system for web opinion mining. In *Proceedings of the 15th ACM SIGKDD International Conference on Knowledge Discovery and Data Mining*, Paris, France.

Thorsten Joachims. 1999. Making large-scale SVM learning practical. In B. Schölkopf, C. Burges, and A. Smola, editors, *Advances in Kernel Methods - Support Vector Learning*. MIT-Press.

Jason S. Kessler, Miriam Eckert, Lyndsie Clark, and Nicolas Nicolov. 2010. The ICWSM 2010 JDPA sentiment corpus for the automotive domain. In *4th International AAAI Conference on Weblogs and Social Media Data Workshop Challenge (ICWSM-DWC)*, Washington, D.C.

Kamal Nigam and Rayid Ghani. 2000. Analyzing the effectiveness and applicability of co-training. In *Proceedings of the Ninth International Conference on Information and Knowledge Management*, McLean, VA.

Kamal Nigam, Andrew Kachites Mccallum, Sebastian Thrun, and Tom Mitchell. 1999. Text classification from labeled and unlabeled documents using EM. *Machine Learning*, 39:103–134.

Bo Pang and Lillian Lee. 2004. A sentimental education: Sentiment analysis using subjectivity summarization based on minimum cuts. In *Proceedings of the 42nd Annual Meeting on Association for Computational Linguistics*, Barcelona, Spain.

Ellen Riloff and Janyce Wiebe. 2003. Learning extraction patterns for subjective expressions. In *Proceedings of the Conference on Empirical Methods in Natural Language Processing (EMNLP)*, Sapporo, Japan.

Hiroya Takamura, Takashi Inui, and Manabu Okumura. 2006. Latent variable models for semantic orientations of phrases. In *Proceedings of the 11th Conference of the European Chapter of the Association for Computational Linguistics (EACL)*, Trento, Italy.

Partha Pratim Talukdar and Fernando Pereira. 2010. Experiments in graph-based semi-supervised learning methods for class-instance acquisition. In *Proceedings of the 48th Annual Meeting of the Association for Computational Linguistics (ACL)*, pages 1473–1481, Uppsala, Sweden.

Songbo Tan, Xueqi Cheng, Yufen Wang, and Hongbo Xu. 2009. Adapting naive Bayes to domain adaptation for sentiment analysis. In *Proceedings of the 31st European Conference on Information Retrieval (ECIR)*, Toulouse, France.

Wei Wang and Zhi-Hua Zhou. 2007. Analyzing co-training style algorithms. In *Proceedings of the 18th European Conference on Machine Learning*, Warsaw, Poland.

Janyce Wiebe and Ellen Riloff. 2005. Creating subjective and objective sentence classifiers from unannotated texts. In *Proceedings of the 6th International Conference on Intelligent Text Processing and Computational Linguistics (CICLing)*, Mexico City, Mexico.

Janyce Wiebe, Rebecca Bruce, and Thomas O'Hara. 1999. Development and use of a gold standard data set for subjectivity classifications. In *Proceedings of the 37th Annual Meeting of the Association for Computational Linguistics (ACL)*, College Park, MD.

Janyce Wiebe, Rebecca Bruce, Matthew Bell, Melanie Martin, and Theresa Wilson. 2001. A corpus study of evaluative and speculative language. In *Proceedings of the 2nd ACL SIGdial Workshop on Discourse and Dialogue*, Aalborg, Denmark.

Janyce Wiebe, Theresa Wilson, Rebecca Bruce, Matthew Bell, and Melanie Martin. 2004. Learning subjective language. *Computational Linguistics*, 30(3):277–308.

Kiduk Yang, Ning Yu, and Hui Zhang. 2007. WIDIT in TREC-2007 blog track: Combining lexicon-based methods to detect opinionated blogs. In *Proceedings of the 16th Text Retrieval Conference (TREC)*, Gaithersburg, MD.

Hong Yu and Vasileios Hatzivassiloglou. 2003. Towards answering opinion questions: Separating facts from opinions and identifying the polarity of opinion sentences. In *Proceedings of the Conference on Empirical Methods in Natural Language Processing (EMNLP)*, Sapporo, Japan.

Ning Yu and Sandra Kübler. 2010. Semi-supervised learning for opinion detection. In *Proceedings of the IEEE/WIC/ACM International Conference on Web Intelligence and Intelligent Agent Technology*, volume 3, pages 249–252, Toronto, Canada.

Wei Zhang and Clement Yu. 2007. UIC at TREC 2007 blog track. In *Proceedings of the 16th Text Retrieval Conference (TREC)*, Gaithersburg, MD.

A Normalized-Cut Alignment Model for Mapping Hierarchical Semantic Structures onto Spoken Documents

Xiaodan Zhu
Institute for Information Technology
National Research Council Canada
Xiaodan.Zhu@nrc-cnrc.gc.ca

Abstract

We propose a normalized-cut model for the problem of aligning a known hierarchical browsing structure, e.g., electronic slides of lecture recordings, with the sequential transcripts of the corresponding spoken documents, with the aim to help index and access the latter. This model optimizes a normalized-cut graph-partitioning criterion and considers local tree constraints at the same time. The experimental results show the advantage of this model over Viterbi-like, sequential alignment, under typical speech recognition errors.

1 Introduction

Learning semantic structures of written text has been studied in a number of specific tasks, which include, but not limited to, those finding semantic representations for individual sentences (Ge and Mooney, 2005; Zettlemoyer and Collins, 2005; Lu et al., 2008), and those constructing hierarchical structures among sentences or larger text blocks (Marcu, 2000; Branavan et al., 2007). The inverse problem of the latter kind, e.g., aligning certain form of already-existing semantic hierarchies with the corresponding text sequence, is not so much a prominent problem for written text as it is for spoken documents. In this paper, we study a specific type of such a problem, in which a hierarchical browsing structure, i.e., electronic slides of oral presentations, have already existed, the goal being to impose such a structure onto the transcripts of the corresponding speech, with the aim to help index and access spoken documents as such.

Navigating audio documents is often inherently much more difficult than browsing text; an obvious solution, in relying on human beings' ability to read text, is to conduct a speech-to-text conversion through automatic speech recognition (ASR). Implicitly, solutions as such change the conventional speaking-for-hearing construals: now speech can be *read* through its transcripts, though, in most cases, it was not intended for this purpose, which in turn raises a new set of problems.

The convenience and efficiency of reading transcripts (Stark et al., 2000; Munteanu et al., 2006) are first affected by errors produced in transcription channels for various reasons, though if the goal is only to browse salient excerpts, recognition errors on the extracts can be reduced by considering ASR confidence scores (Xie and Liu, 2010; Hori and Furui, 2003; Zechner and Waibel, 2000): trading off the expected salience of excerpts with their recognition-error rate could actually result in the improvement of excerpt quality in terms of the amount of important content being correctly presented (Zechner and Waibel, 2000).

Even if transcription quality were not a problem, browsing transcripts is not straightforward. When intended to be read, written documents are almost always presented as more than uninterrupted strings of text. Consider that for many written documents, e.g., books, indicative structures such as section/subsection headings and tables-of-contents are standard constituents created manually to help readers. Structures of this kind, even when existing, are rarely aligned with spoken documents completely.

This paper studies the problem of imposing a

Proceedings of the Fifteenth Conference on Computational Natural Language Learning, pages 210–218,
Portland, Oregon, USA, 23–24 June 2011.

known hierarchical browsing structure, e.g., the electronic slides of lecture recordings, onto the sequential transcripts of the corresponding spoken document, with the aim to help index and hence access the latter more effectively. Specifically, we propose a graph-partitioning approach that optimizes a normalized-cut criterion globally, in traversing the given hierarchical semantic structures. The experimental results show the advantage of this model over Viterbi-like, sequential alignment, under typical speech recognition errors.

2 Related work

Flat structures of spoken documents Much previous work, similar to its written-text counterpart, has attempted to find certain *flat* structures of spoken documents, such as topic and slide boundaries. For example, the work of (Chen and Heng, 2003; Ruddarraju, 2006; Zhu et al., 2008) aims to find slide boundaries in the corresponding lecture transcripts. Malioutov et al. (2007) developed an approach to detecting topic boundaries of lecture recordings by finding repeated acoustic patterns. None of this work, however, has involved hierarchical structures of a spoken document. Research has also resorted to other multimedia channels, e.g., video (Liu et al., 2002; Wang et al., 2003; Fan et al., 2006), to detect slide transitions. This type of research, however, is unlikely to recover semantic structures in more details than slide boundaries.

Hierarchical structures of spoken documents Recently, research has started to align hierarchical browsing structures with spoken documents, given that inferring such structures directly from spoken documents is still too challenging. Zhu et al. (2010) investigates bullet-slide alignment by first sequentializing bullet trees with a pre-order walk before conducting alignment, through which the problem is reduced to a string-to-string alignment problem and an efficient Viterbi-like method can be naturally applied. In this paper, we use such a sequential alignment as our baseline, which takes a standard dynamic-programming process to find the optimal path on an M-by-N similarity matrix, where M and N denote the number of bullets and utterances in a lecture, respectively. Specifically, we chose the path that maps each bullet to an utterance to achieve the highest total bullet-utterance similarity score; this path can be found within a standard $O(MN^2)$ time complexity.

A pre-order walk of the hierarchical tree is a natural choice, since speakers of presentations often follow such a order in developing their talk; i.e., they often talk about a bullet first and then each of its children in sequence. A pre-order walk is also assumed by Branavan et al. (2007) in their table-of-content generation task, a problem in which a hierarchical structure has already been assumed (aligned) with a span of written text, but the title of each node needs to be generated.

In principle, such a sequential-alignment approach allows a bullet to be only aligned to one utterance in the end, which does not model the basic properties of the problem well, where the content in a bullet is often repeated not only when the speaker talks about it but also, very likely, when he discusses the descendant bullets. Second, we suspect that speech recognition errors, when happening on the critical anchoring words that bridging the alignment, would make a sequential-alignment algorithm much less robust, compared with methods based on many-to-many alignment. This is very likely to happen, considering that domain-specific words are likely to be the critical words in deciding the alignment, but they are also very likely to be mis-recognized by an ASR system at the same time, e.g., due to out-of-vocabulary issue or language-model sparseness. We will further discuss this in more details later in our result section. Third, the hierarchical structures are lost in the sequentialization of bullets, though some remedy could be applied, e.g., by propagating a parent bullet's information onto its children (Zhu et al., 2010).

On the other hand, we should also note that the benefit of formulating the problem as a sequential alignment problem is its computational efficiency: the solution can be calculated with conventional Viterbi-like algorithms. This property is also important for the task, since the length of a spoken document, such as a lecture, is often long enough to make *inefficient* algorithms practically intractable.

An important question is therefore how to, in principle, model the problem better. The second is how time efficient the model is. Malioutov and Barzilay (2006) describe a dynamic-programming version of a normalized-cut-based model in solving a topic segmentation problem for spoken documents. Inspired by their work, we will propose a model based on graph partitioning in finding the correspondence between bullets and the regions of transcripts that discuss them; the proposed model runs in polynomial time. We will empirically show its benefit on both improving the alignment performance over a sequential alignment and its robustness to speech recognition errors.

3 Problem

We are given a speech sequence $U = u_1, u_2, ..., u_N$, where u_i is an utterance, and the corresponding hierarchical structure, which, in our work here, is a sequence of lecture slides containing a set of slide titles and bullets, $B = \{b_1, b_2, ..., b_M\}$, organized in a tree structure $T(\Re, \aleph, \Psi)$, where $\Re$ is the root of the tree that concatenates all slides of a lecture; i.e., each slide is a child of the root $\Re$ and each slide's bullets form a subtree. In the rest of this paper, the word *bullet* means both the title of a slide (if any) and any bullet in it, if not otherwise noted. $\aleph$ is the set of nodes of the tree (both terminal and non-terminals, excluding the root $\Re$), each corresponding to a bullet b_m in the slides. Ψ is the edge set. With the definitions, our task is herein to find the triple (b_i, u_j, u_k), denoting that a bullet b_i is mapped to a region of lecture transcripts that starts from the jth utterance u_j and ends at the kth, inclusively. Constrained by the tree structure, the transcript region corresponding to an ancestor bullet contains those corresponding to its descendants; i.e., if a bullet b_i is the ancestor of another bullet b_n in the tree, the acquired boundary triples (b_i, u_{j_1}, u_{k_1}) and (b_i, u_{j_2}, u_{k_2}) should satisfy $j_1 \leq j_2$ and $k_1 \geq k_2$. Figure 1 shows a slide, its structure, and the correspondence between one of its bullets and a region of transcribed utterances (the root that concatenates all such slides of a lecture together is not shown here).

4 A graph-partitioning approach

The generative process of lecture speech, with regard to a hierarchical structure (here, bullet trees), is characterized in general by a speaker's producing detailed content for each bullet when discussing it, during which sub-bullets, if any, are talked about re-

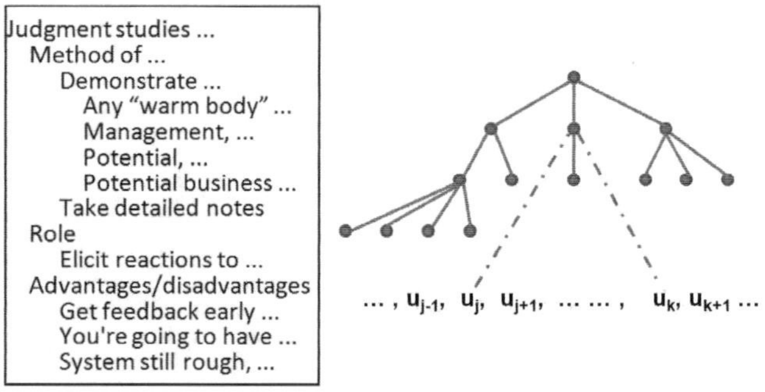

Figure 1: A slide, its tree structure, and the correspondence between one of its bullets and a region of transcribed utterances $(u_j, u_{j+1} ..., u_k)$.

cursively. By its nature of the problem, words in a bullet could be repeated multiple times, even when the speaker traverses to talk about the descendant bullets in the depth of the sub-trees. In principle, a model would be desirable to consider such properties between a slide bullet, including all its descendants, and utterance transcripts, as well as the constraints of bullet trees. We formulate the problem of finding the correspondence between bullets and transcripts as a graph-partitioning problem, as detailed below.

The correspondence between bullets and transcribed utterances is evidenced by the similarities between them. In a graph that contains a set of bullets and utterances as its vertices and similarities between them as its edges, our aim is to place boundaries to partition the graph into smaller ones in order to obtain triples, e.g., (b_i, u_j, u_k), that optimize certain criterion. Inspired by the work of (Malioutov and Barzilay, 2006; Shi and Malik, 2000), we optimize a normalized-cut score, in which the total weight of edges being cut by the boundaries is minimized, normalized by the similarity between the bullet b_i and the entire vertices, as well as between the transcript region $u_j, ..., u_k$ and the entire vertices, respectively.

Consider a simple two-set case first, in which a boundary is placed on a graph $G = (V, E)$ to separate its vertices V into two sets, A and B, with all the edges between these two sets being removed. The objective, as we have mentioned above, is to minimize the following normalized-cut score:

$$Ncut(A,B) = \frac{cut(A,B)}{assoc(A,V)} + \frac{cut(A,B)}{assoc(B,V)} \quad (1)$$

where,

$$cut(A,B) = \sum_{a \in A, b \in B} w(a,b)$$

$$assoc(A,V) = \sum_{a \in A, v \in V} w(a,v)$$

$$assoc(B,V) = \sum_{b \in B, v \in V} w(b,v)$$

In equation (1), $cut(A,B)$ is the total weight of the edges being cut, i.e., those connecting A with B, while $assoc(A,V)$ and $assoc(B,V)$ are the total weights of the edges that connect A with all vertices V, and B with V, respectively; $w(a,b)$ is an edge weight between a vertex a and b.

In general, minimizing such a normalized-cut score has been shown to be NP-complete. In our problem, however, the solution is constrained by the linearity of segmentation on transcripts, similar to that in (Malioutov and Barzilay, 2006). In such a situation, a polynomial-time algorithm exists. Malioutov and Barzilay (2006) describe a dynamic-programming algorithm to conduct topic segmentation for spoken documents. We modify the method to solve our alignment problem here, which, however, needs to cope with the bipartite graphs between bullets and transcribed sentences rather than symmetric similarity matrices among utterances themselves. We also need to integrate this in considering the hierarchical structures of bullet trees.

We first consider a set of sibling bullets, $b_1, ..., b_m$, that appear on the same level of a bullet tree and share the same parent b_p. For the time being, we assume the corresponding region of transcripts has already been identified for b_p, say $u_1, ..., u_n$. We connect each bullet in $b_1, ..., b_m$ with utterances in $u_1, ..., u_n$ by their similarity, which results in a bipartite graph. Our task here is to place $m-1$ boundaries onto the bipartite graph to partition the graph into m bipartite graphs and obtain triples, e.g., (b_i, u_j, u_k), to align b_i to $u_j, ..., u_k$, where $b_i \in \{b_1, ..., b_m\}$ and $u_j, u_k \in \{u_1, ..., b_n\}$ and $j <= k$. Since we have all descendant bullets to help the partitioning, when constructing the bipartite graph, we actually include also all descendant bullets of each bullet b_i, but ignoring their orders within each b_i. We will revisit this in more details later. We find optimal normalized cuts in a dynamic-programming process with the following recurrence relation:

$$C[i,k] = \min_{j \le k}\{C[i-1,j] + D[i,j+1,k]\} \quad (2)$$

$$B[i,k] = \arg\min_{j \le k}\{C[i-1,j] + D[i,j+1,k]\} \quad (3)$$

In equation (2) and (3), $C[i,k]$ is the optimal/minimal normalized-cut value of aligning the first i sibling bullets, $b_1, ..., b_i$, with the first k utterances, $u_1, ..., b_k$, while $B[i,k]$ records the backtracking indices corresponding to the optimal path yielding the current $C[i,k]$. As shown in equation (2), $C[i,k]$ is computed by updating $C[i-1,j]$ with $D[i,j+1,k]$, for all possible j s.t. $j \le k$, where $D[i,j+1,k]$ is a normalized-cut score for the triple (b_i, u_{j+1}, u_k) and is defined as follows:

$$D[i,j+1,k] = \frac{cut(A_{i,j+1,k}, V \setminus A_{i,j+1,k})}{assoc(A_{i,j+1,k}, V)} \quad (4)$$

where $A_{i,j+1,k}$ is the vertex set that contains the bullet b_i (including its descendant bullets, if any, as discussed above) and the utterances $u_{j+1}, ..., u_k$; $V \setminus A_{i,j+1,k}$ is its complement set.

Different from the topic segmentation problem (Malioutov et al., 2007), we need to remember the normalized-cut values between any region $u_j, ..., u_k$ and any bullet b_i in our task, so we need to use the additional subscript i in $A_{i,j+1,k}$, while in topic segmentation, the computation of both $cut(.)$ and $assoc(.)$ is only dependant on the left boundary j and right boundary k. Note that the similarity matrix here is not symmetric as it is in topic segmentation, but m by n, where m is the number of bullets, while n is the number of utterances.

For any triple (b_i, u_{j+1}, u_k), there are two different types of edges being cut: those between $B_{in} \stackrel{\text{def}}{=} \{b_i\}$ (again, including b_i and all its descendant bullets) and $U_{out} \stackrel{\text{def}}{=} \{u_1, ..., u_j, u_{k+1}, ..., u_m\}$, as well as those between $B_{out} \stackrel{\text{def}}{=} \{b_1, ..., b_{i-1}, b_{i+1}, ..., b_m\}$ and $U_{in} \stackrel{\text{def}}{=} \{u_{j+1}, ..., u_k\}$. We discriminate these two types of edges. Accordingly, $cut(.)$ and

$assoc(.)$ in equation (4) are calculated with equation (5) and (6) below by linearly combining the weights of these two types of edges with λ, whose value is decided with a small held-out data.

$$cut(A_{i,j+1,k}, V \setminus A_{i,j+1,k}) = \lambda \sum_{b \in B_{in}, u \in U_{out}} w(b,u) + (1-\lambda) \sum_{b' \in B_{out}, u' \in U_{in}} w(b',u') \quad (5)$$

$$assoc(A_{i,j+1,k}, V) = \lambda \sum_{b \in B_{in}, u \in V} w(b,u) + (1-\lambda) \sum_{b' \in U_{in}, u' \in V} w(b',u') \quad (6)$$

In addition, different form that in topic segmentation, where a segment must not be empty, we shall allow a bullet b_i to be aligned to an empty region, to model the situation that a bullet is not discussed by the speaker. To do so, we made j in equation (2) and (3) above to be able to equal to k in the subscript, i.e., $j \leq k$. Specifically, when $j = k$, the set $A_{i,j+1,k}$ has no internal edges, and $D[i, j+1, k]$ is either equal to 1, or often not defined if $assoc(A_{i,j+1,k}, V) = 0$. For the latter, we reset $D[i, j+1, k]$ to be 1.

A visual example of partitioning sibling bullets b_1, b_2, and b_3 is shown in Figure 2, in which the descendant bullets of them (here, b_4, b_5, and b_6) are also considered. Note that we only show direct children of b_1 here, while, as discussed above, all descendant bullets, if any, will be considered.

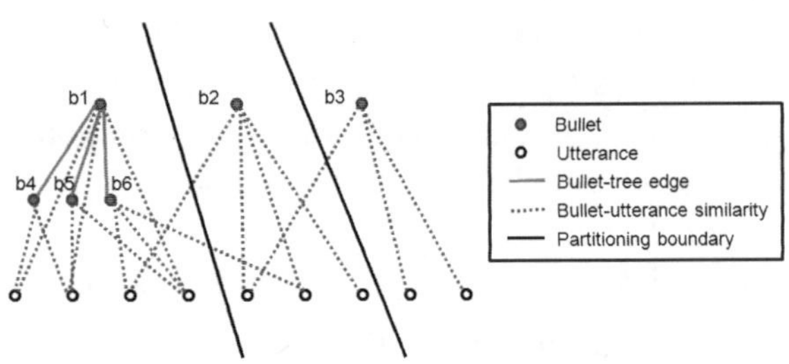

Figure 2: A visual example of partitioning sibling bullets b1, b2, and b3.

Up to now, we have only considered partitioning sibling bullets by assuming the boundaries of their parent on lecture transcripts have already been given, where the sibling bullets and the corresponding transcripts form a bipartite graph. When partitioning the entire bullet trees and all utterances for a lecture, the graph contains not only a bipartite graph but also the hierarchical trees themselves. We decouple this two parts of graph by a top-down traversal of the bullet trees: starting from the root, for each node on the bullet tree, we apply the normalized-cut algorithm discussed above to find the corresponding regions of transcripts for all its direct children, and repeat this process recursively. In each visit to partition a group of sibling bullets, to allow the first child to have a different starting point from its parent bullet (the speaker may spend some time on the parent bullet itself before talking about each child bullet), we inserted an extra child in front of the first child and copy the text of the parent bullet to it. Note that in each visit to partition a group of sibling bullets, the solution found is optimal on that level, which, again, results in a powerful model since all descendant bullets, if any, are all considered. For example, processing high-level bullets first is expected to benefit from the richer information of using all their descendants in helping find the boundaries on transcripts accurately. Recall that we have discussed above how to incorporate the descendant bullets into this process. It would also dramatically reduce the searching space of partitioning lower-level bullets.

As far as computational complexity is concerned, the graph-partitioning method discussed above is polynomial, $O(MN^2)$, with M and N denoting the number of bullets and utterances in a lecture, respectively. Note that M is often much smaller than N, $M \ll N$. In more details, the loop kernel of the algorithm is computing $D[i, j, k]$. This in total needs to compute $\frac{1}{2}(MN^2)$ values, which can be pre-calculated and stored before dynamic-programming decoding runs; the later, as normal, is $O(MN^2)$, too.

5 Experiment set-up

5.1 Corpus

Our experiment uses a corpus of four 50-minute third-year university lectures taught by the same instructor on the topics of human-computer interaction (HCI), which contain 119 slides composed of

921 bullets prepared by the lecturer himself. The automatic transcripts of the speech contain approximately 30,000 word tokens, roughly equal to a 120-page double-spaced essay in length. The lecturer's voice was recorded with a head-mounted microphone with a 16kHz sampling rate and 16-bit samples, while students' comments and questions were not recorded. The speech is split into utterances by pauses longer than 200ms, resulting in around 4000 utterances. The slides and automatic transcripts of one lecture were held out to decide the value of λ in differentiating the two different types of edges being cut, as discussed in Section 4. The boundaries between adjacent slides were marked manually during the lectures were recorded, by the person who oversaw the recording process, while the boundaries between bullets within a slide were annotated afterwards by another human annotator.

5.2 Building the graphs

The lecture speech was first transcribed into text automatically with ASR models. The first ASR model is a baseline with its acoustic model trained on the WSJ0 and WSJ1 subsets of the 1992 development set of the Wall Street Journal (WSJ) dictation corpus, which contains 30 hours of data spoken by 283 speakers. The language model was trained on the Switchboard corpus, which contains 2500 telephone conversations involving about 500 English-native speakers, which was suggested to be suitable for the conversational style of lectures, e.g., by (Munteanu et al., 2007; Park et al., 2005). The whole model yielded a word error rate (WER) at 0.48. In the remainder of this paper, we call the model as ASR Model 1.

The second model is an advanced one using the same acoustic model. However, its language model was trained on domain-related documents obtained from the Web through searching the words appearing on slides, as suggested by Munteanu et al. (2007). This yielded a WER of 0.43, which is a typical WER for lectures and conference presentations (Leeuwis et al., 2003; Hsu and Glass, 2006; Munteanu et al., 2007), though a lower WER is possible in a more ideal condition (Glass et al., 2007), e.g., when the same course from the previous semester by the same instructor is available. The 3-gram language models were trained using the CMU-CAM Language Modelling Toolkit (Clarkson and Rosenfeld, 1997), and the transcripts were generated with the SONIC toolkit (Pellom, 2001). The out-of-vocabulary rates are 0.3% in the output of ASR Model 1 and 0.1% in that of Model 2, respectively.

Both bullets and automatic transcripts were stemmed and stop words in them were removed. We then calculated the similarity between a bullet and an utterance with the number of overlapping words shared, normalized by their lengths. Note that using several other typical metrics, e.g., cosine, resulted in a similar trend of performance change—our conclusions below are consistent under these situations, though the specific performance scores (i.e., word offsets) are different. Finally, the similarities between bullets and utterances yielded a single M-by-N similarity matrix for each lecture to be aligned, with M and N denoting the number of bullets in slides and utterances in transcripts, respectively.

5.3 Evaluation metric

The metric used in our evaluation is straightforward—automatically acquired boundaries on transcripts for each slide bullet are compared against the corresponding gold-standard boundaries to calculate offsets measured in number of words. The offset scores are averaged over all boundaries to evaluate model performance. Though one may consider that different bullets may be of different importance, in this paper we do not use any heuristics to judge this and we treat all bullets equally in our evaluation.

Note that topic segmentation research often uses metrics such as P_k and WindowDiff (Malioutov et al., 2007; Beeferman et al., 1999; Pevsner and Hearst, 2002). Our problem here, as an alignment problem, has an exact 1-to-1 correspondence between a gold and automatic boundary, in which we can directly measure the exact offset of each boundary.

6 Experimental results

Table 1 presents the experimental results obtained on the automatic transcripts generated by the ASR models discussed above, with WERs at 0.43 and 0.48, respectively, which are typical WERs for lectures and conference presentations in realistic and less controlled situations. SEQ-ALN in the table stands for the Viterbi-like, sequential alignment discussed above in section 2, while G-CUT is the graph-partitioning approach proposed in this paper. The values in the table are the average word-offset scores counted after stop-words having been removed.

	WER=0.43	WER=0.48
SEQ-ALN	15.22	20.38
G-CUT	13.41	16.77
Offs. Reduction	12%	18%

Table 1: The average word offsets of automatic boundaries from the gold-standard.

Table 1 shows that comparing these two polynomial-time models, G-CUT reduces the average offsets of SEG-ALN under both WERs. On the transcripts with 0.48 WER, the average word-offset score is reduced by approximately 18% from 20.38 to 16.77, while for the transcripts with WER at 0.43, the offset reduction is 12%, from 15.22 to 13.41. Since both models use exactly the same input similarity matrices, the differences between their results confirm the advantage of the modeling principle behind the proposed approach. Although the graph-partitioning model could be extended further, e.g., with the approach in (Zhu et al., 2010), our primary interest here is the principle modeling advantage of this normalized-cut framework.

The results in Table 1 also suggest that the graph-partitioning model is more robust to speech recognition errors: when WERs increase from 0.43 to 0.48, the error of G-CUT increases by 25%, from 13.41 to 16.77, while that of SEQ-ALN increases by 44%, from 15.22 to 20.38. We due this to the fact that the graph-partitioning model considers multiple alignments between bullets, including their descendants, and the transcribed utterances, where mismatching between bullet and transcript words, e.g., that caused by recognition errors, is less likely to impact the graph-partitioning method, which bases its optimization criterion on multiple alignments, e.g., when calculating $cut(.)$ and $assoc(.)$ in equation (5) and (6). Recall that the ASR Model 2 includes domain-specific Web data to train the language models, which were acquired by using bullet words to search the Web. It is expected to increase the recognition accuracy on domain words, particularly those appearing on the slides. Therefore, Model 2 is likely to particularly increase the correct matching between bullets and transcript.

The results in Table 1 also show the usefulness of better ASR modeling on the structure-imposing task here. As discussed in the introduction section earlier, browsing automatic transcripts of long spoken documents, such as lectures, is affected by both speech recognition errors and lack of browsing structures. Table 1 shows that the improvement in solving the first problem also helps the second.

Last, from a pragmatic viewpoint of system development, the graph-partitioning algorithm is simple to implement: the essence of equation (2)-(6) is to find the optimal normalized-cut score characterized by computing $D[i, j+1, k]$ and updating the formulae with it, which is not much more complicate to build than the baseline. Also, the practical speed difference between these two types of models is not obvious on our dataset.

7 Conclusion

This paper proposes a graph-partitioning approach for aligning a known hierarchical structure with the transcripts of the corresponding spoken document through optimizing a normalized-cut criterion. This approach models the basic properties of the problem and is quadratic-time. Experimental results show both its advantage on improving the alignment performance over a standard sequential-alignment baseline and its robustness to speech recognition errors, while both take as input exactly the same similarity matrices. From a pragmatic viewpoint of system development, this graph-partitioning-based algorithm is simple to implement. We believe immediate further work such as combining the normalized-cut model with CYK-like dynamic programing to traverse the semantic trees in alignment could help us further understand the problem, though such models need much more memory in practice if not properly optimized and have a higher time complexity. Also, topic-segmentation (cohesion) models can be naturally combined with the alignment model discussed here. We will study such problems as our immediate future work.

References

D. Beeferman, A. Berger, and J. Lafferty. 1999. Statistical models for text segmentation. *Machine Learning*, 34(1-3):177–210.

S. Branavan, Deshpande P., and Barzilay R. 2007. Generating a table-of-contents: A hierarchical discriminative approach. In *Proc. of Annual Meeting of the Association for Computational Linguistics*.

Y. Chen and W. J. Heng. 2003. Automatic synchronization of speech transcript and slides in presentation. In *Proc. International Symposium on Circuits and Systems*.

P. Clarkson and R. Rosenfeld. 1997. Statistical language modeling using the cmu-cambridge toolkit. In *Proc. of ISCA European Conf. on Speech Communication and Technology*, pages 2707–2710.

Q. Fan, K. Barnard, A. Amir, A. Efrat, and M. Lin. 2006. Matching slides to presentation videos using sift and scene background. In *Proc. of ACM International Workshop on Multimedia Information Retrieval*, pages 239–248.

R. Ge and R. J. Mooney. 2005. A statistical semantic parser that integrates syntax and semantics. In *Proc. of Computational Natural Language Learnine*, pages 9–16.

J. Glass, T. Hazen, S. Cyphers, I. Malioutov, D. Huynh, and R. Barzilay. 2007. Recent progress in the mit spoken lecture processing project. *Proc. of Annual Conference of the International Speech Communication Association*, pages 2553–2556.

C. Hori and S. Furui. 2003. A new approach to automatic speech summarization. *IEEE Transactions on Multimedia*, 5(3):368–378.

B. Hsu and J. Glass. 2006. Style and topic language model adaptation using hmm-lda. In *Proc. of Conference on Empirical Methods in Natural Language Processing*.

E. Leeuwis, M. Federico, and M. Cettolo. 2003. Language modeling and transcription of the ted corpus lectures. In *Proc. of IEEE International Conference on Acoustics, Speech and Signal Processing*.

T. Liu, R. Hjelsvold, and J. R. Kender. 2002. Analysis and enhancement of videos of electronic slide presentations. In *Proc. IEEE International Conference on Multimedia and Expo*.

W. Lu, H. T. Ng, W. S. Lee, and L. S. Zettlemoyer. 2008. A generative model for parsing natural language to meaning representations. In *Proc. of Empirical Methods in Natural Language Processing*, pages 783–792.

I. Malioutov and R. Barzilay. 2006. Minimum cut model for spoken lecture segmentation. In *Proc. of International Conference on Computational Linguistics and Annual Meeting of the Association for Computational Linguistics*.

I. Malioutov, A. Park, R. Barzilay, and J. Glass. 2007. Making sense of sound: Unsupervised topic segmentation over acoustic input. In *Proc. of Annual Meeting of the Association for Computational Linguistics*, pages 504–511.

D. Marcu. 2000. The theory and practice of discourse parsing and summarization. The MIT Press.

C. Munteanu, R. Baecker, G. Penn, E. Toms, and E. James. 2006. Effect of speech recognition accuracy rates on the usefulness and usability of webcast archives. In *Proc. of ACM Conference on Human Factors in Computing Systems*, pages 493–502.

C. Munteanu, G. Penn, and R. Baecker. 2007. Web-based language modelling for automatic lecture transcription. In *Proc. of Annual Conference of the International Speech Communication Association*.

A. Park, T. Hazen, and J. Glass. 2005. Automatic processing of audio lectures for information retrieval. In *Proc. of IEEE Conf. on Acoustics, Speech, and Signal Processing*, pages 497–500.

B. L. Pellom. 2001. Sonic: The university of colorado continuous speech recognizer. *Tech. Rep. TR-CSLR-2001-01, University of Colorado*.

L. Pevsner and M. Hearst. 2002. A critique and improvement of an evaluation metric for text segmentation. *Computational Linguistics*, 28:19–36.

R. Ruddarraju. 2006. *Indexing Presentations Using Multiple Media Streams*. Ph.D. thesis, Georgia Institute of Technology. M.S. Thesis.

J. Shi and J. Malik. 2000. Normalized cuts and image segmentation. *IEEE Trans. Pattern Anal. Mach. Intell.*, 22.

L. Stark, S. Whittaker, and J. Hirschberg. 2000. Finding information in audio: A new paradigm for audio browsing and retrieval. In *Proc. of International Conference on Spoken Language Processing*.

F. Wang, C. W. Ngo, and T. C. Pong. 2003. Synchronization of lecture videos and electronic slides by video text analysis. In *Proc. of ACM International Conference on Multimedia*.

S. Xie and Y. Liu. 2010. Using confusion networks for speech summarization. In *Proc. of International Conference on Human Language Technology and Annual Meeting of North American Chapter of the Association for Computational Linguistics*.

K. Zechner and A. Waibel. 2000. Minimizing word error rate in textual summaries of spoken language. In *Proc. of Applied Natural Language Processing Conference and Meeting of the North American Chapter of the Association for Computational Linguistics*, pages 186–193.

L. S. Zettlemoyer and M. Collins. 2005. Learning to map sentences to logical form: Structured classification with probabilistic categorial grammars. In *Proc. of Uncertainty in Artificial Intelligence*, pages 658–666.

X. Zhu, X. He, C. Munteanu, and G. Penn. 2008. Using latent dirichlet allocation to incorporate domain knowledge for topic transition detection. In *Proc. of Annual Conference of the International Speech Communication Association.*

X. Zhu, C. Cherry, and G. Penn. 2010. Imposing hierarchical browsing structures onto spoken documents. In *Proc. of International Conference on Computational Linguistics.*

Bayesian Tools for Natural Language Learning

Invited talk

Yee Whye Teh
Gatsby Computational Neuroscience Unit, UCL
ywteh@gatsby.ucl.ac.uk

In recent years Bayesian techniques have made good inroads in computational linguistics, due to their protection against overfitting and expressiveness of the Bayesian modeling language. However most Bayesian models proposed so far have used pretty simple prior distributions, chosen more for computational convenience than as reflections of real prior knowledge.

In this talk I will propose that prior distributions can be powerful ways to put computational linguistics knowledge into your models, and give two examples from my own work. Firstly, hierarchical priors can allow you to specify relationships among different components of your model so that the information learned in one component can be shared with the rest, improving the estimation of parameters for all. Secondly, newer distributions like Pitman-Yor processes have interesting power-law characteristics that if used as prior distributions can allow your linguistic models to express Zipf's Law and Heap's Law.

I will round up the talk with a discussion of the viability of the Bayesian approach, in a future where we have too much data, making the natural language learning problem more a computational rather than a statistical one.

Proceedings of the Fifteenth Conference on Computational Natural Language Learning, page 219,
Portland, Oregon, USA, 23–24 June 2011.

Composing Simple Image Descriptions using Web-scale N-grams

Siming Li, Girish Kulkarni, Tamara L Berg, Alexander C Berg, and Yejin Choi
Department of Computer Science
Stony Brook University
NY 11794, USA
{silli, gkulkarni, tlberg, aberg, ychoi}@cs.stonybrook.edu

Abstract

Studying natural language, and especially how people describe the world around them can help us better understand the visual world. In turn, it can also help us in the quest to generate natural language that describes this world in a human manner. We present a simple yet effective approach to automatically compose image descriptions given computer vision based inputs and using web-scale n-grams. Unlike most previous work that summarizes or retrieves pre-existing text relevant to an image, our method *composes* sentences entirely from scratch. Experimental results indicate that it is viable to generate simple textual descriptions that are pertinent to the specific content of an image, while permitting creativity in the description – making for more human-like annotations than previous approaches.

1 Introduction

Gaining a better understanding of natural language, and especially natural language associated with images helps drive research in both computer vision and natural language processing (e.g., Barnard et al. (2003), Pastra et al. (2003), Feng and Lapata (2010b)). In this paper, we look at how to exploit the enormous amount of textual data electronically available today, web-scale n-gram data in particular, in a simple yet highly effective approach to compose image descriptions in natural language. Automatic generation of image descriptions differs from automatic image tagging (e.g., Leong et al. (2010)) in that we aim to generate complex phrases or sentences describing images rather than predicting individual words. These natural language descriptions can be useful for a variety of applications, including image retrieval, automatic video surveillance, and providing image interpretations for visually impaired people.

Our work contrasts to most previous approaches in four key aspects: first, we *compose* fresh sentences from scratch, instead of retrieving (Farhadi et al. (2010)), or summarizing existing text fragments associated with an image (e.g., Aker and Gaizauskas (2010), Feng and Lapata (2010a)). Second, we aim to generate textual descriptions that are truthful to the specific content of the image, whereas related (but subtly different) work in automatic caption generation creates news-worthy text (Feng and Lapata (2010a)) or encyclopedic text (Aker and Gaizauskas (2010)) that is contextually relevant to the image, but not closely pertinent to the specific content of the image. Third, we aim to build a general image description method as compared to work that requires domain specific hand-written grammar rules (Yao et al. (2010)). Last, we allow for some creativity in the generation process which produces more human-like descriptions than a closely related, very recent approach that drives annotation more directly from computer vision inputs (Kulkarni et al., 2011).

In this work, we propose a novel surface realization technique based on web-scale n-gram data. Our approach consists of two steps: (n-gram) phrase selection and (n-gram) phrase fusion. The first step – *phrase selection* – collects candidate phrases that may be potentially useful for generating the description of a given image. This step naturally accommodates uncertainty in image recognition inputs as

Proceedings of the Fifteenth Conference on Computational Natural Language Learning, pages 220–228,
Portland, Oregon, USA, 23–24 June 2011. ©2011 Association for Computational Linguistics

Figure 1: The big picture of our task to automatically generate image description.

well as synonymous words and word re-ordering to improve fluency. The second step – *phrase fusion* – finds the optimal compatible set of phrases using dynamic programming to compose a new (and more complex) phrase that describes the image. We compare the performance of our proposed approach to three baselines based on conventional techniques: language models, parsers, and templates.

Despite its simplicity, our approach is highly effective for composing image descriptions: it generates *mostly* appealing and presentable language, while permitting creative writing at times (see Figure 5 for example results). We conclude from our exploration that (1) it is viable to generate simple textual descriptions that are germane to the specific image content, and that (2) world knowledge implicitly encoded in natural language (e.g., web-scale n-gram data) can help enhance image content recognition.

2 Image Recognition

Figure 1 depicts our system flow: a) an image is input into our system, b) image recognition techniques are used to extract visual content information, c) visual content is encoded as a set of triples, d) natural language descriptions are generated.

In this section, we briefly describe the image recognition system that extracts visual information and encodes it as a set of triples. For a given image, the image recognizer extracts *objects*, *attributes* and *spatial relationships* among objects as follows:

1. Objects: including *things* (e.g., bird, bus, car) and *stuff* (e.g., grass, water, sky, road) are detected.
2. Visual attributes (e.g., feathered, black) are predicted for each object.
3. Spatial relationships (e.g., on, near, under) between objects are estimated.

In particular, object detectors are trained using state of the art mixtures of multi-scale deformable parts models (Felzenszwalb et al., 2010). Our set of objects encompasses the 20 PASCAL 2010 object challenge [1] categories as well as 4 additional categories for *flower, laptop, tiger*, and *window* trained on images with associated bounding boxes from Imagenet (Deng et al., 2009). Stuff detectors are trained to detect regions corresponding to non-part based object categories (sky, road, building, tree, water, and grass) using linear SVMs trained on the low level region features of (Farhadi et al., 2009). These are also trained on images with labeled bounding boxes from ImageNet and evaluated at test time on a coarsely sampled grid of overlapping square regions over whole images. Pixels in any region with a classification probability above a fixed threshold are treated as detections.

We select visual attribute characteristics that are relevant to our object and stuff categories. Our attribute terms include 21 visual modifiers – adjectives – related to color (e.g. blue, gray), texture (e.g. striped, furry), material (e.g. wooden, feathered), general appearance (e.g. rusty, dirty, shiny), and shape (e.g. rectangular) characteristics. The attribute classifiers are trained on the low level features of (Farhadi et al., 2009) using RBF kernel SVMs. Preposition functions encoding spatial relationships between objects are hand designed to evaluate the spatial relationships between pairs of regions in an image and provide a score for 16 prepositions (e.g., above, under, against, in etc).

[1] http://pascallin.ecs.soton.ac.uk/challenges/VOC/voc2010/

From these three types of visual output, we construct a meaning representation of an image as a set of triples (one triple for every pair of detected objects). Each triple encodes a spatial relation between two objects in the following format: <<*adj1, obj1*>, *prep*, <*adj2, obj2*>>. The generation procedure is elaborated in the following two sections.

3 Baseline Approaches to Surface Realization

This section explores three baseline surface realization approaches: language models (§3.1), randomized local search (§3.2), and template-based (§3.3). Our best approach, *phrase fusion using web-scale n-grams* follows in §4.

3.1 Language Model Based Approach

For each triple, as described in §2, we construct a sentence. For instance, given the triple <<*white, cloud*>, *in*, <*blue, sky*>>, we might generate *"There is a white cloud in the blue sky"*.

We begin with a simple decoding scheme based on language models. Let t be a triple, and let V^t be the set of words in t. We perform surface realization by adding function words in-between words in V^t. As a concrete example, suppose we want to determine whether to insert a function word x between a pair of words $\alpha \in V^t$ and $\beta \in V^t$. Then, we need to compare the length-normalized probability $\hat{p}(\alpha x \beta)$ with $\hat{p}(\alpha\beta)$, where $\hat{p}$ takes the n'th root of the probability p for n-word sequences. We insert the new function word x if $\hat{p}(\alpha x \beta) \geq \hat{p}(\alpha\beta)$ using the n-gram models, where the probability of any given sequence $w_1, ..., w_m$ is approximated by

$$p(w_1, ..., w_m) = \prod_{i=1}^{m} p(w_i | w_{i-(n-1)}, ..., w_{i-1})$$

Note that if we wish to reorder words in V^t based on n-gram based language models, then the decoding problem becomes an instance of asymmetric traveler's salesman problem (NP-hard). For brevity, we retain the original order of words in the given triple. We later lift this restriction using the web-scale n-gram based phrase fusion method introduced in §4.

3.2 Randomized Local Search Approach

A much needed extension to the language model based surface realization is incorporating parsers to

```
Begin Loop (until T iterations or convergence)
    Choose a position i to revise at random
    Choose an edit operation at random
    If the edit yields a better score by LM and PCFG
        Commit the edit
End Loop
```

Table 1: Pseudo code for a randomized local search approach. A possible edit operation includes *insertion*, *deletion*, and *replacement*. The score of the current sentence is determined by the multiplication LM-based probability and PCFG-based probability.

enforce long distance regularities for more grammatically correct generation. However, optimizing both language-model-based probabilities and parser-based probabilities is intractable. Therefore, we explore a randomized local search approach that makes greedy revisions using both language models and parsers. Randomized local search has been successfully applied to intractable optimization problems in AI (e.g., Chisholm and Tadepalli (2002)) and NLP (e.g., White and Cardie (2002)).

Table 1 shows the skeleton of the algorithm in our study. Iterating through a loop, it chooses an edit location and an edit operation (insert, delete, or replace) at random. If the edit yields a better score, then we commit the edit, otherwise we jump to the next iteration of the loop. We define the score as

$$score(X) = \hat{p}^{LM}(X)\hat{p}^{PCFG}(X)$$

where X is a given sentence (image description), $\hat{p}^{LM}(X)$ is the length normalized probability of X based on the language model, and $\hat{p}^{PCFG}(X)$ is the length normalized probability of X based on the probabilistic context free grammar (PCFG) model. The loop is repeated until convergence or a fixed number of iterations is reached. Note that this approach can be extended to simulated annealing to allow temporary downward steps to escape from local maxima. We use the PCFG implementation of Klein and Manning (2003).

3.3 Template Based Approach

The third approach is a template-based approach with linguistic constraints, a technique that has often been used for various practical applications such as summarization (Zhou and Hovy, 2004) and dia-

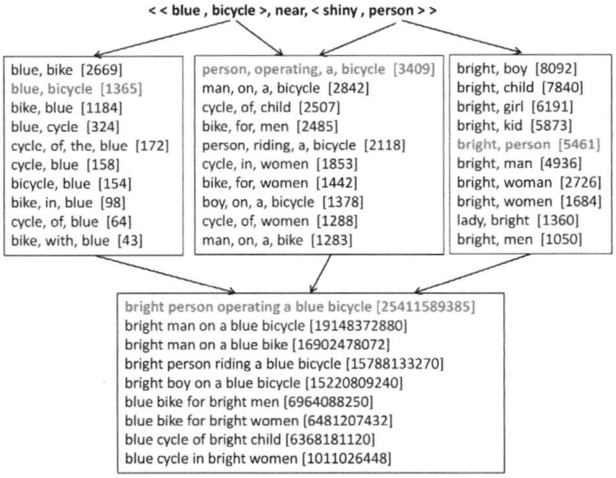

Figure 2: Illustration of phrase fusion composition algorithm using web-scale n-grams. Numbers in square brackets are n-gram frequencies.

logue systems (Channarukul et al., 2003). Because the meaning representation produced by the image recognition system has a fixed pattern of *<<adj1, obj1>, prep, <adj2, obj2>>*, it can be templated as *"There is a [adj1] [obj1] [prep] the [adj2] [obj2]."* We also include templates that encode basic discourse constraints. For instance, the template that generated the first sentences in Figure 3 and 4 is: [PREFIX] [#(x_1)] [x_1], [#(x_2)] [x_2], ... and [#(x_k)] [x_k], where x_i is the name of an object (e.g. "cow"), #(x_i) is the number of instances of x_i (e.g. "one"), and PREFIX $\in$ {"This picture shows", "This is a picture of", etc}.

Although this approach can produce good looking sentences in a limited domain, there are many limitations. First, a template-based approach does not allow creative writing and produces somewhat stilted prose. In particular, it cannot add interesting new words, or replace existing content words with better ones. In addition, such an approach does not allow any reordering of words which might be necessary to create a fluent sentence. Finally, hand-written rules are domain-specific, and do not generalize well to new domains.

4 Surface Realization by Phrase Fusion using Web-scale N-gram

We now introduce an entirely different approach that addresses the limitations of the conventional approaches discussed in §3. This approach is based on web-scale n-gram, also known as Google Web 1T data, which provides the frequency count of each possible n-gram sequence for $1 \leq n \leq 5$.

4.1 [Step I] – Candidate Phrase Selection

We first define three different sets of phrases for each given triple *<<adj1, obj1>, prep, <adj2, obj2>>*:

- $\mathcal{O}_1 = \{(x, f) \mid x$ is an n-gram phrase describing the **first** object using the words $adj1$ and $obj1$, and f is the frequency of $x\}$
- $\mathcal{O}_2 = \{(x, f) \mid x$ is an n-gram phrase describing the **second** object using the words $adj2$ and $obj2$, and f is the frequency of $x\}$
- $\mathcal{R} = \{(x, f) \mid x$ is an n-gram describing the **relation** between the two objects using the words $obj1$ and $obj2$, and f is the frequency of $x\}$

We find n-gram phrases for $\mathcal{O}_1$, $\mathcal{O}_2$, and $\mathcal{R}$ from the Google Web 1T data. The search patterns for $\mathcal{O}_1$ is:

- $[adj_1]$ $[\clubsuit]^{n-2}$ $[obj_1]$
- $[obj_1]$ $[\clubsuit]^{n-2}$ $[adj_1]$

where $[\clubsuit]$ is a wildcard word, and $[\clubsuit]^{n-2}$ denotes a sequence of n-2 number of wildcard words in a n-gram sequence. For wildcards, we only allow a limited set of function words, and verbs in the gerund form[2] for reasons that will become clearer in the next step – phrase fusion in §4.2.

Note that it is the second pattern that allows interesting re-ordering of words in the final sentence generation. For instance, suppose $adj1$=green, $obj1$=person. Then it is more natural to generate a phrase using the reverse pattern such as, *"person in green"* or *"person wearing green"* than simply concatenating $adj1$ and $obj1$ to generate *"green person"*. Similarly, given $obj1$=bicycle and $obj2$=man, generating a phrase using the reverse pattern, e.g., *"man with a bicycle"* would be more natural than *"bicycle with a man"*. Our hypothesis is that such ordering preference is implicitly encoded in the web-scale n-grams via frequencies.

It is worthwhile to note that our pattern matching is case sensitive, and we only allow patterns that are

[2]We treat words with suffix "ing" as gerund for simplicity.

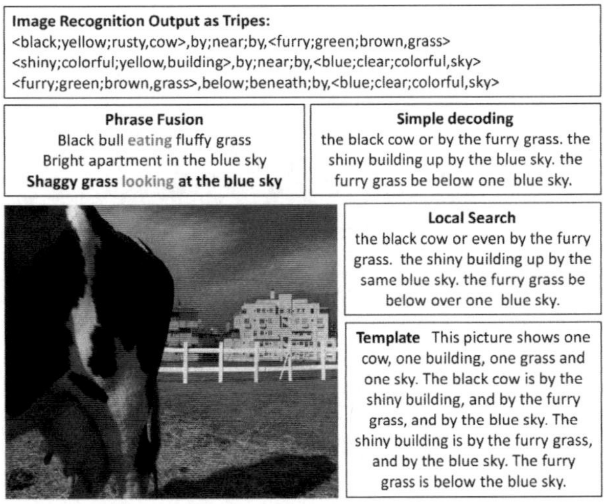

Figure 3: Comparison of image descriptions

all lower-case. From our pilot study, we found that n-grams with upper case characters are likely from named entities, which distort the n-gram frequency distribution that we rely on during the phrase fusion phase. To further reduce noise, we also discard any n-gram that contains a character that is not an alphabet.

Accommodating Uncertainty We extend candidate phrase selection in order to cope with uncertainty from the image recognition. In particular, for each object detection obj_i, we include its top 3 predicted modifiers adj_{i1}, adj_{i2}, adj_{i3} determined by the attribute classifiers (see §2) to expand the set $\mathcal{O}_1$ and $\mathcal{O}_2$ accordingly. For instance, given adj_i =(shiny or white) and obj_i = sheep, we can consider both <shiny,sheep> and <white,sheep> pairs to predict more compatible pairs of words.

Accommodating Synonyms Additionally, we augment each modifier adj_i and each object name obj_i with synonyms to further expand our sets $\mathcal{O}_1$, $\mathcal{O}_2$, and $\mathcal{R}$. These expanded sets of phrases enable resulting generations that are more fluent and creative.

4.2 [Step II] – Phrase Fusion

Given the expanded sets of phrases $\mathcal{O}_1$, $\mathcal{O}_2$, and $\mathcal{R}$ described above, we perform phrase fusion to generate simple image description. In this step, we find the best combination of three phrases, $(\hat{x_1}, \hat{f_1}) \in \mathcal{O}_1$, $(\hat{x_2}, \hat{f_2}) \in \mathcal{O}_2$, and $(\hat{x_R}, \hat{f_R}) \in \mathcal{R}$ as follows:

$$(\hat{x_1}, \hat{x_2}, \hat{x_R}) = \text{argmax}_{x_1,x_2,x_R} score(x_1, x_2, x_R) \quad (1)$$

$$score(x_1, x_2, x_R) = \phi(x_1) \times \phi(x_2) \times \phi(x_R) \quad (2)$$

$$s.t.\ \hat{x_1}\ and\ \hat{x_R} \text{ are compatible}$$

$$\&\quad \hat{x_2}\ and\ \hat{x_R} \text{ are compatible}$$

Two phrases $\hat{x_i}$ and $\hat{x_R}$ are compatible if they share the same object noun obj_i. We define the phrase-level score function $\phi(\cdot)$ as $\phi(x_i) = f_i$ using the Google n-gram frequencies. The equation (2) can be maximized using dynamic programming, by aligning the decision sequence as $\hat{x_1} - \hat{x_R} - \hat{x_2}$.

Once the best combination – $(\hat{x_1}, \hat{x_2}, \hat{x_R})$ is determined, we fuse the phrases by replacing the word obj_1 in the phrase $\hat{x_R}$ with the corresponding phrase $\hat{x_1}$. Similarly, we replace the word obj_2 in the phrase $\hat{x_R}$ with the other corresponding phrase $\hat{x_2}$. Because the wildcard words – [♣] in §4.1 allow only a limited set of function words and gerund, the resulting phrase is highly likely to be grammatically correct.

Computational Efficiency One advantage of our phrase fusion method is its efficiency. If we were to attempt to re-order words with language models in a naive way, we would need to consider all possible permutations of words – an NP-hard problem (§3.1). However, our phrase fusion method is clever in that it probes reordering only on selected pairs of words, where reordering is likely to be useful. In other words, our approach naturally ignores most word pairs that do not require reordering and has a time complexity of only $O(K^2 n)$, where K is the maximum number of candidate phrases of any phrase type, and n is the number of phrase types in each sentence. K can be kept as a small constant by selecting K-best candidate phrases of each phrase type. We set $K = 10$ in this paper.

5 Experimental Results

To construct the training corpus for language models, we crawled Wikipedia pages that describe our object set. For evaluation, we use the UIUC PASCAL sentence dataset[3] which contains upto five human-generated sentences that describing 1000 images. Note that all of the approaches presented in

[3]http://vision.cs.uiuc.edu/pascal-sentences/

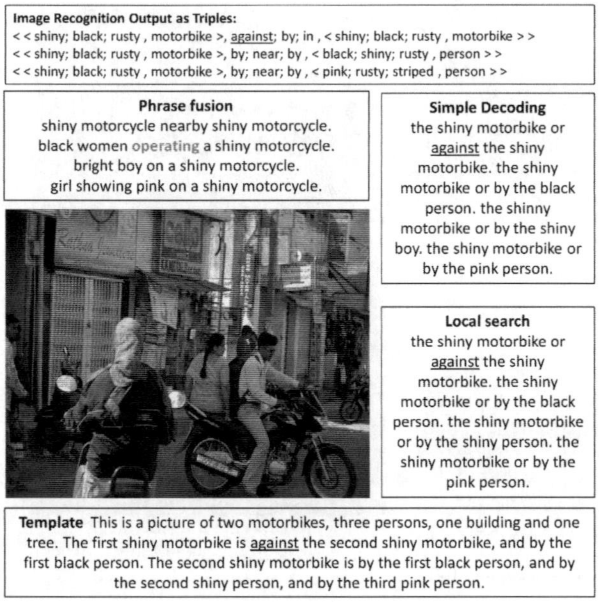

Figure 4: Comparison of image descriptions

Section 3 and 4 attempt to insert function words for surface realization. In this work, we limit the choice of function words to only those words that are likely to be necessary in the final output.[4] For instance, we disallow function words such as "who" or "or".

Before presenting evaluation results, we present some samples of image descriptions generated by 4 different approaches in Figure 3 and 4. Notice that only the PHRASE FUSION approach is able to include interesting and adequate verbs, such as *"eating"* or *"looking"* in Figure 3, and *"operating"* in Figure 4. Note that the choice of these action verbs is based only on the co-occurrence statistics encoded in n-grams, without relying on the vision component that specializes in action recognition. These examples therefore demonstrate that world knowledge implicitly encoded in natural language can help enhance image content recognition.

Automatic Evaluation: BLEU (Papineni et al., 2002) is a widely used metric for automatic evaluation of machine translation that measures the n-gram precision of machine generated sentences with respect to human generated sentences. Because our task can be viewed as machine translation from images to text, BLEU (Papineni et al., 2002) may seem like a reasonable choice. However, there is larger inherent variability in generating sentences from images than translating a sentence from one language to another. In fact two people viewing the same picture may produce quite different descriptions. This means BLEU could penalize many correctly generated sentences, and be poorly correlated with human judgment of quality. Nevertheless we report BLEU scores in absence of any other automatic evaluation method that serves our needs perfectly.

[4]This limitation does not apply to TEMPLATE.

	w/o	w/ syn
LANGUAGE MODEL	0.094	0.106
TEMPLATE	0.087	0.096
LOCAL SEARCH	0.100	0.111
PHRASE FUSION (any best)	0.149	0.153
PHRASE FUSION (best w/ gerund)	0.146	0.149
Human	0.500	0.510

Table 2: Automatic Evaluation: BLEU measured at 1

	Creativ.	Fluency	Relevan.
LANGUAGE MODEL	2.12	1.96	2.09
TEMPLATE	2.04	1.7	1.96
LOCAL SEARCH	2.21	1.96	2.04
PHRASE FUSION	1.86	1.97	2.11

Table 3: Human Evaluation: the scores range over 1 to 3, where 1 is very good, 2 is ok, 3 is bad.

The results are shown in Table 2 – first column shows BLEU score considering exact matches, second column shows BLEU with full credit for synonyms. To give a sense of upper bound and to see some limitations of the BLEU score, we also compute the BLEU score between human-generated sentences by computing the BLEU score of the first human sentence with respect to the others.

There is one important factor to consider when interpreting Table 2. The four approaches explored in this paper are purposefully prolific writers in that they generate many more sentences than the number of sentences in the image descriptions written by humans (available in the UIUC PASCAL dataset). In this work, we do not perform sentence selection to reduce the number of sentences in the final output. Rather, we focus on the quality of each generated sentence. The consequence of producing many

Figure 5: Sample image descriptions using PHRASE FUSION: some of the unexpected or poetic descriptions are highlighted in **boldface**, and some of the interesting incorrect descriptions are underlined.

more sentences in our output is overall lower BLEU scores, because BLEU precision penalizes spurious repetitions of the same word, which necessarily occurs when generating more sentences. This is not an issue for comparing different approaches however, as we generate the same number of sentences for each method.

From Table 2, we find that our final approach — PHRASE FUSION based on web-scale n-grams performs the best. Notice that there are two different evaluations for PHRASE FUSION: the first one is evaluated for the best combination of phrases (Equation (1)), while the second one is evaluated for the best combination of phrases that contained at least one gerund.

Human Evaluation: As mentioned earlier, BLEU score has some drawbacks including obliviousness to correctness of grammar and inability to evaluate the creativity of a composition. To directly quantify these aspects that could not be addressed by BLEU, we perform human judgments on 120 instances for the four proposed methods. Evaluators do not have any computer vision or natural language generation background.

We consider the following three aspects to evaluate the our image descriptions: *creativity*, *fluency*, and *relevance*. For simplicity, human evaluators assign one set of scores for each aspect per image. The scores range from 1 to 3, where 1 is very good, 2 is ok, and 3 is bad.[5] The definition and guideline for each aspect is:

[Creativity] How creative is the generated sentence?

1 There is creativity either based on unexpected words (in particular, verbs), or describing things in a poetic way.

2 There is minor creativity based on re-ordering words that appeared in the triple

3 None. Looks like a robot talking.

[Fluency] How grammatically correct is the generated sentence?

1 Mostly perfect English phrase or sentence.

2 There are some errors, but mostly comprehensible.

3 Terrible.

[Relevance] How relevant is the generated description to the given image?

1 Very relevant.

2 Reasonably relevant.

3 Totally off.

[5]In our pilot study, human annotations on 160 instances given by two evaluators were identical on 61% of the instances, and close (difference ≤ 1) on 92%.

Table 3 shows the human evaluation results. In terms of *creativity*, PHRASE FUSION achieves the best score as expected. In terms of *fluency* and *relevance* however, TEMPLATE achieves the best scores, while PHRASE FUSION performs the second best. Remember that TEMPLATE is based on hand-engineered rules with discourse constraints, which seems to appeal to evaluators more. It would be straightforward to combine PHRASE FUSION with TEMPLATE to improve the output of PHRASE FUSION with hand-engineered rules. However, our goal in this paper is to investigate statistically motivated approaches for generating image descriptions that can address inherent limitations of hand-written rules discussed in §3.3.

Notice that the relevance score of TEMPLATE is better than that of LANGUAGE MODEL, even though both approaches generate descriptions that consist of an almost identical set of words. This is presumably because the output from LANGUAGE MODEL contains grammatically incorrect sentences that are not comprehendable enough to the evaluators. The relevance score of PHRASE FUSION is also slightly worse than that of TEMPLATE, presumably because PHRASE FUSION often generates poetic or creative expressions, as shown in Figure 5, which can be considered a deviation from the image content.

Error Analysis There are different sources of errors. Some errors are due to mistakes in the original visual recognition input. For example, in the 3rd image in Figure 5, the color of sky is predicted to be "golden". In the 4th image, the wall behind the table is recognized as "sky", and in the 6th image, the parrots are recognized as "person".

Other errors are from surface realization. For instance, in the 8th image, PHRASE FUSION selects the preposition "under", presumably because dogs are typically under the chair rather than on the chair according to Google n-gram statistics. In the 5th image, an unexpected word "burning" is selected to make the resulting output idiosyncratic. Word sense disambiguation sometimes causes a problem in surface realization as well. In the 3rd image, the word "way" is chosen to represent "path" or "street" by the image recognizer. However, a different sense of way – "very" – is being used in the final output.

6 Related Work

There has been relatively limited work on automatically generating natural language image descriptions. Most work related to our study is discussed in §1, hence we highlight only those that are closest to our work here. Yao et al. (2010) present a comprehensive system that generates image descriptions using Head-driven phrase structure (HPSG) grammar, which requires carefully written domain-specific lexicalized grammar rules, and also demands a very specific and complex meaning representation scheme from the image processing. In contrast, our approach handles images in the open-domain more naturally using much simpler techniques.

We use similar vision based inputs – object detectors, modifier classifiers, and prepositional functions – to some very recent work on generating simple descriptions for images (Kulkarni et al., 2011), but focus on improving the sentence generation methodology and produce descriptions that are more true to human generated descriptions. Note that the BLEU scores reported in their work of Kulkarni et al. (2011) are not directly comparable to ours, as the scale of the scores differs depending on the number of sentences generated per image.

7 Conclusion

In this paper, we presented a novel surface realization technique based on web-scale n-gram data to automatically generate image description. Despite its simplicity, our method is highly effective in generating mostly appealing and presentable language, while permitting creative writing at times. We conclude from our study that it is viable to generate simple textual descriptions that are germane to the specific image content while also sometimes producing almost poetic natural language. Furthermore, we demonstrate that world knowledge implicitly encoded in natural language can help enhance image content recognition.

Acknowledgments

This work is supported in part by NSF Faculty Early Career Development (CAREER) Award #1054133.

References

A. Aker and R. Gaizauskas. 2010. Generating image descriptions using dependency relational patterns. In *ACL*.

K. Barnard, P. Duygulu, N. de Freitas, D. Forsyth, D. Blei, and M. Jordan. 2003. Matching words and pictures. *JMLR*, 3:1107–1135.

Songsak Channarukul, Susan W. McRoy, and Syed S. Ali. 2003. Doghed: a template-based generator for multimodal dialog systems targeting heterogeneous devices. In *NAACL*.

Michael Chisholm and Prasad Tadepalli. 2002. Learning decision rules by randomized iterative local search. In *ICML*, pages 75–82.

J. Deng, W. Dong, R. Socher, L.-J. Li, K. Li, and L. Fei-Fei. 2009. ImageNet: A Large-Scale Hierarchical Image Database. In *CVPR*.

A. Farhadi, I. Endres, D. Hoiem, and D. A. Forsyth. 2009. Describing objects by their attributes. In *CVPR*.

A. Farhadi, M Hejrati, A. Sadeghi, P. Young, C. Rashtchian, J. Hockenmaier, and D. A. Forsyth. 2010. Every picture tells a story: generating sentences for images. In *ECCV*.

P. Felzenszwalb, R. Girshick, D. McAllester, and D. Ramanan. 2010. Object detection with discriminatively trained part based models. *tPAMI*, Sept.

Y. Feng and M. Lapata. 2010a. How many words is a picture worth? automatic caption generation for news images. In *ACL*.

Yansong Feng and Mirella Lapata. 2010b. Topic models for image annotation and text illustration. In *HLT*.

Dan Klein and Christopher D. Manning. 2003. Accurate unlexicalized parsing. In *Proceedings of the 41st Annual Meeting on Association for Computational Linguistics*, pages 423–430. Association for Computational Linguistics.

Girish Kulkarni, Visruth Premraj, Sagnik Dhar, Siming Li, Yejin Choi, Alexander C Berg, and Tamara L Berg. 2011. Babytalk: Understanding and generating simple image descriptions. In *CVPR*.

Chee Wee Leong, Rada Mihalcea, and Samer Hassan. 2010. Text mining for automatic image tagging. In *COLING*.

Kishore Papineni, Salim Roukos, Todd Ward, and Wei jing Zhu. 2002. Bleu: a method for automatic evaluation of machine translation.

Katerina Pastra, Horacio Saggion, and Yorick Wilks. 2003. Nlp for indexing and retrieval of captioned photographs. In *EACL*.

Michael White and Claire Cardie. 2002. Selecting sentences for multidocument summaries using randomized local search. In *ACL Workshop on Automatic Summarization*.

B.Z. Yao, Xiong Yang, Liang Lin, Mun Wai Lee, and Song-Chun Zhu. 2010. I2t: Image parsing to text description. *Proc. IEEE*, 98(8).

Liang Zhou and Eduard Hovy. 2004. Template-filtered headline summarization. In *Text Summarization Branches Out: Pr ACL-04 Wkshp*, July.

Adapting Text instead of the Model: An Open Domain Approach

Gourab Kundu, Dan Roth
University of Illinois at Urbana Champaign
Urbana, IL 61801
{kundu2,danr}@illinois.edu

Abstract

Natural language systems trained on labeled data from one domain do not perform well on other domains. Most adaptation algorithms proposed in the literature train a new model for the new domain using unlabeled data. However, it is time consuming to retrain big models or pipeline systems. Moreover, the domain of a new target sentence may not be known, and one may not have significant amount of unlabeled data for every new domain.

To pursue the goal of an *Open Domain NLP* (train once, test anywhere), we propose *ADUT (ADaptation Using label-preserving Transformation)*, an approach that avoids the need for retraining and does not require knowledge of the new domain, or any data from it. Our approach applies simple label-preserving transformations to the target text so that the transformed text is more similar to the training domain; it then applies the existing model on the transformed sentences and combines the predictions to produce the desired prediction on the target text. We instantiate *ADUT* for the case of Semantic Role Labeling (SRL) and show that it compares favorably with approaches that retrain their model on the target domain. Specifically, this "on the fly" adaptation approach yields 13% error reduction for a single parse system when adapting from the news wire text to fiction.

1 Introduction

In several NLP tasks, systems trained on annotated data from one domain perform well when tested on the same domain but adapt poorly to other domains. For example, all systems of CoNLL 2005 shared task (Carreras and Màrquez, 2005) on Semantic Role Labeling showed a performance degradation of almost 10% or more when tested on a different domain.

Most works in domain adaptation have focused on learning a common representation across training and test domains (Blitzer et al., 2006; DauméIII, 2007; Huang and Yates, 2009). Using this representation, they retrain the model for every new domain. But these are not *Open Domain Systems* since the model needs to be retrained for every new domain. This is very difficult for pipeline systems like SRL where syntactic parser, shallow parser, POS tagger and then SRL need to be retrained. Moreover, these methods need to have a lot of unlabeled data that is taken from the same domain, in order to learn meaningful feature correspondences across training and test domain. These approaches cannot work when they do not have a lot of unlabeled data from the test domain or when the test domain in itself is very diverse, e.g., the web.

The contribution of this paper is a new framework for adaptation. We propose *ADUT (ADaptation Using label-preserving Transformation)* as a framework in which a previously learned model can be used on an out-of-domain example without retraining and without looking at any labeled or unlabeled data for the domain of the new example. The framework transforms the test sentence to generate sentences that have, in principle, identical labeling but that are more like instances from the training domain. Consequently, it is expected that the exist-

Proceedings of the Fifteenth Conference on Computational Natural Language Learning, pages 229–237,
Portland, Oregon, USA, 23–24 June 2011.

ing model will make better predictions on them. All these predictions are then combined to choose the most probable and consistent prediction for the test sentence.

ADUT is a general technique which can be applied to any natural language task. In this paper, we demonstrate its usefulness on the task of semantic role labeling (Carreras and Màrquez, 2005). Starting with a system that was trained on the news text and does not perform well on fiction, we show that ADUT provides significant improvement on fiction, and is competitive with the performance of algorithms that were re-trained on the test domain.

The paper is organized as follows. Section 2 discusses two motivating examples. Section 3 gives a formal definition of our adaptation framework. Section 4 describes the transformation operators that we applied for this task. Section 5 presents our joint inference approach. Section 6 describes our semantic role labeling system and our experimental results are in Section 7. Section 8 describes the related works for domain adaptation. Finally in Section 9 we conclude the paper with a discussion.

2 Motivating Examples

One of the key reasons for performance degradation of an NLP tool is unseen features such as words in the new domain that were not seen in the training domain. But if an unknown word is replaced by a known word without changing the labeling of the sentence, tools perform better. For example, in the task of syntactic parsing, the unknown word *checkup* causes the Charniak parser to make a wrong coordination decision on the sentence

> *He was discharged from the hospital after a two-day checkup and he and his parents had what Mr. Mckinley described as a "celebration lunch" at the cafeteria on the campus.*

If we replace the word *checkup* with its hypernym *examination* which appears in training data, the parse gets corrected. Figure 1 shows both original and corrected parse trees.

For the task of semantic role labeling, systems do not perform well on the predicates that are infrequent in training domain. But if an infrequent predicate is replaced with a frequent predicate from training domain such that both predicates have similar semantic argument structure, the system performs better. Consider the following sentence

> *Scotty gazed out at ugly gray slums.*

The semantic role for the phrase *at ugly gray slums* with respect to predicate *gaze* is *A1*. But the predicate *gaze* appears only once in training data and our model predicts *at ugly gray slums* as *AM-LOC* instead of *A1*. But if *gaze* is replaced with *look* which occurs 328 times in training data and has similar argument structure (in the same VerbNet class as *gaze*), the system makes the correct prediction.

3 Problem Formulation

Let the in-domain distribution be D_i and out-of-domain distribution be D_o. We have a model f trained over a set of labeled examples drawn from D_i. If D_i and D_o are very dissimilar, f will not perform well on examples drawn from D_o. The problem is to get good performance from f on D_o without retraining f.

We define a *Transformation* g to be a function that maps an example e into a set of examples E. So $g : X \rightarrow 2^X$ where X is the entire space of examples. In this paper, we only consider the *Label-preserving Transformations* which satisfy the property that all transformed examples in E have the same label as input example e, i.e., $\forall x \; x \in S_k \Rightarrow g(x) \subset S_k$ where S_k is the set of examples with label k . Let G be a set of label-preserving transformation functions. $G = \{g_1, g_2, \ldots, g_p\}$.

At evaluation time, for test example d, we will apply G to get a set of examples T_1. Let $T_2 = \{d' \in T_1 : D_i(d') > D_i(d)\}$. So all examples in T_2 have same label as d but have a higher probability than d to be drawn from the in-domain distribution. So f should perform better on examples in T_2 than on d. For each $d' \in T_2$, f will produce scores for the output labels. The scores will be combined subject to constraints to produce the final output.

4 Transformation Functions

After applying a transformation function to get a new sentence from an input sentence, we remember the mapping of segments across the original

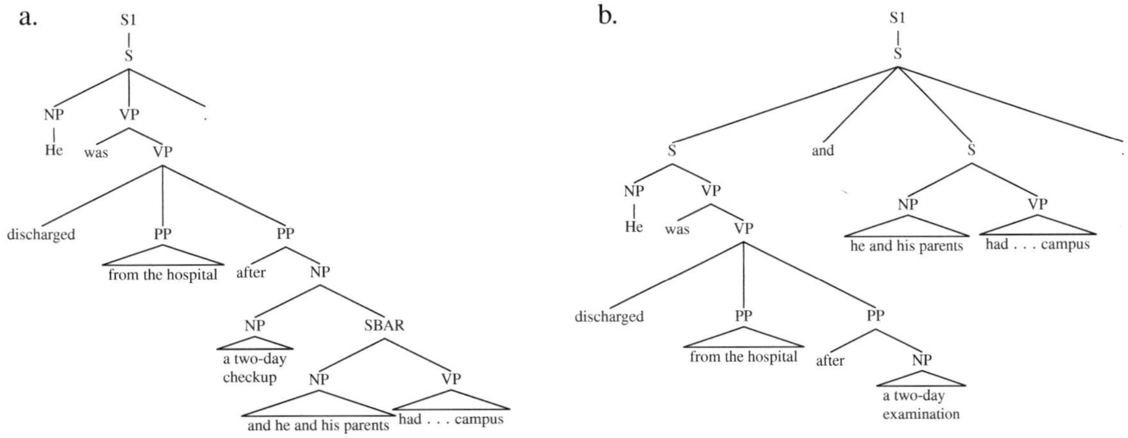

Figure 1: a. Original Parse tree b. Corrected Parse tree after replacement of unknown word *checkup* by *examination*

and transformed sentence. Thus, after annotating the transformed sentence with SRL, we can transfer the roles to the original sentence through this mapping. Transformation functions can be divided into two categories. The first category is *Transformations From List* which uses external resources like WordNet, VerbNet and Word Clusters. The second is *Learned Transformations* that uses transformation rules that have been learned from training data.

4.1 Transformation From List

I. Replacement of Predicate:

As noted in (Huang and Yates, 2010), 6.1% of the predicates in the Brown test set do not appear in WSJ training set and 11.8% appear at most twice. Since the semantic roles of a sentence depend on the predicate, these infrequent predicates hurt SRL performance on new domains. Note that since all predicates in PropBank are verbs, we will use the words *predicate* and *verb* interchangeably.

We count the frequency of each predicate and its accuracy in terms of F1 score over the training data. If the frequency or the F1 score of the predicate in the test sentence is below a threshold, we perturb that predicate. We take all the verbs in the same class of VerbNet[1] as the original verb (in case the verb is present in multiple classes, we take all the classes). In case the verb is not present in VerbNet, we take its synonyms from WordNet. If there is no synonym in WordNet, we take the hypernyms.

From this collection of new verbs, we select verbs that have a high accuracy and a high frequency in training. We replace the original verb with each of these new verbs and generate one new sentence for each new verb; the sentence is retained if the parse score for the new sentence is higher than the parse score for the original sentence.[2] VerbNet has defined a set of verb-independent thematic roles and grouped the verbs according to their usage in frames with identical thematic roles. But PropBank annotation was with respect to each verb. So the same thematic role is labeled as different roles for different verbs in PropBank. For example, both *warn* and *advise* belong to the same VerbNet class (37.9) and take thematic roles of *Recipient* (person being warned or advised) and *Topic* (topic of warning or advising). But *Recipient* was marked as *A2* for *warn* and *A1* for *advise* and *Topic* was marked as *A1* for *warn* and *A2* for *advise* in PropBank annotation. Semlink[3] provides a mapping from the thematic role to PropBank role for each verb. After the SRL annotates the new sentence with PropBank roles for the new verb, we map the PropBank roles of the new verb to their corresponding thematic roles and then map the thematic roles to the corresponding PropBank roles for the original verb.

II. Replacement and Removal of Quoted Strings:

Quoted sentences can vary a lot from one domain to another. For example, in WSJ, quoted sentences are like formal statements but in Brown, these are like informal conversations. We generate the transformations in the following ways:

1) We use the content of the quoted string as one

[1] http://verbs.colorado.edu/ mpalmer/projects/verbnet.html

[2] Parse score is the parse probability returned by Charniak or Stanford parser.

[3] http://verbs.colorado.edu/semlink/

sentence. 2) We replace each quoted string in turn with a simple sentence (*This is good*) to generate a new sentence. 3) If a sentence has a quoted string in the beginning, we move that quoted string after the first NP and VP that immediately follow the quoted string. For example, from the input sentence, *"We just sit quiet", he said.* we generate the sentences 1) *We just sit quiet* 2) *"This is good", he said.* 3) *He said, "We just sit quiet".*

III. Replacement of Unseen Words:

A major difficulty for domain adaptation is that some words in the new domain do not appear in the training domain. In the Brown test set, 5% of total words were never seen in the WSJ training set.

Given an unseen word which is not a verb, we replace it with WordNet synonyms and hypernyms that were seen in the training data. We used the clusters obtained in (Liang, 2005) from running the Brown algorithm (Brown et al., 1992) on Reuters 1996 dataset. But since this cluster was generated automatically, it is noisy. So we chose replacements from the Brown clusters selectively. We only replace those words for which the POS tagger and the syntactic parser predicted different tags. For each such word, we find its cluster and select the set of words from the cluster. We delete from this set all words that do not take at least one part-of-speech tag that the original word can take (from WordNet). For each candidate synonym or hypernym or cluster member, we get a new sentence. Finally we only keep those sentences that have higher parse scores than the original sentence.

IV. Sentence Split based on Stop Symbols:

We split each sentence based on stop symbols like ; and . . Each of the splitted sentences becomes one transformation of the original sentence.

V. Sentence Simplification:

We have a set of heuristics for simplifying the constituents of the parse tree; for example, replacing an NP with its first and last word, removal of PRN phrases etc. We apply these heuristics and generate simpler sentences until no more simplification is possible. Examples of our heuristics are given in Table 1.

Note that we can use composition of multiple transformation functions as one function. A composition $p_1 \odot p_2(s) = \cup_{a \in p_1(s)} p_2(a)$. We apply II⊙I, III⊙I, IV⊙I and V⊙I.

Node	Input Example	Simplified Example	Operation
NP	**He and she** ran.	**He** ran.	replace
NP	**The big man** ran.	**The man** ran.	replace
ADVP	He ran **fast**.	He ran.	delete
PP	He ran **in the field**.	He ran.	delete
PRN	He – **though sick** – ran.	He ran.	delete
VP	He **walked** and ran.	He ran.	delete
TO	I want him **to** run.	I want that he can ran.	rewrite

Table 1: Examples of Simplifications (Predicate is run)

4.2 Learned Transformations

The learned model is inaccurate over verbs and roles that are infrequent in the training data. The purpose of the learned transformation is to transfer such a phrase in the test sentence in place of a phrase of a simpler sentence; this is done such that there exists a mapping from the role of the phrase in the new sentence to the role of the phrase in the original sentence.

Phrase Representation: A phrase tuple is a 3-tuple (t, i, h) where, t is the phrase type, i is the index, and h is the headword of the phrase. We denote by PR the Phrase Representation of a sentence – an ordered list of phrase tuples. A phrase tuple corresponds to a node in the tree. We only consider phrase tuples that correspond to nodes that are (1) a sibling of the predicate node or (2) a sibling of an ancestor of the predicate node. Phrase tuples in PR are sorted based on their position in the sentence. The *index* i of the phrase tuple containing the predicate is taken to be zero with the indices of the phrase tuples on the left (right) sequentially decreasing (increasing).

Transformation Rule: We denote by *Label(n, s)* the semantic role of nth phrase in the PR of the sentence s. Let *Replace*(n_s, n_t, s_s, s_t) be a new sentence that results from inserting the phrase n_s in sentence s_s instead of phrase n_t in sentence s_t. We will refer to s_t as *target sentence* and to n_t as the *target phrase*. Let sp be a sequence of phrase tuples named as *source pattern*. If Label$(n_s, s_s) = r_1$ and Label$(n_t, \text{Replace}(n_s, n_t, s_s, s_t)) = r_2$, then denote $f(r_2) = r_1$. In this case we call the 6-tuple (s_t, n_t, p, sp, n_s, f) a *transformation rule*. We call f the *label correspondence function.*

Example: Consider the sentence s_t = *"But it did not sing."* and the rule τ: $(s_t, n_t, p, sp, n_s, f)$. Let: $n_t = -3$, p = *entitle*,
$sp = [-2, NP, \phi][-1, AUX, \phi][0, V, entitle][1, \phi, to]$
$n_s = -2, f = \{<A0, A2>\} \cup \{<Ai, Ai>|i \neq 0\}$.

The PR of $\tau.s_t$ is {[−4, CC, But] [−3, NP, it] [−2, AUX, did] [−1, RB, not] [0, VB, sing] [1, ., .]}. Consider the input sentence s_s: *Mr. X was entitled to a discount*. with PR of {[−2, NP, X] [−1, AUX, was] [0, V, entitle] [1, PP, to][2, ., .]}. Since $\tau.sp$ is a subsequence of the PR of s_s, τ will apply to the predicate *entitle* of s_s. The transformed sentence is:

s_{tr} = Replace$(\tau.n_s, \tau.n_t, s_s, \tau.s_t)$ = *But Mr. X did not sing.* with PR of {[−4, CC, But] [−3, NP, X] [−2, AUX, did] [−1, RB, not] [0, VB, sing] [1, ., .]}. If the SRL system assigns the semantic role of $A0$ to the phrase *Mr. X* of s_{tr}, the semantic role of *Mr. X* in s_s can be recovered through $\tau.f$ since $\tau.f(A0) = A2 =$ Label$(-2, s_s)$.

While checking if $\tau.sp$ is a subsequence of the PR of the input sentence, ϕ in each tuple of $\tau.sp$ has to be considered a trivial match. So τ will match the sentence *He is entitled to a reward.* with PR = {[−2, NP, He] [−1, AUX, is] [0, V, entitle] [1, PP, to][2, ., .]} but will not match the sentence *The conference was entitled a big success.* with PR = {[−2, NP, conference] [−1, AUX, was] [0, V, entitle] [1, S, **success**][2, ., .]} (mismatch position is bolded). The index of a phrase tuple cannot be ϕ, only the head word or type can be ϕ and the rules with more ϕ strings in the source pattern are more general since they can match more sentences.

Algorithm 1 GenerateRules

1: Input: predicate v, semantic role r, Training sentences D, SRL Model M
2: Output: set of rules R
3: $R \Leftarrow$ GetInitialRules(v, r, D, M)
4: **repeat**
5: $J \Leftarrow$ ExpandRules(R)
6: $K \Leftarrow R \cup J$
7: sort K based on accuracy, support, size of source pattern
8: select some rules $R \subset K$ based on database coverage
9: **until** all rules in R have been expanded before
10: **return** R

The algorithm for finding rules for a semantic role r of a predicate v is given in Algorithm 1. It is a specific to general beam search procedure that starts with a set of initial rules (Line 3, detail in Algorithm 2) and finds new rules from these rules (Line 5, detail in Algorithm 3). In Line 7, the rules are sorted by decreasing order of accuracy, support and number of ϕ strings in the source pattern. In Line 8, a set of rules are selected to cover all occurrences of the semantic role r with the predicate v a specific number of times. This process continues until no new rules are found. Note that these rules need to be learned only once and can be used for every new domain.

Algorithm 2 GetInitialRules

1: Input: predicate v, semantic role r, Training sentences D, SRL-Model M
2: Output: Set of initial rules I
3: $I \Leftarrow \phi$
4: $T \Leftarrow \{s \in D : \text{length}(s) <= e\}$
5: $S \Leftarrow \{s \in D : s$ has role r for predicate $v\}$
6: $M \Leftarrow$ Set of all semantic roles
7: **for** each phrase p_1 in $s_1 \in S$ with gold label r for predicate v **do**
8: **for** each phrase p_2 in $s_2 \in T$ labeled as a core argument **do**
9: **if** $s_1 \neq s_2$ and p_1 and p_2 have same phrase types **then**
10: $\tau \Leftarrow$ empty rule
11: $\tau.s_t \Leftarrow s_2, \tau.p \Leftarrow v$
12: $\tau.n_t \Leftarrow$ index of p_2 in PR of s_2
13: $\tau.n_s \Leftarrow$ index of p_1 in PR of s_1
14: $\tau.sp \Leftarrow$ phrase tuples for phrases from p_1 to v and two phrases after v in PR of s_1
15: $L \Leftarrow \phi$
16: **for** each sentence $s_3 \in D$ with predicate v **do**
17: **if** $\tau.sp$ is a subsequence of PR of s_3 **then**
18: $x \Leftarrow$ replace$(\tau.n_s, \tau.n_t, s_3, \tau.s_t)$
19: annotate x with SRL using M
20: $r_1 \Leftarrow$ the gold standard semantic role of the phrase with index $\tau.n_s$ in PR of s_3
21: $r_2 \Leftarrow$ Label$(\tau.n_t, x)$
22: **if** $r_2 \notin L$ **then**
23: insert(r_2, r_1) in $\tau.f$
24: $L = L \cup \{r_2\}$
25: **end if**
26: **end if**
27: **end for**
28: **for** each role $j \in M - L$ **do**
29: insert(j, j) in $\tau.f$
30: **end for**
31: $I \Leftarrow I \cup \{\tau\}$
32: **end if**
33: **end for**
34: **end for**
35: **return** I

The algorithm for generating initial rules for the semantic role r of predicate v is given in Algorithm 2. Shorter sentences are preferred to be target sentences(Line 4). A rule τ is created for every (p_1, p_2) pair where p_1, p_2 are phrases, p_1 has the semantic role r in some sentence s_1, p_2 is labeled as a core argument($A0 - A5$) in some sentence in T and the phrase types of p_1 and p_2 in their respective parse trees are same(Lines 7 − 9). Every sentence s_3 in training corpus with predicate $\tau.p$ is a potential candidate for applying τ(Line 16) if $\tau.sp$ is a subsequence of PR of s_3(Line 17). After applying τ to s_3, a transformed sentence x is created(Line 18). Lines $20-26$ find the semantic role r_2 of the transferred phrase from SRL annotation of x using model M and create a mapping from r_2 to the gold standard role r_1 of the phrase in s_3. L maintains the set of semantic roles for which mappings have been created. In lines $28-30$, all unmapped roles are mapped to themselves.

The algorithm for creating new rules from a set of existing rules is given in Algorithm 3. Lines $4-13$ generate all immediate more general neighbors of the current rule by nullifying the headword or phrase type element in any of the phrase tuples in its source pattern.

Algorithm 3 ExpandRules

1: Input: a set of rules R
2: Output: a set of expanded rules E
3: $E \Leftarrow \phi$
4: **for** each phrase tuple c in the source pattern of $r \in R$ **do**
5:     **if** c is not the tuple for predicate **then**
6:         create a new rule r' with all components of r
7:         mark the head word of c in the source pattern of r' to ϕ
8:         add r' to E
9:         create a new rule r'' with all components of r
10:         mark the phrase type of c in the source pattern of r'' to ϕ
11:         add r'' to E
12:     **end if**
13: **end for**
14: **return** E

5 Combination by Joint Inference

The transformation functions transform an input sentence into a set of sentences T. From each transformed sentence t_i, we get a set of argument candidates S_i. Let $S = \bigcup_{i=1}^{|T|} S_i$ be the set of all arguments. Argument classifier assigns scores for each argument over the output labels(roles) in S that is then converted into a probability distribution over the possible labels using the softmax function (Bishop, 1995). Note that multiple arguments with the same span can be generated from multiple transformed sentences.

First, we take all arguments from S with distinct span and put them in S'. For each argument *arg* in S', we calculate scores over possible labels as the sum over the probability distribution (over output labels) of all arguments in S that have the same span as *arg* divided by the number of sentences in T that contained *arg*. This results in a set of arguments with distinct spans and for each argument, a set of scores over possible labels. Following the joint inference procedure in (Punyakanok et al., 2008), we want to select a label for each argument such that the total score is maximized subject to some constraints. Let us index the set S' as $S'^{1:M}$ where $M = |S'|$. Also assume that each argument can take a label from a set P. The set of arguments in $S'^{1:M}$ can take a set of labels $c^{1:M} \in P^{1:M}$. Given some constraints, the resulting solution space is limited to a feasible set F; the inference task is: $c^{1:M} = \arg\max_{c^{1:M} \in F(P^{1:M})} \sum_{i=1}^{M} score(S'^i = c^i)$.

The constraints used are: 1) No overlapping or embedding argument. 2) No duplicate argument for core arguments A0-A5 and AA. 3) For C-arg, there has to be an arg argument.

6 Experimental Setup

In this section, we discuss our experimental setup for the semantic role labeling system. Similar to the CoNLL 2005 shared tasks, we train our system using sections 02-21 of the Wall Street Journal portion of Penn TreeBank labeled with PropBank. We test our system on an annotated Brown corpus consisting of three sections (ck01 - ck03).

Since we need to annotate new sentences with syntactic parse, POS tags and shallow parses, we do not use annotations in the CoNLL distribution; instead, we re-annotate the data using publicly available part of speech tagger and shallow parser[1], Charniak 2005 parser (Charniak and Johnson, 2005) and Stanford parser (Klein and Manning, 2003).

Our baseline SRL model is an implementation of (Punyakanok et al., 2008) which was the top performing system in CoNLL 2005 shared task. Due to space constraints, we omit the details of the system and refer readers to (Punyakanok et al., 2008).

7 Results

Results for ADUT using only the top parse of Charniak and Stanford are shown in Table 2. The Baseline model using top Charniak parse (*BaseLine-Charniak*) and top Stanford parse (*BaseLine-Stanford*) score respectively 76.4 and 73.3 on the

[1] http://cogcomp.cs.illinois.edu/page/software

WSJ test set. Since we are interested in adaptation, we report and compare results for Brown test set only. On this set, both *ADUT-Charniak* and *ADUT-Stanford* significantly outperform their respective baselines. We compare with the state-of-the-art system of (Surdeanu et al., 2007). In (Surdeanu et al., 2007), the authors use three models: Model 1 and 2 do sequential tagging of chunks obtained from shallow parse and full parse. Model 3 assumes each predicate argument maps to one syntactic constituent and classifies it individually. So Model 3 matches our baseline model. *ADUT-Charniak* outperforms the best individual model (Model 2) of (Surdeanu et al., 2007) by 1.6% and Model 3 by 3.9%. We also tested another system that used cluster features and word embedding features computed following (Collobert and Weston, 2008). But we did not see any performance improvement on Brown over baseline.

System	P	R	F1
BaseLine-Charniak	69.6	61.8	65.5
ADUT-Charniak	72.75	66.1	**69.3**
BaseLine-Stanford	70.8	56.5	62.9
ADUT-Stanford	72.5	60.0	65.7
(Surdeanu et al., 2007)(Model 2)	71.8	64.0	67.7
(Surdeanu et al., 2007)(Model 3)	72.4	59.7	65.4

Table 2: Comparing single parse system on Brown.

All state-of-the-art systems for SRL are a combination of multiple systems. So we combined *ADUT-Stanford*, *ADUT-Charniak* and another system *ADUT-Charniak-2* based on 2nd best Charniak parse using joint inference. In Table 3, We compare with (Punyakanok et al., 2008) which was the top performing system in CoNLL 2005 shared task. We also compare with the multi parse system of (Toutanova et al., 2008) which uses a global joint model using multiple parse trees. In (Surdeanu et al., 2007), the authors experimented with several combination strategies. Their first combination strategy was similar to ours where they directly combined the outputs of different systems using constraints (denoted as *Cons* in Table 3). But their best result on Brown set was obtained by treating the combination of multiple systems as a meta-learning problem. They trained a new model to score candidate arguments produced by individual systems before combining them through constraints (denoted as *LBI* in Table 3). We also compare with (Huang and Yates, 2010) where the authors retrained a SRL model using HMM features learned over unlabeled data of WSJ and Brown.

System	P	R	F1	Retrain
(Punyakanok et al., 2008)	73.4	62.9	67.8	×
(Toutanova et al., 2008)	NR	NR	68.8	×
(Surdeanu et al., 2007) (Cons)	78.2	62.1	69.2	×
(Surdeanu et al., 2007) (LBI)	81.8	61.3	70.1	×
ADUT-combined	74.3	67.0	**70.5**	×
(Huang and Yates, 2010)	77.0	70.9	**73.8**	✓

Table 3: Comparison of the multi parse system on Brown.

Table 3 shows that *ADUT-Combined* performs better than *(Surdeanu et al., 2007) (Cons)* when individual systems have been combined similarly. We believe that the techniques in (Surdeanu et al., 2007) of using multiple models of different kinds (two based on sequential tagging of chunks to capture arguments whose boundaries do not match a syntactic constituent) and training an additional model to combine the outputs of individual systems are orthogonal to the performance improvement that we have and applying these methods will further increase the performance of our final system which is a research direction we want to pursue in future.

We did an ablation study to determine which transformations help and by how much. Table 4 presents results when only one transformation is active at a time. We see that each transformation improves over the baseline.

The effect of the transformation of *Replacement of Predicate* on infrequent verbs is shown in Table 5. This transformation improves F1 as much as 6% on infrequent verbs.

The running time for *ADUT-Charniak* on Brown set is 8 hours compared to SRL training time of 20 hours. Average number of transformed sentences generated by *ADUT-Charniak* for every sentence from Brown is 36. The times are calculated based on a machine with 2x 6-Core Xeon X5650 Processor with 48G memory.

Transformation	P	R	F1
Baseline	69.6	61.8	65.5
Replacement of Unknown Words	70.6	62.1	**66.1**
Replacement of Predicate	71.2	62.8	**66.8**
Replacement of Quotes	71.0	63.4	**67.0**
Simplification	70.3	62.9	**66.4**
RuleTransformation	70.9	62.2	**66.2**
Sentence Split	70.8	62.1	**66.2**
Together	72.75	66.1	**69.3**

Table 4: Ablation Study for ADUT-Charniak

Frequency	Baseline	Replacement of Predicate
0	64.2	**67.8**
less than 3	59.7	**65.1**
less than 7	58.9	**64.8**
all predicates	65.5	**66.78**

Table 5: Performance on Infrequent Verbs for the Transformation of *Replacement of Predicate*

8 Related Work

Traditional adaptation techniques like (DauméIII, 2007; Chelba and Acero, 2004; Finkel and Manning, 2009; Jiang and Zhai, 2007; Blitzer et al., 2006; Huang and Yates, 2009; Ando and Zhang, 2005; Ming-wei Chang and Roth, 2010) need to retrain the model for every new domain. In (Umansky-Pesin et al., 2010), there was no retraining; instead, a POS tag was predicted for every unknown word in the new domain by considering contexts of that word collected by web search queries. We differ from them in that our transformations are *label-preserving*; moreover, our transformations aim at making the target text resemble the training text. We also present an algorithm to learn transformation rules from training data. Our application domain, SRL, is also more complex and structured than POS tagging.

In (McClosky et al., 2010), the task of multiple source parser adaptation was introduced. The authors trained parsing models on corpora from different domains and given a new text, used a linear combination of trained models. Their approach requires annotated data from multiple domains as well as unlabeled data for the new domain, which is not needed in our framework. In (Huang and Yates, 2010), the authors trained a HMM over the Brown test set and the WSJ unlabeled data. They derived features from Viterbi optimal states of single words and spans of words and retrained their models using these features. In (Vickrey and Koller, 2008), a large number of hand-written rules were used to simplify the parse trees and reduce syntactic variation to overcome feature sparsity. We have several types of transformations, and use less than 10 simplification heuristics, based on replacing larger phrases with smaller phrases and deleting unnecessary parse tree nodes. There are also some methods for unsupervised semantic role labeling (Swier and Stevenson, 2004), (Abend et al., 2009) that easily adapt across domains but their performances are not comparable to supervised systems.

9 Conclusion

We presented a framework for adaptating natural language *text* so that *models* can be used across domains without modification. Our framework supports adapting to new domains without any data or knowledge of the target domain. We showed that our approach significantly improves SRL performance over the state-of-the-art single parse based system on Brown set. In the future, we would like to extend this approach to other NLP problems and study how combining multiple systems can further improve its performance and robustness.

Acknowledgements This research is sponsored by the Army Research Laboratory (ARL) under agreement W911NF-09-2-0053 and by the Defense Advanced Research Projects Agency (DARPA) Machine Reading Program under Air Force Research Laboratory (AFRL) prime contract no. FA8750-09-C-0181. Any opinions, findings, conclusions or recommendations are those of the authors and do not necessarily reflect the view of the ARL, the DARPA, AFRL, or the US government.

References

Omri Abend, Roi Reichart, and Ari Rappoport. 2009. Unsupervised argument identification for semantic role labeling . In *Proceedings of the ACL*.

Rie Kubota Ando and Tong Zhang. 2005. A framework for learning predictive structures from multiple labeled and unlabeled data . *Journal of Machine Learning Research.*

Christopher Bishop. 1995. *Neural Networks for Pattern recognition, chapter 6.4: Modelling conditional distributions.* Oxford University Press.

John Blitzer, Ryan McDonald, and Fernando Pereira. 2006. Domain adaptation with structural correspondence learning. In *Proceedings of the Conference on Empirical Methods in Natural Language Processing (EMNLP).*

Peter F. Brown, Peter V. deSouza, Robert L. Mercer, Vincent J. D. Pietra, and Jenifer C. Lai. 1992. Class-based n-gram models of natural language. *Computational Linguistics*, 18(4):467–479.

Xavier Carreras and Lluís Màrquez. 2005. Introduction to the conll-2005 shared task: Semantic role labeling . In *Proceedings of CoNLL.*

Eugene Charniak and Mark Johnson. 2005. Coarse-to-fine n-best parsing and maxent discriminative reranking. In *Proceedings of ACL.*

Ciprian Chelba and Alex Acero. 2004. Little data can help a lot. In *Proceedings of the Conference on Empirical Methods in Natural Language Processing (EMNLP).*

Ronan Collobert and Jason Weston. 2008. A unified architecture for natural language processing: Deep neural networks with multitask learning. In *Proceedings of ICML.*

Hal DauméIII. 2007. Frustratingly easy domain adaptation. In *Proceedings of the the Annual Meeting of the Association of Computational Linguistics (ACL).*

Jenny R. Finkel and Christopher D. Manning. 2009. Hierarchical bayesian domain adaptation . In *Proceedings of NAACL.*

Fei Huang and Alexander Yates. 2009. Distributional representations for handling sparsity in supervised sequence-labeling . In *Proceedings of ACL.*

Fei Huang and Alexander Yates. 2010. Open-domain semantic role labeling by modeling word spans. In *Proceedings of ACL.*

Jing Jiang and ChengXiang Zhai. 2007. Instance weighting for domain adaptation in nlp. In *Proceedings of ACL.*

Dan Klein and Christopher D. Manning. 2003. Fast exact inference with a factored model for natural language parsing. In *Proceedings of NIPS.*

Percy Liang. 2005. Semi-supervised learning for natural language. *Masters thesis, Massachusetts Institute of Technology.*

David McClosky, Eugene Charniak, and Mark Johnson. 2010. Automatic domain adaptation for parsing. In *Proceedings of NAACL.*

Michael Connor Ming-wei Chang and Dan Roth. 2010. The necessity of combining adaptation methods. In *Proceedings of the Conference on Empirical Methods in Natural Language Processing (EMNLP)*, Massachusetts, USA.

Vasin Punyakanok, Dan Roth, and Wen tau Yih. 2008. The importance of syntactic parsing and inference in semantic role labeling. *Computational Linguistics*, 34(2).

Mihai Surdeanu, Lluís Màrquez, Xavier Carreras, and Pere R. Comas. 2007. Combination strategies for semantic role labeling. *Journal of Artificial Intelligence Research*, 29:105–151.

Robert S. Swier and Suzanne Stevenson. 2004. Unsupervised semantic role labelling. In *Proceedings of Empirical Methods in Natural Language Processing.*

Kristina Toutanova, Aria Haghighi, and Christopher D. Manning. 2008. A global joint model for semantic role labeling. *Computational Linguistics*, 34:161–191.

Shulamit Umansky-Pesin, Roi Reichart, and Ari Rappoport. 2010. A multi-domain web-based algorithm for pos tagging of unknown words . In *Proceedings of Coling.*

David Vickrey and Daphne Koller. 2008. Sentence simplification for semantic role labeling. In *Proceedings of the ACL-HLT.*

Learning with Lookahead: Can History-Based Models Rival Globally Optimized Models?

Yoshimasa Tsuruoka[†*] **Yusuke Miyao**[‡*] **Jun'ichi Kazama**[*]
[†] Japan Advanced Institute of Science and Technology (JAIST), Japan
[‡] National Institute of Informatics (NII), Japan
[*] National Institute of Information and Communications Technology (NICT), Japan
tsuruoka@jaist.ac.jp yusuke@nii.ac.jp kazama@nict.go.jp

Abstract

This paper shows that the performance of history-based models can be significantly improved by performing lookahead in the state space when making each classification decision. Instead of simply using the best action output by the classifier, we determine the best action by looking into possible sequences of future actions and evaluating the final states realized by those action sequences. We present a perceptron-based parameter optimization method for this learning framework and show its convergence properties. The proposed framework is evaluated on part-of-speech tagging, chunking, named entity recognition and dependency parsing, using standard data sets and features. Experimental results demonstrate that history-based models with lookahead are as competitive as globally optimized models including conditional random fields (CRFs) and structured perceptrons.

1 Introduction

History-based models have been a popular approach in a variety of natural language processing (NLP) tasks including part-of-speech (POS) tagging, named entity recognition, and syntactic parsing (Ratnaparkhi, 1996; McCallum et al., 2000; Yamada and Matsumoto, 2003; Nivre et al., 2004). The idea is to decompose the complex structured prediction problem into a series of simple classification problems and use a machine learning-based classifier to make each decision using the information about the past decisions and partially completed structures as features.

Although history-based models have many practical merits, their accuracy is often surpassed by globally optimized models such as CRFs (Lafferty et al., 2001) and structured perceptrons (Collins, 2002), mainly due to the *label bias problem*. Today, vanilla history-based models such as maximum entropy Markov models (MEMMs) are probably not the first choice for those who are looking for a machine learning model that can deliver the state-of-the-art accuracy for their NLP task. Globally optimized models, by contrast, are gaining popularity in the community despite their relatively high computational cost.

In this paper, we argue that history-based models are not something that should be left behind in research history, by demonstrating that their accuracy can be significantly improved by incorporating a *lookahead* mechanism into their decision-making process. It should be emphasized that we use the word "lookahead" differently from some literature on syntactic parsing in which lookahead simply means looking at the succeeding words to choose the right parsing actions. In this paper, we use the word to refer to the process of choosing the best action by considering different sequences of future actions and evaluating the structures realized by those sequences. In other words, we introduce a lookahead mechanism that performs a search in the space of future actions.

We present a perceptron-based training algorithm that can work with the lookahead process, together with a proof of convergence. The algorithm enables us to tune the weight of the perceptron in such a way that we can correctly choose the right action for the

Proceedings of the Fifteenth Conference on Computational Natural Language Learning, pages 238–246,
Portland, Oregon, USA, 23–24 June 2011.

State	Operation	Stack	Queue
0			I saw a dog with eyebrows
1	shift	I	saw a dog with eyebrows
2	shift	I saw	a dog with eyebrows
3	reduce$_L$	saw(I)	a dog with eyebrows
...			
4		saw(I) dog(a)	with eyebrows
5	shift	saw(I) dog(a) with	eyebrows
6	shift	saw(I) dog(a) with eyebrows	
7	reduce$_R$	saw(I) dog(a) with(eyebrows)	
8	reduce$_R$	saw(I) dog(a, with(eyebrows))	
5'	reduce$_R$	saw(I, dog(a))	with eyebrows
6'	shift	saw(I, dog(a)) with	eyebrows
7'	shift	saw(I, dog(a)) with eyebrows	
8'	reduce $_R$	saw(I, dog(a)) with(eyebrows)	
9'	reduce $_R$	saw(I, dog(a), with(eyebrows))	

Figure 1: Shift-reduce dependency parsing

current state at each decision point, given the information obtained from a search.

To answer the question of whether the history-based models enhanced with lookahead can actually compete with globally optimized models, we evaluate the proposed framework with a range of standard NLP tasks, namely, POS tagging, text chunking (a.k.a. shallow parsing), named entity recognition, and dependency parsing.

This paper is organized as follows. Section 2 presents the idea of lookahead with a motivating example from dependency parsing. Section 3 describes our search algorithm for lookahead and a perceptron-based training algorithm. Experimental results on POS tagging, chunking, named entity recognition, and dependency parsing are presented in Section 4. We discuss relationships between our approach and some related work in Section 5. Section 6 offers concluding remarks with some potential research directions.

2 Motivation

This section describes an example of dependency parsing that motivates the introduction of lookahead in history-based models.

A well-known history-based approach to dependency parsing is *shift-reduce parsing*. This algorithm maintains two data structures, *stack* and *queue*: A stack stores intermediate parsing results, and a queue stores words to read. Two operations (actions), *shift* and *reduce*, on these data structures construct dependency relations one by one.

For example, assume that we are given the following sentence.

I saw a dog with eyebrows.

In the beginning, we have an empty stack, and a queue filled with a list of input words (State 0 in Figure 1). The *shift* operation moves the left-most element of the queue to the stack. In this example, State 1 is obtained by applying *shift* to State 0. After the two *shift* operations, we reach State 2, in which the stack has two elements. When we have two or more elements in the stack, we can apply the other operation, *reduce*, which merges the two stack elements by creating a dependency relation between them. When we apply *reduce*$_L$, which means to have the left element as a dependent of the right element, we reach State 3: The word "I" has disappeared from the stack and instead it is attached to its head word "saw".[1] In this way, the shift-reduce parsing constructs a dependency tree by reading words from the queue and constructing dependency relations on the stack.

[1] In Figure 1, $H(D_1, D_2, \ldots)$ indicates that $D_1, D_2, \ldots$ are the dependents of the head H.

Let's say we have now arrived at State 4 after several operations. At this state, we cannot simply determine whether we should *shift* or *reduce*. In such cases, conventional methods rely on a multi-class classifier to determine the next operation. That is, a classifier is used to select the most plausible operation, by referring to the features about the current state, such as surface forms and POSs of words in the stack and the queue.

In the lookahead strategy, we make this decision by referring to future states. For example, if we apply *shift* to State 4, we will reach State 8 in the end, which indicates that "with" attaches to "dog". The other way, i.e., applying *reduce*$_R$ to State 4, eventually arrives at State 9', indicating "with" attaches to "saw". These future states indicate that we were implicitly resolving PP-attachment ambiguity at State 4. While conventional methods attempt to resolve such ambiguity using surrounding features at State 4, the lookahead approach resolves the same ambiguity by referring to the future states, for example, State 8 and 9'. Because future states can provide additional and valuable information for ambiguity resolution, improved accuracy is expected.

It should be noted that Figure 1 only shows one sequence of operations for each choice of operation at State 4. In general, however, the number of potential sequences grows exponentially with the lookahead depth, so the lookahead approach requires us to pay the price as the increase of computational cost. The primary goal of this paper is to demonstrate that the cost is actually worth it.

3 Learning with Lookahead

This section presents our framework for incorporating lookahead in history-based models. In this paper, we focus on *deterministic* history-based models although our method could be generalized to non-deterministic cases.

We use the word "state" to refer to a partially completed analysis as well as the collection of historical information available at each decision point in deterministic history-based analysis. State transitions are made by "actions" that are defined at each state. In the example of dependency parsing presented in Section 2, a state contains all the information about past operations, stacks, and queues as

Input
  d: remaining depth of search
  S_0: current state
Output
  S: state of highest score
  v: highest score

function SEARCH(d, S_0)
  if $d = 0$ **then**
    return $(S_0, \boldsymbol{w} \cdot \phi(S_0))$
  $(S, v) \leftarrow (\text{null}, -\infty)$
  for each $a \in$ POSSIBLEACTIONS(S_0)
    $S_1 \leftarrow$ UPDATESTATE(S_0, a)
    $(S', v') \leftarrow$ SEARCH($d-1, S_1$)
    if $v' > v$ **then**
      $(S, v) \leftarrow (S', v')$
  return (S, v)

Figure 2: Search algorithm.

well as the observation (i.e. the words in the sentence). The possible actions are *shift*, *reduce*$_R$, and *reduce*$_L$. In the case of POS tagging, for example, a state is the words and the POS tags assigned to the words on the left side of the current target word (if the tagging is conducted in the left-to-right manner), and the possible actions are simply defined by the POS tags in the annotation tag set.

3.1 Search

With lookahead, we choose the best action at each decision point by considering possible sequences of future actions and the states realized by those sequences. In other words, we need to perform a *search* for each possible action.

Figure 2 describes our search algorithm in pseudo code. The algorithm performs a depth-first search to find the state of the highest score among the states in its search space, which is determined by the search depth d. This search process is implemented with a recursive function, which receives the remaining search depth and the current state as its input and returns the state of the highest score together with its score.

We assume a linear scoring model, i.e., the score of each state S can be computed by taking the dot product of the current weight vector $\boldsymbol{w}$ and $\phi(S)$, the feature vector representation of the state. The

1: **Input**
2: C: perceptron margin
3: D: depth of lookahead search
4: S_0: current state
5: a_c: correct action
6:
7: **procedure** UPDATEWEIGHT(C, D, S_0, a_c)
8: $(a^*, S^*, v) \leftarrow (\text{null}, \text{null}, -\infty)$
9: **for each** $a \in$ POSSIBLEACTIONS(S_0)
10: $S_1 \leftarrow$ UPDATESTATE(S_0, a)
11: $(S', v') \leftarrow$SEARCH(D, S_1)
12: **if** $a = a_c$ **then**
13: $v' \leftarrow v' - C$
14: $S_c^* \leftarrow S'$
15: **if** $v' > v$ **then**
16: $(a^*, S^*, v) \leftarrow (a, S', v')$
17: **if** $a^* \neq a_c$ **then**
18: $\boldsymbol{w} \leftarrow \boldsymbol{w} + \phi(S_c^*) - \phi(S^*)$

Figure 3: Perceptron weight update

scores are computed at each leaf node of the search tree and backed up to the root.[2]

Clearly, the time complexity of deterministic tagging/parsing with this search algorithm is $O(nm^{D+1})$, where n is the number of actions needed to process the sentence, m is the (average) number of possible actions at each state, and D is the search depth. It should be noted that the time complexity of k-th order CRFs is $O(nm^{k+1})$, so a history-based model with k-depth lookahead is comparable to k-th order CRFs in terms of training/testing time.

Unlike CRFs, our framework does not require the locality of features since it is history-based, i.e., the decisions can be conditioned on arbitrary features. One interpretation of our learning framework is that it trades off the global optimality of the learned parameters against the flexibility of features.

3.2 Training a margin perceptron

We adapt a learning algorithm for margin perceptrons (Krauth and Mezard, 1987) to our purpose of optimizing the weight parameters for the lookahead search. Like other large margin approaches such as support vector machines, margin perceptrons are known to produce accurate models compared to perceptrons without a margin (Li et al., 2002).

Figure 3 shows our learning algorithm in pseudo code. The algorithm is very similar to the standard training algorithm for margin perceptrons, i.e., we update the weight parameters with the difference of two feature vectors (one corresponding to the correct action, and the other the action of the highest score) when the perceptron makes a mistake. The feature vector for the second best action is also used when the margin is not large enough. Notice that the feature vector for the second best action is automatically selected by using a simple trick of subtracting the margin parameter from the score for the correct action (Line 13 in Figure 3).

The only difference between our algorithm and the standard algorithm for margin perceptrons is that we use the states and their scores obtained from lookahead searches (Line 11 in Figure 3), which are backed up from the leaves of the search trees. In Appendix A, we provide a proof of the convergence of our training algorithm and show that the margin will approach at least half the true margin (assuming that the training data are linearly separable).

As in many studies using perceptrons, we average the weight vector over the whole training iterations at the end of the training (Collins, 2002).

4 Experiments

This section presents four sets of experimental results to show how the lookahead process improves the accuracy of history-based models in common NLP tasks.

4.1 Sequence prediction tasks

First, we evaluate our framework with three sequence prediction tasks: POS tagging, chunking, and named entity recognition. We compare our method with the CRF model, which is one of the de facto standard machine learning models for such sequence prediction tasks. We trained L1-regularized first-order CRF models using the efficient stochastic gradient descent (SGD)-based training method presented in Tsuruoka et al. (2009). Since our main in-

[2]In actual implementation, it is not efficient to compute the score of a state from scratch at each leaf node. For most of the standard features used in tagging and parsing, it is usually straight-forward to compute the scores incrementally every time the state is updated with an action.

terest is not in achieving the state-of-the-art results for those tasks, we did not conduct feature engineering to come up with elaborate features—we simply adopted the feature sets described in their paper (with an exception being tag trigram features tested in the POS tagging experiments). The experiments for these sequence prediction tasks were carried out using one core of a 3.33GHz Intel Xeon W5590 processor.

The first set of experiments is about POS tagging. The training and test data were created from the Wall Street Journal corpus of the Penn Treebank (Marcus et al., 1994). Sections 0-18 were used as the training data. Sections 19-21 were used for tuning the meta parameters for learning (the number of iterations and the margin C). Sections 22-24 were used for the final accuracy reports.

The experimental results are shown in Table 1. Note that the models in the top four rows use exactly the same feature set. It is clearly seen that the lookahead improves tagging accuracy, and our history-based models with lookahead is as accurate as the CRF model. We also created another set of models by simply adding tag trigram features, which cannot be employed by first-order CRF models. These features have slightly improved the tagging accuracy, and the final accuracy achieved by a search depth of 3 was comparable to some of the best results achieved by pure supervised learning in this task (Shen et al., 2007; Lavergne et al., 2010).

The second set of experiments is about chunking. We used the data set for the CoNLL 2000 shared task, which contains 8,936 sentences where each token is annotated with the "IOB" tags representing text chunks. The experimental results are shown in Table 2. Again, our history-based models with lookahead were slightly more accurate than the CRF model using exactly the same set of features. The accuracy achieved by the lookahead model with a search depth of 2 was comparable to the accuracy achieved by a computationally heavy combination of max-margin classifiers (Kudo and Matsumoto, 2001). We also tested the effectiveness of additional features of tag trigrams using the development data, but there was no improvement in the accuracy.

The third set of experiments is about named entity recognition. We used the data provided for the BioNLP/NLPBA 2004 shared task (Kim et al., 2004), which contains 18,546 sentences where each token is annotated with the "IOB" tags representing biomedical named entities. We performed the tagging in the right-to-left fashion because it is known that backward tagging is more accurate than forward tagging on this data set (Yoshida and Tsujii, 2007).

Table 3 shows the experimental results, together with some previous performance reports achieved by pure machine leaning methods (i.e. without rule-based post processing or external resources such as gazetteers). Our history-based model with no lookahead was considerably worse than the CRF model using the same set of features, but it was significantly improved by the introduction of lookahead and resulted in accuracy figures better than that of the CRF model.

4.2 Dependency parsing

We also evaluate our method in dependency parsing. We follow the most standard experimental setting for English dependency parsing: The Wall Street Journal portion of Penn Treebank is converted to dependency trees by using the head rules of Yamada and Matsumoto (2003).[3] The data is split into training (section 02-21), development (section 22), and test (section 23) sets. The parsing accuracy was evaluated with auto-POS data, i.e., we used our lookahead POS tagger (depth = 2) presented in the previous subsection to assign the POS tags for the development and test data. Unlabeled attachment scores for all words excluding punctuations are reported. The development set is used for tuning the meta parameters, while the test set is used for evaluating the final accuracy.

The parsing algorithm is the "arc-standard" method (Nivre, 2004), which is briefly described in Section 2. With this algorithm, state S corresponds to a parser configuration, i.e., the stack and the queue, and action a corresponds to shift, reduce$_L$, and reduce$_R$. In this experiment, we use the same set of feature templates as Huang and Sagae (2010).

Table 4 shows training time, test time, and parsing accuracy. In this table, "No lookahead (depth = 0)" corresponds to a conventional shift-reduce parsing method without any lookahead search. The results

[3]Penn2Malt is applied for this conversion, while dependency labels are removed.

	Training Time (sec)	Test Time (sec)	Accuracy
CRF (L1 regularization & SGD training)	847	3	97.11 %
No lookahead (depth = 0)	85	5	97.00 %
Lookahead (depth = 1)	294	9	97.19 %
Lookahead (depth = 2)	8,688	173	97.19 %
No lookahead (depth = 0) + tag trigram features	88	5	97.11 %
Lookahead (depth = 1) + tag trigram features	313	10	97.22 %
Lookahead (depth = 2) + tag trigram features	10,034	209	97.28 %
Structured perceptron (Collins, 2002)	n/a	n/a	97.11 %
Guided learning (Shen et al., 2007)	n/a	n/a	97.33 %
CRF with 4 billion features (Lavergne et al., 2010)	n/a	n/a	97.22 %

Table 1: Performance of English POS tagging (training times and accuracy scores on test data)

	Training time (sec)	Test time (sec)	F-measure
CRF (L1 regularization & SGD training)	74	1	93.66
No lookahead (depth = 0)	22	1	93.53
Lookahead (depth = 1)	73	1	93.77
Lookahead (depth = 2)	1,113	9	93.81
Voting of 8 SVMs (Kudo and Matsumoto, 2001)	n/a	n/a	93.91

Table 2: Performance of text chunking (training times and accuracy scores on test data).

clearly demonstrate that the lookahead search boosts parsing accuracy. As expected, training and test speed decreases, almost by a factor of three, which is the branching factor of the dependency parser.

The table also lists accuracy figures reported in the literature on shift-reduce dependency parsing. Most of the latest studies on shift-reduce dependency parsing employ dynamic programing or beam search, which implies that deterministic methods were not as competitive as those methods. It should also be noted that all of the listed studies learn structured perceptrons (Collins and Roark, 2004), while our parser learns locally optimized perceptrons. In this table, our parser without lookahead search (i.e. depth = 0) resulted in significantly lower accuracy than the previous studies. In fact, it is worse than the deterministic parser of Huang et al. (2009), which uses (almost) the same set of features. This is presumably due to the difference between locally optimized perceptrons and globally optimized structured perceptrons. However, our parser with lookahead search is significantly better than their deterministic parser, and its accuracy is close to the levels of the parsers with beam search.

5 Discussion

The reason why we introduced a lookahead mechanism into history-based models is that we wanted the model to be able to avoid making such mistakes that can be detected only in later stages. Probabilistic history-based models such as MEMMs should be able to avoid (at least some of) such mistakes by performing a Viterbi search to find the highest probability path of the actions. However, as pointed out by Lafferty et al. (2001), the per-state normalization of probabilities makes it difficult to give enough penalty to such incorrect sequences of actions, and that is primarily why MEMMs are outperformed by CRFs.

Perhaps the most relevant to our work in terms of learning is the general framework for search and learning problems in history-based models proposed by Daumé III and Marcu (2005). This framework, called LaSO (Learning as Search Optimization), can include many variations of search strategies such as beam search and A* search as a special case. Indeed, our lookahead framework could be regarded as a special case in which each search node con-

	Training time (sec)	Test time (sec)	F-measure
CRF (L1 regularization & SGD training)	235	4	71.63
No lookahead (depth = 0)	66	4	70.17
Lookahead (depth = 1)	91	4	72.28
Lookahead (depth = 2)	302	7	72.00
Lookahead (depth = 3)	2,419	33	72.21
Semi-Markov CRF (Okanohara et al., 2006)	n/a	n/a	71.48
Reranking (Yoshida and Tsujii, 2007)	n/a	n/a	72.65

Table 3: Performance of biomedical named entity recognition (training times and accuracy scores on test data).

	Training time (sec)	Test time (sec)	Accuracy
No lookahead (depth = 0)	1,937	4	89.73
Lookahead (depth = 1)	4,907	13	91.00
Lookahead (depth = 2)	12,800	31	91.10
Lookahead (depth = 3)	31,684	79	91.24
Beam search ($k = 64$) (Zhang and Clark, 2008)	n/a	n/a	91.4
Deterministic (Huang et al., 2009)	n/a	n/a	90.2
Beam search ($k = 16$) (Huang et al., 2009)	n/a	n/a	91.3
Dynamic programming (Huang and Sagae, 2010)	n/a	n/a	92.1

Table 4: Performance of English dependency parsing (training times and accuracy scores on test data).

sists of the next and lookahead actions[4], although the weight updating procedure differs in several minor points. Daumé III and Marcu (2005) did not try a lookahead search strategy, and to the best of our knowledge, this paper is the first that demonstrates that lookahead actually works well for various NLP tasks.

Performing lookahead is a very common technique for a variety of decision-making problems in the field of artificial intelligence. In computer chess, for example, programs usually need to perform a very deep search in the game tree to find a good move. Our decision-making problem is similar to that of computer Chess in many ways, although chess programs perform min-max searches rather than the "max" searches performed in our algorithm. Automatic learning of evaluation functions for chess programs can be seen as the training of a machine learning model. In particular, our learning algorithm is similar to the supervised approach (Tesauro, 2001; Hoki, 2006) in that the parameters are optimized based on the differences of the feature vectors realized by the correct and incorrect actions.

[4]In addition, the size of the search queue is always truncated to one for the deterministic decisions presented in this paper. Note, however, that our lookahead framework can also be combined with other search strategies such as beam search. In that case, the search queue is not necessarily truncated.

In history-based models, the order of actions is often very important. For example, backward tagging is considerably more accurate than forward tagging in biomedical named entity recognition. Our lookahead method is orthogonal to more elaborate techniques for determining the order of actions such as easy-first tagging/parsing strategies (Tsuruoka and Tsujii, 2005; Elhadad, 2010). We expect that incorporating such elaborate techniques in our framework will lead to improved accuracy, but we leave it for future work.

6 Conclusion

We have presented a simple and general framework for incorporating a lookahead process in history-based models and a perceptron-based training algorithm for the framework. We have conducted experiments using standard data sets for POS tagging, chunking, named entity recognition and dependency parsing, and obtained very promising results—the accuracy achieved by the history-based models enhanced with lookahead was as competitive as globally optimized models including CRFs.

In most of the experimental results, steady improvement in accuracy has been observed as the depth of the search is increased. Although it is not very practical to perform deeper searches with our current implementation—we naively explored all possible sequences of actions, future work should encompass extending the depths of search space by introducing elaborate pruning/search extension techniques.

In this work, we did not conduct extensive feature engineering for improving the accuracy of individual tasks because our primary goal with this paper is to present the learning framework itself. However, one of the major merits of using history-based models is that we are allowed to define arbitrary features on the partially completed structure. Another interesting direction of future work is to see how much we could improve the accuracy by performing extensive feature engineering in this particular learning framework.

Appendix A: Convergence of the Learning Procedure

Let $\{x^i, a^i_c\}_{i=1}^K$ be the training examples where a^i_c is the correct first action for decision point x^i, and let $\mathcal{S}^i$ be the set of all the states at the leaves of the search trees for x_i generated by the lookahead searches and $\mathcal{S}^i_c$ be the set of all the states at the leaves of the search tree for the correct action a^i_c. We also define $\overline{\mathcal{S}^i} = \mathcal{S}^i \setminus \mathcal{S}^i_c$. We write the weight vector before the k-th update as $\boldsymbol{w}^k$. We define $S^*_c = \underset{S\in\mathcal{S}^i_c}{\operatorname{argmax}}\, \boldsymbol{w}\cdot\phi(S)$ and $\overline{S^*} = \underset{\overline{S}\in\overline{\mathcal{S}^i}}{\operatorname{argmax}}\, \boldsymbol{w}\cdot\phi(\overline{S})$[5]. Then the update rule can be interpreted as $\boldsymbol{w}^{k+1} = \boldsymbol{w}^k + (\phi(S^*_c) - \phi(\overline{S^*}))$. Note that this update is performed only when $\phi(S_c)\cdot\boldsymbol{w}^k - C < \phi(\overline{S^*})\cdot\boldsymbol{w}^k$ for all $S_c \in \mathcal{S}_c$ since otherwise S^* in the learning algorithm cannot be a state with an incorrect first action. In other words, $\phi(S_c)\cdot\boldsymbol{w} - \phi(\overline{S^*})\cdot\boldsymbol{w} \geq C$ for all $S_c \in \mathcal{S}_c$ after convergence.

Given these definitions, we prove the convergence for the separable case. That is, we assume the existence of a weight vector $\boldsymbol{u}$ (with $||\boldsymbol{u}|| = 1$), $\delta\ (> 0)$, and $R\ (> 0)$ that satisfy:

$$\forall i, \forall S_c \in \mathcal{S}^i_c, \forall \overline{S} \in \overline{\mathcal{S}^i} \quad \phi(S_c)\cdot\boldsymbol{u} - \phi(\overline{S})\cdot\boldsymbol{u} \geq \delta,$$
$$\forall i, \forall S_c \in \mathcal{S}^i_c, \forall \overline{S} \in \overline{\mathcal{S}^i} \quad ||\phi(S_c) - \phi(\overline{S})|| \leq R.$$

The proof is basically an adaptation of the proofs in Collins (2002) and Li et al. (2002). First, we obtain the following relation:

$$\begin{aligned}\boldsymbol{w}^{k+1}\cdot\boldsymbol{u} &= \boldsymbol{w}^k\cdot\boldsymbol{u} + (\phi(S^*_c)\cdot\boldsymbol{u} - \phi(\overline{S^*})\cdot\boldsymbol{u})\\ &= \boldsymbol{w}^k\cdot\boldsymbol{u} + \delta \geq \boldsymbol{w}^1\cdot\boldsymbol{u} + k\delta = k\delta.\end{aligned}$$

Therefore, $||\boldsymbol{w}^{k+1}\cdot\boldsymbol{u}||^2 = ||\boldsymbol{w}^{k+1}||^2 \leq (k\delta)^2$ — (1). We assumed $\boldsymbol{w}^1 = \mathbf{0}$ but this is not an essential assumption.

Next, we also obtain:

$$\begin{aligned}||\boldsymbol{w}^{k+1}||^2 &\leq ||\boldsymbol{w}^k||^2 + 2(\phi(S^*_c) - \phi(\overline{S^*}))\cdot\boldsymbol{w}^k\\ &\quad + ||\phi(S^*_c) - \phi(\overline{S^*})||^2\\ &\leq ||\boldsymbol{w}^k||^2 + 2C + R^2\\ &\leq ||\boldsymbol{w}^1||^2 + k(R^2 + 2C) = k(R^2 + 2C) \text{— (2)}\end{aligned}$$

Combining (1) and (2), we obtain $k \leq (R^2 + 2C)/\delta^2$. That is, the number of updates is bounded from above, meaning that the learning procedure converges after a finite number of updates. Substituting this into (2) gives $||\boldsymbol{w}^{k+1}|| \leq (R^2 + 2C)/\delta$ — (3).

Finally, we analyze the margin achieved by the learning procedure after convergence. The margin, $\gamma(\boldsymbol{w})$, is defined as follows in this case.

$$\begin{aligned}\gamma(\boldsymbol{w}) &= \min_{x_i} \min_{S_c\in\mathcal{S}^i_c, \overline{S}\in\overline{\mathcal{S}^i}} \frac{\phi(S_c)\cdot\boldsymbol{w} - \phi(\overline{S})\cdot\boldsymbol{w}}{||\boldsymbol{w}||}\\ &= \min_{x_i} \min_{S_c\in\mathcal{S}^i_c} \frac{\phi(S_c)\cdot\boldsymbol{w} - \phi(\overline{S^*})\cdot\boldsymbol{w}}{||\boldsymbol{w}||}\end{aligned}$$

After convergence (i.e., $\boldsymbol{w} = \boldsymbol{w}^{k+1}$), $\phi(S_c)\cdot\boldsymbol{w} - \phi(\overline{S^*})\cdot\boldsymbol{w} \geq C$ for all $S_c \in \mathcal{S}_c$ as we noted. Together with (3), we obtain the following bound:

$$\begin{aligned}\gamma(\boldsymbol{w}) &\geq \min_{x_i} \frac{\delta C}{2C + R^2}\\ &= \frac{\delta C}{2C + R^2} = \left(\frac{\delta}{2}\right)\left(1 - \frac{R^2}{2C + R^2}\right)\end{aligned}$$

As can be seen, the margin approaches at least half the true margin, $\delta/2$ as $C \to \infty$ (at the cost of infinite number of updates).

[5] S^*_c and $\overline{S^*}$ depend on the weight vector at each point, but we omit it from the notation for brevity.

References

Michael Collins and Brian Roark. 2004. Incremental parsing with the perceptron algorithm. In *Proceedings of ACL*, pages 111–118.

Michael Collins. 2002. Discriminative training methods for hidden markov models: Theory and experiments with perceptron algorithms. In *Proceedings of EMNLP*, pages 1–8.

Hal Daumé III and Daniel Marcu. 2005. Learning as search optimization: Approximate large margin methods for structured prediction. In *Proceedings of ICML*, pages 169–176.

Yoav Goldbergand Michael Elhadad. 2010. An efficient algorithm for easy-first non-directional dependency parsing. In *Proceedings of NAACL-HLT*, pages 742–750.

Kunihito Hoki. 2006. Optimal control of minimax search results to learn positional evaluation. In *Proceedings of the 11th Game Programming Workshop (GPW)*, pages 78–83 (in Japanese).

Liang Huang and Kenji Sagae. 2010. Dynamic programming for linear-time incremental parsing. In *Proceedings of ACL*, pages 1077–1086.

Liang Huang, Wenbin Jiang, and Qun Liu. 2009. Bilingually-constrained (monolingual) shift-reduce parsing. In *Proceedings of EMNLP*, pages 1222–1231.

J.-D. Kim, T. Ohta, Y. Tsuruoka, Y. Tateisi, and N. Collier. 2004. Introduction to the bio-entity recognition task at JNLPBA. In *Proceedings of the International Joint Workshop on Natural Language Processing in Biomedicine and its Applications (JNLPBA)*, pages 70–75.

W Krauth and M Mezard. 1987. Learning algorithms with optimal stability in neural networks. *Journal of Phisics A*, 20(11):L745–L752.

Taku Kudo and Yuji Matsumoto. 2001. Chunking with support vector machines. In *Proceedings of NAACL*.

John Lafferty, Andrew McCallum, and Fernando Pereira. 2001. Conditional random fields: Probabilistic models for segmenting and labeling sequence data. In *Proceedings of ICML*, pages 282–289.

Thomas Lavergne, Olivier Cappé, and François Yvon. 2010. Practical very large scale CRFs. In *Proceedings of ACL*, pages 504–513.

Yaoyong Li, Hugo Zaragoza, Ralf Herbrich, John Shawe-Taylor, and Jaz S. Kandola. 2002. The perceptron algorithm with uneven margins. In *Proceedings of ICML*, pages 379–386.

Mitchell P. Marcus, Beatrice Santorini, and Mary Ann Marcinkiewicz. 1994. Building a large annotated corpus of English: The Penn Treebank. *Computational Linguistics*, 19(2):313–330.

Andrew McCallum, Dayne Freitag, and Fernando Pereira. 2000. Maximum entropy markov models for information extraction and segmentation. In *Proceedings of ICML*, pages 591–598.

Joakim Nivre, Johan Hall, and Jens Nilsson. 2004. Memory-based dependency parsing. In *Proceedings of CoNLL*, pages 49–56.

Joakim Nivre. 2004. Incrementality in deterministic dependency parsing. In *ACL 2004 Workshop on Incremental Parsing: Bringing Engineering and Cognition Together*, pages 50–57.

Daisuke Okanohara, Yusuke Miyao, Yoshimasa Tsuruoka, and Jun'ichi Tsujii. 2006. Improving the scalability of semi-markov conditional random fields for named entity recognition. In *Proceedings of COLING/ACL*, pages 465–472.

Adwait Ratnaparkhi. 1996. A maximum entropy model for part-of-speech tagging. In *Proceedings of EMNLP 1996*, pages 133–142.

Libin Shen, Giorgio Satta, and Aravind Joshi. 2007. Guided learning for bidirectional sequence classification. In *Proceedings of ACL*, pages 760–767.

Gerald Tesauro, 2001. *Comparison training of chess evaluation functions*, pages 117–130. Nova Science Publishers, Inc.

Yoshimasa Tsuruoka and Jun'ichi Tsujii. 2005. Bidirectional inference with the easiest-first strategy for tagging sequence data. In *Proceedings of HLT/EMNLP 2005*, pages 467–474.

Yoshimasa Tsuruoka, Jun'ichi Tsujii, and Sophia Ananiadou. 2009. Stochastic gradient descent training for l1-regularized log-linear models with cumulative penalty. In *Proceedings of ACL-IJCNLP*, pages 477–485.

Hiroyasu Yamada and Yuji Matsumoto. 2003. Statistical dependency analysis with support vector machines. In *Proceedings of IWPT*, pages 195–206.

Kazuhiro Yoshida and Jun'ichi Tsujii. 2007. Reranking for biomedical named-entity recognition. In *Proceedings of ACL Workshop on BioNLP*, pages 209–216.

Yue Zhang and Stephen Clark. 2008. A tale of two parsers: investigating and combining graphbased and transition-based dependency parsing using beam-search. In *Proceedings of EMNLP*, pages 562–571.

Learning Discriminative Projections for Text Similarity Measures

Wen-tau Yih **Kristina Toutanova** **John C. Platt** **Christopher Meek**
Microsoft Research
One Microsoft Way
Redmond, WA 98052, USA
{scottyih,kristout,jplatt,meek}@microsoft.com

Abstract

Traditional text similarity measures consider each term similar only to itself and do not model semantic relatedness of terms. We propose a novel discriminative training method that projects the raw term vectors into a common, low-dimensional vector space. Our approach operates by finding the optimal matrix to minimize the loss of the pre-selected similarity function (e.g., cosine) of the projected vectors, and is able to efficiently handle a large number of training examples in the high-dimensional space. Evaluated on two very different tasks, cross-lingual document retrieval and ad relevance measure, our method not only outperforms existing state-of-the-art approaches, but also achieves high accuracy at low dimensions and is thus more efficient.

1 Introduction

Measures of text similarity have many applications and have been studied extensively in both the NLP and IR communities. For example, a combination of corpus and knowledge based methods have been invented for judging word similarity (Lin, 1998; Agirre et al., 2009). Similarity derived from a large-scale Web corpus has been used for automatically extending lists of typed entities (Vyas and Pantel, 2009). Judging the degree of similarity between documents is also fundamental to classical IR problems such as document retrieval (Manning et al., 2008). In all these applications, the vector-based similarity method is the most widely used. Term vectors are first constructed to represent the original text objects, where each term is associated with a weight indicating its importance. A pre-selected function operating on these vectors, such as cosine, is used to output the final similarity score. This approach has not only proved to be effective, but is also efficient. For instance, only the term vectors rather than the raw data need to be stored. A pruned inverse index can be built to support fast similarity search.

However, the main weakness of this term-vector representation is that different but semantically related terms are not matched and cannot influence the final similarity score. As an illustrative example, suppose the two compared term-vectors are: {*purchase*:0.4, *used*:0.3, *automobile*:0.2} and {*buy*:0.3, *pre-owned*: 0.5, *car*: 0.4}. Even though the two vectors represent very similar concepts, their similarity score will be 0, for functions like cosine, overlap or Jaccard. Such an issue is more severe in cross-lingual settings. Because language vocabularies typically have little overlap, term-vector representations are completely inapplicable to measuring similarity between documents in different languages. The general strategy to handle this problem is to map the raw representation to a common *concept* space, where extensive approaches have been proposed. Existing methods roughly fall into three categories. Generative topic models like Latent Dirichlet Allocation (LDA) (Blei et al., 2003) assume that the terms are sampled by probability distributions governed by hidden topics. Linear projection methods like Latent Semantic Analysis (LSA) (Deerwester et al., 1990) learn a projection matrix and map the original term-vectors to the dense low-dimensional space. Finally, metric learning approaches for high-dimensional spaces have

Proceedings of the Fifteenth Conference on Computational Natural Language Learning, pages 247–256,
Portland, Oregon, USA, 23–24 June 2011.

also been proposed (Davis and Dhillon, 2008).

In this paper, we propose a new projection learning framework, Similarity Learning via Siamese Neural Network (S2Net), to discriminatively learn the concept vector representations of input text objects. Following the general Siamese neural network architecture (Bromley et al., 1993), our approach trains two identical networks concurrently. The input layer corresponds to the original term vector and the output layer is the projected concept vector. Model parameters (i.e., the weights on the edges) are equivalently the projection matrix. Given pairs of raw term vectors and their labels (e.g., similar or not), the model is trained by minimizing the loss of the similarity scores of the output vectors. S2Net is closely related to the linear projection and metric learning approaches, but enjoys additional advantages over existing methods. While its model form is identical to that of LSA, CCA and OPCA, its objective function can be easily designed to match the true evaluation metric of interest for the target task, which leads to better performance. Compared to existing high-dimensional metric learning methods, S2Net can learn from a much larger number of labeled examples. These two properties are crucial in helping S2Net outperform existing methods. For retrieving comparable cross-lingual documents, S2Net achieves higher accuracy than the best approach (OPCA) at a much lower dimension of the concept space (500 vs. 2,000). In a monolingual setting, where the task is to judge the relevance of an ad landing page to a query, S2Net also has the best performance when compared to a number of approaches, including the raw TFIDF cosine baseline.

In the rest of the paper, we first survey some existing work in Sec. 2, with an emphasis on approaches included in our experimental comparison. We present our method in Sec. 3 and report on an extensive experimental study in Sec. 4. Other related work is discussed in Sec. 5 and finally Sec. 6 concludes the paper.

2 Previous Work

In this section, we briefly review existing approaches for mapping high-dimensional term-vectors to a low-dimensional concept space.

2.1 Generative Topic Models

Probabilistic Latent Semantic Analysis (PLSA) (Hofmann, 1999) assumes that each document has a document-specific distribution θ over some finite number K of topics, where each token in a document is independently generated by first selecting a topic z from a multinomial distribution $\text{MULTI}(\theta)$, and then sampling a word token from the topic-specific word distribution for the chosen topic $\text{MULTI}(\phi_z)$. Latent Dirichlet Allocation (LDA) (Blei et al., 2003) generalizes PLSA to a proper generative model for documents and places Dirichlet priors over the parameters θ and ϕ. In the experiments in this paper, our implementation of PLSA is LDA with maximum a posteriori (MAP) inference, which was shown to be comparable to the current best Bayesian inference methods for LDA (Asuncion et al., 2009).

Recently, these topic models have been generalized to handle pairs or tuples of corresponding documents, which could be translations in multiple languages, or documents in the same language that are considered similar. For instance, the Poly-lingual Topic Model (PLTM) (Mimno et al., 2009) is an extension to LDA that views documents in a tuple as having a shared topic vector θ. Each of the documents in the tuple uses θ to select the topics z of tokens, but could use a different (language-specific) word-topic-distribution $\text{MULTI}(\phi_z^L)$. Two additional models, Joint PLSA (JPLSA) and Coupled PLSA (CPLSA) were introduced in (Platt et al., 2010). JPLSA is a close variant of PLTM when documents of all languages share the same word-topic distribution parameters, and MAP inference is performed instead of Bayesian. CPLSA extends JPLSA by constraining paired documents to not only share the same prior topic distribution θ, but to also have similar fractions of tokens assigned to each topic. This constraint is enforced on expectation using posterior regularization (Ganchev et al., 2009).

2.2 Linear Projection Methods

The earliest method for projecting term vectors into a low-dimensional concept space is Latent Semantic Analysis (LSA) (Deerwester et al., 1990). LSA models all documents in a corpus using a $n \times d$ document-term matrix $\mathbf{D}$ and performs singular value decomposition (SVD) on $\mathbf{D}$. The k biggest singular values are then used to find the $d \times k$ projection matrix. Instead of SVD, LSA can be done by applying eigen-decomposition on the correlation matrix between terms $\mathbf{C} = \mathbf{D}^T\mathbf{D}$. This is very similar to principal component analysis (PCA), where a covariance matrix between terms is used. In practice, term vectors are very sparse and their means are close to 0. Therefore, the correlation matrix is in fact close to the covariance matrix.

To model pairs of comparable documents, LSA/PCA has been extended in different ways. For instance, Cross-language Latent Semantic Indexing (CL-LSI) (Dumais et al., 1997) applies LSA to concatenated comparable documents from different languages. Oriented Principal Component Analysis (OPCA) (Diamantaras and Kung, 1996; Platt et al., 2010) solves a generalized eigen problem by introducing a noise covariance matrix to ensure that comparable documents can be projected closely. Canonical Correlation Analysis (CCA) (Vinokourov et al., 2003) finds projections that maximize the cross-covariance between the projected vectors.

2.3 Distance Metric Learning

Measuring the similarity between two vectors can be viewed as equivalent to measuring their distance, as the cosine score has a bijection mapping to the Euclidean distance of unit vectors. Most work on metric learning learns a Mahalanobis distance, which generalizes the standard squared Euclidean distance by modeling the similarity of elements in different dimensions using a positive semi-definite matrix $\mathbf{A}$. Given two vectors $\mathbf{x}$ and $\mathbf{y}$, their squared Mahalanobis distance is: $d_{\mathbf{A}} = (\mathbf{x} - \mathbf{y})^T\mathbf{A}(\mathbf{x} - \mathbf{y})$. However, the computational complexity of learning a general Mahalanobis matrix is at least $O(n^2)$, where n is the dimensionality of the input vectors. Therefore, such methods are not practical for high dimensional problems in the text domain.

In order to tackle this issue, special metric learning approaches for high-dimensional spaces have been proposed. For example, high dimension low-rank (HDLR) metric learning (Davis and Dhillon, 2008) constrains the form of $\mathbf{A} = \mathbf{U}\mathbf{U}^T$, where $\mathbf{U}$ is similar to the regular projection matrix, and adapts information-theoretic metric learning (ITML) (Davis et al., 2007) to learn $\mathbf{U}$.

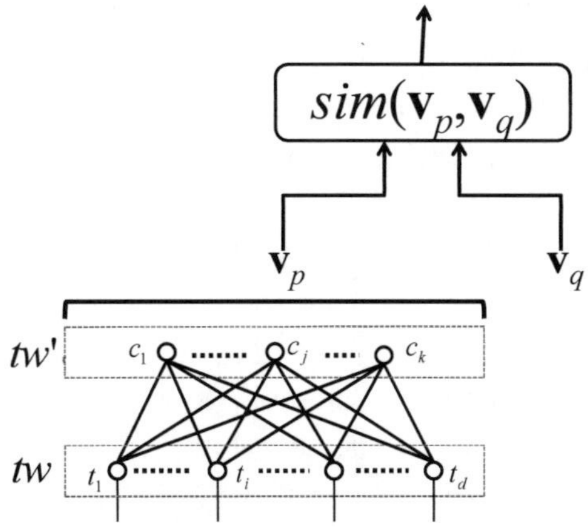

Figure 1: Learning concept vectors. The output layer consists of a small number of concept nodes, where the weight of each node is a linear combination of all the original term weights.

3 Similarity Learning via Siamese Neural Network (S2Net)

Given pairs of documents with their labels, such as binary or real-valued similarity scores, our goal is to construct a projection matrix that maps the corresponding term-vectors into a low-dimensional *concept* space such that similar documents are close when projected into this space. We propose a similarity learning framework via Siamese neural network (S2Net) to learn the projection matrix *directly* from labeled data. In this section, we introduce its model design and describe the training process.

3.1 Model Design

The network structure of S2Net consists of two layers. The input layer corresponds to the raw term vector, where each node represents a term in the original vocabulary and its associated value is determined by a term-weighting function such as TFIDF. The output layer is the learned low-dimensional vector representation that captures relationships among terms. Similarly, each node of the output layer is an element in the new concept vector. In this work, the final similarity score is calculated using the cosine function, which is the standard choice for document similarity (Manning et al., 2008). Our framework can be easily extended to other similarity functions as long as they are differentiable.

The output of each concept node is a linear combination of the weights of all the terms in the original term vector. In other words, these two layers of nodes form a complete bipartite graph as shown in Fig. 1. The output of a concept node c_j is thus defined as:

$$tw'(c_j) = \sum_{t_i \in V} \alpha_{ij} \cdot tw(t_i) \quad (1)$$

Notice that it is straightforward to add a non-linear activation function (e.g., sigmoid) in Eq. (1), which can potentially lead to better results. However, in the current design, the model form is exactly the same as the low-rank projection matrix derived by PCA, OPCA or CCA, which facilitates comparison to alternative projection methods. Using concise matrix notation, let $\mathbf{f}$ be a raw d-by-1 term vector, $\mathbf{A} = [\alpha_{ij}]_{d \times k}$ the projection matrix. $\mathbf{g} = \mathbf{A}^T\mathbf{f}$ is thus the k-by-1 projected concept vector.

3.2 Loss Function and Training Procedure

For a pair of term vectors $\mathbf{f}_p$ and $\mathbf{f}_q$, their similarity score is defined by the cosine value of the corresponding concept vectors $\mathbf{g}_p$ and $\mathbf{g}_q$ according to the projection matrix $\mathbf{A}$.

$$sim_{\mathbf{A}}(\mathbf{f}_p, \mathbf{f}_q) = \frac{\mathbf{g}_p^T \mathbf{g}_q}{||\mathbf{g}_p|| ||\mathbf{g}_q||},$$

where $\mathbf{g}_p = \mathbf{A}^T\mathbf{f}_p$ and $\mathbf{g}_q = \mathbf{A}^T\mathbf{f}_q$. Let y_{pq} be the true label of this pair. The loss function can be as simple as the mean-squared error $\frac{1}{2}(y_{pq} - sim_{\mathbf{A}}(\mathbf{f}_p, \mathbf{f}_q))^2$. However, in many applications, the similarity scores are used to select the closest text objects given the query. For example, given a query document, we only need to have the comparable document in the target language ranked higher than any other documents. In this scenario, it is more important for the similarity measure to yield a good ordering than to match the target similarity scores. Therefore, we use a pairwise learning setting by considering a pair of similarity scores (i.e., from two vector pairs) in our learning objective.

Consider two pairs of term vectors $(\mathbf{f}_{p_1}, \mathbf{f}_{q_1})$ and $(\mathbf{f}_{p_2}, \mathbf{f}_{q_2})$, where the first pair has higher similarity. Let Δ be the difference of their similarity scores. Namely, $\Delta = sim_{\mathbf{A}}(\mathbf{f}_{p_1}, \mathbf{f}_{q_1}) - sim_{\mathbf{A}}(\mathbf{f}_{p_2}, \mathbf{f}_{q_2})$. We use the following logistic loss over Δ, which upper-bounds the pairwise accuracy (i.e., 0-1 loss):

$$L(\Delta; \mathbf{A}) = \log(1 + exp(-\gamma\Delta)) \quad (2)$$

Because of the cosine function, we add a scaling factor γ that magnifies Δ from $[-2, 2]$ to a larger range, which helps penalize more on the prediction errors. Empirically, the value of γ makes no difference as long as it is large enough[1]. In the experiments, we set the value of γ to 10. Optimizing the model parameters $\mathbf{A}$ can be done using gradient based methods. We derive the gradient of the whole batch and apply the quasi-Newton optimization method L-BFGS (Nocedal and Wright, 2006) directly. For a cleaner presentation, we detail the gradient derivation in Appendix A. Given that the optimization problem is not convex, initializing the model from a good projection matrix often helps reduce training time and may lead to convergence to a better local minimum. Regularization can be done by adding a term $\frac{\beta}{2}||\mathbf{A} - \mathbf{A}_0||^2$ in Eq. (2), which forces the learned model not to deviate too much from the starting point ($\mathbf{A}_0$), or simply by early stopping. Empirically we found that the latter is more effective and it is used in the experiments.

4 Experiments

We compare S2Net experimentally with existing approaches on two very different tasks: cross-lingual document retrieval and ad relevance measures.

4.1 Comparable Document Retrieval

With the growth of multiple languages on the Web, there is an increasing demand of processing cross-lingual documents. For instance, machine translation (MT) systems can benefit from training on sentences extracted from parallel or comparable documents retrieved from the Web (Munteanu and Marcu, 2005). Word-level translation lexicons can also be learned from comparable documents (Fung and Yee, 1998; Rapp, 1999). In this cross-lingual document retrieval task, given a query document in one language, the goal is to find the most *similar* document from the corpus in another language.

4.1.1 Data & Setting

We followed the comparable document retrieval setting described in (Platt et al., 2010) and evaluated S2Net on the Wikipedia dataset used in that paper. This data set consists of Wikipedia documents

[1]Without the γ parameter, the model still outperforms other baselines in our experiments, but with a much smaller gain.

in two languages, English and Spanish. An article in English is paired with a Spanish article if they are identified as comparable across languages by the Wikipedia community. To conduct a fair comparison, we use the same term vectors and data split as in the previous study. The numbers of document pairs in the training/development/testing sets are 43,380, 8,675 and 8,675, respectively. The dimensionality of the raw term vectors is 20,000.

The models are evaluated by using each English document as query against all documents in Spanish and *vice versa*; the results from the two directions are averaged. Performance is evaluated by two metrics: the Top-1 accuracy, which tests whether the document with the highest similarity score is the true comparable document, and the Mean Reciprocal Rank (MRR) of the true comparable.

When training the S2Net model, all the comparable document pairs are treated as positive examples and all other pairs are used as negative examples. Naively treating these 1.8 billion pairs (i.e., 43380^2) as independent examples would make the training very inefficient. Fortunately, most computation in deriving the batch gradient can be reused via compact matrix operations and training can still be done efficiently. We initialized the S2Net model using the matrix learned by OPCA, which gave us the best performance on the development set[2].

Our approach is compared with most methods studied in (Platt et al., 2010), including the best performing one. For CL-LSI, OPCA, and CCA, we include results from that work directly. In addition, we re-implemented and improved JPLSA and CPLSA by changing three settings: we used separate vocabularies for the two languages as in the Poly-lingual topic model (Mimno et al., 2009), we performed 10 EM iterations for folding-in instead of only one, and we used the Jensen-Shannon distance instead of the L1 distance. We also attempted to apply the HDLR algorithm. Because this algorithm does not scale well as the number of training examples increases, we used 2,500 positive and 2,500 negative document pairs for training. Unfortunately, among all the hyper-parameter settings we tested, HDLR could not outperform its initial model, which was the OPCA matrix. Therefore we omit these results.

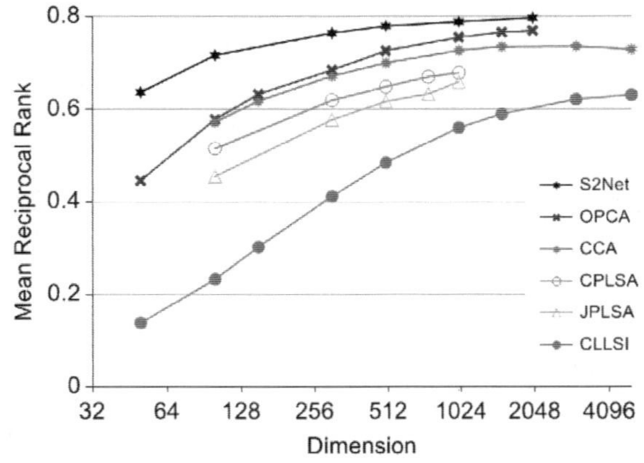

Figure 2: Mean reciprocal rank versus dimension for Wikipedia. Results of OPCA, CCA and CL-LSI are from (Platt et al., 2010).

4.1.2 Results

Fig. 2 shows the MRR performance of all methods on the development set, across different dimensionality settings of the concept space. As can be observed from the figure, higher dimensions usually lead to better results. In addition, S2Net consistently performs better than all other methods across different dimensions. The gap is especially large when projecting input vectors to a low-dimensional space, which is preferable for efficiency. For instance, using 500 dimensions, S2Net already performs as well as OPCA with 2000 dimensions.

Table 1 shows the averaged Top-1 accuracy and MRR scores of all methods on the test set, where the dimensionality for each method is optimized on the development set (Fig. 2). S2Net clearly outperforms all other methods and the difference in terms of accuracy is statistically significant[3].

4.2 Ad Relevance

Paid search advertising is the main revenue source that supports modern commercial search engines. To ensure satisfactory user experience, it is important to provide both relevant ads and regular search

[2] S2Net outperforms OPCA when initialized from a random or CL-LSI matrix, but with a smaller gain. For example, when the number of dimensions is 1000, the MRR score of OPCA is 0.7660. Starting from the CL-LSI and OPCA matrices, the MRR scores of S2Net are 0.7745 and 0.7855, respectively.

[3] We use the unpaired t-test with Bonferroni correction and the difference is considered statistically significant when the p-value is less than 0.01.

Algorithm	Dimension	Accuracy	MRR
S2Net	2000	**0.7447**	**0.7973**
OPCA	2000	0.7255	0.7734
CCA	1500	0.6894	0.7378
CPLSA	1000	0.6329	0.6842
JPLSA	1000	0.6079	0.6604
CL-LSI	5000	0.5302	0.6130

Table 1: Test results for comparable document retrieval in Wikipedia. Results of OPCA, CCA and CL-LSI are from (Platt et al., 2010).

results. Previous work on ad relevance focuses on constructing appropriate term-vectors to represent queries and ad-text (Broder et al., 2008; Choi et al., 2010). In this section, we extend the work in (Yih and Jiang, 2010) and show how S2Net can exploit annotated query–ad pairs to improve the vector representation in this monolingual setting.

4.2.1 Data & Tasks

The ad relevance dataset we used consists of 12,481 unique queries randomly sampled from the logs of the Bing search engine. For each query, a number of top ranked ads are selected, which results in a total number of 567,744 query-ad pairs in the dataset. Each query-ad pair is manually labeled as *same*, *subset*, *superset* or *disjoint*. In our experiment, when the task is a binary classification problem, pairs labeled as *same*, *subset*, or *superset* are considered relevant, and pairs labeled as *disjoint* are considered irrelevant. When pairwise comparisons are needed in either training or evaluation, the relevance order is *same* > *subset* = *superset* > *disjoint*. The dataset is split into training (40%), validation (30%) and test (30%) sets by queries.

Because a query string usually contains only a few words and thus provides very little content, we applied the same web relevance feedback technique used in (Broder et al., 2008) to create "pseudo-documents" to represent queries. Each query in our data set was first issued to the search engine. The result page with up to 100 snippets was used as the pseudo-document to create the raw term vectors. On the ad side, we used the ad landing pages instead of the short ad-text. Our vocabulary set contains 29,854 words and is determined using a document frequency table derived from a large collection of Web documents. Only words with counts larger than a pre-selected threshold are retained.

How the data is used in training depends on the model. For S2Net, we constructed preference pairs in the following way. For the same query, each relevant ad is paired with a less relevant ad. The loss function from Eq. (2) encourages achieving a higher similarity score for the more relevant ad. For HDLR, we used a sample of 5,000 training pairs of queries and ads, as it was not able to scale to more training examples. For OPCA, CCA, PLSA and JPLSA, we constructed a parallel corpus using only relevant pairs of queries and ads, as the negative examples (irrelevant pairs of queries and ads) cannot be used by these models. Finally, PCA and PLSA learn the models from all training queries and documents without using any relevance information.

We tested S2Net and other methods in two different application scenarios. The first is to use the ad relevance measure as an *ad filter*. When the similarity score between a query and an ad is below a pre-selected decision threshold, this ad is considered irrelevant to the query and will be filtered. Evaluation metrics used for this scenario are the ROC analysis and the area under the curve (AUC). The second one is the ranking scenario, where the ads are selected and ranked by their relevance scores. In this scenario, the performance is evaluated by the standard ranking metric, *Normalized Discounted Cumulative Gain* (NDCG) (Jarvelin and Kekalainen, 2000).

4.2.2 Results

We first compare different methods in their AUC and NDCG scores. *TFIDF* is the basic term vector representation with the TFIDF weighting ($tf \cdot \log(N/df)$). It is used as our baseline and also as the raw input for S2Net, HDLR and other linear projection methods. Based on the results on the development set, we found that PCA performs better than OPCA and CCA. Therefore, we initialized the models of S2Net and HDLR using the PCA matrix. Table 2 summarizes results on the test set. All models, except TFIDF, use 1000 dimensions and their best configuration settings selected on the validation set.

TFIDF is a very strong baseline on this monolingual ad relevance dataset. Among all the methods we tested, at dimension 1000, only S2Net outperforms the raw TFIDF cosine measure in every evaluation metric, and the difference is statistically sig-

	AUC	NDCG@1	NDCG@3	NDCG@5
S2Net	**0.892**	**0.855**	**0.883**	**0.901**
TFIDF	0.861	0.825	0.854	0.876
HDLR	0.855	0.826	0.856	0.877
CPLSA	0.853	0.845	0.872	0.890
PCA	0.848	0.815	0.847	0.870
OPCA	0.844	0.817	0.850	0.872
JPLSA	0.840	0.838	0.864	0.883
CCA	0.836	0.820	0.852	0.874
PLSA	0.835	0.831	0.860	0.879

Table 2: The AUC and NDCG scores of the cosine similarity scores on different vector representations. The dimension for all models except TFIDF is 1000.

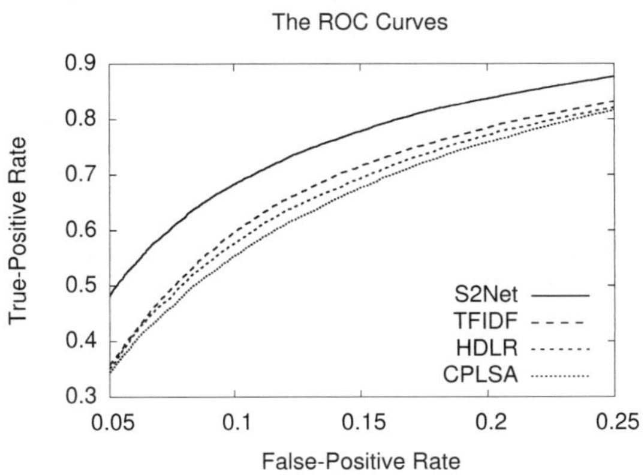

Figure 3: The ROC curves of S2Net, TFIDF, HDLR and CPLSA when the similarity scores are used as ad filters.

nificant[4]. In contrast, both CPLSA and HDLR have higher NDCG scores but lower AUC values, and OPCA/CCA perform roughly the same as PCA.

When the cosine scores of these vector representations are used as ad filters, their ROC curves (focusing on the low false-positive region) are shown in Fig. 3. It can be clearly observed that the similarity score computed based on vectors derived from S2Net indeed has better quality, compared to the raw TFIDF representation. Unfortunately, other approaches perform worse than TFIDF and their performance in the low false-positive region is consistent with the AUC scores.

Although ideally we would like the dimensionality of the projected concept vectors to be as small as possible for efficient processing, the quality of the concept vector representation usually degrades as well. It is thus interesting to know the best trade-off point between these two variables. Table 3 shows the AUC and NDCG scores of S2Net at different dimensions, as well as the results achieved by TFIDF and PCA, HDLR and CPLSA at 1000 dimensions. As can be seen, S2Net surpasses TFIDF in AUC at dimension 300 and keeps improving as the dimensionality increases. Its NDCG scores are also consistently higher across all dimensions.

4.3 Discussion

It is encouraging to find that S2Net achieves strong performance in two very different tasks, given that it is a conceptually simple model. Its empirical success can be attributed to two factors. First, it is flexible in choosing the loss function and constructing training examples and is thus able to optimize the model directly for the target task. Second, it can be trained on a large number of examples. For example, HDLR can only use a few thousand examples and is not able to learn a matrix better than its initial model for the task of cross-lingual document retrieval. The fact that linear projection methods like OPCA/CCA and generative topic models like JPLSA/CPLSA cannot use negative examples more effectively also limits their potential.

In terms of scalability, we found that methods based on eigen decomposition, such as PCA, OPCA and CCA, take the least training time. The complexity is decided by the size of the covariance matrix, which is quadratic in the number of dimensions. On a regular eight-core server, it takes roughly 2 to 3 hours to train the projection matrix in both experiments. The training time of S2Net scales roughly linearly to the number of dimensions and training examples. In each iteration, performing the projection takes the most time in gradient derivation, and the complexity is $O(mnk)$, where m is the number of distinct term-vectors, n is the largest number of non-zero elements in the sparse term-vectors and k is the dimensionality of the concept space. For cross-lingual document retrieval, when $k = 1000$, each iteration takes roughly 48 minutes and about 80 iterations are required to convergence. Fortunately, the gradient computation is easily parallelizable and further speed-up can be achieved using a cluster.

[4]For AUC, we randomly split the data into 50 subsets and ran a paired-t test between the corresponding AUC scores. For NDCG, we compared the DCG scores per query of the compared models using the paired-t test. The difference is considered statistically significant when the p-value is less than 0.01.

	TFIDF	HDLR	CPLSA	PCA	$S2Net_{100}$	$S2Net_{300}$	$S2Net_{500}$	$S2Net_{750}$	$S2Net_{1000}$
AUC	0.861	0.855	0.853	0.848	0.855	0.879	0.880	0.888	0.892
NDCG@1	0.825	0.826	0.845	0.815	0.843	0.852	0.856	0.860	0.855
NDCG@3	0.854	0.856	0.872	0.847	0.871	0.879	0.881	0.884	0.883
NDCG@5	0.876	0.877	0.890	0.870	0.890	0.897	0.899	0.902	0.901

Table 3: The AUC and NDCG scores of S2Net at different dimensions. PCA, HDLR & CPLSA (at dimension 1000) along with the raw TFIDF representation are used for reference.

5 Related Work

Although the high-level design of S2Net follows the Siamese architecture (Bromley et al., 1993; Chopra et al., 2005), the network construction, loss function and training process of S2Net are all different compared to previous work. For example, targeting the application of face verification, Chopra et al. (2005) used a convolutional network and designed a contrastive loss function for optimizing a Eucliden distance metric. In contrast, the network of S2Net is equivalent to a linear projection matrix and has a pairwise loss function. In terms of the learning framework, S2Net is closely related to several neural network based approaches, including autoencoders (Hinton and Salakhutdinov, 2006) and finding low-dimensional word representations (Collobert and Weston, 2008; Turian et al., 2010). Architecturally, S2Net is also similar to RankNet (Burges et al., 2005), which can be viewed as a Siamese neural network that learns a ranking function.

The strategy that S2Net takes to learn from labeled pairs of documents can be analogous to the work of distance metric learning. Although high dimensionality is not a problem to algorithms like HDLR, it suffers from a different scalability issue. As we have observed in our experiments, the algorithm can only handle a small number of similarity/dissimilarity constraints (i.e., the labeled examples), and is not able to use a large number of examples to learn a better model. Empirically, we also found that HDLR is very sensitive to the hyperparameter settings and its performance can vary substantially from iteration to iteration.

Other than the applications presented in this paper, concept vectors have shown useful in traditional IR tasks. For instance, Egozi et al. (2008) use *explicit semantic analysis* to improve the retrieval recall by leveraging Wikipedia. In a companion paper, we also demonstrated that various topic models including S2Net can enhance the ranking function (Gao et al., 2011). For text categorization, similarity between terms is often encoded as kernel functions embedded in the learning algorithms, and thus increase the classification accuracy. Representative approaches include *latent semantic kernels* (Cristianini et al., 2002), which learns an LSA-based kernel function from a document collection, and work that computes term-similarity based on the linguistic knowledge provided by WordNet (Basili et al., 2005; Bloehdorn and Moschitti, 2007).

6 Conclusions

In this paper, we presented S2Net, a discriminative approach for learning a projection matrix that maps raw term-vectors to a low-dimensional space. Our learning method directly optimizes the model so that the cosine score of the projected vectors can become a reliable similarity measure. The strength of this model design has been shown empirically in two very different tasks. For cross-lingual document retrieval, S2Net significantly outperforms OPCA, which is the best prior approach. For ad selection and filtering, S2Net also outperforms all methods we compared it with and is the only technique that beats the raw TFIDF vectors in both AUC and NDCG.

The success of S2Net is truly encouraging, and we would like to explore different directions to further enhance the model in the future. For instance, it will be interesting to extend the model to learn nonlinear transformations. In addition, since the pairs of text objects being compared often come from different distributions (e.g., English documents vs. Spanish documents or queries vs. pages), learning two different matrices instead of one could increase the model expressivity. Finally, we would like to apply S2Net to more text similarity tasks, such as word similarity and entity recognition and discovery.

References

Eneko Agirre, Enrique Alfonseca, Keith Hall, Jana Kravalova, Marius Pasca, and Aitor Soroa. 2009. A study on similarity and relatedness using distributional and WordNet-based approaches. In *Proceedings of HLT-NAACL*, pages 19–27, June.

Arthur Asuncion, Max Welling, Padhraic Smyth, and Yee Whye Teh. 2009. On smoothing and inference for topic models. In *UAI*.

Roberto Basili, Marco Cammisa, and Alessandro Moschitti. 2005. Effective use of WordNet semantics via kernel-based learning. In *CoNLL*.

David M. Blei, Andrew Y. Ng, Michael I. Jordan, and John Lafferty. 2003. Latent dirichlet allocation. *Journal of Machine Learning Research*, 3:993–1022.

Stephan Bloehdorn and Alessandro Moschitti. 2007. Combined syntactic and semantic kernels for text classification. In *ECIR*, pages 307–318.

Andrei Z. Broder, Peter Ciccolo, Marcus Fontoura, Evgeniy Gabrilovich, Vanja Josifovski, and Lance Riedel. 2008. Search advertising using web relevance feedback. In *CIKM*, pages 1013–1022.

Jane Bromley, James W. Bentz, Léon Bottou, Isabelle Guyon, Yann LeCun, Cliff Moore, Eduard Säckinger, and Roopak Shah. 1993. Signature verification using a "Siamese" time delay neural network. *International Journal Pattern Recognition and Artificial Intelligence*, 7(4):669–688.

Chris Burges, Tal Shaked, Erin Renshaw, Ari Lazier, Matt Deeds, Nicole Hamilton, and Greg Hullender. 2005. Learning to rank using gradient descent. In *ICML*.

Y. Choi, M. Fontoura, E. Gabrilovich, V. Josifovski, M. Mediano, and B. Pang. 2010. Using landing pages for sponsored search ad selection. In *WWW*.

Sumit Chopra, Raia Hadsell, and Yann LeCun. 2005. Learning a similarity metric discriminatively, with application to face verification. In *Proceedings of CVPR-2005*, pages 539–546.

Ronan Collobert and Jason Weston. 2008. A unified architecture for natural language processing: deep neural networks with multitask learning. In *ICML*.

Nello Cristianini, John Shawe-Taylor, and Huma Lodhi. 2002. Latent semantic kernels. *Journal of Intelligent Information Systems*, 18(2–3):127–152.

Jason V. Davis and Inderjit S. Dhillon. 2008. Structured metric learning for high dimensional problems. In *KDD*, pages 195–203.

Jason V. Davis, Brian Kulis, Prateek Jain, Suvrit Sra, and Inderjit S. Dhillon. 2007. Information-theoretic metric learning. In *ICML*.

Scott Deerwester, Susan Dumais, George Furnas, Thomas Landauer, and Richard Harshman. 1990. Indexing by latent semantic analysis. *Journal of the American Society for Information Science*, 41(6):391–407.

Konstantinos I. Diamantaras and S.Y. Kung. 1996. *Principal Component Neural Networks: Theory and Applications*. Wiley-Interscience.

Susan T. Dumais, Todd A. Letsche, Michael L. Littman, and Thomas K. Landauer. 1997. Automatic cross-linguistic information retrieval using latent semantic indexing. In *AAAI-97 Spring Symposium Series: Cross-Language Text and Speech Retrieval*.

Ofer Egozi, Evgeniy Gabrilovich, and Shaul Markovitch. 2008. Concept-based feature generation and selection for information retrieval. In *AAAI*.

Pascale Fung and Lo Yuen Yee. 1998. An IR approach for translating new words from nonparallel, comparable texts. In *Proceedings of COLING-ACL*.

Kuzman Ganchev, Joao Graca, Jennifer Gillenwater, and Ben Taskar. 2009. Posterior regularization for structured latent variable models. Technical Report MS-CIS-09-16, University of Pennsylvania.

Jianfeng Gao, Kristina Toutanova, and Wen-tau Yih. 2011. Clickthrough-based latent semantic models for web search. In *SIGIR*.

G. E. Hinton and R. R. Salakhutdinov. 2006. Reducing the dimensionality of data with neural networks. *Science*, 313(5786):504–507, July.

Thomas Hofmann. 1999. Probabilistic latent semantic indexing. In *SIGIR '99*, pages 50–57.

K. Jarvelin and J. Kekalainen. 2000. Ir evaluation methods for retrieving highly relevant documents. In *SIGIR*, pages 41–48.

Dekang Lin. 1998. Automatic retrieval and clustering of similar words. In *Proc. of COLING-ACL 98*.

Christopher D. Manning, Prabhakar Raghavan, and Hinrich Schütze. 2008. *Introduction to Information Retrieval*. Cambridge University Pres.

David Mimno, Hanna W. Wallach, Jason Naradowsky, David A. Smith, and Andrew McCallum. 2009. Polylingual topic models. In *EMNLP*.

Dragos Stefan Munteanu and Daniel Marcu. 2005. Improving machine translation performance by exploiting non-parallel corpora. *Computational Linguistics*, 31:477–504.

Jorge Nocedal and Stephen Wright. 2006. *Numerical Optimization*. Springer, 2nd edition.

John Platt, Kristina Toutanova, and Wen-tau Yih. 2010. Translingual document representations from discriminative projections. In *EMNLP*.

Reinhard Rapp. 1999. Automatic identification of word translations from unrelated English and German corpora. In *Proceedings of the ACL*, pages 519–526.

Joseph Turian, Lev Ratinov, and Yoshua Bengio. 2010. Word representations: a simple and general method for semi-supervised learning. In *ACL*.

Alexei Vinokourov, John Shawe-taylor, and Nello Cristianini. 2003. Inferring a semantic representation of text via cross-language correlation analysis. In *NIPS-15*.

Vishnu Vyas and Patrick Pantel. 2009. Semi-automatic entity set refinement. In *NAACL '09*, pages 290–298.

Wen-tau Yih and Ning Jiang. 2010. Similarity models for ad relevance measures. In *MLOAD - NIPS 2010 Workshop on online advertising*.

Appendix A. Gradient Derivation

The gradient of the loss function in Eq. (2) can be derived as follows.

$$\frac{\partial L(\Delta, \mathbf{A})}{\partial \mathbf{A}} = \frac{-\gamma}{1+\exp(-\gamma\Delta)}\frac{\partial \Delta}{\partial \mathbf{A}}$$

$$\frac{\partial \Delta}{\partial \mathbf{A}} = \frac{\partial}{\partial \mathbf{A}} sim_{\mathbf{A}}(\mathbf{f}_{p_1}, \mathbf{f}_{q_1}) - \frac{\partial}{\partial \mathbf{A}} sim_{\mathbf{A}}(\mathbf{f}_{p_2}, \mathbf{f}_{q_2})$$

$$\frac{\partial}{\partial \mathbf{A}} sim_{\mathbf{A}}(\mathbf{f}_p, \mathbf{f}_q) = \frac{\partial}{\partial \mathbf{A}} \cos(\mathbf{g}_p, \mathbf{g}_q),$$

where $\mathbf{g}_p = \mathbf{A}^T\mathbf{f}_p$ and $\mathbf{g}_q = \mathbf{A}^T\mathbf{f}_q$ are the projected concept vectors of $\mathbf{f}_q$ and $\mathbf{f}_q$. The gradient of the cosine score can be further derived in the following steps.

$$\begin{aligned}
\cos(\mathbf{g}_p, \mathbf{g}_q) &= \frac{\mathbf{g}_p^T\mathbf{g}_q}{\|\mathbf{g}_p\|\|\mathbf{g}_q\|} \\
\nabla_{\mathbf{A}}\mathbf{g}_p^T\mathbf{g}_q &= (\nabla_{\mathbf{A}}\mathbf{A}^T\mathbf{f}_p)\mathbf{g}_q + (\nabla_{\mathbf{A}}\mathbf{A}^T\mathbf{f}_q)\mathbf{g}_p \\
&= \mathbf{f}_p\mathbf{g}_q^T + \mathbf{f}_q\mathbf{g}_p^T \\
\nabla_{\mathbf{A}}\frac{1}{\|\mathbf{g}_p\|} &= \nabla_{\mathbf{A}}(\mathbf{g}_p^T\mathbf{g}_p)^{-\frac{1}{2}} \\
&= -\frac{1}{2}(\mathbf{g}_p^T\mathbf{g}_p)^{-\frac{3}{2}}\nabla_{\mathbf{A}}(\mathbf{g}_p^T\mathbf{g}_p) \\
&= -(\mathbf{g}_p^T\mathbf{g}_p)^{-\frac{3}{2}}\mathbf{f}_p\mathbf{g}_p^T \\
\nabla_{\mathbf{A}}\frac{1}{\|\mathbf{g}_q\|} &= -(\mathbf{g}_q^T\mathbf{g}_q)^{-\frac{3}{2}}\mathbf{f}_q\mathbf{g}_q^T
\end{aligned}$$

Let a, b, c be $\mathbf{g}_p^T\mathbf{g}_q$, $1/\|\mathbf{g}_p\|$ and $1/\|\mathbf{g}_q\|$, respectively.

$$\begin{aligned}
\nabla_{\mathbf{A}}\frac{\mathbf{g}_p^T\mathbf{g}_q}{\|\mathbf{g}_p\|\|\mathbf{g}_q\|} =& -abc^3\mathbf{f}_q\mathbf{g}_q^T - acb^3\mathbf{f}_p\mathbf{g}_p^T \\
&+ bc(\mathbf{f}_p\mathbf{g}_q^T + \mathbf{f}_q\mathbf{g}_p^T)
\end{aligned}$$

Author Index